Aid and Reform in Africa
Lessons from Ten Case Studies

Edited by

Shantayanan Devarajan
The World Bank

David R. Dollar
The World Bank

Torgny Holmgren
Ministry of Foreign Affairs, Sweden

The World Bank
Washington, D.C.

Cover design by Drew Fasick and Ultra Designs.

Library of Congress Cataloging-in-Publication Data

Aid and reform in Africa : a report from ten countries / edited by Shantayanan
Devarajan, David Dollar, Torgny Holmgren.
     p. cm.
     Includes bibliographical references and index.
     ISBN 0-8213-4669-5
     1. Economic assistance—Africa. 2. Africa—Economic policy. I. Devarajan,
Shantayanan, 1954– II. Dollar, David. III. Holmgren, Torgny, 1954–

HC800 .A628 2000
338.96—dc21   00-050359

Contents

Box

Tables

FIGURES

Foreword

Three years ago, in 1998, we published a study, *Assessing Aid*, from which two themes emerged. First, effective aid requires the right timing, and second, it requires the right mix of money and ideas. This volume builds upon the lessons learned from that study.

In 1999 I outlined a proposal for a comprehensive development framework, a key element of which—and the one I feel most strongly about—is **ownership**. I have always argued, and continue to argue, that a development program must be country-owned, not owned by donors or the World Bank. The ten case studies that make up this volume also show that country ownership is the way to make assistance effective.

These studies of aid and reform in Africa confirm that when aid supports a country-owned development strategy, it can lead to sustained growth and poverty alleviation. The case studies also show that when reform is imposed from abroad, even as a quid pro quo for aid, it is not sustainable. In other words, this book provides empirical foundations for the new development partnership, with donors supporting country-owned programs with their knowledge, ideas, and money.

Each recipient country of aid in Africa has demonstrated different results in the reforms it has undertaken. Two have grown rapidly and reduced poverty. Two others, as this volume outlines, have shown significant reform in recent years, but it may be too early to judge sustainability. In yet other countries, matters have changed little, or they have even become worse.

The divergent outcomes have resulted from several factors, all of which are elaborated upon in the case studies. It is significant that the authors of the case studies are all nationals of the countries themselves, writing in collaboration with members of the donor community.

Together, and with outside support, Africans *can* and *will* address their challenges—in their own ways—for lasting results. This message was underscored by all the 22 African presidents I met on my last trip to Africa. And this is why the subject of aid and reform is so crucial to Africa.

Even a cursory gleaning of development statistics will make clear the scale of the problems that Africa faces, and the challenges that must be overcome. Let me present just a few.

Between 1990 and 1998, the number of people living in poverty actually **increased** in Sub-Saharan Africa, from 242 to 291 million people. And while the number of people living on less than a dollar a day—in absolute poverty—declined in this period by five percentage points the world over, in Africa the change was barely discernible.

Even with faster economic growth, the number of people living on less than a dollar a day will increase from nearly 291 million in 1998 to nearly 330 million in 2008. Under conditions of slower growth and rising inequality, that number could be as high as 406 million.

In 17 of the 48 countries in Sub-Saharan Africa, life expectancy **declined** between 1990 and 1998, while it went up from age 63 to age 65 in all developing countries. Africa is home to 70 percent of the adults, and 80 percent of the children, living with HIV in the world. Of the nearly 22 million people who have died from AIDS and AIDS-related diseases, 17 million have been Africans. It is estimated that by the year 2014, the population of the world will be 7 billion. Of the increase, nearly a quarter—240 million—will be in Sub-Saharan Africa.

To deal with the challenges that these problems pose—and those of coping with a rapidly globalizing digital economy—aid must be effective for reform to take hold. The lessons drawn from the studies of the relationship between aid and reform in Africa become critical to its people, and to their future.

This book also reflects the World Bank's new style of research. Just as *Voices of the Poor* taught us about poverty, the authors of the case studies in this book teach us about how aid really affects reform in Africa. The studies capture the richness, the texture, and nuances of aid and reform. And the conclusions show that we are not afraid to be critical of ourselves.

The authors of the studies in *Aid and Reform in Africa* deserve to be commended. This volume represents the World Bank doing what it does best: asking hard questions; building on 55 years of experience; reaching out to partners; pushing the frontiers of knowledge; delivering results; and doing all this while keeping its eyes on the main goal—a world free of poverty.

James D. Wolfensohn
President
The World Bank

Acknowledgments

This book has enjoyed an unusual degree of collaboration. We would like to express our gratitude to Paul Collier, who encouraged us to undertake the project, helped us frame the study, and provided invaluable advice and support throughout the process. We are also grateful to Alan Gelb and Kwesi Botchwey for comments and suggestions at various stages of the manuscript. We benefited from the research assistance of Charles Chang and Jacqueline Vanderpuye-Orgle, and the logistical support of Raquel Luz, Emily Khine, Shanaz Khan and Rina Bonfield. Finally, our thanks go to the World Bank publications team and to Catherine Sunshine, who did an excellent job of editing the manuscript.

For helpful comments, we are grateful to participants at the following workshops and seminars, where the papers were presented: Frankfurt, Germany, June 7–8, 1999; Washington, D.C., September 27, 1999; Dar es Salaam, Tanzania, November 18–19, 1999; Nairobi, Kenya, September 19, 2000; and Clermont-Ferrand, France, September 20–21, 2000.

Finally, for financial assistance, we are grateful to the World Bank's Research Support Budget, and the governments of France, Germany, the Netherlands, Norway, Sweden, and Switzerland.

Overview

Since the early 1980s, virtually every African country has received large amounts of aid aimed at stimulating policy reform. The results have varied enormously. Ghana and Uganda were successful reformers that grew rapidly and reduced poverty. Côte d'Ivoire and Ethiopia have shown significant reform in recent years, but it remains to be seen if this is sustained. In other countries, policies changed little or even got worse. This book synthesizes the findings from 10 case studies that investigate whether, when, and how foreign aid affected economic policy in Africa.

The 10 countries covered in the study reveal the range of African policy experience. The countries are shown in figure 1.1, which relates foreign aid in the 1990s to a measure of overall economic policy (the World Bank's Country Policy and Institutional Assessment). This is a broad measure of economic policy that covers macroeconomic management, as well as effectiveness of the public sector in providing the services that are essential for growth and poverty reduction (see box 1.1). All of these countries received large amounts of aid; all had structural adjustment programs with the international financial institutions. Yet the policy outcomes are quite diverse. Ghana and Uganda achieved sustained good policy (and good economic outcomes). The other eight countries did not. In examining their cases, it is useful to divide them into three groups: the post-socialist reformers (Ethiopia, Mali, and Tanzania), the mixed reformers (Côte d'Ivoire, Kenya, and Zambia), and the nonreformers (the Democratic Republic of Congo [formerly Zaire], and Nigeria). These categorizations do not reflect policy changes in the past one or two years; nor are they meant to be an assessment of current policy. The case studies look at the reform process during the 1980s and 1990s. The average policy ratings for the 1990s give an indication of the pace of reform during the period covered by the studies.

What constitutes "good policy" and how to measure it are somewhat controversial. Development experience and research have established a

1

FIGURE 1.1 AID AND POLICY IN THE 1990S

Aid as a percentage of GDP (1991–97)

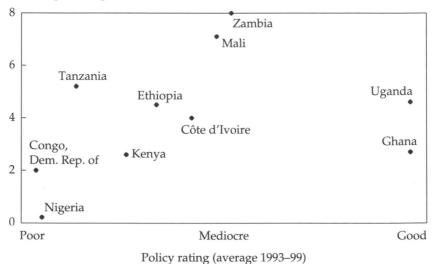

Policy rating (average 1993–99)

fair amount of knowledge about policies that promote growth and reduce poverty: absence of high inflation, functioning foreign exchange
and financial markets, openness to foreign trade, effective rule of law,
and delivery of key services such as education. There remain, however,
policy areas about which we know less and about which there is ongoing debate. Openness of the capital account and school vouchers for poor
children are two examples. Nevertheless, we know enough about development policies to make a fair assessment of the quality of policies across
countries and over time. We emphasize, however, that learning about
development policy is an ongoing process. In fact, one of the main roles
of effective aid is to support countries' learning about good policy, both
drawing on existing knowledge and creating new knowledge. Finally,
the notion that we are doing a reasonable job of measuring policy across
countries is supported by the fact that our broad measure of policy pre-
dicts fairly well the gross domestic product (GDP) growth rates of the
four categories of countries in our study. The successful reformers have
grown well in the 1990s; the nonreformers have gone backwards rapidly; and the performance of the other groups is in between (figure 1.2).

     That the 10 countries in our study all received large amounts of aid,
including conditional loans, yet ended up with vastly different policies
suggests that aid is not a primary determinant of policy. That is the conclusion of a number of recent cross-country statistical studies summarized

Box 1.1 Measuring Economic Policy

The measure of policy used in the figures throughout this paper is a broad one. Conceptually, it measures the extent to which government policy creates a good environment for broad-based growth and poverty reduction. In practice, it has four components:

- *Macroeconomic policies:* whether fiscal, monetary, and exchange rate policies provide a stable environment for economic activity
- *Structural policies:* the extent to which trade, tax, and sectoral policies create good incentives for accumulation by households and firms
- *Public sector management:* the extent to which public sector institutions effectively provide services complementary to private initiative, such as the rule of law (functioning of the judiciary, police), infrastructure, and social services
- *Social inclusion:* the extent to which policy ensures the full participation of the society through social services that reach the poor and disadvantaged, including women and ethnic minorities.

Figure 1.2 Policy and Growth in the 1990s

Real GDP per capita growth (1990–96)

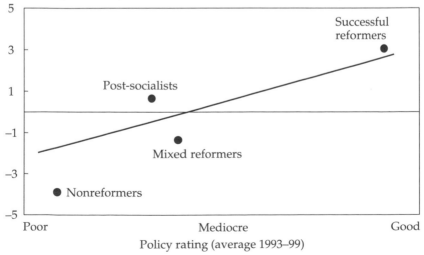

Policy rating (average 1993–99)

in the World Bank report *Assessing Aid* (1998). Specifically, Burnside and Dollar (2000) found that the amount of aid countries received had no effect on the quality of their macroeconomic policies. Dollar and Svensson (2000) investigated the determinants of the success or failure of reform programs supported by adjustment assistance. They found that reform outcome could be predicted by underlying political-economy variables such as length of tenure of the government and whether the leader was democratically elected. Variables under donors' control had no influence on the success or failure of reform. Other studies have found no systematic relationship between aid and policy (Killick 1991; Ranis 1995; Mosley, Harrigan, and Toye 1995).

More generally, recent literature indicates that policy formulation depends primarily on domestic political-economy factors (Rodrik 1996; van de Walle and Johnston 1996). There is no consistent relationship between aid and reform. It is important to emphasize, though, that cross-country studies reveal what is true *on average*. The average relationship is likely to disguise the fact that aid supported policy reform in some cases and sustained poor policy in others (Sachs 1994). The purpose of country studies is to delve more deeply into the relationship between aid and reform, capturing the nuances of both successful and stalled reforms. More specifically, our study addresses the following questions:

- Are there common characteristics of successful and failed reformers that enable us to understand better the political economy of reform?
- Do donors tailor their assistance to different types of countries and to different phases in the reform process, or just provide undifferentiated assistance?
- Have large amounts of financial aid to countries with poor policy sustained the bad policies?
- Has aid played a useful role in the successful reformers? If so, how?

These are important questions for the development community. Improvements in economic policy are the key to more rapid growth and poverty reduction in Africa and elsewhere in the developing world. How can foreign aid best support these improvements? If policy is truly independent of aid, then—to have the maximum impact on poverty reduction—aid should be allocated on the basis of how poor countries are and the observed quality of their economic policy. Collier and Dollar (1999) estimate the poverty-efficient allocation of aid, assuming that aid has no effect on policy. But the effect of aid on growth and poverty reduction increases with the quality of policy. For a given level of poverty, therefore, aid should rise with the quality of policy (figure 1.3). Figure 1.3 also shows the actual allocation of aid in 1996, after controlling for the level of poverty and for population. Donors tend to concentrate their assis-

FIGURE 1.3 ACTUAL AID, POVERTY-EFFICIENT AID, AND POLICY

Aid as percentage of GDP

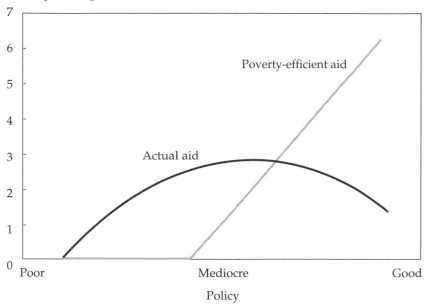

tance in countries with mediocre policies and actually discriminate against poor countries that have reformed. A number of factors account for this concentration of assistance in countries with weak policies, but one of them is the expectation that aid can spur policy reform and thus have a big payoff in these cases. Our study asks whether this pattern of aid allocation makes sense: that is, has the large amount of aid to countries with weak policies actually led to reform?

The main findings from the 10 case studies are that:

- Policy formation is primarily driven by domestic political economy. It is hard to find simple generalizations about successful and failed reformers, but one striking fact is that countries that have truly severe economic and political crises (Ghana, Uganda, Nigeria, and the Democratic Republic of Congo) tend to move to the extremes, either developing coherent reform movements or declining rapidly. Of these crisis countries, it is the ones rich in natural resources that fell into civil war (Nigeria, the Democratic Republic of Congo). The countries that avoided crises did not fall apart, but have found it hard to develop coherent reform movements that can overcome vested interests who benefit from the perpetuation of poor policies.

- Successful reformers have consultative processes that build consensus for change. However, in our sample there is no relationship between formal democratic institutions and good economic policy.
- Large amounts of aid to countries with bad policy sustained those poor policies. The funding allowed the delay of reform. Attaching conditions to the aid in these cases has not successfully led to policy change, nor has it delayed the disbursement of funds.
- Aid played a significant and positive role in the two sustained reformers (Ghana, Uganda). It helped with ideas, though in both cases there was also strong local talent formulating policy. In these cases, finance grew as policy improved and increased the benefits of reform, helping to sustain political support.
- In general, donors have not discriminated effectively among different countries and different phases of the reform process. Donors tend to provide the same package of assistance everywhere and at all times. The lessons from the Ghana and Uganda cases are that donors should concentrate on technical assistance and other soft support without large-scale budget or balance of payments support in the phase before governments are serious about reform. If a reform movement develops, finance can be increased as policies actually improve. In the early stage of serious reform, political leaders and technocrats actually welcome conditionality in order to bind themselves to policy change. Once the reform movement is well entrenched, conditionality becomes less useful because it limits participation and disguises ownership.

In summary, if donors thought that they had no effect on policy at all, the rational way to allocate aid would be based on how poor countries are and the observed quality of their policies. Our study shows that this approach is also the best way to ensure that aid has a positive effect on policy. It avoids disbursing large-scale finance into bad policy environments, where the funds can actually sustain corrupt and incompetent governments. It puts resources into the good policy environments in which financial assistance has a positive effect, increasing the benefits of good policy and sustaining political support for reform. In addition to quantity, the composition of aid is important. In the pre-reform period, technical assistance and policy dialogue are most supportive of policy reform. During periods of rapid reform, policy dialogue is important, as is finance. This is the phase in which conditional loans tend to be useful and effective. At a later stage of reform, conditionality is less useful, while finance remains important. By altering both the quantity and composition of aid, donors could more systematically support genuine policy reform in the developing world.

The remainder of this overview chapter is organized as follows. The next section examines the political economy of reform in the 10 countries covered by the case studies. The third section then looks at the pattern of aid to the countries. In the fourth section we link the two previous sections and investigate the effect of aid on reform. Section 5 concludes.

POLITICAL ECONOMY OF REFORM IN 10 AFRICAN STATES

At the beginning of the 1980s, the typical African country was following a "statist" model of development, with government intervention in almost every sector of the economy. Most notable were government restrictions on foreign trade (import tariffs, quotas, and export restrictions), maintenance of an overvalued exchange rate, and production in the hands of public enterprises. Not only did these policies fail to improve living standards in Africa—despite substantial amounts of foreign aid—but they seemed to exacerbate the effects of the external shocks of the 1970s. A consensus emerged in the donor community that improving economic policy in Africa was the highest priority (see, for example, World Bank 1982). Many donors, including the World Bank, began channeling their aid toward "structural adjustment programs"—loans and grants aimed at inducing governments to reform their policies.

Twenty years later, there does not seem to have been a systematic relationship between the volume of aid and the extent to which African countries reformed their economic policies. Some countries, such as Ghana and Uganda, undertook sustained reforms; others, such as Kenya, Tanzania, and Côte d'Ivoire, reformed in fits and starts; while others, notably Nigeria and the Democratic Republic of Congo, deteriorated. Yet, all of these countries received large amounts of aid. Clearly, therefore, the process of policy reform was significantly affected by domestic factors. In this section, we investigate what those factors were, and how they spurred or hampered policy reform. In particular, we look at the roles of crises, technocrats, ideology, leadership, and institutions.

It Takes a Crisis

It is difficult to find a case where reform occurred without a crisis. In January 1983, inflation in Ghana was over 100 percent. Meanwhile, Nigeria announced it was expelling 1.2 million Ghanaians—10 percent of Ghana's population—back to their homeland. Brush fires caused by a recent drought destroyed much of the cocoa crop. An aid mission to "friendly" socialist countries in 1982 generated no financial support. The country had no choice but to undertake a stabilization and structural adjustment program supported by the International Monetary Fund

(IMF) and the World Bank. In short, Ghana embraced serious reform only after it had exhausted all other options.

Similarly, in Uganda in 1986, the banking system was insolvent; the country had two weeks of imports in reserves; and inflation was 300 percent. The government had little choice but to restart the IMF program.

When a country is in a crisis, even those who benefited from the distorted policy regime begin to suffer.[1] The crisis in Ghana galvanized political support for reforms from those who were most severely hurt by the previous regime. An unlikely coalition of neo-Marxist students, urban workers, and lower-ranking army officers formed the nucleus of a pro-reform group. While the army as a whole may have supported earlier regimes, the 1981–83 crisis caused a split between the higher and lower ranks. Jerry Rawlings, the flight-lieutenant who led the December 31, 1981 coup, came from the lower ranks.

In Mali, likewise, most of the significant reforms occurred when the government's "back was against the wall"—when civil servants had not been paid for eight months (1988), when cotton prices fell sharply (1992), or when a drought led to unprecedented power cuts (1999).

The other mixed reformers in our 10 countries either did not have a crisis or had other options when faced with a crisis—and chose to exercise them. For instance, Kenya was rescued from the first oil crisis by the coffee boom of the mid-1970s. Zambia met the first copper crisis of 1974 with commercial borrowing, and thereby avoided having to negotiate policy reforms with the Bretton Woods institutions. That Zambia's reforms in the early 1990s came out of a "honeymoon" period, not a crisis, may have something to do with the weak implementation and stop-go nature of those reforms. Moreover, Côte d'Ivoire continued to receive aid from France even when its policies were extremely poor. Only when the spigot was turned off in 1993 did Côte d'Ivoire face its first real crisis and undertake its first real reform.

Second, leadership in a crisis matters. How the chief executive responds to pressure from vested interests can make a difference. Fearing that structural adjustment programs would cut their food subsidies, urban workers in Zambia opposed these reforms until 1991. President Kaunda, who faced opposition to reform from his own political party and bureaucracy, felt his political base would be undermined by reforms.[2] But urban workers supported the Ghanaian and Ugandan reform programs, not least because the programs were championed by the head of state in both countries. Ugandan president Museveni's support for the reform program did not waver even when the International Coffee Agreement collapsed and the 1990–91 Gulf War sent oil prices skyrocketing. Ayittey (1989) observes that when the stature of the head of state is inextricably linked to the state of the economy, reform requires immense cour-age, since it implies failure as a leader (Houphoüet-Boigny of Côte d'Ivoire and Nyerere of Tanzania are examples).

Third, the complexity of many of these reforms makes it difficult to judge before the fact who will win and who will lose. The private sector in Kenya supported price decontrol, even if the ensuing trade liberalization may have hurt some firms. The business community in Ghana was too diffuse to either support or oppose the Economic Recovery Program: they did not benefit from the earlier regime, and probably suffered under trade liberalization. In short, rather than instilling a status quo bias (Fernandez and Rodrik 1991), uncertainty about reform outcomes may— in a crisis atmosphere—break down vested interests.

A final point about crisis is that the combination of economic crisis and the existence of significant natural resources provides a fertile ground for civil war and political disintegration (Collier and Hoeffler 2000). Thus, in Nigeria and the Democratic Republic of Congo, economic crisis resulted in civil wars in which different groups vied for control of the resources.

Backsliding

Just as every reform episode in Africa is preceded by a crisis, it is followed by reform slippage. In Ghana, an 80 percent wage increase to civil servants in 1992 undermined the macroeconomic program. A value added tax (VAT) introduced in 1995 had to be rescinded because of political opposition. The VAT was reintroduced in 1998 with significantly lower rates. Uganda's stabilization program began slipping in 1991–92, with the fiscal deficit approaching 10 percent of GDP and inflation rising. The donors cut back assistance that year, and the IMF/World Bank program was delayed.

The reasons for this backsliding become more apparent when we examine the experience of mixed reformers. In Tanzania, there was retrogression in the early 1990s because the second-generation reforms—civil service reform, budget management, privatization—were much more intrusive. They required fundamental changes to public sector institutions, something that the first-generation reforms, such as trade liberalization or exchange rate devaluation, did not. Even in a star performer like Uganda, public sector reform has yet to happen. Zambia's reform program has been undermined by falling copper prices and a severe drought in 1994–95. But here too the intrusiveness of the second-generation reforms is a factor. Zambia has privatized 224 of the 275 parastatals, but the government's inability to privatize the copper mine, ZCCM, brought negotiations with the international financial institutions to a standstill. In Kenya's case, the first-generation reforms—trade liberalization, price decontrol, and exchange rate flexibility—were undertaken by a small circle of reformers in the Central Bank and Ministry of Finance. They were ill-equipped to undertake the next round of reforms, which were of a structural and institutional nature, and required much broader consultation, at the very least with line ministries. After adopting an ambitious reform program in 1992, Ethiopia may be going through its backsliding phase now (the war with Eritrea did not help). Privatization, corruption, and transparency are all issues the government has been reluctant to address, and may lead to a stalemate with the donor community. Despite major strides in macroeconomic and trade policy reform, Mali has been unable to privatize many inefficient and loss-making public enterprises.

Technocrats

Any reform program has winners and losers in the short run, and the losers will attempt to block the policy change. It takes disinterested economic analysis to gauge whether on balance the economy will benefit from the reforms. Countries with a strong cadre of economists would therefore have an edge. For instance, the appointments of Joe Abbey and Kwesi Botchwey to the National Economic Review Committee in Ghana contributed to the success of the economic program. Sensitive to popular sentiment against devaluation, Botchwey was able to sell the program as one of bonuses and surcharges that accomplished the same thing. But it is important to note that in Ghana the technocrats began to lose power after the 1992 parliamentary elections, when elected legislators and not a group of highly skilled but unelected technocrats began designing policies. In Uganda as well, technocrats such as Emmanuel Tumusiime-Mutebile have played a critical role in developing the reform program.

Technocrats alone, however, cannot ensure reform. Kenya had some of the best, but its reform record is very mixed. Technocrats anticipated all the public sector reform issues in Kenya in the 1990s through their sessional paper series. But without political support from the leadership, they have been unable to accomplish much. The same was true in Zambia in 1986, when President Kaunda replaced his economic team, who had just negotiated an adjustment program with the Bank and Fund, with a group of anti-reformers.

Ideology

It is sometimes argued that the resistance to, and impetus for, reforms are driven not by economic analysis but by ideology. This interpretation is especially tempting in Africa, given the legacy of socialist ideology in the continent. The case studies reveal that reality is more complex. One of the most left-leaning governments in Africa, Ghana, is a star reformer. The left-wing factions in Ghana did oppose aid from the West (and, by extension, devaluations and associated reforms). But when the leftist intellectual Samir Amin was brought in to advise the government in 1982, he told them Ghana had no choice but to deal with the international financial institutions. Kenya may have accepted the label of "African socialism" at independence, but its economic policies followed a more market-oriented and foreign investment–friendly path. Nevertheless, its reform record has been mixed. In 1981, Tanzania was unable to present a credible reform package to the World Bank and IMF (despite encouragement from both institutions) because the Nyerere government believed the problems causing the crisis were external and not internal policy weaknesses. Later, however, when the anti-reform minister of planning, Malima, was put in charge of drafting the government's reform package, he became pro-reform.

Institutions

Perhaps the most important lesson that emerges from the 10 case studies is that the way in which societies organize vested interests, technocrats, and the leadership drives the success of reform. It is a fair generalization to say that successful reformers have consultative processes that result in a broad consensus for reform. On the other hand, it is interesting that in our sample there is no relationship between formal democratic institutions and reform. The two strongest reformers—Rawlings and Museveni—came to power through military coups. Authoritarian governments in Nigeria and the Democratic Republic of Congo, on the other hand, never seriously embraced economic reform. The democratic government that replaced Kaunda in Zambia did not make much progress with reform.

While not formally democratic, the Ugandan reform was broadly consultative at every step of the way. President Museveni established the Presidential National Forum to debate reform issues in 1987. The Ugandan Manufacturers Association sponsored seminars and discussion papers in the 1987–89 period. The Presidential Economic Council had open debates on reform and sponsored a December 1989 conference on trade liberalization that has been described as a turning point in public opinion. In Tanzania, when economists at the University of Dar es Salaam began holding public meetings on economic liberalization, party leaders and policymakers had to start listening to the reformist elements in government. That same year (1984), the government allowed own-funded imports, devalued the currency, and increased agricultural prices by about 30 percent.

By contrast, policymaking in Kenya appears to be restricted to a small circle. While prescient, the sessional papers are not debated in Parliament.

As a result, the reforms are not always "owned" by even the line ministries, and other stakeholders are not consulted. The establishment of the Export Promotion Council in 1992 was a step toward involving the business community in policy decisions. Zambia's reforms were pushed through during the "honeymoon period" following multiparty elections. As Finance Minister Kasonde put it, "Necessary but unpopular decisions had to be quick. I was very interested in using the political status of the MMD government to make economic advancements." By moving quickly before opposition to the reforms could mobilize, the Zambian government may have contributed to the backsliding. Interest groups, none of which were consulted before the reforms, slowed down the pace of implementation. Overall, support for the Zambian reforms outside of a few cabinet ministers has been shallow.

FOREIGN AID FOR AFRICAN REFORMERS

Trends and Directions of Foreign Aid

A striking feature in the case studies is the persistence of aid to individual countries. Aid was disbursed at an even level irrespective of policy reforms undertaken (see the appendix for a definition of aid). Two examples run counter to this average trend. The first is the smooth increase in aid to the successful reform countries (Ghana and Uganda), and the second is the trend in the late 1990s toward greater selectivity in aid allocations. In this section we first review those broad trends and then characterize the aid relationship for the four country groups. We conclude by commenting upon some common findings regarding the roles of nonfinancial aid and donor coordination.

One reason why aid is so persistent is that in many cases it was a foreign policy tool rather than a tool for economic development. This has led to a high degree of inertia in bilateral aid flows over the years. Every single reduction of aid levels, however small, was deemed a sign of distrust of the recipient government rather than a judgment of its economic reform program. Alesina and Dollar (forthcoming) find that aid allocations for many bilateral donors have been driven by strategic variables such as colonial relationships and voting patterns in the United Nations. Exceptions to this pattern are the Nordic countries, Canada, and the Netherlands.

In our sample, the post-socialist reformers received the highest GDP share of aid and the mixed reform countries the largest amounts of aid per capita (tables 1.1 and 1.2). Côte d'Ivoire and Zambia top the list with US$74 and US$112 per capita, respectively, in the mid-1990s. The most successful reformers started off with very low aid levels. Aid to Ghana and Uganda increased as they reformed, but by the late 1990s they were getting half as much aid per capita as the mixed reformers. The

TABLE 1.1 TOTAL EFFECTIVE DEVELOPMENT ASSISTANCE
IN RELATION TO GDP, 1978–97
(percent)

	1978–81	*1982–85*	*1986–89*	*1990–93*	*1994–97*
Successful reformers	1.12	1.54	3.62	3.89	3.56
Ghana	1.30	1.56	3.66	2.95	2.43
Uganda	0.94	1.52	3.58	4.83	4.68
Post-socialist reformers	4.89	4.94	6.00	6.05	5.20
Ethiopia	1.85	3.17	4.32	5.32	3.78
Mali	6.00	5.97	7.65	7.06	7.33
Tanzania	6.81	5.69	6.02	5.79	4.49
Mixed reformers	2.36	2.42	3.47	4.95	8.46
Côte d'Ivoire	0.85	0.65	1.22	2.52	5.61
Kenya	2.22	2.38	2.93	2.98	2.18
Zambia	4.00	4.24	6.26	9.36	17.59
Nonreformers	1.34	1.02	1.50	1.14	1.00
Congo, Dem. Rep. of	2.63	1.98	2.90	2.13	1.88
Nigeria	0.05	0.05	0.09	0.15	0.11

Source: Chang, Fernández-Arias, and Servén 1999.

nonreformers, finally, score very low on these measures with Nigeria receiving on average just US$1–$2 per capita in aid, among the lowest in Africa. (Donors give less aid per capita to populous countries, and that is an important factor explaining the low aid to Nigeria.)

The successful market-based reformers received more multilateral aid while the post-socialist countries have mainly received bilateral aid (see table 1.3 in appendix 1.2). The reform programs in Ghana and Uganda started off with an unusually high share of multilateral aid, around 70 percent. Bilateral aid has increased over the years and now accounts for some 50 percent of the aid. An opposite trend can be noted among the post-socialist countries where multilateral aid is on the rise but on a much smaller scale. The mixed reformers received aid from almost all bilateral and multilateral donors, in equal amounts. There is a close association between the stability of aid flows and the share of multilateral versus bilateral aid. Aid levels are more stable in countries where bilateral donors dominate. Where the multilateral donors have had a larger presence, the flow of aid depends more on the actual policies pursued. This holds as long as the international financial institutions have not committed too many funds?as they then tend to lend in order to get paid back.

The interesting exception to the pattern of aid persistence is the aid to Ghana and Uganda, which has risen in lockstep with improvements in policies—at least until the mid-1990s when aid started to taper off. Starting from very low aid levels and an initial period of technical assistance and policy dialogue, financial support took off as policies developed.

TABLE 1.2 TOTAL EFFECTIVE DEVELOPMENT ASSISTANCE
PER CAPITA, 1980–96
(U.S. dollars)

	1978–81	1982–85	1986–89	1990–93	1994–97
Successful reformers	11.6	13.0	27.9	35.3	28.4
Ghana	13.0	12.2	34.3	35.2	31.4
Uganda	10.4	13.6	22.0	35.4	26.3
Post-socialist reformers	19.5	17.6	26.2	28.4	23.1
Ethiopia	7.9	10.3	16.0	19.9	15.1
Mali	33.1	32.1	46.7	46.0	47.4
Tanzania	37.8	26.9	39.8	39.3	29.6
Mixed reformers	26.7	25.6	32.1	43.7	54.2
Côte d'Ivoire	17.9	11.7	21.6	36.8	74.2
Kenya	23.0	28.4	30.2	34.5	24.5
Zambia	50.1	37.4	54.1	82.0	111.7
Nonreformers	4.7	3.7	4.4	2.8	2.0
Congo, Dem. Rep. of	13.3	9.4	15.0	8.9	4.9
Nigeria	0.9	0.7	1.4	2.1	1.4
Aid per capita in Sub- Saharan Africa	23.7	22.5	30.7	37.3	32.3
All ten countries' share of total aid to Sub- Saharan Africa (%)	30.7	29.5	32.9	31.3	34.4

Source: Chang, Fernandez-Arias, and Servén 1999.

Also, the general persistence of aid may be changing in the 1990s.
With increasing aid fatigue, budget cuts in countries of the Organisation
for Economic Co-operation and Development (OECD), the end of the
Cold War, and the introduction of "governance" conditionality, aid funds
have become more movable. The emerging global consensus in the early
1990s on what forms good development policy has, together with research evidence, also helped induce a greater willingness to reallocate
aid in favor of good policies.

Successful Reformers

Ghana and Uganda are among the most successful reformers in Sub-
Saharan Africa during the past 20 years. There are many noticeable similarities in their reform programs as well as in the donors' support of
them. Starting in 1986–87, with a time lag of some four years, Uganda
followed a path more or less identical to the one Ghana had taken. In
fact, a number of Ugandan delegations visited Accra to learn from the
Ghanaian experience.

FIGURE 1.4 AID AND POLICY: SUCCESSFUL REFORMERS

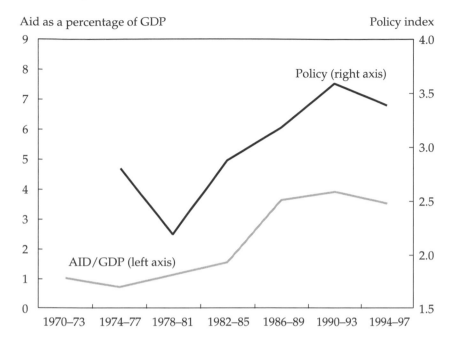

Aid as a percentage of GDP   Policy index

The two countries' new governments—which came to power through military coups—started off with initial programs built on price controls, barter trade, and seeking aid from the Eastern bloc. Neither government was convinced that market-friendly policies were desirable. The policy failures that followed helped trigger the introduction of market-based reform programs. Those programs in turn received good support from the donors, both multilateral and bilateral, after an initial "wait and see" period. Aid volumes picked up in the mid-1980s when the reform programs took off and the level of aid has since then closely matched the policy improvements in lockstep fashion (figure 1.4). However, aid started to taper off in the late 1990s when policies (in Uganda) were still improving. The aid level reached at that stage was far below what other countries in the sample have received (excluding the nonreforming countries).

Lending played the predominant role in the aid program in the 1980s, while grant-based aid has taken over in the 1990s (see figure 1.10 in Appendix 1.2). The shift is closely related to the gradual change from multilateral aid (loans) to bilateral aid (grants).

Policy dialogue with the IMF and the World Bank played a critical role in the early years of reform. Both countries relied in the early stages of reform on small groups of dedicated technocrats and politicians.

Conditional financial aid was later most helpful in pushing the reform agendas and in implementing the reforms. The two countries have a high degree of success in adjustment lending provided by the World Bank, with outcome ratings considerably higher than the average for Africa. Loans to Ghana during the first years of reform were judged as performing better than loans in the 1990s, when the macroeconomic situation deteriorated. The success rate of adjustment lending to Uganda followed an inverse pattern with better outcomes in the 1990s than in the 1980s, when reforms were either rejected or implemented reluctantly.

Post-Socialist Reformers

A common pattern emerges in the reform path among the three post-socialist countries. Tanzania experienced two waves of reform with a period of backsliding in between, and it appears that Ethiopia and Mali are going through a similar cycle. How has aid responded to the different periods of reforms?

Aid volumes did not follow this cyclical pattern but were quite steady over time (figure 1.5). The three countries, particularly Mali and Tanzania, received large amounts of aid irrespective of policy performance.

FIGURE 1.5 AID AND POLICY: POST-SOCIALIST REFORMERS

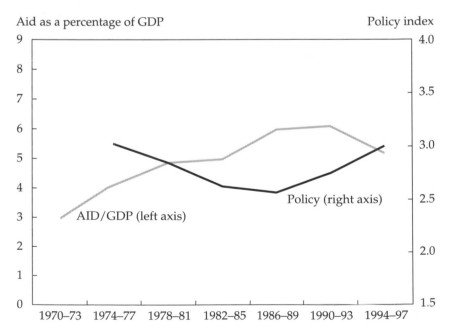

Aid as a percentage of GDP · Policy index

AID/GDP (left axis)

Policy (right axis)

1970–73 1974–77 1978–81 1982–85 1986–89 1990–93 1994–97

When policies deteriorated in the early 1980s, aid in relation to GDP actually increased. The worse the policies got, the more aid they received. From the late 1980s there is a closer correlation between the (improving) policy level and the level of aid in relation to GDP. All three countries have mainly received grant aid (figure 1.11 in Appendix 1.2). Technical assistance (TA) has played an important role, counting for as much as 18 percent of overall aid, the highest share among any of the group of countries studied. Lending accounts for approximately half of the assistance in the 1980s and one-third in the 1990s.

Bilateral aid is two-thirds of total aid but a shift to multilateral aid is gradually taking place. Tanzania has been critically dependent on bilateral donors from the OECD's Development Assistance Committee, and it was mainly bilateral organizations that provided loans to Ethiopia during its socialist period. As a noncolony, Ethiopia did not until recently attract the level of aid it needed and could effectively absorb. The country now receives aid from both multilateral and bilateral donors but many policymakers express a strong preference for greater multilateralization of aid and disbursement in block grants.

Mixed Reformers

Among mixed reformers, aid has moved in inverse relation to policy reforms (figure 1.6). When policies were rather good (1970s and early 1980s) the countries received less assistance than they did when policies started to deteriorate. In the early 1990s, however, both policies and aid levels moved in a synchronized manner. For instance, Côte d'Ivoire received a large inflow of aid after the 1994 devaluation of the CFA franc.

Zambia poses an interesting example of donor behavior. A reformist government came to power in Zambia in 1990. Donors rewarded this locally owned policy process with large increases in aid. Major reforms were initiated, but over time the commitment to reform has waned. Different views among donors have led to counter-cyclical aid flows from bilateral and multilateral donors. The bilateral donors have increasingly tied their aid to political conditionality in the 1990s and have frozen disbursements on occasion. However, the multilateral institutions, stressing economic performance, have not cancelled any loans in the 1990s, while the 1980s was characterized by a stop-go pattern in their relationship with the Zambian government. In the 1980s, in the absence of aid coordination, bilaterals even increased their aid portfolios when Zambia cancelled the agreements with the multilaterals.

Lending has played the key role among aid instruments even though the share has decreased a bit over the years from 70 percent in 1980–81 to 60 percent in 1994–96 (figure 1.12 in Appendix 1.2). The three countries have all been large recipients of adjustment loans. Kenya was in

FIGURE 1.6 AID AND POLICY: MIXED REFORMERS

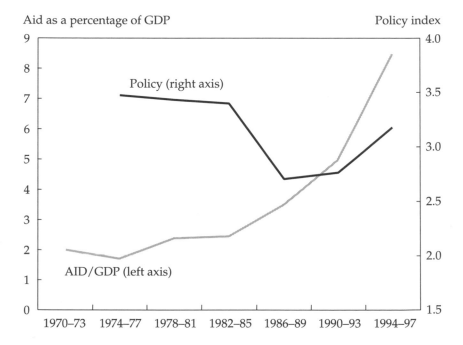

Aid as a percentage of GDP   Policy index

fact the first country in Africa to get structural adjustment funding from the World Bank.

Technical assistance has been very stable, around 16 percent of overall aid. Kenya, with the highest relative share of TA among all countries in the sample, has received over US$3.5 billion of grant TA since 1970.

Nonreformers

Aid flows relative to GDP have been much lower for the Democratic Republic of Congo and Nigeria than for the other countries in the study (figures 1.7 and 1.13 in Appendix 1.2). This is partly due to the two countries' large populations and partly due to their extraordinarily poor economic management over the past 30 years.

Aid flows to Nigeria have also been influenced by that country's oil income, with less aid provided during the oil boom years. Aid, though, has not been nearly as important a component of Nigeria's political economy as it has for other African countries. Debt rescheduling, including the rescheduling of private debt, has been more important.

The Democratic Republic of Congo has made two genuine attempts

FIGURE 1.7 AID AND POLICY: NONREFORMERS

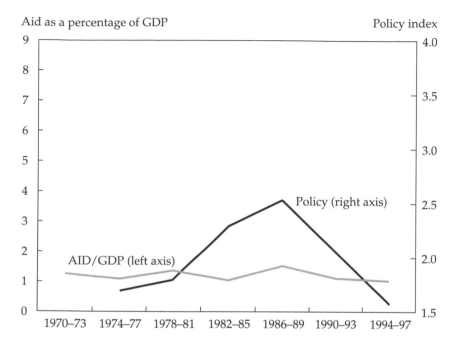

Aid as a percentage of GDP

Policy index

Policy (right axis)

AID/GDP (left axis)

at economic reform since independence, in 1967 and 1983–85. The reform program in the 1980s was supported by an IMF standby arrangement, but little additional support came from the donor community. Improved fiscal management allowed the Democratic Republic of Congo to pay its external debt, resulting in a net transfer of resources to its creditors. This gave strong ammunition to the opponents of fiscal rigor and the reform program was abandoned in late 1985. The donor community, reacting with delay to the net transfer problem, stepped up its assistance and net transfers became positive in 1986 when it was too late.

Both countries have mainly received loans and multilateral aid, with Nigeria having the highest multilateral share of all countries in the sample. Nigeria progressively became more dependent on World Bank loans throughout the period as the country rejected IMF loans and their conditionalities.

Technical Assistance and Nonfinancial Aid

The case studies show that technical assistance works when it responds to genuine demand and is well managed. Unfortunately, a lot of TA has not followed that concept. This is a great loss since TA has accounted for a large share of the aid to the countries studied, some 13 to 18 percent.

TA in general has long had a low rate of success in annual World Bank (Operations Evaluation Department) evaluations. Even though the post-socialist countries have received as much as one-fifth of overall aid as TA, the recipients are surprisingly critical of technical assistance:

> A fundamental problem is that there has been no clear government policy on the role or limits of technical assistance. The government has finally [in 1997] decided to address the problem in a systematic fashion. It has drafted a policy with wide-ranging proposals to restore better use of external resources allocated for technical assistance recruitment and to enhance ownership by the government in the management of these resources. (Tanzania: 300)

But bilateral donors are reluctant to shift responsibilities to the recipient government. They find that Tanzania is doing the right things in terms of policy reforms but that administrative capacity and competence is very low.

Ethiopian policymakers express mixed feelings about some conventional aspects of technical assistance. They support technical assistance where knowledge transfer is programmed, the advice is grounded in Ethiopian conditions, and the country is given some freedom to buy expertise in the free market as needed. However, they tend to look askance especially at those consultants who "parachute in." (Ethiopia: 209)

Demand and management aspects have been the fundamental causes of successful TA. Uganda has made unusually good use of TA. One main reason for this has been that Uganda made greater use of TA when its commitment to reform grew stronger. The success of its reform program can to a large extent be attributed to nonfinancial assistance.

Even if the overall record of TA to Africa is mediocre, policy dialogue and TA have in several cases had a substantial impact on economic policy formulation. The donor community has played a central role in supporting key ministries and agencies and, increasingly, local research institutions. In Kenya, which has received the most technical assistance of all the countries studied,

> TA has undoubtedly influenced the analytical capabilities of Kenyan technocrats and institutions and their approach to analyzing economic issues. . . . Although outsiders may have influenced the priority given to various economic policy issues, it is nevertheless clear that most of the reform agenda implemented over the past 20 years has been developed internally. (Kenya: 475, 506)

Similarly, TA to the Central Bank and the Ministry of Finance in Zambia has provided ammunition to reformist technocrats. But the ownership of the reform process has been weak, and Zambia fits a more general portrait of a country in which policy choices are driven by donor funding rather than domestically formulated policies (Zambia: 587).

Nigeria exposes an interesting aspect of TA. The country has had the basic technocratic capacity to design reforms; TA has never been important in policy design. Any TA would have belied the government's insistence that the reforms were designed by Nigerians for Nigerians. The other nonreforming country, the Democratic Republic of Congo, has, on the other hand, received a fairly large share of its aid as TA (22 percent). In the early 1980s the donor community provided assistance to help run public institutions and the large public enterprise sector. A number of local technicians were trained in various sectors and became the backbone of the economy.

Aid Coordination

In many of the countries studied—all huge recipients of bilateral and multilateral aid—inefficiency in, or lack of, aid coordination over the years is remarkable. The main coordination mechanisms in most countries have been the Consultative Group (CG) meetings and local coordination meetings led by a lead ministry or the World Bank. In addition, the Special Program of Assistance for Africa (SPA) has definitely had a great impact on aid coordination, as have the Paris Club debt reschedulings for countries with heavy debt.

Aid coordination has improved considerably during the 1990s in many countries. The governments are increasingly playing a more active role, in Ghana and Uganda for instance, and the local donor coordination has been intensified. Consultative Group meetings are being held in the field. In Uganda the 1998 CG meeting took place in Kampala for the first time, with broad local participation of the president, cabinet ministers, nongovernmental organizations, civil society, and the media.

Tanzania is at present in the forefront of discussions on a change in the partnership between donors and recipient. The donors and the government agreed on a list of actions in 1997 and there have been significant advances in a number of fields such as establishing government leadership in macroeconomic management. Nevertheless, the donors will probably still have a high degree of control of their own slices of the "joint" programs to make sure that the activities are in accordance with their list of priorities and that the money can be accounted for (Tanzania: 306).

Donor coordination has been an ongoing challenge in Kenya given the multiplicity of multilateral and bilateral donors. Almost all Western donors have been active, putting heavy demands on the time of senior government officials.

HAS AID SUPPORTED REFORM?

Countries that have successfully reformed have had clear political movements leading to these changes, what is often referred to as local "ownership" of reforms. Countries that have made less progress typically have had powerful vested interests blocking change. Either way, economic policies are primarily domestically grown. That was the main message of section 2.

While countries have different political economies and go through different phases of reform, donors tend to do the same things everywhere and at all times—with a few interesting exceptions that we highlighted. But the overall similarity of donor behavior everywhere was one of the strong messages of section 3.

In this section we bring aid and reform together and examine the extent to which aid has influenced policy. The general finding is that different instruments work in different phases of the reform process. If donors use the wrong instrument at the wrong time, it will be either a waste or downright counterproductive.

Since Ghana and Uganda are the countries in the sample that achieved sustained good policy, we can use their experiences to trace out three phases of reform. Figure 1.8 shows the time path of economic policy for

FIGURE 1.8 AID AND POLICY IN REFORMING COUNTRIES

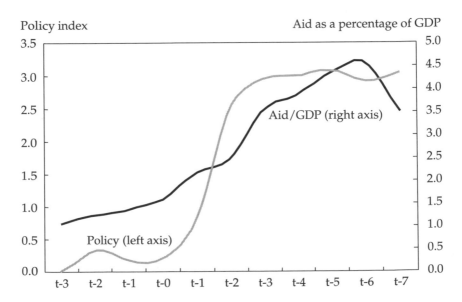

three successful low-income reformers. (Vietnam's experience has interesting parallels with those of Ghana and Uganda, so we have included it in this figure.) Each country has a "pre-reform" phase of very poor economic policy. Then there is a period of rapid reform, in each case associated with a new government. The rapid reform begins in 1983 for Ghana, in 1987 for Uganda, and in 1991 for Vietnam. Within a period of three or four years there is very significant improvement in policy. After that the pace of reform slackens, but in each case the country has put in place policies that are well above average for low-income countries.

All the other countries in our study have had poor policy before reform too. But none has achieved sustained good policy. Where exactly to place countries in this framework can be a matter of some debate. For example, Zambia appeared to be embarking on serious reform with the advent of a new government in 1991, but implementation has fallen short of expectations. Côte d'Ivoire and Ethiopia are arguably in a phase of rapid reform now (that is, since 1994), but it remains to be seen if it will be sustained. Nevertheless, most of the categorizations are quite clear. None of the countries other than Ghana or Uganda progressed beyond a "pre-reform" phase through the end of the 1980s.

It is also useful to ask, what signals the transition from one phase to another? How do we know if a country has started the rapid reform phase? In the case of the successful reformers, the beginning of rapid reform was marked by a new government coming to power. In addition, there are usually some dramatic, "stroke of the pen" reforms that are needed and that signal a real shift to reform. Stabilization, price liberalization, devaluation—these are the classic examples of dramatic changes that signal a new economic regime. As for the shift from the "rapid reform" to the "good policy" phase, this occurs when all of the important macroeconomic reforms have been completed (the above plus fiscal reform and trade liberalization), and then the country moves on to the second-generation reforms. Most of the second-generation reforms require institutional change and reform of the public sector (privatization, civil service reform, judicial reform, and budget reforms to make public expenditures more effective and to increase accountability). In general, these reforms take more time and require more participation than the macroeconomic reforms.

Aid in the Pre-Reform Phase

What is distinctive about the pre-reform phase is that a country has poor policies and no coherent political movement to change the situation. Ghana and Uganda (and Vietnam too) are interesting in that during their pre-reform period they received small amounts of aid from Western donors (shown in figure 1.8), and most of this was in the form of technical assistance. This is not typical of donor behavior. All of the other countries received large amounts of aid in their poor policy periods, including quick-disbursing policy-based loans. (The different treatment for Ghana, Uganda, and Vietnam probably reflects the fact that their governments were politically estranged from the West during their poor policy periods, and for them reform came hand-in-hand with political openings to the West.) What are some of the lessons about aid in the pre-reform period, gleaned from the different case studies?

First, there is general agreement that technical assistance and policy dialogue are often—though not always—useful in this phase. When Ghana was dealing with macroeconomic crisis in the early 1980s, for example, it had well-trained economists to develop policy proposals, and these technocrats found the policy dialogue with the international financial institutions to be helpful in working out plans. A few years later, when Uganda's leaders were looking for new policies, one thing that helped was donor-financed study tours to Ghana. In the successful cases, political leaders learn from other countries and from their own mistakes. Low-key assistance can help with this policy learning, which generally has to take place at a country's own pace. Even in countries that remain in the pre-reform phase for a long time, technical assistance can lay the foundation for policy learning. In Kenya, for example, donors are supporting the Kenyan Institute for Policy Research and Analysis to help develop local capacity for policy analysis and formulation. This kind of capacity building is not going to have a large payoff as long as vested interests block serious reform, but it is an essential foundation if a political movement for change develops.

A second common theme in the case studies is that conditionality does not work in the pre-reform phase in which there is no serious movement for change. Conditional adjustment loans were used in the pre-reform phase in all of the countries. The Zambia study argues forcefully that conditionality was not effective in bringing about change, and that the failure to reform could be tied to powerful vested interests:

> Western donor institutions had insisted since the early 1980s that market mechanisms should replace state controls. The demands and conditions became ever more pronounced and insistent. Zambia's ability to ignore these demands was limited as a result of its financial need and lack of alternative financial sources for securing foreign exchange. . . . In theory, therefore, the leverage of the Western financial institutions and donor governments was high. However, when one looks at the efforts to implement reforms in the 1985–87 period, the lack of influence of the external institutions in the face of unraveling agreements is striking. The implementation of the 1985 structural adjustment program indicated that the international donors were virtually powerless and unable to

interfere after the president changed his economic team in April 1986 from the group who had negotiated the program to some of the strongest critics of a market-based economy. Experiences in Zambia in the 1980s highlight the importance of local ownership of the reform process: The conditionality mechanisms were unable to bring about policy change as these measures were at odds with the economic ideology prevailing at the time, and therefore were not supported by the political leadership. (Zambia: 572)

In Zambia, policy failed to improve—and actually got worse—despite a long series of adjustment loans and a mounting volume of aid (figure 1.9). The Kenya study comes to similar conclusions about the effectiveness of conditionality during a period in which there was no strong commitment to reform:

Did [structural adjustment lending with conditionality] induce the Kenyan government to adopt reforms that it might not otherwise have undertaken? Kenya received huge amounts of aid in return for policy reform agreements—almost US$3 billion over the entire 1970–96 period. How effective was this aid in "buying" reforms? We would argue that at times of severe economic crisis, as in 1980–82 and 1993, the government's need for financial support was

FIGURE 1.9 ZAMBIA: AID AND POLICY

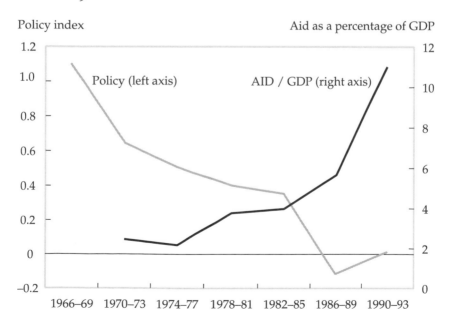

sufficiently desperate that the promise of such support did induce the government to come to agreement relatively quickly on far-reaching reform programs. However, as noted above, these agreements were not always implemented. Sometimes the probability of successful implementation was low from the outset. Other times the lenders or donors may have aligned themselves with well-intentioned technocrats who wished to achieve the results contracted for but lacked the political support to do so. It is our view, therefore, that donor aid can have an influence on the form of agreement reached and on the agreed timetable for implementation, but whether implementation is carried out depends in the end much more on domestic political and economic factors than on donor money. (Kenya: 514)

The impotence of conditionality in the face of powerful vested interests against reforms comes through as well in the case studies of the Democratic Repubic of Congo, Ethiopia, and Nigeria:

The dialogue with technicians and high officials was open and productive. There was a broad consensus on the reform agenda at this level, but, as became increasingly clear, President Mobutu had no intention of making any change in his ways of managing the country. In his view, the reform program was fine as long as it did not impose any limits on his prerogatives. (the Democratic Republic of Congo: 640)
    Consistent with the experiences of many countries, in Ethiopia there appear to be few cases where conditionalities overcame stiff government resistance . . . Aid does not seem to buy good reform when the conditionalities are perceived, rightly or wrongly, to undermine the core of the regime's ideology or its power base. (Ethiopia: 205)
    The Babangida government attempted to address the complex issues that contributed to the impoverishment of Africa's largest country, but failed to implement a coherent program. These failures came about because the logic of austerity and economic reform is anathema to the clientelistic system of Nigerian politics. (Nigeria: 674)

The use of conditional loans in these situations is not merely wasteful; it may actually be harmful. As noted above, Ghana, Uganda, and Vietnam were able to engage in policy learning without a massive aid relationship. Aid and conditionality may actually obstruct this policy learning, as in Zambia:

In aid-dependent countries such as Zambia, donor conditionality undermines genuine policy learning. Once they understand that donors mean to set policy, ministries become passive. Individual officials have negative incentives to disagree with the donors since this will only serve to delay the arrival of the much-needed resources. (Zambia: 587)

A third general point about aid in the poor policy period is that it may have perverse incentive effects. That is, finance may deter reform, and the absence of finance may encourage reform since it removes one easy way out of macroeconomic problems for the government. This argument is particularly applicable to large-scale budget or balance of payments support, which in a bad policy environment may reduce the urgency of reform.

The Côte d'Ivoire, Kenya, the Democratic Republic of Congo, Nigeria, and Tanzania studies all conclude that aid financing in the 1980s actually led to worse economic policies:

The former colonizer [France] paid its ex-colony's debts to save it from default. It can be argued that by so doing, it relieved the pressure for structural adjustments, thereby retarding reform. (Côte d'Ivoire: 379)

Is it possible that a large volume of aid could make it easier for a government to ride out a crisis without undertaking needed reforms? It is probable that the heavy infusion of budget support Kenya received during the 1980s helped the government to finance the budgetary cost of an overstaffed civil service and inefficient public enterprises, thus enabling the government to defer reforms in these areas until the 1990s. (Kenya: 515)

External support . . . was indirectly used to enlarge the capacity of the regime to spend for nondevelopment purposes. The reformers who counted on the help of the international community had great difficulties fighting against the populist sentiments that were stirred up by the regime as a means to better maintain its staying power. (the Democratic Republic of Congo: 644)

Of course, the money provided by donors gave the Babangida government some breathing room. . . . When these inflows combined with the additional oil revenue following the invasion of Kuwait in 1990, it allowed the Babangida government to try to revert to politics as usual. The government did not have enough money to return to the status quo ante but the immediate impetus for adopting the reform program was no longer there. (Nigeria: 674)

Initially aid probably delayed reforms by helping to finance schemes that would have been wholly nonviable without aid backing . . . (Tanzania: 338)

Conversely, several studies note occasions in which the absence of aid finance encouraged reform. In Ghana,

> Five factors help to explain why the PNDC chose to reform . . . First, there was undoubtedly a liquidity crisis. Foreign exchange reserves, trade credit, and medium-term financing had all dried up . . . What gave the government political room to carry out the reform? Not many alternative approaches existed that would generate the financial resources necessary for the economy's recovery. Few Ghanaians needed to be convinced of this fact; for the average citizen who had already suffered more than a decade of economic hardship, it was clear that the old order had failed. (Ghana: 79)

The important point here is that in the absence of large-scale aid, the impact of poor economic policies was clear. The political leaders felt that they had little choice but to undertake serious reform. In Kenya too, reforms such as liberalization of foreign exchange and foreign trade in the early 1990s were introduced when relations between the government and donors were strained and financing was in decline (Kenya: 478).

To summarize conclusions about the pre-reform, poor policy phase: large-scale finance has, if anything, a negative effect, reducing the need to reform; and conditionality has typically failed in the absence of a serious domestic movement for change. Technical assistance and policy dialogue, on the other hand, have helped governments and their civil societies learn about policy from neighbors and from their own experimentation. It is noteworthy that the successful reformers *all had modest aid programs in the pre-reform period.* It should be stressed that the recommendation here is not to withhold all aid from countries with bad policies. Rather, the point is that, in an environment of poor policies, large-scale budget support has sustained those bad policies and has not produced good outcomes.

Aid in the Period of Rapid Reform

The successful reformers have each had a period of three to four years in which very significant policy changes were effected. It is not easy to know in advance when a large reform movement is about to take off, but in most cases the change is brought about by a relatively new government. In the cases of Ghana and Uganda the new governments did not come to power intending to put market-oriented policies into place. But they did come to power intending to improve people's lives and they were open to learning and experimentation. Zambia is an interesting case as well, as a new government came to power in the early 1990s intending to put market-friendly policies into place, yet achieved only limited success.

What can we say about the role of aid during the phase of rapid policy improvement? First, both the Ghana and Uganda studies are quite emphatic that aid finance played an important supporting role. In the case of Ghana, balance of payments support "provided the government with the breathing space it required to contain domestic opposition to market-based reforms. . . . [It] allowed imports that helped fill the shelves of supermarkets and other traders. The filled shelves provided a psychologically-induced breather for the government because . . . people saw this as a sign of better things to come" (Aryeetey and Cox 1997).

Referring back to figure 1.8, it can be seen that in the successful reformers aid flows rose in lockstep with policy improvements. When countries actually reform, finance increases the benefits of those reforms. That is, the growth impact of a particular improvement in policy is enhanced by the flow of aid. There are two reasons for this. Aid increases confidence in the reform program and calls forth greater private investment. Also, it enables the government to provide public services that are complimentary to private investment. By increasing the benefits of reform, aid enhances the likelihood that it will be sustained. As the Ghana study notes,

> Coming back to politics, economic reform proved politically sustainable in the end only because some results emerged quickly . . . (Ghana: 67)

While Ethiopia has not made as much progress with reform, its case nevertheless reveals the importance of aid in consolidating reform once it has started:

> Aid had a minimal impact on growth or poverty in the 1980s since Ethiopia was embroiled in a protracted civil war along with a bold program of building a socialist economy. Market-oriented reforms were initiated in 1990 in response to profound economic and political crises. The reform program initially attracted a sizeable increase in external assistance in support of liberalization, stabilization, and rehabilitation. Subsequent aid helped to deepen reform commitments and supported high growth rates. (Ethiopia: 170)

A second point about the rapid reform phase is that technical assistance and policy dialogue retain their usefulness. "Ownership" of reform means that there is political commitment to change and able technocrats who can work out the details of reform. This layer of technocrats is often rather thin, however, so that the training/policy advice part of aid is quite important. It helps deepen the layer of capable officials and provides useful sounding boards for the technocrats who are working out the details of reform.

When government officials are committed to reform, technical support is often important to actually put reforms into place. A good example of this is the return of nationalized property to private citizens in Uganda, a highly politicized reform but one that was important in establishing the government's commitment to private property rights. While success required support at the political level, it also required foreign technical assistance to bring about a good outcome (Uganda: 128).

Aid is particularly critical in the "rapid reform" phase because of the tendency for backsliding noted in section 2. When Ghana's macroeconomic program deteriorated in the early 1990s, donor support continued because the government had some credibility as a reformer—and Ghana proceeded to undertake major structural reforms. Meanwhile the lack of donor support for debt reduction in the Democratic Republic of Congo's brief reform episode of 1985 may have contributed to that country's rapid reversal.

The third important finding about the rapid reform phase concerns conditionality. If political leaders are committed to reform and technocrats are implementing the changes—with technical advice as needed—one might think that there is no role for conditionality. But both the Ghana and Uganda studies agree that the technocrats actually welcome conditional assistance in this period. This is the one time at which conditional loans tend to be successful and useful. What technocrats are doing with conditional loans in this period is getting clear decisions from political leaders and signaling publicly the seriousness of reform. Thus, in the case of Uganda,

> The conditions helped reform-minded elements in the government push the reform agenda forward with the support of the president. The conditionality was therefore a helpful tool for generating, implementing, and cementing reforms. When the government was in this transition process many reforms were driven by the requirements of conditionality. (Uganda: 136)

In order for conditionality to play this useful role, the key measures that form the conditions for loan disbursement have to be ones that the recipient government truly supports. The Ghana study notes several reasons why conditional loans worked during that country's rapid reform phase:

> The first was the caliber, coherence, and continuity of the Ghanaian team. Its relatively small size, highly qualified staff, and skill at implementing measures allowed some flexible interpretation of conditions. In addition, it appears that the Ghanaian team was usually extremely well prepared. The second reason was the nature of the World Bank and (to a lesser extent) IMF teams. They proved

over time adept at understanding the context in which certain decisions had to be undertaken and gave the Ghanaians some room.
(Ghana: 86)

Thus, to be useful, conditionality must reflect measures that the government wants to carry out, not ones imposed by outside agencies.

A fourth point about the rapid reform phase is more speculative. There
are several pieces of evidence suggesting that the *failure of instruments* in
the pre-reform period limits their utility if a country ever gets serious
about reform. Recall again that rapid reform in Ghana, Uganda, and
Vietnam was not preceded by a period of large-scale Western aid and
failed adjustment loans. Contrast this with Zambia, where a reform government came to power in the early 1990s in an environment of aid dependency and with a long legacy of failed adjustment loans. After years
of failure, it is hard to see how Zambian officials could have used conditional loans in the same manner that Ghana and Uganda did.

Aid in Good Policy Regimes

There are two points to make about the role of aid once good policy has
been achieved—one about volume, the other about composition.

Cross-sectionally, donors tend to discriminate against the poor countries that have put good policy into place. There is also some element of
this in the time-series relationship between aid and policy in Ghana and
Uganda. Aid rose as policy improved, and as noted in the preceding
section, this played a positive role in sustaining reform. However, once
good policy was achieved, aid declined (figure 1.8). There are several
factors at work here. For one thing, policy leveled off, which is almost
inevitable after a period of rapid improvement. Donors like to think that
their money is attached to *policy change,* and in Ghana and Uganda when
policy change slowed down, aid declined. This behavior is not particularly rational given that the level of policies is much higher in these countries than elsewhere in Africa. A second factor may be that donors think
that these countries can now attract private capital flows. However, the
evidence is that poor countries with good policies do not find it easy to
attract private foreign investment. Perceptions of policies and of risk
change slowly. Aid has a high return in Ghana and Uganda as it stimulates growth and poverty reduction. These are exactly the environments
in which high levels of aid flows should be sustained.

A second point about aid in the good policy environments is that donors continue to use conditional assistance, when in fact it has outlived
its usefulness by this point. As noted, conditionality is useful during a
period of rapid reform in which the government is trying to establish its
credibility as a reformer and get macroeconomic policy measures well

entrenched. But there is a cost to using conditionality in this way. To some extent, conditionality disguises the ownership of reforms. And it tends to limit participation in policymaking.

The Uganda study argues that there was strong ownership of reforms by the government, but because of the continued use of conditionality by the donors, many stakeholders in civil society are confused about where reform measures come from. Activists in nongovernmental organizations and private sector representatives interviewed for the case study thought that much of the policy package was imposed from outside (Uganda: 145). If this view is widespread, it reduces the credibility of the reform program. People have a natural and understandable tendency to resent and resist outside pressure. Hence, if the reforms are believed to be primarily externally driven, it is harder for them to take root. A careful reading of the case studies suggests that there is a brief period during which the benefits of conditionality may outweigh the costs; however, once reform measures are well established it is important for the donor community to move away from conditionality so that the local management of reform is clear.

In both Ghana and Uganda, donors have continued to use conditionality well after the end of the rapid reform period. In fact, in Ghana conditionality became more stringent over time, as the overall quality of policies improved:

- Conditions became more numerous. IMF conditions rose from 20 in 1983 to 40–50 in 1988–89. This reflected the Fund's increased involvement in structural issues, some of which the Bank regarded as its turf.
- Conditionality-based lending became more important. The share of policy-based loans rose sharply in Ghana's overall loans from the Bank.
- Conditions became tighter and deeper, and also increasingly specific: for example, personnel cuts in the civil service were explicitly specified (Ghana: 86).

Not only does conditionality disguise the ownership of reform, it also tends to limit the participation in decisionmaking. In Ghana, "the nature of the dialogue and Bank/Fund conditionality favored the use of a small group of technocrats for making decisions" (Ghana: 85). If each major dose of assistance requires detailed agreement on 40 to 50 policy measures, then it is difficult to have wide debate and participation in economic decisionmaking. Finally, conditionality cuts against the grain of the second-generation reforms that even successful reformers find elusive. Public sector reform, for instance, requires a long-term commitment to institution building, something that cannot be achieved by conditionality-based lending. The institution building of the second-generation reforms is also more likely to require wide participation, which as noted is limited by conditionality. Finally, as we stressed in the introduction, with some of the second-generation reforms we simply do not know what is good policy, and the issue for donors is to support genuine policy learning rather than to impose models through conditionality.

CONCLUSIONS

Donors have three basic instruments that they can use to encourage the adoption of good economic policies in developing countries: money, conditionality, and technical assistance/policy dialogue. The 10 case studies in the Aid and Reform in Africa project reveal examples in which each of these has made positive contributions to countries' efforts to improve their policies. However, the striking impression that comes through is that *donors have used these instruments fairly indiscriminately.* That is, donors tend to provide the same types of aid in all cases, when in fact the instruments have different payoffs at different points in the reform process. Using the wrong instrument at the wrong time is at best wasteful, and in some cases may have actually retarded reform. Several of the case studies argue eloquently that aid could have been used more effectively to support reform:

> While the responsibility for the failure of the Democratic Republic of Congo as a state lies squarely with the political elite under President Mobutu, which ruled the country until 1997, it is clear also that the interaction with the international donor community has not been as helpful as it could have been. The major donors were also the major creditors. By financing nonviable projects under commercial credit conditions in the early 1970s, and not providing appropriate debt relief ten years later when the country was in the process of reforming, they contributed to making adjustment difficult to sustain. (the Democratic Republic of Congo: 629)
>
> Successful reform is undergirded by a strong commitment to good governance. This is essential for rebuilding business confidence, including among the growing Ethiopian diaspora. In the final analysis, political reform is a domestic affair. If the government manages to undertake the remaining reforms while building up its capacity for implementation, Ethiopia stands to benefit doubly from an increasingly selective international aid regime and a reinvigorated private sector. Donors can aid this process with a better calibration of aid and reform. (Ethiopia: 212)

In summary, how should donors use their different instruments in order to have the maximum impact on policy change?

Money

If money had no impact on policy at all, the poverty-efficient allocation of aid would be conditioned on the level of poverty and the quality of policies: countries with a better *level* of policy should get more money. This is also the allocation of money that is most likely to have a positive impact on policy. Giving large amounts of money to countries with poor policy has not stimulated reform. In fact, several case studies argue persuasively that money in this situation allows a government to avoid reform. The evidence is that in the poor policy situation, money does not provide broad benefits reflected in growth or poverty reduction. But it has to go somewhere, so presumably it allows the government to finance favored sectors and groups, maintaining support for the inefficient status quo. As the level of policy improves, the evidence is that money begins to have a broad positive effect on the whole economy. That is, it increases the benefits from the better policy environment. In Ghana and Uganda, this effect clearly helped sustain difficult reforms. Thus, money can help improve policies, but the key is to disburse it as actual policy improvement is achieved. In our two successful reform cases, finance increased in lockstep with policy gains.

Conditionality

All of the case studies agree that economic policy is primarily driven by domestic politics, not by outside agents. The key to successful reform is a political movement for change, and donors cannot do very much to generate this:

> What is needed is to develop new ideas about how Nigerian politics should operate, something that the World Bank, the IMF, and the bilateral donors cannot provide. Only the Nigerians can do that. (Nigeria: 675)

However, once reform movements developed in Ghana and Uganda, there was a brief period of rapid reform in which conditionality was welcomed by the government and was useful. It enabled a government that was serious about change to signal and commit to policy measures. To be effective in this way, conditionality must focus on measures that the government believes in and that are truly important. In Ghana and Uganda, the government itself proposed policy conditions to which it should be held.

Using conditionality in other situations has not been productive. In the pre-reform phase in which the government is not committed to reform, conditional loans have generally been a farce in which the government agrees to measures it does not believe in as a way to get funding, fails to carry them out, and then receives the funding from donors anyway. All of the case studies are very negative about this traditional use of conditionality to try to cajole governments to do things that they are really not interested in. These failed adjustment loans have discredited the instrument and made it less useful in the cases in which conditional aid actually could have been helpful. (To the extent that true reformers would like to signal that they are serious about reform, conditional loans are less useful as a signal if they are given indiscriminately to reformers and nonreformers alike.) Conditionality is also less useful once a country has achieved sustained good policy, as in the case of Ghana and Uganda. The ongoing use of conditionality disguises the true ownership of the reform program, takes up valuable government time, and limits participation in the debate and decisionmaking about economic policy. In these cases donors need to find simpler ways of transferring the financial resources that in fact have a high payoff in the good policy environment.

Technical Assistance/Policy Dialogue

Technical assistance or policy dialogue is an instrument that can be useful at any phase of the reform process. If it is well managed, it assists the country in its own policy learning process, that is, learning from other countries and from its own policy experiments. The case studies reveal that TA often is not well managed: it tends to be ineffective if it is supply-driven from the donor side. But in each phase of the reform process there are groups inside and outside of government that are analyzing policy experiences and working out the details of reform, and these groups generally benefit from a dialogue with foreign experts. Where technical assistance has worked well, there has been genuine mutual learning on the part of the local counterpart and the foreign experts.

In sum, foreign aid has often contributed to policy reform, but it could do so more consistently if donors were more selective in the recipients and instruments. With governments that have poor economic policies and no serious interest in reform, donors need to operate on a small scale, providing technical support where there is real demand (perhaps to groups outside of government). In this situation, large-scale finance and conditional loans have not been useful. The development of a reform movement is primarily in domestic hands. If one develops, foreign aid can help consolidate it through financial support and conditionality. Conditionality outlives its usefulness fairly quickly, however, and has the problem that it may disguise domestic ownership of policies and limit participation in decisionmaking. In the low-income countries that have made good progress with policy reform, donors should find simple ways of providing finance without loads of conditionality. Most importantly, rather than reducing support, as they have tended to do in the few countries that have achieved sustained good policy, donors should maintain a high level of finance in these productive environments.

APPENDIX 1.1
DEFINITION OF AID

The term "aid" in this paper is based on a measure called effective development assistance (EDA), recently developed by the World Bank. EDA is defined as the sum of the grants of all development flows disbursed in a given period. It covers grants and the grant equivalent of official loans. In this study we have also included grants tied to technical assistance in this measure. A second concept used is official development finance (ODF), which consists of EDA plus the nongrant component of official loans.

The EDA measure provides a more accurate measure of true aid flows than the standard aid measure known as official development assistance (ODA). ODA consists of financial aid and technical cooperation, where financial aid includes grants and concessional loans having a grant element of at least 25 percent. The measure tends to overestimate aid flows since it includes the full face value of concessional loans.

For further information on the definitions of EDA and ODF see Chang, Fernández-Arias, and Servén (1999).

APPENDIX 1.2
ADDITIONAL DEVELOPMENT FINANCE DATA

TABLE 1.3 RELATIVE SHARES OF TYPES OF AID
(OFFICIAL DEVELOPMENT FINANCE), 1980–96
(percent of total)

Period	Bilateral	Multilateral	Loans	Grants	Technical assistance
	Successful Reformers				
1980–81	48	52	65	21	14
1982–85	28	72	69	20	11
1986–89	37	63	64	26	10
1990–93	46	54	53	34	13
1994–96	48	52	46	38	16
Average	42	58	57	30	13
	Post-Socialist Reformers				
1980–81	74	26	53	32	15
1982–85	77	23	57	29	14
1986–89	68	32	37	45	18
1990–93	57	43	27	53	20
1994–96	56	44	29	49	22
Average	65	35	39	43	18
	Mixed Reformers				
1980–81	49	51	70	13	17
1982–85	48	52	69	16	15
1986–89	55	45	52	30	18
1990–93	55	45	49	33	18
1994–96	45	55	60	28	12
Average	51	49	57	27	16
	Nonreformers				
1980–81	55	45	64	12	24
1982–85	48	52	75	9	16
1986–89	39	61	73	12	15
1990–93	34	66	62	22	16
1994–96	22	78	58	25	17
Average	39	61	68	16	16

Source: OECD.

FIGURE 1.10 TOTAL OFFICIAL DEVELOPMENT FINANCE FLOWS TO SUCCESSFUL REFORMERS, 1980–96

Millions of 1996 constant U.S. dollars

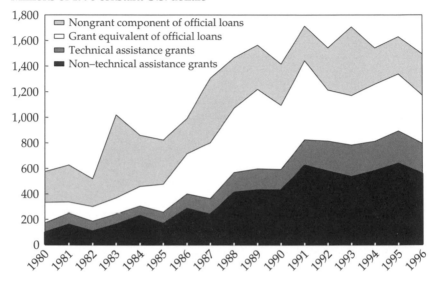

FIGURE 1.11 TOTAL OFFICIAL DEVELOPMENT FINANCE FLOWS TO POST-SOCIALIST REFORMERS, 1980–96

Millions of 1996 constant U.S. dollars

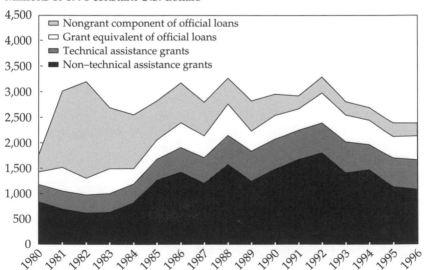

FIGURE 1.12 TOTAL OFFICIAL DEVELOPMENT FINANCE FLOWS
TO MIXED REFORMERS, 1980–96

Millions of 1996 constant U.S. dollars

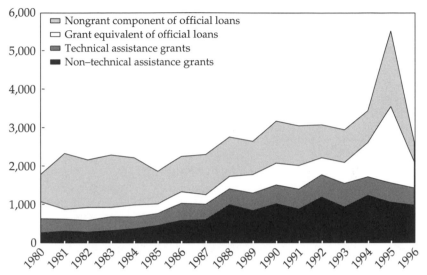

FIGURE 1.13 TOTAL OFFICIAL DEVELOPMENT FINANCE FLOWS
TO NONREFORMERS, 1980–96

Millions of 1996 constant U.S. dollars

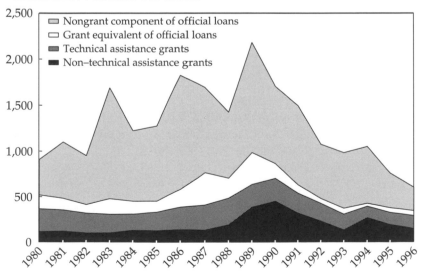

NOTES

1. Grosh (1994) points out that clientelist networks unravel during a general-ized political and economic collapse, whereas during moderate economic dete-rioration, state elites are reluctant to encroach on rent-seeking coalitions.

2. Van de Walle (1994) and Lewis (1996) have described the typical African leader as seeking to placate key constituencies while marginally observing policy conditions to maintain the flow of external resources.

REFERENCES

Alesina, Alberto, and David Dollar. Forthcoming. "Who Gives Aid to Whom and Why?" *Journal of Economic Growth.*

Aryeetey, E., and A. Cox. 1997. "Aid Effectiveness in Ghana." In Jerker Carlsson, Gloria Somolekae, and Nicolas van de Walle, eds., *Foreign Aid in Africa: Learn-ing from Country Experience.* Uppsala, Sweden: Nordic Africa Institute.

Ayittey, George. 1989. "Political Economy of Reform in Africa." *Journal of Eco-nomic Growth* 99 (3): 4–17.

Burnside, Craig, and David Dollar. Forthcoming. "Aid, Policies, and Growth." *American Economic Review.*

Chang, Charles C., Eduardo Fernández-Arias, and Luis Servén. 1999. "Measur-ing Aid Flows: A New Approach." Policy Research Working Paper 2050. World Bank, Development Research Group, Washington, D.C.

Collier, Paul, and David Dollar. 1999. "Aid Allocation and Poverty Reduction." World Bank, Washington, D.C. Processed.

Collier, Paul, and Anke Hoeffler. 2000. "Greed and Grievance in Civil War." Policy Research Working Paper 2355. World Bank, Development Research Group, Washington, D.C.

Dollar, David, and Jakob Svensson. Forthcoming. "What Explains the Success or Failure of Structural Adjustment Programs?" *Economic Journal.*

Fernandez, Raquel, and Dani Rodrik. 1991. Resistance to Reform: The Status Quo Bias in the Presence of Individual-Specific Uncertainty. *American Eco-nomic Review* 81:1146–55, December 1991.

Grosh, Barbara. 1994. "Through the Structural Adjustment Minefield." In Jenni-fer A. Widner, ed., *Economic Change and Political Liberalization in Sub-Saharan Africa.* Baltimore: Johns Hopkins University Press.

Killick, Tony. 1991. "The Development Effectiveness of Aid to Africa." Policy Research Working Paper 646. World Bank, International Economics Depart-ment, Washington, D.C.

Lewis, Peter M. 1996. "Economic Reform and Political Transition in Africa: The Quest for a Politics of Development." *World Politics* 96(49): 99–129.

Mosley, P., J. Harrigan, and J. Toye. 1995. *Aid and Power.* 2d ed. Vol. 1. London: Routledge.

Ranis, Gustav. 1995. "On Fast Disbursing Policy-Based Loans." Department of Economics, Yale University. Processed.

Rodrik, Dani. 1996. "Understanding Economic Policy Reform." *Journal of Economic Literature* 34 (1), March 1996.

Sachs, Jeffrey. 1994. "Life in the Economic Emergency Room." In J. Williamson, ed., *The Political Economy of Policy Reform*. Washington, D.C: Institute for International Economics.

Tumusiime-Mutebile, E. 1995. "Management of the Reform Programme." In P. Langseth, J. Katobor, E. Brett, and J. Munene, eds., *Uganda Landmarks in Rebuilding a Nation*. Kampala: Fountain Publishers.

van de Walle, Nicolas. 1994. "Political Liberation and Economic Policy Reform in Africa." *World Development* 94 (22): 483–500.

van de Walle, Nicolas, and T. Johnston. 1996. *Improving Aid to Africa*. Washington, D.C.: Overseas Development Council.

World Bank. 1982. *Accelerated Development in Sub-Saharan Africa: An Agenda for Action*. Washington, D.C.

———. 1998. *Assessing Aid: What Works, What Doesn't, and Why*. New York: Oxford University Press.

Successful Reformers

Ghana

Yvonne M. Tsikata
Economic and Social Research Foundation
Dar es Salaam, Tanzania

ACRONYMS AND ABBREVIATIONS

AFRC	Armed Forces Revolutionary Council
AGC	Ashanti Goldfields Corporation/Ashanti Goldfields Company Ltd.
BOP	Balance of payments
EDA	Effective development assistance
ERP	Economic Recovery Program
ESAF	Enhanced Structural Adjustment Facility (of the IMF)
GDP	Gross domestic product
GQ	Grant equivalent of a loan
IMF	International Monetary Fund
INCC	Interim National Coordinating Committee
JFM	June Fourth Movement
NATCAP	National Technical Cooperation and Assessment Program
NDC	National Democratic Congress
NDM	New Democratic Movement
NERC	National Economic Review Committee
NPP	New Patriotic Party
NRC	National Redemption Council
NUGS	National Union of Ghana Students
PAMSCAD	Program of Actions to Mitigate the Social Costs of Adjustment
PDC	People's Defence Committee
PNDC	Provisional National Defence Council
PNP	People's National Party
SAP	Structural Adjustment Program
SMC	Supreme Military Council
SOE	State-owned enterprise
SPA	Special Program of Assistance (for Sub-Saharan Africa)
TA	Technical assistance
TUC	Trades Union Congress
VAT	Value added tax
WDC	Workers' Defence Committee

A significant body of work in recent years has focused on the links between foreign aid and the economic performance of countries.[1] Researchers have explored the roles that different types of aid may play in reform—financial versus nonfinancial aid, policy-based versus unconditional aid. They have also examined ways to maximize aid effectiveness and the role of donors in achieving that goal. One troubling conclusion is that "recent cross-country evidence has shown that foreign aid has a strong, positive effect on a country's economic performance if the country has undertaken certain policy and structural reforms. However, the evidence shows that aid in general has not been going to countries that have undertaken these reforms. Donors give less assistance to countries with good policies than to ones with poor or mediocre policies" (Holmgren 1998).

Ghana's experience with foreign aid supports this conclusion. During the 1980s, when it undertook far-reaching economic reforms, Ghana was one of the most successful adjusters. Yet, it received relatively small amounts of aid compared to other African countries. In 1996 it received 2 percent of purchasing power parity GDP in aid, compared to 7 to 8 percent for Mali or Zambia and 4 to 5 percent for Côte d'Ivoire and Tanzania. An important point is that during the 1980s, the volume of aid largely tracked the policy level—it was small when policies were bad, and increased when policies improved. In the 1990s, though, aid to Ghana has declined, while policy slippages—in the larger context—have been modest. Ghana is thus a particularly interesting case for understanding *why* countries choose to reform, and under what circumstances aid is associated with better economic performance.

From a state of economic collapse, Ghana's economy rebounded with sustained economic growth during the first decade of reform. This stellar performance was accompanied by an exponential increase in aid inflows from both bilateral and multilateral sources. The reform program was characterized by a high degree of ownership by top Ghanaian policymakers and the leadership, and was implemented by a high-caliber group of technocrats. The impetus for reform appears to have been both the economic crisis in which the country found itself and an evolution in the thinking of policymakers as they strived for political survival. Aid, especially of the financial kind, was important in sustaining reform. Derailment of economic reform in the 1990s coincided with increased democratization and greater demands on institutional capacity. While economic reforms have resumed, the implementation of structural reforms appears to have become more difficult.

This paper examines the underlying reasons that Ghana chose to reform and the role external assistance may have played in that decision. It analyzes economic policy, institutional and political developments, the main constituencies for reform, and other internal processes that

47

shaped the reforms. It also evaluates the role of aid and donors in initiating, catalyzing, and sustaining reforms. The analysis is based on interviews carried out in Accra in March 1999, as well as on the available literature.

Section 2 describes the different types of aid that Ghana receives and traces the evolution of aid flows. Section 3 places economic policy in Ghana in historical perspective and provides a brief overview of the reforms that took place during the 1980s. Section 4 analyzes the political-institutional framework within which Ghana pursued economic reforms, and the reforms are analyzed in detail in section 5. Section 6 assesses the links between aid and reform and presents conclusions.

AID: COMPOSITION AND TRENDS

This study uses the concept of effective development assistance (EDA) presented in Chang, Fernández-Arias, and Servén (1999). EDA is an aggregate measure of aid flows that combines total grants and the grant equivalents of all official loans. It is computed on a loan-by-loan basis to reflect the financial cost the creditor incurs in making loans on concessional terms. More precisely, EDA is defined as the sum of grant equivalents and grants, excluding technical assistance and any bilateral debt forgiveness. This adjusted measure uses the same conventional grant data but aggregates grant equivalents of loans (GQ) rather than the full face value of all loans deemed concessional. The grant equivalent of a loan is defined as the difference between the present values of the loan's disbursements and stream of expected debt service payments, or the resources that borrowers receive in excess of their interest and repayment obligations. Conceptually, for each loan, this amount is equal to the net loss to the lender—equivalent to a grant. The computation of grant equivalents involves discounting two cash flow streams for each loan's disbursements and interest/amortization payments. It uses discount rates that reflect both the term structure of each loan and the market conditions specific to the loan's currency of issue at the time of valuation. Finally, the paper defines a broader concept of aid, total aid (TOTAID), as EDA plus technical assistance.

Patterns and Trends in Aid

The overall trend in aid to Ghana, as measured by effective development assistance, reflects the country's economic and political history. In that sense, aid flows to Ghana may be said to have been endogenous. Aid flows remained at a low level in the 1970s, a period characterized by chronic domestic economic mismanagement. A default on foreign loans

FIGURE 2.1   TRENDS IN AID TO GHANA, 1970–96

Millions of U.S. dollars

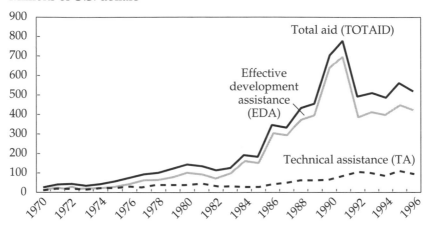

Source: World Bank.

by the military government in 1972 further discouraged foreign assistance.[2]

With the emergence of a democratically elected government in September 1979, aid flows rose for two consecutive years. This trend reversed after the 1981 coup d'etat by the armed forces. Starting in 1985, however, a clear and sustained increase in aid flows occurred as donors perceived greater commitment by government to better economic management and economic reform. Indeed, between 1985 and 1996 total aid flows to Ghana tripled, from US$150.7 million to US$450.8 million in 1995 (see figure 2.1 and table 2.1). However, during the 1980s Ghana was still receiving less aid than most other African countries. The especially rapid increase between 1990 and 1991 was linked to upcoming multiparty democratic elections and was driven primarily by increased grants to support various institution-building activities.

Following the elections, total aid fell, but still remained higher than pre-election levels. The drop was due to fiscal "slippage" in the reform program. This was linked to an 80 percent increase in wages to civil servants, among other factors.[3] The immediate consequence was a suspension of World Bank disbursements between November 1992 and the middle of 1993. This episode was short-lived, and by the end of 1993 both the World Bank and the International Monetary Fund (IMF) were disbursing funds, programs were back on track, and flows resumed to pre-interruption levels. Additional fiscal slippage in 1996, however, led

TABLE 2.1 GHANA: POLICY-BASED LOANS FROM MULTILATERAL
INSTITUTIONS, 1983–96

| | | *IMF* | |
Loan type	Year	*Amount (millions of special drawing rights)*
Standby	1983–84	238.50
Standby	1984–86	180.00
Standby	1986–87	81.80
Extended Fund Facility	1987–90	245.40
Structural Adjustment Facility	1987–90	129.86
Enhanced Structural Adjustment Facility	1988–91	368.10
Enhanced Consultation	1992–95	0.00
Enhanced Structural Adjustment Facility	1995–99	164.40
Total		1,408.10

| | | *World Bank* | |
Loan type	Year	*Amount (millions of U.S. dollars)*
Reconstruction Import I	1983	40.00
Export Rehabilitation I	1984	17.10
Export Rehabilitation II	1984	40.12
Export Rehabilitation III (TA)	1984	17.10
Reconstruction Import II	1985	60.00
Health and Education	1986	15.00
Industrial Sector I	1986	24.95
Industrial Sector II	1986	28.50
Structural Adjustment	1987	80.9
Education Sector	1987	34.5
Structural Adjustment	1987	14.66
Agricultural Services	1987	17.02
Structural Adjustment	1987	34.00
Structural Adjustment Institutional Support	1988	10.80
PAMSCAD	1988	10.60
Financial Sector	1988	100.00
Public Enterprise Assistance	1988	10.50
Cocoa Rehabilitation	1988	40.00
Education Sector Adjustment II	1990	50.00
Structural Adjustment III	1991	13.0
Financial Sector Adjustment II	1991	100.00
Agriculture Sector Adjustment Credit	1992	80.00
Private Sector Development	1994	13.00

Sources: Armstrong 1996; World Bank 1998b.

FIGURE 2.2 GHANA: PERCENTAGE OF EDA LOANS BY CREDITOR,
1970–96

Percent

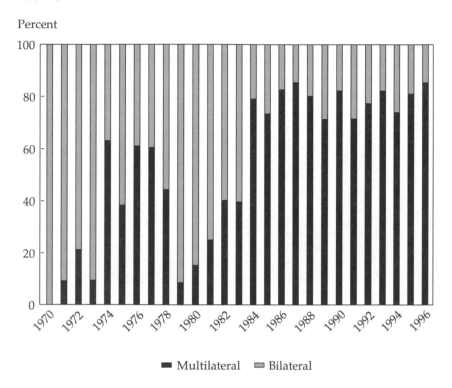

■ Multilateral   ▨ Bilateral

Source: World Bank.

to a temporary derailment of the IMF-supported program under the Enhanced Structural Adjustment Facility.

Multilateral aid has risen dramatically as a share of effective development assistance to Ghana since the late 1970s, when it accounted for less than 10 percent (see figure 2.2). The most dramatic increase occurred in the mid-1980s as the World Bank and IMF supported Ghana's economic reform efforts with a series of adjustment loans and facilities. Between 1983 and 1984 the multilateral share of total aid doubled, to 79.1 percent. While this share has fluctuated since then, it has never fallen below 71 percent; in 1996 it was 85 percent. The increase in multilateral aid relative to bilateral reflects smaller aid budgets for the bilateral donors as well as competing demands from Eastern Europe.

Aid given to different sectors has evolved over time, reflecting both the donors' interests and changes in government priorities. In the first

TABLE 2.2 PHASING AND SEQUENCING OF REFORM POLICIES
IN GHANA, 1983–96

Area of reform	Stabilization (1983–86)	Adjustment (1986–91)	Oscillating reform (1992–96)
Pricing reforms	■ Currency devaluation ■ Removal of price controls ■ Wage restraint ■ Rationalization or deregulation of energy and utility (infrastructure) prices	■ Market-based foreign exchange auction ■ Interest rate liberalization	■ Licensing of foreign exchange bureaus
Fiscal policy	■ Tax reform ■ Consumer subsidies ■ Producer subsidies	■ Medium-term expenditure planning	■ Medium-term expenditure framework
Structural policies	■ Tariff regime simplified and made more uniform ■ Reduction of negative list ■ Removal of import controls	■ Financial sector reforms ■ Investment promotion ■ Divestiture of SOEs	■ Cocoa price to farmers raised ■ All cocoa subsidies for production removed ■ AGC floated ■ Additional SOEs sold/liquidated
Institutional reforms		■ Management of state enterprises ■ Civil service reform ■ Capacity building in core ministries ■ Planning process ■ Statistical and information system improvement	■ Creation of multisector regulatory agency ■ Coordination of donor support for public sector management

Sources: Armstrong 1996; various World Bank and government of Ghana documents.

two years of the Economic Recovery Program, aid served mainly to finance imports (see table 2.2). For the rest of the decade, however, aid
was targeted at balance of payments (BOP) support and the transport
sector, the latter reflecting the tremendous rehabilitation needs. Between
1986 and 1989, balance of payments support averaged just over 50 percent of total aid. During the 1990s, BOP support continued to be important but aid increasingly went to community and social services; between
1993 and 1996 this sector averaged 37.1 percent of total aid. Both agriculture and the transport sector (again) were important recipients of aid
in the late 1990s as well.

Technical assistance (TA) to Ghana declined during the first years of
the reform program (see figure 2.3). This probably reflected the fact that
donor support initially focused on essential BOP support for imports
and reconstruction. Starting in 1986, TA rose steadily, though it remained
a stable or declining share of overall aid until 1990. In the 1990s TA rose
considerably, both in dollar terms and as a share of overall aid, accounting for about one-fifth of the total. This trend can be linked to a growing
realization that the efficiency with which aid is used and the viability of
aid-funded projects depend on strengthened capacity in key institutions.

FIGURE 2.3 COMPOSITION OF TOTAL AID TO GHANA, 1970–96

Percent of total aid

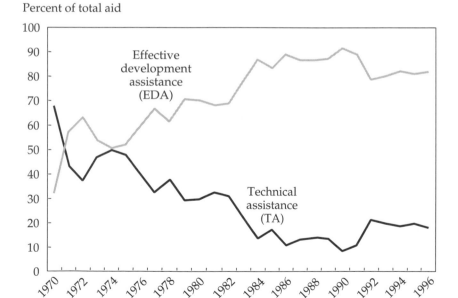

Source: World Bank.

Multilateral Institutions

The World Bank and the IMF have been leaders in providing external support for Ghana's reform efforts. Due to Ghana's perceived commitment to reform and its good results early on, financial support from the Bank and Fund steadily increased. The two institutions collaborated significantly, especially in the early 1980s. The World Bank resumed Consultative Group (CG) donor meetings for Ghana in 1983, and has convened them annually since then to help mobilize large volumes of external assistance for the country. In addition to the CG meetings, the Bank organized a social sector donors' meeting in Vienna in 1986. A meeting of donors to PAMSCAD—the Program of Actions to Mitigate the Social Costs of Adjustment—was held in Geneva in 1988. The biannual meetings of the Special Program of Assistance for Africa (SPA) are used to mobilize aid and coordinate activities. The Bank also took the lead until recently in fostering communication and coordination among the donors. Increasingly, however, the government is playing this role.

Earlier assessment of the World Bank's role in the 1996 Country Assistance Review, as well as recent structured interviews with donor agencies in Accra, indicate that overall the Bank has been successful in its coordination efforts. Nonetheless, the plethora of donor projects and interests means that even stronger government aid coordination efforts are required.

World Bank lending initially focused on rehabilitating Ghana's deteriorated infrastructure, as well as on BOP support. Adjustment lending emerged in response to the need for deeper structural reforms and spanned a number of sectors. Between 1983 and 1994 the Bank committed US$2.4 billion, of which US$1 billion, or about 40 percent, consisted of adjustment lending (Armstrong 1996: 36). If sectoral adjustment lending is included, the adjustment-lending share increases to 42 percent. Table 2.1 gives the list of policy-based loans by the World Bank and the IMF to Ghana since 1983.

These adjustment loans have had a mixed record. In general, however, and certainly during the first years of reform, internal World Bank reviews found the adjustment loans to be performing better than the rest of the portfolio. Agreed policy actions were almost all taken, and with little delay. Agreed studies were carried out, albeit with more delay. The reasons for the success of the early adjustment credits seem to be high commitment on all sides and the administratively simple steps required. The Ghana country assistance review showed that up to 1994, approximately 80 percent of policy-based loans received a satisfactory rating. This was higher than the Bank-wide average of 73 percent, and considerably higher than the 59 percent reported for the Africa region.

Bilateral Aid

Bilateral aid is given for political, strategic, humanitarian, or commercial reasons. It may be intended to meet foreign policy objectives, maintain a historical (usually previously colonial) relationship, or create commercial opportunities. The motivation tends to differ across donor countries, and it is often reflected in the sectors where donors are active and the form in which they choose to give aid.

During the 1970s the most important donors in Ghana were the United Kingdom, the United States, and Canada. Some changes have occurred since then in the ranking of bilateral donors by importance.

Since the early 1980s, the United States has fallen to second place, and Japan has been the largest donor for about a decade. Canada, Denmark, France, Germany, the Netherlands, Spain, and the United Kingdom and also rank high by volume of aid. The rationale for Japanese aid is based on Ghana's importance in the region, its good economic record, and its progress with democratization. In terms of sectors, the Japanese have been most active in infrastructure (fishing harbors, highways, bridges, rural water supply, and electrification) and food aid. One implication of this rise in Japan's importance is that since Japan is not involved with policy-based lending, the Ghanaian government has access to a large volume of nonconditional lending.

The United States had a low-level program between 1982 and 1992, reflecting political tensions between Washington and Accra.[4] With increased democratization in Ghana, its good economic record, and the end of the Cold War, the United States has again become an important bilateral donor. The new U.S. aid paradigm places emphasis on containing and reducing subregional conflicts. U.S. aid goes increasingly to countries in conflict, and tends to taper off as countries do better. The United States is also more interested in the comprehensive framework for reform than previously. Washington has always supported the private sector, but now also examines other indicators of competitiveness such as the exchange rate and inflation. Finally, U.S. agencies bring actors together—Ghanaians with Ghanaians, and Ghanaians with international investors. For example, in October 1997 the U.S. Agency for International Development organized a well-attended conference in North Carolina on investing in Ghana.

Several bilateral donors have provided co-financing for adjustment programs. While bilateral donors often tie their support to either World

Bank or IMF conditions, several of them also negotiate their own bench-marks with the government (for example, Canada).

Donor Coordination

As indicated above, there has historically been a close relationship be-tween the World Bank and other donors in Ghana, with the Bank play-ing a leadership role. After 1986, the Bank's adjustment operations typically attracted substantial co-financing from other donors. In addi-tion to the CG and SPA meetings, the World Bank currently leads the Head of Agencies Meeting in Accra. There are donor sectoral groups and donor lunches, to which ministers and other government officials are invited. Finally, the Bank helps to coordinate the sector investment programs in roads, education, and health. The quality of donor coordi-nation varies by sector. In some, individual interests mean there is still much confusion.

Particularly close collaboration is now evident within the United Nations system in both program planning and operations implementa-tion. The World Bank and U.N. agencies have completed a joint "com-mon country assessment" that provides the overarching framework for the collaboration.

Increasingly, however, the government is taking the lead in setting the agenda for aid/donor coordination meetings on a regular basis. The International Economic Relations Division in the Ministry of Finance is responsible for managing the country's external aid. The Bank of Ghana and the controller and accountant general's office are also important in monitoring aid flows. Problems with disbursement information have ameliorated over the years, but they remain an issue.

Several donors forgave debt or converted debts to grants in the late 1980s and early 1990s. The impact of this debt relief is estimated to have averaged US$30 million from 1990 to 1994.

ECONOMIC REFORM IN PERSPECTIVE

The uninterrupted rule of Jerry Rawlings from the end of 1981 to the present would seem to provide a neat period for analysis. However, one must delve into the late 1960s and the 1970s to understand the economic quandary in which Ghana found itself by 1981 and the nature of the alliances that emerged following the 1981 coup d'etat. This provides background for analysis of the economic policies the government fol-lowed during 1982–96.

Antecedents to the 1981 Macroeconomic Crisis

State-Led Development in the First Republic, 1957–66

At independence in 1957, Ghana was one of the brightest stars in Africa. It enjoyed one of the highest per capita incomes on the continent and was known for its relatively large and well-educated middle class. Economic growth was respectable, averaging 4 percent during the 1960s. This growth was heavily driven by Ghana's most important export, cocoa, which accounted for about 70 percent of foreign exchange earnings. The country was the world's largest producer of cocoa, averaging about a third of world supply in the late 1950s (Killick 1978).

Heavy government intervention in the economy after independence, however, adversely affected economic health. The role of the public sector was greatly enlarged on both the productive and distributive sides. Increasingly Prime Minister Nkrumah carried out more *dirigiste* policies, and in 1961 he officially introduced socialist state-led planning. Deteriorating terms of trade compounded the impact of these policies. Between 1959 and 1965, the world market price of cocoa fell substantially; in fact the 1965 price was only 40 percent of the 1958 level. For all these reasons, large fiscal deficits emerged, the balance of payments deteriorated significantly, and the economy took a nosedive.

Political Turmoil and Short-Lived Reforms, 1966–72

Following a military coup d'etat in February 1966, a new economic team was put in place and attempts were made to reform the economy (see appendix 2.1 for a chronology of events). The National Liberation Council (NLC) reopened negotiations with the IMF, reaching agreement on a standby arrangement in March 1966. The currency was devalued by 43 percent in July 1967, public expenditure was reduced, and the activities of public enterprises were streamlined or eliminated. To address balance of payments difficulties, import controls were tightened and foreign debt payments were rescheduled (Dordunoo and Nyanteng 1997).

Dr. Kofi Busia, a former academic who headed the new civilian government elected in 1969 (the Second Republic), continued these economic reforms. Improving terms of trade enabled the government to reduce significantly the number of goods on the negative list for imports. With a fall in the world price of cocoa in 1971, however, rapid import liberalization was no longer affordable. Both the fiscal and capital accounts deteriorated. In late 1971, the cedi was devalued by 44 percent in an attempt to improve the balance of payments position. Whether this would have achieved that objective will never be known, because less than a month after the devaluation, on January 13, 1972, a military coup d'etat led by Colonel Ignatius Kutu Acheampong overthrew the Busia regime.

Economic Chaos, 1972–79

Under Acheampong and his National Redemption Council (NRC)—later the Supreme Military Council (SMC)—the misguided policies of the First Republic were reintroduced and, indeed, intensified. The NRC revalued the currency by 26 percent, completely at odds with the indications from the parallel market. They imposed stringent import controls, introduced additional price controls, and unilaterally suspended foreign debt servicing.

While favorable terms of trade initially resulted in good economic performance, by 1974 economic decline and decay had begun to set in. Consumer price inflation skyrocketed from 9.6 percent in 1972 to 77.2 percent by 1977. As the exchange rate remained fixed, the cedi was increasingly overvalued, discouraging exports. Government expenditures rose as the state became more heavily involved in production and regulation. These expenditures were financed by complex and high rates of taxation on imports, goods and services, and exports. Ghana experienced continued stagflation in the second half of the 1970s.

More pernicious, perhaps, was the widespread corruption and moral decline that emerged during the rest of the decade. The roots of the corruption lay in the system of import licenses and the high rates of taxation on goods and services. High taxes encouraged rent-seeking behavior (Jebuni, Oduro, and Tutu 1994), while the issuance of chits (associated with the release of goods from state-owned factories) and import licenses became a widespread form of state patronage. During the 1970s, the phrase *kalabule* entered the Ghanaian lexicon.[5] It referred to widespread corruption or a licensed beat-the-system approach to survival (Chazan 1983: 194–97).

The regime had an especially damaging impact on the country's institutions. To begin with, corruption had weakened most state institutions. Civil service employees had to engage in pervasive moonlighting because of inadequate pay. Educated Ghanaians sought better-paying jobs elsewhere in West Africa, as well as in North America and Europe. This brain drain further weakened the universities and other institutions. The diaspora of Ghanaian academics and professionals and the weakening of institutions were to have serious consequences when economic reforms were finally initiated.

As pressure rose from various groups (Association of Professional Bodies, People's Movement for Freedom and Justice, Front for the Prevention of Dictatorship), Acheampong attempted unsuccessfully to form a coalition government of civilians, the military, and the police known as UNIGOV. Under increasing pressures from junior army officers well as civil society, Acheampong's colleagues in the SMC forced him to resign on July 5, 1978.

Lieutenant-General Fred Akuffo took over as head of the revamped Supreme Military Council (SMC II). While some senior officers were dismissed, SMC II prosecuted no one and the UNIGOV concept was still presented as the only model for a transition to "civilian" government. On the economic front, SMC II held preliminary discussions with the IMF but was unable to conclude negotiations. Following widespread strikes in almost every sector of the economy, however, Akuffo finally announced the "unbanning" of political parties on January 1, 1979. Old political groupings and alliances were resuscitated. The People's National Party took over the Convention People's Party/Nkrumahist mantle while the Popular Front Party was the new version of Busia's Progress Party. Assorted smaller parties also entered the fray. General and presidential elections were set for June 18, and Ghana seemed on a smooth path to democratic rule again.

The lower ranks of the armed forces were apparently unhappy with the failure to prosecute SMC officers, even after evidence of corruption. On May 15 Flight Lieutenant Jerry Rawlings and a small group of soldiers conducted what would later be termed a "mutiny or uprising" against the officers. They were unsuccessful and were jailed. Rawlings and the others were subjected to a public trial during which it appears they gained more support from the army rank and file. On June 4, a group of soldiers sprung Rawlings from prison and the "coup" was launched. The new Armed Forces Revolutionary Council (AFRC) indicated that the elections would still go on and stated their intention to hand over power to the elected civilian government in September 1979 as planned. In the meantime, the next three months would be used to "clean house."

On the economic front, the AFRC reimposed price controls on consumables, raised the cocoa price paid to farmers, evacuated some of the rotting cocoa from rural areas with the assistance of students, and collected large amounts of outstanding tax payments during this period. While some of these measures were successful in the short run, many would prove unsustainable (for example, the price controls).

The Limann Era (Third Republic), 1979–81

The new civilian administration of the People's National Party (PNP) led by Dr. Hilla Limann inherited a difficult economic situation. The massive economic decline required tough decisions. It was perhaps not surprising that the new civilian government, having been out of power for several years, seemed to take a long time to make these decisions.

Shillington (1992) reports that some ministers at the time also indicated that they found it difficult to work with a "civil service not used to working within the confines of a strict constitution." In general, the perception was that the administration did not have an economic vision to pull the country out of the malaise. This was illustrated vividly when its budget to Parliament in July 1981 was defeated—a first in independent Ghana's short history.

The situation was also tricky on the political side. Despite the new president's professional credentials, the fact remained that he was a relatively new face in Ghanaian politics.[6] According to Shillington, although the fact that Dr. Limann was not affiliated with any particular political base was a political advantage in the run-up to the election, it probably became a liability once he was in power. In particular, Limann was beholden to the old party hands who had worked hard to ensure his election.[7] By the end of the year, the impression was that the government had come to a "virtual standstill because of the in-fighting" within the PNP.[8]

Increasing public dissatisfaction aggravated the economic and political difficulties.[9] Union strikes increased in all sectors and the incidence of armed robbery (until then uncommon) rose. Left-wing groups such as the June Fourth Movement and the New Democratic Movement became focal points for opposition to the regime.

Under these circumstances, it was perhaps not surprising that the coup d'etat of December 31, 1981 took place. Rumors had been circulating for several weeks in military circles (Shillington 1992: 79). Nonetheless, the immediate rationale for the coup was not purely economic but encompassed moral and populist reasons as well. This was particularly evident in the statements of Flight Lieutenant Jerry Rawlings and members of the new Provisional National Defence Council (PNDC) at the time.

Economic Policy

Dr. Limann and his government, then, came into power under somewhat inauspicious circumstances. In addition, as outlined above, the general economic situation was desperate and financial liquidity precarious. Lax fiscal and monetary control over almost a decade had resulted in hyperinflation. Inflation worsened over the next two years, reaching 77 percent by 1981. Production had contracted in all sectors of the economy. Cocoa exports, which were Ghana's leading foreign exchange earner, had declined, in part because of the absence of basic transport infrastructure to move the harvest to the ports. The shortage of foreign exchange meant that critical spare parts and inputs were in short supply, adversely affecting the performance of the industrial sector. Not surprisingly, both social and physical infrastructure had deteriorated severely.

Following the coup, the PNDC was quick to recognize the seriousness of the situation. It was less quick to act, however. This reflected the internal tug-of-war at the time between various supporters of the regime over the direction of economic policy (discussed farther on). When the struggle was over, a far-reaching program of economic stabilization and reform was introduced. For the rest of the 1980s, Ghana continued to reform its economy and indeed became a leading example of a successfully adjusting country. During the 1990s this momentum slowed somewhat.

Stabilization and Reform, 1983–91

In 1983 the PNDC introduced an Economic Recovery Program (ERP) to stabilize and liberalize the economy. The ERP and its follow-up, the Structural Adjustment Program (SAP), received substantial assistance from the international financial institutions and donors. Rehabilitation of the country's deteriorated ports, roads, and railway was given priority early in the program. Input and produce marketing of most crops was liberalized over the reform period. In general, price controls on goods and ceilings on interest rates were removed. In the decade following the introduction of the ERP, real GDP growth was impressive, averaging 5 percent annually. Real income grew by 2 percent per capita during the decade. Inflation remained high and variable, however, discouraging private investment.

Oscillating Reform, 1992–96

The mostly successful adjustment was partially derailed in 1992, in part because of an election-related wage increase. With loss of fiscal control came macroeconomic instability, reflected, for example, in higher inflation. Much of the 1990s were spent trying to regain sustained fiscal balance. Not surprisingly, the decade was marked by increased difficulties between the government and the Bretton Woods institutions as policy slippage occurred. On the positive side, accelerated government efforts to increase investment paid off in the form of higher investment rates and greater foreign investment.

INSTITUTIONAL FRAMEWORK

The institutional features of Ghana, as well as political developments during the period under review, influenced the economic reform process. To understand how, it is necessary to examine aspects of the underlying political culture, the political economy of reform, and the role of democratization and various interest groups.

Political Culture

From the time of Ghana's independence until the 1981 coup d'etat, the state (and by extension the politicians who ruled the state) was viewed as a provider. This concept, which existed under Nkrumah, was linked to the idea of the head of state as a chief who must take care of his subjects—in essence, a "provider-in-chief." There was a general expectation that the state would provide jobs directly, provide subsidies for enterprises, or even provide free social services.[10] Moreover, at a personal level there was an expectation that members of a family who were well off would provide for others less fortunate. Politicians were no exception to this rule.

During the Acheampong era, this concept evolved into a form of state patronage in which import licenses, chits, and even cars were the give-aways.[11] The beneficiaries were executives of state-owned enterprises (SOEs) and their families and friends, but the largesse was not restricted to them. Even employees of SOEs benefited because in lieu of adequate pay, the government gave them goods that they were expected to sell on the black market.

During the 1980s this system was overturned. The December 31 coup was clearly targeted at those who had been benefiting from *kalabule*. Rawlings felt very strongly that this was a moral issue, and from his speeches, it is clear that he felt these *kalabule* "entrepreneurs" were against the people. The populism of the PNDC made it clear where they stood: with the people.

How did these developments affect economic reform and decisionmaking? The evidence suggests that they helped in the beginning. Clearly, all the rent-seekers and others who had benefited from the system were a ready-made anti-PNDC group. However, the PNDC had effectively, and decisively, broken links with those groups. Hence, they were not a factor initially. Chazan (1991) points out that between 1983 and 1991, the state was insulated from strong interest group demands. She is referring in particular to what she terms the "postcolonial elites" with whom the PNDC had broken. The relationship previous governments had maintained with the urban elite (consulting them, making them part of the decisionmaking process, and ensuring that they were kept happy) was shattered. In its place stood the "people" as represented by the People's Defence Committees (PDCs) and Workers' Defence Committees (WDCs). While this should have complicated decisionmaking in principle, as discussed earlier, by early 1983 decisionmaking was quite centralized, carried out by a small group of technocrats.

The Political Economy of Reform, 1983–91

A key question is *when* and *why* economic policy reform followed the path it did in Ghana, and why it faltered in the early 1990s. This requires

an understanding of the evolution of economic thought in Ghanaian economic policymaking. The discussion draws on the extensive literature
on Ghanaian politics in the past two decades as well as on interviews
carried out in Accra in March 1999.[12]

Support for the regime was especially strong among those who felt
they had not benefited under the previous regime. The establishment of
People's Defence Committees and Workers' Defence Committees that
excluded management also reflected the gap between the "haves" and
"have-nots."

The resulting array of coalitions in support of and against the government was predictable. Urban workers, students, and lower ranks of the
armed forces were especially strong supporters during the first years of
the regime. The workers and students had been highly vulnerable to the
dramatic decline in living standards during the 1970s. In addition, the
unions had clashed with the Limann government during the Third Republic over better pay and working conditions.[13] With respect to labor,
Herbst (1991) notes that the PNDC was against the trade union *leadership*. It perceived that leadership to have sold out its constituents to previous leaders. According to Herbst, the WDCs were an effective
mechanism for reaching union members outside the normal channels.

University students were also an important supporting constituency
at first. Two major groups emerged initially from the student body: the
June Fourth Movement (JFM) and the New Democratic Movement
(NDM). As discussed in Shillington (1992), the NDM was formed in 1980
and consisted primarily of students and academics. The JFM was also
composed entirely of students to begin with, but broadened to include
militant union leaders as well as community groups. Ideologically, both
of these groups were viewed as neo-Marxist. Finally, the lower ranks of
the army were an important supporting group. In large part because of
the June 4 uprising, when he took full responsibility and absolved his
army colleagues, Rawlings was perceived as a "ranks" man.

The most vocal opponents of the new regime were what could be
viewed as the "establishment"—those in the middle and upper managerial classes that the regime was criticizing vociferously. They included
persons who had benefited through their connections from the extensive system of chits, import licenses, and *kalabule* more generally. Among
them were former politicians, traders, and executives in state-owned
enterprises, professionals (including the Ghana Bar Association), and
entrepreneurs.

While there was a sense that little economic progress had occurred
under Limann, redressing this was initially less important in the
coupmakers' minds. This was because real concerns existed about the
consolidation of power militarily in the face of both domestic and external threats. Domestically, the PNDC could not discount the possibility
of a counter-coup by the officer corps of the army. Perceived external

threats centered on Nigeria and the West, in particular the Central Intelligence Agency (CIA).[14]

Once attention turned to economic issues, it was unclear what was to be done. Disagreement quickly emerged among the supporters of the regime as to what path to follow. On the one hand, the more ideological leftists felt that it would be inappropriate for Ghana to be beholden to the same "imperialist" powers they had been denouncing. In their view, Ghana should go it alone, or failing that, draw on resources from the Eastern bloc. On the other hand, there were those who felt that given the dire economic situation, the country would inevitably need some assistance from the West.[15] Because of these differing points of view and the multitude of parallel new institutions (such as the PDCs and WDCs) with ill-defined roles, the entire decisionmaking process lent itself to endless discussions.

In an attempt to coordinate the PDCs and WDCs better, the regime established an Interim National Coordinating Committee (INCC) in February 1982. It comprised JFM activists and members of the People's Revolutionary League of Ghana. While the PNDC retained ultimate policymaking authority, by virtue of its links with people at the grass roots, the INCC became extremely important. This created some tensions. Resolution of these was expected (but did not occur) when Rawlings replaced the INCC with the National Defence Council (NDC), which he chaired, in July 1982. The stated aim was to strengthen the defense committees and bring them under greater control. As we shall see, the underlying tensions between the left-wing elements in the NDC and the PNDC ultimately led to a serious breach.

Deciding on an economic path was complicated by the fact that Rawlings himself was not very ideological, but instead more populist.[16] Regardless of the points of view, what was not in dispute was the nature of the government's financial difficulties. In December 1981, foreign exchange reserves stood at US$125 million, less than two months of import cover. Short-term export credits and other forms of financing had dried up as external creditors downgraded the country's creditworthiness. This situation had undoubtedly worsened given the PNDC's anti-imperialist sentiments. Most foreign donors had halted flows as they adopted a wait-and-see attitude.

The solutions proposed for these difficulties differed according to political background. Initially the leftists appeared to hold sway in the economic debate as orthodox economic reform proposals were shot down.

Shortly after assuming office, the PNDC had appointed a National Economic Review Committee (NERC) to review the economic situation and make recommendations for short- and long-term measures to rehabilitate the economy. Two important members of the committee were Dr. Joe Abbey, previously commissioner of finance under General Akuffo, and Dr. Kwesi Botchwey, the PNDC secretary for finance and economic planning. Dr. Botchwey was previously a lecturer at the University of Ghana and was at the time one of the most influential leftist intellectuals on the university campuses. The NERC technocrats had concluded after a comprehensive review that the government would need to seek external financial assistance and that a stabilization program involving devaluation of the cedi was necessary. Technocrats in the Ministry of Finance had been working on an economic reform program. The committee viewed the upcoming World Bank/IMF annual meetings as an opportunity to present the government's views. Cognizant of the need for PNDC support, Dr. Abbey outlined the program to a full meeting of the PNDC, the Committee of Secretaries, and the National Defence Council in August 1982.

The meeting's reaction to the August 1982 presentation was initially favorable as participants agreed with Dr. Abbey's exposition on the existing (poor) incentives for exporters. They also seemed to agree with the principle of giving exporters bonuses and surcharging importers. However, a seemingly innocuous question about the distinction between the surcharges and devaluation shifted the momentum. Dr. Abbey's (correct) reply that "it was a matter of semantics" highlighted to the leftists that devaluation was an integral part of the program.[17] In the uproar that followed, no decision was made on the economic path, and several weeks of debate followed.

After the August 1982 meeting a new committee was established to reconcile differences, headed by Chris Atim of the JFM and Yao Graham of the NDM. They came up with what has been characterized as a more leftist document, the Alternative Economic Programme. However, this characterization is too simplistic. As reported in Nugent (1996) and confirmed in interviews, the program was remarkably clear-eyed on certain harsh realities: the need for a realistic exchange rate, for example, as well as the need to contain wages and to link wage increases to productivity. The main thrust of the program, however, was linking economic to political development. In the view of the authors, Ghana's problems were deep-seated and demanded a fundamentally different economic path free of imperialist interference. From their viewpoint, it was inconsistent to depend on the West to rescue Ghana. Implicitly then, the program would rely on future assistance from the socialist countries or generation of the country's own resources.

However, it was already obvious that the Ghana's socialist friends could not provide the level of support needed. Aid-seeking missions to "friendly" countries such as Libya, Cuba, Eastern European countries, and the Soviet Union in the first half of 1982 had generated little financial support.[18] Respected leftist intellectuals such as Samir Amin of the Dakar-based Institute for Planning and Development (IDEP) were brought in. However, their conclusion was the same: the government would have to deal with the international financial institutions to finance any economic recovery. Although the Alternative Economic Programme did not have a financing plan and disappeared from the debate, political difficulties remained in implementing any stabilization program because of ideological differences among supporters of the PNDC.

By October 1982, elements of the left wing associated with the National Defence Council were convinced Rawlings had abandoned the revolution and were increasingly frustrated. They set an October 28 date for a planned coup d'etat to remove him. The plot leaked, however, and the coup plotters were met at the barracks by troops loyal to Rawlings. The coup leaders backtracked and sought to make amends. That some WDCs and PDCs had already assembled in anticipation of a successful coup highlighted the potential dangers to Rawlings. On November 23, another coup was attempted, this time by soldiers who had previously supported the PNDC. Rawlings easily crushed the effort. Riding high on this success, he sought to tie the two conspiracies together.[19] The failed coup attempts provided the PNDC with an opportunity to remove those left-wing elements of the JFM opposed to the economic package, as well as perceived political enemies. Several were arrested and others went into exile. The National Defence Committee was dissolved and restructured to ensure tighter control.

While the debate was going on, behind the scenes the economic team continued to design a comprehensive economic policy for discussion with the IMF. With the elimination of those left-wingers opposed to a deal with the IMF and more market-oriented reform, the team now had a chance to begin to put forward an economic reform plan.

In December 1982, Dr. Botchwey, the finance secretary, presented the government's Program for Reconstruction and Development. This program is discussed in more detail below. Pending a formal arrangement with the Fund, financing was arranged through a bridge loan from Standard Chartered Bank in London. Dr. Frimpong-Ansah, a former governor of the Bank of Ghana during the Busia years, and then a senior adviser at Standard Chartered, was crucial in arranging this loan (Frimpong-Ansah 1991; interviews in Accra).

A number of exogenous crises and increasing financial difficulties in early 1983 further narrowed the options for reform and concentrated the minds of government officials. In January 1983, Nigeria announced that it was deporting all foreign nationals who lacked valid immigration papers. An estimated 1.2 million Ghanaians who had taken advantage of Nigeria's oil boom to escape Ghana's economic crisis were forced to pack up hurriedly and return home. Over a two-week period, Ghana's population essentially swelled by 10 percent. At the same time the country was experiencing a serious drought, reducing opportunities for rural employment for the returnees. Bush fires had destroyed much of the cocoa crop.

In April 1983 the Economic Recovery Program was presented in the budget. By this time, political momentum had shifted in favor of the technocrats. The ERP's economic thrust was essentially the same as the government's program announced on December 30, 1982. The main difference was the language: all references to exploitation and anti-imperialism had been dropped. The program was supported by a standby arrangement with the IMF and a multisector rehabilitation credit from the Bank.

By 1984, technocrats held the day. A small group of highly trained professionals made economic decisions. Many in the group already knew each other, and there was a high level of trust among them. The emphasis was on finding meaningful and practical solutions for Ghana's problems, and on "packaging" the reforms for presentation to the PNDC. For the rest of the decade there was remarkable continuity as there was little turnover in the group. The group was also sheltered from the political battles to some extent. This concentrated, centralized decisionmaking worked well in the early stages where there was more of a crisis mode, and quick and flexible decisionmaking was essential. However, it became increasingly difficult to implement reform this way as the decade went on.

This was the result in part of organizational changes in the decisionmaking apparatus that made coordination more complex. In 1985 a National Development Planning Commission was established. The Ministry of Finance reorganized itself in 1986: the Internal Revenue Service and the Customs, Excise and Preventive Service became autonomous agencies, and new departments were added (Toye 1991). In the late 1980s Dr. Abbey, an essential member of the economic team, became Ghana's ambassador to the United Kingdom and subsequently the United States. While the Washington appointment facilitated dialogue with the multilateral institutions, it probably weakened the team.

Coming back to politics, economic reform proved politically sustainable in the end only because some results emerged quickly, and because the government was able to overcome political opposition skillfully through the rest of the decade.

Electoral and Constitutional Changes

In 1991, a confluence of internal and external pressures led the PNDC to call for presidential and parliamentary elections to be held in 1992.[20] Domestic groups agitating for reform included professionals, students, trade unions, and former politicians. The wave of political liberalization sweeping through Africa was a source of external pressure. Finally, greater donor emphasis on governance and use of conditionality to bring about improved governance hastened democratic reform on the continent. Ghana's elections were staggered, with the presidential elections held in November 1992 and the parliamentary elections set to follow in December.

Rawlings won with 58.3 percent of the vote, and the runner-up gained 30.4 percent. Rawlings won more than 50 percent in every region except Ashanti and gained great support in the rural areas. While the opposition parties disputed the results and subsequently boycotted the parliamentary elections, by August 1993 they had officially recognized the government's legitimacy. The next elections, in 1996, by all accounts were fairer and the results were accepted by all. Rawlings and his party (NDC) won again, but with a reduced majority.

The form of government specified in the 1992 constitution avoids concentration of power in the hands of the president and cabinet or indeed any branch of government. It is designed to foster tolerance and the concept of power sharing. A president, a parliament, a cabinet, a council of state, and an independent judiciary share powers.

Legislative functions are vested in the National Parliament, which consists of a unicameral 200-member body plus the president. The structure and the power of the judiciary are independent of all other branches of government. The Supreme Court has broad powers of judicial review; it rules on the constitutionality of any legislative or executive action at the request of any aggrieved citizen. The legal system is based on the constitution, Ghanaian common law, statutory acts of Parliament, and assimilated rules of customary (traditional) law.

The 1992 constitution contains the most explicit and comprehensive provisions in Ghana's post-colonial constitutional history regarding the system of local government as a decentralized form of national administration. These provisions were inspired largely by current law and by the practice of local government under the PNDC.

The right to form political parties is guaranteed—an especially important provision in light of the checkered history of political parties in post-colonial Ghana. The constitution explicitly requires political parties to have a national character and membership, and says they should not be based on ethnic, religious, regional, or other sectoral divisions.

While these changes were well intentioned and indeed necessary, the net result was to make decisionmaking consultative *and* more difficult.

Influence of Democratization on the Pace and Pattern of Reform

The macroeconomic situation in Ghana deteriorated significantly in the early 1990s. Two of the main causes were political: the effect of the political cycle and the role of unions. In the run-up to the multiparty elections, an 80 percent wage hike for all civil servants resulted in large fiscal imbalances and monetary growth. The other major factor was the significant increase in the number of actors involved in economic decisionmaking. Parliament has played an important role in this regard. For example, in 1993 Parliament failed to approve a petroleum tax increase to raise revenues, resulting in worsened fiscal balance. Overall, the time horizon for policy decisions is now shorter. Since elections now require strategic planning, political types rather than technocrats are now ascendant.

The centralized decisionmaking process that had served the country well in the earlier period of reform was possible precisely because decisionmaking and consultation had not been institutionalized. So there was no broad and popular support for macroeconomic reforms. This was not much of an issue under military rule, but became a problem with multiparty democracy.

There were also difficult issues related to second-generation reforms, including privatization, financial sector reform, civil service reform, and taxation. The government faced public (and in some cases violent) protests against reforms. For example, a demonstration against structural adjustment in July 1995 resulted in the deaths of seven people. The new value added tax introduced in March 1995 was withdrawn after riots in two cities. After an extensive public education campaign, it was reintroduced in 1998 (at a lower level of 10 percent rather than the 15 percent recommended by the government).

Ghana's experience thus stands in contrast to the empirical findings of Dollar and Svensson (1998) that democratically elected governments are more likely to reform successfully. Ghana's periods of most rapid reform occurred under a non-elected government. Democracy has complicated the process of reform. But Ghana's experience is also a function of the nature and maturity of democracy in the country. For example, after the opposition boycotted the 1992 parliamentary elections, which they viewed as unfair, there was no real opposition in Parliament. Instead, the opposition parties used lawsuits to capture government attention and as the basis for their dialogue. Consequently, the government spent much time fighting these lawsuits.

Political Parties

The PNDC banned all political parties following the December 31, 1981 coup. With the announcement that elections would be held in 1992, political parties were "unbanned" on May 18, 1992. In practice, however, the parties existed in all but name throughout most of 1990–91. There was a flurry of activity as new parties registered and established themselves. When the dust settled, it could be seen that the major new parties all were essentially alliances of previous political groupings. The most important were the New Patriotic Party (NPP), the People's National Convention, the National Convention Party, the People's Heritage Party, the National Independence Party, and the unregistered People's Party for Democracy and Development (PPDD), which did not contest the election.[21] A group of pro-government clubs and organizations formed the National Democratic Congress (NDC) and nominated Rawlings as their candidate.

More importantly from the viewpoint of economic reform, the economic platforms of most parties were very similar to the ruling PNDC and to each other. For example, the liberal economic position of support for an open market-based economy, for which Busia's Progress Party/ NPP was known, had been appropriated by the PNDC. The presidential candidates of the other three parties also had little disagreement with the broad direction of the Structural Adjustment Program. One was a wealthy entrepreneur who supported market-based reforms. A second had an economic adviser who was Central Bank governor during the Busia era when market-oriented reforms were attempted. The third acknowledged that Nkrumahism and the welfare state were no longer sustainable (Nugent 1996: 243). The push for political decentralization and rural development was already being implemented by the PNDC. Accordingly, the structural adjustment program was never an issue in the campaign. Reflecting the disappearance of economic issues from the agenda, the pre-election debates centered on the human rights record of the PNDC and attacks on Rawlings.

Support for NDC came from a nationwide grassroots network as well as from aspirant businessmen, the rural elite, and those members of the middle class who have benefited from the rapid expansion of the service sectors. This includes, one might add, the cottage industry of aid-fueled projects and consultant assignments. As the incumbent, the PNDC was able to use a form of state patronage to bolster its support. Aid enabled the PNDC to expand access to infrastructure and social services (Nugent 1996: 206). New roads were constructed and existing ones improved all over the country, and the PNDC expanded the electricity grid to several regions.

The New Patriotic Party emerged from the Danquah-Busia tradition.[22] According to Nugent, it represented a "significant section of the Ghanaian elite, chiefly professionals and businessmen, drawn from the Akan heartland of the defunct Progress Party." The Nkrumahist camp was represented by a plethora of divided parties.

In the end, Rawlings won in 1992 (albeit controversially) and in 1996 (more universally accepted) in part because of the weakness of the opposition forces. Especially in 1992, they were often divided. One could also make the case that the NDC won because the opposition parties did not present a convincing alternative economic plan. Furthermore, Rawlings, as head of state for more than a decade, was able to exploit the advantages of incumbency. His name had become a household word, and he had been able to successfully mobilize grassroots support in the tradition of the Convention People's Party,[23] winning favor with a wide range of interest groups, influential chiefs, and local leaders. Helping Rawlings disseminate his message were a well-established nationwide network of Committees for the Defence of the Revolution, the 31st December Women's Movement, other so-called revolutionary organs, and dedicated district secretaries and chiefs. All these had been active long before the fractious political parties—whose rival leaders were hardly known beyond the major cities—had struggled into existence. Clearly, the benefits of incumbency are especially marked in Africa and will continue to be until a sustainable way to finance political parties is found.

Interest Groups

Politically active and influential interest groups in Ghana include the Trades Union Congress (TUC), the National Union of Ghana Students (NUGS), the Ghana Bar Association, the Association of Recognized Professional Bodies, and various Christian organizations such as the Catholic Bishops' Conference and the Christian Council of Ghana. During the early years of the PNDC, the TUC and NUGS were important supporters of the regime, but did not influence economic policy. In later years they became important pressure points for political reform; this in turn influenced economic reform.

In contrast to many other countries, in Ghana the business community was not an important interest group for a number of reasons. First, there was no monolithic "business community." On the one hand, old-time businessmen were resentful of the government and sensitive to its criticism, especially the charges of *kalabule*, even though many of these people had not necessarily benefited greatly under Acheampong or Limann. Many of them suffered under the rapid trade liberalization imposed by the Economic Recovery Program. On the other hand, aspiring entrepreneurs who were benefiting from the liberalization of the economy were grateful for the new opportunities. The second reason was that with increased PNDC scrutiny of tax payment records and the Citizens' Vetting Committee, few business owners were interested in drawing attention to themselves.

The Trades Union Congress

The TUC had a complex relationship with the PNDC regime that varied over time and depended on the specific affiliated union. Of the 17 unions in the TUC, the most important are the Ghana Private Road Transport Union, the Ghana Mine Workers' Union, and the Railway Workers' Union. In the early 1990s total membership of the TUC was more than 650,000.

Between 1982 and 1984, the regime enjoyed widespread support from the unions. With their leadership discredited due to past close association with Acheampong, the workers sympathized with the stated ideals of the PNDC. In April 1982, the Association of Local Unions (ALU)—a group of more militant trade unionists—unseated the TUC leadership and heads of the 17 national unions. An interim management committee made up of radical supporters of the regime replaced it.[24]

How did the government sell and sustain reforms under the ERP to labor? After all, the program implicitly required wage restraint and potential mass retrenchments, which were bound to hurt organized labor. Consequently, it could be viewed as a betrayal of the regime's populist and left-wing credentials. However, the government was able to survive the budget for a number of reasons.

To begin with, the labor leadership was already compromised by its close links with the PNDC. Other important points were Rawlings's personal credibility and the fact that some of the measures were medium-term. Cukierman and Tommasi (1994) contend that policies are more likely to be implemented by "unlikely" leaders (such as populists or left-wingers) than by those viewed as ideologues. If the populace is not fully informed about the short-term costs, then the populist reformer is better placed to implement reforms. People are more likely to be convinced that the reforms are essential to enhance efficiency rather than ideologically motivated (Dollar and Svensson 1998). This was certainly the case in Ghana. Rawlings's public speeches increasingly emphasized the need to be pragmatic, to enhance efficiency and productivity in order to reduce Ghana's dependency. Other reasons that the PNDC survived the budget speech include its concerted attempt to explain the ERP through public seminars, its direct negotiations with the TUC—resulting in a modest increase in the minimum wage—and, to some extent, fear of the government. Ultimately there was still a bit of a political honeymoon, giving Rawlings the benefit of the doubt.

By the end of the year, the fortunes of the ALU workers had changed. TUC elections voted most of them out and put many of the former executives back in power. Some informants for this study believe that workers viewed ALU as too close to the regime. Whatever the reason, the TUC elections marked the beginning of a more confrontational relationship between organized labor and the PNDC. Workers tried to further their economic interests and focused on the issues of the minimum wage, civil service reform, and privatization. They were constrained, however, by the environment. Heightened opportunities for removal of staff weakened their bargaining position. They were also hampered by the fact that they did not have any constructive alternative vision[25] and the political skills of government. Moreover, different unions benefited differently, reducing union unity. In mining, Ashanti Goldfields workers negotiated a wage of US$2 a day compared with much lower wages at state-owned mines.

In the late 1980s the PNDC tried to co-opt moderate elements of the union movement. By the end of the decade, the gap between the union members and their leaders had widened again.

National Union of Ghana Students

The student organization, NUGS, which represented more than 8,000 students at the country's three universities, was also important in the political dynamics. Initially students had been strong supporters of the regime, but over time they became vociferous critics. The students' support dated back to the original June 4 uprising, when they had been more radical and to the left of the AFRC on many issues. In mid-1982, a crucial time, the students had demonstrated on behalf of the government. But by the end of that year the more conservative students had taken control of NUGS, and as a result support for the PNDC diminished.

The change in NUGS support has been linked to student fears over the proposal to institute a two-year National Service before graduation and plans to revive the Student Task Force. In addition, the increased Christian revivalism on campus (and its associated anti-communism) was at odds with the perceived stance of the PNDC ("Ghana: Roots" 1983). By early 1983, NUGS was calling for the PNDC to hand over power to a government of national unity pending new elections, and following the April budget the students engaged in mass demonstrations against the government. At both the University of Ghana and the University of Science and Technology the students clashed with workers.[26] Ultimately the students were unable to muster broad support for their views. They were widely perceived as being elitist and clashes with campus PDCs had not endeared them to the workers.

Apart from their political viewpoint, the students were hostile to education reforms introduced after 1987, which required them to make greater financial contributions. With increasing student protests in 1987 the government closed the university campuses and arrested various student leaders. During much of the following academic year, the universities were in turmoil as student boycotts occurred and the universities were shut down repeatedly. The closures served effectively to neutralize the protests.

POLICY REFORMS

As far as economic policy was concerned, 1979–82 was essentially a period of muddling through. With elimination of the opposition to reform in late 1982, policy changes began in earnest.

Economic Reforms

Economic reform in Ghana can be broken down into three main periods: (a) successful stabilization, from 1983 to 1986; (b) structural adjustment, from 1986 to 1991; and (c) oscillating policy reform, from 1992 to 1996.

Successful Stabilization, 1983–86

The Economic Recovery Program, supported by World Bank loans and three IMF standby arrangements, was the first comprehensive economic policy package in more than a decade. The objectives of the ERP were as follows:

- Reversing the long decline in production of goods and services by realigning relative prices in favor of production and away from trading and rent-seeking activities;
- Reducing and stabilizing the inflation rate;
- Reducing the large budget deficits and improving the fiscal position of government more generally;
- Rehabilitating social and economic infrastructure;
- Eliminating smuggling and black market activities with respect to the currency; and
- Realigning the currency (the cedi) with major currencies (Ghana 1987).

Structural Adjustment, 1986–91

The Structural Adjustment Program, also known as Economic Recovery Program II, was a follow-up intended to focus on more deep-seated structural issues in the economic recovery. Its specific objectives were to:

- Sustain economic growth at between 5 and 5.5 percent a year over the medium term;
- Increase the level of public investment from about 10 percent of national income to about 25 percent by the end of 1989;
- Increase domestic savings from about 7 percent at the end of ERP I to about 15 percent at the end of the decade;
- Further improve the management resources in the public sector;

- Effectively mobilize the resources thus generated to improve the overall well-being of the people of Ghana, particularly the under-privileged, deprived, and vulnerable sectors of the population (Ghana 1987).

The overall assessment of several observers of the Ghanaian economy is that the ERP and SAP were successful in reversing the economic decline that had taken place. Growth moved from negative to positive and the economy was successfully stabilized (Nyanteng 1997; Kapur 1991). Throughout the 1980s Ghana earned high marks for its reform efforts. We now turn to the individual record of the main policy indicators during the reform periods.

Macroeconomic Management. An immediate economic concern of the PNDC was to improve the external payments position and control rampant inflation. From this perspective, the first stage of stabilization was well managed. Indeed, its centerpiece was the correction of the chronically overvalued exchange rate and successful reduction of inflation by 1991.

Exchange Rate. This was an early and important indicator of reform as it was a very visible symbol of the large distortions in the Ghanaian economy. The government introduced innovative reforms in exchange rate management. Over the reform period, the exchange rate became more realistic and flexible. Exchange rate management can be characterized as one of the ultimate policy successes despite the high political risk that accompanied adjustment of the rate. As mentioned earlier, the PNDC inherited a grossly distorted exchange rate. In early 1982, the official cedi–U.S. dollar rate was 2.75:1, while the black market rate was over 19:1 (Chibber and Shafik 1991). A straightforward devaluation was perceived by some to be politically damaging. To get around this problem, the Ghanaian economic team devised a system of "bonuses" and "surcharges." This was of course a de facto devaluation, but it avoided the use of the dreaded "D" word.[27] Over time, the system of bonuses and surcharges was discarded and step devaluation took place. Between 1983 and 1986, the currency was progressively devalued in nominal terms from 2.75 to 90 cedis per U.S. dollar.

In 1986 the government moved closer to a fully flexible exchange rate with the introduction of a retail foreign-exchange auction market. The government allowed the establishment of foreign exchange bureaus in February 1988 as part of the continuing liberalization of the trade and exchange system. This liberalization continued and culminated in the establishment of an inter-bank market for foreign exchange in 1991.

FISCAL POLICY. Fiscal discipline was introduced and, despite periodic slippage, ultimately sustained during 1983–91. The government turned a fiscal deficit of 4 percent into a surplus of 2 percent. Early success in reducing the deficit rested on the ability to increase revenues rather than on expenditure reduction. The Citizens' Vetting Committee succeeded in expanding the tax base, resulting in greater revenue collection, and revenues rose as a share of GDP from 6 percent in 1983 to 14 percent by 1991. The successful fiscal adjustment was instrumental in lowering inflation.

INFLATION. By reducing deficit financing the government removed one source of inflation. In 1981, CPI inflation was 77 percent. It fell to 22 percent by 1986 and dropped further to 9.5 percent in 1992, its lowest level in two decades.

STRUCTURAL POLICIES. Under the ERP, the prevailing extensive web of administered prices and price controls was largely dismantled. Interest rates were liberalized in the financial sector. By 1986 virtually all price controls had been removed. The external trade regime was liberalized rapidly, but progress was slow on the divestiture of state-owned enterprises.

TRADE POLICY. Significant trade liberalization began under the ERP in 1983. Tariffs were simplified and lowered to create a uniform pattern of protection. Initially, the number of rate bands was reduced to three (0 percent, 25 percent, and 30 percent). Import tariffs fell further in 1986 when rates were lowered to 20–25 percent. In addition, the authorities shortened the negative list for imports. While the exchange rate had moved to a more realistic level, this was still far from equilibrium level or the parallel market rate. Accordingly, import controls remained in place until 1986. Overall, by 1986 Ghana was classified as "open" according to the Sachs-Warner index of openness, in contrast to the previous years when it was classified as "closed."

DIVESTITURE OF STATE-OWNED ENTERPRISES. Under the ERP and SAP, progress in reducing the state's role in public enterprises was slow due to vested interests, political sensitivities, and, in some cases, lack of technical capacity. By 1991 the government had divested only 42 of approximately 300 SOEs.

PUBLIC SECTOR MANAGEMENT. Public sector management was not at the forefront of the reform agenda under the ERP. In part, this was because the first stage of stabilization consisted of reforms that were automatic and involved announcements by government rather than detailed implementation. These included, for instance, the removals of price controls and adjustments in the exchange rate. Under the SAP, the government and donors became increasingly concerned about implementation capacity within the public sector, as well as economic policy coordination. Consequently, measures to strengthen key policy functions in the Ministry of Finance and to reform the civil service were part of the SAP. The government launched civil service reform in 1987 with support from the World Bank but its commitment was weak, and targets for retrenchments were not met. The judiciary and the rule of law were even further removed from the agenda during both the ERP and SAP.

Oscillating Policy Reform, 1992–96

This period marked the first major interruption of lending by the multilateral institutions in two decades. Between November 1992 and mid-1993, Ghana's adjustment program veered off track and the World Bank suspended disbursements. *Fiscal dislocation* associated with the large (80 percent) wage increases awarded to civil servants before the 1992 multiparty elections was the main cause of the policy derailment. The immediate effect was the emergence of a fiscal deficit of about 5 percent of GDP in 1992 from a surplus of 1.5 percent in 1991 as the money supply increased by more than 50 percent. In the second half of 1996, reacting to significant fiscal slippage, the IMF delayed negotiation of the second annual Enhanced Structural Adjustment Facility and the Policy Framework Paper for a year. More generally, it appeared that the government faced increasing difficulties in implementing additional structural reforms.

Ghana survived these temporary suspensions because of strong support from the bilateral donors. By the early 1990s, Ghana had become the ultimate test of structural adjustment and donors were unwilling to see it fail. Canada (which had always been supportive), Japan (which did not generally get into policy discussions), and the United Kingdom in particular all exerted pressure on the multilateral institutions.

During this period the government struggled to reduce *inflation,* which continued to be high and variable. Contributory factors were the creeping fiscal deficits and associated growth in the money supply, which remained high despite a decline from 57 percent in 1992 to 31 percent in 1996.

With respect to *trade policy*, the government introduced a number of incentives targeted at exporters to redress the worsening external payments position. The pace of divestiture of SOEs accelerated. Fiscal considerations led the government to sell shares in Ashanti Goldfields (AGC) on the Ghana and London stock exchanges. The government followed the sale of AGC with many other offerings. The privatization program picked up, and by 1997, more than a third of the 300 public enterprises had been sold or liquidated.

With respect to *public sector management*, by 1994 all parties acknowledged that donor efforts to enhance capacity had been largely ineffective. The government launched the National Institutional Renewal Program (NIRP) in late 1994 to coordinate various public sector reforms (financial management, performance improvement, and pay).

In the mid-1990s the government made progress on defining the regulatory framework and including the enforcement of contracts and property rights. A liberal Investment Act (1994), a Free Zones Act (1995), the Statutory Corporations (Conversion to Companies) Act (1995), and the National Communications Act (1996) facilitated this. In addition, a multisector regulatory agency has been created to facilitate further private sector activity. The World Bank has supported many of these initiatives. Table 2.2 summarizes the sequencing of individual reforms in the 1983–96 period.

High turnover on the economic teams of the World Bank and the government did not facilitate policy reform during the 1990s. A number of World Bank internal reorganizations and the proliferation of projects (and hence task managers) led to a lack of continuity that Ghanaian officials found frustrating. In addition, some officials felt tensions between Bank and IMF staff prevented clear guidance on a number of policy issues, such as civil service reform.

In sum, Ghana's progress and evolution becomes evident when its record of macroeconomic management and structural reforms between the 1970s and the mid-1990s is compared to that of other African countries. On the fiscal side, Ghana's fiscal deficit was significantly higher than the average for the rest of Africa in the 1970s; it surpassed 11 percent in 1976, more than double the average of the continent. Beginning in 1982, Ghana's fiscal position improved tremendously, and from 1983 to 1991 it registered smaller deficits (and eventually larger surpluses) than the rest of the continent. While Ghana's fiscal deterioration in 1992 resulted in a larger deficit than average, by the mid-1990s it was registering surpluses and was again performing above the Africa-wide average.

The story on *inflation* reflects the struggle to contain inflationary pressures that Ghana has faced throughout its reform efforts. Ghana started the reform program with inflation that had been significantly higher than the rest of Africa for almost a decade. While inflation was eventually reduced below the continent average in 1991–92, the fiscal dislocation and other pressures after that caused inflation to exceed the average again.

On the *trade* side, Ghana made early and rapid progress compared to other African countries. While it was classified as "closed" according to the Sachs-Warner definition in 1980, by 1985 it was one of only four countries in Africa (out of 36) that was classified as "open." By 1996 several other countries were classified as "open" (14 of 36). The World Bank's Country Policy and Institutional Assessment ratings for 1998 bear out Ghana's superior macroeconomic management and record of accomplishment in structural reform. In both cases, Ghana scored above the average for countries in Africa.

Triggers for Reform

When and why countries choose to reform is an issue that interests many researchers. Five factors help to explain why the PNDC chose to reform when it did in 1983. The first two provided the immediate impetus for reform, while the last three have to do with the political dynamics that gave the government needed political space to carry out the reforms.

First, there was undoubtedly a liquidity crisis. Foreign exchange reserves, trade credit, and medium-term financing had all dried up by early 1983. At the same time, the government faced unavoidable obligations. Several former officials interviewed for this paper alluded to impending oil payments and the need to pay for a new DC-10 aircraft. Second, drought and bush fires, as well as the return of more than 1 million Ghanaian citizens from Nigeria in early 1983, compounded this liquidity crisis. These two factors (the extreme financial crisis, and the exogenous shocks) are central in explaining how the government came to consider reform. In essence, the situation was so desperate that the costs of doing nothing greatly outweighed the costs of reform.

What gave the government political room to carry out the reform? First, not many alternative approaches existed that would generate the financial resources necessary for the economy's recovery. Few Ghanaians needed to be convinced of this fact; for the average citizen who had already suffered more than a decade of economic hardship, it was clear that the old order had failed. Second, the PNDC had credibility with interest groups that could have created difficulties for the government— notably trade unionists and students. These groups were sympathetic and in essence gave the PNDC a policy honeymoon. Other political opposition, both within and outside, had either been eliminated or was demoralized. The PNDC made a huge effort to educate military groups and the Workers' Defence Committees on the rationale for the reforms. Third, the crisis of the returnees created some national unity. Indeed, the situation gave the regime some political cover to accept the World Bank and IMF loans, which were presented as bolstering the government's own efforts to deal with the crisis.

Overall, though, the economic debate that had taken place during 1982 was necessary for the evolution of economic thought from populism to more market-based reforms. It is inconceivable that these reforms could have taken place in 1982; neither Rawlings nor essential members of the PNDC were yet convinced that market-based reforms were necessary.[28] In that sense, the reforms of 1983 were a result *both* of a gradual evolution in the government's thinking and of crises that served as a trigger in the early part of that year.

The evolution of economic thought was to some extent influenced by staff at the World Bank and IMF. Both institutions had highly committed individuals on the macroeconomic country team who were willing to discuss issues with the government in a nonideological fashion. Indeed their commitment to the process led them to recommend the ERP, although officials back in Washington thought the program was too gradual and questioned the government's commitment to reform. Several people interviewed also referred to the efforts of a senior Ghanaian economist at the Bank who was instrumental in analytical discussions.[29] As Ghana was at the forefront of African countries in terms of structural adjustment, there was little learning from the country's neighbors.

Homegrown Policies

As alluded to earlier, different elements in the government attempted different economic reform packages. The contents of the so-called "more leftist" programs have been discussed already.

In December 1982, Secretary for Finance Dr. Botchwey presented the government's Programme for Reconstruction and Development (Ghana 1983). This program "could be seen as a balancing act between the nuts-and-bolts reformism of the National Economic Review Committee and the long-range concerns of the Alternative Economic Programme. In diagnosing the causes of the crisis, Botchwey struck a middle position, highlighting both the vagaries of the international economy and the pursuit of unwise monetary, fiscal, foreign exchange and pricing policies since the 1970s." A broadened tax base, fewer state enterprises, and a more realistic exchange rate were presented as solutions to the crisis. The program also included some statements associated with the language of the left. For example, there were references to ending exploitation and to imposing state control over certain aspects of import-export trade (Nugent 1996: 110).

In short, the reconstruction and development program was broadly similar to the final Economic Recovery Program. The important difference was that the reference to mass mobilization of the people was dropped. In practice, with the expulsion of the Ghanaians from Nigeria and the need to resettle them, food aid from donors was used to mobilize the returnees in the rural areas for assistance with harvesting the cocoa crop.

Ownership

The Economic Recovery Program and the Structural Adjustment Program (to a lesser extent) enjoyed high Ghanaian ownership—if ownership is narrowly defined to mean the *government's* conviction that it had a stake in the program. Ghanaian officials could rightly point out that they had drafted the original program on which the ERP was based.[30] Public statements by the authorities at the time indicated that they took responsibility for the program. In addition, the authorities did a significant amount of background work on one of the important issues: devaluation. The idea of PAMSCAD emerged not only from concerns raised by outside agencies (principally UNICEF, the United Nations Children's Fund), about the social costs of adjustment, but also from government concerns. There was a great deal of back-and-forth discussion between the Bank/Fund teams on the one hand, and the government under the ERP. Within the Bank, the Ghanaians came to be known as "tough negotiators, able to define the limits of which issues they were or were not prepared to take on, and determine how far they could go" (Armstrong 1996: 54). In an external assessment of the World Bank program in Ghana, the reviewer comments that this ownership led to a more gradual program than either the World Bank or the IMF would have preferred. He notes that this was essentially the correct decision, however, given the political economy of the time (Armstrong 1996:54). That is not to say of course that the gradualism was optimal.

In the 1990s, ownership seems to have declined. This may be a result of several factors, including changes in personalities leading to the need to build new relationships of trust, and adjustment fatigue on the part of both Ghanaians and donors. Perversely, Ghana's successful adjustment in the 1980s led to increased donor flows and with them, greater dependency. This has resulted in more donor-driven agendas and less ownership.

Ownership more broadly defined—to include the private sector, civil society, academics, and trade unions—was not even on the agenda in the beginning.[31] There was less participation by civil society in the programs of the 1980s. The political situation affected this stance to some extent. As discussed above, the PNDC was under continuing political pressure throughout most of its tenure, but especially in the first few years. Opening a dialogue on the reform program was viewed as politically dangerous. While some attempt was made to provide a forum to discuss the ERP and SAP during the 1980s, very little real discussion was ultimately achieved.

Some observers interviewed in Accra suggest that the World Bank itself was concerned about having "endless discussions" of the reform process. So, in general, there was little pressure from any source to have wide participation. In the short run this enabled the authorities to move decisively and firmly on a number of potentially controversial economic issues. However, it has been argued elsewhere that the failure to institutionalize the reform underpinned the difficulties the government faced in consolidating reform in the 1990s (Nugent 1996).

With the exception of only one aspect of the reforms, the various interest groups did not influence the design of the two reform packages in the 1980s. The exception was the social costs of adjustment, particularly as they affected the poor. Given the PNDC's heritage, however, it seems that one reason criticisms of the SAP in this regard were taken seriously was that there was genuine worry about how the poorest people were being affected. To put it another way, it is hard to imagine the PNDC at the time agreeing to such a program targeted at the middle class. In addition, external agencies, notably UNICEF, were instrumental in bringing the issue to the forefront. In 1988 the donor-funded PAMSCAD initiative was introduced. PAMSCAD targeted vulnerable communities, most of them rural, and self-help projects within them. To the extent possible, local materials, technology, and labor were to be used. In total US$87 million was initially committed for PAMSCAD.

THE LINK BETWEEN AID AND REFORM

The overall objective of this study is to assess *whether* and *how* aid influenced reforms in Ghana. Exposures to ideas and policy conditionality, discussed below, are two of the channels through which aid can influence the decision to reform. We conclude by assessing what the Ghana case study suggests about the larger project's three hypotheses:

- Governments choose to reform, or regress, independent of the aid relationship;
- Nonfinancial aid has a better impact than financial aid on generation of policy reforms;
- Financial aid works when policy reforms and institution building are underway.

Generation and Implementation of Reforms

Generation of Ideas

Ideas for the ERP and SAP were generated through a partnership between a small group of technocrats in Ghana and a similar group in the World Bank and the IMF. The Bank in particular carried out high-quality macroeconomic analysis that informed the government's decisions and was viewed as useful in the policy dialogue in the mid-1980s (Armstrong 1996). This was especially important given that the intellectual environment for economists in Ghana had become increasingly barren during the 1970s with the departure of many economists and the closed nature of the economy. On the other hand, since the work of the World Bank was often devoid of any sense of the political economy of reform, the Ghanaian team was critical in providing the context and parameters of reform. This partnership is viewed as having worked well. Both external reviewers and internal Bank audits judged that the first and second Bank structural adjustment credits had met their objectives quite well.

Once we move from the macroeconomic to the sector level, it appears that World Bank economic and sector work was uneven in quality or entirely absent. In these cases, reform suggestions were unconvincing to government officials. The Country Assistance Review on Ghana cites the areas of privatization and public enterprise reform as examples of this phenomenon. From this viewpoint, the poorer project performance in these areas was not surprising.[32]

Notwithstanding the importance of World Bank economic analysis in the mid-1980s, given the financial constraints at the time, financial aid was clearly crucial and more important in sustaining the program. While some of the technical work may have helped to persuade officials on particular issues, this would have been a hollow victory in the absence of financial resources that they could use to revive the economy.

In addition to formal economic analysis, particular *individuals* outside the system were important.[33] As alluded to earlier, key Ghanaians working overseas (at the World Bank and at IDEP in Dakar) were also viewed by some policymakers as critical to formulating ideas. The academics by contrast did not influence the reform process very much. They seemed to have had a healthy dose of skepticism about how long the regime would last. The clashes with students, which led to the shutting down of the universities, did not create favorable conditions for dialogue between the government and the academics.

What is striking is that sources of ideas on reform tended to be available to a rather small group of people within Ghana initially. One conclusion to be drawn is that if these ideas are to be disseminated and discussed beyond government partners, then the supporting studies must be made widely available. The Bank's recent move toward making its documents more accessible is an important step in this direction.

Technical Assistance

Technical assistance by donors has had a mixed record and the overall impact appears weak. The Ghanaian civil servants interviewed perceived technical assistance rather negatively. There was a feeling that it arrived

late in the reform process and was not properly designed. One Ghanaian policymaker who has dealt with several technical assistance projects
characterized TA as "excessively paid consultants from the countries
funding that same technical assistance with little or no appreciation for
the political and institutional dynamics." Similar comments were common among working-level staff interviewed in Accra. Recent comments
by the former minister for finance and economic planning, Dr. Botchwey,
echo this characterization, suggesting that junior and senior staff shared
these views.[34]

The National Capacity Assessment of 1996 found that "Ghana's capacity to handle various technical and managerial activities in most sectors of
the economy has worsened in the last two decades." Efforts to rebuild
capacity, it said, had not been successful. The report identified "lack of
investment in the institutions/processes that form capacity" and the "slow
destruction of the enabling environment for maintaining existing capacities" as the core underlying reasons for the decline (Ghana 1996).

Technical assistance in Ghana has suffered from a number of difficulties. One of the most serious has been the lack of coordination by donors, resulting in duplication of efforts. The United Nations Development
Program's National Technical Co-operation and Assessment Program
(NATCAP) was supposed to improve the effectiveness of TA. However,
as of 1996, the NATCAP program in Ghana was having difficulties achieving this objective and was apparently receiving little support from other
donors. As of 1996, there was no formal aid coordination mechanism for
TA. Attempts to have Ghanaian professionals living overseas return to
work in the civil service has had mixed results. These "returnees" have
engendered substantial resentment among Ghanaian civil servants because of their better working conditions.

Sustainability

Aid to Ghana was very important in sustaining reforms. As Ghana implemented wide-ranging reforms in the mid-1980s, it gained the attention
and admiration of bilateral and multilateral donors. Aid flows to Ghana
increased accordingly, as many donors were eager to support a "win-
ner" that was making tough decisions—especially in a continent where
success stories were rare. As outlined above, the amount of aid to Ghana
grew exponentially during the 1980s. Initially a great deal of this support was for balance of payments and rehabilitation. Over time, donors
moved into sectors. This massive aid flow was instrumental in offsetting
the terms-of-trade decline that Ghana faced in the late 1980s. Aid, in
essence, allowed Ghana to escape the potentially contractionary effects
of a reduction in absorption.

Aid also helped to sustain reforms during the ERP and SAP by reducing their political costs. Two examples discussed in Aryeetey and Cox illustrate this point. First, balance of payments support "provided the government with the breathing space it required to contain domestic opposition to market-based reforms . . . [It] allowed imports that helped fill the shelves of supermarkets and other traders. The filled shelves provided a psychologically-induced breather for the government because . . . people saw this as a sign of better things to come" (Aryeetey and Cox 1997). The second specific example is PAMSCAD. While the implementation of the program was disappointing for a number of reasons, it still indicated that the government was concerned about the rural poor and "silenced opponents."

Finally, to the extent that aid (and the programs it supported) resulted in faster economic growth, rehabilitation of the country's roads, and revitalized exports, it helped the government stay the course.

On the other hand, aid may have inadvertently reduced the long-term sustainability of reform in some instances. The nature of the dialogue and Bank/Fund conditionality favored the use of a small group of technocrats for making decisions. In the context of a non-elected government, the net effect was to discourage consultation. The donors were also directly culpable. Rothchild (1991) reports that the very success of the PNDC in implementing reform led many donors and the IMF to ignore political opposition for the first few years of reform.

One hypothesis in the literature on aid is that strong institutions imply stronger sustainability of reforms. In the case of Ghana, the aid-institutions-sustainability nexus does not meet conventional expectations. Reforms thrived initially despite the absence of strong institutionalized decisionmaking. Aid did not have a positive effect on institutions during the first years of reform because donors focused on (short-term) *outcomes*, not processes. Given the political environment in Ghana, achieving these favorable outcomes was dependent on the "inner circle" approach that implied keeping other institutions out of the decisionmaking process.

Conditionality

Conditionality and the manner in which it was implemented were important in sustaining policy reform during the ERP and SAP.

Aryeetey and Cox (1997) discuss how the government often used the existence of conditionalities to gain leverage when negotiating with local groups. The example they give is education sector reform, which was pushed through rapidly with little discussion. Domestic complaints were greeted with the response that World Bank requirements on disbursements and conditionality necessitated that approach.

The nature of conditionality changed in a number of specific ways between 1983 and 1996:

- *Conditions became more numerous.* IMF conditions rose from 20 in 1983 to 40–50 in 1988–89 (Martin 1991: 245). This reflected the Fund's increased involvement in structural issues, some of which the Bank regarded as its turf.
- *Conditionality-based lending became more important.* The share of policy-based loans rose sharply in Ghana's overall loans from the Bank.
- *Conditions became tighter and deeper,* and also increasingly specific: for example, personnel cuts in the civil service were explicitly specified (Martin 1991).

These conditionalities were not as onerous as they could have been, for two important reasons. The first was the caliber, coherence, and continuity of the Ghanaian team. Its relatively small size, highly qualified staff, and skill at implementing measures allowed some flexible interpretation of conditions. In addition, it appears that the Ghanaian team was usually extremely well prepared.[35] The second reason was the nature of the World Bank and (to a lesser extent) IMF teams. They proved over time adept at understanding the context in which certain decisions had to be undertaken and gave the Ghanaians some room. An example of this two-way dialogue was the introduction of the exchange rate auction. With the support of the Bank, the PNDC convinced the IMF to allow it to "manage" the auction in order to conserve foreign exchange. Instead of pure speculative bidding, it introduced a number of measures that ultimately reduced the number of bids made or accepted. These included "Dutch" bidding in which the successful bidder paid the rate it bid, as well as strict eligibility and documentation requirements.

In addition to this "flexible implementation," the World Bank also redesigned conditions or delayed them if they seemed not to be working. For example, cost recovery in the health sector fell in this category (Martin 1991).

The willingness to engage the Ghanaians in discussions and to allow this kind of slippage was due to a confluence of factors. There was undoubtedly a sense that the government was committed to reform and had sustained it longer than any other country in Sub-Saharan Africa. Bilateral donors who were pleased with Ghana also exerted significant pressure on the international financial institutions. It seems that this flexibility also enabled the government to carry out reforms that were feasible, generated greater sustainability, and strengthened policy reform. By contrast, since the mid-1990s the international financial institutions have seemed less accommodating, at precisely the time when the government has to carry out more consultation with Parliament. From interviews with donors, this change appears to be a consequence of slippage in the early 1990s and hence disillusionment. This "tougher conditionality" has resulted paradoxically in the likelihood of more slippage, not necessarily because the government is not committed, but because of the need to bring others along.

The World Bank and the IMF had a close working relationship during the Economic Recovery Program and the Structural Adjustment Program. This being the pre–Policy Framework Paper era, the closeness was all the more remarkable. Ghana was one of six countries chosen for an enhanced Bank-Fund collaboration pilot. Therefore, closer and more frequent communication took place between staff in the two institutions working on Ghana relative to other member countries.

Despite this close relationship, the IMF and the World Bank did not always coordinate their conditionality well. For example, small farmers and the private sector were expected to lead sustained growth and the Bank programs were designed accordingly. However, the devaluation and tight credit policies recommended by the IMF made it difficult for small farmers and entrepreneurs to obtain the necessary credit to purchase foreign exchange on the auction for imported capital goods (Martin 1991). The Bank staff members felt that the Fund's monetary targets were too tight and began questioning them openly in discussions with the government.[36] Another example of poor conditionality coordination was cocoa producer pricing, where over time higher cocoa prices resulted in a trade-off between fiscal and incentive objectives.

Selectivity

In the case of Ghana, donors initially took a wait-and-see attitude regarding the PNDC and its commitment to reform. As already shown, it was not until 1985—two years after the reforms began—that bilateral donors and the international financial institutions committed appreciably greater resources to the Ghana programs. By then, it was clear that the government was willing and able to undertake difficult reforms and there was a scramble to reward Ghana accordingly. This led to Ghana becoming the success story that everyone wanted to shower with aid based on its good policy environment.

When the policy environment worsened in the early 1990s, many donors were unwilling or found it difficult to withhold aid. This may have reflected not only donor reluctance to label Ghana a "bad performer," but also the belief that the government, which up to then had been a reliable partner, was facing genuine political difficulties.

Information on the evolution of the composition of aid to meet country circumstances is not easy to document and varies across donors.

Nonetheless, some observations can be made. During the early to mid-1980s the World Bank had an appropriate mix of analytical work and financial assistance. A great deal of lending was underpinned by analysis that laid out the case for particular policy recommendations (Armstrong 1996: 52). During the late 1980s and early 1990s, there was more need for technical assistance and fresh ideas as the institutional requirements of adjustment increased, and as program design became more complicated. However, the Bank, among others, was late in providing this and the technical assistance that it offered was often ineffective (Armstrong 1996: 103).

With the advent of multiparty democracy, several donors began providing a new kind of support. Financial and technical assistance to support elections became part of aid. In the run-up to the 1996 elections, all the major donors participated in meetings of the Inter-Party Advisory Committee, which was an important forum for discussion and consensus building. Altogether, the donor community gave US$12.3 million to the National Electoral Commission to "facilitate free and fair elections" by enhancing the capacity of the NEC. A wide range of donors contributed: the United States, Canada, the European Union, Germany, the Netherlands, and China (Ninsin 1998: 185–202).

A recent innovation is the move toward sector programming of aid. Pilots of this approach are already in place for the health and education sectors. The sector approach marks recognition by donors that the multiplicity of actors in particular sectors with different procurement and disbursement procedures as well as different strategies has not served the country or the donors well.

Finally, with multiparty democracy and the increased importance of civil society, donors seem to be emphasizing aid that can facilitate internal dialogue and debate and help the adjustment to democracy. The Bank is shifting its mix of instruments toward non-lending policy advisory services in Ghana. These include, for example, World Bank Institute support for consensus building in civil society and short "just-in-time" technical advice. According to the Country Assistance Strategy, this shift is partly in recognition of the need for vigorous communication and discussion of policies given an active media and parliamentary opposition. Canada and the United States also provide nonfinancial aid aimed at strengthening civil society. U.S. aid particularly targets research and business organizations.

Conclusion

At the beginning of the reform program, even one of the program's strongest supporters perceived the link between aid and reform as something of a chicken and egg question. World Bank lending to Ghana had been suspended (no new loans approved between June 1981 and January 1983) pending macroeconomic reform. Nevertheless, an important internal Bank document also noted that "the Ghanaian authorities' receptivity and interest in pursuing an economic dialogue with the Bank was very much dependent upon an early resumption of Bank lending" (Armstrong 1996). On that basis it was felt that supporting the (however gradual) ERP was an important way of gaining credibility for the Bank that could be parlayed into future advice.

To conclude, let us revisit our three hypotheses. The first asserts that countries choose to reform or regress independent of aid. Ghana's experience shows that aid *was* an important part of the decision to reform as the government anticipated that aid would enable it to meet its economic and political objectives. Aid was also important in *sustaining* reform as it offset economic shocks, generated demonstration effects, and reduced political pressure. The earlier discussion of the political economy considerations underlying reform and the episodes of policy regression in the early 1990s suggest that aid cannot, however, buy reform. It raises an interesting question as to whether potential aid cutoffs by donors hold any credibility for countries that donors have "invested" in heavily, such as Ghana.

The second hypothesis posits that nonfinancial aid (technical cooperation, advisory services, and analytical work) has a better impact than financial aid on the generation of policy reforms in bad policy environments. The first round of reforms in Ghana included rehabilitation of basic infrastructure and balance of payments support. Both of these required more cash than intellect. Indications are that the lack of donor finance during the poor policy period was an important consideration in the decision to reform. But this paper has also shown that the macroeconomic policy dialogue was useful to the reformers. In addition, their implementation requirements were not as onerous as some later reforms. While the mid-1980s economic and sector work that the World Bank carried out was important in the economic dialogue, it is unlikely that it would have generated reforms in the absence of finance. After all, the authorities had already convinced themselves of the basic framework for stabilization.

The third and final hypothesis is that financial aid works when policy reforms and institution building are underway. Ghana's experience suggests that already existing policy reforms are probably necessary (though not sufficient) for financial aid to work effectively. The existence of the reforms or a program for reforms implies prior commitment by the government and indicates that debate regarding reform's merits or demerits has taken place already. Institution building appears to be neither necessary nor sufficient *in the short run* for financial aid to work. The Economic Recovery Program was implemented in a situation where extremely weak institutions inherited from the previous regime were the norm. Yet, the ERP gets high marks for its ability to introduce effectively a wide-ranging set of economic policies. The reason, as discussed above, was the high-caliber (though small) group of policymakers who remained in place for a long period. This was, however, a unique situation. With the inevitable transition in the group and the need to institutionalize decisionmaking, it has proven more difficult to use reform-based aid effectively.

Our study suggests that the relationship between democracy and reform in Ghana has been complex. Donors have expended much energy and resources pushing democratization, in the belief that political and economic liberalization go hand in hand. Ghana's experience illustrates that democratization will not necessarily lead to good economic policy.

APPENDIX 2.1
GHANA: CHRONOLOGY OF POLITICAL
AND ECONOMIC DEVELOPMENTS

6 March 1957	Ghana wins independence from Britain; Nkrumah is prime minister.
1 July 1960	Inauguration of the First Republic.
24 February 1966	Coup d'etat by National Liberation Council overthrows Nkrumah.
22 August 1969	National Liberation Council hands over power to civilians. Second Republic inaugurated. Busia and Progress Party rule.
13 January 1972	Coup d'etat led by Acheampong and the National Redemption Council.
October 1975	National Redemption Council superseded by Supreme Military Council.
5 July 1978	Palace coup; Akuffo overthrows Acheampong, and Supreme Military Council II emerges.
4 June 1979	Uprising by junior officers; Armed Forces Revolutionary Council comes to power.
18 June 1979	Elections.
24 September 1979	Inauguration of Third Republic. Limann is president.
June 1981–January 1983	IDA lending suspended to Ghana.
31 December 1981	Coup d'etat by Rawlings's Provisional National Defence Council.
28–29 October 1982	Attempted coup.
23 November 1982	Attempted coup.
30 December 1982	Secretary for finance and economic planning announces Program for Reconstruction and Development.
January 1983	1.2 million Ghanaians expelled from Nigeria.
April 1983	Budget outlines Economic Recovery Program to be supported by financial assistance from World Bank and IMF.
19 June 1983	Coup attempt.
November 1983	First Consultative Group meeting for Ghana in 13 years.
November 1984	People's Defence Committees and Workers' Defence Committees replaced by Committees for the Defence of the Revolution.
18 May 1992	Ban on political parties lifted.
3 November 1992	Presidential elections. Rawlings wins.
29 December 1992	Parliamentary elections, boycotted by opposition.
Late 1992–early 1993	Adjustment credit tranche releases withheld.
7 January 1993	Fourth Republic inaugurated.

1994	Tranche releases withheld on World Bank Financial Sector Adjustment Credit and Agricultural Sector Adjustment Credit due to privatization delays.
1996	Presidential and parliamentary elections. Rawlings wins 57 percent of popular vote. National Democratic Congress wins 66 percent of parliamentary seats. Opposition accepts results.
1996	ESAF negotiations suspended due to slippage.

APPENDIX 2.2
ADDITIONAL DEVELOPMENT FINANCE DATA

TABLE 2.3 GHANA: EFFECTIVE DEVELOPMENT ASSISTANCE, 1980–96
(millions of U.S. dollars)

Year	TOTAID	EDA	GQ	Grants	TA	GQ (bilateral)	GQ (multi-lateral)
1970	22.3	7.2	1.7	5.5	15.2	0.0	1.7
1971	37.1	21.1	12.7	8.4	15.9	1.2	11.6
1972	40.3	25.4	17.6	7.8	15.0	3.7	13.9
1973	37.9	20.3	14.7	5.5	17.7	1.4	13.3
1974	39.7	19.9	7.9	12.0	19.8	5.0	2.9
1975	53.5	27.7	19.8	7.8	25.9	7.6	12.2
1976	67.8	40.3	20.4	20.0	27.5	12.5	7.9
1977	88.9	59.7	34.1	25.7	29.2	20.6	13.4
1978	98.3	60.9	30.5	30.4	37.5	13.5	17.0
1979	118.9	83.5	51.8	31.7	35.4	4.4	47.4
1980	140.2	97.8	75.3	22.5	42.4	11.5	63.8
1981	131.4	89.0	55.4	33.7	42.3	13.9	41.5
1982	110.7	76.1	46.2	29.8	34.6	18.6	27.6
1983	130.3	101.2	55.0	46.2	29.2	21.8	33.2
1984	189.4	164.1	58.3	105.8	25.3	46.1	12.2
1985	181.3	150.7	76.1	74.6	30.6	55.9	20.2
1986	345.0	306.1	172.6	133.5	39.0	142.8	29.8
1987	336.9	290.8	190.3	100.5	46.1	162.7	27.6
1988	436.6	376.6	206.0	170.7	60.0	165.2	40.8
1989	454.1	394.7	186.3	208.4	59.4	132.9	53.3
1990	707.4	645.3	196.5	448.7	62.1	161.8	34.8
1991	779.6	697.6	227.6	470.0	82.0	162.9	64.8
1992	489.2	386.7	168.9	217.8	102.5	130.7	38.2
1993	507.3	409.3	186.9	222.4	98.0	153.9	33.1
1994	483.3	395.1	176.8	218.3	88.2	130.7	46.1
1995	559.1	450.8	212.6	238.2	108.3	172.4	40.2
1996	523.0	426.5	207.7	218.8	96.5	177.3	30.4

Notes: TOTAID = Effective development assistance + TA (GQ + grants + TA).
EDA = Effective development assistance (GQ + grants).
GQ = Grant equivalent of ODA loan.
TA = Technical assistance.
Source: Chang, Fernández-Arias, and Servén 1999.

TABLE 2.4 GHANA: EDA LOANS AND DONOR GRANTS BY SECTOR, 1980–96
(millions of U.S. dollars)

Year	Balance of payments support	Communication	Social services	Construction	Current imports	Electricity, gas and water production	Financial, insurance, real estate, business	General purpose contributions	Manufacturing	Mining, quarrying	Other contributions	Trade, restaurants, lodging	Transport and storage
1970	0.00	0.00	0.40	0.00	1.30	0.00	0.00	0.00	0.00	0.00	0.00	0.00	0.00
1971	0.00	0.00	5.47	0.00	6.11	1.11	0.00	0.00	0.00	0.00	0.00	0.00	0.00
1972	0.00	0.00	4.40	0.00	8.27	4.69	0.00	0.00	0.00	0.00	0.00	0.00	0.00
1973	0.00	0.00	4.90	0.00	7.65	1.61	0.00	0.00	0.18	0.00	0.00	0.00	0.00
1974	0.00	0.00	1.19	0.00	0.90	0.86	0.00	0.00	4.10	0.00	0.00	0.00	0.05
1975	1.46	0.00	1.55	0.00	1.18	4.69	0.00	0.00	2.36	0.00	0.00	0.00	7.12
1976	3.01	-0.02	1.84	0.00	2.79	1.09	0.00	0.00	2.29	0.00	0.00	0.00	7.65
1977	6.88	-0.01	0.21	0.00	2.95	9.44	0.03	0.00	2.96	0.00	0.00	0.00	9.22
1978	0.63	-0.03	2.17	0.00	1.24	19.35	0.00	0.00	3.09	0.00	0.00	0.00	2.39
1979	0.28	1.63	3.78	0.00	17.51	15.68	-0.02	0.00	6.04	0.00	0.00	0.00	0.12
1980	2.20	-0.15	2.80	0.00	26.26	24.62	0.07	0.88	13.27	0.00	0.00	0.00	0.14
1981	0.00	-0.06	5.75	0.00	20.36	12.33	0.04	0.00	4.58	0.00	0.00	0.00	10.04
1982	0.00	0.03	2.76	0.00	1.85	24.64	1.12	0.00	2.80	0.00	0.00	0.00	7.61
1983	0.00	0.05	15.90	0.00	15.56	10.05	3.94	0.00	1.51	0.00	0.00	1.23	4.73
1984	1.41	1.85	4.04	1.03	20.37	6.59	3.72	0.00	1.93	0.00	4.39	0.00	9.88
1985	19.27	1.67	3.30	0.51	8.08	8.13	4.70	0.00	2.11	-1.02	6.60	0.00	19.31
1986	73.31	0.12	6.85	16.10	9.93	8.12	2.54	0.00	6.50	-1.27	23.35	0.00	24.22
1987	89.39	0.32	7.75	10.83	4.31	16.56	-0.01	0.00	7.59	-2.28	14.61	0.93	34.36
1988	94.22	16.03	13.20	3.86	5.33	19.49	-1.88	0.00	12.67	-1.56	4.33	1.12	26.73
1989	110.21	7.05	11.62	4.97	2.91	8.20	-0.50	0.00	6.32	5.60	1.32	0.00	23.10
1990	121.62	1.70	14.44	6.45	4.11	15.26	-0.03	0.00	7.05	2.55	0.00	0.00	11.77
1991	94.91	2.97	64.15	6.83	0.00	15.21	-0.04	0.00	12.62	5.39	0.00	0.00	16.13
1992	22.60	2.34	19.06	6.95	0.00	12.87	0.00	0.00	8.13	4.23	0.00	0.00	24.18
1993	21.78	2.12	70.74	6.14	0.00	10.20	29.55	0.00	3.87	2.36	0.00	0.00	19.01
1994	28.07	1.68	57.41	10.81	0.00	9.99	33.92	0.00	4.09	3.42	0.00	0.00	23.93
1995	9.61	0.71	79.04	14.17	0.00	15.19	3.97	10.06	1.11	3.21	0.00	0.00	32.52
1996	3.45	1.26	84.81	12.99	0.00	35.24	1.65	10.63	0.12	1.16	0.00	0.00	36.17

Source: Chang, Fernández-Arias, and Servén 1999.

NOTES

1. See, for example, van de Walle and Johnston (1996); Dollar and Burnside (1997); World Bank (1998); Dollar and Svensson (1998).

2. In January 1972 Colonel I. K. Acheampong took power in a coup d'etat. One of the first actions of his National Redemption Council was to repudiate several of the country's foreign debts. A popular cry at the time was *"yentua, yentua"* (we won't pay, we won't pay).

3. The policymakers interviewed expressed differing opinions as to whether the fiscal targets were missed solely or even primarily because of the wage increase.

4. The Ghanaian government accused the United States of trying to overthrow it, and subsequent events lent some credence to these accusations. In 1985, a sting operation involving an American CIA agent resulted in the exchange of a Ghanaian intelligence agent arrested in the United States for several Ghanaian CIA operatives. In March 1986 a ship carrying American mercenaries headed for Ghana was arrested off the coast of Brazil.

5. Frimpong-Ansah (1991) notes that the word is assumed to derive from the Hausa *kara bude* meaning "keep it quiet" or "hide it."

6. Dr. Limann's academic qualifications included a B.Sc. from the London School of Economics, a master's degree in constitutional law, and a doctorate in political science from the University of Paris. He had also served as Ghana's representative to the International Labour Organisation and the World Health Organization.

7. The initial choice, Imoru Egala, who founded the PNP, was under a 12-year ban from public office dating to 1969. He was appealing this ban at the time of the election and was hence ineligible to run for president.

8. Limann confirmed this in a 1982 interview (*West Africa*, 10 May). In response to a question regarding the virtual paralysis of the government, he responded: "Yes. For more than two weeks we did nothing but these continual meetings, the whole day. I was really angry . . . I warned them that this was not going to do them or anybody any good."

9. In the second half of 1981, PNP high-level functionaries begun to fight among themselves over the issue of future party policy in the run-up to the next election. This resulted in a member of the PNP national executive committee issuing a writ in the Accra High Court in November 1981 to restrain the party hierarchy (chairman, general secretary, and publicity) "from railroading through party policy in advance of the national party congress." While the case was ultimately settled out of court, the three officers were ordered to refund within 21 days any monies they had received on behalf of the party. This was followed by the revelation that a senior member of the PNP had received a commission worth 2.7 million pounds sterling on a currency printing contract that was going to cost 22 million pounds total.

10. This role of the state, which has been common in Africa and elsewhere, does not necessarily depend on ideology. Two countries with very different economic

philosophies—South Africa and Tanzania—each used public sector employment to fulfill their social contract with the people. In the case of South Africa under apartheid the state essentially provided guaranteed lifetime jobs for Afrikaners, while in Tanzania the underlying rationale was to fulfill a socialist vision.

11. See Frimpong-Ansah (1991: 110–11) and Ocquaye (1980) for accounts of the system of state patronage during this era.

12. The literature includes, for example, Hansen (1991), Herbst (1991), Ninsin (1998), Nugent (1996), Rothchild (1991), Shillington (1992), and Yeebo (1991).

13. Striking workers from the Ghana Industrial Holdings Corporation were dismissed following their occupation of the Parliament buildings in June 1990. The organization set up to support the sacked workers, the Workers' Solidarity Front, later transformed itself into the Association of Local Unions. This in turn became a militant alternative to the Trades Union Congress.

14. There was some basis for these fears. The government of Nigeria had cut off oil supplies to Ghana during the AFRC era (1979). Having gone through its own political transition, the new Nigerian democratic government was worried about the "contagiousness" of Ghana's coup. The anti-imperialist rhetoric of the PNDC and its close ties with Libya and Cuba worried the Americans. Subsequently, evidence emerged around the time of the "spy swap" showing that the CIA had been actively involved in trying to topple Rawlings during the first few years of PNDC existence.

15. Some policymakers interviewed interpreted the fact that the secretary of finance was the last position to be filled as evidence both of PNDC awareness of the position's importance and of the struggle among PNDC supporters.

16. Chazan (1991) points out that "[while] the ideologues . . . stressed the significance of the capture of the state as the first step toward revolutionary change, emphasis [was] placed by Rawlings on moral rectitude, accountability, reciprocity, and ethical reform. While other leaders of the PNDC underlined the revolutionary nature of the regime, Rawlings expressed himself in missionary and prophetic terms. The former employed the tools of class analysis, whereas Rawlings consistently focused on the people in relation to officialdom. But since the influence of the neo-Marxist intelligentsia on the political education of Jerry Rawlings was still strong at this time, the class-based view prevailed."

17. The description of this meeting is based on interviews with key persons present at the meeting and on Shillington (1992).

18. While financial aid was not forthcoming from most of these countries, Libya played a crucial role by providing 28,000 metric tons of crude oil in July 1982. Over the next six months 12 such consignments were provided, each on free credit for a year and interest-free repayment after that.

19. Nugent (1996) describes some links between the two coups and suggests that some alliances had emerged between unlikely bedfellows.

20. The PNDC had held local government elections in 1988, but they also intensified pressure for national elections.

21. The National Convention Party entered into an alliance with the NDC, earning it a vice-presidential slot.

22. Dr. J. B Danquah was an important leader in the United Gold Coast Convention political party before independence. Nugent (1996) uses the "Busia-Danquah tradition" to refer to a political tendency that veers to the right, relatively speaking.

23. The Convention People's Party was political successful in the late 1950s and early 1960s and was known for its ability to mobilize effectively at the rural grassroots level.

24. This section draws on Jeffrey Herbst, "Labor in Ghana Under Structural Adjustment: The Politics of Acquiescence," in Rothchild (1991).

25. Rothchild (1991: 184) suggests that they lacked analytical skills to take on the government.

26. Nugent (1996) reports that some of these anti-student protests may have been stage-managed. Nonetheless, it appears undeniable that the students were unable to rally mass support for their cause.

27. In a 1989 interview (*Africa News*, 23 January), Dr. Botchwey indicated that approaching the exchange rate adjustment this way was a hard sell to the IMF.

28. Shillington (1992) describes the evolution of Rawlings's economic thinking over this period.

29. This person, a respected Harvard-trained economist, had been an adviser to Limann in 1981 while on leave from the World Bank. He was a friend of key advisers in the PNDC and was invited, on several occasions, to advise the government on economic policy. In addition, he was valued for his perspective on how certain policies would play at the Bank and Fund given his familiarity with the two institutions.

30. This view contrasts with Martin (1991) who claims that the government officials were too busy providing the IMF with data to carry out economic analysis.

31. Aryeetey (1997: 79) notes that even the World Bank's definition of "'ownership' laid particular emphasis on the commitment of the leadership . . . this probably explains why the Bretton Woods institutions did little to encourage the government to consult other institutions."

32. These results are in line with a study by Deninger, Squire, and Basu (1998) that found that prior analytic economic and sector work improved project outcomes and had a high payoff.

33. One World Bank resident representative (a respected academic before joining the Bank) taught courses at the university. He was viewed very favorably for his ability and willingness to engage both policymakers and academics at the University of Ghana in economic issues that had no easy answers.

34. These findings regarding technical assistance are similar to those of Aryeetey and Cox (1997).

35. According to one member of the negotiating team, position papers were always prepared in advance and an internal consensus was reached before negotiations. The Ghanaian team also sometimes arrived early in Washington to consult with Ghanaian economists at the World Bank and the IMF.

36. Personal communication from World Bank staff member.

REFERENCES

Abbey, J. L. S. 1989. "On Promoting Successful Adjustment: Some Lessons from Ghana." 1989 Per Lecture. Per Jacobssen Foundation, Washington, D.C.

Armstrong, R. P. 1996. "Ghana Country Assistance Review: A Study in Development Effectiveness." World Bank, Operations Evaluation Department, Washington, D.C.

Aryeetey, E., and A. Cox. 1997. "Aid Effectiveness in Ghana." In J. Carlsson, G. Somolekae, and N. van de Walle, eds., *Foreign Aid in Africa: Learning from Country Experiences*. Uppsala, Sweden: Nordic Africa Institute.

Chang, Charles C., Eduardo Fernández-Arias, and Luis Servén. 1999. "Measuring Aid Flows: A New Approach." Policy Research Working Paper 2050. World Bank, Development Research Group, Washington, D.C.

Chazan, N. 1983. *An Anatomy of Ghanaian Politics: Managing Political Recession, 1969–82*. Boulder: Westview.

————. 1991. "The Political Transformation of Ghana under the PNDC." In D. Rothchild, ed., *The Political Economy of Recovery*. Boulder: Lynne Rienner.

Chibber, Ajay, and Nemat Shafik. 1991. "The Inflationary Consequences of Devaluation with Parallel Markets: The Case of Ghana." In Ajay Chibber and S. Fischer, eds., *Economic Reform in Sub-Saharan Africa*. Washington, D.C.: World Bank.

Cukierman, Alex, and Mariano Tommasi. 1994. "Why Does It Take a Nixon to Go to China?" Harvard University. Processed.

Deininger, K., L. Squire, and S. Basu. 1998. "Does Economic Analysis Improve the Quality of Foreign Assistance?" *World Bank Economic Review* 12 (September): 385–418.

Dollar, D., and C. Burnside. 1997. "Aid, Policies, and Growth." Policy Research Working Paper 1777. World Bank, Development Research Group, Washington, D.C.

Dollar, D., and J. Svensson. 1998. "What Explains the Success or Failure of Structural Adjustment Programs?" Policy Research Working Paper 1938. World Bank, Development Research Group, Washington, D.C.

Dordunoo, C., and V. K. Nyanteng. 1997. "Overview of Ghanaian Economic Development." In V. K. Nyanteng, ed., *Policies and Options for Ghanaian Economic Development*. Legon, Ghana: Institute of Statistical, Social and Economic Research, University of Ghana.

Frimpong-Ansah, J. H. 1991. *The Vampire State in Africa: The Political Economy of Decline in Ghana*. London: James Currey.

"Ghana: Roots of Student Protest." 1983. *West Africa* (6 June): 1343–45.

Ghana. 1983. "The PNDC's Programme for Reconstruction and Development." Statement by the PNDC secretary for finance and economic planning on radio and television on December 30, 1982. Information Services Department, Accra.

————. 1987. "National Programme for Economic Development" (revised). Accra.

————. 1996. "National Capacity Assessment." Accra.

Haggard, S., and S. B. Webb, eds. 1994. *Voting for Reform: Democracy, Political Liberalization, and Economic Adjustment.* New York: Oxford University Press.

Hansen, E. 1991. *Ghana under Rawlings: Early Years.* Lagos and Oxford: Malthouse Press.

Herbst, J. 1991. "Labor in Ghana under Structural Adjustment: The Politics of Acquiescence." In D. Rothchild, ed., *The Political Economy of Recovery.* Boulder: Lynne Rienner.

————. 1993. *The Politics of Reform in Ghana, 1982–1991.* Berkeley: University of California Press.

Holmgren, T. 1998. "Aid and Reform in Africa: Terms of Reference." World Bank, Development Research Group, Washington, D.C. Processed.

Husain, I., and R. Faruqee, eds. 1994. *Adjustment in Africa: Lessons from Country Case Studies.* World Bank Regional and Sectoral Studies. Washington, D.C.: World Bank.

Jebuni, C., A. Oduro, and K. A. Tutu. 1991. "Trade and Payments Liberalization and Economic Performance in Ghana." Paper presented at the African Economic Research Consortium workshop, Nairobi, Kenya. December.

————. 1994. "Trade and Payments Regime and the Balance of Payments in Ghana." *World Development* 22 (8).

Kapur, I., M. T. Hadjimichael, P. Hilbers, J. Schiff, and P. Szymczak. 1991. "Ghana: Adjustment and Growth, 1983–91." Occasional Paper 86. International Monetary Fund, Washington, D.C.

Killick, T. 1978. *Development Economics in Action: A Study of Economic Policies in Ghana.* New York: St. Martin's Press.

Martin, M. 1991. "Negotiating Adjustment and External Finance: Ghana and the International Community, 1982–1989." In D. Rothchild, ed., *The Political Economy of Recovery.* Boulder: Lynne Rienner.

Ninsin, K., ed. 1998. *Ghana: Transition to Democracy.* Legon, Ghana: Freedom Publications.

Nowak, M., R. Basanti, B. Horvath, K. Lochar, and R. Prem. 1996. "Ghana, 1983–1991." In M. T. Hadjimichael, M. Nowak, R. Sharer, A. Tahari, and a staff team from the Africa Department, eds., *Adjustment for Growth: The African Experience.* Occasional Paper 143. International Monetary Fund, Washington, D.C.

Nugent, P. 1996. *Big Men, Small Boys and Politics in Ghana.* Accra: Asempa Publishers, Christian Council of Ghana.

Nyanteng, V. K. 1997. *Policies and Options for Ghanaian Economic Development.* Legon, Ghana: Institute of Statistical, Social and Economic Research, University of Ghana.

Ocquaye, M. 1980. *Politics in Ghana, 1972–79.* Accra: Tornado Publications.

Rothchild, D., ed. 1991. *The Political Economy of Recovery.* SAIS African Studies Library. Boulder: Lynne Rienner.

Sackey, H. A. 1998. "External Aid and Real Exchange Rate in a Developing Economy: The Ghanaian Situation." Paper presented at the African Economic Research Consortium workshop, Nairobi, Kenya.

Shillington, K. 1992. *Ghana and the Rawlings Factor*. London: Macmillan.

Toye, J. 1990. "Ghana's Economic Reforms, 1983–87: Origins, Achievements and Limitations." In James Pickett and H. Singer, eds., *Towards Economic Recovery in Sub-Saharan Africa: Essays in Honour of Robert Gardiner*. London and New York: Routledge.

———. 1991. "Ghana." In Paul Mosley, Jane Harrigan, and John Toye, eds., *Aid and Power: The World Bank and Policy-Based Lending*. Vol. 2. London and New York: Routledge.

van de Walle, N., and T. A. Johnston, eds. 1996. *Improving Aid to Africa*. Policy Essay 21. Washington, D.C.: Overseas Development Council.

World Bank. 1998a. *Assessing Aid: What Works, What Doesn't, and Why*. New York: Oxford University Press.

———. 1998b. "Ghana: Country Assistance Strategy." Washington, D.C.

Yeebo, Z. 1991. *Ghana: The Struggle for Popular Power. Rawlings: Saviour or Demagogue*. London: New Beacon Press.

Younger, S. 1992. "Aid and the Dutch Disease: Macroeconomic Management When Everybody Loves You." *World Development* 20 (11): 1587–97.

Uganda

Torgny Holmgren
Ministry of Foreign Affairs, Sweden

Louis Kasekende
Michael Atingi-Ego
Daniel Ddamulira
Bank of Uganda
Kampala, Uganda

ACRONYMS AND ABBREVIATIONS

AfDB	African Development Bank
ADF	African Development Fund
CG	Consultative Group
CPIA	Country Policy and Institutional Assessment
EDA	Effective development assistance
EPRC	Economic Policy Research Centre
ERC	Economic and Recovery Credit
ERP	Economic Recovery Program
ESAF	Enhanced Structural Adjustment Facility (of the IMF)
GDP	Gross domestic product
HIPC	Heavily indebted poor countries
ICOR	Incremental capital-output ratio
IDA	International Development Association (of the World Bank Group)
IMF	International Monetary Fund
MFPED	Ministry of Finance, Planning and Economic Development
NGO	Nongovernmental organization
NRM	National Resistance Movement
ODA	Official development assistance
ODF	Official development finance
PEC	Presidential Economic Council
SAC	Structural Adjustment Credit
SAD	Sector Adjustment Credit
SAF	Structural Adjustment Facility (of the IMF)
SAL	Structural Adjustment Loan
sh	Uganda shilling
SIL	Sector Investment Loan
TA	Technical assistance
TAL	Technical Assistance Loan
UDN	Uganda Debt Network
UMA	Uganda Manufacturers Association
UNDP	United Nations Development Programme
UNICEF	United Nations Children's Fund
URA	Uganda Revenue Authority

U ganda's development over the last two decades makes a fascinating case study of the causes of policy reforms and the links between aid and reforms. Starting from an unstable, uncertain, and insecure economic situation, the country has managed to develop a successful reform program. Aid has certainly been part of this development. This study seeks to determine what role it has played and what lessons can be learned from the Ugandan experience.

Uganda received an increasing amount of aid from 1980 to 1995, after which aid started to level off. Until recently aid was provided mainly as loans from multilateral institutions, in contrast to the typical pattern for African countries. Bilateral assistance and grants only came to play the predominant role in the 1990s. Roughly half of total assistance since the mid-1980s has been associated with structural adjustment programs. Technical assistance makes up a large fraction of the aid and has amounted to about one-third of the grants. In addition, Uganda was the first country to receive support through the Heavily Indebted Poor Countries (HIPC) Debt Initiative. Aid coordination improved considerably during the 1990s, with the government playing a more active role and with intensified local donor coordination.

Uganda's reform program has been one of the most successful in Sub-Saharan Africa. The gross domestic product (GDP) grew by an average 6.4 percent during 1987–96, and inflation has been reduced from more than 100 percent in 1987 to single-digit figures. The government has achieved both stabilization and substantial decontrol of the economy. While its early stance was marked by rejection of market-based reforms (1986), followed by reluctant implementation (1987–92), the government has since then moved to full ownership of such reforms. The basic factors behind the success of the reforms include strong political leadership, a process of learning from mistakes, evolving government commitment, and in recent years, broadening domestic ownership of reforms. A more active policy dialogue is now taking place involving the Parliament, the private sector, trade unions, nongovernmental organizations, the media, and other actors. The challenge ahead is to further develop and sustain the reform program as well as to broaden and deepen the domestic ownership.

Aid in various forms helped to support the generation and implementation of the policy reforms. When the government reluctantly introduced market-based reforms, the policy dialogue, advisory services, training, and technical assistance provided by donors were of critical importance, both for the decisions to reform and for the direction of the reforms. The Ugandan government has made unusually good use of technical assistance. Study visits to countries within and outside the region, notably Ghana, were also very valuable during this period.

103

When the government decided to reform in the late 1980s, financial aid and conditionality became a powerful tool. Conditionality, which earlier had been regarded as externally imposed, was now used by reformers within the government to help push the reforms forward. It was pivotal in generating, implementing, and cementing the reforms. With a very weak revenue base, the financial support was, and still is, necessary for implementation of most reforms. Since 1992, however, government ownership of the reforms has meant that conditionality has become less relevant for inducing reforms. From the donors' perspective, policy dialogue and advisory services can once again become the most important instruments for supporting the generation of reforms.

This study is based on a review of current literature, analysis of aid and policy data, and interviews conducted in Kampala in March 1999 (see appendix 3.2). It consists of five parts. Section 2, which follows, describes aid flows to Uganda, highlighting aid linked to the support of policy reforms. Section 3 provides an overview and analysis of the country's economic policy and institutional development. Section 4 addresses the overall question of the links between aid and reform in Uganda, and section 5 concludes by presenting some of the lessons drawn.

AID TO UGANDA

In this paper the term *aid* will refer to effective development assistance (EDA).[1] This measure captures the true grant element of aid flows more accurately than does the commonly used official development assistance (ODA). We will also use the measure official development finance (ODF), which in addition includes nongrant components of official loans, in order to capture all official flows. In this way we include all grants and loans to Uganda that are undertaken by the official sector in order to promote economic development and welfare. Loans from the International Monetary Fund (IMF) for structural adjustment programs, in the form of the Structural Adjustment Facility (SAF) and Enhanced Structural Adjustment Facility (ESAF), are included in our analysis, as are technical assistance grants. But we exclude assistance mobilized directly by nongovernmental organizations and any form of military assistance given to Uganda.[2]

Official Aid Flows

Uganda's post-independence experience with aid flows can be divided into three periods: 1962–78, 1979–85, and 1986–97 (see table 3.6 in Appendix 3.1). Commitments were tiny during the first period, amounting only to US$357 million (4 percent of total aid since independence). A

Figure 3.1 Official Development Finance Flows to Uganda, 1980–96

Millions of 1995 U.S. dollars

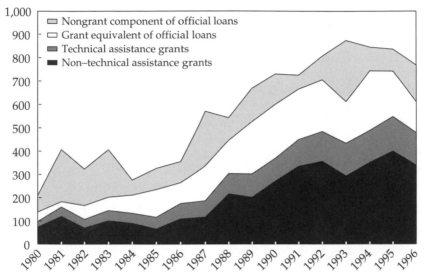

Note: The figure shows official development finance (ODF) as well as effective development assistance (EDA) for 1980-96. The three lower graphs add up to EDA, and all graphs together show ODF.
Source: World Bank.

striking feature of these years is the low level of support from multilateral donors, especially the World Bank, and the general absence of Western countries. Very few bilateral donors committed resources to Uganda. Factors that discouraged the interest of Western donors in this era included the nature of the political regimes in Uganda, the tendency of the regimes to lean toward socialism, and poor macroeconomic management. Only after the fall of Idi Amin in 1979 did the World Bank and a number of European bilateral donors step in. This marked the second phase of aid relationships.

The third phase and the real take-off in terms of aid volume occurred in the mid-1980s, when the current reform program started. Yoweri Museveni and the National Resistance Movement (NRM) assumed power in January 1986. The economy had at that time shrunk by more than 20 percent from its peak value in 1970, and inflation had an annual rate in excess of 240 percent. As shown in figure 3.1, Uganda has received an increasing amount of aid since 1986. The first half of the 1980s was characterized by a rather steady flow of EDA, around US$150 million to US$200 million a year (1995 U.S. dollars). A sharp upturn began in 1987, with continuous growth in annual aid flows until 1995, when aid started to level out. Official loans made up the major part of ODF in the 1980s, while grants, including technical assistance, have taken over that role in the 1990s.

Support from multilateral sources has dominated official development finance over the years, but it has decreased from 3:1 to 1:1 in relation to the bilateral flows over the 16-year period studied. Bilateral ODF flows became larger than the multilateral flows in 1996. This had already been the situation with regard to EDA flows since 1991 (except for 1992).

Multilateral institutions have thus controlled the aid scene for a number of years in Uganda. They have set the tone for the types of aid to be provided and sectors to be supported. With bilateral flows now larger than multilateral flows it remains to be seen whether the bilateral organizations will determine the direction of aid in the future.

Financial Aid

The distribution of financial aid between loans and grants has been fairly even over the period as a whole, with 48 percent loans and 52 percent grants including technical assistance.[3] As shown in table 3.1, loans dominated the aid flows during the 1980s, when they accounted for some 50–60 percent of the annual ODF flows. Grants have, however, increased steadily over the years and outnumber loan disbursements since 1990. The overall grant program took a giant leap in 1987–88 when it almost doubled in size compared to the 1986 figure. Since 1991 the average level of the grant program is US$455 million a year.

Bilateral donors channel their aid mainly as grants, which on average have been 2.5 times the size of the grants by the multilateral institutions. The increase in grants as a share of total aid during this period can be attributed to two factors: (a) the increase in the number of bilateral donors (mainly the Nordic countries), and (b) the government's deliberate decision in 1992 to control its debt by limiting financing of its activities first to grants and then to concessional loans with a grant element of at least 75 percent.

The multilateral institutions have directed a large part of their assistance as policy-based lending oriented to reform. Fast-disbursing support for policy reforms has played a significant role in aid to Uganda, especially in 1987–92 when the basis of the reform program was taking shape. During this period, as discussed in more detail below, financial aid and conditionality were critical in driving the reform program. Bilateral donors in turn have provided substantial co-financing to the adjustment operations. For example, World Bank Structural Adjustment

TABLE 3.1 UGANDA: TOTAL DISBURSEMENTS ON LOANS AND GRANTS (ODF), 1980–96
(millions of current U.S. dollars)

Type of aid	1980	1981	1982	1983	1984	1985	1986	1987	1988	1989	1990	1991	1992	1993	1994	1995	1996
Loans	95.8	207.3	173.1	199.4	106.4	153.5	135.5	317.4	207.3	321.1	343.5	258.9	305.7	391.4	323.7	288.2	288.5
Grants	82.7	134.3	85.0	110.5	98.9	84.3	131.6	153.8	262.8	264.2	351.3	421.4	458.0	383.9	443.7	547.3	478.6
Total	178.5	341.6	258.1	309.9	205.3	237.8	267.1	471.2	470.1	585.3	694.8	680.3	763.7	775.3	767.4	835.5	767.1

Source: Chang, Fernández-Arias, and Servén 1999.

TABLE 3.2 WORLD BANK AND IMF POLICY REFORM LOANS
TO UGANDA, 1980–98

		World Bank (millions of U.S. dollars)		
Loan	Type	Amount approved	Approval year	Closing year
Reconstruction Credit	ERC	72.5	1980	1982
Technical Assistance	TAL	8.0	1980	1985
Reconstruction Credit II	SAL	70.0	1982	1985
Technical Assistance II	TAL	51.3	1983	1992
Agricultural Rehabilitation Sector Adjustment Credit	SAD	66.1	1983	1992
Reconstruction III	SAL	50.0	1984	1987
Economic Recovery Credit	SAL	65.0	1987	1991
Technical Assistance III	TAL	18.0	1988	1995
Public Enterprises	TAL	15.0	1988	1995
Economic Recovery I/II Supplement	SAL	26.7	1989	—
Economic Recovery Credit II	SAL	125.0	1990	1993
Poverty and the Social Cost of Adjustment	SIL	28.0	1990	1995
Agricultural Sector Adjustment	SAD	115.0	1990	1996
Structural Adjustment Credit I	SAL	125.0	1991	1994
Economic and Financial Management Technical Assistance	TAL	29.0	1992	1999
Institutional Capacity Building	TAL	36.4	1992	2000
Financial Sector Adjustment Credit	SAD	100.0	1993	1997
Structural Adjustment Credit II	SAL	80.0	1994	1996
Structural Adjustment Credit III	SAL	125.0	1997	1999
Education Sector Adjustment Credit	SAD	80.0	1998	—

(continued on next page)

Credits (SAC I and III) through the International Development Association were co-financed with US$69.4 million and US$50.0 million respectively. Table 3.2 lists all IMF and World Bank loans for policy reforms during the period 1980–98.

Balance of payments support and IMF disbursements together have accounted for approximately 50 percent of the official development lending during the study period. Table 3.3 shows the amount of import support provided in the 1990s as part of the overall balance of payments support. The support corresponds to approximately one-quarter of overall ODF during those years. The social sectors accounted for 15 percent of the aid flows, while the primary sectors (agriculture, forestry, fishing), power and electricity, manufacturing, and transport accounted for

TABLE 3.2—*continued*

| Loan | Time | Year | International Monetary Fund (1980–84 in millions of SDR, 1987–97 in millions of U.S. dollars) | |
			Amount approved	Amount drawn
Standby Operation	1 year	1980	12.5	12.5
Trust Fund Loan	1 year	1980	22.3	22.3
Compensatory Financing Facility	1 year	1980	25.0	25.0
Compensatory Financing Facility	1 year	1981	45.0	45.0
Standby I	1 year	1981/82	112.5	112.5
Standby II	1 year	1982/83	112.5	112.5
Standby III	1 year	1983/84	95.0	65.0
Structural Adjustment Facility	2 years	1987	69.7	49.8
ESAF	3 years	1989	179.3	179.3
ESAF, additional arrangement	1 year	1992	39.8	39.8
ESAF	3 years	1994	180.0	180.0
ESAF	3 years	1997	138.0	78.0[a]

— Not available.

Note: ERC = Economic Recovery Credit. SAL = Structural Adjustment Loan/Credit. SAD = Sector Adjustment Credit. TAL = Technical Assistance Loan. SIL = Sector Investment Loan. ESAF = Enhanced Structural Adjustment Facility.

a. Disbursements until end of 1998.

Sources: World Bank; IMF.

6–7 percent each over the period (see table 3.15 in Appendix 3.1 for a detailed sector distribution).

Uganda has also received commodity support from the United States, Denmark, Japan, Austria, and the World Food Programme. Since 1987, a total of US$99 million has been committed. The management of commodity aid was very weak before 1992. It was only then, following the merger of the Finance Ministry and the Planning Ministry, that the new Ministry of Finance and Economic Planning[4] was able to incorporate all the funds generated from the various commodity aid programs into the budgeting framework.

Nonfinancial Aid

Technical assistance (TA) grants are the only category of nonfinancial aid that is registered in the official development aid statistics.[5] TA grants have expanded from about 10 percent of all ODF flows to Uganda in the

TABLE 3.3   UGANDA: IMPORT SUPPORT, 1991/92–1996/97
(millions of U.S. dollars)

Source of aid	1991/92	1992/93	1993/94	1994/95	1995/96	1996/97
Multilateral	77.62	62.94	101.04	115.90	54.37	69.09
Bilateral	108.10	120.56	53.79	63.11	31.76	41.71
Total	198.60	196.43	194.65	220.17	138.32	164.10

Source: Bank of Uganda.

early 1980s to 16–17 percent on annual basis since 1992. However, the relative share of TA reached a peak in 1986 shortly after the new government came to power (see tables 3.7 and 3.8 in Appendix 3.1).

TA made up almost one-third of total grants during the period 1980–96. Bilateral TA grants have increased from 40 percent of all TA grants in the mid-1980s to more than 70 percent since 1994 (see table 3.14 in Appendix 3.1). The United States, the United Kingdom, and Germany are the main bilateral providers of TA, accounting for nearly two-thirds of the total. Since 1991, Denmark, the Netherlands, and Sweden have also been substantial providers of grant-based TA. The United Nations Development Programme (UNDP) and the United Nations Children's Fund (UNICEF) have been responsible for 76 percent of the total multilateral grant-based TA. Both institutions increased their TA substantially in 1988–89.

Technical assistance can take the form of freestanding TA loans or can be part of project loans. The World Bank provided six freestanding TA loans to Uganda between 1980 and 1996 for a total amount of US$158 million, corresponding to 12.3 percent of total funds committed by the Bank (see table 3.2). Five of these operations had as their central objective to help core economic ministries and agencies design and implement economic reforms, and to strengthen systems and capacities within those agencies.

Evaluations show that Uganda has made unusually good use of technical assistance, especially TA directed to the finance and planning ministries and the Bank of Uganda. We will discuss this further in the section on financial versus nonfinancial aid, and examine the impact of nonfinancial aid on the policy formulation process.

Debt Relief

Uganda has been burdened by heavy debt for the last 15 years. The debt ratios were extremely high in the early 1990s, with total debt-to-export ratios over 1,400 percent and debt-service ratios over 60–70 percent, well above what are commonly regarded as sustainable debt levels (see figure 3.2).

The external debt increased in lockstep with the economic reform program during the 1980s. The total debt stock increased by some 16–17 percent annually toward the end of the decade. At the end of June 1996, public and publicly guaranteed external debt amounted to US$3,147 million, or 62.7 percent of GDP. Uganda has borrowed mainly from multilateral institutions. They accounted for most of the external debt at that time (76 percent), followed by non–Paris Club bilateral creditors (11 percent), Paris Club creditors (10 percent), and commercial creditors (3 percent). Among the multilateral institutions, the International Development Association (IDA) of the World Bank Group was the single largest creditor (53 percent), followed by the IMF (12 percent), and the African Development Bank (IDA 1997).

Because of its severe debt and its credible reform program, Uganda became the first country to be declared eligible for assistance under the Heavily Indebted Poor Countries (HIPC) Debt Initiative.[6] Uganda reached the "decision point" in April 1997 and the "completion point" one year later, receiving relief of close to US$650 million (US$350 million in net present value) from its external creditors. Assistance by IDA

FIGURE 3.2 UGANDA: DEBT INDICATORS, 1980–97

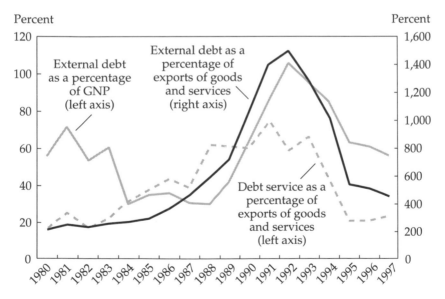

Source: World Bank.

under the HIPC Initiative was conditional on structural and social development performance criteria agreed with the government and monitored under IDA-supported programs.

The bilateral creditor governments in the Paris Club have agreed to debt rescheduling for Uganda on six occasions since 1980 (see table 3.17 in Appendix 3.1). Uganda was the first country to receive debt rescheduling on Naples terms in February 1995, corresponding to a reduction in eligible debt of 67 percent in net present value terms.

The government is now committed to borrowing only on highly concessional terms and grant financing as part of its strategy to achieve debt reduction and sustainability. The effort is also reflected in table 3.18 in Appendix 3.1, which shows an increase in donors' debt relief disbursements from US$12.9 million in 1991/92 to US$53.31 million in 1996/97. Before the introduction of the HIPC Initiative, repayment of multilateral debt was eased by a number of bilateral donors through the Multilateral Debt Fund. Disbursements from this fund equaled the magnitude of debt relief eventually provided under the HIPC Initiative annually.

On commercial debt, in February 1993 Uganda concluded an agreement sponsored by the IDA Debt Reduction Facility to purchase US$153 million of eligible principal debt owed to commercial banks. The debt was bought back at 12 cents per dollar, at a total cost of US$22.6 million.

Bilateral and Multilateral Institutions

Bilateral Aid

The bilateral donors have accounted for 50 to 60 percent of total aid (EDA) to Uganda during the 1990s. Bilateral assistance took a dramatic turn upward in 1988, when EDA more than doubled from its 1987 level of US$83 million. The shift was closely related to the improvements in political arrangements with the new government from 1986 on, and the change in economic policy that occurred in mid-1987. The government's economic reforms clearly paid off in terms of more aid flowing in, and the donors adapted quickly to the improved circumstances for utilizing aid. This change occurred just as the Cold War was coming to an end, prompting some donors to re-evaluate their geostrategic reasons for aid allocations.

Bilateral donors have extended their assistance principally in the form of grants (see figure 3.3). Grants including technical assistance accounted for 85 percent of ODF between 1980 and 1996. The share has grown even stronger in the 1990s, with grants amounting to 89 percent of total bilateral flows. Technical assistance makes up about one-quarter of this. Since aid from the bilateral donors has increased in size, in both absolute and relative numbers, Uganda now receives aid on softer terms than before.

FIGURE 3.3 UGANDA: ODF AND EDA FROM BILATERAL DONORS, 1980–96

Millions of 1995 U.S. dollars

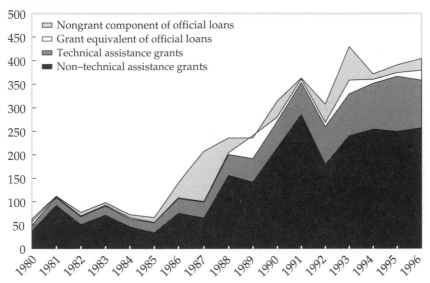

Source: World Bank.

Some 21 countries have been active donors since 1986, with a core group of seven countries that each provided more than US$10 million annually during the 1990s (tables 3.9 and 3.10 in Appendix 3.1 list all donors to Uganda). Before 1988 only four donors had annual programs of more than US$10 million (the United Kingdom, the United States, Germany, and Italy). The United Kingdom remains the largest bilateral donor, mainly because of the historical ties, and the United States stands second in grant allocation to Uganda over this period (1989–96). Other significant donors are Germany, Denmark, Sweden, the Netherlands, and Japan.

Multilateral Institutions

The International Development Association of the World Bank Group is the most important creditor to Uganda. IDA dominates not only multilateral aid to Uganda but also the total aid flow. IDA accounted for approximately 20 percent of total aid to Uganda during the period. IDA, the IMF, and the European Union are responsible for 65–75 percent of the multilateral financing. Other multilateral organizations with material programs in Uganda are the African Development Fund, UNDP, UNICEF, the United Nations High Commission for Refugees, and the World Food Programme (see tables 3.9 and 3.10 in Appendix 3.1).

Figure 3.4 indicates that financing by multilateral institutions, like that of bilateral donors, took a giant step in the mid-1980s. ODF financing almost doubled between 1986 and 1987, from just under US$162 million to US$300 million, but toward the end of the period it flattened out at a level of about US$400 million a year in disbursements. A decline in support in real terms can be noted in 1996, when disbursements by the European Union and IDA diminished sharply.

The multilateral institutions essentially provide assistance in the form of loans. Lending has on average accounted for 72 percent of the multilateral ODF flows. However, the European Union has provided most grants among all donors (including bilateral donors) to Uganda, totaling an average of US$39 million per year in 1980–96. In 1992 alone Uganda received an equivalent of US$156 million from the European Union, largely because of the collapse of world coffee prices.

Figure 3.4 Uganda: ODF and EDA from Multilateral Institutions, 1980–96

Millions of 1995 U.S. dollars

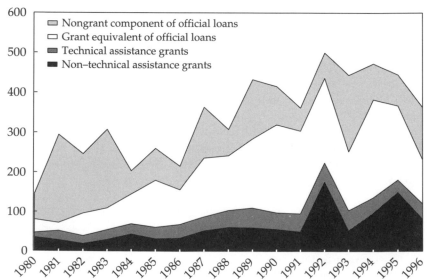

Source: World Bank.

Aid Coordination

A considerable improvement in the government's coordination of aid has taken place in the 1990s. Today, all coordination is handled by the Aid Liaison Department in the Ministry of Finance, Planning and Economic Development (MFPED). Previously, there existed at least five coordinating units in different ministries, making coordination very scattered. Furthermore, in 1995 the Parliament passed an External Loans Act that stated that only the Ministry of Finance could raise foreign borrowings on behalf of the government. This has also helped reinforce discipline in the government's aid coordination efforts. Improved coordination has led to aid being more accurately reflected in the budget than before. At the same time donors tend to channel more of their funding as budget support, for instance through the Poverty Action Fund.

All government projects are subject to screening and approval by the Development Committee. The Aid Liaison Department then identifies potential donors for projects approved by the committee. However, donor-funded projects are still to a large extent initiated through direct contacts between line ministries and donors. Sector coordination is often managed by line ministries even if the Ministry of Finance sometimes calls for tripartite discussions with line ministries and donors to help shape sector programs and ascertain that they are consistent with the overriding reform objectives. The Finance Ministry is also involved in all final negotiations with donors. More recently the ministry has been insisting that donor support should be discussed in the context of sector-wide dialogue on policy reforms and investment programming and the rolling Medium Term Expenditure Frameworks. It has also instituted quarterly meetings with donors, nongovernmental organizations, and the media to report on the Poverty Action Fund.

Consultative Group (CG) meetings chaired by the Wold Bank are routinely held every 12 to 15 months. The meetings have focused on the reform program and financing needs as well as on topics such as poverty, social sectors, debt, and corruption. In December 1998 the CG meeting took place in Kampala for the first time. The meeting had broad participation of donors (16 bilateral and 18 multilateral organizations), cabinet ministers, other government officials, nongovernmental organizations, stakeholders, and the media. The president took part in almost the entire meeting. The participation of a wide range of stakeholders in the local CG meetings is in line with the World Bank's Comprehensive Development Framework. Any continuation of locally held broad-based meetings will primarily depend on the government's interest and leadership.

The government and the donors meet quarterly in local coordination meetings chaired by the minister of finance or the Treasury secretary in the periods between CG meetings. The group sometimes meets to discuss thematic issues. Donors meet among themselves monthly under the chairmanship of the World Bank resident representative. The heads of the United Nations agencies also meet monthly to coordinate U.N. activities in Uganda. In addition, a number of ad-hoc sector working groups are in place, each led by a donor with particular interest in or knowledge of the sector concerned. Those groups also include government representatives, and their meetings provide a forum for the exchange of information and in some cases for formulation of joint strategies. Some donors said in interviews that the gap between the World Bank-IMF and the bilateral donors in terms of their assessment of the overall situation in Uganda had narrowed lately thanks to the intensified coordination. This also resulted in the preparation of joint donor statements at the CG meeting held in Kampala in 1998.

POLICY REFORMS AND INSTITUTIONAL DEVELOPMENT

Economic Policy 1980–98

From 1980 to 1985

Development finance literature links economic performance measured in terms of GDP growth to a healthy and vibrant financial sector (see, for example, McKinnon 1973; Shaw 1973; Fry 1995). However, the link between the financial and real sectors in Uganda has been weak. This is largely attributed to the weakness in the financial sector itself, poor credit culture among borrowers, and the financial repression that existed during the 1970s and 1980s. Furthermore, after years of decay in the 1970s a number of business enterprises lacked a credit history and suffered from low rates of capacity utilization and lack of working capital despite sound prospects over the medium term. There was need for a residual direct support from government to bolster such enterprises as a way of kick-starting the productive sector of the economy.

Between 1970 and 1980, the financial markets in Uganda were distinguished by regulation and lack of robust financial policies. Price controls that were applied to the goods and financial markets without regard to market conditions resulted in, first, the misallocation of resources to sectors that appeared productive only because they were highly protected, and second, the emergence of informal markets (Atingi-Ego and Matthews 1994; Kasekende and Atingi-Ego 1996; Kasekende and Malik 1993).

Consequently, the basic indicators of financial development added up to a rather discouraging picture. Real interest rates continued be negative, and the returns on formal financial assets declined. The result was disintermediation in the formal financial system with the savings and investment ratios declining. Investment became biased toward short-term projects, largely because of the increased variability in the rate of returns caused by high inflation levels.

To restart growth the government had to place high priority on re-establishing macroeconomic stability. In addition, both working and long-term finances had to be secured from external sources. This culminated in the first standby agreement with the IMF in 1981 that was aimed at restoring macroeconomic stability. The arrangement emphasized polices to encourage the mobilization of domestic resources. To this end, inflation had to be contained through an agreed reduction in overall budget deficit, domestic credit to government, stabilizing the value of the shilling, and a recovery in the productive capacity of the economy. Selective credit policies of the authorities resulted in the crowding out of some private sector agents and the government tried to bridge this gap by mobilizing some donor resources for on-lending though certain commercial banks. In addition, government sought to use the interest rate policy to increase domestic savings and hence loanable funds, so as to meet the credit needs of the private sector in the economy.

There was, however, little progress in improving the tax structure and tax collection. This combined with weak expenditure controls and growing military opposition brought about a deterioration in budgetary discipline in 1984–85, resulting in expansionary fiscal policies. The government accumulated huge expenditure arrears equivalent to 21 percent of total expenditure commitments, and then stepped up the issue of long-term bonds to finance the arrears. The available monetary policy instruments could not effectively mop up the overhang in domestic liquidity and this built up inflationary pressure on domestic prices and on the floating exchange rate.[7] In response to the rapid depreciation, the government tightened restrictions on the exchange system. These developments led to violation of the benchmarks of the monetary programs agreed by the government and the IMF, and as a result the program with the IMF collapsed in 1984.

Afterward, economic performance deteriorated. Real GDP declined by 10 percent between 1984 and 1985, inflation bounced back from double digits in 1984 to triple digits by 1985, and an overvalued exchange rate reduced the export base to a single export—coffee. Import volumes also declined, reflecting the reduced capacity of the economy to finance imports even to obtain essential intermediate goods and spare parts.

The principal lesson of this period was that the stabilization program was not accompanied by commitment on the part of the government to institute fiscal and monetary policy reforms to curb inflation,[8] improve public service delivery, and allocate resources to productive enterprises.

These were the main causes of economic instability in the first place and ought to have been addressed.

From 1986 to 1998

The economy of Uganda suffered from serious policy reversals in 1985–86. The foreign exchange constraint tightened, budgetary discipline worsened, and the institutional framework suffered from further dislocation. Inflation skyrocketed to the triple-digit range, reaching 296 percent in 1986, while deposit rates remained at about 35 percent. A number of problems observed in the early 1980s re-emerged with greater severity. Unregulated agencies in foreign exchange (the *kibanda* market) strengthened in their management of foreign exchange (Kasekende and Ssemogerere 1991), and a number of residents preferred foreign exchange–denominated assets to the shillings-denominated assets (Kasekende and Malik 1994).

1986: TURNING POINT. The government that took office in January 1986 faced daunting challenges in almost all facets of the economy. There was the problem of liquidity overhang and runaway inflation at a time of huge financial requirements to rehabilitate the economy. The banking system was insolvent despite the urgent need to encourage productive investment. Foreign exchange reserves could hardly cover two weeks of import requirements. Many firms lacked working capital and were not creditworthy. The system for procurement and processing of cash crops was highly inefficient, and the mismanagement of credit resulted in the nonpayment of farmers.

The new government invited a team of international economists and a number of influential local academics, entrepreneurs, and others to carry out an in-depth study of the economy and advise on the best way to restart economic growth. The team was asked to provide a comprehensive macroeconomic framework for the country's rehabilitation and development and to identify a mechanism and projects for sound management and development of the economy over the long term.

There was lack of consensus among team members on certain key areas of macroeconomic management, in particular the choice between a closed and open economy. A minority report of the study recommended revaluing the shilling from shs 50 to shs 14 per U.S. dollar. The argument, to use the exchange rate as a nominal anchor to inflation, was in line with the thinking of the new government. Indeed, the government chose the closed model and opted for a revaluation as recommended in the minority report. Implementing these recommendations turned out to be a serious mistake, as they fueled macroeconomic instability and worsened external viability. In addition, the government also began a program built on price controls and ideas about barter trade with Libya, North Korea, and similar countries. The "Washington consensus" was regarded as an imperialistic policy package.[9] There was, however, disagreement within the government about which type of reform program to follow. The government chose a "control" model despite opposition from critics who argued strongly that such a strategy would fail. The opponents of the reform program were nonetheless kept in the government; this later proved to be a very wise decision that benefited the economy (Tumusiime-Mutebile 1995).

Macroeconomic imbalances meanwhile intensified and all indicators pointed to a further deterioration in the economy. It became evident that the "control" model was doomed to fail. This failure, however, became a landmark in the policymaking process in that officials were reshuffled and the direction of policy choices changed. It also softened the official attitude toward the once-unpopular market policies and paved the way for liberalization. In other words, a congruence of events and the failure of the 1986 recommendations to deliver economic stability led to a reassessment of policies.

1987–91 Economic Reforms

As mentioned above, the initial economic policies of 1986 were inconsistent and by 1987 it was evident that a new program was needed. The exchange rate and inflation levels were out of control and the whole situation was steadily deteriorating. Faced with these problems, the government resumed dialogue with IMF and the World Bank, seeking their assistance in designing and implementing an economic recovery program. The main objectives of the reform program were to promote long-term growth through substantial investment in order to rehabilitate physical assets and the infrastructure. Policy reforms were needed to promote structural changes, whose implementation would depend on mobilization of necessary external resources.

The president provided the highest level of backing for the new economic reforms, although there was still some reluctance within the government. Government officials were sent to training programs and to Ghana on study tours to prepare for the new reform program. After protracted negotiations with the IMF, the government decided to start an Economic Recovery Program (ERP) in May 1987, supported by the IMF and the World Bank. The ERP had the following broad objectives:

- Economic growth of at least 5 percent per year in order to permit growth of real per capita GDP of at least 3 percent per year. This was to be achieved through improved producer incentives, agricultural produce marketing, and increased industrial capacity utilization.
- Restoration of price stability.

- Halting and reversing the deterioration in the balance of payments through restructuring of debt, export promotion, and increased capacity utilization in the import substitution industries.
- Strengthening the institutional framework.

Key to the reform package was a national currency reform. The government introduced a new currency at a rate of exchange of one new shilling to 100 old shillings. It also imposed a 30 percent conversion tax on all shilling holdings (currency in circulation and deposits). The exchange rate was simultaneously devalued by 76.6 percent and the government said that in the future the exchange rate would be adjusted whenever necessary.

Not all policymakers were fully convinced that the stabilization and structural adjustment programs were the right policies. Advocates of the reform process engaged in education and persuasion during 1987–89. To influence public opinion, they sponsored seminars and prepared public discussion papers (Tumusiime-Mutebile 1995). On the policy front, the Presidential Economic Council (PEC) played a crucial role during the initial period of the country's reform efforts. The council, chaired by the president, is a decisionmaking rather than advisory body. It greatly assisted reform advocates by holding open debate on the policies, and it also provided an important forum for discussion of major economic policy proposals requiring immediate attention. Proponents and opponents of reforms were invited to articulate and defend their points of view in the PEC. Interviews with government officials indicated that technocrats also used the PEC as a forum to convince the president of the need for reform. To this end the council secretary had a certain degree of independence in shaping the agenda and inviting people to meetings, which helped in pushing through reform efforts (Lamont 1995).

The leadership of the government remained committed to the reforms despite some lingering reluctance among officials and exogenous shocks to the economy (collapse of the International Coffee Agreement and rising oil prices due to the Gulf War). As part of the reform process, the government convened a consultative conference in December 1989 to critically discuss the state of Uganda's economy. All stakeholders in the economy were invited and the conference turned out to be another landmark in the reform process. It laid the foundation for a radical liberalization of the foreign exchange market system by legalizing the parallel *(kibanda)* market, which internal observers viewed as a key reform. The government made this decision entirely on its own, with no conditionality from the IMF or World Bank (Tumusiime-Mutebile 1995). The most important outcome of the meeting may have been the widespread support, including that of the president, for the economic reforms that emerged (IMF 1998).

The rehabilitation of the economy relied to a large extent on donor support to finance the required increase in import volume. This in turn contributed to a worsened debt situation, as mentioned. The government's Economic Recovery Program was supported by about 25 policy-based credits from the World Bank, amounting to more than US$1 billion in the five-year period 1987–92. The lending started with two Economic Recovery Credits focusing first on stabilization and later on demand management, including interest rate reform and measures to contain the fiscal deficit, trade liberalization and revitalization of the private sector, and public sector management. A Structural Adjustment Credit (SAC I) in 1991 supported coffee sector reforms, improvements in the trade regime, increased revenue mobilization, civil service reform, and actions to speed up operations of the Departed Asians Property Custodian Board.

The principal results of the economic reform program implemented between 1987 and 1991 included: (a) a lowering of the inflation rate from an average of 190 percent per year to about 28 percent per year by 1991; (b) a revival of the GDP growth rate to an average of 6.3 percent per year over 1988–91; and (c) a slow recovery of exports, and of private and public sector investment.

The program for 1990–91 specifically provided for the strengthening and development of the banking industry and the generation of up-to-date and accurate information on the balance sheets of financial institutions. Following the legalization of the parallel market foreign exchange bureaus were licensed in July 1990 to trade in foreign exchange. Interest rates were further reviewed to provide adequate incentives for domestic resource mobilization and term lending.

AFTER 1992: FULL OWNERSHIP. In 1991 and 1992, the government implemented wide-ranging policies intended to eliminate the structural and financial bottlenecks that had constrained progress in economic stabilization. These included the excessive growth in domestic credit during the 1991/92 financial year, which resulted from weaknesses in monitoring the program and failure to take appropriate corrective measures as the problems emerged. Prominent among the problems was the monetization of the budget deficit, which averaged 10.2 percent of GDP in 1991/92 compared to 3.5 percent the previous year. Consequently, government expenditure measured as a percentage of GDP rose from 16 percent in 1990/91 to 23 percent in 1991/92; this caused inflation to surge to 58 percent on annualized rate by March 1992. This in turn led to violation of the benchmarks in the monetary program and the delay of the IMF/World Bank program. Donors delayed disbursements in 1991 pending implementation of some reforms (foreign exchange auction), and this caused the fiscal crisis.

The experience made clear the increasing dependence of the budget on foreign savings and the need for a tool to make the budget flexible. It also showed the need to widen the range of instruments in economic management, particularly monetary policy instruments, and to move faster into market-oriented policies.

These lessons provided an opportunity to reassess the policy environment, and led the government to reform the management of its fiscal and monetary policies. The following reforms were implemented to strengthen the conduct of fiscal and monetary policy:

- The president announced that borrowing from the Bank of Uganda constituted indiscipline, and broad reform policies were introduced in the financial sector.
- A cash budget rule was adopted beginning April 1992 and a cash-flow management committee was instituted, including officials from the Bank of Uganda and the Ministry of Finance and Economic Planning. The flexible management of the budget greatly helped to reduce financial imbalances and provide adequate resources to the banking sector to support private sector credit.
- The Bank of Uganda was mandated to auction Treasury bills as necessary to achieve the monetary targets. A decision was also made to review interest rates regularly to ensure real interest rates of at least 4 percent on 12-month deposits.
- More market-oriented methods were introduced in the management and allocation of foreign exchange and determination of the exchange rate.
- The government linked the one-year deposit rate, the lending rates on credit to the agricultural sector, and the interest rates on term credits to the auction-determined discount rate in an effort to strengthen resource mobilization and efficient allocation of resources. This took effect in October 1992. All other interest rates were completely decontrolled. Interest rates were fully liberalized in 1993/94.
- Beginning in 1992/93, the Reserve Money Program was developed as a key instrument in liquidity management and implementing monetary policy.

Between 1993 and 1998, then, management of the economy was largely dictated by the lessons drawn from the slippage that occurred in 1991. Another important factor was institutional reform, namely the president's decision to strengthen the economic team by combining the ministries of Finance and Economic Planning into one. In fact, the team from the Ministry of Planning that had contributed immensely to the reform efforts took over the leadership of the combined ministry. Thanks to this merger, the government strengthened its commitment to macroeconomic stability, and ownership of the reform program deepened. The continuity and long tenure of the economic team has turned out to be critical in the process leading to full ownership of the reform program and Uganda's entry into a period of sustained reforms.

Following the restoration of macroeconomic stability, a new three-year ESAF program was agreed with the IMF in 1994. The program focused on structural reforms, fiscal objectives, and reserves accumulation. The government introduced tax rate changes, established an independent revenue authority, abolished the export tax on coffee, and removed the monopoly of the Coffee Marketing Board. Under this program, the IMF and other donors sought to finance the deepening of reforms, especially the structural and institutional reforms (discussed below). The World Bank followed up with a second Structural Adjustment Credit, also in 1994.

The results of implementing the above policies between 1992 and 1998 have been quite satisfactory:

- Private sector investments in Uganda increased from 9 percent of GDP in 1991/92 to 13 percent in 1998/99.
- Growth rate of real GDP increased to an average of 7.6 percent per year.
- Inflation declined to 8 percent, down from 190 percent over the period 1987–91.
- The current account deficit was narrowed from 6 percent in 1992 to 4 percent in 1996, measured as current account deficit/GDP (including grants).
- Monetary deepening (M2/GDP) was experienced, from 8.2 percent in 1992 to 11.7 percent in 1996.
- Foreign exchange cover, measured in terms of months of imports cover, increased from two to about five months.

All these measures resulted in lower inflation levels and satisfactory growth rates, as shown in figure 3.5.

The IMF and Uganda agreed on a new ESAF in 1997. It focused on maintaining macroeconomic stability, private sector promotion, export-oriented growth, and structural and institutional reforms to further reduce impediments to growth and job creation. Uganda accepted the obligations of Article VIII and removed current account restrictions, and went to full capital account convertibility in 1997. In the same year the World Bank approved a third Structural Adjustment Credit. The credit aimed at stabilization and the acceleration of economic growth through fostering long-term fiscal sustainability, involving a more efficient tax system as well as better management of public expenditures.

FIGURE 3.5 INFLATION AND GROWTH IN UGANDA, 1980–96

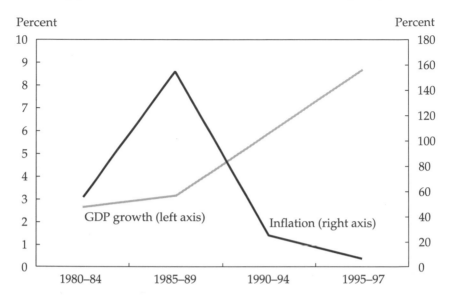

Source: World Bank.

Growth and Poverty Trends

GROWTH. As stated above, Uganda has recorded reasonable economic growth rates between 1986 and 1998, averaging 6.5 percent per year. Before this period, Uganda had suffered from massive economic mismanagement that led to total collapse of the productive capacity of the economy. A very important requirement for the economic revival of the country was the adoption of proper macroeconomic management policies. Indeed, economic growth in Uganda in recent years owes much to the adoption of prudent macroeconomic policies by the government as discussed above. Growth in Uganda has been driven by recovery in agricultural production and an increase in capacity utilization in the industrial sector. However, sustained growth can only be expected through investment by both the private and public sectors.

The recovery of the agricultural sector since 1987 followed government recognition of the sector's potential to lead the country's recovery and the economic reforms undertaken to realize this potential. Monetary and nonmonetary agriculture together accounted for about 54.8 percent of GDP in 1987. Efforts were made to remove the main constraints to agricultural production and diversification (Kasekende and Atingi-Ego

1999). These included the lack of foreign exchange to import agricultural inputs, as well as monopoly and other institutional inadequacies in the marketing of the output. The removal of some of these constraints, together with the peace prevailing in most parts of the country, led to increased land use and high agricultural production. Output in agriculture grew by 62 percent between 1986 and 1998. The turnaround has mainly benefited rural people, who produce mostly on small land holdings.

In the industrial sector, the initial effort was geared toward increasing capacity utilization of the existing factories. Low capacity utilization had resulted from lack of foreign exchange for the importation of spare parts and raw materials. Measures taken to revive this sector included the introduction of the Open General License and Special Import Program in 1988, both of which were intended to allocate scarce foreign exchange to priority areas. Success has been achieved in this area, with the manufacturing sector recording average growth of 12.74 percent per year between 1989/90 and 1998/99 and increasing its share of GDP by more than 4 percentage points. Table 3.4 highlights the monetary GDP performance in selected sectors of the Ugandan economy in1989/90 and 1998/99.

A significant change associated with the reform period has been the shift of production from the public to the private sector. This is expected to lead to sustained growth and poverty reduction. The share of private capital formation increased from 7 percent of GDP in 1989/90 to 13 percent in 1998/99. At the same time public capital formation declined from 7 percent of GDP to 5 percent during the same period.

POVERTY. Poverty reduction has been a major concern of government during the reform period. Both human and financial resources have been

TABLE 3.4 UGANDA: GROWTH PATTERNS SINCE 1989

Sector	Average growth 1989/90 – 1998/99 (percent)	Share of GDP (percent)	
		1989/90	1998/99
Agriculture	5.98	24.3	23.1
Manufacturing	12.74	5.4	9.6
Construction	10.46	5.1	7.3
Trade	8.41	11.0	13.1
Hotels and restaurants	12.10	1.1	1.8
Transport and communication	9.03	4.1	5.2
Total GDP	6.40	51.0	60.1

Source: Uganda Bureau of Statistics.

deployed to tackle poverty at all levels, in both the urban and rural areas. Government recognizes that poverty reduction can be addressed in two ways in addition to maintaining macroeconomic stability. The first is by putting in place an environment that promotes investment and fast economic growth, in order to provide employment opportunities to the population and increase their incomes. Second, the government believes that there are additional intervention measures that can also work directly to alleviate poverty. The two approaches are seen as complementing each other in the fight against poverty.

Given the high level of macroeconomic instability during the initial period of the reform effort, the government concentrated on programs that would promote stability and efficient use of national resources. The structural adjustment programs supported by the IMF and World Bank were used as the framework for economic management. During the latter part of 1980s, there were no direct interventions aimed at reducing poverty. A special Program to Alleviate Poverty and the Social Costs of Adjustment was designed at the turn of the decade when it was recognized that some vulnerable groups would not benefit in the short run from the Economic Recovery Program. The World Bank supported the program with a credit of US$28 million. It was basically intended to mitigate the social costs that arose from demand management measures of government (particularly fiscal tightening), associated with the adjustment programs.

With economic stability restored for the past few years, the government is now focusing its efforts on poverty reduction through direct intervention. This is contained in a Poverty Eradication Action Plan that was developed by government in 1997. Key features include programs aimed at improving the road network, agricultural modernization, universal primary education, primary health care, and promotion of the private sector. Government plans to increase spending on those sectors that are believed to have a direct impact on the quality of life of poor Ugandans. To further boost the Poverty Action Fund, government has directed all savings on debt repayment arising from the HIPC Initiative toward the priority sectors—an indication of its determination to fight poverty. The savings from HIPC are in the region of US$40 million per year, and donors are expected to contribute an additional US$40 million to the fund.

The government strongly believes that provision of security is key to ensuring that the poorest members of society enjoy the benefits of growth. In addition, the Poverty Eradication Action Plan emphasizes improved governance through enhanced transparency and accountability for resources directed to the Poverty Action Fund. As an example, resources released for the primary education program are advertised in the daily newspapers, and the regular donor meetings on the Poverty Action Fund receive financial reports on the fund's receipts and disbursements.

Although there are several gaps in poverty data, there is some evidence of a reduction in the level of poverty in Uganda following years of steady economic growth. The household budget survey of 1997 indicates improvements in the living conditions of the poor. The report indicates that household expenditure increased by 128 percent in the rural areas, while in the urban areas average household expenditure increased even faster, by 133 percent between 1992 and 1996. In addition, the report shows that the share of iron-roofed houses in total residential houses increased from 38 percent in 1991 to 48 percent by 1996. Reflecting increases in income, the share of food and beverages in total household expenditure has fallen by 5 percentage points, from 60 to 55 percent during the same period.

Institutional Development and the Governance System

The restoration of economic growth was largely supported by the adoption of prudent macroeconomic policies that initially increased the utilization of existing capacity; after 1992–93, new investments also played a role. However, according to Kasekende and Atingi-Ego (1999), this kind of growth will taper off as spare capacity diminishes, and therefore new capacity will have to be generated if current growth rates are to be sustained. This calls for increased investment-GDP ratios and incremental capital-output ratios (ICORs). It is very likely that with poor service delivery in either the public or the private sector or both, the associated ICORs will be lower than would be the case with efficient service delivery. Consequently, increased investment-GDP ratios need to be accompanied by efficient public service delivery in order to tap the maximum ICORs. In line with this, some institutional reforms have been undertaken in an attempt to increase the effectiveness of service delivery through building relevant institutions.

Institutional Development

PRIVATE SECTOR DEVELOPMENT. In line with the recommendation that the role of government in production and the allocation of productive resources should be reduced, some institutional reforms were undertaken to increase the effectiveness of the private sector. These included, among others, civil service reforms, public sector reform, and a framework for market determination of prices of productive resources (for example, the exchange rate). Investment laws and procedures were streamlined in order to attract both domestic and foreign investors. To this end, a new Investment Code Act (1991) replaced the Foreign Investment Act (1977), and the Industrial Licensing Act (1969) was abolished. The Investment Code Act sought to attract, promote, and facilitate investment, provide fiscal incentives, protect foreign and local investors, and introduce a mechanism for the repatriation of dividends and fees. In 1991 the Uganda Investment Authority was created to administer the new investment code and also to act as a one-stop investment center for investors.

Contentious issues such as the Departed Asians Property Custodian Board had to be resolved as a step toward reaffirming government respect for private property rights. By 1994, a total of 640 out of 690 claims by noncitizens and 1,860 out of 2,000 claims by citizens had been verified and property returned to the original owners. This was a good performance given that the non-returned properties were either not claimed or the verification needed more time. By 1996 this process was cleared. It is worth noting that this is an area in which technical assistance played a large role, and it also demonstrated the role of support for a reform at the highest political level.

In addition to drawing on technical assistance, reform-minded technocrats have used conditionality in order to overcome pockets of resistance to reforms. In some cases they have asked for specific conditions to be embedded in the support programs. It was therefore not uncommon to see structural benchmarks in the performance criteria of the ESAF programs being used as a means of speeding up reforms. This may be seen as a step in the right direction insofar as deepening the reforms is concerned. There have, however, been reports of less transparent reform undertakings in the privatization of some state-owned enterprises. Those few cases notwithstanding, most Ugandans appear to have embraced the idea of privatization.

With respect to the exchange rate and trade policy reform, the government in 1991 was more than committed to conform to Article VIII of the IMF agreement, which stipulated that no restrictions be placed on international transactions. By July 1990, the authorities had already legalized the buying and selling of foreign currencies in the foreign exchange bureaus at a market-determined rate. Further reforms in the financing of international trade were implemented in January 1992 following the government's replacement of the Open General License and Special Import Program with the weekly foreign exchange auction of donor-provided import support funds. What is important here is that the donor aid flows provided the needed foreign exchange for the weekly private sector foreign exchange auction, thus boosting private sector confidence. Finally, in 1993, the auction and the surrender requirements were abolished and replaced with a unified foreign exchange system with the commercial banks and foreign exchange bureaus as the key institutions in the market. In addition, in July 1997 the capital account of the balance of payments was opened up in an attempt to increase private capital inflows.

Other measures taken to revamp export earnings included the liberalization of export commodity marketing. A number of private companies and cooperative unions were licensed to compete with the once monopolistic marketing boards. The main result has been the on-spot delivery of cash for value offered by the producers, as opposed to the earlier practice of issuing promissory chits. On the macroeconomic front, the central bank financing of the marketing boards was often associated with the injection of high-powered money into the system and this was a principal cause of the inflationary episodes in Uganda. Since the liberalization of marketing arrangements, the competition in marketing has completely ended this type of financing. As part of the government's commitment to economic stabilization, a coffee stabilization tax was imposed when world market prices for coffee surged during the 1994–95 coffee boom. This was to ensure that the exchange rate did not appreciate markedly and adversely affect competitiveness of the export sector.

Government also took steps to create institutions that could help to promote the growth of the private sector. These actions included:

- Provision of an appropriate legal framework that strengthens commercial jurisdiction, reinforces property rights, and facilitates settlement of business disputes
- Support for the development of well-organized groups representing various interests in the private sector
- Establishment of a properly functioning financial system and safety net in order to meet liquidity needs of the private sector and minimize liquidity crises, for example through deposit insurance schemes. The financial sector reforms were also necessary because the high intermediation costs were retarding private sector development.

POLICY DIALOGUE. Since 1987, a few institutions and organizations have become active in the policy dialogue. These include the Parliament, the independent Economic Policy Research Centre at Makerere University, the Uganda Manufacturers Association, the Private Sector Foundation, unions such as the National Organization of Trade Unions, nongovernmental organizations (mainly through Uganda Debt Network), and, to a lesser extent, the Uganda Farmers Association.

The *Parliament* acts as a useful instrument and watchdog. Major economic policy changes are now being reviewed and adopted by the Parliament. It has been especially active in the field of privatization and resisted, for instance, the privatization of Uganda Commercial Bank. It has also exposed cases of corruption, leading to impeachment, removal, or reshuffling of cabinet ministers and resulting in greater transparency and accountability in public administration.

Research institutions can potentially play a strong role in the identification of problem areas and in deepening the domestic policy dialogue. Institutions such as the Economic Policy Research Centre (EPRC) could become facilitators for the internal dialogue on policy issues as well as local watchdogs, roles often undertaken by the World Bank today in driving the dialogue on policy reforms. Rather than having a voice of its own in the policy debate, EPRC would plan a catalytic role, providing analytical input for the process and bringing together the different stakeholders to debate the various issues.

The *private sector* enjoys the respect of the government, which supports private sector participation in policy formulation. A transition has taken place since 1987, when the private sector was regarded mainly as a subject for government regulation. Current thinking on private sector development is discussed with the private sector before new policies are developed and proposed by the government. The Uganda Manufacturers Association (UMA) has evolved into a key institution representing the interests of the private sector. Over the years, it has developed a strong partnership with government in policy formulation. In 1991 it spearheaded the setting up of the Presidential Forum, which includes all key stakeholders in policymaking and the private sector. However, the role of the forum has recently waned. The private sector through UMA participates in the budget process, which has been well received by the government and the president. UMA has participated on a number of occasions in determining the speed and sequencing of the trade reform program. Academic researchers and local consultants have also taken part in the policymaking process through UMA.

Private sector representatives emphasized in interviews that the government should not make any rules for the sector without consulting them. Some also complained that even though the sector rightly is engaged in policy discussion, its real influence is rather marginal. The private sector and the government agree on many points, but members of the UMA said that the government is unwilling to listen seriously to the private sector when the two sides disagree (interview, UMA, 1999). Officials at the Ministry of Finance and Economic Planning responded that someone has to make the final decision, weighing all factors, and that not all actors could be equally satisfied with the outcome. The policies implemented reflect inclusion of concerned parties in the process, if not always a consensus. Private sector representatives also said in interviews that there needs to be an element of competition in the political system so that private sector participants can voice their concerns to different parties if their ideas are not reflected in actual policymaking. "Once you lack competition you risk being patronized."

Other private sector actors are the Private Sector Foundation and the Uganda Exporters' Association. The Uganda National Chamber of Commerce and Industry is not as active in lobbying, although it has some political influence through members of Parliament (IMF 1998).

The *farmers* are barely active in the policy dialogue. The Uganda Farmers Association only participates to a very limited extent in the discussion. However, the key institution charged with spearheading agricultural sector reforms is the Agricultural Secretariat in the Bank of Uganda. It was set up with financing from IDA, which provided resident advisers while consultants came from the U.N. Food and Agriculture Organization and the World Bank, and other local researchers were recruited as needed. The secretariat is credited with restructuring of both coffee and cotton subsectors as well as the land reform.

Nongovernmental organizations (NGOs) have also become more involved in policy discussions. A large number of local and foreign NGOs are active in the country, an estimated 1,500 to 2,000 organizations, making coordination very difficult. Nevertheless, NGOs have made their voices heard on the debt issue in particular through the Uganda Debt Network (UDN). The government has called UDN for consultation on policy issues, but the network's representatives found the meetings often to be information dissemination by the government rather than real consultations. As with the private sector, many NGOs welcome the opening of dialogue but find that their influence on policy formulation continues to be minimal.

There apparently exists a political will to involve NGOs and other stakeholders in the policy dialogue, but more investments seem to be needed on both sides to form this partnership. A group consisting of NGOs and the government has been formed to monitor the Poverty Action Fund. NGOs attended the CG meeting in December 1998 but were not engaged in its preparation; this made their participation in the meeting less effective, according to NGO sources.

Some donors expressed doubts in interviews as to whether NGOs and the private sector can contribute effectively to the policy dialogue. According to this view the NGOs are in many cases too consensus-oriented and the private sector is still too dependent on the government to be active critical voices in the debate. NGO representatives believe on the other hand that a major constraint to active participation is lack of consultation by donors. They say that instead of holding discussions with and relying only on the government, donors should meet with NGOs, the private sector, research institutions, and others as they formulate their support strategies. Aid organizations should focus on the civil society, private sector, and autonomous institutions in addition to the government.

Public Sector Management

The government realized in 1992 that the successful achievement of macroeconomic stability would rest largely on the control of inflation.

To this end, monetization of the budget deficit would have to be reduced, and fiscal discipline based on tax administration and control of government expenditures would have to be implemented. A thoroughgoing reform of the civil service would also be necessary. In light of these objectives, the government undertook major efforts on tax reform and this led to creation of the Uganda Revenue Authority (URA). The decision to establish the URA outside the existing civil service structure was intended to allow the entity much better terms of employment and tools to effectively carry out its duties of increasing tax collection. As of 1999, the tax-to-GDP ratio is nearly 12 percent, up from 6 percent at the time the URA was created. Financial assistance toward the creation of the URA came from the United Kingdom, UNDP, and the World Bank through IDA.

A civil service reform was badly needed in order to establish a well-paid, motivated, and efficient civil service while at the same time strengthening the government's ability to deliver services to the population. As a first step toward achieving this objective, in 1992 the number of ministries was reduced from 38 to 21. Under the Structural Adjustment Credit, the downsizing of the civil service was made possible through, first, the displacement of irregularly employed staff and the elimination of ghost workers, and second, retrenchment, natural attrition, and continued control over recruitment. As a result of these measures, by the end of 1993 the number of civil service employees on the payroll was reduced to 170,000, down from the 270,000 recorded in July 1991. In addition, approximately 50,000 soldiers were demobilized.

To solidify this reform, donor-funded technical assistance to government helped to establish a computerized payroll and begin a system of personnel management. Once again, the commitment of government to civil service reform was very important because there was intense social pressure against this government policy. Equally important was the financial assistance of US$13 million, administered by IDA, that the donors provided to pay retrenchment packages. As a result of these policy measures, civil service pay more than tripled. In addition, a number of donors helped to provide salary top-ups, though this policy has recently been discontinued.

Equity of Public Expenditures

Public expenditure reforms were designed to address the inadequate spending on the social sector and economic infrastructure. Beginning in fiscal 1991, the budget increased allocation toward so-called Priority Program Areas. Since then, these areas have been protected from expenditure cuts. Overall, improvements and transparency in public expenditure programs have been achieved largely through (a) keeping the expenditures within sustainable limits; (b) strengthening annual recurrent expenditure programming; and (c) monitoring actual expenditure through releases.

The development budgets were rationalized through the screening of new projects, improving quality at entry points, and identifying the necessary funding. Beginning in 1995, projects under public investment programs also received their full allocation of counterpart funds.

Public spending on basic services such as health and education generally increased between 1990 and 1995, largely because the budgetary allocations to these services were protected. In their study, Ablo and Reinikka (1998) attempted to determine whether the increase in budgetary allocations translated into enhanced delivery of health and education services. They found that school enrollment had increased by 60 percent during 1990–95, contradicting earlier reports by the Education Ministry that school enrollment had not gone up despite the budgetary increase. This in turn cast doubt on the reliability of the officially reported data. This finding may be supported by the view that improved social, economic, and political conditions allowed more parents to send their children to school at the same time as the central government increased the contributions to the primary schools.

Another finding of the study was that increased budget allocations might not matter in a situation where existing institutions are weak. Governance and accountability are key in ensuring that budgetary allocations result in expenditure outlays for the projects they are intended to benefit. But the study confirmed hypotheses of poor governance and accountability. Competing needs within the sector, or at various levels of government itself, lead to the misuse of public funds. The survey showed that not all the budgetary allocation to increased teacher salaries filtered through to the intended beneficiaries. The institutional context and incentives also played a role across the sectors. Schools were found to keep relatively good records on enrollment and financial flows, but this was not the case with the health centers. This can be attributed to the role of the Parent Teacher Associations (PTAs) that were the main financiers of the primary schools and, generally speaking, insisted on accountability from the schools. It is, however, doubtful whether under the current system of Universal Primary Education, which abolished the financing from the PTAs, the schools will continue to keep relatively good records.

Table 3.5 compares budgetary allocations to different sectors of the economy in the 1960s and the 1990s. The data reveal the increasing emphasis on education and security at the expense of agriculture and infrastructure. The health sector's share has hardly changed, and given the reduced share of agriculture there are worries that the fight against poverty may be weakened. The government, however, recognizes the problem of poverty in the country and the urgent need to eradicate it as part

TABLE 3.5 UGANDA: SECTOR DISTRIBUTION OF BUDGETARY ALLOCATION, 1965–70 AND 1994–99
(percent of total)

Sector	1965/66	1966/67	1967/68	1968/69	1969/70	1994/95	1995/96	1996/97	1997/98	1998/99
Agriculture	8.20	10.00	10.50	8.50	9.60	2.60	1.50	1.40	1.30	1.50
Education	12.30	12.20	6.30	8.11	9.40	19.80	18.80	21.80	23.40	22.70
Health	6.90	7.80	8.00	4.30	9.60	6.50	6.40	6.50	5.50	6.40
Road/works	5.10	4.60	6.30	8.30	9.50	4.30	4.30	6.80	4.90	6.90
Law/order	11.00	10.70	10.60	8.90	9.70	8.90	9.70	8.60	7.50	6.70
Defense	10.00	9.20	11.60	9.50	10.70	17.20	16.50	16.50	14.00	13.50
Other	46.50	45.50	46.70	52.39	41.50	40.70	42.80	38.40	43.40	42.30
Total	100	100	100	100	100	100	100	100	100	100

Source: Government of Uganda, "Background to the Budget,"1970/71, 1995/96, and 1998/99.

of sustainable development. This is seen in the increased budgetary allocation for education, mainly through the Universal Primary Education scheme. This represents the greatest social service investment toward poverty eradication to date. To ease constraints on the marketing of rural produce, the government eliminated monopoly marketing arrangements, decontrolled producer prices, and increased budgetary allocations toward road works. It has drawn up a 10-year road sector development program that includes road rehabilitation and expansion. Government's focus in the health sector is toward preventive health care. The national immunization program has been vigorously pursued and this has led to a reduction in child mortality. Planning is underway to set up a community health department in every hospital, and government is currently developing a Health Policy White Paper and a National Health Plan Framework.

Governance and the Political System

Dictatorship, corruption, centralization, and personalization of power have characterized Uganda's political history. In the 1960s, the regime then in power abolished the federal system enshrined in the 1962 constitution and put in place a contested constitution that created an over-centralized system of governance. The decade of the 1970s was marked by military dictatorship, while the first half of the 1980s witnessed civil wars. Beginning in 1986, political stability was restored throughout the country, although beginning in the late 1980s insurgency in the northern part of the country, and more recently in the western part, eroded the stability. The insurgency notwithstanding, progress has been made in adhering to tenets of good governance. A homegrown constitution was recently promulgated following some amendments in the draft constitution by the constituent assembly. The draft constitution that the assembly debated was a summary of ideas that a constitutional commission had collected from Ugandans from all walks of life. This constitution is now the pillar of political system and governance in the country.

The government has attempted since 1986 to politically empower its people. The direct election of local leaders in 1997 and 1998, for instance, provided an opening for Ugandans to demand accountability from their elected leaders. However, the process is still far from complete, and is constrained by persistent high levels of illiteracy and poverty as well as lack of civic competition. The presidential and parliamentary elections held in 1996 and the local government elections of 1997 and 1998 reflected these problems. The system of secret ballot and adult suffrage still needs to be extended to elections at all levels. According to the Uganda Human Development Report (UNDP 1998), the presidential elections were marred by widespread vote-buying that was fueled by the high levels of poverty among the majority of the rural electorate. As a result, the electorate did not fully exercise their voting rights under the law.

AID AND REFORM

The Impact of Aid on Reforms

We have seen that poor economic policies and social disturbance led to a huge decline in the economy in the latter part of the 1970s. By the early 1980s a reform mentality was beginning to take hold, and the country ran a relatively strong economic program based on fiscal consolidation in 1981–83. The IMF and the World Bank released standby and reconstruction credits during this period and a Consultative Group meeting was convened in 1982. Although delayed, the credits gave rise to fruitful dialogue on economic policy and management issues (World Bank 1998a). However, during 1983 the fiscal program started to loosen and the program went off track in 1984–85.

Since the present government came to power in 1986, Uganda has gone through three distinct phases of reform: 1986, when the government rejected market-based reforms; 1987–92, when it implemented reforms reluctantly; and from 1992 on, characterized by full government ownership of the reform program. Aid in various forms has supported reforms undertaken during these three phases. Technical assistance, training, and policy dialogue were the key ingredients in shaping the reform program. An IMF representative interviewed in Kampala remarked, "In the early days of the NRM government, IMF and the World Bank more or less ran a macroeconomic classroom with the president" (interview, IMF, Kampala, 1999).

During the period of reluctant reforms (1987–92), nonfinancial assistance was important but the conditionality linked to financial support probably had an even greater impact on the reform efforts. The conditions helped reform-minded elements in the government push the reform agenda forward with the support of the president. The conditionality was therefore a helpful tool for generating, implementing, and cementing reforms. When the government was in this transition process many reforms were driven by the requirements of conditionality (Tumusiime-Mutebile 1995). Many of the reforms were of a defensive nature, repairing aspects of the economy that had been destroyed over the preceding 15 years. Donor support was also critical in helping to build capacity. A World Bank representative interviewed in Kampala said, "The World Bank stayed on in 1986–88 even during periods when it did not fully subscribe to the policies undertaken by the government. This strengthened the credibility and trustworthiness of the relationship" (interview, World Bank, Kampala, 1999).

Since 1992, with full ownership of the reform program, conditionality no longer plays a decisive role in inducing reform undertakings. The government has taken over the design of the reform agenda, and the success of the reform program during this period can largely be attributed to this strengthened government ownership. The financial support is still needed, along with debt rescheduling through HIPC, but from the donors' perspective policy dialogue can once again be the single most important instrument in supporting generation of reforms.

Uganda has had good relations with its donors due to the agreement on the need for reforms. There has been "broad acceptance of the measures required to bring them about"; moreover, "conditionality was never 'imposed,' it was an economic necessity" (Tumusiime-Mutebile 1995). After some six or seven years of reform efforts the government was able to design reforms proactively, sometimes running ahead of the donors in this respect. Examples include the exchange rate reforms, capital account liberalization, and decentralization. All in all, during the period 1989–98 the government implemented far-reaching measures that substantially reduced the role of government in the economy. The financial sector and the trade and foreign exchange regimes were substantially liberalized. These measures did involve wide consultations and discussions with donor agencies as well as substantial preliminary work by government and the stakeholders. This reveals not only government attempts to own the reform process but also to involve key players in the design of economic policy.

Uganda has experienced a smooth relationship between aid and policies since the mid-1980s. Figure 3.6 traces the relationship between aid/ GDP and the World Bank's Country Policy and Institutional Assessment (CPIA). The latter is a broad measure of economic policy that covers macroeconomic management, as well as the effectiveness of the public sector in improving services that are essential for growth and poverty reduction.[10] A distinct change in the policy index can be noted in 1987–88, when the new government radically changed its course. This triggered large amounts of financial aid, and more bilateral donors became active in Uganda. This was also the period, according to government officials, when aid played its most decisive role in shaping policy. Technical assistance and especially financial aid and the conditionality linked to it helped push the balance in favor of the reformers in government during this period of reluctance (1987–92). However, when the government acquired full ownership of its reform program from 1992 onwards, the aid/GDP ratio started to decline. To have maximum effect on poverty reduction, aid should instead have increased at least in tandem with the policy improvements. Other studies show that Uganda and countries

FIGURE 3.6 UGANDA: AID AND POLICY, 1970–96

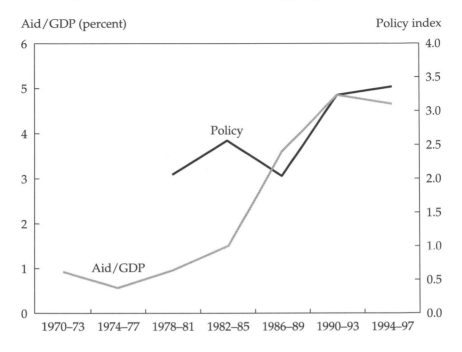

Source: World Bank.

with similar characteristics get less aid than they ought to if effective poverty alleviation is indeed the overarching goal of foreign aid.[11]

Surprisingly, IMF, IDA, and the European Commission lowered their disbursement in nominal terms drastically in 1996. That does not necessarily indicate a permanent shift, and it will require a few years more to assess the situation.

Audits and follow-up of World Bank adjustment lending point in the direction of rather successful operations during the 1990s. The overall rating for Structural Adjustment Credits I and II (1991–94 and 1994–96) are tentatively set at satisfactory to highly satisfactory, while the institutional development impact of the operations would be partial to substantial (World Bank 1997, 1999). The degree of government commitment to reform is closely correlated to the outcome ratings. The success rate of adjustment lending follows closely the improvements in government ownership, with better outcome in the 1990s than in the 1980s when reforms were either rejected or implemented reluctantly. Four of the six adjustment operations supported by the World Bank during the period have been deemed successful, which is a high rating compared to similar operations in most other African countries.

Financial Aid versus Nonfinancial Aid

Financial Aid

Meaningful reforms start, in general, with the government acting of its own accord. Ideally, aid donors should then come in and refine and redirect the reforms. If donors dictate reforms there is a high risk of unsustainable results. When the government of Uganda prepares reforms it starts by discussing them internally and with the IMF and the World Bank. Officials of the Ministry of Finance, Planning and Economic Development interviewed in Kampala in 1999 claimed that they focus on how to get the reforms right rather than on finding potential financial support for the reforms. Reforms should not be triggered by the prospects of acquiring funding, or at least this should happen very seldom. This is probably more true for the period after 1992 than it was in the late 1980s, when the government adopted the IMF program because it needed to obtain access to donor funds (IMF 1998).

Funding is nevertheless needed in almost every case where reforms are undertaken, even if it is not the main cause of the reform. Most reforms implemented in Uganda could not have been implemented without donor support. At the same time, there were a few reforms undertaken that did not depend on financial assistance, such as the liberalization of coffee marketing, the primary education program, and decentralization to the district level (interviews, MFPED, 1999). In the end, the commitment to reform can be measured by the political will to sustain the reforms. One example is the national pride in keeping inflation down, which would have been unthinkable ten years ago (interview, IMF, Kampala, 1999).

Nonfinancial Aid

A key principle of the aid and reform relationship is that ideas "stick" but projects do not. Ideas—about good governance, trade liberalization, or lowering inflation, for example—may take time to become accepted, but once established they can have sustainable effects. Individual projects on the other hand can have an immediate impact, but this effect may be short-lived or taper off over time. The key challenge for donors is therefore to support ideas in order to help reforms take off.

Experience suggests that nonfinancial aid should come first, while financial aid has a more important role to play later in the process by supporting the chosen path. This principle is probably more applicable in cases where there is greater government ownership of the reform program.

Technical assistance has had a great impact on capacity building in Uganda, especially in relation to the Ministry of Finance and Economic Planning and the Bank of Uganda. Local observers also said that the success of the Ugandan reforms to a large extent can be attributed to nonfinancial aid (interview, EPRC, 1999).

The commitment to technical assistance is critical for its success, as is the government's vision and its capacity to articulate its needs. There needs to be a well-articulated demand for the advice. A committed government will benefit from the assistance and bring the right people in. Successful TA also depends on the culture of the ministry, the availability of the local staff, and the behavior of the expatriate adviser.

Furthermore, policy dialogue and analytical work, in particular by the World Bank and IMF together with the government, have played a critical role in terms of setting the agenda and formulating priorities in the reform program. The consultation process has helped give broad exposure to the reform ideas and justify the priorities. For example, World Bank economic and sector work has been critical in the recent focus on poverty eradication (interview, World Bank, Kampala, 1999).

Uganda has a reputation for making good use of TA. TA has been effective and internalized. In the case of the Finance Ministry, its officials said, technical assistance has had a true advisory role and has been integrated in the policymaking process. The ministry has also benefited from donor-provided allowances for training and salaries for local professionals. Young Ugandan economists have learned a lot from the expatriates. The long-term effects of TA can be noted in the increased levels of skills, knowledge, and policy reforms compared to ten years ago (interview, MFPED, 1999).

According to IMF representatives, in general the Fund's nonfinancial support can help trigger reforms while its funding seldom does so. "It is critical that the outcome of TA can be measured, otherwise there is an imminent risk for failure. Performance criteria should therefore be built into the programs" (interview, IMF, Kampala, 1999).

In annual ratings by the Operations Evaluation Department of the World Bank, technical assistance projects often score very low. In general it is hard to find successful TA projects, especially in Africa. However, the department's audit of the second and third technical assistance projects in Uganda found that they had been rather successful.

The two projects had the twin objectives of facilitating the short-term design and implementation of economic reform measures and fostering long-term institutional development and capacity building related to improving economic management. The principal lesson was that management matters most. TA II (1983–92) had a marginally satisfactory outcome, while TA III (1988–94) had a highly satisfactory outcome. The main shortcomings of TA II were that the overall political and institutional environments were not conducive to either short-term policy reforms or long-term institutional development. The strengths of TA III were that all of its components were highly relevant, that the borrower was strongly committed to achieving project objectives, and that project management on both the government and World Bank sides was good. The correlation between the success rate and the timing of the two operations is consistent with general findings of this study: that the commitment to and ownership of the reform program was being established and strengthened during this period. It seems plausible that Uganda made better use of TA when its own commitment to reform grew stronger.

Conditionality

Government officials claim that it is solely a domestic decision whether or not to reform. Conditionality can tip the balance in favor of a reform program but cannot by itself induce the reforms. When the government believes that conditions facilitate a program's objectives then conditionality can come to reflect a negotiated understanding between the government and the donor. Conditionality becomes part of a consensus-building process in which the government and donors together design the reforms. Such consensus-oriented conditionality has increasingly come to characterize the Uganda reform program over the years.

Conditionality was used by the reformers within the government to help convince others of the advantages of the planned reforms during the period of reluctant reform (1987–92). The proponents of conditionality also found that it introduced a necessary rule-based system with checks, balances, and benchmarks to measure progress. In some cases the reformers even asked the Bretton Woods institutions (primarily the World Bank) to introduce certain conditions that they wished to have included. In this way coffee liberalization (abolishing the floor price of coffee), which was resisted by the then-minister of agriculture, came to be included as a condition in Structural Adjustment Credit II by the World Bank. In certain cases the government has also taken reforms a step farther than required by the conditionality in the loan contracts. Trade liberalization, for instance, went farther than the conditions in the World Bank's adjustment loans (interview, MFPED, 1999).

As discussed earlier, in a situation with established government ownership conditionality tends to become less relevant, especially given the huge increase lately in the number of conditions linked to each loan. Tumusiime-Mutebile (1995) believes that "there is no reason why sound economic management should be driven, or even constrained, by conditionalities attached to donor assistance." On the contrary, conditionality can have negative effects if loans and credits are overloaded with conditions.

IMF and World Bank representatives in Kampala said that the role of the two institutions is to strengthen the hands of the reformers (interviews, IMF and World Bank, Kampala, 1999). The Washington institutions and the reformers often have the same objectives and they seldom disagree on issues in the context of conditionality. Analytical work and conditionality have in many cases been a fruitful combination for setting the agenda, and conditionality works more ex post and functions as benchmarking. One school of thought is that conditionality needs to be precise and defined in numeric terms to be effective, making IMF programs more useful than World Bank conditional lending.

Several NGOs and private sector representatives, on the other hand, say that the government of Uganda has had to agree to the policies proposed and accept conditionality in order to receive financial aid. "The government owns the reform program but the program is based on IMF-World Bank conditionality rather than local participation. The government adapts to the donors' priorities and there are still significant policy conditions" (interviews, UDN and UMA, 1999). Some NGOs were grateful for certain donor conditions such as the social sector spending targets linked to the HIPC Initiative, but they also criticized donors for not sticking to their conditions and for being too weak in penalizing nonfulfillment.

Triggers for Reform

Leadership

Political leadership, government commitment, and domestic ownership are key to any reform program. Aid and external support can only be complementary in the process. In the end the success of policy reforms comes down to political leadership. This has to a large extent proven to be the case for Uganda, where a strong leadership has gradually given rise to a deepened government commitment as well as broader domestic ownership.

The government's capacity to learn from its own mistakes has also been decisive for the formulation of the reform program. In the early days of his presidency Museveni rejected market-based solutions and did not want to deal with the IMF. A congruence of events and the poor economic performance in 1986 led to a reassessment of policies in 1987. The country was in a post-conflict situation and had terms-of-trade problems arising from a slump in coffee prices and other circumstances. All these factors contributed to a rethinking of policies, and they were certainly more critical than external "pressure" in triggering the new reform program in 1987. Policy formulation benefited from a process of "learning by doing."

Since the period of reluctance, and especially since the 1989 national conference on the economy and the 1992 cabinet restructuring, reforms have been driven by strong leadership with a core team at the Ministry of Finance, Planning and Economic Development. Most important is that the economic team has continued intact over the years, and that the president himself has taken an active interest in the reform program.

As stated above it has also been claimed that the president and the government have decided to reform, irrespective of potential aid. This is probably more true for the period since 1992 than it was during the period of reluctant reforms, when aid and conditionality apparently played a critical role in the reform program.

Learning from Neighbors

Education, training, seminars, and study tours have been important in the generation of reform ideas, according to the government. This has included visits to other countries with successful reform experiences. Ghana has played a notable role in Uganda's generation of ideas and reforms; several delegations from different ministries have been sent to Accra to learn from the Ghanaian program. Today other African countries are sending delegations to Kampala for the same type of advice and learning.

Government Ownership

Endogenous forces have to a large extent driven the reform agenda. There have been very few policy reversals. During the early reform program, beginning in 1987, it was primarily the Ministry of Planning and Economic Development and reform-minded members of the cabinet who drove the reform program. The base for the reform program has widened considerably since then. What used to be debate within an inner circle in the late 1980s has now in many instances become a broad-based dialogue involving many stakeholders.

The same goes for the government budget, which is now made with the participation of many actors. The budget process takes off with a two-day seminar in which donors, NGOs, and other stakeholders take part, resulting in broader understanding and ownership of the budget. Decentralization and district focus have contributed to a closer involvement of stakeholders in the budget process.

Further evidence that government ownership is essential to a successful program is the fact that program implementation is still slowest in areas where disagreements exist between the government and the international financial institutions. This was the case, for instance, with regard to civil service reform.

In the early years of reform there was a considerable goodwill toward the reform undertakings, which had few losers. The public sector was small, government employees could hardly survive on their salaries, and there was no large protected import substitution sector. The cost of adjustment has been relatively low in Uganda (IMF 1998; Tumusiime-Mutebile 1995), as a result of the country's particular circumstances when it entered into the reform program. In a post-conflict situation with a rundown economy, Uganda had hardly any price controls or subsidies on essential commodities in place, so there was no need to liberalize prices or remove subsidies to the detriment of poorer groups. Food consumption had remained robust over the years, thanks to fertile soils. However, the gains of the reform program could be questioned if the income gap between different groups is widening. IMF (1998) finds that policy change has brought only limited benefits to many poor Ugandans because of their initial dependence on subsistence agriculture. The government's Poverty Eradication Action Plan of 1997 stated that "regardless of the stable and conducive macroeconomic environment the poor households have not fully benefited from the macroeconomic stability."

Participatory Process

Public dialogue is very active in Uganda and the government is now more open to discussion with a greater degree of openness. Reform policies have been more internalized by both civil servants and those outside government. The discussion on reforms in the society has become fairly open in this new era of "government by workshop" (interview, World Bank, Kampala, 1999). The Ministry of Finance for its part "advocates inclusion of stakeholders in the reform dialogue. It strengthens the understanding and outcome of the reforms and makes them less reversible" (interview, Tumusiime-Mutebile, 1999).

If the next step is to move from government ownership to strengthened domestic ownership, this process of inclusion needs to be deepened and broadened. In the end it relies not only on the political will of the government to open up, but also on capacity building among the stakeholders to prepare them for this role. A broadening of ownership is particularly necessary now that the reform program is shifting its main focus from macroeconomic reforms to public service delivery.

Nonetheless, tensions still exist between the government and outside stakeholders. Persons outside government voiced criticisms in interviews to the effect that the government holds seminars, meets with task forces, and so forth, but that those activities do not influence real policymaking. "There is a political will to involve stakeholders but investments are also needed in order to form the partnership" (interview, Coopibo-Uganda, 1999). Representatives of stakeholders also stressed that it is important for outside actors to keep their independence and retain their role for policy lobbying. There are few well-organized groups, and those that exist often lack the necessary capacity, skills, and equipment to express their thoughts convincingly.

Capacity Building

Donor support for capacity building has to a large extent focused on the key players in policy formulation—the Ministry of Finance and the Bank of Uganda. In order to keep up with an evolving reform agenda and deepen the ownership of reforms, however, there is a need to expand capacity in other ministries and agencies as well. "If line ministries are constrained by capacity, they are not only inferior in generating ideas, but also in the dialogue with donors as well as within the government in the budget process" (interview, PRESTO, 1999). Limited institutional capacity is still regarded as a potential risk by the World Bank in implementation of the structural adjustment credits.

Capacity building is also needed among NGOs and different stakeholders to prepare them to take an active and well-informed role in the policy discussion. Furthermore, the knowledge necessary to identify, review, and analyze government policies would strengthen the domestic ownership of the reforms. Many of those interviewed said that the policy dialogue should be based on facts rather than beliefs. Such capacity building would also help to improve aid effectiveness, since a great deal of aid is channeled through NGOs.

LESSONS OF UGANDA'S REFORM PROCESS

A primary lesson to be drawn from the period since 1987 is that ownership of a reform program is critical to its success. The time element also suggests that reforms are a long process that requires political stability and macroeconomic continuity in addition to patience and transparency. It is important to note that over the last 12 years, many stakeholders have become involved in the broad-based dialogue with government regarding the reforms. Organized groups such as the Parliament, the private sector (notably the Uganda Manufacturers Association), NGOs, the press, and academics are now greatly involved in the policy debates about future reforms. However, there is still a problem in that only a few well-organized groups exist and these typically lack capacity to articulate their positions forcefully and convincingly using empirical analysis.

Homegrown programs continued to be implemented in this period. The government initiated measures for which donors mainly provided financing and technical assistance. The Ugandan authorities have emphasized pro-developmental and poverty-reducing strategies in addition to good macroeconomic policies. These have included the introduction of universal primary education, for which substantial resources from both multilateral and bilateral sources have been mobilized, as well as other initiatives such as the drafting and promulgation of a homegrown constitution.

Second, on the basis of the Uganda experience we contend that macroeconomic and political stability trigger increased donor interest in the reform program. And the development of and commitment to a good reform program open an avenue for providing financing with less conditionality.

With respect to key lessons learned from Uganda's experience of reform, our findings tend to agree with some earlier ones, such as those contained in the World Bank Implementation Completion Report on Uganda's SAC I and II. This report concludes, first, that the programs' focus and internal coherence improved the performance of government and the private sector environment. It says that as the first-generation problems are tackled, new issues emerge that may call for a simultaneous macroeconomic stabilization supplemented by microeconomic and sector reforms. Consequently, the unfinished reform agenda calls for continued balance of payments support and adjustment.

Secondly, institutional capacity is a very important determinant of success in implementation. Political support notwithstanding, sustainable deployment of available managerial talent through donor-financed technical assistance and related programs has been useful in ensuring successful implementation of structural adjustment programs. Accordingly, the future reform program needs to incorporate appropriate institutional building of local capacity. The design of future programs should seek to increase understanding and ownership of the reforms by all key stakeholders in the private sector, the NGO community, and the country's political leadership.

APPENDIX 3.1
UGANDA: DATA AND STATISTICS

The External Aid Co-ordination Department in the Ministry of Finance, Planning and Economic Development in Kampala maintains a database on external aid to Uganda, including commitments, aid terms, disbursement, and the sectors receiving assistance. However, the department has not published aid statistics regularly. UNDP in Uganda produces an annual "Development Co-operation Report" that provides comprehensive data on external development assistance to Uganda. This report has been produced in collaboration with the government since 1995. In order to increase government ownership of the report, UNDP has supported the participation of the Ministry of Finance in the report's production.

TABLE 3.6 AID COMMITMENTS (ODA) TO UGANDA, 1962–97
(thousands of U.S. dollars)

Creditor/donor	1962–71	1972–78	1979–85	1986–97
European Union	—	—	100,564	692,547
EU countries	—	—	100,824	1,942,793
North America	—	—	23,296	458,537
Russia	19,746	—	—	255
Eastern Europe	—	—	9,034	34,930
Japan	—	—	—	197,241
China	—	—	—	175,618
Asia (excluding Japan)	—	—	8,000	93,512
Arab countries	—	99,430	20,415	167,343
Other bilaterals	—	—	—	49,109
IMF	—	182,368	307,365	507,594
World Bank	—	—	206,323	1,694,324
African Development Bank	4,284	23,640	133,867	476,381
Other multilaterals	—	27,090	216,864	700,245
Total	24,030[a]	332,527	1,126,552	7,190,428

— Not available.
a. The disbursement for this period differs significantly from the US$94.08 million reported in the government of Uganda's "External Debt Management Report" of 1991. The totals for other periods are comparable.
Source: Aid Data Unit, Ministry of Finance, Planning and Economic Development.

TABLE 3.7 UGANDA: OFFICIAL DEVELOPMENT FINANCE, 1980–98
(millions of U.S. dollars)

	1980	1981	1982	1983	1984	1985	1986	1987	1988	1989	1990	1991	1992	1993	1994	1995	1996
All sources																	
Gross disbursement on official loans	95.8	207.3	173.1	199.4	106.4	153.5	135.5	317.4	207.3	321.1	343.5	258.9	305.7	391.4	323.7	288.2	288.5
Non-technical assistance grants	61.6	100.7	55.5	76.6	66.5	47.4	81.6	96.4	187.1	176.5	257.5	314.2	336.2	259.7	319.0	399.1	338.5
Technical assistance grants	21.1	33.6	29.5	33.9	32.4	36.9	50.0	57.4	75.7	87.7	93.8	107.2	121.8	124.2	124.7	148.2	140.1
Total official development finance	178.5	341.6	258.1	309.9	205.3	237.8	267.1	471.2	470.1	585.3	694.8	680.3	763.7	775.3	767.4	835.5	767.1
Bilateral sources																	
Gross disbursement on official loans	11.2	3.0	7.3	5.8	6.8	8.3	24.9	89.4	30.7	38.7	41.1	8.9	45.3	89.5	18.0	24.4	46.0
Non-technical assistance grants	31.6	77.4	40.7	54.3	34.4	24.6	56.7	53.8	134.9	124.3	204.5	268.1	169.7	213.2	231.2	249.5	257.3
Technical assistance grants	11.1	13.6	13.5	15.0	12.8	15.4	23.7	28.0	38.4	43.5	53.6	63.8	76.0	78.9	88.5	116.7	100.7
Total official development finance	53.9	94.0	61.5	75.1	54.0	48.3	105.3	171.2	204.0	206.5	299.2	340.8	291.0	381.6	337.7	390.6	404.0
Multilateral sources																	
Gross disbursement on official loans	84.5	204.3	165.7	193.7	99.6	145.2	110.6	228.0	176.6	282.4	302.4	250.0	260.4	301.9	305.6	263.8	242.5
Non-technical assistance grants	30.0	23.3	14.8	22.3	32.1	22.8	24.9	42.6	52.2	52.2	53.0	46.1	166.5	46.5	87.8	149.6	81.2
Technical assistance grants	10.0	20.0	16.0	18.9	19.6	21.5	26.3	29.4	37.3	44.2	40.2	43.4	45.8	45.3	36.2	31.5	39.4
Total official development finance	124.5	247.6	196.5	234.9	151.3	189.5	161.8	300.0	266.1	378.8	395.6	339.5	472.7	393.7	429.6	444.9	363.1

Note: The grant equivalent of a $100 million loan disbursement is $20 million when the loan is 20 percent concessional.
Source: Chang, Fernández-Arias, and Servén 1999.

TABLE 3.8 UGANDA: EFFECTIVE DEVELOPMENT ASSISTANCE, 1980-96
(millions of U. S. dollars)

	1980	1981	1982	1983	1984	1985	1986	1987	1988	1989	1990	1991	1992	1993	1994	1995	1996
All sources																	
Grant equivalents of loan disbursements	35.0	19.4	47.5	43.0	58.4	87.2	87.4	124.0	123.1	195.8	219.9	202.8	209.1	158.5	231.3	194.2	132.2
Non-Technical assistance grants	81.8	100.7	55.5	76.6	68.5	47.4	81.6	96.4	187.1	176.5	257.5	314.2	336.2	259.7	319.0	399.1	338.5
Technical assistance grants	22.1	33.8	28.5	33.9	32.4	36.9	50.0	57.4	75.7	07.7	93.8	107.2	121.8	124.2	124.7	148.2	140.1
Total effective development assistance	117.7	153.7	132.5	154.4	157.3	171.5	199.0	277.8	385.0	460.0	571.2	624.2	867.1	542.4	875.0	741.5	610.8
Bilateral sources																	
Grant equivalents of loan disbursements	8.3	2.1	1.5	1.5	2.2	0.7	1.3	1.2	3.5	43.3	9.0	7.1	8.5	28.2	7.6	8.0	21.1
Non-technical assistance grants	31.6	77.4	40.7	54.3	54.4	24.0	85.7	53.8	134.9	124.3	204.5	200.1	100.7	213.2	231.2	240.6	257.3
Technical assistance grants	11.1	13.6	13.5	16.0	12.8	15.4	23.7	26.0	38.4	43.5	53.6	83.8	76.0	78.9	86.6	116.7	100.7
Total effective development assistance	49.0	93.1	55.7	70.8	49.4	40.7	81.7	83.0	176.8	211.1	267.1	339.0	254.2	318.3	327.3	374.2	379.1
Multilateral sources																	
Grant equivalents of loan disbursements	28.7	17.3	46.0	42.3	58.2	86.5	66.2	122.7	119.7	152.6	210.9	195.7	200.7	132.3	223.7	186.2	111.1
Non-technical assistance grants	30.0	23.3	14.8	22.3	32.1	22.8	24.9	42.8	52.2	52.2	53.0	46.1	166.5	46.5	87.8	149.6	81.2
Technical assistance grants	10.0	20.0	16.0	18.8	19.6	21.5	28.2	29.4	37.3	44.3	40.2	43.4	45.8	45.3	38.2	31.5	39.4
Total effective development assistance	68.7	60.6	76.8	83.5	107.9	130.8	117.4	194.7	208.2	248.0	304.1	285.2	413.0	224.1	347.7	367.3	231.7

Note: The grant equivalent of a $100 million loan disbursement is $20 million when the loan is 20 percent concessional
Source: Chang, Fernández-Arias, and Servén 1999.

TABLE 3.9 UGANDA: TOTAL OFFICIAL DEVELOPMENT FINANCE BY CREDITOR, 1980–96
(millions of U. S. dollars)

Source	1980	1981	1982	1983	1984	1985	1986	1987	1988	1989	1990	1991	1992	1993	1994	1995	1996
Bilateral	53.9	84.0	61.5	75.1	54.0	48.3	105.3	171.2	204.0	206.5	299.2	340.8	291.0	381.6	337.7	390.6	404.0
Multilateral	124.5	247.6	198.5	234.9	151.3	189.5	161.8	300.0	266.1	378.8	395.6	339.5	472.7	393.7	429.6	444.9	383.1
Total	178.5	341.6	258.1	309.9	205.3	237.8	267.1	471.2	470.1	586.3	694.8	680.3	763.7	775.3	767.4	835.5	787.1
Bilateral																	
Australia	1.8	3.2	4.6	4.2	3.5	0.3	0.2	0.1	0.6	0.6	0.5	0.5	0.9	1.0	1.3	1.2	1.6
Austria	0.1	0.1	0.0	0.0	0.1	0.0	0.1	0.1	0.1	11.4	2.1	2.8	4.3	17.2	13.1	15.4	15.3
Belgium	0.2	0.5	0.2	0.4	0.3	1.7	0.2	0.5	0.5	0.4	10.6	0.8	0.9	1.5	1.9	5.3	1.8
Canada	0.9	3.3	4.9	2.0	6.5	2.6	1.7	2.1	21.8	6.6	7.1	5.3	9.1	3.7	4.7	1.6	1.7
Denmark	1.7	1.2	1.3	2.3	2.6	0.8	2.8	4.9	11.6	15.6	25.4	32.4	37.1	45.4	53.0	60.1	68.0
Finland	0.2	1.2	0.8	0.9	0.1	0.4	1.6	0.7	0.4	7.8	1.5	1.5	1.5	0.5	0.3	1.3	1.1
France	12.0	2.1	3.0	0.9	3.1	0.8	0.9	1.1	1.1	7.0	8.9	8.8	9.8	4.8	3.5	10.3	13.7
Germany, Fed. Rep. of	8.4	11.4	7.7	29.4	3.5	4.4	12.9	18.4	19.9	19.9	27.0	34.2	23.0	45.3	29.5	47.2	40.1
Ireland	0.0	0.0	0.0	0.0	0.1	0.0	0.1	0.1	0.2	0.1	0.1	0.1	0.3	0.6	2.0	5.0	4.9
Italy	0.1	1.0	1.0	1.9	5.2	7.1	30.0	18.4	23.4	13.0	15.8	14.1	13.5	14.4	5.6	3.6	7.0
Japan	0.1	1.0	1.5	4.1	5.6	3.2	3.1	0.6	9.5	1.1	9.5	14.9	14.6	39.7	41.0	23.9	49.8
Luxembourg	0.0	0.0	0.0	0.0	0.0	0.0	0.0	0.0	0.0	0.0	0.0	0.0	0.1	0.0	0.0	0.0	0.0
Netherlands	4.3	21.1	2.1	7.3	4.6	1.9	6.3	2.2	3.6	3.1	3.8	22.9	15.1	23.1	25.5	31.8	32.6
New Zealand	0.0	0.0	0.0	0.0	0.0	0.0	0.0	0.0	0.0	0.0	0.0	0.0	0.0	0.0	0.1	0.1	0.0
Norway	0.4	1.2	7.0	1.2	1.1	1.2	2.2	2.7	3.5	4.5	7.4	5.2	8.2	13.3	18.8	20.5	20.5
Portugal	0.0	0.0	0.0	0.0	0.0	0.0	0.0	0.0	0.0	0.0	0.0	0.0	0.0	0.0	0.0	0.0	0.0
Spain	0.0	0.0	0.0	0.0	0.0	0.0	0.0	2.1	2.7	5.1	0.0	4.4	13.8	15.8	1.8	0.2	13.8
Sweden	2.4	3.8	0.4	0.7	0.2	0.0	1.9	4.0	11.2	16.3	14.5	34.3	29.0	16.6	25.4	25.3	32.7
Switzerland	0.7	0.8	0.5	0.5	0.3	0.3	1.8	1.8	9.0	3.1	12.5	7.2	8.3	7.3	0.8	8.9	0.7

United Kingdom	8.7	30.8	18.6	9.7	10.6	15.1	24.4	23.8	52.8	40.7	38.0	51.5	40.1	54.8	52.0	85.4	82.2
United States	13.0	8.0	2.0	4.0	3.0	5.0	4.0	14.0	18.0	21.1	59.4	51.7	22.0	57.0	51.0	48.0	28.0
Arab countries	1.3	0.1	0.1	0.2	0.2	0.1	0.0	0.0	0.0	28.5	40.0	50.0	15.5	0.2	0.2	0.1	0.1
Unspecified	1.6	3.0	6.1	5.4	3.3	3.8	11.3	75.6	14.8	2.2	17.0	0.4	23.0	19.5	6.7	14.4	7.6
Total	53.9	94.0	81.5	75.1	54.0	48.3	105.3	171.2	204.0	206.5	299.2	340.8	291.0	381.6	337.7	390.8	404.0
Multilateral																	
AfDB	4,1	6.6	8.0	8.7	7.4	32.0	5.2	8.8	2.7	5.3	0.0	2.4	3.0	2.5	0.2	6.7	9.7
ADF	0.0	0.0	8.1	0.0	0.0	0.0	0.8	2.0	21.2	38.1	11.5	20.1	32.1	25.7	17.9	32.0	32.3
EEC	25.1	13.1	11.4	17.8	22.0	17.2	17.8	32.3	38.8	38.4	38.0	27.9	158.1	29.8	53.5	108.3	46.1
EIB	0.0	0.0	7.4	2.2	0.0	0.0	0.0	0.0	1.8	0.0	0.2	1.5	0.7	7.9	2.0	0.0	2.9
IDA	1.1	15.4	31.1	32.6	58.2	91.8	62.1	112.0	73.9	97.7	208.1	136.5	155.7	141.1	223.2	159.8	123.5
IFAD	0.0	0.0	0.5	6.4	0.0	6.8	9.8	3.5	0.0	0.0	0.0	3.7	3.5	8.5	3.8	2.8	4.0
IFC	0.0	0.0	0.0	9.8	0.0	2.3	0.0	0.0	0.0	0.0	0.0	0.0	0.0	0.0	0.0	0.0	0.0
IMF	77.9	144.8	93.8	113.8	21.5	0.0	0.0	58.8	73.6	51.1	81.2	78.4	58.1	0.0	52.5	55.0	63.2
Other U N	0.2	0.1	1.5	0.4	0.5	0.8	0.7	1.2	5.8	5.8	5.0	2.3	1.4	0.9	1.2	2.1	2.5
UNDP	3.3	13.9	8.4	6.8	7.0	8.3	7.0	8.8	12.7	15.6	16.2	17.1	18.0	14.8	11.8	7.1	19.0
UNFPA	0.2	0.1	0.0	0.1	0.2	0.2	0.2	0.4	0.8	2.5	3.0	3.2	2.6	2.1	4.5	4.8	2.9
UNHCR	2.9	1.7	1.3	4.4	5.4	3.8	10.5	7.5	5.8	6.2	2.5	4.0	5.5	8.0	16.3	19.8	21.1
UNICEF	3.1	3.9	4.4	6.1	5.4	7.6	8.2	7.0	9.4	12.5	11.8	14.9	18.5	17.2	16.3	14.2	13.0
UNTA	0.3	0.3	0.4	1.3	1.1	1.2	1.1	1.5	1.2	1.8	1.3	1.9	1.3	2.1	1.8	3.4	1.7
WFP	4.9	12.7	9.7	9.9	13.5	7.7	9.2	14.3	15.4	15.0	16.5	18.1	10.8	17.0	18.4	23.6	14.3
Arab agencies	0.0	0.0	0.0	0.0	0.1	0.0	0.0	0.0	0.2	0.8	0.9	0.1	0.1	0.3	0.2	0.0	0.0
Unspecified	1.4	35.2	10.5	14.9	9.1	9.3	31.3	43.9	3.0	89.8	3.4	7.5	9.2	118.2	5.7	6.7	8.9
Total	124.5	247.8	198.5	234.9	151.3	189.5	161.8	300.0	288.1	378.8	305.8	330.6	472.7	303.7	420.8	444.0	363.1

Note: Official development finance = gross disbursements on all official loans + official grants.
Source: Chang, Fernández-Arias, and Servén 1999.

TABLE 3.10 UGANDA: TOTAL EFFECTIVE DEVELOPMENT ASSISTANCE BY CREDITOR, 1980–96
(millions of U. S. dollars)

Source	1980	1981	1982	1983	1984	1985	1986	1987	1988	1989	1990	1991	1992	1993	1994	1995	1996
Bilateral	49.0	93.1	55.7	70.8	49.4	40.7	81.7	83.0	178.8	211.1	287.1	339.0	264.2	318.3	327.3	374.2	379.1
Multilateral	68.7	80.8	76.8	83.5	107.9	130.8	117.4	194.7	209.2	249.0	304.1	285.2	413.0	224.1	347.7	367.3	231.7
Total	117.7	153.7	132.5	154.4	157.3	171.5	199.0	277.8	385.9	480.0	571.2	824.2	887.1	542.4	675.0	741.5	810.8
Bilateral																	
Australia	1.8	3.2	4.6	4.2	3.5	0.3	0.2	0.1	0.6	0.6	0.5	0.5	0.9	1.0	1.3	1.2	1.8
Austria	0.1	0.1	0.0	0.0	0.1	0.0	0.1	0.1	0.1	10.1	1.8	2.5	4.3	12.0	11.2	10.8	14.3
Belgium	0.2	0.5	0.2	0.4	0.3	1.7	0.2	0.5	0.6	0.4	10.8	0.6	0.9	1.5	1.9	5.3	1.8
Canada	0.9	3.3	4.9	2.0	8.5	2.8	1.7	2.1	21.8	8.6	7.1	5.3	9.1	3.7	4.7	1.6	1.7
Denmark	1.7	1.2	1.3	2.3	2.6	0.8	2.8	4.9	11.8	15.8	25.4	32.4	37.1	45.4	53.0	60.1	68.0
Finland	0.2	1.2	0.6	0.9	0.1	0.4	1.8	0.7	0.4	5.9	1.5	1.5	1.5	0.5	0.3	1.3	1.1
France	8.3	2.1	2.8	0.9	2.5	0.8	0.9	1.1	1.1	2.1	7.4	8.7	4.9	4.8	3.5	10.3	13.7
Germany, Fed. Rep. of	8.4	11.4	7.7	29.4	3.5	4.4	12.9	15.8	18.7	19.9	27.0	34.2	23.0	37.9	29.5	47.2	40.1
Ireland	0.0	0.0	0.0	0.0	0.1	0.0	0.1	0.1	0.2	0.1	0.1	0.1	0.3	0.6	2.0	5.0	4.9
Italy	0.1	1.0	1.0	1.9	4.9	7.1	30.0	18.4	18.2	10.8	15.8	13.1	11.7	10.2	5.5	3.6	7.0
Japan	0.1	1.6	1.5	4.1	5.6	3.2	3.1	0.6.	9.5	1.1	9.5	14.9	14.6	28.0	38.7	23.9	40.4
Luxembourg	0.0	0.0	0.0	0.0	0.0	0.0	0.0		0.0	0.0	0.0	0.0	0.1	0.0	0.0	0.0	0.0
Netherlands	4.3	21.1	2.1	7.3	4.8	1.9	8.3	2.2	3.5	3.1	3.5	22.9	15.1	23.1	25.5	31.8	32.6
New Zealand	0.0	0.0	0.0	0.0	0.0	0.0	0.0	0.0	0.0	0.0	0.0	0.0	0.0	0.0	0.1	0.1	0.0
Norway	0.4	1.2	7.0	0.0	1.1	1.2	2.2	2.7	3.5	4.5	7.4	5.2	8.2	13.3	18.8	20.5	20.5
Portugal	0.0	0.0	0.0	0.0	0.0	0.0	0.0	0.0	0.0	0.0	0.0	0.0	0.0	0.0	0.0	0.0	0.0
Spain	0.0	0.0	0.0	0.0	0.0	0.0	0.0	-0.1	-0.1	0.0	0.0	1.6	5.0	6.2	0.6	0.2	6.0
Sweden	2.4	3.8	0.4	0.7	-.2	0.0	1.9	4.0	11.2	16.3	14.5	34.3	29.0	16.6	25.4	26.3	32.7
Switzerland	0.7	0.8	0.5	0.5	0.3	0.3	1.8	1.8	9.0	3.1	12.5	7.2	9.3	7.3	0.6	8.9	0.7

United Kingdom	6.7	30.8	18.8	8.3	8.6	10.8	12.0	13.4	50.0	40.7	36.0	51.5	40.1	64.0	52.0	85.4	62.2
United States	13.0	8.0	2.0	4.0	3.0	5.0	4.0	14.0	16.5	18.9	46.0	51.4	22.0	57.0	51.0	49.0	29.0
Arab countries	1.3	0.1	0.1	0.2	0.2	0.1	0.0	0.0	0.0	28.5	40.0	50.0	15.5	0.2	0.2	0.1	0.1
Unspecified	0.4	2.1	0.8	1.5	0.7	0.3	0.1	0.8	0.7	26.8	0.3	3.1	1.8	-5.4	1.6	2.8	1.7
Total	49.0	93.1	55.7	70.8	49.4	40.7	81.7	83.0	176.8	211.1	287.1	339.0	264.2	318.3	327.3	374.2	379.1
Multilateral																	
AIDB	0.2	0.8	1.4	2.2	1.5	0.7	0.3	0.9	0.1	0.1	0.0	0.1	0.2	0.0	0.0	0.1	0.3
ADF	0.0	0.0	6.9	0.0	0.0	0.0	0.8	1.0	15.9	28.0	0.1	14.5	23.4	18.2	12.2	21.6	21.8
EEC	25.1	12.7	10.4	16.9	21.4	18.8	17.5	32.1	38.5	36.4	36.0	27.9	156.1	29.6	53.5	106.3	46.1
EIB	0.0	0.0	1.2	1.7	0.0	0.0	0.0	0.0	0.8	0.0	0.1	0.7	0.3	4.6	1.5	1.0	1.7
IDA	0.5	13.4	27.3	28.4	50.6	77.4	52.8	91.2	58.7	75.8	180.0	104.8	115.5	102.8	157.7	110.7	84.5
IFAD	0.0	0.0	0.4	5.2	0.0	5.3	7.5	2.6	0.0	0.0	0.0	2.5	2.5	4.5	2.4	1.7	2.5
IFC	0.0	0.0	0.0	-1.4	0.0	-0.3	0.0	0.0	0.0	0.0	0.0	0.0	0.0	0.0	0.0	0.0	0.0
IMF	27.9	0.2	0.0	0.0	0.0	0.0	0.0	24.3	37.4	48.1	41.4	73.1	51.8	0.0	48.2	51.0	0.0
Other UN	0.2	0.1	1.5	0.4	0.5	0.8	0.7	1.2	5.8	5.6	5.0	2.3	1.4	0.0	1.2	2.1	2.5
UNDP	3.3	13.9	8.4	6.6	7.0	8.3	7.0	8.8	12.7	15.6	18.2	17.1	18.0	14.8	11.8	7.1	19.0
UNFPA	0.2	0.1	0.0	0.1	0.2	0.2	0.2	0.4	0.8	2.5	3.0	3.2	2.8	2.1	4.5	4.6	2.9
UNHCR	2.9	1.7	1.3	4.4	5.4	3.8	10.5	7.5	5.8	6.2	2.5	4.0	5.5	8.0	16.3	19.8	21.1
UNICEF	3.1	3.9	4.4	6.1	5.4	7.6	6.2	7.0	9.4	12.5	11.8	14.9	16.5	17.2	16.3	14.2	13.0
UNTA	0.3	0.3	0.4	1.3	1.1	1.2	1.1	1.5	1.8	1.8	1.3	1.9	1.3	2.1	1.8	3.4	1.7
WFP	4.9	12.7	9.7	9.9	13.5	7.7	9.2	14.3	15.4	15.0	16.5	18.1	10.8	17.0	18.4	23.6	14.3
Arab agencies	0.0	0.0	0.0	0.0	0.1	0.0	0.0	0.0	0.2	0.8	0.9	0.1	0.1	0.3	0.2	0.0	0.0
Unspecified	0.1	0.5	3.5	1.7	1.2	1.8	3.9	1.4	6.3	0.5	1.3	0.0	6.9	2.1	1.8	1.1	0.5
Total	68.7	60.6	78.8	83.5	107.9	130.8	117.4	194.7	209.2	249.0	285.2	304.1	285.2	413.0	224.1	347.7	231.7

Note: Effective Development Assistance = grant equivalents of official loan disbursements + official grants.
Source: Chang, Fernández-Arias, and Servén, 1999.

TABLE 3.11 UGANDA: TOTAL DISBURSEMENTS ON LOANS BY CREDITOR, 1980–96
(millions of dollars)

Source	1980	1981	1982	1983	1984	1985	1986	1987	1988	1989	1990	1991	1992	1993	1994	1995	1996
Bilateral	11.2	3.0	7.3	5.8	6.8	8.3	24.9	89.4	30.7	38.7	41.1	8.9	45.3	89.5	18.0	24.4	46.0
Multilateral	84.5	204.3	165.7	193.7	99.6	145.2	110.6	228.0	176.6	282.4	302.4	250.0	260.4	301.9	305.6	263.8	242.5
Total	95.8	207.3	173.1	199.4	106.4	153.5	135.5	317.4	207.3	321.1	343.5	258.9	305.7	391.4	323.7	288.2	288.5

Source: World Bank.

TABLE 3.12 TOTAL GRANT EQUIVALENTS OF LOAN DISBURSEMENTS BY CREDITOR, 1980–96
(millions of U.S. dollars)

Source	1980	1981	1982	1983	1984	1985	1986	1987	1988	1989	1990	1991	1992	1993	1994	1995	1996
Bilateral	6.3	2.1	1.5	1.5	2.2	0.7	1.3	1.2	3.5	43.3	9.0	7.1	8.5	26.2	7.6	8.0	21.1
Multilateral	28.7	17.3	46.0	42.3	56.2	86.5	66.2	122.7	119.7	152.6	210.9	195.7	200.7	132.3	223.7	186.2	111.1
Total	35.0	19.4	47.5	43.9	58.4	87.2	67.4	124.0	123.1	195.8	219.9	202.8	209.1	158.5	231.3	194.2	132.2

Sources: World Bank; Chang, Fernández-Arias, and Servén 1999.

TABLE 3.13 UGANDA: TOTAL NON-TECHNICAL ASSISTANCE GRANTS BY CREDITOR, 1980–96
(millions of dollars)

Source	1980	1981	1982	1983	1984	1985	1986	1987	1988	1989	1990	1991	1992	1993	1994	1995	1996
Bilateral	31.6	77.4	40.7	54.3	34.4	24.6	56.7	53.8	134.9	124.3	204.5	268.1	169.7	213.2	231.2	249.5	257.3
Multilateral	30.0	23.3	14.8	22.3	32.1	22.8	24.0	42.6	52.2	52.2	53.0	46.1	166.5	46.5	87.8	149.6	81.2
Total	61.6	100.7	56.5	76.6	66.5	47.4	81.6	96.4	187.1	176.5	257.5	314.2	336.2	259.7	319.0	399.1	338.5

Source:OECD.

TABLE 3.14 UGANDA: TOTAL TECHNICAL ASSISTANCE GRANTS BY CREDITOR, 1980–96
(millions of dollars)

Source	1980	1981	1982	1983	1984	1985	1986	1987	1988	1989	1990	1991	1992	1993	1994	1995	1996
Bilateral	11.1	13.6	13.5	15.0	12.8	15.4	23.7	28.0	38.4	43.5	53.6	63.8	76.0	78.9	88.5	116.7	100.7
Multilateral	10.0	20.0	16.0	18.9	19.6	21.5	26.3	29.4	37.3	44.2	40.2	43.4	45.8	45.3	36.2	31.5	39.4
Total	21.1	33.6	29.5	33.9	32.4	36.9	50.0	57.4	75.7	87.7	93.8	107.2	121.8	124.2	124.7	148.2	140.1

Source: OECD.

TABLE 3.15 UGANDA: DISBURSEMENTS ON OFFICIAL LOANS BY SECTOR, 1980–96
(millions of U.S. dollars)

Sector	1980	1981	1982	1983	1984	1985	1986	1987	1988	1989	1990	1991	1992	1993	1994	1995	1996
Agriculture, forestry, fishing	0.6	0.2	1.5	14.5	7.5	19.2	24.2	35.9	19.2	25.4	15.9	20.0	14.5	17.8	20.0	17.1	28.5
Balance of payments support	0.0	48.4	36.8	26.4	35.4	49.1	16.8	34.7	41.3	157.8	125.3	75.2	79.8	60.1	57.0	2.7	2.9
IMF disbursements	77.9	144.6	93.8	113.8	21.5	0.0	0.0	58.8	73.5	51.4	81.2	78.4	56.1	0.0	52.5	55.9	63.2
Contributions to finance current imports	0.0	0.0	1.3	0.0	2.0	0.0	0.0	0.0	0.0	0.0	1.1	4.1	12.7	40.0	5.8	2.1	22.9
Community, social, personal, and environmental services	0.8	3.6	11.8	8.5	9.4	15.6	44.8	11.3	7.5	14.5	38.3	20.2	69.6	132.3	51.2	117.7	48.1
Manufacturing	2.8	3.4	13.0	15.9	11.5	27.6	21.6	21.7	15.1	20.3	15.6	16.0	10.5	16.2	12.1	12.6	11.3
Electricity, gas, and water production	0.9	0.0	1.6	6.6	1.5	8.9	18.0	24.9	11.5	10.8	12.1	15.7	18.4	32.6	33.8	30.6	32.8
Transport and storage	12.7	3.8	2.4	0.0	1.7	5.7	3.1	16.5	24.0	32.5	29.5	21.4	22.5	13.5	12.5	9.2	32.0
Other	0.1	1.5	10.9	13.7	15.9	27.4	7.0	113.6	15.2	8.4	24.5	7.9	21.6	78.9	66.3	40.3	46.8
Total	95.8	207.3	173.1	199.4	106.4	153.5	135.5	317.4	207.3	321.1	343.5	258.9	305.7	391.4	323.7	288.2	288.5

Source: World Bank.

TABLE 3.16 UGANDA: DEBT TABLES, 1980–95

(millions of dollars)

	1980	1981	1982	1983	1984	1985	1986	1987	1988	1989	1990	1991	1992	1993	1994	1995
Debt Restructurings																
Total amount of debt rescheduled (current US$)	0.0	..	..	..	..	0.0	0.0	60.7	22.8	60.2	17.8	8.8	99.6	37.8	0.0	172.3
Debt stock rescheduled (current US$)	0.0	..	..	..	..	0.0	0.0	0.0	0.0	0.0	0.0	0.0	0.0	0.0	0.0	143.1
Principal rescheduled (current US$)	0.0	..	..	..	..	0.0	0.0	47.7	13.3	18.2	3.5	3.8	54.9	24.2	0.0	0.0
Official	0.0	..	..	..	..	0.0	0.0	11.4	7.3	10.1	3.5	3.6	30.6	10.8	0.0	0.0
Private	0.0	..	..	..	..	0.0	0.0	36.3	6.0	8.1	0.1	0.2	24.3	13.4	0.0	0.0
Interest rescheduled (current US$)	0.0	..	..	..	..	0.0	0.0	11.1	9.1	10.5	1.0	2.7	37.9	10.1	0.0	30.4
Official	0	..	..	..	..	0	0	5.5	8.3	8	1	2.7	24.2	9.4	0	30.4
Private	0	..	..	..	..	0	0	5.5	0.8	2.6	0	0	13.7	0.7	0	0
Principal forgiven (current US$)	..	..	..	..	..	5.7	0.0	16.6	40.8	0.2	51.2	0.5	13.7	16.0	5.9	0.0
Memo: Interest forgiven (current US$)	..	..	..	..	..	0.8	0	0.2	0	0.1	0.6	0.5	1.5	18.8	0	0.7
Debt stock reduction (current US$)	0.0	..	..	..	..	0.0	0.0	0.0	0.0	0.0	0.0	0.0	0.0	138.9	0.0	41.5
of which debt buyback (current US$)	0.0	..	..	..	..	0.0	0.0	0.0	0.0	0.0	0.0	0.0	0.0	17.3	0.0	0.0
Debt Stock-Flow Reconciliation																
Total change in debt stocks (DOD, current US$)	..	..	..	..	..	..	..	..	..	253.8	406.9	194.3	150.3	101.3	342.8	201.5
Net flows on debt total (NFL, current US$)	115.8	176.5	177.6	151.4	63.5	74.7	81.3	337.8	91.0	231.7	277.2	167.2	236.6	243.5	224.1	185.6
Net change in interest arrears (current US$)	..	..	..	..	..	..	..	..	..	17.0	26.3	18.5	-20.3	-9.6	9.5	-22.1
Interest rescheduled (capitalized) (current US$)	..	..	..	..	..	..	..	..	..	10.6	1.1	2.7	37.9	10.1	0.0	30.4
Debt forgiveness or reduction (current US$)	..	..	..	..	..	..	..	..	..	-0.2	-51.2	-0.5	-13.7	-137.6	-6.9	-41.5
Cross-currency valuation (current US$)	..	..	..	..	..	..	..	..	..	-20.2	54.2	-12.6	-43.4	-10.1	34.3	6.3
Residual	..	..	..	..	..	..	..	..	..	14.9	86.3	19.0	-48.5	5.0	81.8	42.8
Debt Ratios																
External debt (% of exports of goods and services)	209.4	257.3	228.3	265.6	266.3	301.9	383.5	473.1	580.6	716.2	1,050.0	1,395.6	1,501.3	1,172.6	1,012.5	535.7
External debt (% of GNP)	55.6	71.4	53.9	60.4	30.3	35.5	36.4	30.8	29.8	42.0	61.1	85.1	105.6	96.5	85.6	62.8
Total debt services (% of exports of goods and services)	17.4	25.0	15.6	22.7	32.0	32.0	44.1	39.4	62.2	61.3	59.5	74.4	58.5	65.8	45.2	20.5

Source: World Bank, Global Development Finance 1999.

TABLE 3.17 UGANDA: MULTILATERAL DEBT AGREEMENTS WITH OFFICIAL CREDITORS, 1980–97

| Date of agreement | Contract cutoff date | Consolidation period for current maturities | | Consolidation includes | | Share of debt consolidated (percent) | Amount consolidated (millions of U.S. dollars) | Repayment terms[a] | |
		Start date	Length (months)	Arrears	Previously rescheduled debt			Maturity (years/ months)	Grace (years/months)
18 Nov. 81	1 July 81	1 July 81	12	Y		90	63	9/0	4/6
1 Dec. 82	1 July 81	1 July 82	12			90	16	9/0	4/6
19 June 87	1 July 81	1 July 87	12	Y	Y	100	102	14/6	6/0
26 Jan. 89	1 July 81	1 Jan. 89	18	Y	Y	100	86	Menu	Menu
17 June 92	1 July 81	1 July 92	17	Y	Y	100	172	Menu	Menu
20 Feb. 95	1 July 81	1 Feb. 95	Stock	Y	Y	100	110	Menu	Menu

a. Maturity is measured here from the end of the consolidation period to the date of the final amortization payment; the grace period is the time between the end of the consolidation period and the date of the first amortization payment. The secretariat of the Paris Club measures grace and maturity from the midpoint of the consolidation period. "Menu" terms refer to the options agreed to at the 1988 Toronto economic summit meeting.
Source: World Bank, *Global Development Finance 1997* (table A3.2). Data compiled from World Bank Debtor Reporting System and International Monetary Fund data.

TABLE 3.18 UGANDA: DEBT RELIEF, 1991–97
(millions of U.S. dollars)

Type of creditor	1991/92	1992/93	1993/94	1994/95	1995/96	1996/97
Multilateral (EEC)			3.00		2.00	
Bilateral	12.90	12.93	36.35	41.20	50.20	53.31
Multilateral Debt Fund					37.84	48.33
Total	12.90	12.93	39.35	41.20	90.04	101.64

Source: Bank of Uganda.

APPENDIX 3.2
INTERVIEWS IN UGANDA, MARCH 1999

Government of Uganda
(Ministry of Finance, Planning and Economic Development)

Emmanuel Tumusiime-Mutebile, Permanent Secretary, Secretary to the
Treasury.
Damoni Kitabire, Director of Economic Affairs.
Keith J. Muhakanizi, Economic Adviser to the Minister.
Oode Obella, Agricultural Commissioner, Aid Liaison Department.
Ocailap Patrick, Assistant Commissioner, Aid Liaison Department.

Makerere University

Patrick Asea, Professor, Economic Policy Research Centre (EPRC).
Fred Opio, Professor, Economic and Policy Research Centre (EPRC).
Germina Ssemogerere, MA, Economics and Planning.

Private Sector

Dr. William Kalema, Chairman, Uganda Manufacturers Association (UMA).
Emmanuel Buringuriza, Assistant Manager, Business Uganda Develop-
ment Scheme, Private Sector Foundation Project.
Yonasani B. Kanomozi, Director, Community Management Services.

Nongovernmental Organizations

Zie Gariyo, Coordinator, Uganda Debt Network (UDN).
Kevin Akoyi Makokha, Country Representative, Coopibo-Uganda.
Bruce Mazzie, Chief of Party, Private Enterprise Support, Training, and
Organizational Development Project (PRESTO).
Sarah Kitakule, Senior Adviser, Policy Regulation and Reform, PRESTO.
Carolyn Elliott-Farino, Project Administrator, PRESTO.

IMF, Kampala

Zia Ebrahim-Zadeh, Resident Representative.

World Bank, Kampala

Randolph Harris, Resident Representative.
Robert Blake, Senior Resident Economist.

Bilateral Donors

Jens Rasmussen, Deputy Counselor, Royal Danish Embassy.
Martin Koper, First Secretary, Embassy of the Netherlands.

NOTES

1. EDA is defined in this paper as the sum of grant equivalents and grants, including technical assistance grants. Debt forgiveness is excluded. ODF is the sum of EDA and the nongrant component of official loans. For further information on the definitions see Chang, Fernández-Arias, and Servén (1999).

2. Appendix 3.1 contains information on locally produced aid data.

3. Financial aid normally includes grants and concessional loans having a grant element of at least 25 percent. In this discussion of loans and grants we use the ODF concept, which means that "loans" includes gross disbursement of official loans, and "grants" includes non–technical assistance grants as well as technical assistance grants. The aim of the study is not to analyze aid flows per se but rather to examine the relationship between donor behavior, as manifested in aid flows, and recipient country reforms.

4. The Finance and Planning ministries have been separated and merged during the period of the study as follows. 1980–92: Ministry of Finance, Ministry of Planning and Economic Development; 1992–96: Ministry of Finance and Economic Planning; 1996–98: Ministry of Finance, Ministry of Planning and Economic Development; 1998 onwards: Ministry of Finance, Planning and Economic Development. The abbreviation MFPED is used throughout the text when discussing the current joint ministry.

5. Nonfinancial aid includes technical assistance grants to nationals of aid-recipient countries who are receiving education or training, and payments for consultants, advisers, administrators, and the like, serving in aid-recipient countries. The statistics in the study are based on this definition of stand-alone technical assistance grants. In the analysis of the aid-reform relationship we also take into account loan-based technical cooperation, technical assistance components in project loans, advisory services, policy dialogue, and similar nonmonetary measures.

6. Eligibility under the HIPC Initiative is based on the net present value of debt/exports and the debt-service ratio at the "completion point" and beyond in the range of 200–250 percent and 20–25 percent respectively.

7. The government unified the dual exchange regime in 1984. See Kasekende and Ssemogerere (1991) for a full discussion of the exchange rate regimes in 1981–85.

8. Related to expenditure controls, revenue collection, and effective conduct of monetary policy.

9. The Washington consensus refers to a set of internationally agreed measures that are normally implemented during policy reform, including fiscal discipline, financial and trade liberalization, deregulation, taxation and public expenditure adjustments, and privatization.

10. The CPIA, which measures the extent to which government policy creates a good environment for broad-based growth and poverty reduction, has four components: macroeconomic policies, structural policies, public sector man-

agement, and equity. The equity component measures the extent to which policy ensures the full participation of the society through social services that reach the poor and safety nets targeted to the disadvantaged.

11. Collier and Dollar (1998) indicate that Uganda should have received 3.68 percent aid/GDP in a poverty-efficient allocation in 1996, while it actually received 3.34 percent.

REFERENCES

Ablo, E., and R. Reinikka. 1998. "Do Budgets Really Matter? Evidence from Public Spending on Education and Health in Uganda." Policy Research Working Paper 1926. World Bank, Development Research Group, Washington, D.C.

Atingi-Ego, M., and K. Matthews. 1996. "Demand for Narrow and Broad Money in Uganda." *African Review of Money, Banking and Finance. Supplementary Issue on Savings and development* 1 (2).

Bigsten, A. and S. Kayizzi-Mugerwa. 1992. "On Structural Adjustment in Uganda." *Canadian Journal of Development Studies* 13 (1): 57–75.

Brett, E.A. 1995. "Adjustment policy and institutional reform: rebuilding organizational capacity in Uganda." In P. Langseth, J. Katobor, E. Brett, and J. Munene, eds., *Uganda Landmarks in Rebuilding a Nation*. Kampala: Fountain Publishers.

Chang, C., E. Fernández-Arias, and L. Servén. 1999. "Measuring Aid Flows: A New Approach." Policy Research Working Paper 2050. World Bank, Development Research Group, Washington, D.C.

Collier, P., and D. Dollar. 1999. "Aid Allocation and Poverty Reduction." Policy Research Working Paper 2041.World Bank, Development Research Group, Washington, D.C.

Fry, M. 1995. "Savings, Growth and Financial Repression." Paper presented at the Money, Macroeconomic and Finance Research Group Meeting at the London Business School. May.

Harvey, C., and M. Robinson. 1994. "The Design of Economic Reforms in the Context of Political Liberalization: Uganda Case Study." Institute of Development Studies, University of Sussex, U.K. Processed.

IDA (International Development Association). 1997. "Uganda: Preliminary Document on the Initiative for Heavily Indebted Poor Countries." Washington, D.C.

IMF (International Monetary Fund). 1995. "Uganda: Adjustment with Growth, 1987–94." Washington, D.C.

———. 1998. "External Evaluation of the ESAF." Washington, D.C.

Kasekende, L., and M. Atingi-Ego. 1996. "Financial Liberalisation and Its Implications for the Domestic Financial System: The Case of Uganda." Final research paper submitted to the African Economic Research Consortium workshop, Nairobi. May 24–30.

————. 1999. "Enhancing and Sustaining Growth in Africa: Uganda's Macroeconomic Management." EAGER/PSGE study (Equity and Growth through Economic Research/Public Strategies for Growth with Equity).

Kasekende, L., and M. Malik. 1994. "The Financial System, Saving and Investment in Uganda." Paper presented to the U.N. Economic Commission for Africa, Addis Ababa.

Kasekende, L., and G. Ssemogerere. 1994. "Exchange Rate Unification and Economic Development: The Case of Uganda 1987–1992." *World Development* (22) 1183–98.

Lamont, T. 1995. "Economic Planning and Policy Formulation in Uganda." In P. Langseth, J. Katobor, E. Brett, and J. Munene, eds., *Uganda Landmarks in Rebuilding a Nation*. Kampala: Fountain Publishers.

McKinnon, R. 1973. "Money and Capital in Economic Development." Brookings Institution, Washington, D.C.

Shaw, Edward. 1973. *Financial Deepening in Economic Development.* New York: Oxford University Press.

Tumusiime-Mutebile, E. 1995. "Management of the Reform Programme." In P. Langseth, J. Katobor, E. Brett, and J. Munene, eds., *Uganda Landmarks in Rebuilding a Nation*. Kampala: Fountain Publishers.

Uganda. 1991. "External Debt Management Report." Prepared by S.G. Warburg Co. Ltd.

————. 1997. "Poverty Eradication Action Plan." Ministry of Planning and Economic Development, Kampala.

————. 1998. "Policy Framework Paper 1998/99 to 2000/01." Kampala.

UNDP (United Nations Development Programme). 1998. *Uganda Human Development Report.*

World Bank. 1997. "Implementation Completion Report. Uganda: Structural Adjustment Credits I and II (SAC1 and SAC2)." Africa Regional Office.

————. 1998a. "The World Bank's Experience with Post-Conflict Reconstruction. Volume IV: Uganda Case Study." Report No. 17769. Washington, D.C.

————. 1998b. *Assessing Aid: What Works, What Doesn't, and Why.* New York: Oxford University Press.

————.1999. "Preliminary Performance Audit Report. Uganda: First Structural Adjustment Credit and Second Structural Adjustment Credit." Operations Evaluation Department, Washington, D.C.

Post-Socialist Reformers

Ethiopia

Berhanu Abegaz
The College of William and Mary
Williamsburg, Virginia

ACRONYMS AND ABBREVIATIONS

AfDB	African Development Bank
CBE	Commercial Bank of Ethiopia
CPIA	Country Policy and Institutional Assessment
CRS	Creditor Reporting System (of the World Bank)
DAC	Development Assistance Committee (of the OECD)
DRS	Debtor Reporting System (of the World Bank)
EDA	Effective development assistance
EDT	Total external debt, including short-term and use of IMF credit
EPRDF	Ethiopian People's Revolutionary Democratic Front
ESAF	Enhanced Structural Adjustment Facility (of the IMF)
ETB	Ethiopian birr
EU	European Union
FIG	Financial and industrial group
FDI	Foreign direct investment
GDP	Gross domestic product
GTZ	German Agency for Technical Cooperation
HIPC	Heavily indebted poor countries
IDA	International Development Association (of the World Bank Group)
IMF	International Monetary Fund
LDOD	Long-term debt outstanding and disbursed
MEDAC	Ministry of Economic Development and Cooperation
NBE	National Bank of Ethiopia
NFR	Non-factor receipts
NGO	Nongovernmental organization
ODA	Official development assistance
OECD	Organisation for Economic Co-operation and Development
PADEP	Peasant Agricultural Development and Extension Program
PFP	Policy Framework Paper
SAC	Structural Adjustment Credit
SAF	Structural Adjustment Facility (of the IMF)
SDOD	Short-term debt outstanding and disbursed
SDP	Sector development program
SIP	Sector investment program
SOE	State-owned enterprise
SPA	Special Program of Assistance (for Sub-Saharan Africa)
TGE	Transitional Government of Ethiopia
TPLF	Tigray People's Liberation Front
U.N.	United Nations
UNESCO	United Nations Educational, Scientific, and Cultural Organization
UNICEF	United Nations Children's Fund
UNDP	United Nations Development Programme
UNFPA	United Nations Population Fund
WFP	World Food Programme
WHO	World Health Organization
WPE	Workers' Party of Ethiopia

The primary concern of this paper is the relationship between development aid and the process of economic reform in Ethiopia in 1980–98. However, a few words on issues pertaining to aid effectiveness and selectivity provide a useful context.

Development aid involves the transfer of resources from official or private institutions to low-income economies in the form of loans on concessional terms, technical assistance, and outright grants. The effectiveness of official development assistance has recently been the focus of comprehensive cross-national studies, most notably by the Task Force on Concessional Flows (Cassen 1994) and the World Bank (1998b). The Cassen report, relying primarily on country case studies, concluded that, first, the majority of official aid intended for long-term development has been successful; and second, aid has not necessarily gone where it is used most efficiently. For example, South Asia has lost its share of aid to Africa, where aid works relatively less well. The recent World Bank study, focusing on domestic factors, notes that (a) financial assistance has a big, positive impact where recipients have already undertaken sensible economic reforms; (b) financial aid flows do not discriminate between recipients with good policy and recipients with mediocre policy; (c) financial aid is generally fungible, thereby making the assessment of aid effectiveness difficult; (d) program finance enhances the prospects of success for sectoral and project aid; (e) nonfinancial aid is more effective than money in inducing nonreforming governments to seriously contemplate removing distortionary policies; and (f) effective aid often comes as a package of finance and ideas that fosters the emergence of good institutions and sound policies.

These findings, together with the decline of aid by one-third in the 1990s, have triggered a serious rethinking of the optimal composition and recipient-selectivity of aid programs. This trend is particularly of concern for Sub-Saharan Africa, where aid intensity is high and aid effectiveness is low (van de Walle and Johnston, 1996; World Bank 1994, 1998b; O'Connell and Soludo 1998). The mixed record on the effectiveness of external economic assistance to Ethiopia is reviewed in Maxwell (1998) and IDS/IDR (1996) for European Union aid; in World Bank (1997a) for the International Development Association (IDA) loan portfolio; and in Clay, Molla, and Habtewold (1998) for food aid.

External economic assistance has played an important role in the economic development programs of successive Ethiopian governments since 1960. The primary objectives of donors in Ethiopia have been the promotion of economic growth through support for investment and reform, alleviation of the unacceptably high rate of absolute poverty, and reduction of the vulnerability of the economy to adverse natural and terms-of-trade shocks. Other donor motives, especially geostrategic ones, have also generated military assistance, which at times has dwarfed development aid and threatened to nullify the latter's positive impact.

Ethiopia managed to attract more than US$17 billion in official development assistance in 1980–97. The annual inflow of some 16 percent of gross domestic product (GDP) was divided equally between multilateral donors, on the one hand, and bilateral donors as well as foreign nongovernmental organizations, on the other. The country today is heavily indebted to the tune of US$10 billion, almost equally split between Russia and members of the Development Assistance Committee (DAC) of the Organisation for Economic Co-operation and Development (OECD).

The main conclusions of this paper can be summarized as follows. Aid had a minimal impact on growth or poverty in the 1980s since Ethiopia was embroiled in a protracted civil war along with a bold program of building a socialist economy. Market-oriented reforms were initiated in 1990 in response to profound economic and political crises. The reform program initially attracted a sizeable increase in external assistance in support of liberalization, stabilization, and rehabilitation. Subsequent aid helped to deepen reform commitments and supported high growth rates. The residual *dirigisme* of the ruling party, however, appears to frustrate the enactment of important second-generation reforms.

The rest of the paper is organized as follows. Section 2 presents a brief country background, focusing on the economic profile of Ethiopia, while section 3 contains data on the level, source, and composition of aid. The political economy of institutional and policy reform under the Derg and Ethiopian People's Revolutionary Front governments is discussed in section 4. Section 5 sets forth hypotheses concerning the relationship between aid and reform, and section 6 offers a summary and conclusions. A chronology of reforms undertaken during the period under review is included as an appendix.

COUNTRY BACKGROUND

Ethiopia has a number of peculiar characteristics that must be kept in mind when evaluating the record on the role of aid in the country's development strategy. They include marked demographic and ecological diversity, an extremely high rate of absolute poverty and economic insecurity, a predominantly subsistence and coffee-based monocrop economy, and an old but resilient state plagued by autocratic rule and endemic social unrest.

The country's 60 million people are highly diverse in ethnic, religious, and geographic terms. According to census figures (Ethiopia 1998b), there are more than 80 distinct ethnic groups. However, two groups of equal size, the Oromo and the Amhara, together account for more than two-thirds of the population. About 60 percent of Ethiopians are Christian, a third are Muslims, and the remainder adhere to various indigenous religions. In the urban areas there is distinct occupational specialization among the various ethnic groups. Ecological diversity is unusually high, with 18 agro-ecological zones, and there is marked contrast between the densely settled mixed farming regions of the temperate central highlands and the transhumant lowlands.

Ethiopia is arguably the poorest country of its size in the world by almost all measures of poverty. Despite its good agricultural endowments, it has yet to achieve sustained food security. A 1981–82 survey found that nearly 90 percent of the population was below the poverty line of US$2 per day. In 1995–96, 43 percent of farm households were food insecure. Famines, regional and nationwide, occur with distressing frequency, thereby converting much of the transitory poverty into chronic poverty (Ramachandran 1997; Clay, Molla, and Habtewold 1998). The worst rural poverty is found in the famine-prone northern highlands, especially in parts of Tigray and Wollo, and in the lowlands along the country's international borders, most notably, the Afar, Somali, Borana, Gedeo, and Omo areas. Interestingly, the rate of urban poverty may very well have approached the level of rural poverty in the 1990s. Middlebrook and Corzato (1999) document poverty in Addis Ababa. An assessment of the relationship between growth and poverty reduction is frustrated by the lack of reliable data on the historical trends of poverty rates.

The country's social indicators reflect its low per capita income. Half the population does not have access to health facilities within 10 kilometers. Life expectancy at less than 50 years is below the average for Sub-Saharan Africa, as are school enrollment ratios. Only 40 percent of primary school–age children are enrolled in primary schools and just 15 percent of eligible students attend secondary schools.

Ethiopian economic data are generally incomplete or inconsistently reported, especially for periods longer than five years. I have constructed a number of economic series for the period under review, piecing together the more reliable birr-based series from disparate sources.[1] The basic macroeconomic indicators are reported in table 4.1. They are averaged over distinct subperiods paralleling notable reforms or shocks to the economy (see also appendix 4.2). Seven time segments are identified in order to capture major institutional changes or policy episodes: 1980–83 (*zemetcha* years), 1984–85 (nationwide famine), 1986–89 (central planning), 1990–91 (liberalization and political change), 1992–94 (recovery and stabilization), 1995–97 (structural reforms), and 1998–2001 (sector development programs).

The growth rate of real GDP during the study period was modest but respectable. The predominantly agricultural economy (agriculture ac-

TABLE 4.1 ETHIOPIA: BASIC ECONOMIC INDICATORS, PART A

Indicator	1980–83	1984–85	1986–89	1990–91	1992–94	1995–97	1998–00[a]
Annual average growth (%) (in 1990 birr)							
Real GDP	5.5	–5.3	5.3	3.0	7.6	7.8	2.5
Population	2.8	2.8	3.0	3.1	2.9	2.9	3.0
GDP per person	2.7	–8.1	2.3	–0.1	4.7	4.9	–0.5
Exports	8.8	28.0	3.1	–18.0	89.4	12.1	3.2
Imports	3.8	3.3	–1.2	–32.6	–16.9	12.6	5.4
Gross domestic investment	30.0	–40.2	0.0	–5.0	32.3	27.5	—
Money supply, M1	12.2	17.0	10.7	19.6	13.0	4.4	10.0
GDP deflator	6.5	26.0	0.8	21.4	11.7	3.4	2.4
Consumer price index[b]	3.8	29.1	4.2	35.7	5.7	–4.3	3.8
As percentage of GDP							
Gross domestic investment	12.5	13.8	16.7	11.5	12.9	18.0	20.3
Private consumption	78.8	78.6	75.4	76.5	84.8	81.7	80.0
Government consumption	15.5	16.3	16.4	17.9	11.6	12.0	11.0
Net exports and NFR	–6.8	–8.8	–8.0	–6.5	–9.6	–11.8	–11.7
Gross domestic savings	5.7	5.0	8.7	5.4	3.3	6.2	8.5

TABLE 4.1 ETHIOPIA: BASIC ECONOMIC INDICATORS, PART B

Levels	1980	1997
Real GDP (millions of 1990 birr)	13,485	28,361
Population (millions)	38	60
GDP per person (millions of 1990 birr)	358	473
Real exports (millions of 1990 birr)	1,912	4,238
Real imports (millions of 1990 birr)	10,555	20,033
Exchange rate (ETB/US$)	2.1	6.5
Quality of life indicators		
Poverty rate		
Below US$1/day (% of population)	46.0	44.0 (1995)
Poverty gap[c] (% of GDP)	12.4	—
Below US$2/day (% of population)	89.0	—
Poverty gap (% of GDP)	42.7	—
Under-5 mortality rate (per thousand)	213.0	177.0
Gross enrollment ratio (ages 6–23, %)	16.0	18.0

— Not available.

a. Projected based on constant factor cost in the 1998 Policy Framework Paper (Ethiopia 1998a).

b. The consumer price index (CPI) is for Addis Ababa only, and excludes housing cost. A national CPI was introduced in 1995–96. For 1990–97, the growth rates of the three price indicators are as follows: GDP deflator, 8.9 percent; CPI, 6.9 percent; and food price index, 12.4 percent. The complete data for the GDP-based inflation rate are as follows: 1970–98, 7.8 percent; 1970–75, 4.8 percent; 1976–80, 15.0 percent; 1980–90, 5.2 percent; 1991–92, 21.0 percent; 1993–98, 3.6 percent.

c. Size of income transfer needed to lift the poor above the poverty line, expressed as a fraction of GDP.

Sources: IMF 1998b, 1999a; World Bank 1995, 1999b; UNDP 1998.

counts for 55 percent of GDP) faced a number of shocks, including two waves of systemic change as well as fluctuations in commodity prices, civil strife, and droughts. During "normal" years, real per capita income grew at an annual rate of between 2.6 percent and 3.3 percent. The corresponding growth rate for GDP was 5.5 percent in the 1980s and 6.2 percent in the 1990s. These improvements, though hard to disentangle, are attributable to good weather, higher coffee prices, and allocational efficiency gains from the *zemetcha* (mass mobilization) campaigns, economic liberalization, and substantial inflows of development assistance.

When the crisis years of 1984–85 and 1990–91 are included, however, real GDP grew at an annual rate of only 2.6 percent between 1980 and 1997—replicating the performance of the 1970s. Agricultural growth, which carries half the sectoral weight, averaged 0.6 percent per year in the 1980s and 3.0 percent in the 1990s. According to the International Monetary Fund (IMF), the annual average growth rate of real GDP for 1970–98 was 2.86 percent. In light of the high rate of population growth, variously estimated at 2.5 to 3.0 percent per year, the average Ethiopian is at best as well off today as she was in 1970. On the other hand, the record on macroeconomic stability has been enviable. The inflation rate rarely exceeded single digits (the annual average was 7.8 percent for 1970–98), and the fiscal deficit was kept within manageable levels with some exceptions (see tables 4.1 and 4.2).

AID: LEVEL, TYPES, AND SOURCES

This case study uses two broad measures of official aid. The first, net official development assistance (ODA), is the sum of official grants (including technical assistance and food aid) and concessional loans with a grant element of at least 25 percent. It is calculated net of amortization payments. The second, effective development assistance (EDA), is the sum of discounted official grants and the grant equivalent of concessional loans, that is, the dollar value of the grant element. Dissatisfied with the shortcomings of net ODA, Chang, Fernández-Arias, and Servén (1999) constructed EDA as a superior measure of the real cost of aid to donors (though not necessarily to the recipient).

Size of Aid Flows

The data on the time pattern of resource flows to Ethiopia show some inconsistency even between the DRS (which appears to include portions of aid from the Council for Mutual Economic Assistance) and CRS databases.[2] I rely primarily on CRS data. Alternative measures of aid will also be used as shown in table 4.3.

TABLE 4.2 ETHIOPIA: FISCAL TRENDS, 1980–99

	Baseline:				
Revenue/expenditure	*1980–85*	*1986–90*	*1991–95*	*1996–97*	*1998–99*
Revenue and expenditure (% of GDP)					
Total revenue	15.4	24.6	17.8	21.5	20.2
Domestic	15.2	21.0	15.0	17.9	16.7
External grants	0.2	3.6	2.8	3.6	3.6
Total expenditure	20.5	31.7	23.1	23.8	24.9
Recurrent	—	22.1	14.8	13.5	13.9
Capital	—	9.6	8.2	10.4	11.0
Fiscal deficit (cash basis)					
Before grants	–5.3	–10.7	–8.1	–5.9	–7.8
After grants	–5.1	–7.1	–5.3	–2.2	–4.3
Average GDP (millions of current birr)	10,841	15,790	29,523	43,335	45,204
Allocation of expenditure (% of total)					
General administration	—	7.2	10.7	10.8	—
Defense	—	30.8	10.6	7.9	18.0
Economic infrastructure	—	5.6	10.7	16.5	—
of which: Roads	—	1.9	5.0	10.3	—
Economic development	—	24.4	23.1	22.0	—
of which: Agriculture	—	7.9	7.4	6.6	—
Social Services	—	15.9	23.2	25.1	—
of which: Education	—	9.5	14.1	15	—
of which: Health	—	3.3	5.1	6.4	—
Other	—	16.1	21.6	17.9	—
of which: Interest and charges	—	4.8	10.5	8.6	—
of which: External assistance	—	6.1	2.8	0.0	—
Total expenditure (millions of birr)	—	4,937	6,808	10,471	11,917

— Not available.

Sources: 1998–99 baseline data from World Bank 1998a, vol. 1, tables 1.2 and 3.1. All other data from IMF 1998b; World Bank 1999d.

Ethiopia's ODA receipts exceeded US$17 billion in nominal terms (US$23 billion in real terms) during 1980–97. This comes out to US$1.0 billion (nominal) or US$1.3 billion (real) of annual inflow. In 1996 prices, the annual inflow of net ODA3 (including loans, grants, technical assistance, and food aid) to Ethiopia averaged US$1.2 billion per year in the 1980s. It rose to US$1.4 billion per year in 1991–96 before slowing subsequently. In constant dollars, the pattern is M-shaped with peaks occurring in 1985 (famine effect) and 1992 (honeymoon effect). This pattern suggests that the ODA premium for the ambitious reform program of the 1990s has been a modest increase of 17 percent.

TABLE 4.3 ETHIOPIA: OFFICIAL DEVELOPMENT ASSISTANCE, 1980–97
(millions of U.S. dollars)

Year	Net ODA1: loans + grants[a] (CRS)	Net ODA loans[b] (CRS)	Net ODA grants (CRS)	IDA credits (DRS)	IMF credits (DRS)	FDI[c] (DRS)	Technical assistance (CRS)	Food aid (CRS)	Net ODA2[d] (DRS)	Net ODA3[e] (CRS)	Debt service (DRS)	ODA deflator (CRS)
1980	212	43	169	28	9	0	44	30	274	286	45	0.53
1981	245	46	199	28	73	0	64	54	1,251	363	58	0.51
1982	200	40	160	28	26	2	53	38	1,625	291	76	0.49
1983	339	126	213	42	0	–3	64	41	1,016	444	107	0.49
1984	361	75	286	41	0	5	81	91	929	533	130	0.47
1985	710	92	619	50	0	0	104	167	1,296	981	159	0.48
1986	629	67	563	38	41	–1	115	175	1,108	919	224	0.60
1987	627	134	493	86	0	–3	147	91	1,000	865	248	0.69
1988	963	188	775	75	0	2	197	157	1,263	1,317	309	0.75
1989	749	132	617	70	0	0	234	97	902	1,080	304	0.74

1990	1,020	161	858	74	0	12	254	195	1,201	1,469	236	0.83
1991	1,097	110	988	59	0	6	206	265	1,565	1,568	138	0.86
1992	1,182	106	1,076	112	20	6	190	222	1,484	1,594	109	0.91
1993	1,094	361	733	230	30	7	171	118	1,136	1,383	95	0.89
1994	1,076	311	764	150	20	3	126	48	958	1,250	112	0.93
1995	888	246	642	84	0	8	167	125	837	1,180	154	1.02
1996	850	227	623	142	21	5	202	70	657	1,122	347	1.00
1997	637	72	565	65	0	5	168	75	723	880	99	0.92

Note: CRS = Creditor Reporting System (OECD database), DRS = Debtor Reporting System (World Bank database).

a. Net ODA loans + grants (= financial aid)

b. Loan disbursements, net of amortization.

c. Foreign direct investment (private). The FDI figures are gross underestimates. During 1992–98, the Ethiopian Investment Authority approved 163 projects worth US$1.4 billion (mainly Saudi and European). Of these, only 21 projects are operational and another 49 projects are under implementation (see UNCTAD/ICC 1999, tables 5 and 6).

d. Net flows on debt + grants + technical assistance + food aid. ODA2 and ODA3 are the broadest measures of aid given the sometimes dubious assumption that food aid releases dollars for investment that would otherwise have financed essential food imports. Food aid (93 percent of which comes in the form of grains) has recently been equivalent to a quarter of national grain sales (Clay, Molla, and Habtewold 1998).

e. Net ODA loans + grants + technical assistance + food aid.

Sources: DRS data from World Bank 1999c. CRS data from OECD 1999.

In terms of aid intensity, the relevant figures are as follows. The ODA3-to-GNP ratio rose from 12 percent in the 1980s to 23 percent in the 1990s, yielding an average of 16 percent for 1980–97. In per capita terms, receipts rose from US$15/$23 (nominal/real) in the 1980s to US$27/$30 in the 1990s, for a period average of US$20/$26 during 1980–97.

The table shows other interesting patterns of aid flow. First, the share of grants in net cash disbursements rose substantially to exceed 50 percent after 1985. Second, debt service levels reached their peak, in absolute terms and relative to exports, in the second half of the 1980s. Third, Ethiopia relies heavily on ODA from four multilateral sources (the International Development Association, the European Union, the African Development Bank, and the United Nations) and a handful of European bilateral donors (mainly the Nordic countries, Germany, and Italy). Although it has managed to obtain a steady average annual flow of US$275 million in trade credit, Ethiopia remains distinctly unattractive to private investment from abroad.

Foreign direct investment (FDI) has remained low, falling far below East African levels even in absolute terms (UNCTAD/ICC 1999). Data from the Ethiopian Investment Authority show significant FDI inflows in 1997 and 1998. The cumulative investment capital of the 200 approved projects for the period 1993–99 was Birr 8.5 billion (US$1.1 billion). However, only 21 projects with an investment capital of Birr 3.2 billion (US$400 million) are currently in operation (IMF 1999b).

Data on EDA (table 4.4) confirm much of the trend captured by the conventional measures. The "effective" grant equivalent (GEQ) of concessional ODA loans averages 30 percent. This proportion rose from about 21 percent in the 1980s to 46 percent in the 1990s, which compares unfavorably with an average grant element of 70 percent for 1991–97 (see figures 4.1 and 4.2). In real terms, the size of EDA loans was on average twice as high in the post-socialist period as in the socialist period. In terms of grant equivalency, bilateral loans declined to modest levels in the 1990s. Finally, the share of technical assistance in total aid was 20 percent—below the Sub-Saharan Africa average of 25 percent (see O'Connell and Soludo 1998, table 1).

Sources and Uses of Aid

Being a non-colony, Ethiopia did not until recently attract the level of development assistance that it needed and could absorb effectively. It was, nonetheless, the largest recipient of the modest U.S. economic assistance to Sub-Saharan Africa during 1961–76. The Commission of the European Communities under Lomé was especially generous, providing grants of US$2.5 billion (in terms of 1990 dollars) during 1976–94 (Maxwell 1998: 105). Other multilateral agencies (notably IDA and the

TABLE 4.4 ETHIOPIA: EFFECTIVE DEVELOPMENT ASSISTANCE, 1980–96
(millions of U.S. dollars)

Year	TEDA	EDA1	EDA2	GEQ	Grants	TA	GEQ: multilateral	GEQ: bilateral	TA/EDA2
1980	239	165	209	40	125	44	26	14	21
1981	444	326	390	191	135	64	33	157	16
1982	269	178	231	71	107	53	32	39	23
1983	406	302	365	152	150	64	50	102	18
1984	553	281	362	76	205	81	42	34	22
1985	923	651	756	137	514	104	65	72	13
1986	855	564	680	117	447	115	49	69	17
1987	742	504	651	158	346	147	95	63	23
1988	1,097	737	934	159	578	197	93	66	21
1989	848	517	751	134	383	234	83	51	31
1990	1,175	726	980	122	604	254	97	25	26
1991	1,347	876	1,082	95	781	206	81	8	19
1992	1,393	981	1,171	95	886	190	119	8	16
1993	1,098	809	980	247	562	171	246	0	17
1994	964	790	916	152	638	126	152	0	14
1995	898	606	773	131	475	167	125	0	22
1996	850	578	780	158	420	202	158	0	26

Notes: TEDA = Total effective development assistance (= GEQ + grants + TA+ food aid). EDA1 = Effective development assistance (= GEQ + grants). EDA2 = Effective development assistance (= EDA1 + TA). GEQ = Grant equivalent of an ODA loan. TA = Technical assistance (= technical cooperation).
Source: Chang, Fernández-Arias, and Servén 1999.

FIGURE 4.1 ETHIOPIA: AVERAGE GRACE PERIOD AND MATURITY
OF ODA LOANS

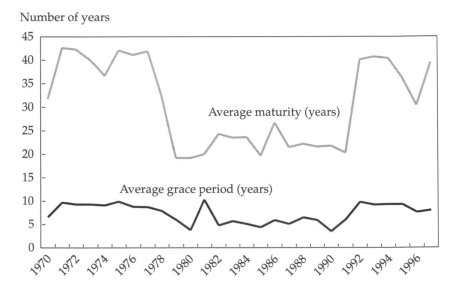

Source: OECD 1999.

African Development Bank) and bilateral donors (especially Italy and
Sweden) provided the bulk of the external assistance. The United Nations agencies, most notably the United Nations Development
Programme (UNDP) and the World Food Programme (WFP), were also
active. WFP alone provided US$600 in food assistance during 1990–93.

Between 1980 and 1997, 60 percent of grants in cash or in kind came
from Europe and another 20 percent from the U.N. agencies. Since the
mid-1990s, there has been a gradual decline in commitments by the European Union (EU) and Italy. This trend has been countered by increased
support from IDA, Germany, and the United States. Japan, the Netherlands, and Canada also increased their aid in the 1990s. The Nordic countries as a group present an interesting model of stable and predictable
aid to Ethiopia (table 4.5).

Nearly all the concessional loans come from two multilateral institutions: the International Development Association of the World Bank
Group, and the African Development Fund of the African Development
Bank (AfDB). The former made its first African loan to Ethiopia in 1950.
The latter began its lending program to Ethiopia in 1975 (as did the European Community), and it has beefed up its commitments in the past
five years (AfDB 1996).

FIGURE 4.2 ETHIOPIA: AVERAGE GRANT ELEMENT AND SHARE
OF MULTILATERAL DEBT

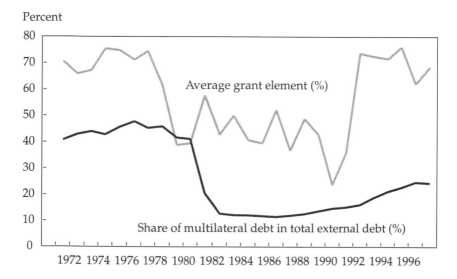

Percent

Source: OECD 1999.

The CRS data reveal other interesting patterns concerning assistance to Ethiopia from the Development Assistance Committee of the OECD. The share of DAC bilateral aid in net ODA1 fell from 60 percent in 1991–93 to 45 percent in 1994–97. ODA accounts for 98 percent of official development finance from all sources. One-third of technical cooperation grants come from non-DAC sources. And there has been a noticeable decline of both net disbursements and commitments since 1995.

The distribution of aid disbursement by sector provides useful information on the priorities of donors, creditors, and the two Ethiopian governments. Table 4.6 presents data on bilateral commitments by purpose. For net loans and grants from all sources, the gap between commitments and actual disbursements is generally small, except during the second half of the 1980s when the surge in external support began on the heels of the 1984 famine. The table shows that bilateral ODA commitments are largely accounted for by expenditures on social infrastructure, program aid, and production sectors. Program assistance was especially strong, accounting for nearly half of bilateral resources, during the unstable years of 1985–93. Production sectors such as industry and agriculture received much less, as is often the case in Sub-Saharan Africa.

TABLE 4.5 ETHIOPIA: NET ODA LOANS AND GRANTS BY CREDITOR OR DONOR, 1970–97
(millions of U.S. dollars)

| Year | Loans | | | Grants[b] | | | | | | | | |
	All loans	ADF[a]	IDA	All grants	European Community	United Nations	Germany	Italy	United States	Nordic countries[c]	Japan	Netherlands
1970	14	0	3	26	0	4	4	3	7	6	0	0
1975	63	0	19	71	8	16	6	3	9	12	1	3
1980	43	3	28	169	32	48	10	8	20	33	1	4
1981	46	11	28	199	42	67	11	15	4	23	3	4
1982	40	7	26	160	27	58	11	4	3	21	1	3
1983	126	12	41	213	47	15	10	14	8	25	3	3
1984	75	5	39	286	58	64	29	12	21	30	4	9
1985	92	17	48	619	103	108	27	63	146	49	8	8
1986	67	15	35	563	85	90	24	134	94	54	7	8
1987	134	23	82	493	93	103	27	98	8	59	16	7
1988	188	17	72	775	134	156	38	158	69	86	14	23
1989	132	28	66	617	45	192	41	119	26	74	13	11
1990	161	43	69	858	102	203	46	131	53	97	11	25
1991	110	41	54	988	159	367	48	77	88	88	18	26
1992	106	50	106	1,076	292	239	204	41	68	87	11	29
1993	361	117	225	733	123	183	50	12	131	80	48	34
1994	311	61	156	764	182	76	89	41	122	62	44	33
1995	246	82	77	642	82	107	76	27	70	76	63	40
1996	227	79	128	623	53	117	81	40	56	72	50	60
1997	72[d]	24	50	565	42	142	58	32	60	75	37	35

a. African Development Fund (of the African Development Bank, AfDB)
b. Two other less generous but still important DAC donors not listed here are Canada and the United Kingdom.
c. Sweden, Norway, Denmark, and Finland.
d. This figure is too low (taken as it appeared in the source).
Source: OECD 1999.

TABLE 4.6 ETHIOPIA: BILATERAL ODA COMMITMENTS
BY PURPOSE, 1973–97
(millions of U.S. dollars)

Year	Total commit-ment[a]	Infra-structure + program	Infrastructure			Program[b]		Prod-uction sectors
			Total	Social	Economic	Total	Food	
1973	32	21	20	13	7	2	0	2
1974	42	10	10	4	5	0	0	21
1975	67	51	38	29	9	14	8	16
1976	17	12	5	5	0	7	7	5
1977	31	17	7	6	1	9	9	13
1978	53	26	18	3	15	8	8	10
1979	42	23	5	5	0	18	18	7
1980	48	29	6	6	0	23	23	12
1981	80	49	8	8	0	41	36	25
1982	69	56	31	31	0	25	25	8
1983	76	46	10	6	4	36	36	16
1984	202	114	41	8	32	73	73	52
1985	308	206	61	24	37	145	145	45
1986	231	162	22	17	5	140	140	26
1987	361	127	43	31	12	84	84	62
1988	486	336	164	64	101	172	135	78
1989	278	144	48	25	24	96	90	82
1990	353	197	38	29	9	159	157	37
1991	210	170	16	7	8	154	150	20
1992	430	266	106	95	11	160	155	33
1993	368	233	79	67	12	154	111	64
1994	306	169	119	74	45	50	50	48
1995	566	273	147	104	43	126	85	58
1996	393	221	156	142	13	65	46	98
1997	295	180	103	82	21	77	65	46

a. Reported total commitment does not always equal the sum of its components (e.g. 1988).
b. Program aid includes food aid and balance of payments and budget support. Remainder categories include action relating to debt, emergency assistance, multisectoral aid, and unspecified.
Source: OECD 1999.

External Debt: Stock and Service

At the end of 1997, Ethiopia's external debt stock (EDT)—nearly all of which was public debt—was estimated at US$10.0 billion (see table 4.7). The distribution of debt by ownership is as follows. Some 62 percent is owed to bilateral lenders, mainly to Russia for military purchases during the Soviet era. Multilateral creditors accounted for over one-third of

TABLE 4.7 ETHIOPIA: TOTAL DEBT STOCKS, 1980–97
(millions of U.S. dollars)

Year	EDT	Total LDOD	IDA: LDOD	SDOD	IMF	Arrears[a]	Export credit
1980	824	688	249	57	79	2	—
1981	1,842	1,638	276	59	145	2	—
1982	3,280	3,051	302	68	161	2	120
1983	3,845	3,649	342	63	134	2	177
1984	4,220	4,054	379	68	98	2	279
1985	5,206	5,057	437	77	71	1	297
1986	6,134	5,967	486	83	84	1	323
1987	7,364	7,191	601	98	76	55	389
1988	7,704	7,515	658	134	55	16	372
1989	7,842	7,700	718	112	30	69	323
1990	8,634	8,483	824	145	6	279	311
1991	9,119	8,843	883	276	0	1,088	292
1992	9,341	9,003	964	319	19	1,780	239
1993	9,703	9,287	1,187	368	49	2,105	235
1994	10,067	9,570	1,373	424	72	3,204	234
1995	10,309	9,775	1,470	461	74	4,067	239
1996	10,078	9,484	1,555	502	92	4,784	300
1997	10,079	9,427	1,532	565	87	5,298	237

— Not available.
Note: The above include ruble-denominated defense loans from the former Soviet Union. The Ministry of Finance put the external debt as of June 1998 much lower at US$7.8 billion, of which US$4.1 billion was owed to Russia.
EDT = Total debt stocks, including short-term debt and use of IMF credit.
LDOD = Long-term debt outstanding and disbursed.
SDOD = Short-term debt outstanding and disbursed.
a. Arrears include principal and interest.
Source: World Bank 1999c.

the total. IDA, with a portfolio of $1.5 billion, owns half of the multilateral debt. Private creditors claim the remaining 5 percent of the total debt stock. The data also show that short-term debt accounts for less than 5 percent of the total debt stock.

Until recently, Ethiopia has had a record of remarkable diligence in servicing its debt. Arrears of both principal and capitalized interest increased substantially after 1990, reaching a whopping 53 percent of EDT by 1998. The real debt stock per capita in the 1990s was about six times as high as aid flow per capita (US$180 as against US$30).

In net present value terms, the servicing of Ethiopia's external debt burden is quite unsustainable (Ghani and Zang 1995). In current value terms, debt service payments averaged 27 percent of GNP in the 1980s before falling to 23 percent in the 1990s. International reserves were, in fact, down to less than one month of imports in 1988–91. At the beginning of 1998, the debt inclusive of arrears to Russia represented 963 percent of exports (see table 4.8) or 159 percent of GNP. The forecasts in Policy Framework Paper 5 (PFP5) show that the debt-to-export ratio will fall to 265 percent in 2001 (Ethiopia 1998a).

Ethiopia was granted debt relief on enhanced Toronto terms by the Paris Club in December 1992. The relief involved debt cancellation of US$101 million and debt rescheduling of US$271 million. Ethiopia also bought back some of its commercial debt (US$226 million) in 1995 at a rate of 8 cents per dollar, utilizing the World Bank's debt buyback facility. The preliminary review of eligibility for the Heavily Indebted Poor Countries (HIPC) Debt Initiative has been completed for Ethiopia.

TABLE 4.8 ETHIOPIA: DEBT STOCKS AND DEBT SERVICE INDICATORS, 1980–97

(percent)

Year	CL/EDT	RES/MGS (months)	RES/TDS	EDT/XGS	TDS/XGS	EDT/GNP
1980	68	4	585	140	8	16
1981	78	5	643	326	10	36
1982	84	3	367	610	14	60
1983	86	3	192	666	19	64
1984	85	1	84	674	21	74
1985	86	2	136	932	28	78
1986	86	3	148	891	33	88
1987	87	2	90	1,150	39	99
1988	86	1	48	1,189	48	101
1989	87	1	40	1,035	40	99
1990	87	1	23	1,276	35	127
1991	84	1	77	1,667	25	172
1992	84	3	247	2,037	24	169
1993	84	4	527	1,889	19	158
1994	84	6	526	1,788	20	209
1995	85	7	529	1,277	19	180
1996	86	5	211	1,224	42	169
1997	86	3	507	963	10	159

Note: Includes ruble-denominated defense loans from the former Soviet Union.
CL/EDT = Concessional loans to total external debt.
RES/MGS = International reserves to imports of goods and services.
RES/TDS = International reserves to total debt service.
EDT/XGS = Total debt service to exports of goods and services.
EDT/GNP = Total external debt to gross national product.
Source: World Bank 1999c.

Finalization of the debt relief package is pending settlement of the Ethiopia-Eritrea conflict (World Bank 1999d; IMF 1999b).

Ethiopia also stands to benefit from the more generous Cologne summit declaration on HIPC. The annual saving from debt relief, however, appears to be modest given the recent trends of resorting to arrears. Assuming a 70 percent reduction in debt service payments from debt relief, the money that would be available for additional social spending is about US$50 million to US$100 million (that is, given the wide range of estimated annual debt service payment of US$150 million to US$350 million in recent years). Ethiopia also continues to press for a major write-off of Russian debt.[3]

Timing and Stability of Aid Flows

In a world of imperfect markets, the impact of aid on growth depends in part on its timing and degree of instability, that is, whether it is predictable or not. In the case of Ethiopia, the critical policy focus is on the quantity (and quality) of investment. Foreign aid, which accounts for more than one-fifth of GNP, finances nearly half the capital expenditure in the federal budget. Furthermore, in the spirit of two-gap models, an important determinant of changes in Ethiopian capital-good imports is the time path of foreign exchange earnings from exports (Etherington and Yainshet 1988; Lensink and Morrissey 1999; World Bank 1998a).

A glance at figures 4.3 and 4.4 shows some interesting patterns in this regard. First, the variation in the growth rate of net ODA1 is much higher than that of exports (or GDP). Generally, multilateral aid is more stable than bilateral aid, and project aid is steadier than program aid.

Second, the correlation between the growth rates of export revenues and ODA (grants and loans) is low and negative (Pearson r = –0.25). This means that the changes in the flow of aid do not have a systematically countervailing relationship with fluctuations in export earnings. This can be attributed to a number of factors, including the changing share of nonproject aid and the bunching of aid receipts relative to commitments, which are driven largely by bureaucratic dynamics. It also means that ODA flows are not entirely geared to stabilizing the overall supply of foreign exchange.

Third, the level of total receipts (inclusive of ODA, other official flows, and private flows) does compensate for the volatility of export earnings (r = –0.57) so that total foreign exchange flows are reasonably stable. As shown in figure 4.4, this produces the expected synchronization between total foreign exchange receipts and the import bill.

Two inferences can be drawn from this cursory overview. Increases in the share of program aid, by stabilizing total foreign exchange inflows, would help to reduce growth-retarding uncertainty for investors (Lensink

FIGURE 4.3 ETHIOPIA: GROWTH RATES OF GDP, EXPORTS, AND NET ODA

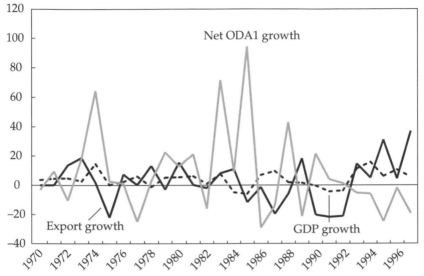

Annual growth rate (%)

Net ODA1 growth

Export growth

GDP growth

Note: Calculated in 1996 U.S. dollars.
a. Net ODA1 refers only to financial aid (grants and net loans) to make it comparable to export earnings. It averaged US$500 million (or US$700 million in 1996 prices) during 1970–97.
Sources: IMF 1998 (for GDP); World Bank 1999c (for imports and exports); OECD 1999 (for ODA, receipts, and deflator).

and Morrissey 1999; Collier and Gunning 1999). Furthermore, the rising share of nonproject aid may bring more flexibility, but at the expense of aid predictability since the tap may be more easily turned on and off by disgruntled donors.

INSTITUTIONAL DEVELOPMENT AND POLICY REFORM

During the period under consideration, Ethiopia underwent two waves of radical economic reform: one revolutionary and anti-market in orientation, and the other more modest and mixed-economy in orientation. The former reflects the pervasive influence of the left-wing student movement, and the latter a reluctant retreat from socialist economic ideas by the products of the same movement. The chronology of institutional and policy reforms introduced by the two regimes is shown in appendix 4.2.

FIGURE 4.4 ETHIOPIA: SOURCES AND USES OF FOREIGN EXCHANGE

Millions of U.S. dollars

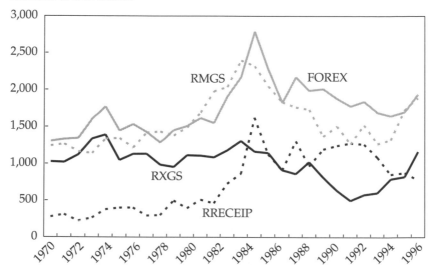

RRECEIP = All foreign exchange receipts from ODA and non-ODA sources, excluding exports.
FOREX = Total foreign exchange inflows, including export earnings.
RXGS = Exports of goods and services.
RMGS = Imports of goods and services.
Sources: IMF 1998 (for GDP); World Bank 1999c (for imports and exports); OECD 1999 (for ODA, receipts, and deflator).

Institutional Transformation under the Derg

The period between 1974 and 1990 was one of revolutionary turmoil following the coup d'etat against the monarchy, civil wars, a war with Somalia, and an experiment with agrarian socialism. By the end of the 1970s, the broad outline of a quasi-socialist economy was in place: all land, extra houses, and large as well as medium private enterprises were nationalized without compensation. Owner-cultivators and sharecroppers were given use rights (usufruct) to land in lieu of their customary freehold or communal ownership rights. The rural population was then organized into peasant associations. These state-sponsored associations were soon to serve as stepping stones for the establishment of producer cooperatives or quasi-collective farms. Much of inter-regional wholesale and retail trade in key staples and important industrial goods was reserved for parastatals.

The military regime's vision of state-led industrialization included an over-zealous "villagization" campaign, to facilitate political control as well as the delivery of social services; an ambitious but poorly planned program of "resettlement" of the drought-vulnerable population; and a program of import substitution for key industrial goods. By mid-1988 villagization had grouped 12 million people—one-third of the rural population—in more than 12,000 large villages (Clapham 1988: 251).

Though briefly distracted by the devastating 1984–85 national famine, when GDP contracted by 13.2 percent, the Derg consolidated its power in the second half of the decade. It formulated a Ten-Year Perspective Economic Plan (1985–94) with an unrealistic expectation of receiving foreign aid to finance more than half of the planned investment (World Bank 1987; Griffin 1992). The plan nevertheless provided a more consistent framework for medium-term and annual plans than the previous disparate-projects approach. The economy rebounded briefly but spectacularly at the rate of 9.3 percent and 13.8 percent in 1986 and 1987 respectively. To its credit, the government also expanded elementary and secondary education and rural health clinics at unprecedented rates. The ambitious literacy campaign was awarded a UNESCO prize. However, two-thirds of the adult population remains illiterate today.

The military regime also belatedly established a socialist party, the Workers' Party of Ethiopia (WPE), with military officers and the upper echelon of the civil service at its core. Ethiopia finally joined the "people's democracies" of the Soviet bloc in 1987 with the declaration of the People's Democratic Republic of Ethiopia under a constitution ratified by national referendum.

The Derg intensified the administrative centralization program of the monarchy under a unitary state, and implemented an unprecedented degree of state ownership and control of the modern sector of the economy. The country's 15 regions were reorganized into 30 administrative units. Imitating the nomenklatura systems of the socialist states, the regime established parallel networks of government and party organs down to the level of the *kebelle* (neighborhood), all controlled by WPE functionaries. The Derg also introduced a still enduring cadre system of party control of the economic, military, and administrative sectors of the state bureaucracy.

A number of developments accentuated the "normal" level of crisis in the waning days of war socialism, which eventually led to policy reforms. First, the burden of financing a huge army was too high for the feeble domestic economic base to support, especially since the Soviet Union was itself beset by a profound crisis after 1988. Second, the idea of socialism was discredited internationally and domestically. Third, the economic consequences of the campaigns of villagization, resettlement, and producer cooperatives proved disastrous for an already impoverished population. The economy cumulatively shrank by 7.0 percent during and immediately after the height of the civil war, in 1988–92. While most captive civil servants could do little to arrest the double squeeze on salaries of pay freezes and double-digit inflation, small producers increasingly resorted to the age-old but inefficient methods of survival—informal exchange and subsistence production.

The IDA maintained a modest portfolio of loans (US$35 million annually) during 1976–86. It confined its funding to economic and sector work (technical assistance and country economic memoranda), and financing of selected social services, transportation and communication, and the important coffee sector. Loan disbursement rose to US$52 million per year during 1989–90 with an agreement to support an agricultural extension and credit program called the Peasant Agricultural Development and Extension Program (PADEP). As shown in table 4.6, the government managed to obtain a respectable level of grant money in the 1980s (on a per year basis):US$70 million from the EC-EU, US$68 million from Italy, US$135 million from the Nordic countries, US$25 million from Germany, and US$41 million from the United States, mostly food aid. Data on economic aid from the Council for Mutual Economic Assistance are sketchy but it was rather modest (US$30 million in 1983) and came primarily in the form of project aid (Clapham 1988).[4]

The Derg seriously considered liberalization after 1988 although the implementing legislation was not in place until the WPE Congress of March 1990, a year before the regime's demise (Haile Mariam 1990). The impetus appears to have come from the pressure created by the steady gains of the northern rebel movements as well as the disappointing economic results of agricultural cooperatives and parastatals in the distributive sector. The reforms were in the nature of "perfection of control" rather than significant concessions to the market. Their significance lies in the dynamic they created for further reform.

The most notable measures were the following. Inheritable use rights were granted on nationalized land, membership in producer cooperatives became voluntary (which led to their spontaneous dismantling by jubilant cooperators), many prices were decontrolled, and the draconian restrictions on private trade were grudgingly lifted. The liberalization of the grain market, the most important market in Ethiopia, paved the way for a steady although still incomplete integration of inter-regional markets.

Most foreign owners of nationalized enterprises did, under pressure from the international financial institutions and bilateral donors, eventually receive compensation. Most citizens whose property was confiscated are still awaiting restitution. As we will see below, these issues keep coming up in the policy dialogue with multilateral donors and in the lingering complaints of the business community.

Institutional Reform under the EPRDF

The year 1991 was a watershed for reform: a coalition led by two liberation fronts ended the civil war victoriously. The province of Eritrea became an independent state in 1993.[5] A transitional government of Ethiopia (TGE) was formed in Addis Ababa by a loosely affiliated assortment of liberation fronts known as the Ethiopian People's Revolutionary Democratic Front (EPRDF). The Tigray People's Liberation Front (TPLF), which serves as the vanguard of the coalition, accounts for most of the senior government leadership.

This was a rather unusual conclusion for a civil war. Groups at the periphery in effect gained exclusive control of the state machinery. The country is still contending with all the contradictions entailed in such a dispensation for both victor and loser (Bevan 1994; Chole 1993). The large national army of 500,000 was disbanded and replaced by EPRDF's own army (Dercon and Ayalew 1998). The civil service was trimmed by about a quarter; many were fired for political reasons. Despite a secular decline in real wages and compression of the salary structure, the 300,000-strong civil service accounts for one-third of formal-sector employment in Ethiopia (IMF 1999b).

The TGE proceeded to decree a number of important institutional reforms in 1991–94, before the national election. The administrative structure of the country was revamped once again, this time into nine federal units (*killils*) and special administrations in the two richest cities (Addis Ababa and Dire Dawa). The regional states were further divided into 66 zones comprising 556 *woredas* or units of local government with about 100,000 people each.

The 1994 Ethiopian Constitution enshrined an ethnic-based federalism. After the 1995 "administratively fair, yet uncompetitive" elections (World Bank 1998c), a bicameral parliament dominated by the EPRDF assumed power under the newly created Federal Democratic Republic of Ethiopia. The federal constitution is Soviet-like in granting to any ethnic group the right to self-determination "including and up to secession." While the idea of a decentralized governmental structure finds broad support, the wisdom of gerrymandering districts to create ethnic fiefdoms remains a highly contentious issue in Ethiopian politics.

Ethiopia today employs an unusual form of fiscal federalism. The large vertical imbalance between the revenue-raising power of the federal government (which collects some 80 percent of revenues) and the responsibilities of the regions is bridged by unrestricted block grants. These subsidies are based on a formula that purports to reflect a region's population, development level, and local revenue generation. The advantages of responsiveness to local needs which would normally result from decentralization are, therefore, diminished by the lack of performance-based reciprocity, inter-regional gaps in technocratic capacity, and the relative neglect of the special needs of municipalities (World Bank 1999a).

Policy Reform under the EPRDF

A few months after assuming state power, the EPRDF issued its first economic program (Ethiopia 1991). The program proposed to deepen the price decontrol and domestic trade liberalization introduced by the previous government. It advocated continuation of state ownership and control of industry, finance, modern services, and land. The leadership's vision of the post-socialist economy, though amended after 1993, remains one of a "state-led market economy" with mixed ownership and active regulation to stem market failures.

The first Policy Framework Paper (PFP), covering 1992–93, marked the formal start of an extensive stabilization and structural adjustment program for poverty reduction and transition to a market economy. Key elements of the various rounds of the first-stage reforms included (see appendix 4.2):

- Prudent fiscal policies (mainly through retrenchment of the army and civil servants, tax reform, and lower defense spending) and monetary policies (limiting monetization of the fiscal deficit)
- A substantial correction of the overvalued nominal exchange rate
- Decontrol of many prices
- Liberalization of the foreign trade and foreign exchange regime
- Autonomy of state-owned enterprises (SOEs) and privatization of small and medium enterprises
- Financial market reform, including the licensing of six local private banks and seven insurance companies so far, and interest-rate (except for deposit rate) liberalization
- A liberal investment code with an investment authority that is organized as a "one-stop shop."

The last two PFPs have paid greater attention to agriculture and rural development, social sectors, infrastructure, energy, export and private sector development, and the financial sector. A civil service reform program is also underway. It encompasses the areas of financial management, judicial reform, human resource management, top management systems, human resource management, and service delivery.

The government adopted a three-year adjustment program in mid-1996 under the IMF's Enhanced Structural Adjustment Facility (ESAF). In addition to the stabilization program, which was also supported by a Structural Adjustment Credit (SAC I) loan from IDA, it introduced structural reform measures aimed at liberalizing the economy. All retail prices, except petroleum, have been decontrolled. Export taxes were eliminated except on coffee, and in that case license fees for exporters were reduced. Measures to revive the private sector included allowing domestic private participation in freight forwarding and clearing, and in banking and insurance activities. The parastatal monopoly in coffee marketing was effectively abolished by allowing the private sector into coffee trading, marketing, and exports.

Maximum import duties were lowered from 230 percent to 40 percent, and to a weighted average of 21.5 percent by 1998. The negative list used to determine eligibility for imports through the foreign exchange auction has been reduced. Exporters of goods and services are now allowed to retain 10 percent of foreign exchange earnings. The government also issued a new labor code that incorporates much international practice in the areas of employment conditions and compensation; it eliminated the monopoly power of some official marketing and trade corporations, and completed the decontrol of agricultural prices. The investment code was revised four times in as many years and presently allows greater private sector participation, including in public utilities where the state enjoys a de facto monopoly. In addition, a number of modest measures have been taken to promote exports.

Ethiopian public enterprises have historically been commercially (if not always economically) profitable, and their privatization does have important fiscal implications. For example, they accounted for 90 percent of federally collected revenues in 1996, with a full 40 percent coming from just 10 of the largest SOEs (World Bank 1998a:46–47). Nonetheless, the Ethiopian Privatization Agency has recently stated that, during 1993–98, it undertook the divestiture of 176 firms (three-quarters of them retail shops and hotels) at a total price of 2.5 billion birr, or US$330 million. Financing and the inefficient land-lease policy are the major constraints on the planned case-by-case privatization of 120 large enterprises over the next three years.

Some 16 of the enterprises were sold to foreign capital. The largest investor, the Saudi conglomerate of Midroc Ethiopia, which accounted for 64 percent of privatization receipts, paid US$172 million for the Lega Dembi Gold Mines and another US$90 million for ten agro-processing enterprises. It also owns the new Sheraton Addis and a network of construction, service, and financial establishments (UNCTAD/ICC 1999).

The birr has been allowed to float, as a result of which the ETB/US$ exchange rate rose from about 2 in mid-1992 to about 8 in mid-1999. This flexibility has resulted in the convergence of the official, auction, and parallel market exchange rates. The real exchange rate depreciated significantly as a result of the nominal devaluation and disinflation. The growth rate of the GDP deflator declined from 21 percent to 3 percent between 1991 and 1997. With additional support for improvements on the supply side, these reforms will result in a marked improvement in the competitiveness of Ethiopian exports.

A number of tax policy reforms and other government revenue enhancement measures were also introduced. The number of income tax brackets was reduced and the top marginal tax rate was lowered from 85 percent to 40 percent. Revenue mobilization, at less than 15 percent of GDP, remains inadequate. Tax arrears and corruption (notably in Customs, parts of Inland Revenue, and at the regional level) continue to be major problems, as is the 1960-vintage commercial code (World Bank 1998a, 1998c).

Reform Dialogue: Government and Stakeholders

A striking feature of the landscape of reform in Ethiopia is the absence of an *institutionalized* mechanism for subjecting economic policy proposals to discussion or debate between the government and the various business and civic organizations. The dearth of public information and the limited public participation in policy deliberation makes Ethiopia an odd man out among such progressive reformers as Uganda and Ghana.

The marginalization of important stakeholders (opposition parties, various chambers of commerce and sectoral associations, farmers' groups, the independent press, professional associations, trade unions, local nongovernmental organizations, the academic community, and the like) reflects the autocratic legacies of the country's political systems. Successive governments have prevented, co-opted, or marginalized nascent civil society institutions. This has had several unsavory consequences. The business community is impelled to resort to corruption; the "watchdog" role of an independent, informed press is weakened; the sense of ownership of the reforms by the public is foregone; effective oversight by Parliament is undermined; and issues of distributional fairness across regions or sectors become overly politicized.

Recent research on aid effectiveness and sustainability of reforms points to a number of conclusions. First, equitable growth is predicated on sound macroeconomic fundamentals, good budget management, and institutional reforms that foster the mobilization of underutilized resources. Second, the sustainability of good reforms, in turn, depends on domestic ownership as manifested by the commitments of the leadership and the citizenry to the reforms along with the capacity to implement them. Third, good governance ultimately undergirds the above in the form of an accountable executive, a professional bureaucracy, the rule of law, a stable and transparent policymaking process, and an engaged civil society (World Bank 1998a; Leonardo and others 1999).

The formal decisionmaking framework under the current EPRDF government is clear enough. The overall development strategy and policy

direction are apparently scrupulously debated within the central committee of the EPRDF. The prime minister's office is the focal point of
coordination on major policy decisions between the executive branch
and the legislative branch (EPRDF congresses and the Parliament, which
is controlled by the ruling party). The Ministry of Economic Development and Cooperation (MEDAC) is the main gateway for donors. Line
ministries and regional planning bureaus also have varying levels of
input. Any loan secured has to be signed off by the Council of Ministers.

Donors focusing on program support and sector programs have found
this arrangement slow but expedient since it lends itself to efficient technocratic relations with unambiguous lines of authority. However, the
Ethiopian governance system, by short-circuiting broad participation,
undermines the sustainability of reforms in the long run. The easy phase
of reform (involving rehabilitation, liberalization, and stabilization) seems
to have enjoyed the tacit support of most sectors of the population, consulted or not. Second-generation reforms involving ownership of land,
large state enterprises, party-owned business groups, and competition
policy are, however, too contentious for the viability of a model based
on diktat.

The angst of the business community and other stakeholders is eloquently expressed by the well informed, if sometimes overly critical,
economics correspondent of the *Addis Tribune,* a respected weekly. The
assessment is worth quoting at length since it aptly captures the agenda
for future policy debate:

> It is no wonder that in Ethiopia today several risible economic poli-
> cies and practices are in effect: Individuals cannot own land; houses
> and other properties confiscated by the predatory Derg regime con-
> tinue to be in the possession of the present government; the official
> policy of ethnic bias prompts leaders to allocate disproportionate
> amounts of public resources to favoured regions; the mixing of
> politics with business is flagrantly practised; privatization of na-
> tionalized enterprises is going on without any regard to the issue
> of compensation; back-breaking increases have been made in rents
> on government-owned (but previously privately-owned) commer-
> cial premises; unprecedently high taxes are levied on rental income
> and capital gains; *bona fide* franco valuta imports are prohibited;
> private foreign exchange bureaus are not allowed; foreign partici-
> pation in the banking and insurance sector is banned; directed credit
> is commonplace; top-notch university lecturers and experienced
> civil servants have been dismissed or forced into early retirement;
> peasants critical of official economic policy and political thinking
> have been disposed of their plots of land; commercial farming is
> eyed with suspicion; and peasant agriculture is being saturated

with fertilizer to the neglect of irrigation. Similar deficiencies are easily observed in the political arena as well, but there is no need to go into them here as they are quite well-known. (Addis Tribune 1998e)

Donors, including usually outspoken bilaterals, have chosen to bifurcate economic conditionality and political conditionality. Their complaints appear to have been largely confined to the more programmatic issues of public sector efficiency, transparency, and a blanket appeal for stakeholder participation and respect for basic human rights. A number of donors, for example, suspended program aid in 1999 for fear that fungible resources might be diverted to finance the Ethio-Eritrean war, which claimed 20 percent of the 1999 budget (World Bank 1999d; IMF 1999b; Economist 1999). Given the current outpouring of pan-Ethiopian patriotism, many hope that the EPRDF administration will take advantage of this opportunity to establish a more inclusive governance system.[6]

Donor Assistance Strategy

Given the importance of multidonor participation, in terms of both ideas and money, to the post-Derg reform programs, it is useful to take a brief look at the goals and strategies of the donor community. I draw heavily on the World Bank's Country Assistance Strategy since it is well documented.

The highlights of reform measures pursued by the multilateral institutions and multidonor conferences are presented in appendix 4.2. The history of reform in the past three decades and the ODA data reviewed earlier both suggest that, with the exception of the international financial institutions, donors on the whole have been unable or unwilling to effect a close linkage between aid and reform, perhaps for fear of punishing the poor.

Ethiopia enjoys a good relationship with the community of multilateral and bilateral donors. IDA assistance was devoted in the early phase of the TGE reform program to economic recovery, structural adjustment, and the preparation of policy framework papers as well as technical documents. It then switched emphasis in 1997 to sector investment programs (SIPs), primarily externally funded and spanning five to ten years. Other multilateral donors active in these programs include the African Development Bank, the European Union, and the United Nations agencies. Several bilateral donors also provide active support for these programs.

Overall, the donor assistance strategy for use of aid to Ethiopia has been directed at four policy clusters. The first cluster focuses on policy dialogue together with economic and sector work designed to emphasize the importance of macroeconomic stability, private sector development, and improvements in capacity for implementing projects or policies. A number of studies, including five public expenditure reviews and an equal number of PFPs, have provided a coherent framework for linking project funding with sector and program aid in a forward-looking manner (World Bank 1997a).

A second cluster is devoted to infrastructure development with a special emphasis on expanding the road network and the supply of electricity. The third cluster concentrates on growth-enhancing support for agriculture (mainly improved seeds and fertilizer), exports (designed to diversify the export basket and reduce dependence on large flows of aid), and small enterprises. A fourth cluster of reforms is aimed at the alleviation of poverty with the help of ambitious sector investment programs in education and health and modest projects in the areas of population, gender equality, food security, and water supply.

SIPs have a number of defining characteristics. They are sector-wide in scope; they provide a coherent framework for sector policy; they put local stakeholders in the driver's seat; they let all donors sign on; they enjoy common implementation arrangements with a multiyear horizon and transparency; and they require minimal long-term foreign technical assistance (Rose 1985; Lister 1998). Presently, there are SIPs in three priority sectors: transport (roads subsector), education, and health. They are integrated into the government's budget and implemented by government agencies in collaboration with the private sector, especially in health and road building.[7] Similar initiatives in the areas of energy and food security are in the making.

The formal mechanisms for aid coordination in Ethiopia are strong, at both the external and country levels. At the external level, aid coordination is carried out through Consultative Group meetings, four of which have been held since 1992. The multidonor meetings of the Special Program of Assistance for Africa, also held biennially since 1992, provide a useful forum for aid coordination and review of country performance. At the country level, MEDAC is the overall coordinator of all external assistance delivery to Ethiopia. Other key participants include the prime minister's office, the Ministry of Finance, the National Bank of Ethiopia, and the Council of Ministers. Frequent consultation between local representatives of donors and the government is now routine.

More than 15 donor countries are active in Ethiopia. Their areas of emphasis include relief and rehabilitation, food aid, social sector development, infrastructural development, and adjustment support in collaboration with the multilateral development institutions. Germany, Japan, Italy, the United States, the Nordic countries, the Netherlands, and Canada are the leading bilateral donors (see table 4.5). Those giving smaller amounts include the United Kingdom, France, Switzerland, Austria, Australia, China, and the Republic of Korea.[8]

Many nongovernmental organizations (NGOs) are also active in Ethiopia although their number is low by the standards of other African countries. According to the Federal Disaster Prevention and Preparedness Commission, there are 310 registered NGOs (one-third of which are foreign) operating in the country. They are active in the areas of relief and rehabilitation as well as in development programs geared toward education, health, water supply, agriculture (most notably the Sasakawa/ Global 2000 Program), and off-farm income-generating activities for poor households. The combined annual budget of NGOs in Ethiopia is variously estimated in the range of US$150 million. A new "Code of Conduct for NGOs in Ethiopia" was signed by 165 NGOs in March 1999. This followed a period of friction with the government, which is accused of, among other things, favoring party-affiliated NGOs.

Donor Assessment of Reform Record

A World Bank mission to socialist Ethiopia recalls an oft-repeated observation regarding the perplexing gap between the potential and the actual performance of the Ethiopian economy:

> Ethiopia has some comparative advantages stemming from its size, natural resources, location, and its competent civil service . . . Ethiopia has generally avoided heavily bank-financed deficit spending and consequent inflation. The country's external debt burden has so far been kept within manageable bounds, and in (favorable) contrast to the experience of many African countries, its rates of capacity utilization in industry have been quite high. Its record of project implementation has been relatively good, and its technocrats and civil servants have a reputation for honesty, dedication and competence. These are indeed important strengths and successes of economic management to build upon. (World Bank 1987: 3)

The report goes on to explain this paradox of high potential and low achievement in terms of "initial conditions" of poverty and underdevelopment, vulnerability to numerous internal and external shocks, and the misguided economic policies of the Derg government. Carefully noting that it had no quarrels with socialism per se, the mission made a strong plea for policy reform in the name of economic efficiency.

The first full-scale single-country evaluation of European Community/European Union aid was conducted on Ethiopia in 1995, covering the previous 20 years (IDS/IDR 1996; Maxwell 1998). It reached the following conclusions, among others: (a) the effectiveness of EU aid was undermined by the unfavorable policy environment and the numerous shocks to the economy; (b) there was a mixed pattern of success (infrastructure, water, energy, Shoa province PADEP, sectoral import program for agriculture) and failure (rural water supply, soil conservation, food aid, Stabex); (c) there was a gradual "learning by doing" on the part of the EU, since the agency was inadequately prepared but also contractually constrained to engage in policy dialogue, especially under Lomé I and Lomé II; and (d) the bias of the Ethiopian governments toward overcentralization and overstandardization was not vigilantly countered. The review recommends a unified Ethiopian program instead of a multiplicity of instruments and a long chain of decisionmaking back to Brussels, and greater emphasis on policy dialogue with the government.

Recent World Bank reports suggest a much more upbeat assessment regarding the first-generation or "Washington consensus" reforms under the new government (that is, reconstruction, stabilization, liberalization, and some privatization). First, the leadership is described as knowledgeable and committed to serious economic reform.[9] Second, policymakers are said to exhibit a strong sense of "ownership" of the reform programs—a point proudly underscored by the prime minister himself (Zenawi 1999). Ownership here means irreversibility of commitment to the reforms, and the capacity to implement them. Third, the economic record, in terms of growth and stability, has so far been impressive.

The reports also express some concerns. Loan portfolio performance, despite significant improvements through the 1980s, still receives an only "satisfactory" rating. Although the government has shown a steep learning curve in implementing promised reforms, it continues to confront a number of problems. Tax collections (especially income and domestic sales) are narrowly based and backlogged even in relatively developed areas such as Addis Ababa. The overregulated government system breeds corruption, although not on a grand scale comparable to many other African countries. The civil service is underpaid and initiatives from below undervalued; and the judicial system remains woefully inadequate (World Bank 1998a, 1998c). The net effect is that absorptive capacity (defined narrowly as the current rate of disbursement) is increasingly becoming a binding constraint on the full utilization of pledged aid.

That is not to say that donors are always efficient. A recent assessment of the three SIPs laments the fall in external financing to less than half of what was promised (Ethiopia 1999). Concerns about the unreliability of ODA disbursements are also reflected in the strong preference expressed by regional governments for predictable federal subsidies over earmarked foreign aid of similar amounts. The relatively low effectiveness of EU aid is also partly attributed to the EU's weakness in policy dialogue and the callous neglect by the EU bureaucracy of the importance of good local administrative resources to oversee the implementation process (Maxwell 1998). Poor food aid targeting has meant that only half of the food-insecure households benefit from grain distribution (Clay, Molla, and Habtewold 1998).

The leadership is seen to be especially attracted to the East Asian model of development, and the dual-track and gradualist Chinese approach to post-socialist reform. Ethiopia, however, lacks many of the ingredients of East Asian success: a government committed more to nurturing than controlling weak markets, a highly meritocratic and politically insulated technocracy, high rates of saving and investment, a reservoir of off-farm production capability comparable to China's dynamic township and village enterprises, a region with lots of positive economic spillovers, and a much less fractious polity (Wade 1990; World Bank 1993; Woo 1998).

The government has now begun to confront, albeit less decisively, the second generation of reforms in the areas of financial deepening, competition, managerial capacity, transfer of technology, diversification of exports, and labor-intensive private small enterprises (Stiglitz 1998). The World Bank laments the reluctance to go all-out for a radical transformation into a market economy in these terms:

> The careful consideration of policy options and the "ownership" that it reflects are welcome but, in general, the Government tends to be over-cautious in undertaking the second generation of reforms that are needed now. The boldness and decisiveness of the initial phase of reforms has given way to an all-round cautiousness on virtually all fronts in the next phase. Also weaknesses in implementation capacity need to be addressed if the absorption of concessional resources is to rise substantially and the economy is to move to the "frontier" of the balance between stabilization and growth. (World Bank 1997a: 10)

The IMF expresses similar sentiments in more specific terms:

> After a number of ambitious "first-generation" reforms in the early years of the present regime, the structural reform effort slowed somewhat in subsequent years. An anti-export bias persisted in the trade regime, exchange and trade regulations remained burdensome, foreign direct investment was limited to a narrow range of activities, and capacity building in the government was constrained by slow implementation of the civil service reform. Moreover, despite the establishment of the Ethiopian Privatization Agency in 1994, the sale of SOEs continued to be undertaken at a slow pace. The rudimentary state of the financial sector and the outdated reach of the legal and regulatory framework also hindered private sector development. (IMF 1999b: 20)

Some Ethiopian economists have suggested that financial stability has been attained largely through budgetary restraint and significant increases in aid flows (Chole 1993, 1994; Degefe and Nega 1999/2000; Addis Tribune 1998c). Achieving sustained and broad-based growth requires greater emphasis on a positive supply response. It is also worth noting here that the relevant standard for judging the efficacy of the current policy stance is no longer the dismal record of the Derg regime. Domestically, the relevant frame of reference ought to be the goal of doubling real per capita income every 10 to 15 years. This presupposes a growth rate of 8 percent per year during the period. Externally, the benchmark should be the incentives provided to foreigners relative to those of countries that compete most directly with Ethiopia for investment or export markets.

One challenge is to raise the discouraging domestic saving rate (6 percent) and the modest investment rate from 18 percent to at least 25 percent of GDP. This, in turn, cannot be accomplished with increased tax effort alone. Accelerating reforms in such areas as land use, banking, and transparency would improve Ethiopia's competitiveness by providing an unambiguous signal to the overcautious private sector that the government is committed to an open, rule-based market economy (UNCTAD/ICC 1999; World Economic Forum 1998).

The upshot is that Ethiopia is at a crossroads between the easy phase of liberalization and the hard phase of deep institutional reform. The post-1990 record shows that the country has made a decisive break with its socialist past in many, but not all, respects. Price controls have been largely dismantled, tax and tariff rates lowered, and the inflation rate kept low. The EPRDF government's strong sense of ownership of the reforms has until recently resulted in well-coordinated donor assistance, which has focused on sector investment programs in roads, health, and education.

The momentum of reform seems to have been adversely affected by the 1998–2000 intermittent war along the border with Eritrea. It has certainly diverted the attention of senior policymakers from issues of long-term development. Aside from the loss of tens of thousands of lives, the conflict is estimated to have cost the central government directly as much as US$1.5 billion. The switching of port traffic from Assab to Djibouti, the destruction of farms, the disruption of regional domestic trade, the reductions in outlays for capital expenditure and economic services, the temporary surcharges on key imports, and the disruption of flights for Ethiopian Airlines are additional economic costs borne by a fragile economy. On top of this, donors suspended virtually all aid save emergency assistance and projects already underway. It is, therefore, by no means clear that the good record in macroeconomic liberalization can be sustained much less replicated at the microeconomic level given the inevitable need to kick-start the reform process.

THE RELATIONSHIP BETWEEN AID AND REFORM

The relationship between aid and reform, especially when it involves institutional transformation, is profoundly political. It involves redistribution of power within society, and therefore calls for both positive and normative analyses. The comments below are based on the history of the government's preferred policy posture and the negotiated reform measures actually undertaken, and what I was able to glean from various donor reports or gather from interviews primarily with government officials in March 1999.

A more nuanced treatment of the political economy of Ethiopian reform calls for an intimate knowledge of policy debates within the ruling party and the nature of negotiations between the donors and the government. Compared to the case of other African reformers, the identification of pro-reform and anti-reform policy elites is made more difficult (and perhaps moot) by the opaque nature of the decisionmaking process under the collective model of party governance that currently prevails in Ethiopia.

The Aid and Reform in Africa project, of which this paper is a part, sets out to test three hypotheses: (a) governments choose to reform, or regress, independent of the aid relationship; (b) nonfinancial aid has a better impact than financial aid on the generation of policy reforms; and (c) financial aid works when policy reforms and institution building are already underway. The overall conclusion is that the aid-reform linkage in Ethiopia is rather complex: aid appears to have induced or cemented some reforms but not others; and the optimal sequencing of the forms of assistance (money or ideas) or the efficient timing of aid is often hard to establish in the absence of a clear counterfactual. Selected examples will be used to illustrate these issues.

Where Aid Succeeds in Inducing Reform

In countries like Ethiopia, aid is likely to induce and lock in new reform or broaden existing reform when the foreign exchange constraint is binding and (a) the payoffs to both the government and citizens are demonstrably high, or (b) the payoffs to the rulers are high even though the "masses" get little, or (c) successful reforms are introduced progressively and delicately so that even a reluctant government can conveniently claim ownership. The payoff to the ruling elite may take the form of directing externally funded projects and off-budget expenditures to favored regions or sectors, shifting fungible resources to politically favored but low-return activities, and misappropriation of public funds where corruption is rampant. It also depends on the presence of a crisis situation (thereby generating intense pressure in favor of high-stake reforms) at the time reforms are seriously contemplated (Grindle and Thomas 1991).

In the case of Ethiopia, the willingness to engage in meaningful reform seems to have prevailed since 1988. The Derg approached Western donors with hat in hand once it became clear that Soviet bloc aid was about to end and that the socialist experiment had failed. The treadmill of modest reforms did not impress potential donors, however.[10] Major bilateral donors such as Italy displayed little interest in pushing for reform, and more reform-minded ones like Sweden limited their efforts to projects that skirted policy barriers to reach the poor directly. The IMF and the World Bank were active in the preparation of PFP1 under the Derg, but it was not implemented because the government balked, particularly at the requirement of a substantial devaluation of the birr (Chole 1994).

In the post-socialist period, quick-disbursing and highly fungible aid initially followed the restoration of peace and the enactment of policies focused on stabilization and rehabilitation. Subsequent aid financed jointly designed sector programs, financial reform, and improvements in public sector management.

The EPRDF government was quite keen to obtain funds for essential imports, emergency recovery, and rehabilitation (Bevan 1994; World Bank 1997b; Maxwell 1998). Despite an initially poor loan portfolio performance, there was mutual eagerness among donors and the government to push for significant increases in quick-disbursing loans and grants during 1991–93. While calling for a convincing strategy for marketization, a consortium of donors orchestrated by the World Bank provided US$680 million for the Economic Recovery and Reconstruction Program, followed by a US$250 million structural adjustment credit (World Bank 1997b).

The significant evolution in official thinking (or calculation) becomes most evident when one contrasts the EPRDF government's initial apprehensiveness about a rapid marketization of the economy, as expressed in "Economic Policy of Ethiopia during the Transition Period" (Ethiopia 1991), with the latest reform measures agreed to in PFP5, "Ethiopia: Policy Framework Paper 1998/99–2000/01" (Ethiopia 1998a). The 1991 policy paper, acknowledging the failures of the Derg regime, committed the TGE to deepening the liberalization initiated earlier by the Derg in the areas of road transport, domestic retail (but not wholesale) trade, and rural labor markets. It also put great emphasis on reconstruction of war-torn regions and rehabilitation of infrastructure.

Critical decisions concerning external trade and foreign exchange system reform, financial reform, privatization of public enterprises, and land

and civil service reform were postponed until after the 1995 national election. Many of these issues were sidestepped even after the end of the transitional period, as we will see below.

The potential leverage at the disposal of the major donors (notably the World Bank, AfDB, EU, Germany, Italy, Sweden, and the United States) is indicated in part by the level of aid intensity. In 1996 Ethiopia received 5 percent of the net ODA of approximately US$17 billion to Sub-Saharan Africa. This works out to US$16 per capita, one of the lowest per capita aid levels among countries of similar size. It is, however, 16 percent of Ethiopia's GNP, above the average for Sub-Saharan Africa.[11] In the 1990s the aid share in GNP averaged 23 percent. Since total government expenditure is a quarter of GNP, these figures imply that ODA flows were equivalent to 90 percent of budgetary expenditure. Aid currently finances as much as half of the capital budget and one-sixth of federal government revenue (see table 4.2).

During 1992–94, the World Bank made it clear that the coordinated support for recovery and stabilization was being provided with the expectation that it would be followed with an expanded program of assistance tightly leashed to a number of policy "triggers." It is fair to say that many of the structural reforms would not have been considered seriously, much less fully implemented, without the infusion of substantial policy loans and grants (Abegaz 1994; Chole 1994; World Bank 1997a).

The contents of successive PFPs clearly show that a number of policy measures are conspicuous by their recurrence. At donor insistence, the investment code was revised four times in as many years to bring it closer to best practice among African reformers. The foreign exchange system was progressively pushed beyond episodic devaluations to include auctions and an interbank market. The international financial institutions are currently pushing for the phasing out of the auction system and full current account convertibility (more on this below). The government has reluctantly committed itself to the privatization of large SOEs although PFP5 still calls for improved modality that includes transparency in utilization of the proceeds. The persistent call for rationalizing the decentralized budgetary system, including the introduction of rolling public investment plans, is beginning to be heeded. Finally, the call for a comprehensive food security plan is being taken seriously and might result in a full-fledged sector program.

While the government initiated most of these reforms, the prima facie evidence suggests that donor pressure has made a critical difference in transforming many of them into more than piecemeal measures. How far the aid leverage could have been deployed by a "united front" of donors in an effort to buy even more ambitious reforms is nonetheless hard to establish.

Where Aid Fails to Generate Reform

Cases where aid, for various reasons, failed to produce more than marginal reforms are more readily identifiable. Consistent with the experiences of many countries, in Ethiopia there appear to be few cases where conditionalities overcame stiff government resistance (Collier and others 1997; Leonardo and others 1999). The following examples pertain to disagreements involving national security issues, or the regime's power base, or its view of the optimal mix between the public sector and the private sector (as in the case of certain conditionalities of the IMF).

The threat of a reduction or withdrawal of aid appears on the whole ineffective whenever Ethiopia is in the midst of a major national crisis. When the Derg declared Ethiopian socialism, some multilateral donors (notably the World Bank) and important bilateral donors (the United States) withheld much of their already meager assistance to the country, losing potential leverage in the process. The United States went further and refused delivery of weapons already paid for. Facing secessionist rebellions at home and an invasion by Soviet-armed Somalia, the regime sought and received massive (mostly military) assistance from the Soviet Union itself. In the spirit of the Cold War, the two superpowers ended up switching sides. Many informed Ethiopians blame shortsighted Carter Administration policy for unwittingly aiding in the transformation of an otherwise reformist committee of noncommissioned officers into one controlled by a dictator (Mengistu Haile Mariam) with a grandiose vision of garrison socialism. Similar threats in early 1999 by most donors to suspend program aid, which were soon carried out, have been bitterly resisted by the EPRDF government.

Aid also does not seem to buy good reform when the conditionalities are perceived, rightly or wrongly, to undermine the core of the regime's ideology or its power base. Although the World Bank and other major donors understandably regret the lingering mindset of control over facilitation in the bureaucracy, slippage in economic management, and inefficiencies in the land lease system, they have also chosen to sidestep or soft-pedal some of the more fundamental institutional or policy reforms needed to solve them. That is probably because they know that these and other reforms are unpalatable to the government (World Bank 1997b).

A notable policy issue that is conspicuous by its absence from the economic reform agenda is the question of private ownership of agricultural and urban lands. Ethiopia had a long history of private ownership of land in a multitude of tenure forms (freehold, kinship, village, parish, clan, crown). In all these institutional forms, wealth was based less on ownership title than on entitlements (customary or legal) to the produce from the land. European-type feudal estates or Asian-type widespread landlessness were rare. This explains in large part why the nationalization of land, which transferred use rights to producers, had such a negligible impact on output or productivity.

Officials put the case against the granting of freehold tenure in terms of the need for access to land for all in order to ensure economic security for the rural poor (Zenawi 1999). The government's longstanding promise to hold a national referendum on land ownership has yet to materialize (Ethiopia 1991). Its current strategy of "agricultural development–led industrialization" focuses instead on long-term leases and such shortcuts as supplying fertilizer and improved seeds.

The experience of Ethiopia and other countries, however, demonstrates that the economic case against reprivatization is unconvincing (Deininger and Feder 1998). The linking of land access to residency, the inability to use land as collateral, and the insecurity that arises from loss of land as a result of periodic redistributions (due to demographic pressure or as political punishment) have stifled agricultural development. Labor mobility has been reduced or frozen. Optimal farm sizes fail to emerge as the efficient farmers who produce much of the marketable surplus cannot increase their farm size in a country where 20 percent of farmers account for 80 percent of grain sales. More alarmingly, investment in permanent improvements of the land is discouraged. Finally, off-farm activities that would absorb those who choose to mortgage or sell their subsistence plots (some 60 percent cultivate less than one hectare) are stymied.

A secure private land title (individual and communal) is, of course, a necessary but not sufficient condition for a green revolution to occur. This is far from the case of a "dry prairie" awaiting the drenching rains of private incentives to bloom. Ownership reforms will have to be complemented by a more efficient marketing system and enhanced access to modern inputs. Support in the form of public infrastructural investment, credit, and extension services remains minimal. The inescapable fact is that the most effective anti-poverty program is one that reinvigorates rural development by harnessing the willingness of Ethiopian farmers to embrace demonstrably profitable innovations (Howard and others 1998; Degefe and Nega 1999/2000).

In the urban areas, some half a million poorly maintained housing units remain in government hands. The urban land leasehold system, whose inefficiency and corruption are the subject of perennial complaints by the business community, has contributed to a severe shortage of commercial space and housing. Addis Ababa, whose municipal limit boasts plenty of land, continues to suffer an unacceptably high rate of open and disguised unemployment; many of the jobless have secondary or even tertiary education. The binding constraint here is one of finance or institutional infrastructure rather than a shortage of disciplined and easily trainable labor (UNCTAD/ICC 1999; Middlebrook and Corzalo 1999; Addis Tribune 1988a).

A second area of policy contention that has received little attention in the dialogue between the government and the various donors is the concern regarding the growing number of enterprises that are surreptitiously owned by the ruling party. While the use of political power by "big men" to accumulate personal wealth and grease a patrimonial system is all too common throughout Africa, the phenomenon of an extensive network of party-controlled enterprises is a rather new development in Ethiopia.[12]

According to several unpublished reports and reports in the private press, the reliability of which cannot be fully ascertained, a large number of enterprises wholly or partially owned by EPRDF are being organized into interlocking financial and industrial groups (FIGs). Their assets are estimated in the range of 1 billion to 2 billion birr. They are said to be registered in the name of various individuals, NGOs, or regional governments. Most of the TPLF business concerns are reportedly under the supervisory umbrella of the Endowment Fund for the Rehabilitation of Tigray, whose major divisions are headed by senior party members (Aynekulu 1996a, 1996b; "Ethiopian Non-Governmental Business" 1999).

Some of the largest EPRDF companies or their affiliates are as follows: in agriculture, Hiwot Agricultural Mechanization, Zeleke Agricultural Mechanization, Tesfa Livestock, and Rahwa Goat and Sheep Export; in finance and trade, Wegagen Bank, Africa Insurance, Guna Trading House, Ambassel Trading House, Dinsho Plc, Wondo Trading, and Dedebit Credit and Savings Institution; in industry and mining, Meskerem Investment, Ezana Mining, Sheba Tannery, Almeda Textiles and Garment, Addis Pharmaceuticals, Mesfin Industrial Engineering, Beruh Chemical, and Dashen Brewery; in construction, Addis Construction, Sur Construction, and Mesebo Building Materials; in transport, Trans-Ethiopia, Blue Nile Transport, and Express Transit; and in services, Mega-Net Corporation and Experience Ethiopia Travel.[13]

The concern about the role of these holdings is multifaceted. First, such firms in effect create two distinct private sectors—one that is politically connected, and another that is not. The former can exploit political connections (through party cadres in the bureaucracy) to practice unfair competition for government business and to engage in rent-seeking in the form of tailored state subsidies or protection and insider privatization. These firms can also potentially be used to undermine the economic position of the party's political opponents, all without violating the letter of the law. Second, the government's near monopoly over the banking system lends itself to directing credit to favored enterprises on less than commercial terms. Third, one can only wonder how the existence of these organizational economic assets has shaped the government's attitude toward future reforms, especially in banking, the commercial code, and the judiciary. If party- and bank-organized FIGs are here to stay, damage from rent-seeking and stripping of public assets may be minimized with an introduction of enforceable antitrust and fair competition legislation along the lines of Russia or Korea (Johnson 1997).

A third illustration of the limits of aid as leverage comes from financial-sector reform which, along with land policy and Party-affiliated businesses, constitutes the "third rail" of Ethiopian political economy. The three-year $127 million ESAF loan (1996–99) was not fully implemented because of a row between the government and the IMF (IMF 1998a). The midterm review of the ESAF was allowed to lapse at the end of 1997 over a number of disagreements between the government and the IMF (Addis Tribune 1998b). The Fund released the second annual disbursement in November 1998 on account of the good overall record on macroeconomic stability, and in exchange for limited concessions in the foreign exchange regime (see appendix 4.2 and Ethiopia 1998a).

The IMF argues that the low level of financial intermediation and poor securities markets in Ethiopia, even by African standards, are due to largely policy-imposed "structural rigidities." The barriers to financial deepening include: the near-monopoly of the banking system held by the Commercial Bank of Ethiopia (CBE), including the requirement that SOEs do their banking exclusively with the CBE; poor collatoralization of assets, largely tied to market failures linked to the land-lease system; a misguided ban on foreign banks, insurance companies and stand-alone forex bureaus; and inadequate bank supervision and prudential oversight. Concern was also expressed about weakening external accounts and lackluster tax collection which threaten Ethiopia's advance to the decision point of the HIPC Initiative (IMF 1999B; Demeksa 1999; Harvey 1996).

The government's reluctance to undertake rapid financial reform appears to reflect two concerns. For one, the authorities rightly view radical liberalization of the banking system and the capital account as a risky proposition for countries like Ethiopia with weak regulatory and judicial systems. The recent experience of transition economies and emerging markets provides an important cautionary tale. Furthermore, policymakers seem frustrated by the unrealistic expectation of donors that a country with limited capacity can satisfactorily implement four ambitious sets of interconnected reforms simultaneously: fiscal devolution, civil service reform, sector development programs, and banking reform. The other reason is that a less-transparent control of key financial institutions constitutes an important leverage for the ruling party. Again, where economics meets politics, the resistance against sensible reform is likely to be strong.

The Ethiopian experience suggests that aid followed rather than led the initial wave of reforms. Since then, a good mix of technical and financial assistance has had the effect of coaxing the government to move closer to the limits allowed by its own ideological or narrow organizational interests.

The sequencing of Ethiopian reform is the traditional one of progression from the easy and immediately necessary to the hard. The reform program began with emergency recovery and stabilization and moved on to marketization and modest privatization. While other post-socialist reformers (Tanzania and Mali, for example) have made some headway in the transition between first-generation and second-generation reforms, Ethiopia continues to hesitate as it ponders the difficult jump into a full-fledged market economy.

The Coupling of Money and Ideas

Nonfinancial assistance, in the form of policy dialogue, analytical work (country memoranda, specialized sector studies, policy framework papers, public expenditure surveys, public finance management, and statistical work), and the provision of equipment and training can make a critical difference when it is focused on upgrading domestic capability. Ideas concerning the virtuous circle of openness, stability, and growth or the importance of a medium-term economic framework for rationalizing overall policy are certainly being internalized in Ethiopia.

Some Ethiopian policymakers, however, express mixed feelings about some conventional aspects of technical assistance. They support technical assistance where knowledge transfer is programmed, the advice is grounded in Ethiopian conditions, and the country is given some freedom to buy expertise in the free market as needed. However, they tend to look askance especially at those consultants who "parachute in." These complaints are also familiar in other African countries (Berg 1993).

Technical cooperation can certainly be useful even in nonreforming economies, since it can often help minimize damage from distortionary policies. The small nonfinancial assistance provided during the Derg years (about 15 percent of net ODA) was indeed helpful in upgrading technocratic skills. It was, however, too modest in size (and not tied to the prospect of a big aid inflow) to tip the balance in favor of what amounted to a regime-undermining systemic reform. The environment was such that open criticism by reform-minded civil servants would have been reckless (Griffin 1992; World Bank 1987). Anecdotal evidence suggests, however, that various segments of the bureaucracy strove to minimize economic damage by selective and slow implementation of misguided policies.

Recent multilateral assistance to Ethiopia has had a high policy content and a good analytical foundation. Technical assistance has recently accounted for some 20 percent of ODA, about two-thirds of the level for developing countries (O'Connell and Soludo 1998: table 1). Aside from the expected problems of inexperience and staff turnovers, the new administration is praised for fulfilling the numerous conditionalities of the structural adjustment program faithfully. Ethiopia is nonetheless far from the policy frontier compared to its competitors, and analytical work and policy dialogue are judged to be at the formative stages (World Bank 1997a, 1997b).[14]

Reforming the Donor-Beneficiary Relationship

The fashionable rhetoric of full partnership notwithstanding, both the donor-recipient relationship (for grants) and the donor-client relationship (for soft loans) are fraught with inequality in Africa (van de Walle and Johnston 1996). Donors typically come armed with money, superior analytical capability (but inferior knowledge of local conditions), and the mentality of a generous but calculating patron. Aid bureaucracies are partly motivated by narrower incentives such as maximizing disbursement rates even at the cost of quality. Anecdotal evidence suggests that the behavior of some officials from bilateral aid agencies betrays an unwillingness to maximize the pass-through of funds while insisting on micromanaging the aid relationship.[15]

For policymakers in countries like Ethiopia, where a strong sense of confidence and ownership prevails, some policy conditions and excessive documentation requirements appear as wasteful diversions of scarce administrative resources. In interviews, many express a clear preference for greater multilateralization of aid, a guaranteed flow of aid under a negotiated framework, and disbursement in the form of block grants (earmarked or unrestricted budget support known as channel 1 funds) to the extent possible (also see Maxwell 1998).

A negotiated framework, these officials argue, provides flexibility of implementation while permitting donors to concentrate on the "rules of the game" and on "evaluating outcomes." Evaluation is, however, frustrated by the multiplicity of often conflicting output indicators akin to the "success indicator problem" of Soviet planning.

Finally, while there are many donor conferences, there is no Africa-wide forum for channeling the collective views or reform proposals of recipient countries. In addition to delinking development aid from narrow foreign policy or commercial objectives, there are a number of issues to be addressed, including recipient input concerning the amount and form of technical assistance and the uneasy roles of mushrooming NGOs.

CONCLUDING THOUGHTS

Post-socialist economic reform in Ethiopia has so far been undertaken in two stages: rehabilitation, stabilization, and basic liberalization during

1990–95; and infrastructure-oriented SIPs, financial liberalization, and improvements in public sector management during 1996–98. Aid, flowing at an annual average of US$1.3 billion (in constant dollars) followed the first phase of homegrown reforms as a reward for good behavior. Well-coordinated aid in the form of policy dialogue and analytical work, as well as money, also played an important role in jointly forging the second phase of reform, this time as much by persuading as by rewarding.

Despite the significant accomplishments of the past six years, there is a substantial opportunity to further revamp the still regimented economy. Such measures would include restoring private ownership of most land; reforming the banking system by breaking up the CBE and granting autonomy to the National Bank of Ethiopia (NBE); a vigorous competition policy with respect to large SOEs and party-owned businesses; and reform of the governance system, both the political and bureaucratic aspects. Many of these reforms have frontloaded costs and backloaded benefits that render them unappealing to myopic policymakers. They may also entail concentrated opportunity costs to the ruling party but diffused benefits to the electorate.

Multinational agencies often pose the basic question of reform in Africa in terms of rescuing nascent markets from the bundle of contradictions that characterize the post-colonial state: "authoritarian and yet fragile; highly centralised yet dispersed; overdeveloped in size yet underdeveloped in function; trumpeting national unity yet controlled by narrow personal cliques; nationalistically resistant to outside political pressures but weakly subordinate to economic ones" (Africa Confidential 1999: 5). While the Ethiopian state is old and resilient, it does share the African pattern of a center that is too weak to centrally plan a socialist economy or to "govern" the market effectively. It is nevertheless strong enough for capricious interventions which, among other things, raise transaction costs substantially and stimulate growth-retarding informality.

The Achilles heel of Ethiopian development (and reform) is its inability to nurture an equitable political system that secures lasting peace at home and stability in the Horn of Africa. In March 1978, Ethiopia won a bloody border war with Somalia. March 1990 saw the country's return to a market economy in the midst of a raging civil war between an alliance of two liberation fronts and the Derg government. Almost a decade later, in March 1999, an even bloodier war was re-ignited between the two erstwhile allies.

More than US$6 billion worth of Soviet bloc and Western arms supplies to the impoverished Horn of Africa region has left a legacy of chronic violence and mutual destabilization. The region has witnessed two of Africa's most mechanized wars in just two decades. The resumption of a war economy is once again accompanied by a major famine in the northern provinces affecting 5 million to 6 million people. The economic distress is compounded by an intensifying AIDS pandemic. External destabilization and incessant domestic conflicts produce myopia born of a heightened sense of insecurity, destruction of capital (physical and social) and information, militarization of life, and mutual distrust. The two contradictory faces of external aid, one destructive and the other constructive, have yet to be explicitly contrasted in the assessment of aid to Ethiopia.

It is no wonder, then, that Ethiopia presents a classic case of an economy with great potential struggling to overcome a "low-level equilibrium trap." The hopeful signs—periodic spurts of growth, driven mainly by positive shocks such as favorable weather or higher coffee prices and aid flows—prove fleeting time and again. One consequence of this is the desire of both educated Ethiopians and those with capital to emigrate. Another is the strong preference by risk-averse capital for myopic investments that produce quick profits. Such an environment is invariably inimical to long-term investment and growth (Collier and Gunning 1999; Bevan 1994; Chole 1993).

All is not lost, however, and talk of aid triage (a severe form of selectivity) by some donors is rather misplaced. The past six years have shown that, with peace and modest economic reforms, the economy is capable of expanding at more than twice the rate of population growth. This growth record has been facilitated by a remarkable degree of macroeconomic stability.

One lesson from successful open economies is that, while sustained stability is necessary for investment, removing the remaining barriers to growth on the supply side is just as essential. The domestic capability that is being built up in Ethiopia with the help of external assistance will have to be aimed at exploiting the untapped opportunities at home and abroad (especially the underutilized Middle Eastern, Lomé, and GSP market outlets). The bridge between domestic capability and opportunity is supplied by sufficiently deep economic reform. Successful reform is, in turn, undergirded by a strong commitment to good governance. This is essential for rebuilding business confidence, including among the growing Ethiopian diaspora.

In the final analysis, political reform is a domestic affair. As the disappointing response to the highly liberal investment code amply demonstrates, a country that treats its citizens fairly is also a country that is attractive to foreign capital. If the government manages to undertake the remaining reforms while building up its capacity for implementation, Ethiopia stands to benefit doubly from an increasingly selective international aid regime and a reinvigorated private sector. Donors can aid this process with a better calibration of aid and reform.

APPENDIX 4.1
ETHIOPIA: CHRONOLOGY OF POLITICAL
AND ECONOMIC DEVELOPMENTS

1974–75	A military junta led by NCOs (Derg) overthrows the monarch in a creeping coup d'etat. The Derg proclaims socialism and nationalizes all land, medium and large enterprises, and extra houses.
1975–84	The Derg uses *zemetcha* campaigns to implement land redistribution, establish peasant cooperatives and urban *kebelles*, and consolidate state control of the economy and polity. A major border war with Somalia results in the switching of superpower alliance toward the Soviet Union. Nationwide famine affects millions of people, resulting in relief efforts worldwide. The era of favorable terms of trade for primary exports ends.
1987–89	Ten-Year Perspective Economic Plan is introduced. Ethiopia is formally declared a socialist "people's democracy." Workers Party of Ethiopia is established. Villagization and resettlement campaigns intensify. Civil war in the northern part of the country escalates.
1990–91	WPE Congress announces the decision to liberalize prices and make membership in the cooperatives voluntary. Peasants dismantle producer cooperatives. EPRDF and EPLF guerrilla alliance overthrows WPE government. Transitional Government of Ethiopia formed.
1992–93	Stabilization and rehabilitation program undertaken. Province of Eritrea formally secedes from Ethiopia (1993).
1994–97	Major economic reforms introduced, including liberalization, stabilization, and structural adjustment; significant gains are achieved in terms of growth and stability. Ethnic-based federal system introduced under a new constitution.

1998–2000   Ethiopia and Eritrea fight three rounds of a costly border war.

Most official loans and grants suspended pending end of the conflict.

Prolonged drought and a major famine plagues the country once again.

Looming HIV/AIDS crisis enters the national agenda.

Ruling EPRDF wins nearly all seats in the 2000 parliamentary elections.

APPENDIX 4.2
ETHIOPIA: CHRONOLOGY OF MAJOR
ECONOMIC REFORMS, 1974–98

1974–78	Derg nationalizes all land, modern enterprises, and extra houses.
	Peasant associations (rural *kebelles*) established.
	Urban neighborhood associations (urban *kebelles*) established.
	Rural cooperative proclamation issued.
1979–83	Lower and advanced producer cooperatives established.
	State commercial monopolies control trade and transportation sectors.
	State industrial enterprises rationalized and expanded.
	Economic *zemetcha* (mass mobilization) campaigns launched.
1984–89	Resettlement and villagization programs expanded.
	National famine relief efforts.
	Ten-year Perspective Economic Plan introduced.
1990–91	Land-use rights become inheritable.
	Limited price decontrols introduced.
	Producer cooperatives decollectivized.
	Private interregional trade permitted.
	Demobilization of 455,000 soldiers after EPRDF takeover in mid-1991.
1991–95	Stabilization of prices and reduction of budget deficit.
	Rehabilitation and reconstruction of civil war damage.
	Economic Recovery and Rehabilitation Program.
	Structural adjustment program under SAC and SAF:

- Decontrol of most prices
- Foreign exchange auctions
- Reduction of import tariffs
- Decentralized land-lease system
- Entry of private banks
- Treasury bill market
- Establishment of Ethiopian Privatization Agency

First generation of civil service reform:
- Salary reform
- Retrenchment of government employees

Birr currency area established with Eritrea.

Ethiopian Investment Authority established.

1996–98   Sector development programs in health, education, roads, energy.

System of fiscal federalism introduced with nine regional states.

Structural adjustment program under ESAF.

With respect to the *financial sector:*
- Decontrolled lending rate, but floor for deposit rate.
- Abolished automatic surrender of forex, and 10 percent retention.
- Established interbank market, though not yet active.

With respect to the *foreign exchange and trade system:*
- Raised the frequency of forex auctions, reduced most restrictions, and permitted bank-run forex bureaus.
- Eliminated most restrictions on current account transactions.
- Eliminated forex surrender requirements and permitted a 10 percent retention of export proceeds.
- Lowered average tariff to 19.5 percent and reduced tariff bands to eight.
- Ended parastatal monopoly on customs clearing and forwarding services.

With respect to *export promotion and development:*
- Ceased price verification on non-coffee exports
- Allowed exporters to engage in all implicit forms of foreign credit except formal loan agreements

With respect to *privatization:*
- Completed privatization of 175 enterprises.
- Brought 12 SOEs to point of sale.
- First phase of privatization brought in Birr 2.8 billion for the extrabudgetary privatization fund.
- Second phase envisages sale of 115 corporatized SOEs.
- Government to retain over 50 of the largest, profitable SOEs.

With respect to *private sector development:*

- Abolished subsidies for and ban on private trade in fertilizers.
- New legal and regulatory framework and authority.
- Foreclosure law introduced.
- Further liberalization of the foreign investment code.

With respect to the *civil service reform program* of 1996:

- New directives on financial and debt management, and procurement by federal government.
- Budget management and control manuals prepared.
- Outstanding challenges: quality of staff, performance-based incentives, and corruption.

Sources: Abegaz 1994; World Bank 1997a, 1999d; IMF 1999b; Ethiopia 1996, 1998a.

APPENDIX 4.3 ETHIOPIA: HIGHLIGHTS OF DONOR ASSISTANCE STRATEGY, 1980–2001

	Policy and capacity development	Adjustment and growth	Physical infrastructure	Poverty and human services	Agriculture and environment
1980–91	Technical assistance planning agency CEM	Coffee processing IMF standby (1981–82)	Energy Transport/telecom. Towns/urban	Education V–VII Family health	Irrigation PADEP
1992–94	CG1–2 (1992, 1994) SPA PFP1–PFP3 PER1	Economic recovery and reconstruction program SAC I and SAF Private sector development	Road rehabilitation Calub Gas Gilgel Gibe hydro	Food security	Improved seeds Fertilizer
1995–2001	CG3–4 (1996, 1998) PFP4–PFP5 SIP (or SDP) MTEF/PIP PER2–PER6	ESAF (1996–99) Export promotion SME development Rail rehabilitation	Power distribution Water supply Road SIP Energy Women's rights	Family planning Social rehabilitation Education SIP Health SIP Conservation	Sale of state retail Support services Research and training Food security

CG   Consultative Group (multidonor conferences)
SAC Structural Adjustment Credit
SME Small and medium enterprises
PFP Policy Framework Paper
MTEF Medium-term Economic Framework

SIP   Sector investment program
ESAF Extended Structural Adjustment Facility
CEM Country economic memorandum
PER   Public expenditure review
PIP   Public investment plan

Sources: World Bank 1992, 1995, 1997a; USAID 1999; Maxwell 1998; IMF 1999b; Ethiopia 1998a.

NOTES

1. For this reason, the growth rates reported here do differ (mostly insignificantly) from those reported in official publications for shorter periods. The Ethiopian economy is among the least researched in Africa.

2. DRS is the Debtor Reporting System of the World Bank database; CRS is the Creditor Reporting System of the OECD database.

3. The 1997 accord between Russia and the Paris Club calls for an upfront discount of 80 percent on the stock of debt owed and the application of Naples terms to the remainder (which means another 67 percent reduction in NPV terms of the remainder 20 percent). If these assumptions hold—that is, a 90 percent write-off of Russian debt—the debt stock will fall to US$2.8 billion and the debt service to 184 percent of exports by 2001. Almost all of the Russian debt, now valued at US$4.8 billion, is military-related.

4. The projects included Komolcha Textile Mill, Mugher Cement Works, Nazret Tractor Assembly, and Melka Wakena hydroelectric project.

5. The terms under which the province of Eritrea (3.5 million people) formally seceded from Ethiopia in 1993 turned out to be of strategic importance for both countries in economic terms. Notable issues such as border demarcation, access to seaports, division of assets and the national debt, and equitable treatment of each other's citizens were either postponed or handled in a manner that was widely perceived as prejudicial to Ethiopia's interests. These inequities are generally believed to be at the root of the 1998–99 border war between the two countries.

According to the Ethio-Eritrean agreements on economic and political cooperation, Assab and Massawa were to be free ports; goods, capital, and labor would move freely; and the Ethiopian birr was to serve as a common currency. However, the two countries had contrasting strategies of development, harmonization of macroeconomic policy was slow, and some 150,000 Eritrean nationals resident in Ethiopia were accorded equal treatment with Ethiopians without full reciprocity by Eritrea. These loopholes produced an estimated 1 billion birr of debt incurred by the Eritrean monetary authorities to their Ethiopian counterparts, a substantial foreign exchange leakage due to re-exports by Eritrea of birr-purchased Ethiopian export products and participation of Eritrean agents in foreign exchange auctions in Addis, rising charges for port services, and the like (Addis Tribune 1998d).

The arrangements were de facto terminated in 1998, with Ethiopia switching its major port to Djibouti and requiring trade in hard currency upon the introduction of the Eritrean nakfa in 1997. The immediate consequences of the war for Ethiopia and Eritrea have included deportation of each other's citizens on grounds of national security, tens of thousands of casualties on both sides, displacement of half a million people, and diversion of development funds (from investment and debt service funds in the case of Ethiopia) for the acquisition of sophisticated weaponry—not to mention an estimated daily expenditure of US$1 million by each to prosecute the war (Economist 1999; Ethiopia 1999).

6. According to the 1999 reports of Amnesty International, Human Rights Watch, and the Ethiopian Human Rights Council, there are more than 10,000 political prisoners in Ethiopia, most being held without formal charge or trial. The second national parliamentary elections were held in 2000.

7. The donors for the transport (road sector) SIP include the European Union, the Department for International Development of the U.K., the German Agency for Technical Cooperation and the German Development Bank, the Nordic Development Fund, and the Japan International Cooperation Agency. The education sector SIP was a cooperative effort of AfDB, Finland, Germany, Ireland, Italy, Sweden, the United States, UNESCO, UNICEF, and UNDP. Finally, the health sector SIP was partially funded by AfDB, the EU, Finland, Ireland, Italy, the Netherlands, Norway, Sweden, Austrian Development Cooperation, UNDP, UNICEF, UNFPA, the United States, and WHO.

8. There are "national flag" patterns here as in other African countries. The United States, for example, limited its cumulative aid of more than US$1 billion in 1984–94 to emergency food assistance and rehabilitation. It has since expanded its menu to include development assistance in the areas of education, health, food security, and democratization (USAID 1999). The German aid program, channeled mainly through GTZ, emphasizes skills transfer, poverty alleviation, food security, resource management, and selected social development programs.

9. The most recent Country Assistance Strategy (World Bank 1997: 2) points out that, notwithstanding the unfortunate ethnic flavor to politics, the developmentalist nature of the government is reflected in "an exceptionally strong sense of 'ownership' of economic policies and to probity in their implementation. Policymakers are given to very serious consideration of policy options, do not make policy commitments lightly and have a solid track record of delivering on those they do. The Prime Minister [Meles Zenawi] himself is very keenly involved in economic management and has an impressive grasp of economic issues to an extent that the label of an outstanding economic technocrat could be applied to him without much exaggeration."

10. The conflict over the Peasant Agricultural Development and Extension Program (PADEP) provides a good illustration. Drawing on the experience of the minimum package extension programs of the previous government and the successful training and visit system in India, IDA offered as much as US$400 million in the early 1980s to provide modern inputs and advice in potentially surplus-producing districts. This was conditional on government action to raise farmgate prices and to remove draconian restrictions on private trade. The Derg refused on account of its different priorities and ideological commitments. These terms, however, were accepted in principle by the same government at the end of 1987 and limited funding became available once the crisis of agrarian socialism became undeniable (Clapham 1988). In 1989, IDA disbursed US$77 for PADEP I.

11. The comparable DAC figures for Ethiopia's peer group in 1996 were as follows: Ghana, US$38 per capita or 11 percent of GNP; Kenya, US$22 or 7 percent; Uganda, US$25 or 13 percent; Zambia, US$40 or 11 percent. For other comparative figures from early 1990–95, which make Ethiopia's aid intensity even lower, see O'Connell and Soludo (1998: table 4).

12. This phenomenon of cadre capitalism, familiar from the early years of the KMT in Taiwan, is also ubiquitous in the Sudan and Eritrea in the 1990s. Although the 1994 Ethiopian constitution prohibits political organizations from engaging in profit-making activities, the public is keenly aware of the prominence of these corporations. For example, a recent World Bank mission on corruption observes:

"Private sector and civil society representatives told the mission that political parties belonging the EPRDF, especially the Tigrayan People's Liberation Front (TPLF), have established companies which can include banks and insurance companies. There is a common perception among some in the business community that these companies have preferential treatment over private sector companies with respect to government contracts, government-controlled credit facilities, import and export licenses, and customs clearances. The mission was not able independently to confirm these allegations.

"Government interlocutors explained that a number of organizations developed during the seventeen years of struggle against the Dergue, acquiring assets and property. Once the war was won, the winning side had to decide what to do with them. Since holding companies are not provided for in Ethiopian law, the EPRDF created foundations under which the party-affiliated companies (and NGOs) are located. The intention of such companies and NGOs is to provide benefits to the survivors of war—wounded, widows, orphans, handicapped, etc. Several of the party-affiliated organizations are headed by party members. These organizations are not allowed to acquire institutions which have been or are being privatised (World Bank 1998c: 7)."

Senior government officials insist that the firms do not receive any special favors from the government (Zenawi 1999). Another argument advanced in their favor is that, being large, these firms compete solely with foreign enterprises. They therefore play little role in displacing the domestic private sector (author's interview with Ato Neway Gebreab, chief economic advisor to the prime minister).

13. Other TPLF-affiliated NGOs that are active investors in the front companies include the Tigray Development Association Endowment Fund for Relief and Reconstruction of Tigray, and the Relief Society of Tigray. The rest are owned or co-owned by the other allied parties of the EPRDF coalition: Amhara National Democratic Movement, Oromo People's Democratic Organization, and South Ethiopia People's Democratic Movement.

14. Ethiopia's overall CPIA (Country Policy and Institutional Assessment) score of 3.7 for 1998 is on par with Ghana (3.6), but behind such reform leaders as Botswana (4.4) and Uganda (4.2). The subcategory scores for Ethiopia (compared

with the Africa-wide average) are as follows: 4.3 (3.2) for macroeconomic management; 3.1 (3.1) for sustainable and equitable growth; 3.8 (2.9) for reduction of inequality; and 3.9 (2.8) for public sector management. The 1998 *Africa Competitiveness Report* ranks Ethiopia low in overall competitiveness (17 out of 23), but high for the optimism of the business community (5 out of 20) and for its FDI protection regime (World Economic Forum 1999).

15. A senior policymaker in a line ministry recently told me of an encounter with a representative of a bilateral agency who suggested that funds be deposited in the name of the minister. When told that such a practice is not permissible in Ethiopia, the response was that it is indeed common elsewhere in Africa. A director of the Economic Commission for Africa calls this phenomenon "a race to the bottom": such donors seek out the least demanding recipients, and Africans are almost invariably blamed for the resulting aid ineffectiveness. From the donor perspective, the challenge of managing an aid program in the complex environment of countries like Ethiopia is aptly captured by the metaphor "hitting a moving target from a moving platform" (Maxwell 1998: 107).

REFERENCES

Abegaz, Berhanu. 1994. "Ethiopian Economic Reform." In Berhanu Abegaz, ed., *Essays on Ethiopian Economic Development*. Aldershot, U.K.: Avebury.
Addis Tribune ("by our economic correspondent/commentator"). 1998a. "Yet Another 5-Year Action Plan—This Time Around for Addis Ababa." 20 February.
———. 1998b. "Latest Talks Between Ethiopia and IMF Fail to Lift ESAF Suspension." 13 March.
———. 1998c. "Foreign Aid is Propping up the Ethiopian Economy." 10 April.
———. 1998d. "Unfair Economic Advantages Eritrea Enjoyed from Its Hegemonic Relationship with Ethiopia." 31 July.
———. 1998e. "Ethiopia's Alarming Brain Drain." 12 December.
Africa Confidential. 1999. "Africa Scrambles for Africa." 40(1):2–5.
AfDB (African Development Bank). 1996. "Ethiopia: 1996–98 Country Strategy Paper." Abidjan.
Aynekulu, Awualom. 1996a. "The Emerging Monopolies of the TPLF." *Ethiopian Register* (July): 20–32.
———. 1996b. "The Emerging Monopolies of the TPLF, Part 2." *Ethiopian Register* (August): 14–22.
Berg, Elliot. 1993. *Rethinking Technical Assistance and Capacity Building in Africa.* New York: United Nations Development Programme.
Bevan, David. 1994. "Economic Aspects of Ethiopian Transition to Peace." In Jean-Paul Azam, David Bevan, Paul Collier, Stefan Dercon, Jan Willem Gunning, and Sanjay Pradhan, "Some Economic Consequences of the Transition

from Civil War to Peace." Policy Research Working Paper 1392. World Bank, Development Research Group, Washington, D.C.

Cassen, Robert. 1994. *Does Aid Work?* New York: Oxford University Press.

Chang, Charles C., Eduardo Fernández-Arias, and Luis Servén. 1999. "Measuring Aid Flows: A New Approach." Policy Research Working Paper 2050. World Bank, Development Research Group, Washington, D.C.

Chole, Eshetu. 1993. "The Dismal Economy: Current Issues of Economic Reform and Development in Ethiopia." *Ethiopian Journal of Economics* 2(1): 37–72.

———. 1994. "A Preliminary Appraisal of Ethiopia's Economic Reforms, 1991–93." In Harold Marcus, ed., *New Trends in Ethiopian Studies*, vol. 2. Trenton, N.J.: Red Sea Press.

Clapham, Christopher. 1988. *Transformation and Continuity in Revolutionary Ethiopia*. Cambridge: Cambridge University Press.

Clay, Daniel, Daniel Molla, and Debebe Habtewold. 1998. "Food Aid Targeting in Ethiopia." Grain Market Research Program Working Paper 12. MEDAC, Addis Ababa.

Collier, Paul, and Jan Willem Gunning. 1999. "Explaining African Economic Performance." *Journal of Economic Literature* 37 (March): 64–111.

Collier, Paul, P. Guillaumont, S. Guillaumont, and J. W. Gunning. 1997. "Redesigning Conditionality." *World Development* 25 (9): 1399–1407.

Degafe, Befekadu, and Berhanu Nega, eds. 1999/2000. *Annual Report on the Ethiopian Economy*. Addis Ababa: United Printers for the Ethiopian Economic Association.

Deininger, Klaus, and Gershon Feder. 1998. "Land Institutions and Land Markets." Policy Research Working Paper 2014. World Bank, Development Research Group, Washington, D.C.

Demeksa, Bulcha. 1999. "Revising the Banking Sector." *Addis Tribune*, July 30.

Dercon, Stefan, and Daniel Ayalew. 1998. "Where Have All the Soldiers Gone: Demobilization and Reintegration in Ethiopia." *World Development* 26 (9): 1661–75.

The Economist. 1999. "Africa's Forgotten War." 15 May.

Etherington, Dan, and Alasebu Yainshet. 1988. 'The Impact of Income Terms of Trade for Coffee on Capital Goods Imports and Investment in Ethiopia." *Eastern Africa Economic Review* 4 (1): 48–52.

Ethiopia. 1991. "Economic Policy of Ethiopia during the Transitional Period." Prime Minister's Office, Addis Ababa.

———. 1992, 1993, 1994, 1996, 1998a. "Ethiopia: Policy Framework Paper." Ministry of Finance and National Bank, Addis Ababa.

———. 1998b. "The 1994 Population and Housing Census of Ethiopia." Central Statistical Office, Addis Ababa.

"Ethiopian Non-Governmental Business: Companies Controlled by or Associated with EPRDF-Member Organizations." 1999. Anonymous document. Addis Ababa. Processed.

Ghani, Ejaz, and Hyoungsoo Zang. 1995. "Is Ethiopia's Debt Sustainable?" Policy Research Working Paper 1525. World Bank, Development Research Group, Washington, D.C.

Griffin, Keith, ed. 1992. *The Economy of Ethiopia*. London: Macmillan.

Grindle, Merilee, and John Thomas. 1991. *Public Choices and Policy Change: The Political Economy of Reform in Developing Countries*. Baltimore: Johns Hopkins University Press.

Haile Mariam, Mengistu. 1990. "Report by Mengistu Haile Mariam: Resolutions Adopted by the 11th Plenum of WPE." Workers' Party of Ethiopia, Addis Ababa.

Harvey, Charles. 1996. "Banking Reform in Ethiopia." Working Paper 37. Institute of Development Studies, Sussex, U.K.

Howard, Julie, Mulat Demeke, Valerie Kelly, Mywish Maredia, and Julie Stepanek. 1998. "Can the Momentum Be Sustained? An Economic Analysis of the MOA/SG2000's Experiment with Improved Cereals Technology in Ethiopia." MEDAC, Addis Ababa.

IDS/IDR (Institute of Development Studies/ Institute for Development Research). 1996. *An Evaluation of Development Cooperation Between the European Union and Ethiopia, 1976–1994*. 7 vols. Addis Ababa.

IMF (International Monetary Fund). 1988a. "IMF Approves Second Annual ESAF Loan for Ethiopia." Press release 98/51. October.

———. 1998b. *International Financial Statistics 1998*. Washington, D.C.

———. 1998c. *Ethiopia: Statistical Appendix*. IMF Staff Country Report 9816. Washington, D.C.

———. 1999a. *International Financial Statistics*. February supplement. Washington, D.C.

———. 1999b. *Ethiopia: Recent Economic Developments*. IMF Staff Country Report 99/98. Washington, D.C.

Johnson, Juliet. 1997. "Russia's Emerging Financial-Industrial Groups." *Post-Soviet Affairs* 13 (4): 333–65.

Lensink, Robert, and Oliver Morrissey. 1999. "Aid Instability as a Measure of Uncertainty and the Positive Impact of Aid on Growth." University of Nottingham.

Leonardo, José, Hartwig Schafer, and Gaspar Frontini. 1999. "Towards a More Effective Conditionality: An Operational Framework." *World Development* 27 (2): 285–99.

Lister, Stephen. 1998. "Implementing Sector Development Programs in Ethiopia." Consultant's draft report. Addis Ababa.

Maxwell, Simon. 1998. "Effectiveness of European Aid to Ethiopia." In Marjorie Lister, ed., *European Union Development Policy*. New York: St. Martin's Press.

Middlebrook, P., and F. Corzato. 1999. "Displaced, Disempowered and Distressed: A Focus on Poverty in Addis Ababa." Draft. World Bank, Washington, D.C.

O'Connell, Stephen, and Charles Soludo. 1998. "Aid Intensity in Africa." Working Paper Series 3-99. Centre for African Economies, Oxford University.

OECD (Organisation for Economic Co-operation and Development). 1999. *Geographic Distribution of Financial Flows to Aid Recipients*. Paris.

Ramachandran, Mahadevan. 1997. "Food Security: Economics of Famine, Food Aid and Market Integration in Ethiopia." University Microfilms International, Ann Arbor, Mich.

Rose, Tore 1985. "Aid Modalities: Sector Aid as an Instrument in Sub-Saharan Africa." In T. Rose, ed., *Crisis and Recovery in Sub-Saharan Africa*. Paris: Organisation for Economic Co-operation and Development.

Stiglitz, Joseph. 1998. "More Instruments and Broader Goals: Moving Toward the Post-Washington Consensus." 1998 WIDER Annual Lecture, Helsinki, Finland.

UNCTAD/ICC (United Nations Conference on Trade and Development and International Chamber of Commerce). 1999. *An Investment Guide to Ethiopia: Opportunities and Conditions*. New York: United Nations.

UNDP (United Nations Development Programme). 1998. *Human Development Report 1998*. New York: Oxford University Press.

USAID (United States Agency for International Development). 1999. "Ethiopia: Congressional Presentation." Washington, D.C.

van de Walle, Nicolas, and Timothy A. Johnston. 1996. *Improving Aid to Africa*. Policy Essay 21. Washington, D.C.: Overseas Development Council.

Wade, Robert. 1990. *Governing the Market: Economic Theory and the Role of Government in East Asian Industrialization*. Princeton: Princeton University Press.

Woo, Wing Thye. 1998. "Why China Grew." In Peter Boone, Stanislaw Gomulka, and Richard Layard, eds., *Emerging from Communism: Lessons from Russia, China, and Eastern Europe*. Cambridge: MIT Press.

World Bank. 1987. "Ethiopia: Recent Economic Developments and Prospects for Recovery and Growth." Washington, D.C.

————. 1992, 1995, 1997a. "Ethiopia: Country Assistance Strategy." Washington, D.C.

————. 1993. *The East Asian Miracle: Economic Growth and Public Policy*. New York: Oxford University Press.

————. 1994. *Adjustment in Africa: Reforms, Results, and the Road Ahead*. New York: Oxford University Press.

————. 1995. *World Tables 1995*. Washington, D.C.

————. 1997b. "Ethiopia: Implementation Report on Structural Adjustment Credit (SAC I)." Washington, D.C.

————. 1998a. *Ethiopia: Review of Public Finances*. 2 vols. Washington, D.C.

————. 1998b. *Assessing Aid: What Works, What Doesn't, and Why*. New York: Oxford University Press.

————. 1998c. "Ethiopia: Anti-Corruption Report." Washington, D.C.

————. 1999a. "Ethiopia: Regionalization Study." Washington, D.C.

————. 1999b. *World Development Report 1999/2000*. New York: Oxford University Press.

————. 1999c. *Global Development Finance 1999*. Washington, D.C.

————. 1999d. "Ethiopia Public Expenditure Review: Aide Memoire." 1999 PER Mission, Addis Ababa.

World Economic Forum. 1998. *Africa Competitiveness Report 1998*. Geneva.

Zenawi, Meles. 1998. "Interview." *The Financial Times*, 2 March.

Mali

Patrick Guillaumont
Sylviane Guillaumont Jeanneney
Jacky Amprou
Auvergne University
Clermont-Ferrand, France

Oumar Cheick Sidibé
Ministry of Economic Affairs, Mali

ACRONYMS AND ABBREVIATIONS

AFD	Agence Française de Développement
BCEAO	Banque Centrale des Etats de l'Afrique de l'Ouest
BEAC	Banque des Etats de l'Afrique Centrale
CCCE	Caisse Centrale de Coopération Economique
CFA	Communauté financière africaine (franc zone)
CFAF	CFA franc
CFDT	Compagnie Française des Textiles (French Textile Company)
CMDT	Compagnie Malienne pour le Développement des Textiles (Malian Textile Development Company)
CPS	Contribution pour prestation de service (service charge)
DAC	Development Assistance Committee (of the OECD)
DFI	Droit fiscal d'importation (fiscal import tax)
DNAE	Direction Nationale des Affaires Economiques (National Directorate of Economic Affairs)
EDA	Effective development assistance
EDM	Société d'Energie du Mali (Mali Electricity Company)
ESAF	Enhanced Structural Adjustment Facility (of the IMF)
GNP	Gross national product
HIPC	Heavily indebted poor countries
IAS	Impôt sur les affaires et services (tax on goods and services)
IDA	International Development Association (of the World Bank Group)
IMF	International Monetary Fund
ISCP	Impôt spécial sur certains produits (special tax on certain products)
ODA	Official development assistance
ODF	Official development finance
OECD	Organisation for Economic Co-operation and Development
OHADA	Organization for the Harmonization of Business Law in Africa
OPAM	Office de Commercialisation des Produits Agricoles du Mali (Mali Agricultural Products Office)
OSRP	Office de Stabilisation et de Régulation des Prix (Price Stabilization and Regulation Office)
PASEP	Public Enterprise Sector Adjustment Program (Programme d'Ajustement du Secteur des Entreprises Publiques)
PRED	Economic Reform and Development Program (Programme pour la Réforme Economique pour le Développement)
PRMC	Programme de Restructuration des Marchés Céréaliers (Cereals Market Restructuring Program)
PRODEC	Program for the Development of Education
SAF	Structural Adjustment Facility (of the IMF)
SAP	Structural adjustment program
SDR	Special drawing right (of the IMF)
SGS	Société Générale de Surveillance
SOMIEX	Société Malienne d'Import-Export (Malian Import-Export Company)
TOF	Total gross official flows (from the public sector)
USAID	U.S. Agency for International Development
VAT	Value added tax
WAMU	West African Monetary Union
WAEMU	West African Economic and Monetary Union

In the case of Mali, analysis of the relationship between aid and economic policy reform is particularly interesting on several counts.

First, Mali was, and still is in relative terms, one of the top 10 aid recipients in the world. In 1997, net flows of official development aid represented 18.4 percent of GNP, 77.2 percent of investments, and 47.5 percent of imports of goods and services (World Bank 1999c: 353). It should be noted that the "aid intensity" ratio as a function of the country's 1997 gross national product (GNP) corresponds roughly to the average over the past 10 years.

Second, Mali has a long history of reforms that have dealt with the monetary regime, trade policy, and public sector management. After having embarked shortly after its independence upon a socialist experiment that included the creation of a separate currency, controls over foreign exchange and external trade, and widespread state control over economic activities, Mali rejoined the franc zone in 1967 and the West African Monetary Union (WAMU) in 1984, and then helped to create the West African Economic and Monetary Union (WAEMU) in 1994. These radical institutional changes were, as we shall see, followed at irregular intervals by a great number of economic reforms both macroeconomic and structural in nature.

Third, and perhaps because of the two preceding factors, Mali has been the object of particular interest on the part of donors interested in improving their procedures and the efficacy of their aid. Thus, at the initiative of the Development Assistance Committee (DAC) of the Organisation for Economic Co-operation and Development (OECD), a novel experiment in the local coordination of external aid was set up under the name Aid Review (*revue de l'aide*). It gave rise first to an evaluation report (OECD 1998), followed by regular and joint examinations of aid operations conducted by the main dispensers of aid at the local level. Mali was once again chosen to be one of seven countries included in the Structural Adjustment Participatory Research Initiative, in which the recipient government evaluates the adjustment policies in collaboration with the main donors and nongovernmental organizations.

Given the intensity of aid, the number of aid sources, their degree of involvement in the reform process, and the country's longstanding and varied history of reform, Mali was thought to be able to provide some insight into the ways in which aid can or cannot influence economic reform.

The relationship between aid and reform depends on the nature of the aid provided. In the case of adjustment aid, which includes explicit economic policy conditionalities, the linkage can be extremely close. Section 2 of this chapter, which describes the structure and evolution of the external aid that Mali has received, points up the importance, in the total aid picture, of macroeconomic or budgetary aid and of structural or sectoral aid, as well as the general evolution of aid and the cycles it goes through. These last are, as we shall see, quite closely associated with economic policy cycles. It also emerges that, when the evolution and structure of Mali's aid are placed in their context (monetary coopera- tion, external debt, etc.), the links between aid and reform seem to have been mutually reinforcing.

Section 3 deals with Mali's reform experience, its phases, and its ar- eas of application. The pace and effectiveness of reform appear to be greatly influenced by Mali's initial socialist experiment and by the country's place within regional institutions. The sectors where reform has been most effective are macroeconomic reform (that is, budgetary and monetary reform) and economic liberalization, where both external and internal trade are concerned.

Section 4 attempts to derive some lessons from the Malian experience concerning the conditions under which aid can best foster reform. Four hypotheses are presented, dealing with the role of crises, internal con- sensus, aid coordination, and the financing of the costs of reform.

TRENDS AND CYCLES IN AID TO MALI

In order to understand the evolution of aid to Mali, it is useful to refer to different concepts of aid, each of which has a different significance for the study of the aid/reform relationship. Analysis of the evolution of aid then makes it possible to discern recurring "aid cycles." Finally, an analysis of the origin and nature of aid flows supports the hypothesis that the link between aid and reform tends to become stronger over time.

Five Useful Aid Concepts

Five concepts of external aid are used in this study. The first, as defined by OECD's Development Assistance Committee, is official development assistance (ODA). This represents aid flows to developing countries that are provided by public entities, that is, central and local governments, and by multilateral institutions, and that meet two criteria: (a) their main objective is to promote economic development and the well-being of the beneficiary countries (they therefore include technical assistance grants); and (b) the terms are concessional, with a grant element of at least 25 percent. ODA is usually calculated net of amortization. The main disad- vantage of this concept is that it fails to take into account nonconcessional flows, including those of the International Monetary Fund (for example, standby arrangements and enhanced facilities) and the World Bank (a consideration relevant to some countries, but not to Mali).

The second concept, effective development assistance (EDA), devel- oped by Chang, Fernández-Arias, and Servén (1999), is defined as the sum of total grants except technical assistance and the grant equivalents of official loans.[1] This type of aid is calculated on the basis of data from the OECD's DAC, but lumps together the grant equivalents of loans (rather than their face value), including loans with a concessional element of less than 25 percent. This concept, unlike ODA, does not take into account debt adjustments, whether in the form of debt forgiveness or rescheduling. Only concessional flows from the IMF (such as the Structural Adjustment Facility and Enhanced Structural Adjustment Facility) are taken into account here.

Two broader concepts can be introduced here in order to account for the whole of official development finance. The first, calculated on the basis of data gathered by Chang, Fernández-Arias, and Servén (1999), is the aggregate official development finance (ODF). It includes not only effective development assistance (grants and the grant element included in loans), but also the nonconcessional element of loans, technical assistance grants, and the IMF's nonconcessional financing. The other is calculated on the basis of data from OECD's DAC and is referred to as total gross official flows from the public sector (TOF). It includes ODA (gross) as well as other flows from the public sector. The latter are public sector interventions whose main goal is not development-related and which, although they are intended to foster development, have a grant element below 25 percent and are therefore excluded from the ODA category. They are essentially public credits for exports, equity holdings and investments in the public sector portfolio, and nonconcessional IMF and World Bank financing (enhanced facilities and standby agreements). These two aggregates—ODF and TOF—are conceptually equivalent, except for the debt adjustment issue (see figure 5.1). They differ mainly in the statistical sources used.

For purposes of examining the relationship between aid and reform, the value of the ODF or TOF concepts is that they include not only technical assistance (as does the ODA concept), but also the IMF's nonconcessional financing (which ODA does not do). The latter carries macroeconomic conditionalities and was used by Mali from 1971 to 1988. The value of the ODF or TOF concepts also resides in the fact that they deals with *raw* aid flows, that is, those that are subject to negotiation between the country and the donors and that are in this respect liable to influence a government's behavior. At the other end of the spectrum, *net transfers* point up the true contribution that aid flows are making to domestic expenditures, since they deduct amortization *and* interest from the raw amount. This concept is not only of macroeconomic significance, but also represents for governments that portion of external contributions above and beyond that which helps avoid the accumulation of external arrears.

All flows initially expressed in current dollars were deflated by the index established for this purpose by OECD,[2] based on the assumption

FIGURE 5.1 THE DIFFERENT AID CONCEPTS USED
(IN TERMS OF DISBURSEMENTS)

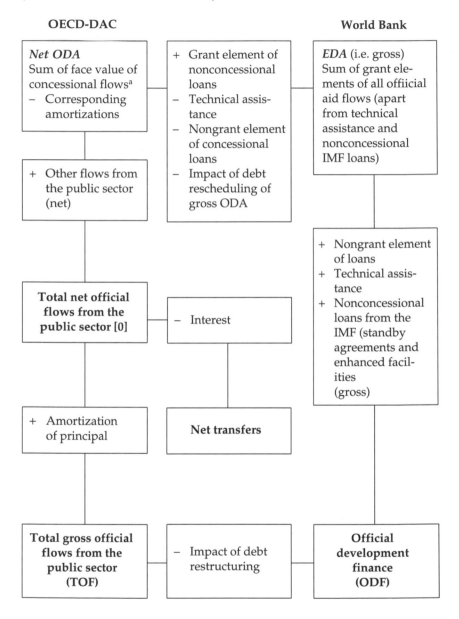

a. Debt restructuring (whether cancellation or rescheduling) is taken into account as a fictive grant (which increases gross ODA) corresponding to normal amortization, which is itself accounted for as an imaginary amortization: gross and net ODA amounts are thus increased by the same amount, which is equal to the fictive, or avoided, amortization.

that 1996 = 100. They represent aid flows in constant (1996) dollars. Figures 5.2 through 5.11 and tables 5.4 through 5.11 in the appendix summarize data relative to the different aid concepts applied in Mali and provide a basis for the commentary that follows.

Aid Intensity: Cycles of Aid and Reform

As indicated in the introduction, aid intensity—that is, the relationship of aid to some other economic aggregate, which may be the GNP, imports, or investment—is particularly high in Mali (see figure 5.3 in the appendix). Over the past 10 years, ODA has represented about 20 percent of GNP, 53 percent of imported goods and services, and 85 percent of investment. These ratios put Mali among the top 10 developing countries in terms of aid intensity.

Although it has always been high, this intensity has experienced fluctuations. As shown in figure 5.3, net ODA as a percentage of GNP rose steadily, from only 10 percent of GNP in 1976 to 32 percent in 1985. It fell again to a low of 14 percent in 1993, and rose to nearly 25 percent in 1994 before declining again. In 1997, it was on the same order of magnitude as in the early 1990s or early 1980s.

However, the wide variations in aid intensity should be interpreted in the light of exchange rate movements. The spike in aid intensity in 1994 is partly due, of course, to the devaluation of the CFA franc, which doubled the CFAF equivalent of external aid to Mali. The fact remains, however, that net ODA in constant dollars increased slightly in 1994 (see figure 5.2 in the appendix). Similarly, the rapid hike in ODA observed between 1981 and 1985 and its subsequent drop starting in 1986 resulted in part from changes in the dollar in relation to the French franc and, therefore, in relation to the CFA franc. Thus, between 1980 and 1983, ODA in dollar terms diminished even though aid intensity increased greatly.

The First Three Cycles: 1962–82

Despite these divergences associated with the trading currency, it is possible to identify several cycles in aid to Mali, which seem closely linked to the country's political situation.

A first cycle was observed during the 1960s, and corresponded to aid flows from Eastern bloc countries during the socialist experiment from 1962–67, which then declined markedly in 1967–68. The reentry into the franc zone occurred at this point, and then the coup d'etat that brought Moussa Traoré to power.

A second aid cycle began in 1969 and peaked in 1975. It corresponded to an economic recovery program that benefited in 1969 and 1971 from two standby agreements with the IMF (which was the first to get involved in the franc zone), and was also undoubtedly related to the external aid connected with the great drought of the early 1970s. Aid levels then fell back down in 1976.

A third cycle peaked in 1980 and ended in 1982 following some economic difficulties. It was at this time that Mali resumed its dialogue with the Bretton Woods institutions.

The Last Three Cycles: 1982–99

Since the early 1980s, three new aid cycles can be discerned in connection with phases of economic policy. These phases will be the main focus of the rest of this study.

The first cycle lasted from 1982 to 1987, with a peak year in 1986. Mali reestablished its relationship with the IMF, signed three standby agreements (in 1982, 1983, and 1985), obtained an agricultural sector adjustment credit (in 1983) from the World Bank, and rejoined WAMU in 1984. But in 1986–87 the agreements with the IMF were suspended (and no adjustment credit was obtained from the Bank). It should be noted that the growth of ODA and its subsequent decline in 1986–87 was not the direct result of changes in flows from the IMF, since those flows were at that time still nonconcessional. Rather, it seemed to be associated with the pace of reforms as reflected in relations with the IMF.

A second cycle began in 1987, peaked in 1989, and ended in 1993. It corresponded initially to a wave of important reforms undertaken from 1987 to 1989 and was marked by a last standby agreement with the IMF in 1988. This was followed immediately by a structural adjustment facility and a structural adjustment credit from the World Bank in 1990. Aid and reform then slowed due to political troubles in late 1991 and the overthrow of the regime in 1992—despite the provision in 1992 of an Enhanced Structural Adjustment Facility (ESAF) from the IMF—and then a suspension of adjustment lending in the franc zone in anticipation of the devaluation. The disbursement of the second tranche of the ESAF was put on hold pending this measure.

A third cycle started to take shape in 1993, first with an increase in aid obtained in 1994–95 as an accompaniment to the devaluation and in support of democratization. This increase was attributable as much to bilateral as to multilateral donors, the latter being a bit more generous. But it was followed by a new decline in 1997 and, as we shall see, by a corresponding decrease in the pace of reform.

The apparent cycles of aid, as identified on the basis of ODA levels, appear again when one applies the concept of official development finance (ODF) (see figure 5.4). In the case of Mali, the proportion of nonconcessional loans is small, with the exception of the IMF's support up to 1988. As became apparent, IMF agreements can play a signal role for other donors, accelerating and slowing the pace of their disbursements.

The Origin and Nature of Inflows:
A Growing Aid-Reform Linkage

The sources and the nature of aid flows to Mali have changed considerably over the past 30 years. Three phenomena characterize this evolution: first, the change in monetary cooperation with France that occurred when Mali joined WAMU in 1984; second, the change in the relative importance of various donors; and, finally, the changing nature of aid in a context of growing indebtedness. These three factors profoundly modified the relationship between aid and reform in Mali.

Changes in Monetary Cooperation

In 1967, Mali, which had withdrawn from the franc zone in 1962, signed a new monetary cooperation agreement with France and reentered the franc zone, without reentering the WAMU. This meant that the Malian franc was henceforth fixed relative to the French franc (one Malian franc = one French centime, a 50 percent devaluation of the Malian franc). The Malian currency became totally convertible into French francs, the guarantee of convertibility being provided by the establishment of a *compte d'opérations* (operations account) within the French treasury where the Central Bank of Mali was supposed to deposit its reserves and where it had unlimited drawing rights. Adherence to agreed-upon rules of monetary issuance was monitored by the Central Bank's board of directors, which included French representatives on equal footing with their Malian counterparts. The operations account, unlike what happened with the Banque Centrale des Etats de l'Afrique de l'Ouest (BCEAO) or the Banque des Etats de l'Afrique Centrale, was in debt from the outset. This was increasingly the case until 1984, when Mali reentered WAMU.[3]

Paradoxically, although France occupied a very important position within the Central Bank of Mali (which had a French general director until 1983 and Malian and French managers serving on an equal footing on the board of directors), it undoubtedly did not wish to impose strict management of monetary policy. Despite the statutory rule stating that the cumulative level of the Central Bank's contributions to the government could not exceed 10 percent of tax revenues, Mali's money supply grew very quickly, through advances to the public treasury as well as through contributions to public enterprises experiencing deficits. In a holdover from the 1960s, these enterprises continue to play an important role in the Malian economy.

Mali's actual entry into WAMU, which had been planned under the 1967 agreement, did not occur until 1984. Mali's currency then became the CFA franc, which replaced the Malian franc without any change in parity between the two currencies. This marked a break in relations between the Central Bank—henceforth the BCEAO—and Mali's public treasury. The variation in the credit of the monetary system to the Malian public treasury had an impact on the money supply that was almost always negative between 1984 and 1992. This change resulted from the fact that the multilateral constraints exerted by other WAMU members proved stronger than the control wielded by France in an exclusively bilateral relationship, as well as from the fact that Mali's macroeconomic policy was the main focus of IMF conditionalities.

Two factors obliged Mali to have recourse to the IMF. The first was that debits from the operations account, according to the franc zone's monetary cooperation agreements, required the debitor to turn to other sources of foreign currencies and thus to the IMF. The second was that Mali needed the IMF to lighten the constraints weighing upon its public finances. Indeed, the help provided in the form of the operations account was in fact balance of payments support, but unlike other multilateral assistance with the same objective, it was not simultaneously supporting public finances, since the flip side of France's guarantee of the Malian franc's convertibility was the statutory limitation of the Central Bank of Mali's contribution to the government. This is why Mali, like most other franc zone countries, resorted to the IMF fairly quickly after the financial situation deteriorated, in 1969 as well as in 1982.

Thus, from one phase to another of Mali's monetary regime, one sees donors playing a growing role in the definition of macroeconomic policy.

As a WAMU member, Mali was obliged to devalue once again in 1994 (by 50 percent). For Mali, the devaluation of the CFA franc was almost an exogenous decision to which it rallied at the 1994 meeting of heads of state of the franc zone in Dakar. But for WAMU members, this meeting was also an opportunity to sign the treaty creating WAEMU (the West African Economic and Monetary Union), which not only implied the creation of a common market, but also provided for multilateral monitoring of budgetary policies, as well as for joint sectoral interventions. This new institutional stage therefore had important economic policy implications for Mali: the influence of aid on policy could now be exerted in part through this regional conduit.

Changes in the Sources of Aid

Tables 5.3 and 5.7 in the appendix show changes in the proportions of various types of aid provided to Mali, starting in 1964 for ODA and in 1975 for ODF. For the 1960s, however, ODA statistics, which are obtained from the OECD, do not include contributions from countries that are not members of the DAC, many of which (such as communist bloc countries and their Arab allies) provided aid that cannot be inventoried under ODA.[4]

THE BILATERAL-MULTILATERAL SPLIT. If one looks at the extremes of table 5.4, that is, the 1964–67 and 1994–97 periods, it would appear that the relative proportions of bilateral and multilateral aid have remained unchanged, at 54 percent and 46 percent respectively. However, during the 30 years in between these percentages fluctuated quite widely. The proportion of bilateral aid increased until 1982–85, when it reached 69 percent (as against 31 percent for multilateral aid), and then declined.

The trend is a little less clear if, instead of considering ODA, one focuses on ODF. This includes non-ODA public flows, bilateral as well as multilateral, and especially, it should be noted, the IMF's contributions through 1988 when the structural adjustment facilities came onstream. Over the last period, the proportion of bilateral financing remained preponderant, at 59 percent, despite its steady 20-year decline.

BILATERAL AID: FRENCH AID DECLINES, BUT REMAINS IMPORTANT. The relative proportion of French aid within ODA, which it naturally dominated in the decade following Mali's independence, diminished steadily to 16 percent of the total in 1994–97. This is still a high proportion, however, and is equivalent to the World Bank's share.

Among the bilateral aid flows, French aid has been closely linked to certain critical phases of economic policy because of the particular history of Mali's monetary regime outlined earlier: Mali's return to the franc zone in 1967, its entry into WAMU in 1984 (over the 1982–85 period, French aid regained its 28 percent share, whereas it had stood at 21 percent over the 1972–81 period), and finally the devaluation of the CFA franc in 1994. French aid also contributes to the fact that the share of bilateral grants (including technical assistance) is much larger than the multilateral share.

Bilateral aid from the United States also played an important role in terms of its volume and relationship to economic reform. Although there was a steady drop in the proportion of ODA coming from North America (from 13 to 8 percent, see appendix table 5.4), the 1988–90 period was characterized by an interesting American experiment in aid in support of economic reform (the PRED program, discussed farther on).

Finally, one should note the significant growth in aid from Japan, which, with 7 percent of total ODA in 1994–97, was the second-ranking bilateral donor, even ahead of the United States (North America as a whole represented 8 percent).

MULTILATERAL AID AND MULTILATERAL DEVELOPMENT FINANCING. Multilateral ODA, although at the same level in 1994–97 as 30 years previously (that is, 46 percent of the total), came from very different sources by the 1990s. During the 1964–67 period, European ODA disbursements represented almost all multilateral aid; in 1994–97 they accounted for only 13 percent of the aforementioned 46 percent (or 28 percent of all multilateral aid). Still, it should be noted that this proportion had fallen between 1982 and 1987 to 7 percent, on average, of total ODA (a drop that would be even more noticeable if the percentage were calculated for ODF, since this period corresponded to significant contributions from the IMF on conditions that were not yet those of ODA).

The fluctuation noted in the relative proportion of European multilateral aid could, at first glance, be interpreted as a political manifestation of a desire to modulate aide as a function of judgments about the country's general policy, since this type of aid rose in the 1990s relative to the 1980s. The fluctuation also reflects the wide swings in aid flows from other sources that brought total ODA to a particularly high level in the 1980s. Total European aid over the 1994–97 period was roughly at its 1972–81 level (table 5.4). It is reasonable to wonder why European aid did not undergo the same fluctuations as other forms of aid.

The main compensatory change that occurred was, of course, the growth of the Bretton Woods institutions, which accounted for 3 percent of total ODA in 1964–67 and for 22 percent 30 years later: 16 percent for the World Bank (in the form of IDA credits) and 6 percent for the IMF. The weight of the IMF, like that of the Bank, is actually more important than these figures indicate, because IMF agreements are a prerequisite for many other types of aid, especially for the World Bank's adjustment operations and those of various other donors, and also because the World Bank acts as the lead bank in various aid areas, as will be seen.

This change naturally helped reinforce the potential link between aid and economic reform, since the aid of the Bretton Woods institutions is, in principle, associated with reform to a greater extent than that of other donors.

Changes in the Nature of Aid and Growing Indebtedness

Like most Sub-Saharan African countries, Mali experienced a financial crisis in the early 1980s due to wide fluctuations in the terms of trade, which had improved in the late 1970s but deteriorated sharply thereafter. The experience of the 1970s had led to an excessively expansive policy characterized by rapid growth of the money supply and in public expenditures. Thus, for the second time, Mali had to implement an adjustment policy with the support of the Bretton Woods institutions. This was a turning point in the evolution of the aid received by the country.

The aid received by Mali since the early 1980s has had three main characteristics. The first is, of course, the increase in nonproject aid, especially for adjustment. However, it is very difficult to isolate statistically the aid flows that are akin to adjustment aid. (Under the heading "General Program Assistance," which is OECD's classification, appendix table 5.5, which deals only with ODA, indicates only a part of the nonproject aid that is subject to economic policy conditionalities. For example, it includes neither the IMF's contributions through 1998, which do not come under ODA, nor sectoral adjustment credits, which are included under other headings.) It should be noted that adjustment aid provided to Mali in the early 1980s came not only from the Bretton Woods institutions, although they predominated, but also from bilateral donors, and especially France through its aid agency or in the form of direct budget aid.[5]

It should also be noted that adjustment aid, which had been on hold just before the devaluation, was very high after that event (in 1994–95), and came as often from multilateral sources as from bilateral ones. But it seems that since then, multilateral aid (for example, from the IMF, World Bank, and European Commission) has predominated in this area.

Second, the growing importance of technical assistance should be noted, as figure 5.4 shows. Based on trends in the overall aid volume, the proportion of technical assistance in total ODA fluctuated, finally ending up in the 1980s at a level above that of the two previous decades. During the 1994–97 period, it reached about 26 percent of total ODA (nearly 40 percent of bilateral ODA, but only 11 percent of multilateral ODA). The weight of technical assistance may in itself be a factor in the stronger link between aid and reform.

Third, although grants are traditionally a large proportion of aid received by Mali (that is, usually more than 50 percent of official development finance, as shown in figure 5.5), this proportion dropped slightly in 1982 and 1983 due to the increase in other contributions. In general, the high proportion of grants has not prevented the growth of external indebtedness, which was particularly severe in the first half of the 1980s, as can be clearly seen in figures 5.10 and 5.11.

Mali is currently counted among the heavily indebted poor countries that are eligible for HIPC initiatives. In late 1998, its total external debt totaled US$1,239 million in net present value, or 220 percent of export receipts for that same year (World Bank 1999a: 103, 106). Figure 5.10 shows how the debt ratio, expressed in face value, has evolved in relation to GNP: the ratio had been around 100 percent between 1984 and 1993, and stayed at a little over 115 percent after the spike due to the devaluation.

The growth of debt, whatever its origin, has increased Mali's dependency on the IMF, with which it had four standby agreements and three structural adjustment facilities between 1982 and 1998 (see appendix table 5.9). The agreements were themselves a precondition for renegotiation of the debt with the Paris Club, which has restructured Mali's public debt four times since 1988 (see appendix table 5.10). Finally, Mali's eligibility for the HIPC Initiative makes it especially important for Mali to adhere to the agreements concluded with the IMF and the World Bank, and therefore increases the potential impact of aid on reform.

It should be noted (see figure 5.9) that the evolution of net transfers hardly differs from that of raw aid flows, although the size of the difference between these two flows naturally becomes more pronounced as indebtedness increases (it currently stands at around one-fifth).

MALI'S COMMITMENT TO REFORM AND SUPPORT FROM EXTERNAL DONORS

Mali's reform experience has been profoundly influenced by its point of departure. Let us recall that, almost immediately after independence, Mali embarked upon an ambitious socialist experiment characterized by state control of the economy and closure to the outside world, through, most notably, withdrawal from the franc zone (1962). The Malian experience was also marked by a strong and traditional inclination toward regional integration. Without going as far back as the ancient empire of Mali, one must remember that, at the time of independence and during the brief period preceding the socialist experiment, Mali joined with Senegal in what was called the Fédération du Mali. Once it reentered the franc zone in 1967, Mali then became involved in various attempts at regional integration in connection with trade (the West African Customs Union, UDAO, and then the West African Economic Community, CEAO) or resource management (the Organization for Development of the Senegal River, OMVS). As previously discussed, its entry into the West African Monetary Union in 1984 provided a durable framework for its policy of regional rapprochement, which was consolidated once again in 1994 with the creation of the West African Economic and Monetary Union. These two factors—the socialist experience of the 1960s and Mali's regional commitment—explain the long history and the pace of reforms undertaken in Mali, as well as the areas in which they have advanced the most (macroeconomic policy and economic liberalization) and those where they have been more uneven (public sector reform and institutional framework). The result is that external aid has exerted more influence on reforms in some sectors than in others.

Here we will examine in turn the pace of reform in Mali since 1980, according to the three "cycles" distinguished previously, looking specifically at the reform of public finances, the reform of external trade, cereals market reform, the reorganization of the cotton sector, and, finally, other areas of public sector reform. As we shall see, aid sources have been closely involved.

The Pace of Reform in Mali Since 1980

Although Mali experienced an initial reform phase upon its reentry into the franc zone in 1967, and with its first IMF agreement shortly thereafter, it was not until the early 1980s that the reforms were incorporated into a general structural adjustment program onto which many sectoral programs were grafted. Mali's main donors participated in these programs.

Since 1980, as was noted previously, three cycles of reforms can be distinguished, corresponding to their start-up (1980–87), acceleration (1987–93), and consolidation (1993–99). During each phase, reforms have dealt simultaneously with incentive structures and with public resource management.

The 1980–87 Period

IMPROVEMENTS IN THE STRUCTURE OF ECONOMIC INCENTIVES. The most important reform had to do with the cereals sector. The Cereals Market Restructuring Program (Programme de Restructuration des Marchés Céréaliers, PRMC) was set up, and the Malian government agreed to liberalize the cereals market (see discussion of the PRMC below).

The distribution monopoly held by some public enterprises also began to erode. SOMIEX (Société Malienne d'Import-Export), which had held the monopoly on external trade since the 1960s, progressively lost it (it was abolished a first time in August 1986, and then reinstated in September). Its monopoly was restricted to 11 products. The monopoly of the cement plant was also eliminated.

MANAGEMENT OF PUBLIC RESOURCES. Several measures were taken, although they were tentative in their content. They dealt either with the administration of public finances (including the reform of budgetary nomenclature), or with the control of expenditures (that is, a reduction in the operating expenditures of certain ministries, a freeze on promotions in the civil service, etc.). Finally, the first indications of government disengagement started to appear with the privatization of public enterprises without any economic importance, namely a brickyard (SOBRIMA) and a tannery (TAMALI).

The end of this period saw the beginning of the restructuring of the Banque de Développement du Mali and of the airline Air Mali. In the latter case, the money-losing routes were eliminated and some aircraft sold off.

The 1988–93 Period

IMPROVEMENTS IN THE STRUCTURE OF ECONOMIC INCENTIVES. The main measures applied in this area during this period were the following:

- Total liberalization of prices between 1988 and 1990, except for hydrocarbons;
- Elimination of the monopoly on hiring held by the National Employment and Manpower Office (Office National de la Main d'Oeuvre et de l'Emploi, ONMOE);
- Revision of the Labor Code;
- Updating of the Commercial Code;
- Liquidation of SOMIEX (in 1988);
- Liberalization of external trade, including most notably the elimination of import/export permits (discussed below);
- Simplification and streamlining of customs tariffs;
- Replacement of the tax on goods and services by a value added tax (VAT).

MANAGEMENT OF PUBLIC RESOURCES. In the area of budgetary policy, the wage bill did indeed diminish due to the voluntary departure of some civil servants. Staff reductions continued through 1993. The different government funds (*fonds de l'Etat*), which constituted annexes to the government budget, were integrated and/or eliminated in accordance with the principle of the single cashier (*unicité de caisse*).

In the area of financial policy, the restructuring of the Bank of Mali was completed and the Postal and Telecommunications Office was divided into three entities: the Postal Checking and Savings Funds (Société des Chèques Postaux), the National Post Office, and the Telecommunications Company of Mali (Société des Télécommunications du Mali). The privatization of enterprises continued at a rapid pace. Enterprises had to be either liquidated, privatized, or rehabilitated. A time frame for this was developed under a special program: the Public Enterprise Sector Adjustment Program (Programme d'Ajustement du Secteur des Entreprises Publiques, PASEP).

A new program for the agricultural sector was initiated. It took into account the restructuring of the cotton production stream, of the Mali Agricultural Products Office (OPAM), and of the different development offices.

The 1994–99 Period

This was a period of consolidation and continuation of reforms already initiated.

IMPROVEMENTS IN THE STRUCTURE OF ECONOMIC INCENTIVES

- All prices were liberalized, including prices of petroleum products;
- In terms of the regulatory framework, trade and administrative tribunals were set up and became operational in three regions of Mali (Kayes, Bamako, and Mopti);
- External trade procedures were simplified through the establishment of the "one window" system (*guichet unique*) for handling all formalities;
- In the context of support to the private sector, a center for handling business-related formalities was set up, and funds were made available to the Private Sector Development Project (Projet de Développement du Secteur Privé, PDSP) for the restructuring of Mali's Chamber of Commerce and Industry;
- In the area of fiscal reform, a Large Enterprises Directorate (Direction des Grandes Entreprises, DGE) was created to monitor enterprises with turnover exceeding 200 million CFAF. In addition, the list of products exempt from the VAT was reduced and an overall reform of income tax was adopted.

MANAGEMENT OF PUBLIC RESOURCES

- The principle of the program budget was adopted. Monitoring of certain expenditures was improved. This mainly concerned the wage bill, for which the use of electronic databases became widespread, and also such budget items as student scholarships, water, electricity, and telephone.
- Education, health, and road maintenance were recognized as priority sectors as far as public expenditures are concerned.
- In the monetary area, external adjustment resulted in devaluation of the CFA franc.
- The privatization of enterprises continued and the government disengaged from all nonstrategic enterprises.
- In the agricultural sector, a performance contract between the government, the cotton company, and producers was signed in June 1994, and the various performance plans between OPAM and the government were renewed.

Phases of Reform and Cycles of Aid

It is interesting to compare the preceding description of the pace of reforms with the aid cycles presented earlier. Unfortunately, we were not able to trace an economic policy indicator like the one established for various countries by Burnside and Dollar. There were two reasons for this: one is that the data are unavailable, which would explain why Burnside and Dollar did not establish such an indicator for Mali. The three indicators they selected and aggregated into an average indicator are not particularly relevant to Mali. Actually, little is known about Mali's inflation rate during the 1960s, and it also jumped in 1994 due to the devaluation after having been low for several years (its increase reflects the reform, or rather a reform, rather than the other way around). The openness indicator developed by Sachs and Warner, a unitary indicator equal to 0 or 1, is ill-suited to grasping the different phases of external trade reform as it will be described. The only thing that could be shown was the evolution of the third indicator—that is, the fiscal balance—but this is too partial to provide a synoptic view of economic policy.

What is striking, on the other hand, is that each new phase of reform (1982–83, 1987–88, 1993–94) was accompanied or immediately followed by an increase in external aid. The slowing down of reform also corresponded more or less to the declining phases of the aid cycle. This parallelism is an indication that, in Mali, aid and reform have not evolved independently of each other. These apparent links at the overall level are examined in more detail in the sections dealing with the main sectors subject to reform.

Reform of Public Finances

The reform of public finances was an essential part of economic reform. It fulfilled both the objective of macroeconomic equilibrium (through a planned reduction in the budget deficit) and the objective of development, since fiscal reform was supposed to help improve the incentive system, whereas improvement in public resource management was aimed at restructuring public expenditures in favor of priority development-related expenditures.

The reform of public finances mobilized most donors. The IMF and World Bank were the most heavily involved, especially through the structural adjustment loan (ESAF) of 1992. This touched off numerous cofinancing packages from the German, Dutch, Swiss, and Norwegian governments, as well as from the European Union and the African Development Bank. The United States and France also contributed to the program at the same time in the form of budgetary aid. The United States first provided budgetary aid in the context of the Economic Recovery Program (1987–88), and then under the Economic Reform and Development Program (Programme pour la Réforme Economique pour le Développement, PRED) of 1991–97, which had its own conditionalities.

The main measures taken in the area of public finance can be grouped into three categories of reform: budgetary administration, taxation, and the structure of public expenditures.

Reforms to Improve Budgetary Administration

During the first phase of reforms, the first task accomplished was the development of a clearer nomenclature for public expenditures. The most important efforts to improve financial administration were implemented from 1988 onwards, however. An important reform goal was to unify the government budget by integrating the supplemental budgets (*budgets annexes*) and special funds into it, and this was done in 1991 for 6 out of the 10 supplemental budgets or special funds.

The intention was also to improve the monitoring and control of budgetary procedures, especially by improving the efficiency of the office responsible for payments to civil servants (Bureau Central de la Solde). Unfortunately, the destruction in 1991 of the equipment and administration facilities of the Ministry of Civil Service greatly slowed the computerization of personnel management. Since 1994, there has been better monitoring of the wage bill, as well as of other public expenditures such as student scholarships, water, electricity, and telephone service.

Considerable progress has also been made in programming and monitoring public investments. The national capacity for programming and monitoring still appears to be weak, however, especially at the level of the line ministries.

Starting in 1994, emphasis was placed mainly on improving tax recovery by strengthening the tax administration and by creating a system of unique taxpayer ID numbers. The Large Enterprises Directorate has been operational since 1994 and has proved effective. However, the computerization of fiscal services is still embryonic and much remains to be done to improve tax collection.

Tax Reform

Tax reform was undertaken mainly under the second reform phase. An important aspect of this reform consisted of replacing the tax on goods and services (*impôt sur les affaires et services*, IAS) by a value added tax, thereby eliminating the IAS's spillover effects and export distortions, since the IAS did not provide for reimbursement of exporters for taxes paid at intermediate stages. Taxation of the informal sector was facilitated by the introduction of the "advance on various taxes" (*avance sur impôts et taxes*, ADIT), which was set at 5 percent of imports and public procurements and deductible from indirect taxes. A new investment code went into effect in June 1991.

This reform of excise taxes obviously complemented the reform of import and export taxes, which was part of the simultaneous liberalization of external trade (see below).

The reform of direct taxes had originally been planned for 1992. The idea was to institute a single private income tax and a single tax on business profits. This reform was postponed because the Malian authorities feared that it might result in a decrease in tax revenues due to their inability to manage a new tax system. The reform of direct taxation was finally achieved in the budget of 1999 with the elimination of the income tax surcharge and the introduction of restructured schedular taxes, including a tax on business revenues, the expansion of the global tax *(impôt synthétique)* to include all businesses having an annual turnover of less than 30 million CFAF, and the introduction of a progressive tax on salaries.

Restructuring of Public Expenditures

The goal of the reform was to contain the wage bill so as to be able to increase spending on education, health, and the maintenance and development of infrastructures.

A lasting cap on the wage bill could not be achieved with a freeze on civil service salaries and hiring alone, as was the case during the first phase of adjustment. A true civil service reform (supported by the SAC) was undertaken in 1989–90. It was aimed at reducing staff numbers through a program of voluntary departures and increasing staff efficiency by adopting new institutional guidelines *(cadres organiques)* and revising the compensation policy applicable to government employees.

The voluntary departures were partially (60 percent) accomplished, but not really under the conditions that had been envisioned initially. Some civil servants who chose to leave came from the priority sectors of education and health. The results of the program for the reinsertion of those leaving (through the creation of businesses) were disappointing and contributed to an increase in the banking system's dubious loans.

The civil service's institutional guidelines were called into question in 1991 by labor unions that had not been involved in their definition, and the new project did not become operational, since it would have involved an increase in the number of civil servants. In 1994 a new civil service statute was adopted, under which salaries are to be based more on merit and less on seniority.

The devaluation of the CFA franc in 1994, which was followed by an increase of only 10 percent in salaries and a resumption in promotions (increasing the total wage bill by 18 percent), contributed greatly to a reduction in civil servants' remuneration in real terms.

Since 1991, the proportion of expenditures devoted to education, health, and infrastructure maintenance has gradually increased. In education, however, a considerable share of funds was absorbed by secondary and higher education (especially student scholarships), and this led to the cancellation in April 1993 of the last two tranches of the World Bank credit for education. The World Bank's new educational adjust-

TABLE 5.1 MALI: BUDGETARY CONVERGENCE CRITERIA
(percent of tax revenues)

	1995	1996	1997	1998	1998 norms
Salaries and compensation	36.5	28.9	28.9	27.0	40.0 max
Internally financed capital expenditures	14.1	14.1	16.3	20.4	20.0 min
Base cash balance	31.6	40.1	25.7	28.2	15.0 min
Variation in internal arrears (billions of CFAF)	−14.0	−19.0	−8.4	−4.0	0.0
Variation in external arrears (billions of CFAF)	0.0	0.0	0.0	0.0	0.0

ment (approved in 1995) includes a substantial program for the development of primary education and for the streamlining of secondary and higher education.

Taken as a whole, all of these interventions, in terms of both receipts and expenditures, resulted in a widely fluctuating budget deficit. In terms of the percentage of GDP, the overall deficit (that is, the government's net financing requirement) experienced, from the beginning of the adjustment period, three years of sharp increase (1985, 1991, 1994) followed by an effort at reduction. Although it reached 18.2 percent of GDP in 1983, it was brought back down in 1996–97 to less than 8 percent of GDP.

Since 1996, Mali's budgetary policy has been subject to multilateral monitoring by WAEMU, whose council of ministers establishes its guidelines. As can be seen from table 5.1, Mali has adhered to all of the budgetary convergence criteria since 1998.

Reform of Foreign Trade

In 1988, Mali reestablished a relationship with the Bretton Woods institutions and embarked upon a vast reform program, one of the most important components of which was the reform of foreign trade. From independence to 1988, foreign trade had been essentially controlled by the government, with a rigid system of quotas and prohibitions. State enterprises had by that time revealed their shortcomings in production, imports, exports, and distribution.

The reform was implemented in three stages.

From 1988 to 1989

All export products received automatic authorization, which had not been the case previously. All import products received automatic authorization, except for sugar, flour, tea, oil, soap, rice, and pharmaceutical products.

From the institutional standpoint, the "one window" approach to international trade was established to facilitate foreign trade procedures.

From 1990 to 1991

Foreign trade documentation was modified. Instead of the import or export certificate, a declaration of "intent to import or export" was established, thus casting off the constraints of foreign trade operations and introducing a simple statistical registration that is more flexible.

The requirement for the stamp of approval of the Foreign Exchange Office was abolished. The Société Générale de Surveillance (SGS) was asked to become involved at the stage where merchandise is loaded. The SGS determines the quantity, quality, and customs value of all merchandise valued at over 3 million CFAF.

At the same time, the following tariff measures went into effect at customs:

- Elimination of the export tax, including the service charge *(contribution pour prestation de service*, CPS).
- Elimination of all administrative prices and price schedules on imports and exports, with the exception of administrative prices for petroleum products.
- Elimination of the tax imposed by the Price Stabilization and Regulation Office (Office de Stabilisation et de Régulation des Prix, OSRP) and its incorporation into the fiscal import tax *(droit fiscal d'importation*, DFI).
- Elimination of the mining fund tax *(taxe fonds minier)* and of the petrostock tax *(taxe petrostock)*.
- Merging of the fuel import tax *(taxe d'importation sur le carburant*, TIC) and the special tax on certain products *(impôt spécial sur certains produits*, ISCP).
- Revision of DFI rates so as to reduce the number of rates to three (0 percent for exempted products, 10 percent for special products, and 25 percent for all other products).
- Revision of the ISCP (or excise tax), which was thenceforth applied to cola nuts, alcoholic beverages, tobacco, cigarettes, vehicles, salt, photographic film, and petroleum products.
- Introduction of a special tax on certain products *(taxe de protection dégressive*, TDP), set at a minimum rate of 40 percent and intended to decrease by 10 percent annually, in such a way as to drop to 0 percent after four years. This was applied to the following products: flour, palm oil, household soap, plastic bags, bottles, flasks,

handicrafts, khaki fabric, printed fabrics, packaging materials, galvanized metal tubs and pails, household items, electronic batter-
ies, pasta, cookies, plaster and matches.

■ Introduction of the flexible import tax (*taxe conjoncturelle
d'importation*), the application of which was limited to rice and sugar.

Since 1992

The final step in the reform of foreign trade was supposed to result in
the abolition of the requirement for declarations of intent to import or
export, and its replacement with simple customs declarations. This measure could not be implemented due to reluctance on the part of the Economic Affairs Directorate to relinquish its prerogative to demand a
declaration of intent.

Customs tariffs were further simplified, to the extent that, by 1998,
import tariff regulations distinguished only three categories of goods
and three types of levy (customs, import tax, and the *contribution pour
prestation de service* or CPS), as shown in table 5.2.

The tariff had to be changed and simplified as of January 1, 2000 in
the context of the WAEMU treaty.

The Cereals Market Restructuring Program (PRMC)

The Situation before the PRMC

With regard to cereals, as in other economic sectors, marketing was still
tightly controlled by the government in the early 1980s. Indeed, the Mali
Agricultural Products Office (Office de Commercialisation des Produits
Agricoles du Mali, OPAM), created in 1965, held the monopoly over
cereals purchases from producer groups and over the sale of these cereals in urban areas and in rural areas experiencing shortfalls. In addition,

TABLE 5.2 MALI: TARIFF STRUCTURE BY RATE CATEGORIES IN 1998
(percent)

	Customs	Import tax	CPS	Total fees
Category 1: critical products[a]	0	0	5	5
Category 2: inter-mediate products and equipment	5	10	5	25
Category 3: other products	5	25	5	35

a. Since August 1997, raw materials, intermediate products, and spare parts intended for
industrial use have been taxed as critical products (category 1).
Source: Data supplied by the Customs Directorate (table reprinted from Chambas and
others 1999).

the Société de Crédit Agricole et d'Equipement Rural (SCAER) had a monopoly on the marketing of agricultural inputs. Producer prices were at the same time controlled by the Price Stabilization and Regulation Office (OSRP), which used a fixed-rate estimate of the costs of transporting, warehousing, and marketing cereals to determine a cost price and then consumer prices, which could be subsidized. It was the same with the price of agricultural inputs.

In reality, OPAM never succeeded in completely controlling the market (Lecaillon and Morrisson 1986). It seems to have handled half of it, at best. Since the towns and the deficit-suffering zones of northern Mali were imperfectly supplied, a private trade in cereals—initially prohibited and then tolerated—sprang up. Farmers participated all the more willingly in this trade as the official producer prices were set at an abnormally low level.

This policy led to an impasse. On the one hand, it had created a considerable deficit in the public and semipublic sectors, and on the other hand, production growth lagged behind that of demand. Thus, the policy contributed at the same time to a deterioration of public finances and in the balance of payments.

This is precisely the diagnostic arrived at by the National Seminar of 1980, which was convened to consider a restructuring of OPAM and the cereals market. Its recommendations were therefore geared to the need to liberalize the cereals market, reorganize OPAM, and change pricing policy. In order to facilitate the implementation of these recommendations, donors agreed to contribute 250,000 tons of cereals (maize equivalent) over five years. These cereals were to be sold by OPAM and the proceeds used to create a Joint Counterpart Fund (Fonds Commun de Contrepartie).

Objectives and Phases of the PRMC

The PRMC went through five phases, each of which was first validated by a national seminar. A joint platform was then developed and became the PRMC's frame of reference.

᠎ PHASE I: 1981–87. In March 1982, a law "setting the rules for the cereals trade" provided a basis for liberalizing this sphere of activity. OPAM's monopoly was thus abolished. Any merchant meeting the criteria of the Commercial Code was free to buy and sell cereals. From 1986 onward, such individuals were free to import cereals (with the exception of rice). OPAM's mandate from that time on was to regulate the market by creating buffer stocks. It entered into purchase contracts with producer groups (at a price that constituted a floor for them) and resold cereals when their selling price reached a ceiling set by the authorities. OPAM's operating expenses were to be maintained for five years at their 1981 level.

The new price policy provided for a gradual increase in producer prices over five years. The purpose of this increase was to encourage production (with a view to food self-sufficiency) and to avoid clandestine exports by bringing prices closer to those prevailing in neighboring countries. The rise in producer prices implied a parallel increase in consumer prices. Because of the political risks, this rise was gradual and the merging of official and black market was also gradual.

PHASES II TO IV: 1988–97. Phase II began in May 1988 with the liberalization of prices for millet, sorghum, maize, and rice, except for rice from zones where rice is grown on perimeters. Rice prices were freed up in the entire country in December 1989.[6] These decisions had been preceded in 1987 by the elimination of all consumer subsidies.

The next phases of the PRMC essentially dealt with reforming OPAM. In accordance with performance contracts signed in 1988, 1990, and 1994, OPAM stopped subsidizing producer prices. Its role was limited to creating buffer stocks (the volume of which was reduced), managing food aid, and providing cereals to areas experiencing shortfalls. OPAM underwent a considerable restructuring. It reduced its staff from 718 to 204, changed its salary policy so as to boost productivity, and strengthened its financial management.

Thanks to the PRMC and the favorable weather conditions of the preceding years, Mali became nearly self-sufficient and food aid was substantially cut back. Mali's cereals deficit zones were supplied mainly out of the country's own production.

PHASE V: 1997–99. OPAM was by this time less and less dependent upon external aid. The government now finances a growing proportion of its operating costs out of its own budgetary resources, and in 2001 all external financing of OPAM should cease.

Phase V had two main objectives. The first was to recognize and deal with emergency situations by establishing a system of enhanced food security (*sécurité alimentaire renforcée*, SAR). More specifically, the idea was to improve the efficiency of the existing system and to create new instruments for preventing major crises (e.g., a monitoring unit and emergency intervention plan).

A second objective was to reduce food security risks over the medium term by improving the conditions in which cereals markets operate. More specifically, the goals were to improve the information system, set up structures for directing production streams, develop new tools suited to a liberalized environment, develop a policy regarding product quality, and, finally, facilitate access to financing for professional operators.

The restructuring of the market, now well underway, should open a modernization phase characterized by greater professionalism on the

TABLE 5.3 RESOURCES FOR MALI'S CEREALS MARKET
RESTRUCTURING PROGRAM, BY PHASE

	Phase I (6 years)	Phase II (3 years)	Phase III (3 years)	Phase IV (3 years)	Phase V (3 years)
External resources	15,377	8,253	5,596	—	3,710
Malian government budget	0	0	0	—	2,810
Total	15,377	8,253	5,596	—	6,520
Annual average	2,563	2,571	1,899	—	2,173

— Not available.
Sources: For phases I, II, and III, Coelos 1994; for phase V, Deme 1999: 36.

part of operators and an improvement in the quality of products and services.

External Support for the PRMC

It is noteworthy that, during the implementation of these different phases, donors have provided the Malian government with substantial resources with which to carry out the reform. Table 5.3 shows the levels of these resources by phase.

During the first three phases, the proportion of resources obtained from the sale of food aid dropped considerably, falling from 87 percent in the first phase to 45 percent in the third phase. Resources corresponding to monetary substitutions for food aid or to direct donor contributions have evolved in the opposite direction: their relative weight went from 13 percent to 55 percent between the first and third phases (Coelos 1994).

The PRMC and the Reform Process

The PRMC has been a key tool in the liberalization of the cereals market. Its success in this area is essentially the result of:

- The commitment of certain Malian authorities to this reform;
- The determination of certain donors to see the reform succeed; and
- The fact that the structural adjustment program (SAP) included among its conditionalities certain measures stipulated in the various joint donor/government platforms.

The PRMC acted as a catalyst in the cereals sector, since it helped the Malian government to implement the SAP measures. This accelerated the liberalization of the cereals market within the larger context of the overall economic liberalization accomplished by means of the IMF's and World Bank's preconditions.

The PRMC also mitigated social tensions over the 1985–88 period. It helped increase producer prices, stimulating production and maintaining consumer prices at reasonable levels.

Reorganization of the Cotton Sector

After having been in the hands of the Compagnie Française des Textiles (CFDT), the development of cotton growing has since 1975 been entrusted to a mixed enterprise (40 percent CFDT, 60 percent Malian government). Its mandate was very broadly defined as the processing of seed cotton into cotton fiber, as well as rural development (and not only cotton development) in its zone of intervention, Mali Sud. From the outset, the Malian Textile Development Company (CMDT) has performed important public service functions such as extension, credit, and transportation, but its performance has been closely associated with that of other organizations involved in this production stream, including SOMIEX, which handles cotton fiber exports, and OSRP, which is responsible for stabilizing the government-determined price paid to producers. This latter entity collected cotton revenues and paid the CMDT and SOMIEX on a fixed-rate basis. Neither of these companies was concerned with the equilibrium of the cotton sector, nor did they have any incentive to reduce costs and increase productivity.

Since cotton represents 50 percent of Mali's exports and is the livelihood of more than 20 percent of the population (Laporte and Monier 1994), the abrupt drop in international cotton prices in 1985 radically modified Mali's economic and financial prospects by causing a large operating deficit in the production stream, which was partially covered by tax exemptions that contributed to reduced budgetary inflows. The cumulative deficits of the 1985–86 and 1987–88 cropping seasons amounted to more than 2 billion CFAF. The seriousness of the crisis forced the Malian authorities to undertake an in-depth reorganization of the production stream to increase its productivity, a move that was all the more crucial because Mali's membership in WAMU made it impossible to use the devaluation to increase productivity by means of a relative price movement.

In 1986, and not only because of the problems with cotton described above, SOMIEX's monopoly was abolished and the CMDT took over cotton fiber exports. Reorganization of the production stream was the subject of the "Sélingué seminar" that gathered together Malian authorities and donors whose proposals were accepted by the government in November 1988. This made it possible, after various preparatory studies, for the government and CMDT to sign their first performance contract in 1989, and a second in 1994.

In order to increase the production stream's productivity, the performance contract stipulated that the CMDT must become an autonomous enterprise assuming financial responsibility for its industrial and commercial activities. Therefore, the CMDT from that time on collected the proceeds from cotton sales and was no longer subject to any export tax. However, the mechanism for setting producer prices and sharing profits (see below) stipulated that CMDT's fees must be capped and that overruns must be debited from profits, while reduced costs were to be a gain for CMDT. On the other hand, CMDT was only obligated to perform tasks related to rural development to the extent that the government provided the corresponding funds. These public service tasks were clearly spelled out in an appendix to the performance contract.

From both the social and economic standpoints, it also seemed desirable for cotton producers to benefit from a purchase price that was profitable (and in keeping with the international price), as well as stable. For this reason, a system of price stabilization was created according to the following principles:

- A minimum producer purchase price was defined.
- To this minimum price, CMDT's stabilized operating expenses were added, along with a portion of amortizations, to arrive at an equilibrium price of cotton fiber for export.
- Profits resulting from an export price above the equilibrium price as defined above were then to be divided four ways, according to a rule established in advance, among the stabilization fund, the producers' rebate, CMDT, and the government.
- If the export selling price was below the equilibrium price, the stabilization fund covered CMDT's minimum expenses. In the event that the fund experienced a lasting shortfall, the plan was to lower the floor price paid to producers (a situation that occurred in 2000).

It should be noted that institutional reform in this production stream has certainly been facilitated by the important donor-financed development project (Mali Sud III) in the main cotton growing area. This project's economic objectives are ambitious and the financial stakes are high (24 billion CFAF, of which 16 billion in foreign aid from France, the World Bank, and the Netherlands). The aim is primarily to promote the diversification of agricultural production and natural resource management, while at the same time preserving land capital for the future, providing training and support to village associations, and, finally, developing new types of management advisory services and methods of disseminating agricultural techniques.

The combination of the cotton sector reform and the development of the Mali Sud project was deemed satisfactory by a World Bank assessment in June 1998.

Other Areas of Public Sector Reform: Varying Degrees of Success

In addition to the three main sectors of reform that have been described, a brief account is given below of three other areas involving the public sector, where progress has been uneven: the reform of the numerous offices created in the past, privatizations, and the reform of judicial institutions.

Reform of Public Offices

Under the socialist policy pursued in the 1960s and 1970s, numerous public offices had been created to manage the various sectors of economic activity. The offices that were performing inefficiently were generally unprofitable. One of the essential policy elements was then to reform them or abolish them. Much has been done in this regard in various ways.

First, the reform of the Rural Development Agencies (Opérations de Développement Rural, ODR) has led to a substantial reduction in their share of the state budget (World Bank 1998b). OTER (Rural Equipment Works Operation) was privatized and became profitable. ODIPAC (Grain and Groundnut Integrated Development Agency) and ODIK (Kaarta Integrated Rural Development Agency) have been abolished. ORS (Segou Rice Agency) has been restructured (unprofitable activities discontinued, action limited to training activities financed from water fees), as has OPSS (Improved Seed Development Agency), so that seeds are no longer produced by the office but by farmers under contract, also with cost recovery. Finally, OHVN (Upper Niger Valley Rural Development Agency) has also been reorganized and has increased its productivity. It should be noted that the cost of these restructurings and in particular the compensation paid to staff who were dismissed was largely financed from various sources of aid.

A more important, older, and in a way symbolic department is the Office du Niger, created in 1932. It also underwent considerable restructuring in the mid-1980s, and some of its activities were transferred to the private sector. Finally, in 1995, a performance contract between the state, the Office du Niger, and the producers confirmed the liberalization of the sector covered by the office. It is now responsible for conducting public service missions (maintenance of secondary roads and advice on rural matters) and for supplying one service—water, for which users pay the actual cost. There has been new private involvement upstream and downstream of rice production, which increased considerably during 1984–90, as soon as the reform was initiated (with a smaller increase during the first half of the 1990s because of the sharp decline in the price of rice).

The reform of the Office du Niger was financed with the help of the principal donors in Mali.

Privatization

As a legacy of the socialist experiment, Mali had a number of public enterprises, including some in the productive sector. Here too, the inefficiency and shortcomings of these enterprises required disengagement by the state, which proved to be more difficult than for the Rural Development Agencies. It was perhaps more difficult to restructure these enterprises, to compensate the staff who were dismissed, and to find buyers on terms acceptable to the Malian authorities.

In any case, the privatization of the Mali Electricity Company (EDM) was not accepted until a major crisis affected electricity supply (see below). The privatization of SOTECMA (the telecommunications company) was postponed, and in the case of SONATEM (National Tobacco and Match Company), which had been seriously mismanaged in the past, foreign capital participation amounting to only 49 percent is currently envisaged. Difficulties remain for the Hôtel de l'Amitié and—more important—for BMCD (Mali Bank for Credits and Deposits).

Restructuring of Public Spending and Promotion of Education

One area that is essential for the long-term development of Mali—education—is still lagging behind. The main aim of the government's long-term (10-year) development strategy for education, called PRODEC, is to achieve a considerable improvement in primary enrollment rates, particularly by increasing the share of the budget allocated to education (26 percent in 2000, compared with 23 percent in 1997). However, disagreements within the government have delayed the implementation of this plan, to which various sources of external financing are ready to provide assistance.

Reform of Judicial Institutions

In this domain, where much remains to be done, external assistance seems to have had some effect: first in the case of PRED, the Economic Reform and Development Program, financed by the U.S. Agency for International Development (USAID) in 1991; second, through French technical assistance within the framework of the Organization for the Harmonization of Business Law in Africa (OHADA); and finally, as a recent conditionality for adjustment assistance (that is, the 1996 ESAF).

As far as the judiciary is concerned, the aim of PRED was to make the investment environment healthier and more stable by creating commercial and administrative courts and studying the advisability of establishing an arbitral tribunal to settle disputes in a manner appropriate to the culture of Mali. During 1994, therefore, PRED assisted the government in the following activities:

- A decree concerning the election and eligibility of members of commercial courts. Following this decree, the overall intellectual level of the judges improved, and the function was opened to categories of persons who previously were excluded, such as haulage contractors, bankers, industrialists, insurers, and brokers. This made it possible to have more specialized commercial courts.
- Adoption of requirements for proper functioning of the courts. To deter any behavior that might impede the correct functioning of the courts, the National Assembly adopted a disciplinary system similar to that applicable to presiding judges. Reference is made to the obligation of due diligence, in order to guarantee speedy consideration of cases.
- Equipment of the commercial courts, administrative courts, and Supreme Court. Typewriters and photocopiers have already been delivered. Computers have been provided to the Supreme Court and the software will be provided for legal databases.
- Adoption of a new Code of Civil, Commercial, and Social Procedure. The code in force dated from August 18, 1961. It was out of date and had many gaps. To facilitate access to the courts by litigants, the principles governing deposits were reviewed thoroughly. The plaintiff is now no longer required to deposit 7 percent of the amount of his claim. In order for his pleas to be receivable, he will simply have to pay a lump sum ranging from 5,000 to 25,000 CFA francs, depending on the amount of the claim. The amount of the deposit was reduced to 3 percent.
- Creation of administrative courts at Kayes, Bamako, and Mopti.
- Ratification of the New York and Washington Conventions so as to attract investment (the former relates to the recognition and enforcement of foreign arbitral awards and the latter relates to the settlement of investment disputes).

It is noteworthy that USAID gave substantial financial assistance to the government through this project.

Five years later, despite the establishment of OHADA, private observers have found that the judiciary is not yet functioning properly. This is why the ESAF is again including it in its program for 1998–99, with the aim of creating commercial courts, effectively applying the OHADA arrangements, expanding the training and inspection of judges, developing a code of ethics for judges to be applied as of 1999, and trying strictly to apply the sanctions against judges who violate the code.

This text, which corroborates the information obtained in Mali, indicates how much remains to be done if the judiciary is to function properly. Indeed, this is the aim of the ten-year program (PRODEJ) being implemented in this area, where it is still too soon to assess the effectiveness of the reform.

WHEN DOES AID FACILITATE REFORM?
FOUR LESSONS FROM THE EXPERIENCE OF MALI

The preceding analysis of aid and reform trends shows that the relationship between them is not simple. Aid and reform have undergone fluctuations that are apparently simultaneous but that do not indicate a one-way causality: aid may either spur reform or respond to reform. Even when donors cannot spur reform, they want to be able to demonstrate the effectiveness of their aid in this area. In Cocteau's famous words: "The scope of these mysteries is beyond us; let us pretend that we organized them." Donors may also quite simply want to reward reformers and perhaps thus encourage other countries to follow suit.

However, the experience of Mali does seem to show a real influence of aid on reform, but with both successes and failures. It appears that aid plays an important but not always decisive role. Its decisiveness depends on whether the political authorities and the local administration "own" the reforms. And the factors conducive to this ownership are precisely the factors that ensure the effectiveness of aid for reform.

Four conclusions, based on Mali's experience, can be drawn from this general principle:

- Aid is more likely to facilitate reform if a critical situation has revealed the need for it.
- Aid is more likely to lead to reform if the stakeholders are aware of its usefulness or if there is scope for mediation between opposing interests.
- Aid is more likely to facilitate reform if there is no disagreement between the various donors on the details of the reform.
- Aid is more likely to facilitate reform if it considerably reduces the costs incurred.

"Back to the Wall": Reform Facilitated by Aid in a Crisis

The first lesson suggested by the Malian experience is that aid is more likely to facilitate reform if the economy as a whole or the sector concerned is in a critical situation. In a crisis, the donors' advice is more easily heard and the drawbacks of not reforming are more obvious. The crisis, whatever its costs, convinces all groups concerned of the need for reform and facilitates ownership of it. Several examples from Mali may illustrate this point.

Unpopularity of Domestic Arrears

It has been seen above that an important aspect of reform concerned the reform of public finances and particularly reduction of the budget deficit. This deficit reduction has been achieved gradually, largely through a payroll decrease resulting from downsizing and a decrease in real civil service wages. Paradoxically, the commitment of the Malian authorities to take the measures that resulted in this improvement was facilitated by the serious consequences of the state's financial difficulties and in particular the arrears in domestic payments, including a large backlog of wages. On three occasions, domestic public arrears were reduced under a program financed by assistance: from 1983 to 1986, from 1988 to 1991, and again after 1994. In 1988, the backlog of civil service wages ranged from three to eight months, depending on the sectors and geographical areas. The trade union grouping itself was then in favor of reform: better to be sure of receiving reduced wages than to face uncertainty in the payment of nominally unaltered wages!

Effect of International Prices

A second example is the impact of the decline in the international price of the principal export, cotton. In 1985–86 and again in 1991–92, the international price of cotton dropped sharply. Because of its repercussions on the whole sector, this decline created a need for widespread restructuring: in 1986, responsibility for cotton exports was taken away from SOMIEX and given to CMDT, and in 1989 a new performance contract defined the obligations of CMDT and created a new stabilization machinery. These reforms in turn made it possible to increase and stabilize the real price paid to the producer and achieve a sizable increase in production.

Energy Shortage and Privatization

The reform of the public enterprise responsible for the distribution of water and electricity has for the last 20 years been the subject of lengthy discussions between donors and the Malian authorities. The situation of the Société d'Energie du Mali (EDM) is characterized by recurring difficulties in balancing electricity supply and demand, resulting in frequent power cuts during the dry season and serious financial difficulties.

The Malian authorities were strongly opposed to privatization, and in 1995 they agreed to the idea of a "global management delegation" entrusted to an international consortium (composed of SAOM International, Electricité de France, and Hydro Quebec International, and financed by the World Bank, the Canadian International Development Agency, and Agence Française de Développement). However, since they did not really own the decision, the Malian authorities found themselves in ongoing disagreement with the management delegation. This undermined the delegation's actions and then led Mali to denounce the agreement at the beginning of 1998.

In April 1998, the Malian government and the donors agreed on the need to privatize the enterprise and on ways of preventing the financial situation from deteriorating too seriously, with reallocation of certain external funding. However, it seems that the steps toward privatization were taken reluctantly by Mali. It was only in February 1999 that a commercial bank was recruited for this purpose.

In the spring of 1999, however, the electricity shortage reached unprecedented proportions, with extended power cuts during the driest season. This had dramatic consequences for many small businesses, as well as for people's living conditions. This acute shortage was attributable to poor maintenance of the power stations and to the questionable choice of a combustion turbine with delays that obliged EDM to empty the Sélingué dam completely in May. In addition, on April 27 the control panel at one of the two power stations caught fire, probably because of poor maintenance.

In the face of this critical situation, there was a change in the Malian government's willingness to undertake a radical reform and in the willingness of the population to accept one. In October 1999, at a meeting with all the donors (including IMF), Mali established a definite timetable for privatization. At the same time, it accepted technical assistance for the interim management and received aid for the purchase of a new power station, so that electricity supply could be restored and privatization would not be jeopardized by the lack of a buyer. But in this case it was definitely the crisis that enabled aid to spearhead reform.

Decline of State Structures and Liberalization of the Cereals Market

Other examples could be given to illustrate this point. In particular, the restructuring of the cereals market was easier to implement in 1981 because farmers were no longer selling to OPAM, which was supposed to have a monopoly, while cereals production was increasing. Earlier the drought in the 1970s and its dramatic consequences had also illustrated the need for far-reaching reform in this sector. The people involved at the time admit that it is not clear whether it was the Malian leaders or their partners who had the idea of the reform which would gradually free prices. In any case, the time was ripe.

Consensus or Mediation:
Reform Facilitated by Aid When Interests Can Be Reconciled

Whatever aid is provided, internal political factors are crucial if the reform is to be effective. Economic policy advice is more likely to be well received if the proposed reforms appear not to disfavor a large segment of the population. Mali's success story, the Cereals Market Restructuring Program, also illustrates this concept: each stage of the reform was validated by a "national platform" at which producers and consumers expressed their views. However, it is not always so easy to reconcile interests and a different approach was adopted depending on whether the prevailing regime was authoritarian or democratic.

Two Opposing Examples:
Liberalization of Foreign Trade and Privatizations

Two opposing examples may be used to illustrate this point: the reform of foreign trade and privatizations. It is noteworthy that in these two areas reform ran counter to the country's initial policy choices favoring a dominant role for the state in the economy. Despite this ideological reluctance, liberalization proved to be much easier than privatization. This is precisely because there were fewer interests opposed to liberalization than to privatization.

During the period 1988–93, the trade liberalization measures were welcomed not only by the government but also by the technical departments responsible for implementing them (in particular the National Directorate of Economic Affairs, DNAE), by the economic operators, enterprises, and traders, and by consumers, who immediately understood that they would benefit. In this way, for example, the monopoly of SOMIEX, which was losing one billion CFA francs a year, was finally brought to an end. All the stakeholders were convinced that the liberalization of distribution would benefit the state, traders, and consumers, even if the company's employees would suffer.

Even in this area, however, some doubts were expressed and resulted in backtracking. This was so, for example, in the case of SOMIEX, as well as with the abolition of the export tax which was a conditionality for the USAID-funded PRED. This tax, which was abolished in 1990 so that the scheduled aid could be disbursed, was restored and then abolished again in 1997 under pressure from USAID.

The large-scale privatization program desired by donors generally encountered obstacles of two types (in addition to ideological resistance). One was connected with the vested interests of the employees of the enterprises to be privatized. The other had to do with the multiplicity of government departments involved.

When the privatization or liquidation of a public enterprise is announced and it is not possible to compensate the workers rapidly, there is a risk of collusion between managers and workers in the enterprise to aggravate the situation of the enterprise and make its privatization more difficult. The disparity in the compensation offered to workers in public enterprises (ranging from 12 to 36 months' wages) was a source of frustration and led certain dismissed workers to sue the government (in 1995, the government had been required by the courts to pay 24 billion CFA francs).

While DNAE was the only technical body responsible for trade liberalization, the office of public enterprises responsible for privatizations is obliged to consult the technical departments of the Ministry of Agriculture, the Ministry of Industry, or the Ministry of Tourism, depending on the sector corresponding to the enterprise to be privatized. In addition, whereas trade liberalization involves only a decision by the government, privatization requires the approval of the National Assembly. This naturally slows down the process, but makes it more difficult to reverse.

There are, however, two cases in which the restructuring of public enterprises succeeded (the Office du Niger and the Office of Hydrocarbons), thanks to the availability of effective technical assistance and the necessary funding.

Reconciliation of Interests under an Authoritarian Regime and under a Democratic Regime

The role of aid in overcoming opposition to reform, whether motivated by vested interests or by principle, differed depending on whether the regime was authoritarian or democratic—in other words, before or after 1991.

When power was essentially concentrated in the hands of the head of state, it was he who mediated between his proreform ministers (generally the ministers of finance and planning), who were more frequently in contact with the Bretton Woods institutions, and the more conservative ministers, who were often in charge of sectoral departments. In this case, the input from outside in some sense bolstered the proreform position, both because it provided arguments in favor and because of the financial benefits of reform.

According to the people who were responsible for the initial reforms, in the 1980s, it seems that many reforms were suggested by the Bretton Woods institutions (for example, introduction of VAT, abolition of Air Mali, increased flexibility in labor law) and that the proreform ministers advocating these ideas were supported intellectually by the donors, although within the party these ministers were accused of being their "yes men."

In this political context, the financial benefit of reform often tipped the scales in its favor at the level of the head of state. This was the case when meat prices were to be decontrolled, against the advice of the minister of animal husbandry (in 1988), and also when the monopoly of SOMIEX, after having been suspended following the president's meeting with the SOMIEX workers in August 1986, was reinstated by the same president the very next month. This was the context in which an IMF negotiator told the minister of finance: "Your country has introduced a number of reforms, but it is one of the countries least supportive of reform."

Starting in 1991, democratization somewhat modified the influence of vested interests on the role of aid in the promotion of reform. Democratization must naturally promote the ownership and internalization of reforms. At the same time, however, the experience of Mali has shown that it slows down this process when certain interests involved are irreconcilable and there is not sufficient mediation capacity at the government level. Two examples can be given of this risk of aid blockage and ineffectiveness.

The first example, which is especially important in view of the low educational level in Mali, is the Program for the Development of Education (PRODEC). After having been negotiated at length by all donors and Malian stakeholders, and although substantial financing had already been mobilized, this program was blocked because of a dispute between the two ministers responsible for education.

Another example, less far-reaching but highly symbolic, was the "pink market"—the central market of Bamako. After having burned, this market was faithfully reconstructed using a donation from France (AFD). More than a year after completion of the reconstruction, it remains unoccupied because of the lack of a policy decision on the method of assigning spaces to traders, who cannot all be accommodated, and lack of a policy of space management. In the meantime, traders and their customers are crowded in unhygienic conditions around the empty space reserved for the market.

The "pink market syndrome" is emblematic of a more general difficulty, noted by several observers, resulting from the slow pace of decisionmaking, even in areas that are crucial for the development of Mali's economy. While the social benefits of consensus have been fully understood, the same cannot be said of the social cost of delays and failure to take decisions. In this context, aid seems to be effective in promoting reform only if it is combined with local capacity to mediate between conflicting interests.

Donor Attitudes: Reform Facilitated by Aid When the Sources of Aid Are Permanently Involved and Coordinated

The third factor determining the contribution of aid to reform is the actual attitude of the donors. Here there appear to be two essential elements. One is the donors' ability to become involved themselves and to involve their Malian counterparts in the reform. The other is their ability to coordinate their advice.

It is in the social sector that the need for projects to be prepared in close collaboration with the Malians is most acute. One example is a health, population, and rural water project in the Kayes region financed by the World Bank in 1985 (Kayes-Bafoulabe-Kenieba project). The goal was to improve access to drinking water by drilling wells and opening health centers, applying the principle of "cost recovery." The project failed because it was not supported by the people. The financed infrastructures rapidly deteriorated and the centers closed.

A second example may be taken from the customs sector. Because of the importance of this category of revenue for the Malian government, donors have tried constantly to improve the collection of customs duties. In 1994 the European Union financed technical assistance to the customs offices, but the results were not up to expectations. On the other hand, in 1995 the Canadian International Development Agency launched a Program for the Improvement of Customs Revenue in close cooperation with the Ministry of Finance. At the request of the customs administration, arrangements were made to improve the working conditions of the relevant staff, particularly by constructing suitably equipped customs offices across the country and by motivating and training customs officers. Partly as a result of this program, revenue increased from 5–6 billion CFA francs a month in 1995 to 11–12 billion a month in 1999.

Another example of the weak effect of aid on reform is provided by the courts. Their reform is one component of the PRED initiative financed by USAID from 1992 to 1997. Apparently the project originated when a Malian lawyer contacted the American aid agency. It was a far-reaching project, since it comprised both reform of laws and regulations and investment in the equipment of the courts (with funding amounting to US$7 million) and seemed to be sound. However, it was designed without the initial participation of the Malian side and implemented by a private U.S. firm that does not seem to have worked sufficiently directly for the Malian government. The functioning of the commercial and administrative courts apparently still leaves much to be desired, because of the reluctance of the private operators to criticize their peers.

Once again, a different example is provided by PRMC, since its success in cereals market restructuring is also due to the continuing support of external financing sources and to the ongoing presence of a technical assistant who was totally involved in the program.

Another efficiency factor to be considered is the coherence of the advice given by the various aid sources. When there are differing points of view, these may be echoed within the administration, resulting in postponement of the reform. It is sometimes claimed that disagreement among donors gives recipient countries more freedom. In fact, however, it delays financing and reform. Two examples illustrate this risk.

The first concerns the program for the improvement of the road infrastructure, an effort that is essential in order to make Mali more accessible and one to which several of the main sources of financing (European Union and World Bank) are prepared to give considerable support. The sticking point is the creation of a road fund to be financed from specific revenues and used to guarantee proper road maintenance. The World Bank and the European Union favor the creation of such a fund; but IMF, which for several years has been persuading the Ministry of Finance of the benefits of a single cashier at the level of the state, is opposed, fearing that the fund would set a precedent for other sectors (such as mines).

Another example of disagreement relates to the status of CMDT, the conditions in which producers may participate in the capital of the company, and, more generally, how to introduce more competition in the sector. The difference of opinion involves, on the one hand, the World Bank, and on the other, France and other European donors, especially the Netherlands. Here too, the stakes are high, since they involve the country's principal export activity, which was one of the main levers of Mali's growth, and since today CMDT seems to be in a worse financial position. Consequently, the negotiation of the new performance contract between CMDT and the government, which was to be signed in September 1999, has fallen behind schedule. This relatively recent difficulty does not detract from the fact that in the past the successful implementation and outcome of the southern Mali operation, in which CMDT played an essential role, benefited greatly from the coordination among donors (Agence Française de Développement, World Bank, Banque Ouest-Africaine de Développement, African Development Foundation, Banque Européenne d'Investissment, the Netherlands, Guinea, and Belgium).

Together with the past experience of the southern Mali project and the cotton sector, PRMC once again provides an example of good coordination of aid.

Lastly, it should be noted that, in budgetary matters, the leadership of IMF, whose support for reform reflects the goals of multilateral monitoring of public finances pursued by WAEMU, was instrumental in the reduction of the budget deficit and the restructuring of public spending.

Generally speaking, it seems useful if in a number of areas one external aid institution can play a lead role and be more particularly responsible for monitoring conditionalities. The very large number of aid sources and the sometimes excessive number of conditions laid down for disbursement considerably complicate the task of the Malian administration and mean that it has to spend an inordinate amount of time responding to donors' conditions. In addition to the 30 or 40 conditions for the structural adjustment loan, there are the conditions for the sectoral programs (as for agriculture or public enterprises) or specific programs (PRMC, PRED). Ideally, all these conditions should be monitored by the Ministry of Finance, which is responsible for mobilizing financial resources. Certain conditionalities are not respected because of lack of monitoring: the Ministry of Finance concentrates essentially on respecting the commitments given to major donors (OECD 1998).

One way of limiting the number of conditionalities is donor coordination, which has developed considerably in Mali in recent years, particularly in major sectors, for programs such as PRODEC and PRODESS (Integrated Health Sector Development Program), and through regular organized consultations.

Coverage of Costs: Reform Facilitated by Aid When Aid Covers Some of the Costs

Mali provides several examples of cases in which, by covering part of the costs of reforms, external funding has been a decisive factor in their adoption and success. For instance, food aid supported the launching of PRMC, thus avoiding a situation in which liberalization is accompanied by an excessive increase in food prices, which would have jeopardized continuation of the program.

Another particularly instructive example is the aid provided by USAID under programs of economic reform. In order to promote the development of the private sector, USAID assumed for one year the temporary shortfall resulting from the reduction (from 15 to 7 percent) of the lump-sum contribution payable by enterprises.

A similar example is the financing (by the World Bank and USAID) of the termination payments due when staff are to be reduced.

On the other hand, the restructuring of public enterprises and, consequently, privatizations have been hindered by the lack of funds to pay prompt compensation to dismissed workers.

A fifth lesson could be learned from the Malian experience. In a way, it intersects with the four others and echoes the initial principle stated at the outset: aid truly contributes to reform only if it is owned in one way or another by the leaders of recipient countries.

Indeed, the Malian experience can be quoted in support of a conditionality of performance to replace the conditionality of means that is still the rule today (on the principle of conditionality of performance, see Guillaumont and Guillaumont 1994, 1995; Collier and others 1997; Guillaumont and Chauvet 1999). The Malian authorities have shown a keen interest in this new way of thinking.

CONCLUSION: RETURN TO INITIAL ASSUMPTIONS

These lessons of the Malian experience provide some kind of response to the three questions that the Aid and Reform in Africa study set out to address.

First, did the Malian governments decide to reform their economic policies independently of the aid relationship? Clearly they did not, but the answer differs depending on whether the regime was the authoritarian one in power before 1991 or the current democratic government. For the reforms that took place before 1991 and which, as noted, were far-reaching, aid strengthened the arguments of the proreformers within the government, in the context of the financial constraints facing the government. During the democratic period, the role of external aid in the reform process changed: aid also contributed to reforms because it reduced their immediate cost to the population. In a way, democratization made the traditional conditionality less effective, since reform requires greater ownership by the political authorities.

Second, does nonfinancial aid have a greater impact than conditional financial aid on the implementation of reforms? The answer to this question depends partly on the answer to the first question. If financial aid were indeed ineffective, then nonfinancial aid would very likely be more effective. However, since we have decided that financial aid is quite effective in the preparation of reforms in Mali, the question concerns the effectiveness of nonfinancial aid *per se*. In Mali, such aid has taken two forms: traditional technical assistance and institutional arrangements.

Technical assistance undoubtedly plays an important role in Mali, in view of the administrative shortcomings in that country. During the mission, it became apparent that its effectiveness depended essentially on the quality of the staff, the ongoing nature of their presence in Mali, and the nature of their functions. Two contrasting examples have been given above (PRMC and PRED).

Institutional arrangements themselves have a considerable influence on the adoption of reforms and their irreversibility. In this connection, it is extremely important that Mali belongs to the franc zone and even more that it was a member of WAMU and is now a member of WAEMU. This was important not only for monetary policy but also for the management of public finances and the easing of foreign trade restrictions. Concerning the latter point, the creation of a regional common market offers some guarantee that reform will be lasting.

Finally, did financial aid work better when reforms of economic policy and capacity building were already underway? The answer to this question is tricky and is not clearly affirmative in the case of Mali. The far-reaching reforms implemented over the past twenty years initially collided with a strong socialist and interventionist tradition inherited from the 1960s. This is why donors often seem to have taken the initiative in reforms and to have played an important role at the beginning of the process.

Conceivably, financial aid should again become effective under the current democratic political regime and in an economy in which most restrictions have been lifted. However, as noted, if aid in this new context is to contribute effectively to reform and development, it must undoubtedly provoke a more rapid and more far-reaching mobilization of political leaders and the administration. This could result from a new type of conditionality, geared more to performance than to instruments.

APPENDIX 5.1
SUMMARY OF DATA FOR COMMENTS
ON AID CONCEPTS IN MALI

FIGURE 5.2 MALI: TOTAL NET OFFICIAL DEVELOPMENT ASSISTANCE

Millions of 1996 constant U.S. dollars

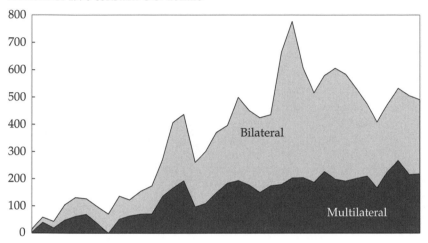

Source: OECD-DAC.

FIGURE 5.3 MALI: AID INTENSITY, 1975–97

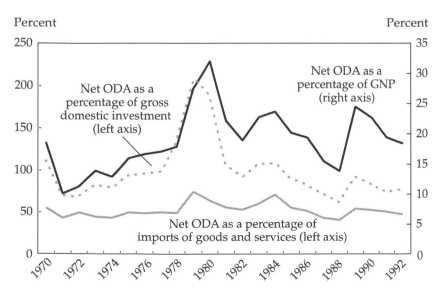

Source: World Bank, *World Development Report 1999.*

FIGURE 5.4 MALI: OFFICIAL DEVELOPMENT FINANCE
(DISBURSEMENTS), 1970–96

Millions of 1996 constant U.S. dollars

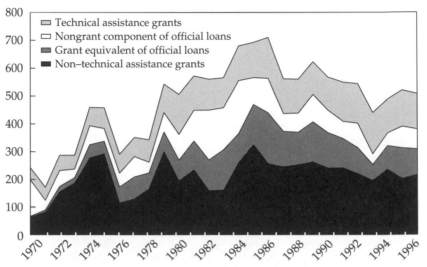

Note: Public lending includes concessional loans from the IMF (SAF and ESAF), as well
as nonconcessional loans (enhanced facility and standby agreement).
Source: Chang, Fernández-Arias, and Servén 1999.

FIGURE 5.5 MALI: COMPOSITION OF FLOWS OF ODF
(DISBURSEMENTS), 1970–96

Millions of 1996 constant U.S. dollars

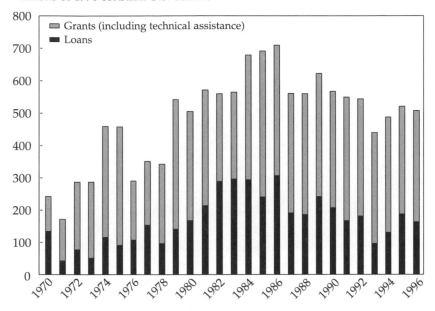

Note: Public lending includes concessional loans from the IMF (SAF and ESAF), as well as nonconcessional loans (enhanced facility and standby agreement).
Source: Chang, Fernández-Arias, and Servén 1999.

FIGURE 5.6 MALI: ODF FROM BILATERAL SOURCES
(DISBURSEMENTS), 1975–96

Millions of 1996 constant U.S. dollars

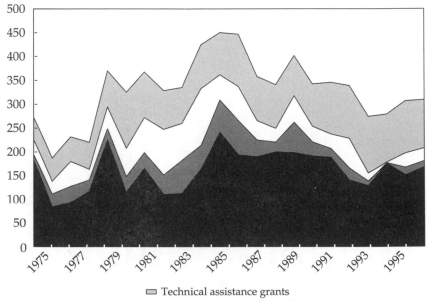

☐ Technical assistance grants
☐ Nongrant component of official loans
▨ Grant equivalent of official loans
■ Non–technical assistance grants

Source: Chang, Fernández-Arias, and Servén 1999.

FIGURE 5.7 MALI: ODF FROM MULTILATERAL SOURCES (DISBURSEMENTS), 1975–96

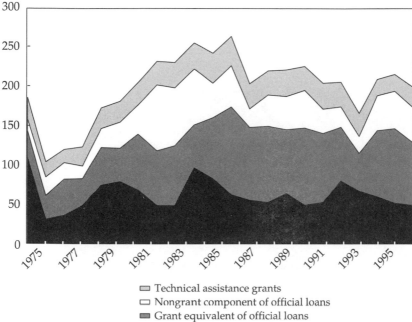

Millions of 1996 constant U.S. dollars

☐ Technical assistance grants
☐ Nongrant component of official loans
▨ Grant equivalent of official loans
■ Non–technical assistance grants

Note: Public lending includes concessional loans from the IMF (SAF and ESAF), as well as nonconcessional loans (enhanced facility and standby agreement).
Source: Chang, Fernández-Arias, and Servén 1999.

FIGURE 5.8 MALI: COMPARISON OF ODF AND TOF, 1970–96

Millions of 1996 constant U.S. dollars

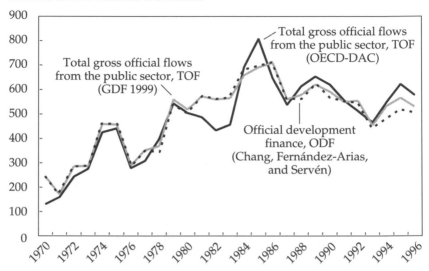

Sources: Chang, Fernández-Arias, and Servén 1999; OECD-DAC; World Bank, Global Development Finance 1999.

FIGURE 5.9 MALI: NET TRANSFERS FROM THE PUBLIC SECTOR, 1975–97

Millions of 1996 constant U.S. dollars

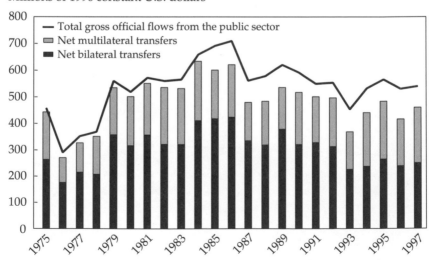

Source: World Bank, Global Development Finance 1999.

FIGURE 5.10 MALI: DEBT RATIOS, 1975–96

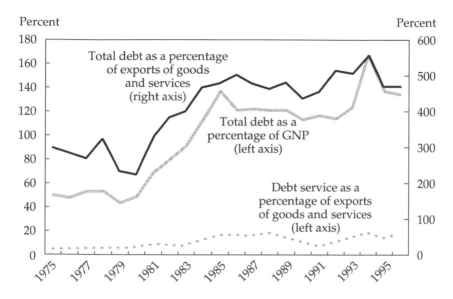

Source: World Bank, *Global Development Finance 1998.*

FIGURE 5.11 MALI: STRUCTURE OF LONG-TERM, PUBLIC, GOVERNMENT-SECURED DEBT OUTSTANDING, 1970–97

Millions of 1996 constant U.S. dollars

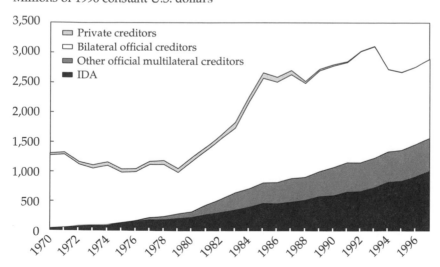

Source: World Bank, *Global Development Finance 1999.*

TABLE 5.4 MALI: NET ODA DISBURSEMENTS, 1964–97

	Annual average in millions of 1996 constant US dollars							
	1964–67	1968–71	1972–81	1982–85	1986–87	1988–90	1991–93	1994–97
Bilateral	61.5	79.7	212.7	399.1	365.7	384.5	278.5	268.9
EU members	46.6	58.5	133.6	248.6	222.2	263.5	181.8	186.2
France	42.7	46.6	74.7	158.6	101.6	134.4	98.1	81.8
North America	14.8	15.8	43.4	70.0	74.9	61.6	61.8	42.3
Japan			5.2	9.4	10.8	21.6	13.4	34.1
Arab		5.3	28.2	54.9	38.4	9.8	1.5	−9.1
Multilateral	53.4	61.4	147.2	176.5	195.3	205.3	192.4	231.4
IDA	2.9	11.4	32.2	41.7	66.5	63.1	63.3	80.3
IMF	0.0	0.0	0.0	0.0	−8.1	10.2	10.4	31.5
European Commission	53.6	33.2	62.5	43.1	40.8	48.1	64.9	62.9
ADB	−3.3		8.9	18.9	32.0	39.6	19.0	21.4
Total	114.9	141.1	359.9	575.6	561.0	589.7	470.8	500.3

	As a percentage of the total							
Bilateral	54	56	59	69	65	65	59	54
EU members	41	41	37	43	40	45	39	37
France	37	33	21	28	18	23	21	16
North America	13	11	12	12	13	10	13	8
Japan	0	0	1	2	2	4	3	7
Arab	0	4	8	10	7	2	0	−2
Multilateral	46	44	41	31	35	35	41	46
IDA	3	8	9	7	12	11	13	16
IMF	0	0	0	0	−1	2	2	6
European Commission	47	24	17	7	7	8	14	13
ADB	−3	0	2	3	6	7	4	4

Source: OECD-DAC.

TABLE 5.5 MALI: ODA COMMITMENTS BY SECTOR, 1973-97

	Annual average in millions of 1996 constant US dollars					
	1973–82	1982–85	1986–87	1988–90	1991–93	1994–97
Infrastructures and social services	40.2	111.2	43.5	93.2	81.3	140.2
Infrastructures and economic services	66.1	103.8	28.8	51.5	34.7	68.9
Production	68.7	91.6	131.8	145.7	75.8	57.4
General assistance program[a]	44.2	51.5	47.4	119.0	98.1	58.6
including IMF and IDA adjustment assistance	0.0	0.0	2.5	79.3	79.2	48.0
Debt restructuring	22.4	44.4	0.0	2.1	0.6	7.8
Emergency aid	7.8	9.7	5.2	0.3	0.6	2.0
Other[b]	17.3	31.9	37.0	36.6	52.0	42.0
Total	266.7	444.2	293.6	448.4	343.2	376.9

	As a percentage of the total					
Infrastructures and social services	15.1	25.0	14.8	20.8	23.7	37.2
Infrastructures and economic services	24.8	23.4	9.8	11.5	10.1	18.3
Production	25.7	20.6	44.9	32.5	22.1	15.2
General assistance program[a]	16.6	11.6	16.1	26.5	28.6	15.5
including IMF and IDA adjustment assistance	0.0	0.0	0.9	17.7	23.1	12.7
Debt restructuring	8.4	10.0	0.0	0.5	0.2	2.1
Emergency aid	2.9	2.2	1.8	0.1	0.2	0.5
Other[b]	6.5	7.2	12.6	8.2	15.1	11.1

a. Includes adjustment programs, food aid programs, and other balance of payments supports.
b. Includes multisectoral aid, support to NGOs, and nonallocated/nonspecific aid.
Source: OECD-DAC Creditor Notification System.

TABLE 5.6 MALI: TECHNICAL ASSISTANCE, 1962–97

	Annual average in millions of 1996 constant US dollars							
	1962–67	1968–71	1972–81	1982–85	1986–87	1988–90	1991–93	1994–97
Bilateral	21.0	30.3	60.9	84.3	101.4	88.1	112.7	106.6
Multilateral	46.0	11.2	22.2	33.1	34.3	31.3	31.0	25.5
Total	67.1	41.5	83.1	117.4	135.8	119.4	143.7	132.1
	As a percentage of the total							
Bilateral	31.4	72.9	73.3	71.8	74.7	73.8	78.4	80.7
Multilateral	68.6	27.1	26.7	28.2	25.3	26.2	21.6	19.3

Source: OECD-DAC.

TABLE 5.7 MALI: OFFICIAL DEVELOPMENT FINANCE
AND ITS COMPONENTS, BY SOURCE, 1975–97

	Disbursements, in millions of 1996 constant US dollars					
	1975–81	1982–85	1986–87	1988–90	1991–93	1994–97
Total official development finance (loans and grants)						
Bilateral	282.0	384.7	402.3	361.6	319.6	298.3
Multilateral	155.6	239.4	233.0	221.6	191.5	207.3
Total	437.6	624.0	635.3	583.3	511.1	505.6
Loans						
Bilateral	71.1	143.4	109.4	77.1	54.2	29.3
Multilateral	67.7	137.0	139.6	134.9	94.0	131.3
Total	138.8	280.4	249.0	212.0	148.2	160.6
Grants (including technical assistance)						
Bilateral	210.8	241.2	292.9	284.5	265.4	268.9
Multilateral	87.9	102.4	93.4	86.7	97.5	76.0
Total	298.7	343.6	386.3	371.2	362.9	345.0
Grants (excluding technical assistance)						
Bilateral	140.4	157.0	191.5	196.4	152.6	165.1
Multilateral	63.9	69.2	59.1	55.4	66.5	53.6
Total	204.3	226.2	250.5	251.8	219.2	218.7
	As a percentage of total official development finance					
Total official development finance (loans and grants)						
Bilateral	64.4	61.6	63.3	62.0	62.5	59.0
Multilateral	35.6	38.4	36.7	38.0	37.5	41.0
Total						
Loans						
Bilateral	16.3	23.0	17.2	13.2	10.6	5.8
Multilateral	15.5	22.0	22.0	23.1	18.4	26.0
Total	31.7	44.9	39.2	36.4	29.0	31.8
Grants (including technical assistance)						
Bilateral	48.2	38.7	46.1	48.8	51.9	53.2
Multilateral	20.1	16.4	14.7	14.9	19.1	15.0
Total	68.3	55.1	60.8	63.6	71.0	68.2
Grants (excluding technical assistance)						
Bilateral	32.1	25.2	30.1	33.7	29.9	32.7
Multilateral	14.6	11.1	9.3	9.5	13.0	10.6
Total	46.7	36.2	39.4	43.2	42.9	43.3

Source: Chang, Fernández-Arias, and Servén 1999; OECD-DAC.

TABLE 5.8 MALI: WORLD BANK ADJUSTMENT CREDITS, 1980–98
(millions of U.S. dollars)

Loans	Type	Date approved	Amount approved	Amount disbursed
Agriculture	SECAC	1983	—	56.6
Public enterprises	SECAC	1988	40	40
Agriculture	SECAC	1990	53	53
Structural adjustment	SAC	1990	70	70
Economic recovery	SECAC	1994	25	25
Education	SECAC	1995	50	50
Economic management	SAC	1996	60	46.1

— Not available.
Note: SAC = Structural Adjustment Credit. SECAC = Sectoral Adjustment Credit.
Source: World Bank.

TABLE 5.9 MALI: IMF ADJUSMENT LOANS

Loans	Duration	Year	Millions of SDR		Millions of U.S. dollars	
			Amount approved	Amount disbursed	Amount approved	Amount disbursed
Standby Agreement I	1 year	1969	—	3.0	—	3.0
Standby Agreement II	1 year	1971	—	4.5	—	4.5
Standby Agreement III	1 year	1982	—	30.3	—	33.5
Standby Agreement IV	2 years	1983	—	40.5	—	43.3
Standby Agreement V	2 years	1985	—	22.8	—	23.1
Standby Agreement VI	2 years	1988	12.7	12.7	17.1	17.1
SAF	3 years	1988	35.6	25.7	47.2	34.1
ESAF	4 years	1992	79.2	79.2	111.5	111.5
ESAF	3 years	1996	62.0	62.0	90.0	90.0

—Not available.
Sources: IMF; *Marchés Tropicaux.*

TABLE 5.10 MALI: MULTILATERAL DEBT RESTRUCTURING AGREEMENTS WITH OFFICIAL CREDITORS, 1980–98

| Date of agreement | Consolidation period | | | Consolidation included | | Portion of debt consoli-date (%) | Amount consolidated (U.S. $ millions) | Repayment terms | |
	Deadline	Start date	Duration	Arrears	Debt already rescheduled			Maturity	Grace period
27 Oct 88	1 Jan 88	1 Jul 88	16	Yes		100	48	Menu[a]	Menu
22 Nov 89	1 Jan 88	1 Nov 99	26		Yes	100	33	Menu	Menu
29 Oct 92	1 Jan 88	1 Oct 92	35	Yes	Yes	100	107	Menu	Menu
20 May 96	1 Jan 88	20 May 96	Stock	Yes	Yes	100	33	Menu	Menu

a. The term "menu" refers to options that were the object of an agreement reached at the 1988 Toronto Summit; for agreements effective as of 1995, the term "menu" refers to the so-called "Naples" options after December 1994.
Source: World Bank, Global Development Finance 1997.

TABLE 5.11 MALI: DEBT RATIOS

	1975–81	1982–85	1986–87	1988–90	1991–93	1994–97
Debt service (% of exports of goods and services)	5	11	17	15	11	15
Total debt (% of exports of goods and services)	282	432	491	461	492	472
Total debt (% of GDP)	47	94	105	103	107	127

Source: World Bank, *Global Development Finance 1999.*

TABLE 5.12 MALI: STRUCTURE OF LONG-TERM, PUBLIC, AND GOVERNMENT-SECURED DEBT OUTSTANDING, 1970–97

	Millions of 1996 constant U.S. dollars						
	1970–71	1972–81	1982–85	1986–87	1988–90	1991–93	1994–97
Official creditors	1282.8	1104.5	2008.7	2569.0	2653.6	2986.0	2761.3
Official bilateral creditors	1241.9	898.4	1334.0	1718.5	1659.7	1806.2	1330.6
Official multilateral creditors	40.7	206.1	674.7	850.6	993.8	1179.8	1430.8
Including IDA	40.7	161.0	380.5	471.5	565.1	685.5	897.9
Private creditors	34.1	56.5	83.2	75.0	25.8	8.2	1.1
Total	1316.9	1161.0	2091.9	2643.9	2679.3	2994.2	2762.4
	As a percentage of total debt outstanding						
Official creditors	97.4	95.1	96.0	97.2	99.0	99.7	100.0
Official bilateral creditors	94.3	77.4	63.8	65.0	61.9	60.3	48.2
Official multilateral creditors	3.1	17.7	32.3	32.2	37.1	39.4	51.8
Iincluding IDA	3.1	13.9	18.2	17.8	21.1	22.9	32.5
Private creditors	2.6	4.9	4.0	2.8	1.0	0.3	0.0

Source: World Bank, *Global Development Finance 1999.*

TABLE 5.13 MALI: STRUCTURE OF TOTAL SERVICE OF LONG-TERM, PUBLIC, AND GOVERNMENT-SECURED DEBT, 1970–97

	Millions of 1996 constant U.S. dollars						
	1970–71	1972–81	1982–85	1986–87	1988–90	1991–93	1994–97
Official creditors	3.7	12.8	33.4	38.1	51.1	51.6	83.5
Official bilateral creditors	3.4	11.0	16.9	22.3	21.9	27.3	43.9
Official multilateral creditors	0.3	1.8	16.6	15.9	29.2	24.3	39.6
Including IDA	0.3	1.1	3.9	5.7	6.7	7.6	13.2
Private creditors	0.3	1.3	6.3	8.8	2.5	1.5	0.2
Total	4.0	14.2	39.8	46.9	53.6	53.2	83.7
	As a percentage of total debt outstanding						
Official creditors	93.1	90.3	84.0	81.3	95.3	97.1	99.7
Official bilateral creditors	86.6	77.4	42.4	47.5	40.9	51.3	52.5
Official multilateral creditors	6.4	13.0	41.6	33.9	54.6	45.7	47.3
Including IDA	6.4	8.0	9.7	12.2	12.5	14.3	15.8
Private creditors	6.9	9.4	15.9	18.7	4.7	2.9	0.3

Source: World Bank, *Global Development Finance 1999.*

NOTES

1. All loans of public origin, except for those having a purely military or defense-related purpose.

2. The deflator is the one calculated by DAC (OECD), and corresponds to the average of the deflators of donor countries that are members of the DAC once prices are expressed in U.S. dollars at the current exchange rate (assuming that 1996 = 100). This average is weighted according to the volume of ODA dispensed by each country in 1996.

3. The account went from 156 million French francs in 1968 to 1,272 million as of December 31, 1983. This debit was not counted in ODA since it bore debtor interest indexed according to the Bank of France's discount rate, nor was it counted under total gross official flows from the public sector (TOF), a more disputable decision that is probably justified because its direct objective was not development, but instead the maintenance of the currency's convertibility.

4. Also, it was sometimes difficult to determine if such aid met ODA criteria due to the secret nature of the conditions and swap agreements associated with it.

5. Until July 1990, the Caisse Centrale de Coopération Economique (CCCE) was providing Mali with concessional loans that complemented budgetary aid. Subsequently, the CCCE only granted "structural adjustment grants" to Mali, as it did with other low-income countries. The CCCE subsequently became the Caisse Française de Développement (CFD), and then the Agence Française de Développement (AFD). Bilateral aid to adjustment also came from U.S., Dutch, and Canadian sources.

6. Liberalization of rice marketing and of its purchase price was a condition of aid granted to the Office du Niger.

REFERENCES

Banque de France. 1998. "Rapport Zone Franc 1998." Paris.

Burnside, C., and D. Dollar. 1997. "Aid, Policies, and Growth." Policy Research Working Paper 1777. World Bank, Development Research Group, Washington, D.C.

Chambas, G., J. L. Combes, P. Guillaumont, S. Guillaumont, and B. Laporte. 1999. "Mali: les Facteurs de Croissance à Long Terme." Draft report. Organisation for Economic Co-operation and Development, Paris.

Chang, C., E. Fernández-Arias, and L. Servén. 1999. "Measuring Aid Flows: A New Approach." Policy Research Working Paper 2050. World Bank, Development Research Group, Washington, D.C.

Coelos. 1994. *Capitalisation de l'expérience du PRMC.* Processed.

Collier P., P. Guillaumont, S. Guillaumont, and J. W. Gunning. 1997. "Redesigning Conditionality." *World Development* 25 (9): 1399–1407.

Deme, M. 1999. "Plan d'Action à Moyen Terme (1997–1999) pour la phase V du PRMC." Processed.

Guillaumont, P., and S. Guillaumont. 1994. "La Zone Franc, les Institutions de Bretton-Woods et la Conditionnalité." In *Bretton Woods, mélanges pour un cinquantenaire.* Paris: Revue d'Economie Financière.

———. 1995. "La Conditionnalité à l'Epreuve des Faits." In Michel Rainelli, ed., *La Négociation Commerciale et Financière Internationale.* Paris: Economica.

Guillaumont, P., and L. Chauvet.1999. "Aid and Performance: A Reassessment." Communication ABCDE Workshop on Aid, Selectivity, and Conditionality. World Bank, Washington, D.C.

Laporte, B., and P. Monier. 1994. "Les mécanismes de stabilisation des prix aux producteurs peuvent-ils faire face à la dévaluation du franc CFA? L'expérience du coton au Mali et du caoutchouc en Côte d'Ivoire." *Marchés Tropicaux* no. 2535 (10 June): 1194–5.

Lecaillon, J., and C. Morrisson. 1986. *Economic Policies and Agricultural Performance: The Case of Mali.* Paris: Organisation for Economic Co-operation and Development.

OECD (Organisation for Economic Co-operation and Development). 1998. "Revue du système international d'aide au Mali. Synthèse et analyse." Provisional report. Paris.

———. 1999a. "Répartition Géographique des Ressources Financières Allouées aux Pays Bénéficiaires de l'Aide." Paris.

———. 1999b. "Activités d'Aide en Afrique. Système de Notification des Pays Créanciers." Paris.

Sachs, J. D., and A. M. Warner. 1995. "Economic Reforms and the Process of Global Integration." Brookings Papers on Economic Activity, vol. 1. Brookings Institution, Washington, D.C.

World Bank. 1994. "Country Assistance Strategy for Mali." Report no. 13746-MLI. Washington, D.C.

———. 1996a. "Implementation Completion Report for the Public Enterprise Institutional Development Project." Report no. 15953. Washington, D.C.

———. 1996b. "Implementation Completion Report for the Structural Adjustment Credit." Report no. 15644. Washington, D.C.

———. 1996c. "Project Completion Report for the Economic Recovery Credit." Report no. 15819-MLI. Washington, D.C.

———. 1998a. "Country Assistance Strategy for Mali." Report no. 17775-MLI. Washington, D.C.

———. 1998b. "Implementation Completion Report for the Agricultural Sector Adjustment/Investment Credit." Report no. 18027-MLI. Washington, D.C.

————. 1998c. "Memorandum of the President on Assistance to the Republic of Mali under the HIPC Debt Initiative." Report no. P-7529-MLI. Washington, D.C.

————. 1999a. *Global Development Finance 1999. Analysis and Summary Tables.* Washington, D.C.

————. 1999b. *World Development Indicators.* Washington, D.C.

————. 1999c. *World Development Report 1999.* Washington, D.C.

Tanzania

Arne Bigsten
Göteborg University
Göteborg, Sweden

Deogratias Mutalemwa
Yvonne Tsikata
Samuel Wangwe
Economic and Social Research Foundation
Dar es Salaam, Tanzania

ACRONYMS AND ABBREVIATIONS

AfDB	African Development Bank
BIS	Basic Industries Strategy
CAS	Country Assistance Strategy
CEM	Country Economic Memorandum
CG	Consultative Group
CIS	Commodity Import Support
CTI	Confederation of Tanzanian Industries
DAC	Development Assistance Committee (of the OECD)
EDA	Effective development assistance
ERP	Economic Recovery Program
ESAF	Enhanced Structural Adjustment Facility (of the IMF)
ESAMI	East and Southern African Management Institute
ESRF	Economic and Social Research Foundation
EU	European Union
GDP	Gross domestic product
IDA	International Development Association (of the World Bank Group)
IFI	International financial institution
IMF	International Monetary Fund
MDF	Multilateral Debt Relief Fund
NBC	National Bank of Commerce
NESP	National Economic Survival Program
NGO	Nongovernmental organization
ODA	Official development assistance
OECD	Organisation for Economic Co-operation and Development
OGL	Open General License
PC	Paris Club
PER	Public Expenditure Review
PFP	Policy Framework Paper
PSRC	Parastatal Sector Reform Commission
REPOA	Research on Poverty Alleviation
SAC	Structural Adjustment Credit
SPA	Special Program of Assistance (for Sub-Saharan Africa)
SPA/JEM	Special Program of Assistance/Joint Evaluation Mission
Tshs.	Tanzanian shilling
UNDP	United Nations Development Programme
USAID	U.S. Agency for International Development

Tanzania has been at the center of development debate since the 1960s. It chose to pursue a development strategy aimed at self-reliance and African socialism, and President Nyerere became a respected spokesman for the whole Third World. This sparked a great deal of positive interest in the Tanzanian experiment, particularly from social democratic governments in Europe, which provided generous aid to the country. However, the Tanzanian experiment ran into trouble, drawing more and more critique from the outside, and donor support was reduced. The ensuing economic crisis and increasing domestic critique eventually led to a policy reversal and the introduction of adjustment measures.

The purpose of this study is to get a better understanding of the causes of policy reform in Tanzania, particularly how aid affected the reform process relative to domestic forces. The study is an exercise in economic history or political economy and is not primarily concerned with the impact of aid on economic outcomes. The study covers mainly the period since the onset of the severe economic crisis in Tanzania in 1979, but to put this in perspective we will also briefly outline the policies pursued before that.

The paper has three main objectives: it examines the nature of external assistance, the causes and path of policy reforms, and the relationship between the aid and reforms. Section 2 examines the different types of aid that Tanzania receives, tracing the size and character of the aid flows, the relationship with multilateral and bilateral donors, and attempts at donor coordination. Section 3 describes the economic policy and institutional framework and analyzes more precisely the causes and implementation of the identified policy reforms as well as the internal dialogue and involvement of different actors. Section 4 assesses the links between aid and reform and presents conclusions.

AID FLOWS TO TANZANIA

The standard concept of aid used in most studies is that of official development assistance (ODA), which consists of financial aid and technical cooperation (also called technical assistance). Financial aid includes grants and concessional loans having a grant element of at least 25 percent. Technical cooperation includes grants to nationals of aid-recipient countries receiving education or training, and payments to consultants, advisers, administrators, and similar persons working on assignments of interest to the recipient countries. However, the standard measure tends to overestimate the aid flow, since it does not provide an accurate measure of the grant element in the official loans. The overestimation is less for Africa than for other regions due to the high grant equivalent in loans to Sub-Saharan Africa, but it is still significant.

Because of these problems the World Bank has produced a new aid measure called effective development assistance (EDA), which provides a more accurate measure of true aid flows than the traditional ODA measure (Chang, Fernández-Arias, and Servén 1999). EDA is the sum of grants and the grant equivalent of official loans, and aims to measure the pure transfer of resources. EDA is defined as the grant equivalents of all development flows in a given period. Grants tied to technical assistance are excluded from EDA, but since we use the grant data from the Development Assistance Committee (DAC) of the Organisation for Economic Co-operation and Development (OECD), they are included in the estimates presented in the following section.

Official Aid Flows

Volume and Composition of Aid

Since independence in 1961, Tanzania has been one of the largest recipients of aid in Sub-Saharan Africa in absolute terms. The country still receives considerably more aid as a percentage of gross domestic product (GDP) than most other countries in the region. Tanzania's share of total aid from all the DAC countries was 8.3 percent during the 1970s by the definition used in this study, and the country was the largest recipient of aid in Sub-Saharan Africa in that period (see table 6.1). This share started to decline in 1981, and by 1985 it was down to 5.8 percent. Nevertheless, Tanzania still ranked as the second-largest beneficiary of aid (after Sudan) during the 1980s. Even more remarkable is that even in the mid-1980s, when the policy environment was very poor in Tanzania, the country received more than twice as much as did Ghana, which was considered at that time to be *the* reformer. This suggests that there is a high degree of inertia in aid flows. Once they are committed, it is difficult to cut a country loose. Tanzania continued to rank second in the 1990s, slightly behind Mozambique.

Between 1970 and 1996, the country received a total of US$16,632 million in foreign aid (see table 6.1). Aid is defined here as the sum of total grants according to the DAC definition plus the grant equivalent of loans according to the EDA definition of the World Bank. Aid has accounted for more than 80 percent of total net inflows of external capital, indicating that private capital flows have been small. The annual volume of aid rose from US$37.7 million in 1970 to a peak of US$1,158.0 million in 1992, but then declined to US$830.5 million in 1996. In per capita terms, Tanzania's aid receipts peaked in the late 1980s and early 1990s at more than US$40. As a share of GDP, aid peaked at 30 percent in 1990, but due to the decline in aid flows and the increase in GDP during

TABLE 6.1 TOTAL AID TO TANZANIA, 1970–96
(millions of U.S. dollars)

Year	Total bilateral	Total multilateral	Total aid	Total aid per capita (US$)	Share of bilateral aid in total aid (%)	Share of Tanzania in total aid to Sub-Saharan Africa (%)
1970	37.70	0	37.70	2.7	100.0	4.6
1971	39.04	0.06	39.10	2.8	99.8	3.8
1972	90.52	1.18	91.70	6.3	98.7	6.3
1973	153.62	1.78	155.40	10.4	98.8	9.6
1974	187.56	7.14	194.70	12.6	96.3	8.0
1975	271.04	32.26	303.30	19.1	89.3	9.8
1976	213.12	44.78	257.90	15.7	82.6	8.9
1977	239.86	67.04	306.90	18.1	78.1	9.3
1978	481.66	51.44	533.10	30.6	90.3	12.0
1979	489.51	67.59	557.10	31.0	87.8	10.5
1980	666.82	94.58	761.40	41.0	87.5	11.2
1981	495.43	165.47	660.90	34.5	74.9	9.5
1982	458.07	176.03	634.10	32.0	72.2	9.2
1983	451.71	132.59	584.30	28.6	77.3	8.4
1984	426.48	107.82	534.30	25.3	79.8	7.3
1985	384.49	98.11	482.60	22.2	79.6	5.8
1986	595.58	194.02	789.60	35.1	75.4	7.9
1987	607.00	144.50	751.50	32.4	80.7	7.1
1988	621.97	421.63	1,043.60	44.5	59.5	8.4
1989	660.73	181.57	842.30	34.1	78.4	6.7
1990	767.78	287.81	1,055.60	41.4	72.7	6.4
1991	775.33	315.37	1,090.70	41.5	71.1	6.9
1992	789.73	368.27	1,158.00	42.7	68.1	7.2
1993	918.51	235.99	1,154.50	42.3	79.5	7.8
1994	642.12	285.08	927.20	32.2	69.2	5.8
1995	622.17	231.83	854.00	28.8	72.8	5.7
1996	569.65	260.85	830.50	27.2	68.5	6.0

Sources: World Bank EDA database and OECD-DAC database. The grant estimates are from OECD and include technical assistance, while estimates of the aid element in loans are from the EDA computations.

the 1990s the share has fallen very significantly since then, to about 13 percent of GDP in 1997.

   These figures can be compared with those of some other countries in the region. Aid to Kenya peaked at 27 percent of GDP in 1993, but fell to 5 percent by 1997. In Uganda aid was 27 percent of GDP in 1992, but fell to 13 percent by 1997. Aid to Zambia declined from 36 percent in 1991 to

17 percent in 1997, while aid to Ghana fell from 14 percent of GDP in 1989 to only 7 percent in 1997 (World Bank 1999c). It is evident that Tanzania is not the only country that is highly dependent on aid. Still, aid dependence has declined significantly during the 1990s.

Tanzania has received aid from more than 50 bilateral sources. This is a high figure, but not unusual for the larger African economies. The Nordic countries (Sweden, Norway, Denmark, and Finland) have been the major donors, accounting for more than 30 percent of the country's total ODA receipts between 1970 and 1996 (see table 6.9 for a breakdown of flows by country). Sweden has provided almost half of that amount for most of this period. The second group of major bilateral donors consists of Germany and the Netherlands, each contributing around 8 percent of total aid over the past 20 years. The third group consists of Canada, the United States, and the United Kingdom, each accounting for about 6 percent of Tanzania's total aid receipts. Italy and Japan became important new donors in the late 1980s. China and the socialist bloc drastically reduced their aid programs for Tanzania starting in the 1980s.

During the 1970s, most of the aid flows to Tanzania came from bilateral sources. Multilateral donors contributed an average of about 10 percent annually. Since the early 1980s, however, the share of multilateral donors has risen considerably. In 1988 the multilateral share of total aid was about 40 percent (see table 6.1). In the case of aid in the form of loans, the contribution of multilateral donors has risen much faster, from an average of less than 5 percent in 1970–75 to more than 85 percent in 1987–96 (see table 6.2). Major multilateral donors include the International Monetary Fund (IMF), the World Bank, the African Development Bank (AfDB), the European Union (EU), the United Nations Development Program (UNDP), and the United Nations High Commission for Refugees, with the World Bank Group's International Development Association (IDA) providing about half of total aid from multilateral donors. Total disbursements on EDA loans are shown in table 6.10. During the reform period the amounts have been in the range of US$200 million to US$350 million per year.

In terms of sectoral distribution, most of the aid in the 1960s and the early 1970s was directed to the agricultural and transport sectors. During the second half of the 1970s the emphasis shifted toward industry and energy. Transport became an important aid recipient in the late 1980s and early 1990s. The general pattern of aid distribution in the 1990s has been (in order of importance): transport and communications, receiving about half of the aid flows, followed by agriculture, human resources development, health, integrated regional development, and energy (Mutalemwa, Noni, and Wangwe 1998). The sectoral allocation of EDA loans is shown in tables 6.11 and 6.12. Much of the loan amount during the reform period has gone to the rehabilitation of infrastructure as well

TABLE 6.2 TANZANIA: EFFECTIVE DEVELOPMENT ASSISTANCE
IN THE FORM OF LOANS, 1970–96
(millions of U.S. dollars)

Year	Total bilateral	Multilateral	EDA as loans	Share of bilateral aid in total aid (%)
1970	10.15	0	10.15	100.00
1971	8.50	0.02	8.48	100.20
1972	46.50	0.59	47.10	98.70
1973	89.73	0.88	90.61	99.00
1974	91.55	3.77	95.32	96.00
1975	98.17	16.88	115.05	85.30
1976	38.68	23.28	61.96	62.40
1977	54.91	36.52	91.44	60.10
1978	49.16	26.87	76.03	64.70
1979	33.59	35.82	69.41	48.30
1980	53.53	49.51	103.03	51.90
1981	58.87	92.70	151.57	38.80
1982	50.62	93.25	143.87	35.20
1983	82.58	71.89	154.46	53.50
1984	48.82	55.98	104.81	46.60
1985	22.54	52.06	74.60	30.20
1986	46.77	95.99	142.76	32.80
1987	11.72	71.96	83.69	14.00
1988	22.70	210.85	233.54	9.70
1989	13.38	90.60	103.98	12.80
1990	23.79	145.08	168.87	14.10
1991	16.78	160.11	176.89	9.50
1992	36.83	187.57	224.39	16.40
1993	9.88	119.74	129.62	7.60
1994	6.28	144.57	150.77	4.34
1995	18.88	117.81	136.69	16.02
1996	3.35	132.33	135.68	2.53

Source: World Bank EDA database.

as manufacturing. The World Bank has been the predominant creditor during this period (see table 6.13). Other donors have been reluctant to make loans to the poor and heavily indebted country, but have chosen to provide grants instead. By comparing tables 6.13 and 6.14 we may note that the grant element of World Bank loans has also increased. Since grants are more fungible than loans (Feyzioglu, Swaroop, and Zhu 1998), it is generally more difficult to reallocate aid from the international financial institutions (IFIs) according to the preferences of the recipient government.

The composition of aid has also shifted over time. For most of the 1960s and 1970s, investment projects assistance made up more than two-thirds of total aid. The preference for project assistance over program aid during this period can be attributed to three factors. First, projects appeared to be easy to plan, design, control, and supervise, and hence promised visible results while allowing for direct accountability. Second, unlike programs, projects are easy to tie to the procurement of goods and services from the donor. Third, projects provided donors with opportunities to bypass national institutions and pursue their own objectives.

Since the mid-1980s, there has been a shift in emphasis from project aid to program aid. Principal reasons for the change include Tanzania's growing balance of payments problems and the declining utilization of capacity in industry. These developments were perceived as evidence that the performance of project assistance had been unsatisfactory, and that import support was critically needed to raise the level of output through greater utilization of enterprise capacities. Another important change has involved a shift toward financing more explicitly the project forms of the government's recurrent budget. This has been a response to the growing awareness that insufficient allocations to the recurrent expenditure in the government budget had become a more serious constraint to the delivery of services than allocations to the development budget.

Trends in Aid Flows

Over the period 1970–96, three broad phases of aid flows to Tanzania can be identified: the expansion phase, from 1970 to 1982; the contraction phase, from 1983 to 1985; and the adjustment phase, from 1986 to 1996. Aid to Tanzania increased more than 20 times (in current dollars) between 1970 and 1982. It decreased by about 25 percent between 1982 and 1985, and then rose again sharply from US$482.6 million in 1985 to a peak of US$1,158 million in 1992.

EXPANSION PHASE: 1970–82. The willingness of donors to extend substantial amounts of aid to Tanzania during the late 1960s and the 1970s can be explained by the development policies the country pursued during this period. The country's emphasis on self-reliance and growth with equity, the targeting of government programs to basic needs, and emphasis on cooperatives and Ujamaa villages motivated many donors to provide aid to Tanzania. Such policies were in line with the thinking of social democrats in the North, notably the Nordic countries, Germany (under Willy Brandt), and Canada; these governments took a positive view of Tanzania's development strategy. The World Bank doubled its lending program to Tanzania between 1973 and 1977 because Robert McNamara, who was president of the World Bank at the time, had adopted a policy of growth with equity that was in line with Tanzania's development strategy under the leadership of President Julius Nyerere (Bagachwa, Mbelle, and van Arkadie 1992).

CONTRACTION PHASE: 1983–85. Toward the end of the 1970s, there was a change in donor attitudes toward Tanzania. Donors became increasingly critical of the country's development strategy. There was growing evidence that in spite of the Arusha Declaration neither socialism nor self-reliance had been achieved, and that the effectiveness of aid had been low.[1] Following the breakdown of negotiations with the IMF in September 1980, the general view among Western donors was that aid to Tanzania could not be effective unless the country agreed to redress inappropriate domestic policies. Despite these developments, the Nordic countries did not abandon Tanzania but continued to provide aid although at a reduced rate. By 1983, however, most donors, including Sweden, had begun to scale down their support and aid flows declined sharply. Ultimately, the sheer magnitude of the crisis, pressure from the IMF, the World Bank, and bilateral donors, and the failure of independent national efforts to revive the economy all combined to persuade the government to adopt a far-reaching Economic Recovery Program (ERP I) in 1986 with IMF and World Bank support.

ADJUSTMENT PHASE: 1986–96. The agreements with the IFIs in 1986—a standby agreement with the IMF and a structural adjustment program with the World Bank—helped to restore donor confidence. Under ERP I, the government adopted a broad range of policies aimed at liberalizing internal and external trade, unifying the exchange rate, reviving exports, stimulating domestic saving, and restoring fiscal sustainability. The ERP enjoyed strong donor support. Bilateral aid resumed, leading to a second aid boom that peaked in 1992 (table 6.1).

The agreement with the IMF was renewed in 1987, 1988, and 1990. In 1989, the reforms entered a second phase under ERP II (1989–91). The new reforms continued earlier efforts at trade and exchange rate liberalization and macroeconomic stabilization, but widened to include reforms in the banking system, agricultural marketing, the parastatal sector, government administration, and the civil service, together with a targeting of the social sectors.

However, during 1993–94 relations between the government and major donors deteriorated over the government's failure to collect counterpart funds under the Commodity Import Support scheme and to increase tax collection efforts generally. There were increasing suspicions of corruption. Donors started to question the effectiveness of their aid, as reflected, for example, in evaluation studies carried out by the Nordic countries and the Netherlands in 1994. The government commitment to reform was also questioned, and its failure to conclude a new Enhanced Structural Adjustment Facility (ESAF) with the IMF worsened donor fears. The government, for its part, felt that the donors' demands were often unrealistic and too intrusive in matters that were essentially domestic. An independent group of local and international advisers was commissioned by Denmark to see how the climate of confidence between the two sides could be restored. The group, headed by Professor Helleiner, produced a report in June 1995 that has become an important policy document in both the donor community and the government (Mutalemwa, Noni, and Wangwe 1998).

Strained relations between the government and donors in 1993–94 had a significant adverse effect on aid flows to Tanzania between 1994 and 1996. Donor confidence was restored and normal aid operations resumed after the new government came to power and, especially, after an ESAF agreement was concluded with the IMF in 1996.

Other Types of Financial Aid

Substantial aid has been disbursed as balance of payments support through the Commodity Import Support (CIS) and the Open General License (OGL) schemes. More and more donors are currently inclined to channel their support through a new Balance of Payments Import Support scheme and the newly introduced Multilateral Debt Relief Fund. A few donors, for example the Japanese, still channel their assistance through the CIS arrangement.

Commodity Import Support

The CIS facility established under ERP I used donor funds to help provide foreign exchange to cushion the impact of devaluation and stimulate agricultural exports. The program was to improve levels of capacity utilization of existing production facilities. The CIS was a tied facility, with donors insisting on procurement of goods from their own countries. Restrictions were also placed on the type of goods that could be imported. Applications for utilization of CIS funds had to be submitted to the Treasury, and after approval importers were required to pay a minimum of 30 percent cash cover on the allocated amount. The remaining 70 percent would be paid on arrival of shipping documents.

The scheme ran into difficulties and many donors decided to abandon it because of the government's failure to account for payment of counterpart funds against the foreign exchange disbursed. It should also be noted that the allocation of CIS reflected donors' preferences in that most donors supported "their" projects, that is, projects they had been responsible for financing in the first place. This meant that allocation did not necessarily follow criteria of efficiency.

The program was in some ways similar to the Marshall Plan that helped Europe recover after World War II. The outcome in Tanzania was not as good, however. There was not yet recognition that many of the industries were obsolete and that new investment would be required to make them competitive.

Open General License

The OGL system was established in the early 1980s to provide a nonadministrative system for allocating foreign exchange for the importation of goods. The system was suspended in 1982 because of a shortage of foreign exchange, but resumed in 1988 with joint financing by the World Bank and other donors. The objective was to support a market-driven program of imports. Importers were free to import the goods they wanted, provided they were eligible under the OGL system. The minimum value of goods to be financed under the OGL facility was US$5,000. The Bank of Tanzania issued import licenses automatically, provided that importers fulfilled all the conditions pertaining to the utilization of funds under the facility. Foreign exchange was allocated by way of an import license, and importers were required to make a down payment and settle the difference on arrival of shipping documents.

However, payment of counterpart funds eventually became a problem, as importers did not pay promptly, and the scheme had to be abandoned. A new nonadministrative system of allocation had to be established in 1993. Attempts by government to collect the overdue counterpart funds in relation to OGL and CIS, estimated at Tshs.160 billion at the end of 1992, have not been successful.

The Economic and Social Research Foundation (ESRF) in Dar es Salaam has evaluated the extent to which Tanzania has implemented recommendations from the Special Program of Assistance/Joint Evaluation Mission (SPA/JEM) project with regard to the CIS and OGL schemes (ESRF 1998). The picture is mixed. There has been some progress, but in other areas, for example debt recovery, little has been achieved.[2]

Balance of Payments/Budgetary Support

In 1993, the government introduced a new system of importation as one of the measures adopted under liberalization of foreign trade. The system provides for importers to declare imports by filling in an import declaration form. Donors, through the Special Program of Assistance (SPA) for Sub-Saharan Africa, agreed to disburse balance of payments import support through a reimbursement method. Under the system, expenditures incurred from the country's own foreign exchange are reimbursed upon presentation of specified import documents. After reimbursement, the Bank of Tanzania promptly pays the equivalent in Tanzanian shillings to the Treasury. The agreement between Tanzania and the United States requires the Bank of Tanzania to deposit the counterpart funds to an account that the U.S. Agency for International Development (USAID) maintains with a local commercial bank. The Bank of Tanzania then sells the foreign exchange arising from donor resources to commercial banks in the Inter-Bank Foreign Exchange Market. This system has resolved the problem of nonpayment of counterpart funds to the government.

In 1998 the donors who were active in providing balance of payments import support through this system were the United Kingdom, the Netherlands, the EU, AfDB, and USAID. In 1993–94 a total of 99.4 percent of the amount pledged was disbursed. The period 1994–96 experienced low disbursement of about 30 percent as most donors withheld disbursement. Thereafter disbursement rates picked up to 58 percent and 50.4 percent in 1996–97 and 1997–98 respectively (Mutalemwa, Noni, and Wangwe 1998).

Debt Rescheduling and Debt Alleviation

Tanzania's external debt has increased from US$4,970 million in 1986 to US$7,931 million in 1997, an increase of 59.9 percent. Actual debt service decreased from US$303 million in 1989 to US$122 million in 1990, then increased to US$233 million in 1997 and dropped again to US$174 million in 1997. Between 1986 and 1997, actual debt service averaged 50 percent of scheduled debt service, and as a result, debt arrears accumulated from US$664 million to US$3,227 million during that period.

Paris Club

Between 1986 and 1997 Tanzania went to the Paris Club (PC) five times. The first meeting took place in 1986, followed by meetings in 1988, 1990, 1992, and 1997. At PC I, Tanzania obtained terms under which 97.5 percent (US$722.9 million) of eligible debts in arrears were rescheduled. PC II and PC III gave Tanzania the opportunity to benefit from Toronto terms, which provided for 33 percent debt reduction. Under PC II, debts worth US$22.3 million were cancelled and US$373 million rescheduled. Debts worth US$18.7 million were cancelled and US$199.4 million was rescheduled within the framework of PC III. At PC IV, the enhanced Toronto terms were applied and debts worth US$182.8 million were cancelled and those worth US$458.3 million were rescheduled. Under PC V, the government received the Naples terms. This made it possible for debts worth US$1,000 million to be eligible for consideration for cancellation and those worth US$700 million to be rescheduled.

HIPC

The Heavily Indebted Poor Countries (HIPC) Debt Initiative was established in 1996 to address multilateral debt. It lays down a set of criteria for providing across-the-board debt relief. Tanzania is one of the countries potentially eligible for HIPC support. In April 2000 IDA and the IMF agreed to support a comprehensive debt reduction package for Tanzania under the enhanced HIPC Initiative. Total relief from all of Tanzania's creditors is worth more than US$2 billion in net present value terms. The whole debt relief operation will translate into debt service relief over time of US$3 billion, or about half of Tanzania's debt service obligations during fiscal years 2001–03 and about a third of debt service obligations thereafter. For the program to be fully implemented Tanzania has to satisfy a number of conditions, including the adoption of a participatory poverty reduction strategy paper.

Multilateral Debt Relief Fund

In July 1998, the government took the initiative of setting up a Multilateral Debt Relief Fund (MDF) which is intended to assist in servicing debt obligations to multilateral financial institutions, notably the IMF. Disbursement of funds is based on actual debt obligations that mature during a specific period. Funds disbursed under the system are deposited into a special MDF account and payments are made when the debt obligations fall due. The budgetary savings arising from this arrangement are to be used by government to enhance expenditures in social sectors, especially health and education. Countries that have shown particular interest in contributing to MDF are Denmark, Finland, Ireland, the Netherlands, Norway, Sweden, and the United Kingdom.

Nonfinancial Aid

Technical Cooperation

Between 1976 and 1996, the volume of technical cooperation resources to Tanzania increased by more than 12 times, from US$21.4 million in 1970 to a peak of US$266.7 million in 1995 (see table 6.15). The share of technical cooperation in total foreign assistance, which was 56 percent in 1970, had dropped to 19 percent by 1975. It rose to 29 percent in 1985 and stabilized at around 30 percent in the 1990s.

Technical assistance has mainly been provided as part of specific projects or programs. In that form it did not address the wider objective of institutional capacity building. Projects have usually been approved by donors on condition that they would be executed by special project implementation units often staffed by highly paid expatriate personnel and selected local experts. This is driven by the urge to speed up implementation, though it frequently sets up parallel management units that duplicate functions that can be performed by existing local institutions. In fact, donors go as far as managing the funds themselves.

The behavior of bilaterals differs little from that of multilaterals in this regard. Both tend to doubt local capacities; the difference is that multilaterals are bound by stricter rules regarding procurement that ensure that the Tanzanian government manages the funds and selection of consultants and experts.

A fundamental problem is that there has been no clear government policy on the role or limits of technical assistance. The government policy is so undefined that responsibility is scattered among five ministries, with uncoordinated procedures for determining priority needs, recruiting expatriates, issuing immigration visas and work permits, extending contracts, training local counterpart and replacement personnel, negotiating donor funding, and evaluating expatriate performance (Mutalemwa, Noni, and Wangwe 1998). Following long-standing criticism of both donors and the government of Tanzania over this matter—which culminated with the Helleiner report of 1995 and a commitment in 1997 to do something to rectify the situation—the government has finally decided to address the problem in a systematic fashion. It has drafted a policy with wide-ranging proposals to restore better use of external resources allocated for technical assistance recruitment and to enhance ownership by the government in the management of these resources. Helleiner asserts in his latest assessment report (March 1999) that donors have started to provide more information upon request concerning their direct expenditures on technical cooperation.

The Role of NGOs and Similar Institutions in Transmission of Ideas

The community of nongovernmental organizations (NGOs) in Tanzania has undergone spectacular growth. While there were about 200 NGOs in the mid-1980s, by 1997 about 8,400 had been registered. The unprecedented growth of civic organizations has made it possible for them to assert themselves more forcefully. They work in coalitions, or individually, to lobby for change, as in the recent case of the movement to influence the land bill. Women's organizations, which make up a significant percentage of all NGOs, have been especially active in this regard. They have been involved in lobbying for the reform of laws pertaining to inheritance, domestic violence, land reform, children's rights, and child abuse. In this struggle they are not influenced by external assistance as such, although some of these issues have become transnational.

The growing strength and influence of NGOs and other civil society associations has not come without conflicts. The government has sought ways to contain the NGOs or control their actions, yet at the same time it has been obliged to temper its concern and to consult them more frequently. More recently, the government has been trying to help them create an umbrella body with which it can engage in dialogue. Independent policy analysis groups have begun to speak out directly or through the media, and the government and donors are starting to listen to them. For example, OXFAM, a British NGO, is working with the Mwalimu Nyerere Foundation, a local NGO, to facilitate a national debate on Tanzania's external debt and possible options. The debate has contributed considerably to the establishment of the Multilateral Debt Relief Fund, with pledges and financial contributions from several bilateral donors.

Relations with Multilateral Institutions

Tanzania has had a mixed relationship with the major multilateral institutions—the World Bank and the International Monetary Fund—over the years. During the 1970s, admiration for the integrity of President Nyerere and the independent development path he was trying to forge led the Bank, in particular, to provide significant financial assistance to Tanzania. By the end of the decade, however, it was clear that the country faced increasing economic difficulties due in part to policy mistakes. Both the external and internal accounts were in imbalance. The crisis worsened as a result of several shocks (the breakup of the East African Community in 1977, the war with Idi Amin's Uganda in 1978–79, the end of the coffee boom in 1978, and the second oil crisis in 1979). It seemed inevitable that some of the Arusha Declaration principles of socialism would have to be abandoned if the economy were to recover.

The period 1978–82 was marked by difficult relationships with multilateral institutions. Tanzania attempted a number of homegrown economic reforms, described below. These were not very successful as the proposed programs were too limited and failed to attract foreign financing. Increasingly, bilateral donors who had always been supportive of Tanzania were offering their financial support conditional on Tanzania making a deal with the IMF.

Finally, in 1986, Tanzania reached agreement on a standby arrangement with the IMF. This agreement paved the way for increased lending by the World Bank and several other donors. Nonetheless, the level of bilateral aid did not recover to pre-1986 levels in real terms. Consequently, as discussed above, compared to the 1970s the multilateral donors have become much more important, accounting for more than 90 percent of effective development loans by 1996 (see table 6.13).

The World Bank has taken the lead in mobilizing aid through the Consultative Group meetings. In December 1997 the meeting was held in Dar es Salaam for the first time and was regarded as generally successful (Helleiner 1999). Holding the CG in Dar enabled the president and the entire cabinet to participate. It also allowed trade unions, NGOs, and the private sector to interact with the donor community. Unfortunately, this positive step toward ownership was set back in 1999. The donors voted narrowly to hold the CG in Paris, arguing that they would be better able to attract high-level representation.

The need for donor coordination has been obvious to donors in Tanzania for a long time. Still, efforts to actually coordinate aid from different donors have seldom progressed beyond the organization of meetings, where donors exchange information with each other and the government. The World Bank has now taken the lead in renewed efforts on donor coordination, co-chairing the monthly joint government-donor meetings with UNDP. In addition, the Bank actively consults with the other donors through the Special Program of Assistance for Africa and the World Bank/IMF annual meetings. Nonetheless, it appears that significant duplication still exists among donors and little progress has been made in standardizing reporting systems and so on. For example, several donors are supporting capacity building in the Ministry of Finance, with little attempt to coordinate such support. Individual donors have their own parallel project management systems that essentially bypass the official channels for aid management. Indeed, the 1999 Public Expenditure Review estimates that more than 70 percent of aid did not enter through the budget in the last fiscal year.

Aid sometimes does not tie in to national priorities or development plans. Attempts are underway to resolve some of these problems through sector-wide approaches in education and health. The recent multidonor-government review missions in these sectors are an encouraging sign.

The World Bank is encouraging government ownership of major components of the macroeconomic policy dialogue. In 1999, for the first time, the government drafted the Policy Framework Paper (PFP) and made significant contributions to the Public Expenditure Review (PER). While the PFP took longer to draft than in the past, because of the need to consult, there seems to be general agreement that this new approach resulted in greater ownership by the government.

World Bank lending during the reform period initially focused on rehabilitation of the country's dilapidated infrastructure, with loans for roads, power, and telecommunications. Tanzania has had several adjustment loans from the World Bank and IMF (see table 6.3). A multisector rehabilitation loan supported macroeconomic adjustment in 1986.

TABLE 6.3   WORLD BANK LOANS TO TANZANIA, 1986–99
(millions of U.S. dollars)

Purpose of loan	Principal	Disbursed	Approval date
Roads Rehabilitation	50.0	58.7	6 May 1986
Power Rehabilitation/Energy	40.0	44.3	6 May 1986
Multisector Rehabilitation I[a]	50.0	54.5	20 November 1986
Multisector Rehabilitation I	46.2	48.0	20 November 1986
Telecommunications II	23.0	24.0	28 May 1987
Multisector Rehabilitation I	30.0	30.1	19 January 1988
Multisector Rehabilitation	26.0	25.4	19 January 1988
Agriculture Exports Rehabilitation I	30.0	17.7	29 March 1988
National Agriculture and Livestock	8.3	8.6	13 December 1988
Industry and Trade Adjustment Credit	135.0	129.2	13 December 1988
Industry and Trade Adjustment Credit	12.5	12.6	13 March 1989
Agriculture Extension	18.4	19.3	21 March 1989
Tree Crops	25.1	19.2	27 June 1989
Industry and Trade Adjustment Credit	10.3	12.0	12 October 1989
Ports Modernization	37.0	31.7	27 February 1990
Health and Nutrition	47.6	42.5	6 March 1990
Agriculture Adjustment Credit	200.0	207.6	29 March 1990
Education Planning and Rehabilitation	38.3	33.8	22 May 1990
Roads I	180.4	157.6	31 May 1990
Agricultural Adjustment Credit	16.1	16.4	13 December 1990
Petrol Rehabilitation	44.0	29.4	15 January 1991
Railways Restructuring	76.0	48.3	13 June 1991
Urban Sector Engineering	11.2	10.9	30 July 1991
Financial Sector	200.0	211.0	14 November 1991
Agricultural Adjustment Credit	11.3	11.8	26 November 1991
Engineering Credit	10.0	10.8	14 January 1992
Forest Resources Management	18.3	18.5	11 February 1992
Financial and Legal Management Project	20.0	15.5	9 July 1992
Financial Sector	11.3	11.4	23 December 1992
Telecommunications III	74.5	47.1	27 April 1993
Power VI	200.0	164.5	6 May 1993
Public Sector Management	34.9	32.0	10 June 1993
Agriculture Sector Management Project	24.5	15.2	20 July 1993
Roads II	170.2	20.4	7 April 1994
Mineral Sector Development	12.5	9.0	28 July 1994
Financial Institutional Development	10.9	10.3	3 August 1995
Urban Sector Rehabilitation	105.0	15.9	23 May 1996
National Extension Project Phase II	31.1	9.0	11 July 1996
River Basin Management	26.3	6.7	11 July 1996
Lake Victoria Environment	10.1	1.7	30 July 1996
Structural Adjustment Credit I	125.0	49.4	20 June 1997
Structural Adjustment Credit I	3.9	3.8	20 June 1997
Human Resource Development I	20.9	5.0	7 October 1997
Structural Adjustment Credit I	2.6	2.5	15 December 1997
Agriculture Research	21.8	2.0	29 January 1998
Tax Administration	40.0	0.0	30 March 1999

Note: Boldface indicates policy-based loan.
a. Projects appearing more than once reflect the release of multiple tranches.
Source: World Bank project files.

Sectoral adjustment was supported through loans for industrial reform (1988) and the agriculture sector (1990). The most recent adjustment lending was the Structural Adjustment Credit in 1997. Loans for improved public sector management and for some reforms in the judiciary appeared relatively late. A public sector management project was approved in 1993, and a financial and legal management project to "improve the legal regulatory framework and to improve the administration of justice" was approved in 1992.

General conditionality in Bank lending has been marked by increased cross-sector conditionality and the use of multiple floating tranches. For example, the most recent adjustment credit consists of five tranches. The first tranche was released when the cross-sectoral conditions of credit effectiveness were met. The other four (floating) tranches were designed to be released when specific sectoral conditions were met for (a) development expenditures and the social sector; (b) divestiture of the National Bank of Commerce; (c) parastatal reform; and (d) petroleum sector liberalization. Conditionality in the Bank adjustment credits has focused on numerical targets. The current adjustment program targets a fiscal balance of 0.9 percent (after grants) of GDP before Board presentation. For example, on trade, earlier adjustment lending targeted the number of items on the negative list for imports, as well as the number of tariff rates and their level. In some cases, the conditions have focused on the preparatory work required for effective implementation. This includes the issuance of terms of reference for consultants, establishment of particular units, drafting of action plans, revision of legislation, and so on. The IMF targets have tended to be more strictly numerical and have focused on macroeconomic indicators such as inflation and money supply growth.

Tanzania seems to be facing more difficulties meeting the conditionality criteria for structural reforms. Privatization and reform of the financial sector have been sticking points in the dialogue with the IMF and World Bank. Targets have been missed on a number of occasions. For example, financial sector reform (involving the privatization of a number of state-owned banks) has dragged on since 1995. These difficulties appear to be partly linked to political pressures and partly to inadequate technical capacity to implement the agreed-upon reforms.

Multilateral lending has worked effectively for those aspects of liberalization that were less complex administratively. For example, agriculture, foreign investment, and external trade have all been progressively liberalized. Less progress, however, has been made in those areas that are more complex administratively and that require more frequent monitoring. For example, privatization of the National Bank of Commerce and civil service reform have taken longer than anticipated. Other general issues that have contributed to slow and unsatisfactory progress in the implementation of projects include the lack of counterpart funds for IDA-financed projects, cross-sector conditionality, and difficulties with Bank procurement procedures. Overall, however, disbursement ratios have risen for the Tanzania portfolio and they are roughly at par with the World Bank average.

The multilateral organizations have been pushing the basic structural adjustment agenda in Tanzania as in other African countries, and during the 1990s the policymakers have largely accepted this. They have also supported local research foundations (such as ESRF and REPOA) financially or through consultant contracts, and this also may be contributing to the generation of ideas. In Tanzania, it seems the university (notably the economics faculty) was very influential in generating new ideas for reform. Economic and sector work by the World Bank on Tanzania has become increasingly infrequent, as projects have overwhelmed the country program. The amount spent on economic and sector work has declined in each of the past four years.[3] There now seems to be a renewed effort to carry out more economic analysis but it remains to be seen whether this will translate into more resources for that work. One exception to this trend was the collaborative Country Economic Memorandum/Poverty Assessment in 1996, which was well funded and involved UNICEF, the World Bank, and bilateral donors.

Relations with Bilateral Donors

During the reform period (1986–96), Tanzania was critically dependent on DAC bilateral donors. As noted above, the socialist bloc and China, which became important donors in the 1970s, drastically reduced their aid programs to Tanzania during the 1980s because of their internal political and economic problems. Within the donor group, three categories of donors can be distinguished:

- The Nordic countries, most of which have Tanzania as their main aid recipient, and which have a long tradition of consulting among themselves on aid issues and of coordinating their actions at head-office and local levels.
- Major industrial countries in the DAC group, including Germany, the Netherlands, Canada, the United States, the United Kingdom, Italy, Japan, Belgium, and (particularly for Tanzania) Ireland.
- A large number of small donors such as the former socialist bloc countries, China, and the bilateral Arab funds.

Since the early 1970s Tanzania has had a very special relationship with the Nordic countries, in particular Sweden. This country has consistently provided substantial resources to Tanzania and has positioned itself at the head of the list of the country's aid donors. By 1983 Tanzania's relations with practically all the bilateral donors were under great strain. The fact that even the strongest supporters scaled down their assistance contributed to the change in the country's policies.

The view among the bilateral donors today is that Tanzania is trying to do the right things in terms of policy reform, but that administrative capacity and competence are very low. This means that donors are reluctant to shift responsibilities to the recipient government, although in principle they realize that this is necessary for aid to be effective and sustainable in the long term. Donors are also reluctant to shift too much of their efforts into building administrative capacity, since this might jeopardize the management and success of their conventional projects. The Swedish slogan is "Partnership in Development," but much remains to be done before this becomes a reality on the ground. There is in any case an improvement in terms of policymaking capacity, insofar as it is now more often the government that writes policy and position papers spelling out the priorities. Previously ministries often referred to World Bank documents when asked about government policy.

There is work underway to design comprehensive sector programs in education, health, roads, water, and local government, but how well these will function will depend both on the capacity of the government (particularly at the local level) and on the willingness of donors to change to another type of control. The latter will depend on the former, which means that it is hard to be optimistic about things changing very much in the short run. Donors will probably maintain a high degree of control of their own slices of the "joint" programs to make sure that the activities are in accordance with their list of priorities and that the money can be accounted for. It is an eternal dilemma in the aid business: on the one hand the donors want to give control to the recipient government, but on the other hand they have to report to their home constituencies, particularly the parliaments, about how the money allocated to aid is used.

This also puts a brake on coordination efforts. Some donors are more willing to go down this road than others are, but it is very hard to believe that all will agree to be coordinated. And this means that aid dependence will persist. The recipient should take a more strict line with the donors to make sure that aid fits in with domestic priorities, but in practice there is still a very flexible attitude to donor demands. Tanzania does not say "no" to donors who are willing to put their money into a project, even though it may be out of line with the government's priorities and hard to finance in the long term.

An efficient partnership or efficient local control requires a well-run bureaucracy, and that in turn requires a competent staff and organization. As long as the government pays very low salaries relative to the private sector, it will find it hard to recruit and retain the best people. On top of this there is a virtual stop on new hiring, which means little new blood coming into the system. Donors are involved in various topping-up exercises, either to key personnel or key units to bring about a more efficient organization, but this in turn complicates the general overhaul of the civil service. The government has set forth principles of civil service reform that include gradually increasing real wages, but they are already behind on the latter count. Given the constraints of the cash budget and the limited ability to collect taxes, it will be very hard to achieve the goals set out in the plan.

One aspect of partnership or increased ownership is that the recipient should shoulder a large part of the recurrent costs of a certain project. Typically it is written in the initial agreement that a certain percentage will be paid by the government and that this will gradually increase. The government is willing to sign agreements like this although it should be clear that in reality they will not be able to pay up. The assumption is that they will deal with that issue when it occurs, and typically the donor does not withdraw from their project but tries to find some way to salvage the project anyway. Thus there is a tendency toward hypocrisy on both sides of the table.

It is also hard to coordinate within the government. In the case of the education program the coordination exercise involves as many as nine ministries, which suggests that in the end it will be hard to get a simple and efficient management structure. A wide range of players and interests are involved on both the donor and the government side, and in a weak system such as the Tanzanian one it will be hard to get the bureaucracy to work well. Moreover, in a wide-spanning aid relationship such as Tanzania's, it should not be surprising to find that the interests of players on both the donor and recipient sides frequently overlap or interlock, thus evolving into relationships that are outside the officially established channels.

One early step toward changing the relationship between donors and the government was taken in September 1996, when the Nordic countries (Denmark, Finland, Norway, and Sweden) entered into a partnership agreement with Tanzania. The agreement required the government to produce a policy platform, respect democracy and human rights, fight against corruption and for good governance, emphasize macroeconomic stability and domestic resource mobilization, and focus government activities on core functions, while civil society and the private sector would complement these efforts. Five general principles for the collaboration were set forth:

- The program must be fully owned by Tanzania and formulated according to Tanzania's visions and policies.
- Tanzania is responsible for the programs and accountable for resources provided.

- There should be shared financing, with the Tanzanian share increasing over time.
- There should be a move from discrete projects to sector program support.
- The Nordic countries should support only those activities to which the government of Tanzania gives priority (Embassy of Sweden 1998: 4–5).

These principles obviously represent a radical break with past practice; but the actual practice is, of course, still a long way from the above. Sweden, for example, has a long list of goals that must be met for aid to be considered at all, so it is somewhat hypocritical to say that the programs must be fully owned and formulated according to Tanzanian priorities. When the government formulates plans, it certainly keeps in mind what the donors want to hear. It is only when transfers are in a general form, for example through transfers to the Multilateral Debt Relief Fund, that one can really talk about ownership. Still, other forms of collaboration can be characterized as partnerships, although the donor is in a much more powerful position than the recipient government. The donor can always threaten to withdraw its money, while the recipient government has no such course of action open to it.

In contrast to the Nordic countries, which have been working behind the scenes to provide encouragement and support to Tanzania, the next category of major donors, led by the United States, the United Kingdom, and Germany, have traditionally taken a hard line in their relations with Tanzania. They have tended to identify more strictly with the IFIs and to trigger their aid disbursements more in line with World Bank and IMF judgments.

However, support for reform considerations is also balanced against a complex set of foreign policy interests. For instance, it has been argued that during the second half of the 1980s, Tanzania did not do well in aid terms with the British government of Margaret Thatcher because of its role as a Frontline state, supporting independence for countries in southern Africa and vocally criticizing Western countries' continued economic ties with South Africa. With the change to a Labour government in the United Kingdom, the country's aid disbursements to Tanzania doubled.

Domestic economic interests of the donors have also been a significant influence. For instance, it has been reported that in the late 1980s U.S. pressure on Japan to reduce its balance of payment surpluses led to a major increase in Japanese aid to developing countries, including Tanzania. Japan then hosted the first Tokyo International Conference on African Development (TICAD I) in 1993, followed by TICAD II in 1998, as an indication of its intention to shape an independent African political and economic cooperation policy. The other main objective of the TICAD conferences was to highlight Africa's development problems and prospects, elevating their importance in the eyes of the international community. Similarly, France in recent years was reported to be planning a significant expansion of its aid program to Tanzania and other countries in order to counterbalance efforts by the United Kingdom and the United States to expand their operations in francophone Africa. As a former colonial power, Germany has maintained a special interest in Tanzania and has, among other things, tended to fund some projects that reflect the historical connection. The Arab funds have continued to provide concessional lending without much policy linkage, except when they are involved in co-financing with the Bretton Woods institutions or the AfDB. In 1988–92, Italian aid to Tanzania rose sharply, mainly because of a large increase in support for projects operated by Italian contractors.

Tanzania's relations with donors came under great strain in 1994–95, toward the end of the government of President Ali Hassan Mwinyi. But recent assessments indicate a substantial improvement in donor relations. A factor that has contributed to this improvement has been cited before in reference to the Helleiner report of June 1995. Following an extensive discussion of the report, an agreement was reached in January 1997 between the donors and the government on a new mode of interaction based on a partnership approach, as discussed below.

Many donors are cautious, slow, and reluctant or unable to make the shift, especially in terms of making contributions to "basket funds" in support of these sectoral programs. The tendency is for each donor to cling to its particular area of specialization (for example, capacity building for private sector development in the case of the United States, integrated rural development in the case of the Irish, and structural adjustment in the case of the Swiss).

However, an overall assessment is that today many bilateral donors see great potential in Tanzania. While they recognize that the country's structural problems persist—an inefficient civil service, a slow rate of project implementation, poor accountability in project management—they seem to be encouraged by an improved policy environment and perceived willingness and determination on the part of the government to implement reforms.

Donor Coordination: Transition in Slow Motion

Tanzania is presently in the forefront of the discussions on transforming the aid relationship into a partnership between donors and recipient. Sida, the Swedish development cooperation agency, carried out an informal evaluation of what has been achieved since the Helleiner workshop in January 1997 (Embassy of Sweden 1999a). The Swedish study reviews the list of aims set out in the agreed minutes of that meeting, and reports on progress or lack of it:

1. *Donors should provide the government of Tanzania with information about planned and actual aid flows.* This has proved to be very difficult to achieve because of the quite different ways of accounting for flows among the various donors. Attempts are again made in this year's Public Expenditure Review.

2. *Donors should follow the Tanzanian government's priorities for development projects and seek to exit from noncore activities.* Tanzania claims that the number of projects has been reduced very significantly from about 1,500 to between 500 and 600, but the information is scanty. It should also be noted that development expenditures in 1997–98 were 60 percent below target. This suggests that the system still absorbs resources inefficiently. The shortfall may be due to, for example, the lack of counterpart funds, failure to meet conditions for the project, or problems in implementation.

3. *Aid coordination should be improved.* The education and health sectors should become test cases for aid coordination modalities. There have been steps in this direction (see, for example, Tanzania 1999), but disagreement among donors as to how to proceed has slowed the process. Still, the education sector development plan has just undergone a very comprehensive appraisal by joint teams composed of, on the one hand, foreign consultants appointed by donors who are active in supporting the sector, and on the other hand, local consultants appointed by the Ministry of Education. The 60 consultants spent two weeks making the appraisal and submitted the report to the ministry. The report will provide input into the negotiations between donors and Tanzania—an example of joint action in the policy reform process.

4. *The Policy Framework Paper should be made public and the government should consult with civil society.* The PFP has been made public, but so far the consultations with civil society have not taken off.

5. *Donor discussions on debt relief and development assistance should be integrated.* A Multilateral Debt Relief Fund has been established, although it is a bit unclear what has been achieved in terms of integrating the discussions.

6. *Steps should be taken to develop the planning and financial management capacity in the Treasury and the Planning Commission.* There are several programs underway that seek to build capacity. The further role of the Planning Commission is unclear, however.

7. *Tanzania should take the lead in the preparation of Policy Framework Papers and Public Expenditure Reviews.* This has happened. Tanzania has taken a lead role in the drafting and discussion of the PFP,

and the relevant ministries are more involved than they were before. The same can be said of the PERs. The work is now done on three levels. First, there is a steering committee that oversees the process at the policy level. This consists of the permanent secretaries in the relevant ministries and is chaired by the permanent secretary in the Ministry of Finance. Second, there are technical advisory groups that oversee the implementation of the technical studies and the PER process. This group consists of senior officials from the relevant ministries and is chaired by the deputy permanent secretary in the Ministry of Finance. Third, there is a working group to monitor and coordinate progress on the technical studies. This is also chaired by the deputy permanent secretary in the Ministry of Finance and includes key personnel from the relevant ministries and representatives of donors and research institutions. This group has met twice a month during the process. There is also a small secretariat, consisting of representatives from the ministries and the World Bank, that provides logistical support and other help. The approach is very participatory and is open to ministries, the research community, and donors. The decentralization of the Public Expenditure Review, the Country Assistance Strategy, the Structural Adjustment Credit, and the Country Economic Memorandum to the local World Bank office seems to have helped to achieve a more consultative approach. The fact that the highly respected professor Benno Ndulu is located at the World Bank office in Dar es Salaam has also helped to improve local control and access.

8. *Information, accounting, and reporting of assistance should be standardized.* This has not been done.
9. *Best practice projects in Africa should be collected and analyzed.* This has not been done by the government, and maybe it should not be its job to do so.
10. *The government's capacity to manage should be enhanced and the donors should be willing to transfer more responsibility to the government of Tanzania.* This is an ongoing process in which Sweden is taking the lead. In practice the process is very slow, however. There is deep concern about the problem of corruption, which makes it hard to transfer responsibility. Unless further steps are taken to control corruption and improve transparency, progress will be difficult to achieve.
11. *With regard to the relationships with the civil service, parallel or topping-up arrangements should be minimized.* Again, not much has happened apart from a report identifying and discussing the problem.
12. *Coordination meetings should be rationalized.* The Ministry of Finance has started quarterly sectoral reviews in some sectors (health, education, and roads) to deal with the donors in a more coordinated way.

13. *The use of technical assistance should be reviewed.* This has not been done.
14. *The recommendations should be followed but by a joint committee.* A development forum has recently started to function after a long period of dormancy.
15. *Further stocktaking should take place at the CG meetings.* This did occur at the CG meeting of December 1997, which was held in Dar. The venue of that meeting also allowed broader participation of Tanzania officials in the CG. The 1999 meeting was also supposed to take place in Dar, but the donors preferred to meet in Paris.

Helleiner himself recently returned to Tanzania to review the progress in implementing the agreed actions. He found that there has been a significant advance (Helleiner 1999), especially in establishing government leadership in macroeconomic management. However, his review also notes that progress at the sectoral level has been slow. An important test of the new relationships has been the introduction of sector-wide programs in education, health, and a refurbished road sector. This calls for a significant change from the traditional approach based on directly controlled projects. It also requires the timely provision of complete information, increased emphasis on sector-wide policies (and the capacity and willingness for frank dialogue on them), the turning over of some budgetary control and procurement functions to a local authority, and, above all, the acceptance of government leadership and ultimate responsibility for the sector program.

In conclusion, much remains to be done for the process to move forward. The ideas from the Helleiner workshop make sense, but there are problems on both the donor and the government side. A general observation is that Tanzania is rather good at launching new initiatives and setting up interesting plans, but has poor capacity for implementing them and living by the new principles once they have been established. This was largely true in the past, when such initiatives were not backed by institutional arrangements to keep the implementation going. With the current emphasis by the government on institutionalization of initiatives, there seems to be a chance for better performance than in the past. Transition in Tanzania does not happened with a "big bang." It is, rather, transition in slow motion. This is of course a concern, because if there is no take-off the system may eventually implode.

POLICY REFORMS AND INSTITUTIONAL DEVELOPMENT

The following sections analyze the causes and processes of the reforms. However, before entering into this discussion we need to provide a brief background of the events leading up to the Tanzanian economic crisis.

We will then provide a chronology of the process of policy reform since 1979, identifying the main phases in the donor-recipient relationship. We look specifically at inflation and fiscal policy (macroeconomic management) and at trade policy (an example of structural policies). The macroeconomic and structural policies considered here have been shown in empirical studies to affect developing countries' growth (Sachs and Warner 1995). But successful development also depends on institutional development, so we discuss institutional reform such as the privatization process and public sector management.

From the Arusha Declaration to Crisis

Following independence in 1961 the government concentrated on the Africanization of the public sector, but otherwise there was continued reliance on the private sector. An import substitution policy served to promote industrial development, but the economy remained fairly open. It continued to be highly dependent on revenue from commodity exports. During 1961–67 per capita income grew by 2 percent per year, the highest rate of any period in independent Tanzania (see table 6.4). This was a time of macroeconomic stability with low inflation and a satisfactory balance of payments, and capital formation increased steadily between 1963 and 1967.

However, the government was not satisfied. It was concerned about the apparent increase in inequality, and found industrial growth to be below

TABLE 6.4 TANZANIA: DATA FOR THE PRE-ARUSHA PERIOD, 1961–67

Indicator	1961	1962	1963	1964	1965	1966	1967
Per capita income growth (%)	–7.5	4.3	1.2	3.6	–0.2	9.9	1.8
Population growth (%)	2.8	2.8	2.9	2.9	2.9	3.0	3.0
Urbanization (%)	4.8	4.9	5.1	5.2	5.3	5.6	5.9
Labor force in agriculture (%)	92.4	92.1	91.9	91.7	91.4	91.2	90.9
Monetary growth (%)	—	21.7	25.6	–15.2	31.8	476.7	13.1
Gross investment (% of GDP)	13.7	11.6	10.7	12.0	13.9	15.1	18.9

— Not available.

Sources: Compiled by Bigsten and Danielsson 1999. Income and investment data from the Bureau of Statistics, Dar es Salaam. Other data from *World Development Indicators 1998*.

expectations, as was the inflow of external resources. President Nyerere felt that a new strategy was necessary to speed up development.

The Arusha Declaration of 1967 was a watershed in Tanzanian political and economic history. The government abandoned the cautious policies pursued up to that point and launched a strategy of "African socialism." There was concern that external dependence was too high, and that steps should be taken to create an internally integrated economy. The necessary structural transformation would be facilitated by increased state control.

By the early 1970s, the government had consolidated its hold on most aspects of formal economic activity. Banking and large portions of the industrial sector had been nationalized, the bulk of international trade and private retail trade had been confined to state agencies, and administered prices had largely replaced market prices. A foreign exchange allocation system was developed in response to the balance of payments crises of the early 1970s, and a National Price Commission was established to set prices for a vast range of commodities. By the mid-1970s, most of the rural population had been forced to resettle in "Ujamaa villages" as part of a strategy to promote cooperative agriculture, and monopoly government marketing boards had replaced peasant marketing cooperatives.

In 1974 the government began to implement its Basic Industries Strategy (BIS) of import-substituting industrialization, but it soon had to postpone it in the balance of payments crisis that accompanied the first oil shock. The external position improved dramatically during the coffee boom (1975–78), and the government revived the BIS in a decision that came to dominate the allocation of foreign exchange and the pattern of domestic investment. Table 6.5 shows that investment was high throughout the 1970s, although it declined somewhat in 1973–75. The investment program was state-led, but many of the investments undertaken in the 1970s were supported by donors. The crisis was heralded by the breakup of the East African Community in 1977 and the rapid depletion of international reserves following the end of the coffee boom in 1978 and an abortive import liberalization that same year.

Donors disagreed about Tanzania in the second half of the 1970s. Several bilateral donors were supportive, while the World Bank and the IMF became more and more critical of policies pertaining to agriculture, domestic pricing, the BIS, and the exchange rate (Collier 1991). Since President Nyerere's position was strong both domestically and with many bilateral donors, he was able to take a hard line with the IFIs.

During 1968–78 growth in per capita income was still positive at 0.7 percent per year (see table 6.5). The growth was led by the public sector, while Tanzanian exports, which continued to be dominated by traditional agricultural exports such as coffee and cotton, stagnated. The policy

TABLE 6.5 TANZANIA: DATA FOR THE PRE-CRISIS PERIOD, 1968–78

Indicator	1968	1969	1970	1971	1972	1973	1974	1975	1976	1977	1978
Per capita income growth (%)	2.1	-0.7	3.0	0.8	2.3	0.5	-0.5	2.9	2.3	-2.7	-1.9
Population growth (%)	3.0	3.0	3.0	3.0	3.0	3.0	3.0	3.0	3.1	3.1	3.1
Urbanization (%)	6.1	6.4	6.7	7.4	8.1	8.7	9.4	10.1	11.0	12.0	12.9
External debt (millions of U.S. dollars)	—	—	212	284	407	619	900	1,170	1,380	1,700	1,970
Labor force in agriculture (%)	90.6	90.3	90.1	89.7	89.3	88.9	88.5	88.1	87.7	87.2	86.7
Monetary growth (%)	17.8	9.2	12.0	18.2	17.7	18.2	22.1	24.4	25.1	20.2	12.6
Gross investment (% of GDP)	18.4	16.3	22.9	26.8	23.6	22.6	21.6	20.8	29.0	29.4	33.8

— Not available.

Sources: Compiled by Bigsten and Danielsson 1999. Income and investment data from the Bureau of Statistics, Dar es Salaam. Other data from World Development Indicators 1998.

environment in Tanzania was hostile to both traditional and nontraditional exports. Government monopolization of marketing in the 1970s undercut the rewards to peasant production for export, while inefficiencies drove down producer prices. Other factors included the relocation of rural producers in the "villagization" drive, the high effective protection of the import-substituting industrial sector, which turned relative prices in favor of the urban areas, and the use of trade controls rather than exchange rate adjustment as a means of adjusting to external shocks. The coffee bonanza concealed the weaknesses of the system for a few years, but when it ended the inefficiencies of the economy became apparent.

Chronology of Policy Reforms 1979–99

In looking at the overall pattern and phases of the reform process, it is possible to identify five policy phases in the last 20 years in Tanzania.

1979–82: Stalemate

After the collapse of the commodity boom of 1975–78, the Uganda war in 1978–79, and the second oil crisis in 1979, the economy faced very severe problems. In response, Tanzania agreed to a standby credit with the IMF in 1979, but after the government failed to observe the agreed budget ceiling the agreement was cancelled. During discussion of the release of the second tranche, the government ordered the head of the visiting IMF mission to leave the country. The minister of finance, Edwin Mtei, was perceived by President Nyerere as being too close to the IMF and was removed. Mtei was succeeded by Jamal, who was less eager to reform the economy. Nyerere made a speech in which he criticized the IMF for trying to set itself up as the "International Ministry of Finance" and rejected its demands. Tanzania then turned to the World Bank for assistance, but although the Bank had been supportive throughout the 1970s, it now refused to support the Tanzanian government. There was then little communication for about two years.

In 1981 the Bank indicated that it could provide quick-disbursing aid if the Tanzanian government undertook certain policy changes and reached an agreement with the IMF. The latter demanded a 50–60 percent devaluation, a significant reduction of the budget deficit, removal or reduction of consumer and producer subsidies, positive real interest rates, and higher agricultural prices and import liberalization. The government proposed some new measures in the National Economic Survival Program (NESP) of 1981, which was essentially part of an application to the IMF. The goals stated in the plan were to increase export revenue and eliminate food shortages through various supply-side measures and to reduce public expenditures. This was to be achieved through tighter state control of public expenditures and increased production. The plan was wholly unrealistic, and the IMF found it to be completely unsatisfactory. Anti-reform elements in Tanzania argued that the causes of the crisis were external problems and not internal policy weaknesses. The government's position was that Tanzania was a structurally weak economy and that the remedies proposed, including the dismantling of the socialist structures and deep cuts in social spending on education, health, and water, would not help to revive the economy. The government was not ready to agree to carry out significant reforms. This partly explains why NESP I (1981) and NESP II (1982) were more exhortations than policy change documents.

Moreover, at this time there were very few senior officers in central ministries capable as a group of undertaking independent macroeconomic and sectoral analysis to generate new ideas and develop new programs to address the crisis. Sufficient local intellectual capacity was not available to make it possible for the government to engage in a meaningful debate with the IFIs or even to counterbalance the ruling party's inclinations toward maintaining the status quo. There was excessive reliance on a handful of expatriate advisers, most of whom preferred to toe the party line. Sometimes these advisers held divergent policy perspectives and it was a task to maintain harmony among them.

The faculty at the University of Dar es Salaam had generally been weakened, either by socialist ideology or by opportunists within the institution who were eager to please the party leadership. To identify with the party could open opportunities for accelerated promotions or for transfer to more remunerative positions in parastatal organizations or political structures. Because of a severe shortage of qualified people, such transfers were frequent at the time and contributed to the lack of consolidation of intellectual policy groups within the government or around it.

1982–85: Hard Internal Debate

The country was now in a desperate situation, with the exchange rate greatly overvalued and exports at very low levels. The bilaterals and the World Bank were trying to find some middle ground and sponsored a technical advisory group with well-known economists, who were asked to come up with a compromise package. The group proposed a more moderate devaluation, but the government did not accept even this. The government used the report to produce its own reform package, which was a dilution of the policy changes proposed by the advisory group. This revision was done by the Planning Ministry, then under Minister Malima, who in 1980–92 was basically anti-reform although he later (1992–94) became more pro-reform. The government turned to the Nordic bilaterals to fill the gap left by the IFIs, but by now they also were becoming more critical and did not provide the extra funds. There was thus a steep decline in aid flows between 1982 and 1985, which was period of extreme economic crisis.

Still, a sign of some movement on the government side was the appointment in 1982 of the prime minister, Cleopa Msuya, as minister of finance. He was more aware of the need to mend fences with the IFIs. Together with Rutihinda, who was the permanent secretary in the Ministry of Finance, Msuya tried within the government to push for reforms. There were similar attempts at the Bank of Tanzania. Still, the supporters of reform in the Ministry of Finance had to work hard to build up support for it within the government. The cabinet was dominated at the time by hard-line left-wingers opposed to the reforms, with Finance Minister Msuya as one of the few advocates of reform. The minister of planning, Malima, was a leading opponent of the reforms, and he quickly brought in Ajit Singh from Cambridge to write a counterproposal to the reform plan. There was a head-on collision between Msuya and Malima, in which the latter even wrote a memo to the president accusing the reformers of being "traitors." The parastatal establishment was also a stumbling block in the process, although some could see that devaluation would make it possible for them to improve their results.

It took time for the government to realize that the parastatals were a problem. First, there were attempts to peg the desired exchange rate at a level that would be sufficient to clear the losses of parastatals. This approach was much in favor in 1983 and 1984. Second, the extreme opponent of the reforms, Malima, submitted a paper to the ruling party suggesting that the problem of parastatals was rooted in the existence of the private sector. The private sector would have to be phased out in order to give room for the parastatals to recover! Apparently he believed that the private sector was doing harm to the parastatals through its dealings with them, for example by supplying them with overpriced goods and services.

Public opposition to the policies of the early 1980s was limited, as most Tanzanians chose instead to withdraw into subsistence activities or find other ways to deal with shortages and regulations. Parallel markets emerged, as did illegal cross-border trade. The rapid expansion of the underground economy as well as capital flight undermined the tax base. Semi-public discussions were started at the behest of the reformers within government. An informal network of economists from the University of Dar es Salaam, together with private consultants and personnel from key ministries such as Agriculture, Transport, Industry and Trade, and the Planning Commission, was set up to provide a forum for debate and to increase the understanding of the politicians and policymakers.

The strong political leadership made it possible to push through important decisions (or to reject others) without proper analysis and debate. Nevertheless, there were courageous individuals, notably Mtei and Msuya, who could put forward reform ideas to the party hierarchy and the cabinet. Such people faced stiff resistance from the party, and, as so often happens, vacillating positions developed within the cabinet depending on who could get the president's ear. But the increasingly precarious social situation arising from severe shortages of consumer goods, especially in the large cities, forced the leadership to search for solutions and ultimately to consider seriously the adoption of more comprehensive reform packages.

Up to 1983 the government essentially preserved existing policies. Instead of introducing measures to deal with the imbalances, the government pursued campaigns against corruption and profiteers. Stewart, Klugman, and Neyapti (1999:82) argue that a side effect of the political stability that characterized Tanzania was that it postponed pressures for economic reforms that were essential for economic development. Adam and others (1994) argue that the backing from a range of bilateral donors also made it possible to delay adjustment.

Nonetheless, a second homegrown structural adjustment program was launched in 1983. It was more ambitious than the previous one, but still did not change any of the major parameters of policy. The program sought to identify a series of structural problems in the economy and then adjust the type of state intervention so that the economy would do better. It was not a matter of liberalization and deregulation. The main aim was to increase agricultural production and exports, and the measures included a modest devaluation. This did have some positive effect on exports and agriculture, but fell far short of closing the gap between the official and parallel rates. There was a further tightening of fiscal and monetary policies, but the measures were still insufficient to reverse the trend.

The situation remained grave, and there was mounting public criticism of the shortages of goods. The increasingly tough security measures against smugglers and profiteers only increased the shortages, and it was mainly the smaller culprits who were sentenced in the end. Campaigns against corruption and profiteers were directed at improving the distribution of goods and curbing the practice of stockpiling since it was believed that hoarding or unfair distribution of goods caused the shortages. When the shortages became worse in spite of the campaigns, the champions of this approach began to realize that the problem was more deeply rooted. This realization influenced the decision to permit partial import liberalization in 1984. In fact, Sokoine, then prime minister, led the campaign against profiteers, and later he also led the initiative toward partial liberalization starting with transport. Imports of pick-ups were allowed and supply improved, and these positive results were used to argue for further import liberalization.

The overall failure of the structural adjustment program was aggravated by two factors. First, the receding aid inflows reduced the already low levels of capacity utilization and thus worsened the shortage of goods. Second, the allocation of whatever foreign exchange was available through CIS tended to favor projects, which earlier had been funded by the respective donors rather than being allocated according to efficiency criteria. The few resources available were spread too thinly to be effective.

In 1984 economists from the University of Dar es Salaam started to hold public meetings at which they advocated liberalization measures. The initial discussions targeted policymakers and politicians and some private sector leaders. These meetings were, of course, against the official party line, but they were supported by the reformers within the government, for example in the Ministry of Finance and the Bank of Tanzania. That same year, in the face of extreme goods shortages, the government finally made a more significant move. It chose to allow own-funded imports, it devalued the currency, and it increased agricultural prices by about 30 percent. There was an export retention scheme, and user charges were introduced in health. This was the first step on the road to the restoration of relations with the IFIs. There was now some improvement in the economy and imports could increase somewhat. The government tried to mend relations with the IMF, which felt that the new reform program was a least a basis for further discussions. Talks were reopened between the government and the IMF at the end of the Nyerere era.

1986–92: Initial Reforms and Aid Boom

The years between 1986 and 1992 saw the second aid boom (the first having occurred in the 1970s).When Mwinyi took over as president some initial steps had already been taken on the reform route with the Economic Recovery Program. The government reached an agreement with the IMF in 1986, which also meant that other donors came back in force. Joint government-donor meetings were initiated and have continued with more or less intensity since then.[4]

ERP I covered the period from 1986 to 1989. The targets were to:

- Increase output of food and export crops through appropriate pricing strategies
- Increase capacity utilization in industry from 20–30 percent to 60–70 percent
- Restore internal and external macroeconomic balance through "prudent" monetary, fiscal, and trade policies

- Reduce inflation from 30 percent to 15–20 percent
- Increase foreign exchange earnings from exports from US$400 million to US$630 million by 1989
- Rehabilitate and maintain basic social services.

The policy instruments to be used included:

- Raising agricultural prices by 5 percent per year or to 60–70 percent of the world market price, and reducing the use of price controls
- Sufficient devaluation to eliminate exchange rate overvaluation by mid-1988, with a subsequent move to market-based allocation of foreign exchange
- Deregulation of both imports and local trade
- Control of public expenditure by continuing the austerity measures started in 1984–85, limiting government recurrent expenditure, reducing deficit financing from the banking system, and rationalizing and reducing parastatal activities and subsidies to them
- Tightening monetary policy by raising interest rates until positive in real terms, adopting tight credit ceilings, and limiting the growth of money supply to 15–20 percent per year
- Improving revenue collection through close monitoring and looking for ways to increase efficiency and broaden the tax base
- Non-price measures to increase agricultural production and steps to improve access to consumer goods, distribution of agricultural inputs, and transport infrastructure; general freeing of consumer goods markets.

The Multisector Rehabilitation Credit agreed in 1986 was funded with US$300 million, half from IDA and half from other donors. It concerned prices, fiscal management, and exchange rate adjustment. The main aim of this program was to increase agricultural production through devaluation and improvements in marketing and transport. The allocation of the funds was left to the government, conditional on compliance with certain macroeconomic conditions that were imposed through the disbursement in tranches. At the end, in 1988, some money went through the OGL. Under the program there was a sharp devaluation, limits on the budget and balance of payments deficits, and limits on domestic credit. Still, the implementation was not as smooth as was hoped initially. The second program entered into was the Industrial Rehabilitation and Structural Adjustment Credit of US$242 million, agreed in December 1988. Its main focus was trade liberalization, tariff and sales tax reforms, and industrial restructuring. Funds were now channeled through the OGL system.

A new agreement covered 1989–92. It consisted of an IMF Enhanced Structural Adjustment Facility (ESAF) plus three different World Bank projects. The ESAF covered liberalization of the foreign exchange market. The other programs were the following:

- The Tanzania Agricultural Adjustment Credit of US$338 million started in 1990, again with IDA as the major source. The main concern was now liberalization of the marketing of agricultural inputs and outputs. The money again went through the OGL system, now with a negative list, indicating that the credit was not restricted to agriculture only.
- The Financial Sector Adjustment Program from 1991 covered US$275 million. This focused on privatization of the banking sector and allowing foreign exchange bureaus and foreign banks to enter the market.
- The Structural Adjustment Credit of 1991 focused on restructuring and privatization of parastatals, reform of the civil service, and further restructuring of the markets for agricultural exports.

Nonetheless, although reforms were undertaken during the second half of the 1980s, the cabinet was still dominated by hard-liners who went along very reluctantly. Former president Nyerere, who had stayed as chairman of Chama Cha Mapinduzi (CCM), the ruling party, made his views known from time to time, but seldom intervened directly. It was just a handful of ministers that really supported the reforms, and the debates in the cabinet were very difficult until the Eastern European collapse. After that, from about 1990 onwards, the tone changed dramatically and the hard-liners essentially conceded defeat. In fact a few of them—such as Gertrude Mongela, Alfred Tandau, and David Mwakawago, all strong in the ruling party—were made ambassadors to various countries, keeping them away from active domestic politics.

Although resistance to reforms has been reduced over time and the purge of the hard-liners was a big step forward, elements of resistance remain and have taken different forms. Since the ruling party conceded ideological defeat in the Zanzibar Resolution in 1991, the opposition to reforms that has surfaced from time to time has been mainly issue-oriented rather than based on specific ideological lines. The opponents of reforms have also changed tactics and have been taking nationalistic lines (in the name of indigenous people or Tanzania in general) rather than ideological lines (in the name of socialism). These tactics have emerged most clearly in relation to the process of privatization.

In the first few years of the 1990s reforms took off. Donor confidence in the government increased significantly, and the IFIs presented very positive reports on Tanzania's achievements. Since that time there has been less emphasis on comprehensive macroeconomic programs and targets; rather, the emphasis has shifted to issues such as privatization and civil service and parastatal reform. The five-year plans were abandoned and were replaced by Policy Framework Papers, rolling plans, and forward budgets.

Public debate in the early 1990s mainly concerned the poor quality of social services, but there was also criticism of the lack of democracy. The adjustment measures initially met with limited public opposition, but in 1992 riots took place at two universities to protest the introduction of cost-sharing measures in association with the World Bank Higher Education Credit.

The government's suppression of civil society has gradually eased. It allowed independent newspapers in 1988 and limited public debate on human rights violations in 1991, and in that year it also reduced the supervisory power of the ruling party over the cooperatives. Labor and cooperative unions received some autonomy after 1990 (Stewart, Klugman, and Neyapti 1999). These reforms made it possible to debate issues that previously had not been allowed. The leadership code was abolished in 1992, and several officials have taken advantage of their newfound freedom in unethical ways. Some of this has been exposed in the press.

Nyerere eventually threw his support behind the introduction of democracy. By this time several opposition parties had been formed in Britain and underground in Tanzania. In 1991 a presidential commission took a survey of attitudes toward the introduction of multiparty democracy and found that 77 percent supported the existing one-party system. However, CCM, the ruling party, succumbed to external pressure and legalized the registration of opposition parties in 1992. CCM continued to win by-elections, although the legitimacy of these was contested. The party still had privileged access to the media and there were accusations of irregularities. The opposition parties were either fragmented in ideological identity or were distinguished by their geographical concentration of membership.

1993–95: Off-Track

In 1992 President Mwinyi appointed Malima as minister of finance. Although the move is hard to explain politically given Malima's background, he seemed to have changed his views on economic reform. The cabinet team also changed. This was the start of a new period of crisis, however, and President Mwinyi seemed less emphatic as a reformer during his second term in office. Some argue that he lost control. During the years 1993–95 reforms veered off track, fiscal policy went out of control, large tax exemptions were granted by the minister of finance, and there was a general feeling that corruption and tax evasion were rampant. Government revenue fell, and the government reverted to heavy borrowing in the Central Bank. Much of the fiscal control and discipline that had been developed since 1986 was lost.

Why did the reform process stagnate? The main reason is probably that the donors shifted their demands to new areas and raised the stakes. Second-generation reforms are more intrusive than first-generation reforms. They demand the closing up of various points of leakage in the system, for example through banking reforms. This confronts vested interests more directly, and the government then seeks to find new ways to allocate rents. For such reforms to be successful, therefore, the government must be fully committed to radical reform, and in this case the government was not fully committed.

Many of the donors now lost faith again. In November 1994 the Nordic donors except Denmark suspended aid payments because of the tax exemptions to politically influential people. The IMF failed to engage the government in meaningful discussions, and in 1994 the Fund cancelled the adjustment program and essentially pulled out. Malima was soon forced to resign as minister of finance, mainly on account of the tax exemption scandals, but also because of his inability to communicate with the IFIs. He was moved to the Ministry of Industries and Trade, but before the elections in 1995 he joined an opposition party and left the government. A new minister of finance, Kikwete, was appointed for a short period. Politically it was important to replace a Muslim with a Muslim to avoid turning it into a religious issue, especially because Malima had often indicated in private that he was the first Muslim minister of finance. The transfer of Malima from Finance was clearly engineered by donors on account of the way CIS funds and exemptions were handled.

In fact, a few months earlier Parliament had tried to fight out these issues and strongly criticized Malima for the exemptions, but he survived. President Mwinyi was not ready to let him go. A few months later, when the donors put their foot down, Mwinyi let Malima go but transferred him to Industries and Trade rather than sacking him. This demonstrates the relative influence of donors compared to that of domestic constituencies. In matters of policy reforms it would appear that donors exert greater influence than local groups. This imbalance has been changing gradually, and is likely to continue changing as ownership of development policy shifts to Tanzania.

1996–99: Back on Track

A number of opposition parties took part in the first multiparty elections, but CCM retained power in 1995 with 62 percent of the vote. The new government was elected in November 1995, and in early 1996 the new president, Mkapa, installed a team and from then on the reforms started again. Mkapa had always been one of the few reformers in the government. The government set off on a shadow program with the IMF for the period January–June 1996, which was successfully implemented. This program was watched carefully by all the donors and earned praise from the IMF. The IMF then came back with a new three-year ESAF and other donors followed. Since then the relations have improved. Still, aid inflows are smaller than they were before the break, due to the general decline in foreign aid.

The agenda introduced by the new government at the end of 1995 largely reflects the agreement that had been reached between Tanzania and donors, as expressed very well in the Helleiner report. Mkapa put high priority on fighting corruption and mending relations with donors. He was also determined to keep the reforms on track. In the first few months of the new government a commission was formed to examine the problem of corruption. Efforts to form a Tanzania Revenue Authority were accelerated, and the TRA was established in July 1996. In order to get the new cabinet to come to grips with economic reforms a workshop was organized for all ministers and principal secretaries in which various aspects of reforms were discussed. Resource persons were drawn from within and outside Tanzania, organized by the president's office (Civil Service Department), the Commonwealth Secretariat, and the East and Southern African Management Institute (ESAMI). The week-long workshop was held in Arusha in January 1996.

The government signed a deal at the Paris Club in January 1997 and has already received Naples terms. In April 2000 Tanzania was included in the HIPC Initiative. Private debt is small and has been reduced mainly by donor-financed debt buybacks. The Multilateral Debt Relief Fund helps the government service its debt to the IFIs.

At the beginning of the new century, the status of the adjustment program is relatively satisfactory. The country performs well on the macroeconomic indicators, but struggles with some of the structural performance indicators.

During 1996–99 there were a few cases in which local constituencies were able to express their interests and influence policy by seeking assistance from policy analysis institutions. First, in 1996 a group of business people felt the tax regime was unfavorable to them. The tax rates were too high and they wanted to convince the government that high taxes were inimical to revenue growth. They sought assistance from ESRF, which did a study that synthesized their views and helped them argue their case. The main argument was that if tax rates were lowered and simplified, compliance would increase and tax revenue would go up. This argument was contrary to what the IMF was advising. However, in the 1996–97 budget the government gave in to some of these demands and the following year more gains were made in that direction. In order to blunt the influence of the IMF on the government the business community representatives even arranged to meet for discussions with the major donors and the IFI representatives. It is not clear how much this helped, but they won some concessions in their favor.

In the second instance, in 1997 the Confederation of Tanzania Industries (CTI) wanted to convince the Dar es Salaam city commission that it could lower tax rates and revenue would not suffer. The CTI approached ESRF to undertake a study of the issue; this yielded recommendations for lowering the tax rates but widening the tax base. The study helped in the negotiations and CTI reached an agreement with the city commission. In the end CTI was happy with the lower rates and the city commission was happy because revenue that year exceeded the previous year's revenue by a considerable margin. In this case as well as the preceding one, the local groups influenced policy by generating ideas and by getting a local policy research institute to help analyze the issues and craft the argument in a manner that could be understood better by policymakers.

Civil society is also beginning to exert some influence on policy, but progress in this direction is still gradual. In the case of the restructuring of the National Bank of Commerce (NBC), the government basically agreed with the World Bank about a three-way split (into trade bank, regional bank, and microfinance bank). This idea was not discussed internally, but was sold to Tanzanian policymakers as the option that would most likely receive prompt support from the World Bank; budget time was approaching and support for the budget was crucial. However, a group of concerned citizens undertook to discuss the matter. The group was organized by the Development Policy Centre and held a one-day meeting at ESRF. After analyzing the options, they concluded that the three-way split was not in the national interest. They wrote a letter to the president requesting him to delay the matter for three months to allow more careful discussion of the options for restructuring the NBC.

In response, the president decided to reopen the discussion and appointed additional members to the steering committee dealing with the issue. Some of the new members came from the citizens' group that had submitted its views to the president. The expanded steering committee developed a recommendation for a two-way split (between microfinance and the rest). This option was adopted and continues to operate. Three of the four new members of the steering committee, who had opposed the three-way split, were subsequently appointed to the boards of the new banks.

In effect, the Tanzanian policy advisers had selected an option that they had been led to believe the World Bank preferred on the assumption that this choice would simplify subsequent negotiations on these issues. On paper it appeared to be a decision by Tanzania's policy analysts and policymakers, but in reality little analysis had been done. The recommendations reflected what Tanzanians perceived to be the position of key people in the World Bank. The objective was to simplify negotiations, and not necessarily to choose the option that was best for Tanzania. What was deemed best for Tanzania was the option that would make it easier to attract aid. When the debate was reopened, the choice changed. Under conditions of genuine ownership of policymaking, the restructuring options would have been discussed openly from the start, and it would not have required a protest note from citizens to start that process. The experience confirms that policy analysts sometimes read the minds of IFI officials through informal discussions and later come up with their "own" policy choices that are in reality a reflection of external influence; but it also shows that civil society is beginning to express its views on policy reforms.

Economic Policy and Growth Outcomes 1979–99

Between 1979 and 1985 per capita income fell by 1.5 percent per year according to official estimates (see table 6.6).[5] However, the estimates are particularly uncertain for this period because the price system was in disarray and many economic activities had moved to the parallel economy. Estimates by Bevan and others (1988) suggest more significant income declines. Manufacturing output collapsed on account of the lack of imports, and agricultural growth declined. Public administration was still growing, although the growth rate had fallen to less than 4 percent. State control of the "commanding heights" of the economy was

TABLE 6.6 TANZANIA: DATA FOR THE CRISIS PERIOD, 1979–85

Indicator	1979	1980	1981	1982	1983	1984	1985
Per capita income growth (%)	0.2	–0.2	–3.7	–2.6	–5.6	0.2	1.4
Population growth (%)	3.1	3.2	3.2	3.2	3.2	3.2	3.2
Urbanization (%)	13.9	14.8	15.4	15.9	16.5	17.0	17.6
External debt (millions of U.S. dollars)	2,070	2,450	2,880	3,130	3,390	3,620	4,030
Interest rate spread (%)	7.5	7.5	8.0	8.0	9.0	9.0	7.8
Labor force in agriculture (%)	86.3	85.6	85.6	85.5	85.4	85.2	85.1
Monetary growth (%)	46.9	26.9	18.1	19.5	17.8	3.7	30.3
Gross investment (% of GDP)	33.6	33.1	28.6	26.0	19.3	20.2	18.7

Sources: Bigsten and Danielsson 1999; *World Development Indicators 1998.*

a central tenet of the Arusha Declaration, and by the late 1970s Tanzania had constructed a very comprehensive parastatal sector (Bagachwa, Mbelle, and van Arkadie 1992). From about 40 entities in 1966, the parastatal sector grew to encompass approximately 450 entities by the mid-1980s, covering the entire range of economic activities. In the manufacturing sector the parastatal firms produced half the output and controlled two-thirds of the fixed assets.

Export performance deteriorated as domestic inflation increased and the government compressed imports through direct foreign exchange rationing rather than accommodating inflation through depreciation. Export data for the crisis period must be interpreted with care, since the black market premium on foreign exchange was high and provided strong incentives for smuggling (Kaufmann and O'Connell 1991). The decline in official exports during the crisis period therefore reflects in part a diversion of exports from official to unofficial channels in response to an increasing parallel premium (it rose from 45 percent at the end of 1978 to more than 800 percent at the end of 1985). Some estimates even put the level of smuggled exports at about 50 percent of official exports (Adam and others 1994).

The period of more significant reforms began in 1986 with a maxi-devaluation and the initiation of a standby agreement with the IMF and a structural adjustment program with the World Bank. The agreements with the IFIs helped restore donor confidence. They came back in force and there was a second aid boom that peaked in the early 1990s. This support was probably needed to make the transformation possible, but it is hard to know for sure what would have happened without this resource inflow. Tanzania was obviously in a desperate situation and would have had to go down the reform route in any case.

The reforms managed to increase growth again (table 6.7). Per capita incomes have so far grown by 0.6 percent per year during the reform period. Agricultural growth increased significantly, and the manufacturing sector turned from a decline of 4 percent per year to positive growth, in spite of the fact that many industries have collapsed in the face of increased import competition. There were strong recoveries in construction, trade, and transport as well. The development of the transport sector may be considered a necessary ingredient in the re-creation of a viable market economy. The lagging sector has been public administration.

Drought and floods undermined agricultural production in 1997. Harvests of coffee and cotton, Tanzania's main exports, were particularly badly hit, undermining the country's trade balance. Economic growth in 1998 is estimated to have been only about 3 percent, barely keeping pace with the population growth of 2.8 percent.

From the Arusha Declaration in 1967 until the reforms in the mid-1980s, policies encouraged public sector investment while they actively

TABLE 6.7 TANZANIA: DATA FOR THE REFORM PERIOD SINCE 1986

Indicator	1986	1987	1988	1989	1990	1991	1992	1993	1994	1995	1996	1997	1998
Per capita income growth (%)	3.4	2.7	1.3	−0.6	3.1	−0.3	−1.3	−4.1	−0.1	0.6	1.4	0.5	1.4
Population growth (%)	3.2	3.2	3.1	3.1	3.1	3.1	3.1	3.0	3.0	2.9	2.8	2.7	2.6
Urbanization (%)	18.2	18.9	19.5	20.2	20.8	22.0	23.2	24.5	25.7	26.9	28.1	29.3	30.5
Current account (% of GDP)			−11.6	−15.5	−18.1	−17.2	−21.8	−24.5	−25.5	−24.4	−15.8	—	—
Exports (% of GDP)			9.8	14.6	13.2	8.5	8.4	15.2	18.5	20.5	21.5	—	—
Imports (% of GDP)			27.3	30.7	35.5	35.3	36.8	44.0	45.4	42.4	36.2	—	—
External debt (millions of U.S. dollars)	4,610	5,490	6,010	5,850	6,410	6,540	6,620	6,800	7,260	7,430	7,410	—	—
Government consumption (% of GDP)			16.8	16.3	17.0	18.4	19.3	19.5	18.1	16.1	13.2	—	—
Gross investment (% of GDP)		23.5	17.4	19.3	28.2	28.5	28.9	26.7	26.4	21.2	23.8	—	—
Domestic saving (% of GDP)			1.3	1.3	0.3	−0.6	−1.6	−2.8	−2.0	0.0	3.4	—	—
Interest rate spread (%)	10.0	11.8	12.2	14.0						18.2	23.6	—	—
Labor force in agriculture (%)	85.0	84.8	84.7	84.5	84.4							—	—
Manufacturing (% of GDP)			8.1	8.1	8.9	9.1	8.5	7.8	7.4	7.3	7.3	—	—
Monetary growth (%)	27.9	32.1	32.6	32.1	41.9	30.1	40.6	39.2	35.3	33.0	8.4	—	—

— Not available.

Sources: Bigsten and Danielsson 1999; World Development Indicators 2000.

discouraged private sector investment by means of a complex system of regulations and licenses (Likwelile 1998). The public sector also received preferential treatment in credit allocation (Ndulu and Hyuha 1984). The public sector dominated investment activity and came to dominate production in major parts of the economy, and trade was confined to a limited number of parastatals (Moshi and Kilindo 1995). There was a preference for large and capital-intensive investment projects, often infrastructure projects, rather than directly productive investments. Gross fixed capital formation stood at 23.7 percent on average during the precrisis period of 1967–78, and then remained above 30 percent of GDP during the first years of the crisis before gradually declining to 18.7 percent in 1985. Investment levels in Tanzania have been high throughout, but there has been a strong shift toward private sector investment in recent years. The relative expansion of private sector investment is partly due to the shift in policy and partly due to the lack of resources to finance public sector investments.

Table 6.8 shows the distribution of investment across sectors during the reform period. Agricultural investments have remained fairly low, although this sector would have been expected to respond more strongly to marketing liberalization measures and improvements in the transport infrastructure. There has been an expansion from low levels in mining, where substantial investments have been made in, for example, gold mines. There has been very little investment in manufacturing for most of the period, which may reflect the lack of profitable investment opportunities in the manufacturing sector as well as lack of faith in the reform measures. If investors are not certain that the new system is going to continue, they usually prefer to put their money in short-term assets such as Treasury bills. The risk rating has improved in Tanzania, but it is still much below that of other countries in the region (Ndulu and Wangwe 1997). Much of the new investment has gone instead into infrastructure, trade, and finance. This is probably a necessary first step to restore the economic and market infrastructure after a long period of decline. We cannot be sure, however, that there will be a substantial recovery of investments in the directly productive sectors, although there are some recent signs of a recovery.

Investment rates have continued to be fairly high in Tanzania, although they are much lower during the reform period than what was implied by the old, nonrevised national accounts. It is obvious that low levels of capital formation cannot explain Tanzania's growth problems. The crucial issue is the quality of investments rather than the quantity. Low quality of investment during the pre-crisis and crisis periods is explained by the highly distorted macroeconomic environment and, in the crisis period, by the government's persistence with the Basic Industries Strategy in the face of collapsing foreign exchange availability. The capacity

TABLE 6.8 TANZANIA: SHARES OF GROSS FIXED CAPITAL FORMATION BY TYPE OF ECONOMIC ACTIVITY AT CURRENT PRICES, BY SECTOR

Sector	1987	1988	1989	1990	1991	1992	1993	1994	1995	1996	1997	Total
Agriculture	0.052	0.039	0.040	0.042	0.049	0.063	0.063	0.063	0.064	0.063	0.097	0.066
Mining	0.030	0.026	0.025	0.032	0.048	0.046	0.041	0.043	0.043	0.043	0.106	0.053
Manufacturing	0.003	0.007	0.002	0.002	0.002	0.003	0.003	0.003	0.003	0.003	0.133	0.026
Electricity and water	0.277	0.213	0.229	0.256	0.237	0.235	0.240	0.244	0.240	0.241	0.111	0.218
Construction	0.182	0.248	0.256	0.178	0.161	0.148	0.152	0.136	0.145	0.144	0.110	0.147
Trade	0.111	0.095	0.098	0.120	0.111	0.116	0.119	0.122	0.119	0.120	0.109	0.116
Transport	0.015	0.051	0.022	0.010	0.010	0.008	0.009	0.010	0.009	0.010	0.111	0.029
Finance and real estate	0.314	0.283	0.288	0.340	0.314	0.324	0.331	0.335	0.330	0.332	0.117	0.290
Public administration	0.016	0.038	0.040	0.020	0.068	0.058	0.042	0.044	0.047	0.044	0.104	0.056
Total	1.000	1.000	1.000	1.000	1.000	1.000	1.000	1.000	1.000	1.000	1.000	1.000

Note: These calculations are taken from national accounts in Tanzanian shillings.
Source: Tanzania Bureau of Statistics, "National Accounts of Tanzania Mainland 1987–1997," 23.

utilization rate in manufacturing was driven below 30 percent in the early 1980s. The first phase of reforms in Tanzania was clearly designed to address the more drastic distortions associated with quota protection and nonmarket pricing of foreign exchange.

A second constraint on investment productivity in Tanzania, however, has been the dominance of the public sector in the allocation of credit. Until the banking sector reforms that began in 1992, the parastatal sector had automatic access to credit from the monopoly commercial banking sector, which in turn had automatic access from the Bank of Tanzania. The vast bulk of NBC's lending was to the parastatal sector; in 1980 the private sector accounted for less than 8 percent of NBC's outstanding loans. The parastatal sector made enormous losses through the 1980s (see Eriksson 1998), representing a large drain not only on the budget but also on credit from the banking sector. The point is simple: without hard budget constraints, relative price changes are not likely to produce significant reallocations of resources or big productivity gains. To a large degree, the parastatals, and particularly the marketing boards and (quasi-public) cooperative unions during the reform period, were able to pass a major portion of the relative price changes they faced into greater losses that were financed by the budget or banking system.

The reforms of Tanzania's financial system have just started, and as yet there is relatively little long-term financing available for private firms. Tanzania Housing Bank has folded and the National Bank of Commerce is being transformed and provides mainly short-term loans. Private investments therefore often have to be financed by foreign money.

Institutional Reforms and Governance

Governance is a crucial constraint on development prospects in Tanzania. Immediately after being elected, President Mkapa set up a commission that produced a 900-page report on corruption and mismanagement, known as the Warioba report. Since then, however, little concrete action has been taken, although some low-level officials were dismissed from the government. There are two main pressure groups, the press and the donors, that are capable of bringing about a change in government policy or forcing the government to take action against malpractice. So far, however, people who misbehave tend not be fired or prosecuted, but are simply transferred to some other activity. The lack of action may be because the elite is a rather tightly knit network. In addition, the Parliament does not really play an independent watchdog role in Tanzania; throughout the country's history its role basically has been to support the government's development efforts.[6]

The civil service reform program was officially launched in July 1991, but it was not until 1993 that the government began designing a program to strengthen management of the public sector. Phase one of the Public Sector Reform Program sought to reduce the scope of government operations to affordable levels, to rationalize the government machinery, to develop an open, objective, and competitive pay structure, to decentralize executive responsibilities to local government, and to improve the quality and performance of civil servants (Tanzania 1998a: 1). The main achievement of phase one was the redefinition of the role of the state. The government is in the process of withdrawing from production activities and is trying to reduce its role to affordable levels and enhance the participation of the private sector and NGOs in service delivery. Between 1993 and 1997 there was a 30 percent reduction in the size of the work force, from 355,000 to 270,000.

The new five-year strategy for public sector management and employment builds on what has been achieved so far, seeking better levels of performance. Efforts will concentrate on strengthening public sector discipline and developing clear lines of responsibility and accountability based on modern management principles. The aim is to deliver quality public services under severe budget constraint.

The new program has an interesting budget-based incentive built in. When a ministry or agency has managed to operationalize a services improvement program on the basis of the performance improvement model, it will be graduated out of the "cash budgeting" exchequer release mechanism. This means that the Ministry of Finance will from the outset commit to fund fully and predictably the approved budget of the organization. This is regarded as a key output of the public financial management reform program, and it seems to be a rational way out of the tight cash budget system. Those that have managed to achieve an effective system will be able to run their operations more smoothly in the future. A second incentive mechanism is that institutions will be allowed to retain a significant portion of the cost savings realized on the implementation of restructuring and private sector rationalization programs. Monitoring and evaluation mechanisms will be strengthened. There is also going to be increased private participation in public sector service delivery.

The crisis years in Tanzania led to a dramatic deterioration of real civil service salaries. By the late 1980s the real salary of a civil servant was only one-fifth of what it was in the early 1970s (Tanzania 1998b: 2). Severe distortions and inequities had developed in the compensation structure, and as a result the morale of the service had deteriorated significantly. Performance was poor, and absenteeism, moonlighting, and corruption were growing.

The government has tried to rectify these distortions by rationalizing the wage scales and increasing the real income levels. Many donors offer remuneration incentives (local cost compensation) in various forms

to civil servants working in their projects. According to a recent estimate, about 1,000 civil servants benefit from local cost compensation
(Guidelines 1988:4) at a cost of 13 billion Tshs. This system of course
may make the donor project function better, but over the long term it
tends to undermine efforts to build capacity in the government sector.
The strategy now is that there shall be a convergence between donor
pays and government salaries over the next five years. In the future a
civil servant who takes up a project job will have to resign from his or
her civil service job. The government's aim is to achieve reasonable and
competitive wages for its employees. For low-level workers the government salaries are often higher than those in the private sector, but for
higher grades the salaries are not competitive. The government will do
away with various kinds of benefits, but housing allowances will remain for top personnel. There will also be medical benefits and post-
employment security.

In the drive toward socialism and political control, the government
had set up a large number of parastatals. This was one of the most dramatic examples of dysfunctional government.[7] The performance problems of the parastatals were at their peak during the crisis period, 1979–85,
but the system remained intact and even expanded after that. Parastatal
losses were growing, but the firms had by now learned how to operate
the system and they were successful in acquiring various forms of finance from the government, banks, and foreign donors. This made it
possible for even chronic lossmakers to survive.

The reforms have gradually changed this. Since reforms in the
parastatal sector initially were very limited while at the same time relative prices changed and competition increased, the losses of the
parastatals grew rapidly. The soft budget constraint delayed structural
adjustment and reduced the effectiveness of stabilization measures. In
1990 the ruling party finally decided to move toward complete private
ownership. The Parastatal Sector Reform Commission (PSRC) was
formed in March 1992, but was not fully operational until mid-1993.

The privatization process has moved more slowly than anticipated.
First the PSRC dealt with the smaller units, but now it has started to
work on larger companies such as the utilities. These were originally
considered to be strategic, and the original idea in 1992 was to bring in
private management and let them work under performance contracts.
This was not as effective as hoped, so from 1996 on private ownership
was sought for the strategic industries including railways, telecommunications, harbors, and Air Tanzania. Of the 383 firms that the PSRC had
on the books when it started, 230 had been dealt with by June 1998.
When its task is completed, the PSRC will be phased out. In the wake of
mounting criticism, especially in the Parliament, that public firms were
being sold to foreigners with no meaningful participation by Tanzani-

ans, the government in 1998 established the Privatization Trust to promote wide-share ownership among citizens.

In sum, there has been progress with regard to the privatization program, which the World Bank has characterized as one of the better in Africa. The dismantling of the parastatals will be concluded within a few years. The problem then becomes one of regulating the various utilities with a virtual monopoly position; the system for handling these issues is still very weak. Thus, efforts to effect a division of responsibilities between the functions of government and those of producers have moved forward, but much remains to be done before this is translated into an efficient industry.

The judiciary is exceedingly weak, although a commercial court is to be instituted. At present it can take years for a firm to get a decision in a lawsuit. The labor laws are obsolete, and even firms that fire dishonest or corrupt workers can be taken to court for expensive trials. This means that they end up having to buy off the dishonest workers that they dismiss.

It seems clear that Tanzania had made considerable progress with regard to the economic policy regime. Each year the World Bank undertakes a policy and institutional assessment that ranks performance with regard to 20 specific indicators in four areas: (a) macroeconomic management and sustainability of reforms; (b) policies of sustainable and equitable growth; (c) policies for reducing inequalities; and (d) public sector management. As expected, Sub-Saharan Africa is the region with the lowest average ranking, but Tanzania ranks above the average for Africa (World Bank 1999a). However, the impact of the reforms on economic performance is still limited. The impact of similar reforms in Uganda, for example, has definitely been better. One reason may be that Uganda stayed on course for a much longer period of time. Uganda under Museveni has had more genuine ownership and commitment than Tanzania, where there have been setbacks and a lack of force in implementation. Tanzania always seems to be on the verge of take-off, but so far it has not happened.

A big problem is that the government lacks the competence to manage an essentially market-dominated economy. The provision of public services remains poor, and corruption has probably increased as a consequence of the low salaries in government. From 1994 onward the relationships with the donors deteriorated again. The donors had, for example, pledged substantial balance of payments support, but on account of their view that the government has not been effective enough in tax collection efforts and other areas, they have withheld substantial amounts. Still, Tanzania has certainly come a long way since 1985. Few countries have undergone such a dramatic change of their entire social and economic set-up in such a short time.

THE RELATIONSHIP BETWEEN AID AND REFORMS

In the late 1970s negotiations with the IMF collapsed, since the demands of the IFIs implied a critique of the fundamentals of the Tanzanian approach based on socialist economic management. We have noted that political resistance to reforms was strong, because the liberalization of the economy represented a U-turn relative to the development strategy that was outlined in the Arusha Declaration. The reforms were seen as counter to the ideology of the ruling party, which therefore resisted them as long as possible. Moreover, the behavior of donors during the crisis was neither uniform nor consistent. It took a long time for donors to take a critical look at Tanzania's post-Arusha economic development policies. The Nordic countries and the Netherlands did not take a clear position in favor of liberal reform and the IMF until 1983.

The economic crisis of the first half of the 1980s, plus the withholding of aid and open donor critique of the policy even by the country's "traditional friends," spurred a debate within the government and also outside it, for example at the university. This external pressure likely helped to tip the balance in favor of domestic groups supporting the reforms. There were small policy changes during the first half of the 1980s, but comprehensive reforms were still resisted. By the mid-1980s, however, the crisis was so acute and the external support so small that the government had to budge.

The reforms, which were undertaken in 1984 and 1985, were done partly in anticipation of the negotiations with IFIs. At one level they were internally generated, but at another level they were undertaken with a view to preparing for negotiations with the IFIs. The retirement of Nyerere as president in 1985 opened the way for the agreement on the Economic Recovery Program of 1986–89 and later on a new ERP for 1989–92. Although some people within the government believed it was an appropriate strategy for the future, many saw it as a temporary setback. Nonetheless it is true that aid made reforms possible, at least in the sense that the government saw reforms as a way to get aid. The agreement on reforms also attracted resources, but it was the initial deprivation of resources that speeded preparations for reform and stimulated the internal debate.

After 1986 the tempo of internal policy debates slowed and reforms were basically directed by the IFIs and donors. The reform measures undertaken were in the standard structural adjustment mold, and the level of ownership decreased. The policy changes that were required in the case of Tanzania were unusually large, however, and all parties involved were not really supportive. There was a lot of foot-dragging, but the reformers gradually increased their influence. After the early 1990s the anti-reformers essentially lost control of the party, but even so it was hard to stay on course. Soon there was slippage in the program again and there seemed to be an increase in corrupt practices, which precipitated a new crisis in donor relations between 1993 and 1995. Donors were also dissatisfied with the government's efforts with regard to revenue collection.

The decline in aid inflows following the deterioration in relations with donors again had a significant impact on Tanzanian behavior. It seems to be the case that aid can more easily induce governments to undertake first-stage reforms, which in Tanzania's case included macroeconomic stabilization and some price liberalization. Aid seems to be less effective in stimulating the more intrusive second-generation reforms such as the freeing up of key markets, institutionalization of the market economy, privatization, and opening to foreign participation. These reforms are more directly in conflict with vested interests than first-generation reforms and are therefore more likely to meet resistance.

Still, the new government, from November 1995, put improvement of donor-Tanzania relations high on the agenda. This time the withdrawal of donor support led to more substantive discussions of the need to enhance ownership of the policy reforms. The post-1986 resumption of aid had eroded ownership of the reform process, while the resumption of aid relations in 1996 came with strong expressions of the need to enhance ownership of the reform process. Donor support to institutions of reform such as the Tanzania Revenue Authority showed that donors were willing to see the problems of revenue collection, which had been central to the collapse of Tanzania-donor relations in 1993–94, resolved through institutional reform. The new government has increased reform efforts, although it has had continual problems in undertaking some of the institutional and structural reforms set out. Structural and institutional reforms are at present high on the agenda, and there have been serious problems in their implementation. Still, it is hard to foresee any reversals of the reforms at this stage, although the effectiveness of many aspects of the reform process is in doubt.

During the reform phase Tanzania has managed to bring about an improvement in its policy environment, and it has seen positive per capita income growth. Still, in spite of an increase in investment, it has not been enough to accelerate growth very much. The returns on investments have been poor, which is an indication that the reforms have not yet fundamentally changed the economic environment. Many reforms are still in the planning stage, and those that have been implemented are often ineffective.

Evaluation of the Impact of Aid on Reforms

Our discussion of the link between aid and reforms in Tanzania has of necessity been tentative. It is virtually impossible to identify a counterfactual pattern of change. The key question is whether aid bought reform, or whether the reforms would have come anyway since they were an economic necessity. Initially aid probably delayed reforms by helping to finance schemes that would have been wholly nonviable without aid backing, but once aid started to decline in the first half of the 1980s, the cutbacks probably speeded up reforms. Of course, a country that is not committed to reform may choose to initiate a reform in order to receive foreign assistance. Then, once aid is disbursed, the recipient may not exert much effort to make the reform succeed. This may well have been the case in Tanzania at that time.

We will consider three aspects of the aid-reform relationship: the impact of aid on the initiation and pace of reform, on the content of policies, and on the effectiveness of implementation.

Generation of reforms has largely originated with the IFIs or donors, hence the concern about lack of ownership as pointed out in the Helleiner report. The donors have also had a significant impact on the pace of reform. Some argue that things would be much slower if no deadlines were set by the IMF. The relationship between the World Bank and the government is good at present, and the World Bank has taken the lead in coordinating donor activities.

The content of policy has largely been the standard structural adjustment package, with limited original input by Tanzanians. The weakness of domestic agents in generating ideas has gone hand in hand with lack of coordination in the management of reforms: reforms have been managed piecemeal, each one carried out by the respective government department in isolation. There has been no effective mechanism for examining reforms as a whole package. It is only recently, after the beginning of efforts to draft the PFP, that a broad perspective on reforms has started to take shape. Added to this is the new initiative to prepare Sector Development Programs, although technical advisers have played an important role in formulating some of these programs.

It should also be realized that local groups have historically been excluded from policy debates and policymaking, which has been regarded as the responsibility of government. As economic and political liberalization takes root, it should become increasingly possible for local groups to play a role in generating ideas for reforms. The various local groups have a better chance now to articulate their interests, and over time they will build the capacity to do so. Given the very strong leadership in the period before the reforms and the fundamentally different development policy framework that was adopted, the process of consensus building toward reform was bound to be difficult. Still, in recent years there has been a more open debate that may help to build national consensus and commitment.

With regard to the content of the policies, there have been improvements during the current government. With the search for direction high on the agenda, the government appointed a team of local experts to craft a development vision for Tanzania. The team submitted its "Vision 2025" document to the government in 1998, which approved and adopted it in May 1999. Some of the issues addressed by the vision document are reduction of aid dependence and promotion of self-reliance (on domestic resources), building capacity to own the development agenda, human development including poverty eradication, building a strong and competitive economy, and broadening and institutionalizing participation in development.

Today it is largely the government that sets sector priorities. Donors push mainly for health and education, while the government is also concerned with roads, water, and other areas. The big problem now is not a lack of insight about what the appropriate policy package is, but the fact that the reforms still are not implemented effectively. It is not easy to determine how much of this ineffectiveness is due to structural characteristics and the generally low level of competence, and how much to the lack of government commitment and lack of support and pressure from the domestic constituency.

There have obviously been several setbacks in the Tanzanian reform process, but it seems unlikely that it would have progressed to its current stage without the pressure from donors. It is not possible to say whether it was technical assistance and policy advice or the financial flows that brought about the change. Since the nonfinancial aid typically is combined with financial aid, it is hard to separate their effects.

The problem of the counterfactual also applies to the issue of whether the reforms can be sustained without aid in the future. The answer to this question also hinges on whether aid is buying reforms that the government otherwise would be unwilling or even unable to undertake, or whether the reforms are done willingly since it is obvious that they are the best option in any case. In the case of Tanzania, aid initially bought reforms that otherwise at least would have been delayed, but in the 1990s it seems more likely that there is some genuine backing for the reform process.

It appears that the ineffectiveness of the system to a considerable extent depends on the aid relationship. There is certainly need both for a more efficient governance structure and for changes in the nature of the donor-recipient relationship. It is not clear exactly how and to what extent changes in the aid relationships can contribute to improvements of the governance structure, but some thoughts on this question follow.

Where to Go?

Collier (1997) contends that the link between aid and reforms in Sub-Saharan Africa is weak and that governments generally have decided to reform due to pressure from domestic political forces, largely independent of the aid relationship and aid conditions. According to this view, it is only a combination of broad, informed, and empowered domestic constituencies and the presence of successful neighbors that will induce reforms. Conditionality therefore should not be used to induce policy change but to ensure that aid goes to environments where it can be effective. The flow of aid should reflect the level of the policy environment. In its review of the ESAF (IMF 1998), the IMF argued that high conditionality programs generally do not do well. When conditionality is tight the recipient country perceives a loss of control over the policy content and the pace of implementation of the reform program. It is also suggested that there is a correlation between the degree of ownership and the success of program implementation.

Aid to Tanzania has bought a certain reform agenda. This does not necessarily mean that the government would follow a strategy of no reform without aid, but it might pursue a strategy more in line with its "real" priorities. It is not easy to discern in what way such a reform agenda would differ from the current one, and therefore also hard to determine its viability. Still, to make the reform process more effective the government should be allowed to take control over priorities, and if donors are not willing to support the agenda—because they believe it to be nonviable or detrimental to development as they see it—they will have to withdraw from supporting the country. There is a problem in implementing this approach, however, as reflected in the slowness of change in donor flows to Tanzania. It is easy to withdraw if the support is of a general nature such as balance of payments or budget support, but once the donor is closely involved in project aid it becomes very difficult to pull out and in so doing probably kill the project. This is actually another argument for more general forms of aid. If the notion of country choice is to become meaningful, there is a need for more general forms of transfers.

It has been pointed out that conditionality is more effective when it focuses on a small range of quantifiable indicators. Still, the number of conditions has not declined much over the years, and they have become increasingly important since the bilaterals now require that the government of Tanzania meet the demands of the IFIs. Here the donor community should move toward conditions that reward good behavior or good policy environments based on expert evaluations, rather than reward promises.

Such a strategy also requires improved donor coordination, since this would make it easier for the government to take control. There is some movement toward more general forms of support, as in the case of the tax reform program where the World Bank put up some money and the donors then provided the rest without their own specific requests. This is not the norm; instead, the donors fall over each other in some areas, such as capacity building in the Ministry of Finance.

Given the magnitude of aid that Tanzania has received, the poor growth record poses an obvious question of aid effectiveness. It is clear on the face of it that aid has not had a strong payoff in terms of growth. Constructing a proper counterfactual is extremely difficult, however. What would have happened if less aid had been given? Aid has clearly exerted two kinds of influence in Tanzania: on the supply of external resources, and on policy formation. Disentangling these effects is crucial for assessing the impact of aid on growth in Tanzania. The answer to the question of whether aid works only in good policy environments is left hanging. The policy environment as we normally define it has certainly improved in Tanzania, but as yet there is no strong evidence that aid has a better growth impact now than in the early stages of the reform period. On the basis of this paper we are therefore not able to say much about the impact of aid on the real economy. Still, aid has unquestionably had a major impact on the reform process in Tanzania.

APPENDIX 6.1
TANZANIA: CHRONOLOGY OF POLITICAL
AND ECONOMIC DEVELOPMENTS

1961	Tanzania wins independence.
1967	Arusha declaration.
1975–78	Coffee boom.
1978–79	Tanzania-Uganda war.
1981	Government proposes new measures in the National Economic Survival Program (NESP I).
1982	NESP II initiated.
1983	Launching of second homegrown structural adjustment program.
1984	Currency devaluation and import liberalization.
1985	Nyerere retires as president.
1986	Maxi-devaluation and initiation of a standby agreement with the IMF and the SAP with the World Bank.
1986–89	ERP I implemented.
1989–92	ERP II.
1991	Financial sector adjustment program implemented.
July 1991	Civil service reform program launched.
March 1992	Parastatal Sector Reform Commission formed.
1992	Riots to protest cost-sharing measures associated with the World Bank higher education credit. Leadership code abolished. Registration of opposition parties legalized.
November 1994	Nordic donors except Denmark suspend aid payments because of tax exemptions.
1994	IMF cancels the adjustment program and essentially pulls out.
1995	First multiparty election.
January–June 1996	Government sets off shadow program with IMF.
July 1996	Tanzania Revenue Authority established.
1996	ESAF agreement with IMF.
September 1996	Nordic countries enter into partnership agreement with Tanzania.
December 1997	Consultative Group meeting.
July 1998	Multilateral Debt Relief Fund established.

TABLE 6.9 TOTAL GRANTS TO TANZANIA BY CREDITOR

(millions of U.S. dollars)

Creditor	1970	1971	1972	1973	1974	1975	1976	1977	1978	1979	1980	1981	1982
Canada	2.3	3.5	3.9	3.5	6.1	14.8	7.4	7.3	92.1	28.6	19.4	27.2	35.2
Denmark	1.5	2.7	4.1	5.5	8.8	6.5	9.7	6.9	19.7	50.1	22.6	32.5	39.1
European Union	0	0	0	0	0	15.1	5.7	10.6	17.8	22.9	22.0	32.2	20.8
Finland	0	1.0	2.1	3.1	5.8	4.5	6.3	5.2	8.0	33.8	17.7	12.8	12.7
France	0	0	0	0	0	0	0	0	0	0	1.6	1.9	2.7
Germany	4.2	3.6	5.6	7.8	10.6	13.8	16.9	18.2	22.4	40.8	209.0	54.5	59.0
Italy	0.5	0	0.1	0.4	0.1	0.2	0.4	0.8	1.1	1.0	1.8	10.7	12.3
Japan	0.7	0.7	0.7	1.0	1.9	3.1	2.9	2.7	3.2	13.8	13.3	17.5	10.9
Netherlands	1.1	0.9	2.6	3.4	5.1	8.1	23.4	35.6	91.5	76.2	81.5	68.9	52.2
Norway	1.4	2.9	3.5	6.9	10.8	17.2	14.5	25.7	30.7	35.1	44.2	40.1	51.9
Sweden	2.1	3.2	9.1	17.5	29.5	54.0	51.2	57.7	114.4	93.4	78.1	76.5	73.8
Switzerland	0.4	0.2	0.2	0.5	0.3	0.4	0.6	0.7	2.0	3.1	14.0	5.5	5.2
United Kingdom	4.3	3.4	3.5	3.4	3.1	8.5	10.4	11.7	19.8	46.5	74.5	56.0	41.2
United States	5.0	4.0	4.0	5.0	7.0	17.0	24.0	17.0	11.0	11.0	21.0	25.0	20.0
World Bank	0	0	0	0	0	0	0	0	0	0	0	0	0
Total	23.5	26.1	39.4	58	89.1	173.4	200.1	433.7	456.3	620.7	461.3	437	

163.2

(continued on next page)

TABLE 6.9—*continued*

Creditor	1983	1984	1985	1986	1987	1988	1989	1990	1991	1992	1993	1994	1995	1996
Canada	33.9	24.7	30.4	27.2	36.0	42.7	37.1	34.7	29.1	31.7	20.2	10.7	25.4	9.2
Denmark	30.2	29.1	40.1	132.5	49.2	77.8	78.7	78.6	89.1	94.8	80.9	76.6	59.1	91.1
European Union	19.2	28.0	28.0	36.7	34.2	34.2	52.7	41.5	37.7	110.8	65.5	85.7	59.2	40.6
Finland	16.9	21.1	16.6	25.0	33.2	67.2	55.4	51.0	40.5	34.8	15.7	22.5	9.4	9.1
France	2.9	1.5	1.3	2.0	2.4	2.6	16.7	3.2	3.0	27.7	20.4	12.2	22.7	5.9
Germany	36.3	49.8	32.4	44.9	60.2	68.1	51.9	61.0	66.0	68.5	72.4	64.4	67.3	58.7
Italy	7.6	9.4	13.7	17.6	76.5	27.5	13.4	16.1	9.1	19.0	266.6	10.2	3.7	3.2
Japan	12.6	18.3	22.9	30.4	40.9	82.6	56.7	43.4	61.1	79.3	99.6	106.7	125.9	109.5
Netherlands	34.7	40.4	36.3	60.5	73.9	78.9	71.8	94.6	63.7	50.5	55.1	57.8	78.6	74.9
Norway	54.8	45.7	45.4	71.8	75.4	79.2	57.6	103.0	85.7	81.9	68.6	50.5	52.3	53.2
Sweden	69.3	55.1	49.0	106.4	76.5	103.6	90.4	149.6	143	93.1	91.0	50.8	45.3	65.2
Switzerland	5.8	6.1	6.1	19.2	17.0	14.5	23.5	19.0	13.9	29.2	11.9	20.0	19.0	15.6
United Kingdom	43.9	29.7	23.0	17.5	38.6	58.7	60.2	30.6	61.8	100.6	37.0	40.4	30.3	66.0
United States	14.0	20.0	19.0	7.0	9.0	14.0	6.0	78.0	133.0	27.0	24.0	24.0	18.0	13.0
World Bank	0	0	0	0	0	0	0	0	0	0	0	0	0	0
Total	382.1	378.9	364.2	598.7	623.0	751.6	672.1	804.3	836.7	848.9	928.9	632.5	616.2	615.2

Note: Includes technical assistance.
Source: OECD-DAC.

TABLE 6.10 TANZANIA: TOTAL DISBURSEMENTS ON ALL EDA LOANS
(millions of U.S. dollars)

Disbursements	1970	1971	1972	1973	1974	1975	1976	1977	1978	1979	1980	1981	1982
All EDA loans	43.354	50.170	92.049	162.551	174.964	254.353	133.353	197.779	162.307	162.466	240.136	554.34	261.041

Disbursements	1983	1984	1985	1986	1987	1988	1989	1990	1991	1992	1993	1994	1995	1996
All EDA loans	350.819	358.528	160.872	227.458	205.825	336.728	194.158	287.737	276.387	350.987	200.445	243.845	218.090	202.769

Source: World Bank EDA database.

TABLE 6.11 TANZANIA: TOTAL DISBURSEMENTS ON EDA LOANS BY SECTOR

(millions of U.S. dollars)

Sector	Creditor type	1970	1971	1972	1973	1974	1975	1976	1977	1978	1979	1980	1981	1982
Agriculture, forestry, fishing	Multilateral	1.280	1.211	0.997	1.868	2.372	18.432	13.905	15.965	15.872	27.009	13.804	27.424	11.892
Agriculture, forestry, fishing	Bilateral	0.968	1.459	1.052	1.142	2.186	10.070	5.221	12.165	8.274	6.013	11.458	13.881	11.440
Balance of payments support	Multilateral	0	0	0	0	0	30.000	0	20.450	0	0	0	10.000	0
Balance of payments support	Bilateral	0	0	0	0	0.968	2.310	2.090	1.512	0	0	0	0	0
Communication	Multilateral	0	0	0	0	0	0	0	0	0	0	0	0	0
Communication	Bilateral	0	0	0	0	0	0	0	0	1.031	6.418	5.310	4.936	3.271
Community, social, personal, and environmental services	Multilateral	0.024	0.483	1.265	3.962	1.952	2.857	4.964	9.650	5.458	9.666	7.741	20.076	41.269
Community, social, personal, and environmental services	Bilateral	0.747	0.568	1.403	2.863	6.058	5.573	8.214	5.391	8.006	5.642	4.619	4.470	2.781
Construction	Bilateral	0	0	0	0	0	0	0	0	1.817	1.259	0.524	0.205	0
Contributions not recorded as DAC	Multilateral	0	0	0	0	0	0	0	0	0	0	0	0	0
Contributions not recorded as DAC	Bilateral	0	0	0	0	0	0	0	0	0	3.173	0	0	0
Contributions to finance current imports	Multilateral	0	0	0	0	0	0	0	0	0	0	0	0	0
Contributions to finance current imports	Bilateral	0	0	0.0670	1.818	2.592	6.928	9.225	6.789	5.634	3.239	16.863	20.383	21.307
Debt reorganization	Bilateral	0	0	0	0	0	0	0	0	0	0	0	0	0

Electricity, gas, and water production	Multilateral	1.242	7.245	9.333	10.012	8.944	3.422	1.814	3.591	6.232	12.316	40.607	14.907	2.730
Electricity, gas, and water production	Bilateral	4.238	7.070	11.321	39.634	21.743	10.690	10.033	10.550	14.342	0.623	10.897	14.827	20.615
Financial, insurance, real estate, business	Multilateral	0	0	1.928	0.817	3.827	6.433	4.818	4.367	8.282	11.136	16.325	10.399	14.050
Financial, insurance, real estate, business	Bilateral	0	0	0.404	0.620	2.401	6.312	6.455	4.533	2.129	1.832	1.602	1.661	1.265
General purpose contributions	Multilateral	0	0	0.223	0.424	0.239	0.713	1.670	10.518	2.699	4.188	3.201	14.224	11.581
General purpose contributions	Bilateral	2.656	3.214	4.320	6.799	8.845	8.371	5.623	5.683	5.785	8.544	14.090	11.545	11.553
Manufacturing	Multilateral	0	0	0	0	0	1.603	15.660	18.090	23.269	14.966	17.399	27.859	43.619
Manufacturing	Bilateral	3.650	2.359	2.556	31.961	40.690	56.571	29.021	45.148	30.314	18.958	34.279	15.987	11.245
Mining, quarrying	Multilateral	0	0	0	0	0	0	0	0	0	0	5.513	23.090	15.005
Mining, quarrying	Bilateral	0	0.017	0.028	0.021	0.016	0.010	0.006	0.003	0.004	0	0	0	0
Not applicable	Bilateral	0	0	0	0	1.259	2.099	1.775	1.356	0.907	0.546	0.325	273.621	0.988
Trade, restaurants, lodging	Multilateral	0	0	0	0	0	0	0	0	0	0	0.732	0.567	2.305
Trade, restaurants, lodging	Bilateral	2.543	1.959	0.792	0.007	0.002	0	0	0	0	0	0	0	0
Transport and storage	Multilateral	8.115	6.384	4.490	0.507	2.300	6.611	2.812	3.689	7.547	3.669	12.060	2.407	4.320
Transport and storage	Bilateral	17.891	18.201	51.870	60.096	68.570	75.348	10.047	18.329	14.705	23.269	22.787	41.871	29.805

(continued on next page)

TABLE 6.11 — *continued*

Sector	Creditor type	1983	1984	1985	1986	1987	1988	1989	1990	1991	1992	1993	1994	1995	1996
Agriculture, forestry, fishing	Multilateral	11.086	16.053	10.668	11.142	3.544	23.400	15.359	88.887	48.920	126.743	32.766	37.582	29.138	37.519
Agriculture, forestry, fishing	Bilateral	9.364	6.060	6.315	5.323	0.217	3.523	0.685	2.081	1.975	0.187	3.304	3.551	2.817	0
Balance of payments support	Multilateral	0	0	0	0	0	0	1.414	2.919	3.094	0	0	0	0	0
Balance of payments support	Bilateral	0	0	0	0	0	0	0	16.902	0.012	0	0	0	0	0
Communication	Multilateral	10.600	5.008	1.767	3.386	5.586	3.385	7.680	5.915	2.611	1.850	1.338	5.100	6.307	27.885
Communication	Bilateral	2.417	1.066	0.406	0.227	0.113	0.047	9.919	11.631	6.329	2.938	0	3.565	1.520	0.069
Community, social, personal, and environmental services	Multilateral	15.934	15.977	14.529	60.670	54.460	192.083	25.324	12.658	25.806	9.920	14.085	35.411	27.664	22.952
Community, social, personal, and environmental services	Bilateral	66.679	8.700	9.527	1.950	1.228	17.144	2.007	0.259	0.066	0.001	0.150	0	0.744	1.074
Construction	Bilateral	9.441	0	1.241	2.462	1.399	0	0	0	0	0.357	0	0	0	0
Contributions not recorded as DAC	Multilateral	0	0	0	0	0	0	0	0	0	0	0	0	1.114	0
Contributions not recorded as DAC	Bilateral	0	0	0	0	0	0	0	0	0	0	0	0	0	0
Contributions to finance current imports	Multilateral	0	0	0	0.329	0.711	1.510	0.185	2.984	7.500	0	0	0	0	0
Contributions to finance current imports	Bilateral	15.116	1.684	0.010	11.241	0.638	0.506	0.349	0.216	0.484	0	0	8	0	0
Debt reorganization	Bilateral	0	6.123	0.750	1.699	1.801	1.329	16.817	5.506	8.249	5.687	7.493	0	0	0

Sector	Type														
Electricity, gas, and water production	Multilateral	3.339	14.298	9.430	18.409	8.464	26.440	15.488	13.218	5.635	5.643	4.454	13.954	57.877	51.547
Electricity, gas, and water production	Bilateral	34.455	26.055	14.870	26.487	2.299	7.687	11.481	12.296	16.125	69.748	4.369	1.350	23.753	2.612
Financial, insurance, real estate, business	Multilateral	8.430	5.510	0.326	2.830	0.001	0	0	0	49.947	46.783	68.679	61.414	14.027	16.941
Financial, insurance, real estate, business	Bilateral	1.238	1.001	2.805	0.383	0	0.068	0.027	0.018	0	0	0	1.103	0	0
General purpose contributions	Multilateral	0.355	2.854	7.860	3.499	4.011	2.168	1.804	0.211	0	0.132	0	0	0	0
General purpose contributions	Bilateral	6.972	4.101	2.447	2.335	4.896	6.673	4.230	7.787	7.113	6.021	0.921	0	0.873	2.947
Manufacturing	Multilateral	44.590	31.453	15.827	12.373	7.836	4.634	52.574	50.576	35.853	21.720	7.152	3.472	1.974	0
Manufacturing	Bilateral	23.279	6.600	0.946	25.068	0.024	1.219	0	1.069	1.787	3.167	0	0	0	0
Mining, quarrying	Multilateral	4.646	0.741	0.573	3.674	1.863	0.661	0	4.556	0.342	0.601	0.411	0	1.535	1.623
Mining, quarrying	Bilateral	34.201	180.532	10.346	5.939	2.374	1.583	0	0	0	0.011	7.935	0	0	0
Not applicable	Bilateral	0.005	0.096	19.167	0.067	75.707	0	0	0	0	0	0	0	0	0
Trade, restaurants, lodging	Multilateral	2.441	1.194	0.002	0.180	0	0	0	0.654	5.209	0	8.038	0	0	0
Trade, restaurants, lodging	Bilateral	0	0	0	0	0	0	0	0	0	0	0	6.203	0	0
Transport and storage	Multilateral	13.566	6.784	17.469	20.908	15.025	24.322	9.928	22.658	41.687	46.203	38.541	57.941	47.617	37.600
Transport and storage	Bilateral	32.665	16.638	13.591	6.877	13.628	18.346	16.219	24.736	7.643	3.275	0.809	5.199	1.130	0

Source: World Bank EDA database.

TABLE 6.12 TANZANIA: TOTAL DISBURSEMENTS BY SECTOR

(millions of U.S. dollars)

Sector	1970	1971	1972	1973	1974	1975	1976	1977	1978	1979	1980	1981	1982
Agriculture, forestry, fishing	2.248	2.670	2.049	3.010	4.558	28.502	19.126	28.130	24.146	33.022	25.262	41.305	23.332
Balance of payments support	0	0	0	0	0.968	32.310	2.090	21.962	0	0	0	10	0
Communication	0	0	0	0	0	0	0	0	1.031	6.418	5.310	4.936	3.271
Community, social, personal, and environmental services	0.771	1.051	2.668	6.825	8.010	8.430	13.178	15.041	13.464	15.308	12.360	24.546	44.050
Construction	0	0	0	0	0	0	0	0	1.817	1.259	0.524	0.205	0
Contributions not recorded as DAC	0	0	0	0	0	0	0	0	0	3.173	0	0	0
Contributions to finance current imports	0	0	0.067	1.818	2.592	6.928	9.225	6.789	5.634	3.239	16.863	20.383	21.307
Debt reorganization	0	0	0	0	0	0	0	0	0	0	0	0	0
Electricity, gas, and water production	5.480	14.315	20.654	49.646	30.687	14.112	11.847	14.141	20.574	12.939	51.504	29.734	23.345
Financial, insurance, real estate, business	0	0	2.332	1.437	6.228	12.745	11.273	8.900	10.411	12.968	17.927	12.060	15.315
General purpose contributions	2.656	3.214	4.543	7.223	9.084	9.084	7.293	16.201	8.484	12.732	17.291	25.769	23.134
Manufacturing	3.650	2.359	2.556	31.961	40.690	58.174	44.681	63.238	53.583	33.924	51.678	43.846	54.864
Mining, quarrying	0	0.017	0.028	0.021	0.016	0.010	0.006	0.003	0.004	0	5.513	23.090	15.005
Not applicable	0	0	0	0	1.259	2.099	1.775	1.356	0.907	0.546	0.325	273.621	0.988
Trade, restaurants, lodging	2.543	1.959	0.792	0.007	0.002	0	0	0	0	0	0.732	0.567	2.305
Transport and storage	26.006	24.585	56.360	60.603	70.870	81.959	12.859	22.018	22.252	26.938	34.847	44.278	34.125

Sector	1983	1984	1985	1986	1987	1988	1989	1990	1991	1992	1993	1994	1995	1996
Agriculture, forestry, fishing	20.450	22.113	16.983	16.465	3.761	26.923	16.044	90.968	50.895	126.93	36.070	41.133	31.955	37.519
Balance of payments support	0	0	0	0	0	0	1.414	19.821	3.106	0	0	0	0	0
Communication	13.017	6.074	2.173	3.613	5.699	3.432	17.599	17.546	8.940	4.788	1.338	8.665	7.827	27.954
Community, social, personal, and environmental services	82.613	24.677	24.056	62.62	55.688	209.227	27.331	12.917	25.872	9.921	14.235	35.411	28.408	24.026
Construction	9.441	0	1.241	2.462	1.399	0	0	0	0	0.357	0	0	0	0
Contributions not recorded as DAC	0	0	0	0	0	0	0	0	0	0	0	0	1.114	0
Contributions to finance current imports	15.116	1.684	0.010	11.570	1.349	2.016	0.534	3.200	7.984	0	0	8	0	0
Debt reorganization	0	6.123	0.750	1.699	1.801	1.329	16.817	5.506	8.249	5.687	7.493	0	0	0
Electricity, gas, and water production	37.794	40.353	24.300	44.896	10.763	34.127	26.969	25.514	21.760	75.391	8.823	15.304	81.63	54.159
Financial, insurance, real estate, business	9.668	6.511	3.131	3.213	0.001	0.068	0.027	0.018	49.947	46.783	68.679	62.517	14.027	16.941
General purpose contributions	7.327	6.955	10.307	5.834	8.907	8.841	6.034	7.998	7.113	6.153	0.921	0	0.873	2.947
Manufacturing	67.869	38.053	16.773	37.441	7.860	5.853	52.574	51.645	37.640	24.887	7.152	3.472	1.974	0
Mining, quarrying	38.847	181.273	10.919	9.613	4.237	2.244	2.668	4.556	0.342	0.612	8.346	0	1.535	1.623
Not applicable	0.005	0.096	19.167	0.067	75.707	0	0	0	0	0	0	0	0	0
Trade, restaurants, lodging	2.441	1.194	0.002	0.180	0	0	0	0.654	5.209	0	8.038	6.203	0	0
Transport and storage	46.231	23.422	31.060	27.785	28.653	42.668	26.147	47.394	49.330	49.478	39.350	63.140	48.747	37.600

Source: World Bank EDA database.

TABLE 6.13 TANZANIA: DISBURSEMENTS ON EDA LOANS BY CREDITOR
(millions of U.S. dollars)

Creditor	1970	1971	1972	1973	1974	1975	1976	1977	1978	1979	1980	1981	1982
African Development Bank	0	0	1.928	4.850	3.983	6.524	1.038	0.574	10.605	1.018	36.233	22.215	8.224
Canada	1.158	1.460	4.646	37.740	17.989	4.871	5.764	1.121	0	0	0	0	0
Denmark	2.368	2.026	1.373	1.067	8.858	8.268	13.426	24.189	21.296	8.632	15.061	2.174	0.524
Finland	0	0	0.481	0.853	0.869	7.212	5.965	3.538	1.846	0	0	0	8.520
France	0	0	0	0	0	0	0	0	0	7.714	25.094	25.571	20.805
Germany	0.042	0.746	1.264	3.322	7.010	10.518	9.480	12.965	23.308	7.689	7.289	3.948	2.239
Italy	2.120	1.142	1.562	1.380	0.601	0.263	0.082	0.019	0	0	4.307	3.899	3.646
Japan	0	0	0	22.385	38.797	31.762	22.377	13.606	15.066	16.556	17.846	36.262	32.107
Netherlands	0	0.206	0.722	2.325	5.055	8.135	7.180	6.207	0.0540	1.578	1.353	1.322	1.467
Norway	0.013	0.013	0	0	0	0	0	0	0	0	1.232	1.396	0.416
Sweden	7.923	10.254	10.833	6.893	4.219	2.223	1.129	0.390	0	0	0	0	0
Switzerland	0	0	0	0	0	0	0	0	0	0	0	0	0
United Kingdom	0	0	0	0.235	0.253	0.129	0.042	0.021	0.565	0.694	0.412	1.123	1.552
United States	4.370	9.472	4.213	2.998	3.261	12.233	5.023	11.820	6.555	9.013	8.471	8.892	8.163
World Bank	10.661	15.323	16.085	12.075	14.161	59.804	39.383	63.367	52.061	72.690	70.104	98.086	107.238
Total	28.655	40.642	43.107	96.123	105.056	151.942	110.889	137.817	131.356	125.584	187.402	204.888	194.901

Creditor	1983	1984	1985	1986	1987	1988	1989	1990	1991	1992	1993	1994	1995	1996
African Development Bank	7.012	10.407	22.772	34.381	0.290	133.204	4.215	0.052	24.402	1.515	13.114	10.908	6.548	51.644
Canada	0	0	0	0	0	0	0	0	0	0	0	0	0	0
Denmark	3.207	2.274	0.034	22.975	0	0	0	0	0	0	0	0	0	0
Finland	0	5.835	0	0.333	0	0	0	0	0	0	0	0	0	0
France	11.627	5.171	1.902	1.507	1.176	0.919	2.216	4.091	4.501	1.450	0	0	0	0
Germany	1.512	0.985	0.654	0	0	0	0.107	0.124	0	0	0	0	0	0
Italy	10.234	24.960	15.168	29.231	20.152	30.813	30.363	36.466	22.503	77.671	5.368	0.214	23.753	2.681
Japan	17.185	4.641	8.899	5.351	0.247	0.102	0.051	5.139	7.912	5.622	7.493	0	0	0
Netherlands	1.320	0.676	0.399	0.141	0.057	0.023	0.014	0	0	0	0	0	0	0
Norway	0.157	0	0	0	0	0	0	0	0	0	0	0	0	0
Sweden	0	0.521	0	0	0	0	0	0	0	0	0	0	0	0
Switzerland	0	0	0	0	0	0	0	0	0	0.357	0	0	0	0
United Kingdom	0.560	0.369	0.231	11.101	0.345	0.180	0.782	18.722	2.147	0.067	3.454	10.599	2.817	0
United States	6.676	4.325	1.859	0.575	0.217	0.052	0	0.261	0	0	0	0	0	0
World Bank	90.251	74.345	45.903	92.730	95.004	137.771	116.284	189.297	180.664	237.796	155.891	183.203	159.774	136.111
Total	149.741	134.509	97.821	198.325	117.488	303.064	154.032	254.152	242.129	324.478	185.320	204.924	192.892	190.436

Source: World Bank EDA database.

TABLE 6.14 TANZANIA: TOTAL GRANT ELEMENT BY CREDITOR

Creditor	1970	1971	1972	1973	1974	1975	1976	1977	1978	1979	1980	1981	1982
African Development Bank	0	0	0.059068	-0.219959	-0.008669	0.672122	-0.00086	-0.00022	4.095906	-0.014364	15.44780	8.960966	1.009146
Canada	0.428885	0.847759	4.077151	32.15810	15.70584	4.312462	4.921095	0.954465	0	0	0	0	0
Denmark	0	0.077785	0.349752	0.605820	6.142921	6.691987	10.60145	19.36068	17.95983	7.178247	13.30686	1.891968	0.453129
Finland	0	0	0.235896	0.428941	0.436987	4.073034	2.070643	0.534894	0.120133	0	0	0	1.176416
France	0	0	0	0	0	0	0	0	0	0.799027	7.499406	6.939984	6.985513
Germany	0	0.358599	0.607601	2.301310	5.388103	8.352197	7.589165	10.29757	17.78176	5.504168	5.298418	2.870716	1.633721
Italy	0	0	0.074119	0.083336	0.040274	0.016187	0.006350	0.001471	0	0	0.114621	0.103763	0.545133
Japan	0	0	0	2.673332	4.663534	3.839221	2.704419	1.650193	3.937501	6.266033	9.210448	22.39592	19.25626
Netherlands	0	0.084988	0.279146	1.112096	3.182486	5.739715	5.200835	4.433109	0.004265	0.960408	0.926012	0.913500	0.920965
Norway	0	0	0	0	0	0	0	0	0	0	0.460238	0.521503	0.155405
Sweden	0.226757	0.182973	-0.029109	0.008076	-0.015288	-0.018836	-0.024991	0.000010	0	0	0	0	0
Switzerland	0	0	0	0	0	0	0	0	0	0	0	0	0
United Kingdom	0	0	0	0.000675	0.000726	0.000370	0.000121	0.000060	0.073153	0.090798	0.053903	0.156812	0.248030
United States	1.510034	2.166728	1.575552	1.336404	1.499387	6.546919	2.712198	6.481516	3.486323	2.944059	2.583836	4.078003	4.577506
World Bank	0	-0.024220	0.530551	1.117831	3.375268	14.71110	21.49838	30.52487	20.46963	31.78776	29.62509	63.81241	81.77445
Total	2.165676	3.694615	7.759730	41.60596	40.41157	54.93648	57.27881	74.23863	67.92851	55.51614	84.52665	112.6455	118.7356

Creditor	1983	1984	1985	1986	1987	1988	1989	1990	1991	1992	1993	1994	1995	1996
African Development Bank	5.931847	9.040213	17.23824	28.35543	0.111428	103.7071	3.255719	0.008935	18.89661	1.145093	9.513868	7.717076	3.927583	35.31172
Canada	0	0	0	0	0	0	0	0	0	0	0	0	0	0
Denmark	2.858558	2.023903	0.029039	20.23753	0	0	0	0	0	0	0	0	0	0
Finland	0	1.887951	0	0.045979	0	0	0	0	0	0	0	0	0	0
France	4.799597	2.375770	1.127927	0.696489	0.342149	0.214480	0.695216	1.283022	1.398497	0.454902	0	0	0	0
Germany	0.968862	0.533921	0.351928	0	0	0	-0.034962	-0.040517	0	0	0	0	0	0
Italy	3.813431	12.21083	6.770602	11.90796	9.694800	15.00536	14.58652	17.50653	10.96460	33.01884	3.532701	0.148883	16.52540	1.593231
Japan	10.03737	2.654794	4.777057	2.451754	0.156750	0.064755	0.032782	0.926615	1.524406	1.123954	1.646417	0	0	0
Netherlands	0.792835	0.395292	0.228568	0.075769	0.034948	0.014101	0.008583	0	0	0	0	0	0	0
Norway	0.058650	0	0	0	0	0	0	0	0	0	0	0	0	0
Sweden	0	-0.096700	0	0	0	0	0	0	0	0	0	0	0	0
Switzerland	0	0	0	0	0	0	0	0	0	0.086695	0	0	0	0
United Kingdom	0.107953	0.053687	0.025175	6.596000	-0.013186	-0.008057	-0.037344	1.835822	-0.140262	0.003590	0.116446	-1.062441	0.270265	0
United States	4.284486	2.907917	1.276863	0.396112	0.149002	0.035562	0	0.037709	0	0	0	0	0	0
World Bank	54.76558	42.79851	28.81201	69.67844	72.43180	107.0718	87.70944	142.7214	136.3662	179.5619	106.7344	132.7891	110.0874	93.21205
Total	88.41918	76.78610	60.63742	140.4414	82.90769	226.1052	106.2159	164.2795	169.0100	215.3950	121.5438	139.5926	130.8107	130.1170

Source: World Bank EDA database.

TABLE 6.15 TECHNICAL ASSISTANCE GRANTS TO TANZANIA AS A SHARE OF TOTAL TA GRANTS
(millions of U.S. dollars)

Recipient	1970	1971	1972	1973	1974	1975	1976	1977	1978	1979	1980	1981	1982
Tanzania	21.4	24.0	34.8	41.2	48.6	60.2	77.0	80.2	106.5	138.6	172.9	176.8	181.2
Total	437.6	503.5	594.5	693.9	786.4	1,015.4	1,038.6	1,106.9	1,378.2	1,687.6	2,206.7	2,206.0	2,072.3

Recipient	1983	1984	1985	1986	1987	1988	1989	1990	1991	1992	1993	1994	1995	1996
Tanzania	173.9	138.7	141.4	163.4	186.7	210.2	202.4	209.4	209.0	236.5	238.9	211.9	266.7	254.2
Total	2,071.5	2,010.0	2,227.4	2,769.6	2,989.1	3,331.1	3,371.6	3,667.6	3,767.8	4,160.8	4,185.5	3,651.7	4,178.1	3,915.8

Source: World Bank EDA database.

NOTES

Thanks for comments are due to Shanta Devarajan and Benno Ndulu.

1. Donors drew this negative conclusion about aid effectiveness even though they were seldom able to establish a causal link between aid and economic outcomes.

2. The ESRF study found that 17 items whose implementation either had not started or was unsatisfactory according a 1996 study have since then been implemented satisfactorily. However, six issues whose implementation was unsatisfactory then remain unsatisfactory to date. The issues that have been satisfactorily addressed include control of leakage through bonded warehouses; determination of management/operations establishing criteria for bonded warehouses; improved supervision of transit trade (including tracking down goods and conducting audits); Zanzibar leakage (tariffs have been harmonized and Zanzibar is now under the same preshipment inspection system); exemptions (rampant exemptions have been reduced and the audit of IPC exemptions has been undertaken, and the audit report is now with Tanzania Revenue Authority for follow-up action). The issues on which little or no progress has been made include CIS debt recovery, enforcement of tax laws and other legal provisions, and prosecutions and recovery of losses through exemptions.

The CIS debts amount to about Tshs. 115.6 billion, owed by the government (Tshs. 12.5 billion), parastatals (Tshs. 72.6 billion), and the private sector (Tshs. 30.0 billion). Except for debts owed by government, many of the outstanding CIS debts have been disputed. The amount of debt that is not in dispute is in the region of Tshs. 15.2 billion. Even this can hardly be collected as most debtors have tended to plead hardship. The study examined the performance in CIS debt recovery and observed that the report submitted by Tanzania Revenue Authority to the Treasury showed some progress, albeit modest. Until December 1997, a total of Tshs. 15.1 billion had been collected. The collection represents 9 percent of the total amount owed. The study could not establish any substantial collections made during the last six months of 1998. Reasons for this poor performance include shortcomings in the legal framework and inadequate information and documentation. Disputes relating to interest rates and exchange rates adopted in the recovery of the debts have also contributed to delays in payments.

3. It is hard to assess the significance of this trend as World Bank procedures for estimating cost only recently moved to dollar budgeting.

4. Raikes and Gibbon (1996) provide an extended discussion of the policy changes during this period.

5. This section draws heavily on Bigsten and Danielsson (1999). Bevan and others (1990) provide an extensive analysis of macroeconomic developments during the crisis period.

6. The government issued a progress report on the implementation of the Warioba report in February 1999 in response to critics. Also, in March 1999 a high-level, three-day retreat on good governance was held. Participants included

senior government officials (permanent secretaries and the heads of governance institutions, such as the accountant and auditor general, and anti-corruption institutions); resource persons (drawn from ESAMI, ESRF, and the University of Dar es Salaam, and selected public institutions such as TRA and the Corruption Prevention Bureau); and a few donors (UNDP, USAID, Sweden, and the Netherlands).

7. Eriksson (1998) provides a detailed discussion of the impact of parastatals on the Tanzanian economy. Moshi (1998) offers evidence of the extent of the budgetary burden that the public enterprises have constituted.

REFERENCES

Adam, C., A. Bigsten, P. Collier, E. Julin, and S. O'Connell. 1994. "Evaluation of Swedish Development Cooperation with Tanzania." Secretariat for Analysis of Swedish Development Assistance, Ministry of Foreign Affairs, Stockholm.

Bagachwa, M., A. Mbelle, and B. van Arkadie, eds. 1992. *Market Reforms and Parastatal Restructuring in Tanzania.* Economics Department and Economic Research Bureau, University of Dar es Salaam.

Bevan, D., A. Bigsten, P. Collier, and J. W. Gunning. 1988. "The Decline in Tanzanian Incomes during the Nyerere Experiment: Evidence from Household Budget Surveys." In W. van Ginneken, ed., *Trends in Employment and Labour Incomes: Case Studies on Developing Countries.* Geneva: International Labour Organization.

Bevan, D., P. Collier, J. W. Gunning, A. Bigsten, and P. Horsnell. 1990. *Controlled Open Economies.* New York: Oxford University Press.

Bigsten, A., and A. Danielsson. 1999. "Is Tanzania an Emerging Economy?" Report to the OECD. Gothenburg and Lund, Sweden. Processed.

Chang, C., E. Fernández-Arias, and L. Servén. 1999. "Measuring Aid Flows: A New Approach." Policy Research Working Paper 2050. World Bank, Development Research Group, Washington, D.C.

Collier, P. 1991. "Aid and Economic Performance in Tanzania." In U. Lele and I. Nabi, eds., *Transitions in Development: Aid Organizations and the Effectiveness of Aid.* New York: St. Martin's Press.

————. 1997. "The Failure of Conditionality." In C. Gwyn and J. Nelson, eds., *Perspectives on Aid and Development.* Washington, D.C.: Overseas Development Council.

Eriksson, G. 1998. "The Soft Budget Constraint: The Emergence, Persistence and Logic of an Institution: The Case of Tanzania 1967–1992." Ph.D. diss. Stockholm School of Economics.

ESRF (Economic and Social Research Foundation). 1998. "SPA/JEM Project: Analysis of Progress and Relevance." Dar es Salaam.

Embassy of Sweden. 1998. "Partnership in Development: Sweden and Tanzania." Dar es Salaam.

————. 1999a. "Informal follow-up of partnership commitments from the Helleiner Workshop in January 1997." Dar es Salaam.

————. 1999b. "PFP, SAC, PER, CEM and CAS in Tanzania." Dar es Salaam.

Feyzioglu, T., V. Swaroop, and M. Zhu. 1998. "A Panel Data Analysis of the Fungibility of Foreign Aid." *World Bank Economic Review* 12 (1):29–58.

Helleiner, G. 1997. "Changing Aid Relationships in Tanzania? A Progress Report, Year-End 1997." Department of Economics, University of Toronto.

————. 1999. "Changing Aid Relationships in Tanzania." Report to the Government of the Republic of Tanzania. Dar es Salaam.

Helleiner, G., T. Killick, N. Lipumba, B. Ndulu, and K-E. Svendsen. 1995. "Report of the Group of Independent Advisers on Development Cooperation Issues Between Tanzania and Its Aid Donors." Royal Danish Ministry of Foreign Affairs, Copenhagen.

IMF (International Monetary Fund). 1997. "The ESAF at Ten Years: Economic Adjustment and Reform in Low-Income Countries." Occasional Paper 156. Washington, D.C.

————. 1998. "Report of the Group of Independent Persons Appointed to Conduct an Evaluation of Certain Aspects of the Enhanced Structural Adjustment Facility." Washington, D.C.

Kaufmann, D., and S. O'Connell. 1991. "The Macroeconomics of the Parallel Foreign Exchange Market in Tanzania." In A. Chibber and S. Fischer, eds., *Economic Reform in Sub-Saharan Africa.* Washington, D.C.: World Bank.

Likwelile, S. 1998. "Private Investment, Macroeconomic Environment and Economic Growth in Tanzania, 1967–1995." African Economic Research Consortium, Nairobi. Processed.

Moshi, H. 1998. "Fiscal and Monetary Burden of Tanzania's Corporate Bodies: The Case of Public Enterprises." Research paper 75. African Economic Research Consortium, Nairobi.

Moshi, H., and A. Kilindo. 1995. "The Impact of Government Policy on Macroeconomic Variables: A Case Study of Private Investment in Tanzania." African Economic Research Consortium, Nairobi.

Mutalemwa, D., P. Noni, and S. Wangwe. 1998. "Managing the Transition from Aid Dependence: The Case of Tanzania." Economic and Social Research Foundation, Dar es Salaam. Processed.

Ndulu, B. 1993. "Exchange Rate Policy and Management in the Context of Economic Reforms in Sub-Saharan Africa." In G. Hansson, ed., *Trade, Growth and Development: The Role of Politics and Institutions.* London: Routledge.

Ndulu, B., and M. Hyuha. 1984. "Investment Patterns and Resource Gaps in the Tanzanian Economy, 1970–82." In N. Lipumba and others, eds., *Economic Stabilisation Policies in Tanzania.* Economics Department and Economic Research Bureau, University of Dar es Salaam.

Ndulu, B., and S. Wangwe. 1997. "Managing Tanzania's Economy in Transition to Sustained Development." Discussion paper 14. Economic and Social Research Foundation, Dar es Salaam.

Nyoni, T. 1997. "Foreign Aid and Economic Performance in Tanzania." Research Paper 61. African Economic Research Consortium, Nairobi.

PricewaterhouseCoopers. 1999. "Tanzania Public Expenditure Review: Health and Education. Summary of Preliminary Findings." Dar es Salaam.

Raikes, P., and P. Gibbon. 1996. "Tanzania: 1986–1994." In P. Engberg-Pedersen, P. Gibbon, P. Raikes, and L. Udsholt, eds., *Limits of Adjustment in Africa: The Effects of Economic Liberalization, 1986–1994.* Oxford: James Currey; Portsmouth, N.H.: Heinemann.

Stewart, F., J. Klugman, and B. Neyapti. 1999. "Socio-Economic Causes of Conflict: A Comparative Study of Kenya, Uganda and Tanzania." Organisation for Economic Co-operation and Development, Paris. Processed.

Tanzania. 1998a. "Public Sector Reform Programme: Strategy and Action Plan, 1998–2003." Draft.

————. 1998b. "Guidelines for the Rationalisation of Donor's Local Cost Compensation." President's office, Civil Service Department, Dar es Salaam. Draft.

————. 1999. "The Education Sector Reform and Development Programme." Ministry of Education, Dar es Salaam.

Wangwe, S. M., and W. Lyakurwa. 1998. "Aid Dependency: The Phasing Out of Projects. A Macro Perspective." Economic and Social Research Foundation, Dar es Salaam, and African Economic Research Consortium, Nairobi.

Wangwe, S. M., and Y. M. Tsikata. 1999. "Macroeconomic Developments and Employment in Tanzania. Report for the ILO." Economic and Social Research Foundation, Dar es Salaam.

World Bank. 1997a. "Tanzania: Policy Framework Paper, 1997/98–1999/2000." Washington, D.C.

————. 1997b. "Tanzania: Country Assistance Strategy." Washington, D.C.

————. 1999a. "Country Policy and Institutional Assessments: Report on the 1998 Ratings." Washington, D.C. Processed.

————. 1999b. "Public Expenditure Review: Tanzania Mission. Draft Aide Memoire." Dar es Salaam.

————. 1999c. *World Development Indicators 1999.* Washington, D.C.

Mixed Reformers

Côte d'Ivoire

Elliot Berg
Patrick Guillaumont
Jacky Amprou
Auvergne University
Clermont-Ferrand, France

Jacques Pegatienan
University of Abidjan, Côte d'Ivoire

ACRONYMS AND ABBREVIATIONS

AFD	Agence Française de Développement
AGEPE	Agence d'Etudes de Promotion d'Emploi
APEXCI	Côte d'Ivoire Export Promotion Agency
BCEAO	Banque Centrale des Etats d'Afrique de l'Ouest
CAISTAB	Caisse de Stabilisation
CFAF	CFA franc
DAC	Development Assistance Committee (of the OECD)
DCGTx	Direction de Control des Grands Travaux
EDA	Effective development assistance
ESAF	Enhanced Structural Adjustment Facility (of the IMF)
EU	European Union
FDI	Foreign direct investment
FSAL	Financial Sector Adjustment Loan
HRDP	Human Resources Development Project
IDA	International Development Association (of the World Bank Group)
IMF	International Monetary Fund
L/J	Legal/judicial
MOJ	Ministry of Justice
NPV	Net present value
ODA	Official development assistance
ODF	Official development finance
OECD	Organisation for Economic Co-operation and Development
OHADA	Organisation pour la Harmonisation des Droits d'Affaires en Afrique (Organization for the Harmonization of Business Law in Africa)
OMOCI	Office de Main d'Oeuvre de la Côte d'Ivoire
PAGE	Projet d'Appui à la Gestion Economique (Economic Management Support Project)
PIP	Public Investment Program
PAGRH	Projet d'Appui à la Gestion des Resources Humaines (Human Resources Management Support Project)
PASCO	Competitiveness and Regulatory Reform Adjustment Program
PDSSIR	Programme de Développement de Secteur Santé Integré (Integrated Health Services Project)
PSD	Private sector development
PMA	Minimum activities package
RCI	République de Côte d'Ivoire
SAL	Structural Adjustment Loan
SECAL	Sectoral Adjustment Loan
SOE	State-owned enterprise
TA	Technical assistance
TOF	Total gross official flows (from the public sector)
TOR	Terms of reference
UMEOA	Union Monetaire Economique Ouest Africaine (West African Monetary and Economic Union)

The République de Côte d'Ivoire (RCI) presents an unusual case in many respects. Few countries have experienced so many reforms over so long a period—22 World Bank adjustment loans since 1980, nine IMF programs, numerous bilaterally financed reform operations; no sector seems to have escaped reformer attention. Between 1994 and 1997 the RCI was the World Bank's biggest adjustment loan customer, the recipient of more than a third of all the Bank's adjustment lending to Africa.

The RCI experience is special also in that it has been marked by a highly contentious relationship with the Bretton Woods institutions. Unlike most countries, whose reform efforts follow acknowledged failures of development policies, the RCI political leadership retained its belief in the validity of its own development model, which had for decades been widely regarded as successful—indeed as an "economic miracle"; it was thought to be only temporarily derailed after 1980. The reform model of the Bretton Woods institutions was viewed to be ideologically based and thus unsuitable.

Two other aspects of the Ivoirian experience are of special interest. To an uncommon extent, the reform process was externally driven. Until the early 1990s, the role of foreign technical assistance, mainly from France, was greater than anywhere else in the world. Reform programs were thus externally conceived in a multiple sense—via French technical assistance working in the RCI government, via membership in the Franc Zone, and via the Bretton Woods institutions that were so strongly present after 1990. Among other effects, this gave rise to especially serious problems of stunted local ownership of the reforms. Moreover, the RCI is often cited as a case where foreign aid retarded reform, notably by allowing delays in needed exchange rate adjustment after 1986.

In this paper we consider sectoral as well as macroeconomic reform. Four areas are considered: trade liberalization, exchange rate policy, health and education sector public expenditures, and legal and judicial reforms. We describe the reform programs and analyze their origins—and to some extent their effectiveness. We assess the extent to which this country experience confirms the hypotheses that inspired the general research on aid and reform in Africa.

The paper is a joint product of the four authors. Each had responsibility for specific sections, working from an outline prepared by the lead author, Elliot Berg. He edited and modified portions of the individual section drafts, but these are presented more or less as drafted by the individual authors. Readers thus will not find compromise or consensus views on contentious issues (though we agree on most of the analysis). Rather, they are allowed to see the diversity of views and approaches among the co-authors.

The paper is organized in seven sections. Section 2 describes aid patterns in Côte d'Ivoire—amounts, types, and origins. This chapter is the work mainly of Jacky Amprou, research associate at the Centre de Recherche sur le Développement International (CERDI), Université de l'Auvergne, Clermont-Ferrand, France. He put the basic tables and graphs together. Jacques Pegatienan of Université d'Abidjan drafted sections on bilateral aid, nonfinancial flows, and aid coordination. The other authors had some input in this section as well.

Section 3 gives an overview of the economic and institutional background to reform, the evolution of policy, and governance characteristics. It broadly follows the outline suggested in the terms of reference (TOR) for the Aid and Reform in Africa project. The main author of this chapter is Jacques Pegatienan.

Sections 4 through 7 consider specific reform experiences and the role of aid. We focus on the four areas suggested in the TOR: macroeconomic policy, trade liberalization, public expenditure reforms in health and education, and legal/judicial system reforms. We try to treat each of these as an integrated reform story. We describe the reform agenda, comment on effectiveness of the reforms, and analyze the role of aid and aid donors in reform conception and processes. The generalizations and hypotheses that are set out in the TOR are addressed in the context of each of the specific reform areas. This seemed the best way to reduce overgeneralization in analyzing the aid-reform relationship. Main conclusions are set out in section 8.

Section 4 focuses on the 1994 devaluation decision. This is a crucially important episode in the RCI reform experience, central to the assessment of aid-reform relationships in that country, and still controversial. We therefore concentrate on it and little else in the area of macroeconomic policy reform. The author of this section is Patrick Guillaumont, director of CERDI at the Université de l'Auvergne.

Section 5, on trade liberalization, is mainly the work of Jacques Pegatienan. Section 6, on public expenditure reforms in education and health, and section 7, on legal/judicial reform, were written by Elliot Berg, as was the concluding chapter.

The research team was in Abidjan between July 31 and August 12, 1999. This timing was not ideal: many relevant people were away on vacation. But we had no other feasible option. The main consequence was that we were unable to see some key actors in the private sector, leaving us with a sketchy understanding of some issues. Mainly for this reason we have little to say about two important reform areas: the restructuring of cocoa and coffee marketing and the privatization/deregulation of maritime transport. This is unfortunate, since the suitability of these reforms is contested by numerous Ivoirians.

The World Bank office in Abidjan provided indispensable support. Special thanks are due to Chantal Dejeu, Acting Country Director, who guided us with a sure hand, and to Mme. Attobra, who organized our complicated schedule of meetings. Thanks are also due of course to all those who took time in August to meet with us. A list of persons interviewed is attached as appendix 7.1. Appendix 7.2 includes the statistical tables.

AID DEFINITIONS, VOLUMES, AND ISSUES

Concepts of external aid abound. The standard or conventional concept is official development assistance (ODA), which is defined by the Development Assistance Committee (DAC) of the Organisation for Economic Co-operation and Development (OECD) as financial flows to developing countries and multilateral institutions provided by official agencies, which meet the following criteria: their main objective is the promotion of economic development and welfare of recipient countries, and they are concessional and convey a grant element of at least 25 percent. ODA includes technical assistance grants and is usually calculated net of amortization (see figure 7.1 and tables 7.1 and 7.2, and table 7.8 in Appendix 7.2).

FIGURE 7.1 CÔTE D'IVOIRE: TOTAL NET ODA, 1970–96

Millions of 1996 constant U.S. dollars

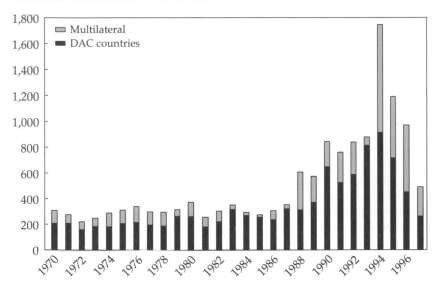

Source: OECD, Geographical Distribution of Financial Flows.

TABLE 7.1 ODA COMMITMENTS TO CÔTE D'IVOIRE, 1975–98
(annual average in thousands of 1996 constant U.S. dollars)

Donors	1975–79	1980–84	1985–89	1990–93	1994–97
Bilateral	147,407	264,242	273,895	839,755	537,281
France	47,575	96,342	111,093	348,263	201,932
European Union members	77,175	132,065	143,116	393,856	267,471
North America	22,657	24,220	9,434	56,651	22,477
Japan	0	11,615	10,252	40,985	45,401
Multilateral	22,018	39,638	3,129	75,305	397,689
IDA	0	0	0	39,647	317,142
European Union	22,018	39,638	479	25,357	68,844
African Development Fund/					
African Development Bank	0	0	2,650	10,301	11,703

Source: OECD Creditor Reporting System.

The main disadvantage of this indicator is that it does not take into account nonconcessional flows. This is an important omission since it means that sizeable financial flows from major multilateral donors are not included, such as regular loans of the World Bank and the African Development Bank and the standby agreements and extended facility loans of the International Monetary Fund (IMF). Another weakness of the net ODA concept is that it does not take account of interest payments on external debt.

TABLE 7.2 CÔTE D'IVOIRE: TOTAL ODA COMMITMENTS
BY SECTOR, 1975–97
(annual average in thousands of 1996 constant U.S. dollars)

	1975–79	1980–84	1985–89	1990–93	1994–97
Social infrastructure and services	25,939	29,069	10,856	63,797	150,779
Economic infrastructure					
and services	28,200	58,517	13,053	60,211	115,478
Production services	40,102	70,616	61,430	75,249	134,043
Commodity aid/general					
program assistance	15,514	11,178	49,876	314,382	235,751
Action relating to debt	0	18,746	24,743	35,034	137,863
Emergency assistance	0	355	0	1,563	643
Other[a]	20,752	20,264	6,133	28,182	38,266

a. Includes multisector/crosscutting, support to NGOs, and unallocated/unspecified.
Source: OECD Creditor Reporting System.

FIGURE 7.2 CÔTE D'IVOIRE: OFFICIAL DEVELOPMENT FINANCE
FLOWS (DISBURSEMENTS), 1970–96

Millions of 1996 constant U.S. dollars

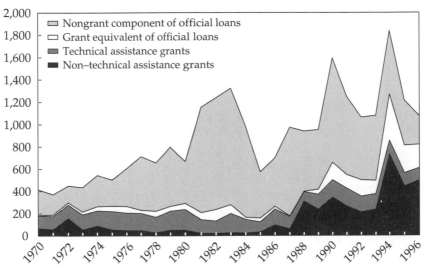

Note: Official loans include IMF concessional loans (SAF and ESAF) and nonconcessional loans (enhanced facility and standby agreement).
Source: Chang, Fernández-Arias, and Servén 1999.

A second concept, developed by World Bank researchers, is effective
development assistance (EDA). It defines aid as the sum of the grant
equivalent of all official loans plus transfers that are full grants, excluding technical assistance (Chang, Fernández-Arias, and Servén 1999).[1] This
adjusted measure uses the conventional grant data (from the OECD's
DAC), but aggregates grant equivalents of loans rather than the full face
value of all loans, even those with less than a 25 percent grant element.
This indicator does not consider debt relief, whether it is in the form of
debt forgiveness or debt rescheduling, as new aid.[2] It retains only the
concessional-window IMF flows (Structural Adjustment Facility loans
and Enhanced Structural Adjustment Facility loans) and discards the
nonconcessional windows loans (standby agreements and Extended
Fund Facility loans).

We present data on EDA as such (figure 7.3 and table 7.9 in Appendix
7.2), and include it in a broader concept: official development finance
(ODF), which includes not only EDA (grants and the grant element of
official loans), but also the nonconcessional part of the loans, technical

Figure 7.3   Côte d'Ivoire: EDA Flows by Type, 1975–96

Millions of 1996 constant U.S. dollars

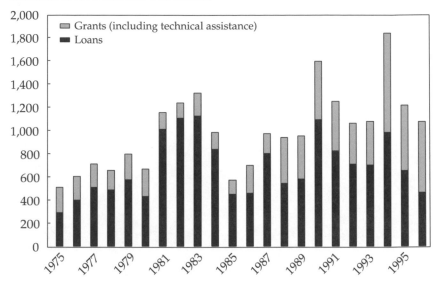

Source: Chang, Fernández-Arias, and Servén 1999.

Table 7.3   Côte d'Ivoire: Total Disbursements on Official Loans by Sector, 1975–96
(millions of 1996 constant U.S. dollars)

	1975–79	1980–84	1985–89	1990–93	1994–96
Agriculture, forestry, fishing	503.1	382.5	553.7	644.8	374.3
Balance of payments support	0.0	820.1	578.2	969.3	783.7
Contribution to finance current imports	0.0	9.3	0.0	51.1	25.9
Social sectors	209.8	380.4	123.7	269.1	493.0
Manufacturing, trade, mining, finance	465.6	493.3	150.0	393.4	246.7
Infrastructure	860.6	796.8	935.6	701.6	133.5
Other	66.2	208.6	63.6	61.5	42.5

Note: Does not include IMF nonconcessional disbursements.
Source: Chang, Fernández-Arias, and Servén 1999.

TABLE 7.4 CÔTE D'IVOIRE: OFFICIAL DEVELOPMENT FINANCE
AND TOTAL DISBURSEMENTS ON LOANS BY CREDITORS, 1975–96
(annual average in millions of 1996 constant U.S. dollars)

	1975–79	1980–84	1985–89	1990–93	1994–96
Total official development finance[a]					
Bilateral	418.8	382.8	296.2	633.3	827.7
Multilateral	236.9	690.3	531.0	611.6	547.3
Total	655.7	1073.1	827.3	1245.0	1375.1
Total disbursements on loan					
Bilateral	254.2	229.0	164.8	371.9	274.8
Multilateral	199.0	673.2	403.3	459.8	425.1
Total	453.2	902.3	568.0	831.7	699.9
Total grants by creditor (inclusive of technical assistance)					
Bilateral	164.6	153.7	131.5	261.4	552.9
Multilateral	37.9	17.1	127.7	151.8	122.3
Total	202.5	170.8	259.2	413.3	675.2
Total non–technical assistance grants					
Bilateral	21.7	18.7	27.5	132.7	443.4
Multilateral	22.3	8.4	118.2	130.4	114.3
Total	44.0	27.1	145.7	263.2	557.7

Sources: Chang, Fernández-Arias, and Servén 1999; OECD-DAC.

assistance grants, and IMF nonconcessional loans (see table 7.4 and figures 7.2, 7.7, and 7.8). Another concept is total gross official flows (TOF), which is derived from the OECD-DAC database and is defined as ODA plus "other official flows." These other flows are transactions by the official sector whose main objective is other than development-motivated, or whose grant element is below the 25 percent threshold that would make them eligible to be recorded as ODA. The main classes of transactions included are official export credits, official sector equity and portfolio investment, and IMF and World Bank nonconcessional loans.

ODF and TOF can be useful for examining the relation between policy reform and external assistance, assuming that the behavior of the government is more influenced by the amount of total cash inflows than by the pattern or composition of those flows (see figure 7.4). We do not rely on them in this paper.

Still another relevant concept is net transfers on aid, which is total net transfers on public and publicly guaranteed long-term debt from official creditors (including net transfers with the IMF) plus disbursements of grants. A related concept, aggregate net transfers, is net transfers on aid

FIGURE 7.4 CÔTE D'IVOIRE: COMPARISON OF ODF AND TOF, 1970–97

Millions of 1996 constant U.S. dollars

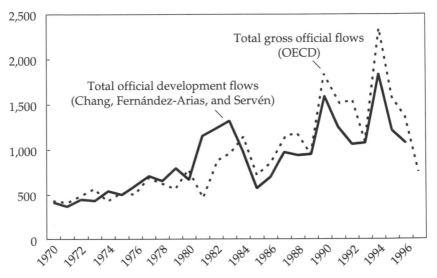

Sources: OECD-DAC; Chang, Fernández-Arias, and Servén 1999.

plus private flows. The World Bank defines it in *Global Development Finance* as net transfers on debt plus foreign direct investment (FDI), plus portfolio equity flows and official grants, minus FDI profits.

The basic aid data are set out in the figures and tables in the text and in appendix 7.3.

Stylized Facts

The following main points emerge from these data and those provided in the statistical appendix.

- *The RCI relied relatively little on aid until recent years.* Up to 1979 the country had access to international money centers, and private capital inflows were substantial (figure 7.9). Modest aid inflows came mainly from France and other European countries; the World Bank had a small presence, and the World Bank Group's International Development Association (IDA) none at all until the 1990s. This changed in the 1980s, though the RCI was not a sizeable aid recipient until the late 1980s (see figure 7.1 and tables 7.1, 7.2, 7.4, and 7.8). From the mid-1960s to the mid-1970s, it received ODA amounting to US$200 million–US$300 million a year (constant 1996 dollars), though total development financial flows were much larger (see tables 7.4, 7.8, and 7.10).

Until the late 1980s, the annual ODA inflow was less than US$300 million in most years (constant 1996 dollars). The amount began to rise in 1988 and 1989, averaged US$800 million annually between 1990 and 1993, then rose dramatically in the two post-devaluation years (1994 and 1995). It reached a peak of almost US$1.8 billion in 1994 before falling back to about US$500 million in 1997. In terms of aid intensity, ODA until the late 1980s was less than 2 percent of GDP, imports, and gross domestic investment. It rose to 10–20 percent in the early and mid-1990s, but returned to under 5 percent with respect to all these indicators in 1997 (figure 7.5).

The largest part of official development flows to RCI was on nonconcessional terms until 1993. Thus while grants amounted to US$200 million or less (1996 dollars) from 1975 to 1987, nongrant equivalents of official loans were two to six times greater (see figures 7.2, 7.7, and 7.8, and table 7.4). It was not until RCI became

FIGURE 7.5 CÔTE D'IVOIRE: AID INTENSITY, 1975–97

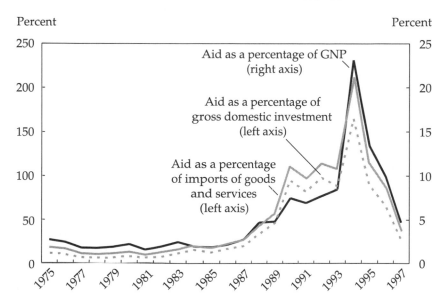

Source: World Bank, *World Development Indicators 1999.*

IDA-eligible in 1994 that grants exceeded nongrants. In 1996 grants made up 80 percent of ODF.

- *The heavy borrowing after 1980 put RCI in the heavily indebted category.* In 1996 the net present value (NPV) of public debt was more than four times the recent average value of exports. Debt service was over 35 percent of exports. The NPV of public debt was 145 percent of GDP and 640 percent of government revenue. Public debt service claimed 52 percent of government revenue.[3] Significant debt relief has been obtained from the Paris Club (table 7.13 in Appendix 7.2). And in 1997 a debt restructuring agreement was signed with commercial creditors to restructure commercial debt that had not been serviced since 1987. Virtually all outstanding commercial commitments were covered. The amount involved is almost US$6.8 billion, of which US$2.4 billion is principal and US$4.4 billion is interest, including arrears and penalties.

- *A dramatic shift took place in the composition of aid after 1990: adjustment loans and grants became dominant,* accounting for almost half the total in 1990–93 (see tables 7.2 and 7.3). The World Bank's shift was particularly strong. In the period 1988–97, adjustment lending accounted for 79 percent of total Bank commitments to the RCI, compared with only 33 percent for the rest of Africa.[4] Project lending suffered. Before 1981, most Bank lending went to agriculture, transport, urban development, and water and sanitation. But the share of these four sectors fell from 76 percent of Bank commitments in 1968–79 to 26 percent in 1994–96.

- *Not only did project lending decline, it also shifted toward projects in support of policy reform*—market liberalization and institutional or capacity development, for example. (See appendix table 7.11 showing World Bank policy loans.)

- *Aggregate aid flows show a sharp rise in the three years immediately following the devaluation of the CFA franc (1994–96), averaging some US$1.25 billion in constant dollars annually.* They declined to less than half a billion dollars in 1997, though this level of concessional assistance was higher than it had been during most of the pre-reform period.

- *Technical assistance (TA) continues to make up a large share of total aid.* Actually, there is some dissonance in the data on technical assistance. Table 7.5 shows an increase in TA grants between 1985–89 and 1994–96. But this seems inconsistent with casual observation— very few expatriate TA providers are seen in government offices— and with trends in TA from France, surely the main provider. The number of French *coopérants* fell from an average of over 2,100 in 1985–89 to 600 in 1994–96 and some 250 in 1998. Part of the explanation is probably found in the financing arrangements for French

TABLE 7.5 CÔTE D'IVOIRE: TECHNICAL ASSISTANCE GRANTS
BY CREDITOR, 1980–96
(annual average in millions of 1996 constant U.S. dollars)

	1975–79	1980–84	1985–89	1990–93	1994–96
Bilateral	142.9	135.1	103.9	128.7	109.5
Multilateral	15.5	8.7	9.6	21.4	8.0
Total	158.5	143.7	113.5	150.1	117.5

Sources: Chang, Fernández-Arias, and Servén 1999; OECD-DAC.

TA, a large part of whose cost was paid for by the RCI itself, which means that the decline in TA numbers would not be matched by a proportional decline in its external financing.

- *The aggregate inflow data show a rapid decline in the second part of the 1990s.* The numbers derived from World Bank/OECD data (see above) show "net transfers on aid," as set out in figure 7.6. These indicate that net transfers on aid were positive in most years during the 1990s, including 1995 and 1996. But after reaching a peak in

FIGURE 7.6 CÔTE D'IVOIRE: NET TRANSFERS ON AID, 1975–97

Millions of 1996 constant U.S. dollars

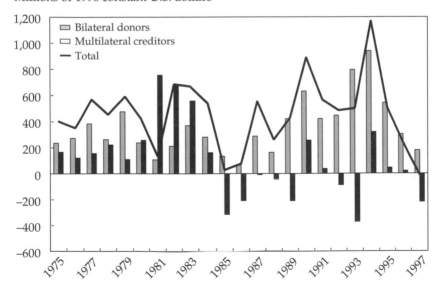

Sources: OECD-DAC; World Bank, *Global Development Finance 1999.*

1994 (the year of the devaluation) they decreased sharply in the following years, becoming negative in 1997. Table 7.6 (from official Ivoirian sources), which refers to net transfers on debt (without grants), shows negative transfers as early as 1995.

Nonfinancial Aid

We turn now to some key issues. *Nonfinancial aid* was especially important in the earlier phases of Ivoirian development. It took the form of technical assistance from France, primarily secondary school and university teachers. Other TA was in health and social development, infrastructures, culture, and scientific research. A total of 31,000 coopérants were present during 1981–95, more than 80 percent of them professors. The number decreased drastically over the years. The rate of decline reached a peak in 1993 (–30.8 percent). As noted above, the number of French coopérants today is a mere 250, of whom 140 are professors, a 58 percent drop from 598 in 1995.[5] Nonetheless, technical assistance overall still seems to comprise almost a quarter of total ODA.

In the 1960s and 1970s one of Côte d'Ivoire's distinctive features was the influence of French TA over the system of decisionmaking in technical administrations as well as in the president's office. In those years, one could find almost no Ivoirian nationals in the position of adviser; France provided most advisers in this pre–structural adjustment period, when the Bretton Woods institutions were absent. President Félix Houphouët-Boigny wanted a gradual replacement of the French, but he wanted good teaching and good administration too, so he continued to employ French technical assistants, paying much of the cost out of local resources. More important, he failed to put in place meaningful and reliable arrangements for the real transfer of technical skills and competencies to Ivoirians.

Resident expatriate technical assistants everywhere tend to develop an informal network of information and influence to which local people have no access. Where there are many expatriate TA people this is exaggerated, and where there are many from one country it is more pronounced still. This was particularly evident in the RCI. Aside from its negative effects on transfer of knowledge, this situation put French *coopérants* in a particularly influential position; dialogue between donors and the government was filtered to a significant extent through the screen of French technicians.

To the extent that foreigners served as technical advisers to the president, to all ministers, and to senior management of state-owned enterprises, ideas generated in the country over a long period could not be of local vintage. French TA deserves credit for bringing about some good results—for example, the vigorous economic growth recorded until the

TABLE 7.6 CÔTE D'IVOIRE: AGGREGATE NET TRANSFERS BY DONOR, 1995–97
(billions of current CFA francs)

	Disbursements				Repayments				Net Transfers			
	1995	1996	1997	Total	1995	1996	1997	Total	1995	1996	1997	Total
IMF	175.1	138.9	0.0	314.0	99.2	58.5	28.4	186.1	75.9	80.4	–28.4	127.9
IBRD and IDA	244.8	253.6	152.7	651.0	305.5	300.6	272.7	878.8	–60.7	–47.0	–120.0	–227.7
UNDP	0.8	1.2	4.6	6.6	0.0	0.0	0.0	0.0	0.8	1.2	4.6	6.6
EU	92.3	74.5	40.3	207.1	17.0	18.1	16.8	52.0	75.2	56.4	23.5	155.1
IFAD	1.7	0.4	1.3	3.4	0.9	1.3	1.9	4.1	0.8	–1.0	–0.6	–0.7
AfDB	45.9	64.1	44.7	154.7	119.2	141.4	131.6	392.3	–73.3	–77.3	–87.0	–237.6
BOAD	19.3	6.5	7.4	33.1	1.2	3.4	3.5	8.0	18.1	3.1	3.9	25.1
Paris Club members	345.9	163.9	71.7	581.5	303.3	237.9	147.6	688.8	42.6	–74.0	–75.9	–107.3
London Club members	0.0	0.0	0.0	0.0	0.0	0.7	6.0	6.7	0.0	–0.7	–6.0	–6.7
Other	31.6	28.5	67.1	127.2	133.6	78.0	71.5	283.1	–102.0	–49.5	–4.4	–155.9
Total	957.2	731.6	389.8	2078.6	979.9	840.0	680.0	2499.9	–22.7	–108.4	–290.2	–421.3

Source: Côte d'Ivoire 1998b: 25.

late 1970s and the relatively strong public administration. By the same token, they have to bear some responsibility for the failures—inadequate attention to knowledge transfer, reliance on approaches and institutions that would prove unsustainable without lavish use of imported manpower, and the maintenance or adoption of inappropriate policies in key sectors like education and health. Education was the single most important area of intervention for French technical cooperation, yet reform made slow progress during their tenure in that sector and is today in much disarray.

After the mid-1980s government officials changed their attitudes toward the use of local human resources. Nowadays, in Côte d'Ivoire, the norm is a local technical adviser. Expatriate, including French, technical advisers are rare, in ministries as well as in the president's and the prime minister's offices. Academics and university professors are more and more associated with the analytical and technical work of the administration. One testimony to the new situation is the fact that there is not a single expatriate technical adviser in the prime minister's office. This is now the rule.

Outside technical influence remains strong, though its origins have shifted. In the era of structural adjustment, the IMF and the World Bank have become powerful advisers to the government. The Bretton Woods institutions' advice is built on an analytical and technical foundation that is usually very impressive, and hence influential in all circles, including that of local technical advisers. Little analytical and technical work is conducted by locals that is not subject to the intellectual influence of the Bretton Woods institutions. But while ideas in general and reform ideas in particular continue to be externally generated, local counterparts are more and more equipped with a capacity to develop home-grown reform ideas, and able to engage in real dialogue with their aid partners.

Bilateral Financial Aid

With respect to bilateral aid, we concentrate on France. Because of that country's close relationship with the RCI, its aid connection merits special attention. France is also a major donor, the third-largest ODA contributor behind the IMF and the World Bank; it provided two-thirds of bilateral aid in 1996, well ahead of Japan's 26 percent and Germany's 5 percent.

French financial assistance to Côte d'Ivoire is accounted for by history, commercial and financial interests, and political strategy. Colonial history and cultural links strengthened the ties with the former colonizer, as did the strong pro-French sentiments of the RCI's first and long-time head of state, President Félix Houphouët-Boigny. The president not only maintained French influence in Côte d'Ivoire, but also championed it in other francophone countries. France has commercial and financial interests in Côte d'Ivoire, which is its second-largest West African market (after Nigeria). The equity capital of Ivoirian modern sector firms is largely French. Large-scale trading businesses are French or French-controlled. Finally, Côte d'Ivoire is a political asset as it is a heavyweight partner in the region.

France provided financial support for the economic development of Côte d'Ivoire. This financial assistance was vital, especially during the difficult years starting in the mid-1980s and in 1990–93, when the country was trying to avoid bankruptcy. The former colonizer paid its ex-colony's debts to save it from default. It can be argued that by so doing, it relieved the pressure for structural adjustments, thereby retarding reform. On the other hand, pressures remained extremely strong, and the country eventually did pursue many reforms. Debate continues on this question, which we review in section 4. As pointed out there, the fact that President Houphouët-Boigny strongly opposed devaluation could not be overlooked.

In the years just before the devaluation, France's influence on policy was diluted by the strong presence of the Bretton Woods institutions. Its influence by no means disappeared, however. Aside from other doors open to it, the strategy of cofinancing most reform programs provided continuing entrée. The mechanism of consultation of cofinanciers was used by France to press its views, dissent from policies, and occasionally provide the political backing that Côte d'Ivoire needed in the negotiations with these institutions. After the devaluation, the role of cofinancier of structural adjustment programs was strengthened. Indeed, the Agence Française de Développement (AFD) spent 600 billion CFA francs in Côte d'Ivoire in the period 1994–98, of which more than half (CFAF 315 billion) was for structural adjustment loans. These resources financed external debt service and internal debt arrears to the private sector.

One of the key implications of the liberalization reforms was a wider opening of the local market to non-French businesses. This challenge was foreseen by France and was met by the extension of CFAF 150 billion in credits to the private sector—25 percent of total AFD assistance between 1994 and 1998. Almost three-fourths of this assistance was in the form of loans to finance the participation of French-controlled firms in the provision of public services—electric power, gas, water, transport (rail and airport), seaport, and toll bridges. (It is not irrelevant that a French firm won the bid privatizing the national telecommunications network.)

There is some feeling among Ivoirians that French aid "unlevels" the private sector playing field. Although a major problem of local companies has always been difficulty of access to credit, French firms engaged in the local market benefit from guarantees to facilitate borrowing. These amounted to CFAF 38 billion in 1994–98, that is 25 percent of AFD assistance to the private sector. Thus it can be argued that the French aid inflows associated with the liberalization reforms reinforced the already strong position of French firms in the economy, especially in key strategic sectors. It should be noted, however, that a somewhat contrary view was expressed by one private sector spokesman, who believed that Levantines and others have won market share from the big French trading houses since the devaluation.

Aid Coordination

In 1991 the government created an institution specialized in the coordination of aid (grants and loans). The objectives of this body were extended in 1994 to cover the monitoring of public investments as well. The institution is the "Comité de mobilisation des financements extérieurs et de suivi des investissements publics," or COMFESIP. Its objectives are to speed up the preparation of funding requests, schedule expected disbursements of exceptional funding, compare scheduled disbursements with liquidity needs of the Treasury, and speed up the implementation of public investment projects. Its main activities are periodic review of the project portfolio, periodic publication of status reports on project implementation, and capacity building in aid management and coordination. It produces a major annual report on aid inflows and disbursements.

COMFESIP is composed of representatives of the main economic and financial units involved in aid management. It is administered by a technical group and a permanent technical secretariat. The technical group includes the prime minister's office and directors of the budget, the Treasury, the planning agency, and the Banque Centrale des Etats d'Afrique de l'Ouest (BCEAO). The permanent technical secretariat is Bureau National d'Etudes de Developpement (BNETD). That comprises the main formal structure on the government side. It produces useful documentation, but it is not clear how effective it is in operational terms—that is, in coordinating actual donor programs. Donors, on their side, have a variety of consultative arrangements, mostly at the sectoral level. These meet informally and produce no reports. In 1997 there were three such groups, each chaired by a lead donor. These groups met monthly in the first semester of 1997, but since then seem to have met sporadically or not at all.

There are informal relations between donors and the COMFESIP secretariat, but roundtables on sectoral issues have been organized to determine strategies and to pledge funding budgets. By mid-1999 four such roundtables had been organized: for environment, health, regional planning and decentralization, and education. Donors use common letters to government to express their concerns and opinions on policy issues.

Despite the fairly extensive formal structure of consultative mechanisms, it is not clear how much genuine consultation takes place. Some incidents suggest that it is highly sporadic and imperfect.

In the health sector, some donors believe true consultation has been minimal, and there does appear to be considerable cross-purpose activity. In agriculture there has not been wholehearted donor consensus with respect to the nature and pace of state withdrawal from cotton, coffee, and cocoa marketing, and this has limited the extent of meaningful coordination. How intensive coordination may be in other sectors is not clear.

POLICY REFORM AND INSTITUTIONAL DEVELOPMENT

The history of Côte d'Ivoire's economic performance can be divided into five periods. The years between 1960 and 1977 were marked by high GDP growth (6–7 percent a year) and general prosperity. Terms of trade and were favorable and stable, and surpluses derived from export revenues financed a high level of public investment. The 1973 oil shock did not slow down growth because the prices of cocoa and coffee rose simultaneously. They achieved record prices in 1976–77, which led to a surge in the rate of public investment financed by the increased revenues of the Caisse de Stabilization (CAISTAB) as well as by foreign borrowing. This period was remarkable for the big size of public investment programs, and their high unit cost and low economic returns (World Bank 1998b).

In 1978–80 financial crisis hit. The situation deteriorated in 1978 with a significant slowdown of the economy as a result of the decline in the prices of cocoa and coffee and consequent fall in public investment. Inflation remained high because of higher import prices caused by the 1979 oil shock and a parallel expansion in the money supply. The rise of interest rates on world capital markets and the sharp deterioration of the terms of trade between 1978 and 1980 induced an increased deficit of the current account in that period. The rise in domestic inflation contributed to the appreciation of the real exchange rate. The demand-driven growth pattern came to an abrupt end (Hopkins 1989). Debt service became so heavy that the government was forced to call on the Bretton Woods institutions for financial assistance.

Between 1981 and 1986 the economy was stabilized, but with recession. The major economic problems facing the country were overexpansion of the public sector with the consequence of declining public savings and rising external debt, a large and ill-conceived Public Investment

Program (PIP), distortions in the structure of price incentives for agricultural products, and excessive protection in industry with induced high costs and low export incentives. These trends led to the erosion of the competitiveness of the economy over the 1970s.

These problems were addressed by a succession of IMF and World Bank loans: an Extended Fund Facility (EFF) agreement with the IMF in 1981 and Fund standby agreements (SBAs) in 1984, 1985, and 1986; and three successive World Bank structural adjustment loans (SALs) in 1981, 1983, and 1986. The stabilization and adjustment measures contained in these loans are described below.

These adjustment programs and policies, coupled with favorable changes in the external environment, had positive results. Despite terms of trade deterioration early in the decade and a drought in 1983, internal balance was restored and competitiveness improved as a result of depreciation of the real exchange rate (the devaluation of the French franc), and tighter fiscal and monetary policies. In 1984 exports increased, the current account moved into surplus, and the growth rate picked up. It increased further in 1985. However, the debt burden increased also: the ratio of foreign debt to GDP that year increased to 84 percent from 41 percent in 1980. In 1986, the real growth of the economy was still positive though lower than population growth.

This improvement was short-lived. From 1987 to 1994 the RCI struggled to avoid bankruptcy. The terms of trade deteriorated in 1987 due to a falling dollar and declining world prices of cocoa and coffee. The growth rate fell, the public investment-to-GDP ratio fell, and the current account was in deficit because of the large interest payments on public debt. The government was forced to suspend its debt service payments in May 1987. No financial assistance came from the World Bank in 1988 because of the absence of an agreement on a macroeconomic framework (Ouayogode and Pegatienan 1994).

Despite the deterioration of the terms of trade and the fall of CAISTAB's revenues after 1986, government maintained the producer price of cocoa and coffee and tried to stock cocoa in an attempt to influence the world market. The result was increased fiscal deficit, accumulation of domestic arrears to the private sector, and an illiquid banking system. During this period intense reform activities were initiated. Two standby agreements were signed with the IMF, one for a year in 1988, a second for two years in 1989. The 1989 program had two main objectives: to reduce producer prices of cocoa and coffee and to cut civil servants' salaries. The producer price measures were implemented; they were halved in September 1989. But social resistance prevented the second objective from being realized. Nonetheless, another standby agreement was signed in 1991 for one year.

Between 1989 and 1991 the World Bank supported the government's reform efforts with six sectoral adjustment loans or credits (SECALs) in the following areas: human resources (the Human Resources Development Project, HRDP), competitiveness (Competitiveness and Regulatory Reform Adjustment Program, PASCO), banking (Financial Sector Adjustment Loan, FSAL), agriculture, water, and energy. Most disbursement on these loans, however, did not occur until 1994, after devaluation.

Notwithstanding the signing of the EFF, SBAs, SALs, and SECALs, and some implementation, such as cutting producer prices and some civil service salaries, financial crisis dominated the early 1990s. The main policy concern was to avoid falling into arrears with the multilateral lenders. In the face of the structural disequilibria caused partly by external shocks and partly by domestic policies, it appeared that the adjustment effort was too little because it concentrated on internal disequilibrium. It also appeared too late, probably because of its political and social costs. It was under these circumstances that the CFA franc was devalued in January 1994.

The post-devaluation years, 1994–98, have been marked by economic recovery. The 50 percent devaluation was aimed at improving the internal and external competitiveness of the economy. It was coupled with measures designed to contain inflationary pressures. The implementation of this policy package improved external competitiveness and economic performance. IMF and World Bank support played a big role in bringing about these results. An Enhanced Structural Adjustment Facility (ESAF) agreement was signed in 1994 and another in 1998 for three years each. Large inflows came from the World Bank via loans signed earlier (the Economic Recovery Credit, HRDP, PASCO, and FSAL) as well as programs in agriculture and transport. Along with and within the framework set by these lead donors, other multilaterals and bilaterals extended their financial assistance to the country as well. As noted in section 1, aid inflows in 1994 amounted to US$1.7 billion, more than twice the pre-devaluation levels, and remained high until 1997.

The positive real growth obtained after devaluation was a dramatic change in comparison with the desperate pre-devaluation situation. (See the economic indicators in table 7.7.) But the recovery is still fragile and poverty issues have only begun to be addressed. According to a World Bank poverty assessment, the rate of headcount poverty increased from 11 percent of the population in 1985 to 31 percent in 1993 and 37 percent in 1995 (World Bank 1997). The last figure is contested, and the four years of 5–6 percent growth since 1995 undoubtedly improved the situation. But there is no room for complacency.

Policy Reforms

Since the inception of the economic and financial crisis in the late 1970s, the reforms undertaken were of different types: macroeconomic, structural, sectoral, and social. The reform in macroeconomic policies was

TABLE 7.7 CÔTE D'IVOIRE: SELECTED ECONOMIC AND FINANCIAL INDICATORS, 1987–96

									Annual percentage changes	
	1987	1988	1989	1990	1991	1992	1993	1994	1995	1996
GDP in real terms	-0.4	1.1	2.9	-1.1	0.0	-0.2	-0.3	2.0	7.1	6.8
GDP per capita	-4.1	-2.3	-1.1	-5.0	-3.8	-4.0	-4.0	-1.9	3.2	3.1
Consumer price index (annual average)	7.0	6.9	1.0	-0.7	1.6	4.2	2.4	32.2	7.7	3.5
External sector on the basis of CFAF										
Export of goods f.o.b.	-20.6	-14.6	5.1	-1.9	-6.6	2.2	-8.5	123.3	20.3	15.0
Import of goods f.o.b.	-3.2	-9.4	8.8	-15.4	10.9	2.0	-3.8	76.7	35.3	20.6
Export volume	-6.0	-4.1	9.4	11.0	-6.9	7.8	-11.0	4.9	70.1	20.3
Import volume	-6.2	-10.2	-0.6	-13.4	9.6	6.8	-8.0	-9.5	37.6	12.4
Terms of trade (deterioration)	-18.1	-11.7	-12.3	-9.5	-1.0	-0.8	—	9.0	14.2	-10.9
Real effective exchange rate (depreciation)	8.3	0.7	-6.8	2.4	-2.8	3.3	-3.1	-34.5	8.3	-2.5
Monetary										
Net domestic assets	5.2	10.1	-8.0	-3.7	-2.1	-0.1	-7.1	-20.0	5.8	0.7
Of which: Government	-2.5	90.1	-1.8	-4.1	2.6	12.9	28.8	-15.9	-1.8	-1.6
Private sector	5.7	-1.6	-5.0	-3.3	-4.0	-9.0	-18.3	10.2	19.9	2.2
Money and quasi-money M2	-1.4	0.2	-7.4	-3.1	0.0	-1.9	-4.3	47.0	17.0	3.0

	Percent of GDP									
Public finances										
Total revenues and grants	—	25.7	21.8	21.5	19.9	20.2	18.1	20.6	22.8	23.2
Total expenditures	—	40.3	38.5	33.4	32.9	31.9	30.0	27.1	26.5	25.3
Overall deficit (–) payment order basis	—	-14.6	-16.6	-12.0	-13.0	-11.7	-11.9	-6.5	-3.7	-2.1
Primary balance	—	-3.1	-5.8	-1.1	-0.8	-0.3	-2.2	3.0	4.9	50.6
Gross domestic investments	11.8	11.5	10.3	8.5	8.6	8.5	7.8	11.1	12.9	13.9
Of which: Central government	5.1	4.7	4.4	3.6	3.4	3.8	3.7	4.1	4.2	4.3
Nongovernment	6.7	6.8	5.9	4.9	5.1	4.7	4.1	7.0	8.7	9.6
Current account balance	-8.6	-11.5	-12.5	-12.2	-11.5	-11.4	-11.0	-1.0	-5.0	-4.8
External public debt	77.0	83.1	93.3	107.3	116.6	127.0	141.9	183.9	157.9	153.5
Government domestic debt							44.6	27.7	25.1	20.9

	Specified units									
GDP at market prices (billions of CFAF)	3,031.7	3,054.5	3,112.8	2,939.3	2,960.0	2,952.1	2,946.2	4,256.0	4,987.7	5,473.6
CFAF per U.S. dollar	300.5	297.9	319.0	272.3	282.1	264.7	283.2	555.2	499.1	511.6
Population (millions)	10.6	11.0	11.4	11.8	12.2	12.7	13.2	13.7	14.2	14.7

Source: IMF.

initiated through the IMF's Extended Facility agreement in 1981 and by six SBAs between 1984 and 1991. These concerned fiscal issues (government revenue recovery and expenditure reduction, rationalization of public investment programs, control of domestic debt, and restructuring of public enterprises), and monetary and financial problems. Over the years, the main objectives of fiscal policy reforms were the elimination of budget deficits and the generation of surplus in the primary budget, in order to pay an increasing share of debt interest and to cover expenditures on physical and social infrastructure. The monetary and financial reforms aimed at reducing domestic credit, maintaining the liquidity of the banking system, and improving the mobilization of domestic savings.

The structural adjustment loans were initiated in the early 1980s. SAL I, in 1981, focused mainly on agricultural pricing and investment policy. SAL II, in 1983, continued to focus on agriculture and added industrial and housing policy. The reform in the industrial sector dealt with export incentives, tariff and nontariff barriers, and the revision of the investment code to include measures favorable to small and medium enterprises. The new housing policy favored lower income housing, reduced the housing benefits for civil servants, and designed mechanisms to cut recurrent housing costs. SAL III, initiated in 1986, aimed at reinforcing the measures of the first two SALs and improving the relative price of tradeables in order to stimulate exports, correcting the urban/rural terms of trade, increasing rural incomes, and encouraging private investment.

After the first three SALs, which were a mixture of structural and sectoral reforms, the first ESAF loan was granted by the IMF in 1994. It had the following objectives: improvement of competition and the regulatory framework, liberalization of the labor market, price decontrol, civil service reduction, accelerated privatization and private sector development, and deregulation of export crop marketing.

Structural adjustment became more specific with sectoral reforms. Between 1991 and 1993 the World Bank supported the three SECALs mentioned earlier, in regulatory reform, financial sector reform, and education and health. The reforms in these sectors were deepened after the 1994 devaluation, and reinforced by a private sector development (PSD) program. Post-devaluation reforms in agriculture aimed at improving farmer incentives and removing the state from export crop production and marketing. Specific measures concerned the following items: the liberalization of cocoa and coffee marketing and the restructuring of CAISTAB, the launching of a new system to allocate export rights by auction, organization of a closer association of the private sector with the management of the cocoa and coffee trade, and liberalization of rice imports.

Far-reaching social sector reforms were introduced in the Human Resources Development Project, the SECAL mentioned earlier. These were reinforced in 1997 by the adoption of a national program for eradicating poverty, with measures designed to increase the rate of school enrollment and literacy, improve basic health care, increase women's participation in development activities, curb rural exodus, and control population growth. It is clear that the RCI undertook, over a 20-year period, a vast program of reforms involving virtually every area of economic policy and most economic institutions. Table 7.11 suggests the substantive range of the reform agendas over the years. Some of these reforms were soundly conceived, others less so. In some—particularly during more recent years—the Ivoirian input was substantial. In most it was slight. Aid and aid donors, and particularly the Bretton Woods institutions, clearly played a significant role in reform conception and design. Despite uneven implementation, the economy is more open than before and more liberal. Instances of unequal or discriminatory treatment persist.

The effects of price liberalization in particular are dampened by information retention by some technical administrations. The perceptible improvements at the macroeconomic level have not yet materialized at the microeconomic level among the urban population, whereas the rural population is probably better off. Significant institutional improvements have also occurred, in the budget process for example, and in export and investment promotion agencies. These favorable changes, however, are balanced by rampant corrupt practices in the administration and by the lack of responsiveness of the political system.

Institutions and Governance

Two institutions play a critical role in the working of the economy and in the reform process: CAISTAB and the CFA monetary union. These institutions were the pillars of a system that worked with remarkable success for two decades. They were supported by France and by the Bretton Woods institutions, and they were deeply anchored in the thinking of President Houphouët-Boigny. All of this made it especially difficult to adapt them when changed circumstances called for reform.

CAISTAB is the marketing board for cocoa and coffee crops. Until September 1989 it applied the principle of never reducing producer prices and of increasing them less than proportionally to rising world prices. The consequence of that asymmetrical behavior was to tax peasants and transfer to the government budget resources generated by the positive difference between world and producer prices. It also financed budgetary losses in cases of negative differentials between the two prices.

CAISTAB was instrumental in the overexpansion of public investment and in the acceleration of state participation in productive and marketing activities. For decades, CAISTAB was a bone of contention in the policy dialogue between Côte d'Ivoire's government and the Bretton Woods institutions.

Côte d'Ivoire's membership in the West African Economic and Monetary Union (Union Monetaire Economique Ouest Africaine, UMEOA) is a determining factor in its exchange rate and fiscal and monetary policies. The UMEOA maintains a fixed rate of exchange between the French franc and the CFA franc. This institutional feature is critical to the evolution of external competitiveness and to adjustment to external shocks. Since for many years a nominal devaluation of the CFAF could not be implemented to reduce real wages and thereby restore external competitiveness, the only way to have that happen was to reduce nominal wages. But opposition to the reduction of civil servants' nominal salaries in 1989 left the government with the option of restoring competitiveness through cuts in public expenditure other than salaries. After a floor was reached in cuts of current expenditure, the government turned to large reductions of public investment, which accelerated the decline of the economy. The 14 countries of the franc zone accepted devaluation of the CFAF in January 1994 to restore external competitiveness. That decision is discussed in detail in section 4.

The government demonstrated a strong political commitment to undertake appropriate development programs that would transform the economy and create new activities. This commitment was expressed by an investment code that granted many incentives to investors, and by the direct participation of the state in productive activities through state-owned enterprises and the creation of physical and human capital. The state intervention and the explosion of the number of parastatals temporarily stimulated economic growth. Unfortunately, this state involvement increased the bureaucratization and the inefficiencies of the economy.

Stability has been an important feature of the RCI political landscape. It was preserved through the autocratic regime of President Houphouët-Boigny, who tolerated no political dissent. Unlike neighboring countries, the RCI lived for decades without a single coup d'etat and there was almost no political violence. This stability built trust and confidence conducive to private investment, especially foreign direct investment. Houphouët also controlled personally the financial resources of the CAISTAB and the decision mechanism on the selection of public investment projects. His control over these resources was a source of considerable economic and political power that he used to consolidate his regime.

In 1990, in the depths of the economic and financial crisis, constitutional changes created a new prime minister position that brought to the forefront BCEAO Governor Alassane Dramane Ouattara. He ruled the country during the illness and until the death of President Houphouët-Boigny in December 1993. It is fair to say that he saved Houphouët's political regime from falling apart. The premiership was a significant political innovation because it guaranteed the continuity of power during the illness of the president. It also had important economic policy implications. The policy dialogue with the Bretton Woods institutions was eased by the positioning of an actor who could be trusted for his technocratic skills and his commitment to reform. To some extent this prevented the collapse of the economy. The 1995 presidential elections ended the transitional period and conferred legitimacy on President Henri Konan Bédié's regime.

President Houphouët-Boigny stayed in power for 40 years. This long political tenure had advantages and disadvantages. The advantages were linked to the fact that his policies were deemed appropriate, given the structure of the economy. Agriculture was made a priority activity, peasants received substantial shares of world prices, and the public investment financed by agricultural revenues created the basic physical and human capital necessary to support productive activities. These policies were implemented for a sufficiently long period with a strong political will and commitment that gave them credibility.

The disadvantage of the long political tenure lay in the fact that the government overextended itself and public investment programs were too ambitious for too long. For decades, President Houphouët, who controlled every economic decision, resisted and postponed needed reforms. He was a fierce opponent of devaluation and there is no question that his long illness and death facilitated the decision to devalue the CFAF, reform the CAISTAB, and launch the privatization spree.

The first attempt at political democratization was the institution in 1980 of municipal and legislative elections within a one-party system. This did not have much impact on the political and economic evolution of the country because political dissent was still not tolerated. The 1990 democratization was prompted by the reaction of civil servants in 1989 to the cutting of their salaries. This contentious salary cut was a critical feature of the "internal adjustment" effort needed to restore fiscal stability and competitiveness. Between 1990 and 1993 scores of political parties were born, a free press appeared, and President Houphouët had in 1990, for the first time, a challenger in an electoral contest. Since 1990 civil society has been organizing itself to voice its concerns and give expression to political dissent. The large number of political parties, the diversified media, and the professional organizations and independent trade unions together act on the government as agents of restraint, in the sense that they critically watch the behavior of political figures and those in public office. So far, this surveillance has been only partially successful in inducing more responsible behavior among government officials.

The multiple parties, independent media, and numerous professional organizations have had only limited influence on the process of policy formulation.

Thus public opinion does not influence the content of policies in decisive ways, because consultation by the government is far from being the rule and those who happen to be consulted rarely find their opinions taken into account. Civil society has little political voice. It lacks cohesiveness. For decades, ethnic and regional cohesion was skillfully preserved by President Houphouët-Boigny. This cohesion was not furthered by President Bédié's policies on ethnicity—his concept of *ivoirité*. The overthrow of Bédié and the popular revolt against military rule late in 1999 were remarkable events, but subsequent ethnic turmoil has paralyzed the economy and put economic reform on hold.

THE CFA PARITY ISSUE

Côte d'Ivoire has undertaken extensive macroeconomic and fiscal policy reforms since 1980, as indicated in the previous section. But by far the most important policy issue concerned the exchange rate—the appropriate relationship between the CFA franc and the French franc. This question dominated policy debate and shaped the economic environment for a decade at least.

The parity issue was central both to aid management and to the pace of reform. So it is essential to look carefully at the donor role in the January 1994 decision to change the parity of the CFAF from one CFAF equals two French centimes, which had been the prevailing rate since 1948, to one CFAF equals one French centime. In addition to being important, this question has also been contentious. It is often cited as a case where aid retarded reform, because aid inflows allowed the RCI government to postpone the inevitable exchange rate devaluation. This section therefore focuses on the devaluation decision.

The decision to devalue the CFAF obviously did not depend on RCI alone, since the CFAF was the common currency of all member countries of the Union Monetaire Ouest Africaine (since 1994, the Union Monetaire et Economique Ouest Africaine part of the franc zone), and the Union statutes required unanimity in such decisions.[6] The French Treasury guarantees the convertibility of the CFAF, and the rules of the monetary arrangement require that the French government be consulted as far as possible about any contemplated change in CFA parity.

Moreover, given the economic weight of Côte d'Ivoire in the Union and the influence of France on the other member countries, it was essential that both Côte d'Ivoire and France agree to the devaluation if the other countries were to go along. If Côte d'Ivoire had opposed devaluation—as did some other member states until the meeting of heads of state in Dakar on January 10–11, 1994, where the decision was made—devaluation would have been impossible.

The decision to devalue was very different from other economic policy measures. Its economic and political significance was considerable, which helps explain why it was so difficult a step to take. Once the decision was taken, implementation had to be immediate and irreversible. Also, it had to be taken at the highest political levels. In the case of Côte d'Ivoire this meant that President Houphouët-Boigny, who had been for years an ardent opponent of devaluation, had to be brought around. As things turned out, due to the illness of the president, the decision to devalue was made by his prime minister, who was then Alassane Ouattara.

Côte d'Ivoire began its adjustment program in 1980, and the parity issue arose at the outset. But the policy context varied substantially over the ensuing 15 years, and with it the attitudes and roles of aid donors. Three periods can be distinguished: an initial period of donor agreement on maintaining parity; a second period when they differed in their recommendations; and a third period when they came together again, in favor of devaluation.

Temporary Consensus on Maintaining Parity: 1980–85

The period of temporary consensus on maintaining the existing parity was 1980–85. Côte d'Ivoire's initial adjustment efforts, at the beginning of the 1980s, were undertaken with the support of the Bretton Woods institutions (see section 1). The Ivoirian authorities, the Bretton Woods institutions, and France agreed on the adjustment strategy to be pursued, which did *not* include devaluation. One indicator of this consensus is that the adjustment loans given by France through the Caisse Française de Coopération Economique explicitly required a previous agreement with the IMF.[7] As for the consensus between Côte d'Ivoire and the aid donors, one manifestation is the fact that the agreements were successfully implemented.

The implementation of a consensus adjustment program was facilitated by the nature of the monetary cooperation agreement with France, and by favorable conditions in international currency markets. The monetary cooperation with France was based on the existence of the operations account maintained by the French Treasury at the Banque Centrale des Etats d'Afrique de l'Ouest (BCEAO), which deposits in this account at least 65 percent of its reserves and can run a deficit without a fixed limit. For the first time since its establishment, the account of the BCEAO was in deficit in 1980, mainly because of the situation of Côte d'Ivoire. The operations account was thus fulfilling the role for which it had been created—that is, to allow franc zone countries to withstand a temporary balance of payments disequilibrium without being forced to abandon convertibility or parity. The operations account gave countries time to implement corrective measures and await a return to more favorable external conditions.

The crisis then facing Côte d'Ivoire was mainly due to falling prices of coffee and cocoa, which had reached exceptionally high levels in 1976–77. The temporary nature of this price boom was not taken account of in macroeconomic policy. A rapid rise in civil service salaries occurred along with an even greater expansion of public investment and external debt. The result was a rapid rise in the public sector deficit, which reached 12 percent of GDP in 1982; it had been zero in 1977. This deficit was not sustainable, given that the regulations of the BCEAO imposed strict limits on its advances to governments. At the same time, Côte d'Ivoire lost its competitiveness, since the real effective exchange rate rose by 30 percent between 1975 and 1980, when it reached its peak (up 24 percent) compared with 1970.[8]

Because of the budgetary roots of the disequilibrium, and because the trade balance remained positive, the stabilization program implemented with the help of the IMF focused, properly, on reform of public finances. Macroeconomic stabilization would allow, by "competitive disinflation," a depreciation of the real exchange rate. As things turned out, the return to competitiveness was smoothed by the devaluations of the French franc and the appreciation of the dollar. And rises in cocoa and coffee prices in 1985 made the budgetary adjustment easier.

The macroeconomic results seemed to validate the policy path adopted. The operations account became positive again in 1985. The public sector deficit was cut beginning in 1983 and turned into a surplus in 1985. The real effective exchange rate depreciated by 34 percent between 1980 and 1985, returning to its 1975 level, while the nominal effective exchange rate only depreciated by about 14 percent.

This exchange rate decline allowed initial moves toward reducing protection, which were incorporated in the second SAL (1983). Quantitative restrictions and reference prices were eliminated and a tariff reform was introduced, which was to reduce the effective protection rate to 40 percent. To this was to be added an export subsidy of 40 percent of value added (for further details see Geourjon 1996: 89). This was to be a mock or indirect devaluation. Doubts existed about whether this measure could be implemented—reasonable doubts as it turned out. That it was proposed suggests that a problem of parity was seen to exist.

Overall, in 1985, Côte d'Ivoire seemed to have returned to a positive growth path after a period of recession. One noteworthy fact during this period is that the real prices paid to producers of coffee and especially of cocoa were maintained, even increased, which brought about a reallocation of income in favor of rural households.

The donor community seemed at the time satisfied with these outcomes. Senior officials of the World Bank even cited the adjustment experience of Côte d'Ivoire up to 1983 as a success story (see, for example, Serageldin 1988).

Breakdown of Consensus: 1986–92

Beginning in 1986 the economic environment turned sharply negative for Côte d'Ivoire. Several external factors contributed, as noted in the previous chapter. The terms of trade became once again unfavorable; and as it turned out this deterioration was the deepest and most durable the country had ever known.[9] The French franc strengthened, the dollar fell, and currencies of big neighboring countries (Ghana and Nigeria, in particular) were devalued.

Confronted with this change in economic conditions the position of the World Bank, and then of the IMF, gradually shifted in favor of devaluation. No official position was announced publicly, but in private, and sometimes even in public, World Bank staff expressed their doubts about the prospects of this new phase of adjustment without devaluation.[10] These publicly expressed opinions were regarded by French officials as untimely and imprudent, certain to exacerbate the loss of confidence and capital flight already observable among Ivoirian economic actors.

During this time, the French authorities never missed an occasion to emphasize their attachment, and that of African governments, to parity maintenance. This was the message given especially during meetings of finance ministers of the franc zone. And, in private, French spokesmen let World Bank management know of their displeasure every time they felt that Bank staff committed an *incartade*—an ill-considered statement or action that was damaging to their official doctrine. These incidents influenced how the devaluation was prepared: French experts worked mainly with those of the IMF. The Bank, which had done so much to bring about acceptance of the idea that devaluation was necessary, was not much involved in preparing the decision.

This discord between the main donors made it very difficult for a long time to engage in quiet, scientific analysis of the costs and benefits of a devaluation for a country like Côte d'Ivoire. Political factors seemed most fundamental in determining the positions adopted. The French government was concerned about the social and political turmoil that might accompany devaluation in countries where France had a military presence. French authorities feared that they would lose the political confidence of African governments and African elites, who would be directly and negatively affected. They feared that the lack of consensus among the countries concerned might lead to a breakup of the franc zone. Indeed many suspected that some partisans of devaluation in the international institutions were using the devaluation issue to undermine the institutions of the franc zone. The French government, finally, was sensitive to the anti-devaluation arguments of some groups of French companies active in Africa, although other enterprises were favorable to parity change.

It is important to recall that on the French side, as early as the end of the 1980s, policy positions were neither uniform nor rigid. Policy discussions were held, secretly, in both the Ministry of Cooperation and the Ministry of Finance. Devaluation had its proponents in various corners of the administration. But none of this was observable; the official position remained firm and clear.

Moreover, French academics said little on the subject and rarely favored devaluation in their writing. In part this was because some of them remained skeptical about the efficacy of adjustment via changes in prices. In part it was because they shared the official concern about disruptive sociopolitical fallout from inflation. Some also continued to believe in the possible success of "competitive disinflation" (or internal adjustment), by which price stability coupled with productivity increases would reestablish equilibrium. Many, finally, convinced about or resigned to the need to devalue, worried about the effects on speculation and capital flight that might flow from pro-devaluation public statements. Thus the advice they might have given on the likely consequences of a devaluation remained unpublished.

Within the World Bank there were also perhaps noneconomic factors underlying their stance. For one thing, Bank staff were not comfortable with the franc zone arrangements and the policies followed by member countries. Many Bank staff members were skeptical about their impact on growth. They believed that the franc zone monetary arrangements lessened adaptability, mainly by removing the exchange rate instrument from the policy arsenal, and that their instruments of monetary and fiscal discipline were often ineffective. They also considered that member countries were exposed to different, not necessarily correlated, external shocks. Finally, they were concerned that Côte d'Ivoire's heavy indebtedness in relation to the Bretton Woods institutions had become unsustainable in the absence of IDA credits.

With respect to Côte d'Ivoire, urban opinion, that of wage earners, was against devaluation. Intellectuals had various, often nuanced, views about the devaluation, and about the franc zone regime. The authorities, until 1992, were strongly opposed to devaluation. Their stance reflected the views of President Houphouët-Boigny, who believed that the declines in cocoa and coffee prices on world markets sprang from a fundamental injustice imposed on his country by the international economic system. Himself a planter, he attached great value to the maintenance of prices paid to producers. He also was a firm believer in maintaining parity of the CFAF. These two policies were to him symbols of the success of Ivoirian development, not to be abandoned.

Given the lack of adequate reserves at the Caisse de Stabilisation, the simultaneous maintenance of coffee and cocoa prices proved impossible. The grave financial crisis that occurred in 1987–88 led to a break between the RCI and the Bretton Woods institutions. The two agreements signed with the IMF in 1987 and 1988 were cancelled, and World Bank lending was suspended until producer prices for the two commodities were reduced. In 1989 President Houphouët-Boigny tried to influence world prices by keeping crops off the market. This did not work. The president had to admit that he had lost the "cocoa battle," and he had to cut producer prices by half. From his perspective, devaluation of the CFAF would have then marked the total victory of international market forces over Côte d'Ivoire.

Despite these conditions, the IMF and the World Bank continued to provide help for stabilization and structural adjustment programs without devaluation. But the implementation of these programs proved very difficult. The IMF loan that emerged from a 1989 agreement was not fully disbursed, nor was the loan attached to a second agreement in 1991. World Bank sectoral loans in 1989–90 were fully disbursed, but not the adjustment loans granted in 1991.

The 1989 Fund program envisaged a vigorous effort to put public finances in order, generating positive budget savings. The Ivoirian government tried in 1990 to impose substantial cuts in civil service salaries. But the announcement of these measures gave rise to serious civil protests, which forced the government to give up on direct salary reductions. Another approach, introduced by Ouattara—first as president of the Interministerial Coordinating Committee and later (after illness disabled President Houphouët-Boigny) as prime minister—resorted to other ways of reducing public expenditure.

The social disruption—including violence—that occurred in 1990 when the government tried to cut salaries served to reinforce doubts, notably in the French aid community, about the right policy to follow. A growing number of observers doubted that factor costs in Côte d'Ivoire could be lowered without devaluation, given the rigidity of nominal wages. At the same time, the violent reaction to the attempt to lower the already low standards of living in urban areas reinforced fears about the political consequences of devaluation.

The conditionality attached to adjustment loans then became ambiguous, as, for example, in the PASCO competitiveness loan granted in 1991. Its purpose was to support a series of reforms aimed at making the Ivoirian economy more competitive, according to the logic of adjustment without devaluation: priority measures dealt with raising productivity. At the same time, it carried as a second-tranche disbursement condition the lowering of the real effective exchange rate to its 1985 level, as calculated by the Fund. However, the real depreciation level thus programmed was such (about 25 percent) that it was not realistically possible without devaluation. In addition, the way the exchange rate was calculated was disputable and risky because it gave too much weight to some primary product exporters that were in situations of extreme monetary disequilibrium, such as Brazil.

Consequently, it became clear that the Fund would not disburse the subsequent tranches, whatever the magnitude of the reforms undertaken elsewhere. The very useful measures agreed to in the sectoral loans were thus diminished in importance. As was predictable, the Bank and the Fund suspended aid to the RCI in 1992, their actions inducing similar responses by other donors. France, on the other hand, continued its adjustment aid (although suspending other aid from the AFD because of payment arrears). However, French adjustment aid was used by Côte d'Ivoire to service its debt to the World Bank.[11] During these years foreign aid defined as net transfers decreased significantly (see figure 7.6).

Did the discordant points of view of donors affect the pace of reform during this period? Looking at the devaluation reform alone, it is clear that the French position postponed its implementation. On the other hand, the decision not to devalue pushed the Ivoirian authorities to introduce, in cooperation with the donors, productivity-raising reforms and reforms in public finance. These were in place and helpful after the devaluation. Examples are the dismantling of quantitative restrictions on imports, the liberalization of most domestic prices, and labor market and judicial system reforms (discussed further below).

Even regional integration was advanced by the pre-devaluation measures—those aimed, for example, at strengthening the monetary union (formation of a multinational banking commission) and at transforming it into an economic union (multilateral monitoring of public finance and gradual moves toward a common market). These changes could be institutionalized when the devaluation took place.

Despite the desirability of these (nondevaluation) reforms, it should be noted that their implementation was surely slowed down when the Fund and the Bank suspended aid after 1992 because of nonperformance on macroeconomic conditionality. The suspension reduced pressures to implement these reforms.

The Decision to Devalue: 1993–94

A whole set of factors came together to bring about the Ivoirian decision to devalue. The analytic and empirical work undertaken in the early 1990s played only a minor role. The various estimates of the appreciation of the real exchange rate were so sensitive to choice of base year and to weighting that they were unconvincing to many decisionmakers. In the Côte d'Ivoire case in particular, the evolution of real and nominal effective exchange rates, as published by the IMF, were highly contestable, since they were so dependent on results of the chaotic evolution of other countries.[12]

In addition, the overvaluation of the CFAF arose less from changes in the real exchange rate than from deterioration of the terms of trade, which in 1992 was in its sixth consecutive year, and from the rising debt burden, which was particularly heavy between 1987 and 1991. Directly and via the budget, these two factors contributed to the pronounced decline of per capita income. Moreover, devaluation rumors forced the Central Bank to maintain a high real rate of interest, which discouraged investment.

As for the many estimates of the degree of overvaluation, they suffered from the same uncertainties as those for real exchange rates, and also from hypotheses about the acceptable size of the current account deficit that were politically based and difficult to justify. These calculations did help give credence to the idea that the parity had become unsustainable. But the decision to devalue was not based directly on these various calculations purporting to estimate the extent of the country's lack of competitiveness.

The decisive factor that led the Ivoirian prime minister and the French authorities to support devaluation was the government's financial condition. Experience had shown the enormous difficulty of improving public finances in a stagnant economic environment. No matter how much effort Côte d'Ivoire made, it could not do without international aid. Confronted with the suspension of adjustment lending by the Bretton Woods institutions, France changed its policy. Whereas French adjustment loans formerly were made only after the aided country had signed an accord with the IMF, in 1991 and 1992 France continued its support, despite the lack of an Ivoirian agreement with the Fund. Côte d'Ivoire was in effect given time to renew its dialogue with its external partners. The French clearly wished to avoid a rupture of relations of franc zone countries with the international economic community.

The decision was prepared, with great discretion, by a small group of civil servants. The political authorities mostly supported the change by this time, although their official posture in defense of the existing parity remained unchanged. The shift in the position of the French government was brought about in part by the power of persuasion of the responsible civil servants and in part by the deteriorating situation within the franc zone and the resulting financial costs being incurred by France. There were also other factors—a complex mixture of a desire to transform French policy toward Africa, fatigue and resignation, and in some cases a sentiment that the devaluation was a kind of deserved punishment for past errors.

In September 1993 Edouard Balladur, then French prime minister, sent a letter to the heads of state of franc zone countries stating that beginning in 1994 France would revert to its former policy on adjustment lending: that is, it would make no such loans in the absence of an agreement with the IMF. This could be interpreted as a signal that France was ready to accept CFAF devaluation. The Ivoirian prime minister, Alassane Ouattara, who had been director of the Africa department of the Fund, and who had lived through the earlier experience with the failed "internal adjustment" effort, was also on board. His agreement was encouraged by the indications that aid donors would be ready to recommence lending at high levels after devaluation.

Ouattara's adherence was officially announced during the meeting of the franc zone heads of state in Dakar in January 1994. It helped win the agreement of all the other states, some of which had been strongly opposed to the change in parity. Côte d'Ivoire used the months before the devaluation to win over other countries of the zone to the devaluation cause, in particular Burkina Faso. The Ivoirian authorities also used the time to prepare an economic policy program to accompany the devaluation. In 1994, net transfers from multilateral institutions to the franc zone countries, especially Côte d'Ivoire, and from bilateral donors as well, reached exceptionally high levels. But it was a transitory gain from the devaluation. As noted in section 2, these flows sharply declined in the following years, with net transfers from multilateral institutions coming close to zero in 1995 and 1996 and becoming negative in 1997 (see figure 7.6).

Three Major Hypotheses

Côte d'Ivoire's choice first not to devalue, then to devalue, can be looked at in light of the three major hypotheses presented in the terms of reference.

First, did the Ivoirian government decide against devaluation, then in its favor, independently of aid relationships? The answer is clearly no. It was external assistance that allowed retention of the existing parity until 1994, and it was the suspension of aid that provoked the devaluation. The data given in section 2 illustrate the precipitous fall in financial inflows on the eve of the devaluation (notably in 1993), and their rise afterward.

Nonetheless, another question has to be asked. In allowing resistance to devaluation and in provoking it later, did aid influence the pace of other reforms? If we consider the first hypothesis from this perspective the response is more complicated. As we saw, some reforms were adopted because of the political option taken to adjust without devaluation, and because this political posture was credible and supported by external donors. But it was no longer credible when these reforms were introduced in a particularly difficult context of bad relations with donors, marked by several suspensions of aid. It is difficult to say, in these circumstances, what was cause and effect in each instance of reluctance to reform and withdrawal of aid.

Consider next the second hypothesis. Did nonfinancial aid have a stronger impact than conditioned financial aid on the decision to devalue? The devaluation decision was made at the highest political levels. It surely could have been influenced by economic ideas, analysis, or the simulations done in Washington or in France on the anticipated effects in the RCI. But given the nature of the decision, its close link to fiscal imperatives, and its eminently political dimension, financial aid surely played the essential role. In other areas (incentive structures, judicial system, and so forth) studies and technical assistance had an important role, but these were for the most part packaged with financial assistance—notably in the framework of structural adjustment loans.

What about the third hypothesis—that financial aid was effective only when reforms were underway? In the present context this means after the devaluation, but not before. This question has meaning only for the periods when aid was not suspended. Certainly economic growth was more rapid after the devaluation than before, but this could be the combined result of the devaluation, the improved terms of trade after the second half of 1993, and the recovery of aid inflow.

It is difficult to attack this question. Multiple elements of economic policy determine the efficiency of aid, not just the devaluation. And nonpolicy factors, notably the external environment, condition aid effectiveness. Before the devaluation, the decline in the terms of trade probably raised the marginal efficiency of an aid dollar in the Côte d'Ivoire, given the strong financial constraints on growth prevailing at that time.

TRADE LIBERALIZATION

Evolution of Trade Policy

Initiation of Industrial Protection: 1960–73

At independence in 1960, Côte d'Ivoire had no industrial base (Côte d'Ivoire 1989). The colonial power neglected the interests of the private sector. The incentive system in place after 1956 favored cheap imports of basic foodstuffs for Europeans and discouraged local transformation of products by imposing high tariffs on raw materials, semifinished inputs, and equipment. In 1959 the RCI government put in place an investment code (law 59-134, September 3, 1959) with a generous incentive system aimed at attracting foreign capital on a selective basis. If granted priority status, investors were exempt from payment of duties on exports and on imports of raw materials entering into exports of finished goods. In addition to these exemptions, priority firms could benefit from a stabilized fiscal regime and an establishment convention for 25 years that granted exoneration from import taxes on raw materials.

Quantitative restrictions were used as an additional instrument to help the installation of industrial firms. They included bans, quotas, and import licensing. Products subject to import licensing had to be screened by a special committee on import control.

The range of government interventions included a complex system of legal price controls.[13] In case of "emergencies" the government could (and did) intervene to block prices of *any* good or service. Prices were blocked in 1967 when the value added tax increased, in 1968 when the minimum wage increased, and in 1969 because the French franc was devalued. Thus, 1966–73 was a period marked by price controls and intermittent imposition of general price ceilings.

Reinforcement of Industrial Protection: 1973–84

Industrial policy was reinforced along two lines: implementation of a strategy of industrial development based on the transformation of local and imported raw materials and protection of the industrial base built on the incentive system of the investment code. A reform was implemented in 1973 that included incentives favoring the import of a wide range of machines and production equipment, incentives to transform timber by taxing its export in raw form, and high import taxes and prohibitions that were used as incentives to promote textile industries. New duties were introduced on exports and imports; the export tax was specifically designed to stimulate domestic transformation.

The use of quantitative restrictions, common during the first episode, was extended after 1973. The instruments used were prohibitions, quotas, and import licensing. The number of products subject to import licensing increased from 86 in 1973 to 310 in 1976 and to 427 in 1982. As a result of these protective measures, the rate of nominal protection increased from 30 percent in 1971 to 32 percent in 1978. The rate of effective protection increased sharply from 39 percent to 76 percent in the same period. Rates of implicit protection were even higher, though they declined during the period (Bohoun 1996).

The government intervened directly in productive activities by investing in state-owned enterprises (SOEs) in order to process agricultural raw materials. The creation of SOEs also was intended to increase local control over industrial activities dominated by French capital. More than 250 SOEs out of 400 listed in 1981 were formed between 1971 and 1980.[14]

Trade Liberalization: 1984–88

In 1984, the investment code and the trade tariff were reformed to reduce the level of industrial protection and to promote industrial exports. The investment code eliminated the exoneration of taxes on imported raw materials granted to priority firms. It also favored location outside of the Abidjan area and facilitated the emergence of small and medium-scale enterprises. The objective was to reduce the rate of nominal protection to a maximum of 40 percent for finished products and 25 percent for raw materials, and the rate of effective protection to a maximum of 40 percent. Thus, low tariffs on equipment and raw materials offered better protection to industry while selectively penalizing the competing foreign products.

Quantitative restrictions were eliminated for products subject to import licensing. In compensation, an import surtax and an entry fiscal surcharge were imposed. An export subsidy was put in place in 1984 to compensate for the overvaluation of the CFAF and to improve the competitiveness of firms.

Despite the general mood favorable to trade liberalization, some increases of tariffs and fiscal taxes on certain products occurred. In 1987 a general tariff increase was imposed. In 1988 the payment of the export subsidy was discontinued. New waves of exonerations and grants of priority status to industrial firms marked the years 1985 to 1988; 54 firms were granted priority status, 30 of them in 1986 alone (Bohoun 1996).

Reversal of Protection: 1988–90

During 1988–90, the deterioration of government revenues prompted a policy shift toward increased protection. In 1989 tariff rates on imports and exports increased from 5 to 10 percent and a new tax (statistical tax) of 2 percent was created. It was estimated that the average tariff rate by 1990 had increased up to its 1983 level (Contamin 1997). Nontariff barriers were reinforced through import controls with the following modalities: creation of a customs value committee, quantitative and qualitative inspection with price comparison, and some prohibitions and import quotas.

Reversal of Liberalization: 1990–93

Starting in 1991, four Sectoral Adjustment Loans (SECALS) were implemented, addressing competitiveness (PASCO), human resources development (HRDP), the financial sector (PASFI), and economic management (PAGE). All to some extent were aimed at increasing industrial competitiveness, though PASCO was most directly targeted that way. The others aimed at improvements in the general institutional environment. New waves of selective trade liberalization occurred. Some tariffs and taxes were eliminated, and others were reduced (those on agricultural and industrial inputs and also on finished products, textiles in particular).

Devaluation and Deepening of Trade Liberalization

The devaluation of the CFAF in 1994 improved significantly the rate of effective protection of the economy. This helped the reduction of nominal protection also needed to limit the inflation generated by devaluation. In 1995, on the basis of 350 tariff positions, the weighted average tariff rate decreased to 29 percent from 37 percent in 1990 (Contamin 1997).

Export promotion was a prominent item in the reform initiated by the devaluation package, with the private sector playing the main role in the new export promotion agency, APEXCI. Critical reforms were also implemented in the agricultural sector. The role of CAISTAB in internal and external marketing of cocoa and coffee was drastically reduced to increase private sector participation and improve the transparency of the external marketing system. The significant change was an auction system for export rights. Some critics claim that this reform gave rise to unanticipated problems involving overbidding and concentration of export rights on a few exporters. The rice marketing system was also liberalized after a difficult dialogue about imports of broken rice. (Many in government feared that unfettered import of broken rice would undermine the domestic rice sector.) Nontariff barriers were eliminated, prices of agricultural products and equipment were liberalized, and effective protection of local production had to be limited to 40 percent. State-owned enterprises in oil palm (PALMINDUSTRIE), sugar (SODESUCRE), and cotton (CIDT) were privatized.

Local opinion acknowledges that trade and price liberalization has been effective, but with some reservations. The playing field is not even; there is some discriminatory and unequal treatment linked to political and family connections. Also there are cases where insufficient information about decontrolled prices subjects small private actors in trading activities to the corrupt practices of civil servants. The business community is favorable to liberalization with equal treatment for everybody. To them tariff reduction appears to be a successful reform area, probably because it was well prepared. But this opinion is not shared by selected influential nonbusiness representatives. The private sector welcomes less government intervention but only a few firms interviewed in a recent survey favored zero public intervention. At the time of the survey (May–

June 1998) spokespersons for 31 percent of the firms questioned thought that liberalization had had a positive impact, 55 percent reported no impact, and only a few (3 percent) indicated a negative impact.

The trade and industrial policy reforms were implemented gradually. The building of the industrial base took place incrementally. The investment code was created in 1959 while the tariff reform was implemented in 1973. These two policy instruments were relied on for many years. They were replaced by a new investment code and a new tariff regime in 1984.

The first set of moves from protectionist policies to liberalization took many years—from the 1960s to 1984. Implementation was gradual because the Ivoirian government was reluctant and resisted the reforms. The government feared a hemorrhage of customs receipts and was preoccupied with finding ways to compensate for the losses of trade-related revenues. There was also the reluctance to make doctrinal jumps, from a controlled economy to a liberalized one, and concern about the costs that might arise.

From the field interviews it appears that implementation is a major problem on the government's end, especially for recent liberalization reforms of cocoa and coffee marketing and CAISTAB. These reforms are widely thought to have been *brutal,* that is introduced too fast. It will, according to some, leave an unorganized rural society facing a volatile world market and oligopsonistic purchasers/exporters. Peasants have not been properly prepared, in this view, and farmer organizations are weak. As will be noted in the concluding section, the experience with coffee marketing liberalization has not confirmed these fears.

Scheduled reform measures were not always taken. In particular, the 1984 liberalization reform featured a simulated devaluation of the CFAF by combining an increase of import tariff and an export subsidy, with the expectation that the first measure would generate sufficient resources to finance the subsidy. The payment of the export subsidy was halted for lack of resources. Overall, the simulated devaluation was credible neither to the Ivoirian administration nor to the private sector. A second reason for this failure had to do with the institutional base: the administration of tax collection in general and the customs administration in particular was weak and of limited efficiency. Even the World Bank management thought that this measure was hastily prepared by its own staff.

The Role of Aid

Trade liberalization was not adopted in reaction to political demands by political elites or local interest groups. The prevailing political sentiment among decisionmakers was to resist these reforms. They were adopted under the pressures of a severe financial crisis caused by a decline of world cocoa and coffee prices and of world demand for exports, losses of foreign exchange and fiscal revenues, and heavy debt burden.

Two types of policy reversals were observed that were also caused by the financial crisis. The first type, reversal to protection, was explained by the losses of foreign exchange and of fiscal revenues due to the fall of prices of cocoa and coffee. This policy reversal highlighted the primacy of short-run financial problems over structural ones; it was adopted under the pressure of the IMF to the dismay of the World Bank, an example of possible conflicts between these two institutions.

The reversal to liberalization, in contrast, was accounted for by the primacy of external competitiveness concerns over worry about short-term revenue losses. These losses were duly recognized as the price to pay to improve income in the medium term because there was no alternative. But selectivity was the rule; no across-the-board tariff reduction was implemented.

Many in government find it difficult to acknowledge that a reform idea is not domestic. The debate over who initiated the policy dialogue is ambiguous and can best be summarized by this phrase, gathered from field interviews: the initiative comes from the government but the government has advisers; indeed the IMF and the World Bank are advisers to the government.

It is clear that trade liberalization was initiated by the World Bank. It was generally opposed by the administration and by a business community used to the shelter of protection and fearful of external competition. At the time of the reform and beyond, the administration was weakened by successive institutional changes and by the departure of highly qualified senior civil servants for positions in the private sector after the merger in 1977 of the Ministry of Planning with the Ministry of Economy and Finance. A weakened administration could not be expected to generate a homegrown reform package. Recently, the World Bank also initiated the reforms of cocoa and coffee marketing and the restructuring of CAISTAB.

The internal dialogue within government about trade liberalization was also difficult as DCGTx (Direction de Control des Grands Travaux), a French-managed parallel administration, overpowered the technical ministries (Ouayogode and Pegatienan 1994). Between 1986 and 1991, DCGTx was formally responsible for economic policies and programs, including the adjustment programs. This agency was generally suspicious of trade liberalization, reflecting French *dirigiste* traditions (and the sentiments of President Houphouët) in this matter.

Parallel markets did exist during episodes of liberalization and policy reversals. Traders, especially women, made frequent trips across the Ghana border and to Nigeria, where prices of the traded goods were competitive. This informal trade in cheap textiles and other manufactured goods harmed the interests of enterprises in the formal sector. But the complaints from formal business organizations did not, apparently, have much impact on the reforms because of the limited dialogue between the administration and the private sector.

In matters of industrial and trade policies, the main actors in the policy dialogue were the government and the World Bank. The World Bank had difficulty convincing President Houphouët-Boigny, the sole decisionmaker in the government, of the necessity to liberalize. He thought that the RCI was sufficiently open and did not need to further open up to the world market. His technical advisers were amused by the effective protection and domestic resource cost calculations, and the conclusions and policy recommendations derived therefrom. They believed them to be too academic to be convincing to either officials or businessmen. This basic skepticism helps explain why the simulated devaluation of 1985–86 lacked credibility and failed.

Since the early 1990s, the influence on economic policymaking of external donors in general and of the Bretton Woods institutions in particular increased and widened because of the deep financial crisis, the illness and death of President Houphouët-Boigny, and the weakness of the present political leadership. The two policy reversals and the deepened post-devaluation liberalization are the net results of interactions between these influences and government's reactions to them and to its own constraints.

The private sector did not play a significant role in the policy dialogue before the privatization program, but it had sufficient influence to cause, in part, the failure of the 1985–86 simulated devaluation. Since the 1994 devaluation and the acceleration of the privatization program, the private sector carries more weight. One example of that is its pressure to eliminate the public export promotion agency (CCIA) and to substitute the privately managed APEXCI. Nonetheless, even in this era of private sector and public sector partnership, government consultation with the private sector, let alone other elements in civil society, is not the norm.

Since 1990, after President Houphouët-Boigny was forced by social and political unrest to open up politically, civil society has been free to voice any concerns, opinions, and dissenting views about government policies. However, the use of these new opportunities by a large number of professional organizations and independent media has not yet proven to have critically influenced the process of policy formulation.

EDUCATION AND HEALTH SECTOR REFORMS

Until the 1980s, reform in the social sectors was not a live issue. The central concern was expansion: providing *more* schooling, *more* health care. This reflected in part the buoyant economy of the two post-independence decades, which generated growth in revenues. It also re-flected President Houphouët's awareness of education's role in economic growth and his view that a well-educated Ivoirian elite was essential to reduce dependence on expatriate skills.

In this period, donors financed mainly infrastructure investments, with some effort at quality improvement; France assisted by providing thou-sands of teachers. Thus the World Bank financed only three education projects prior to 1980, for teacher training and vocational education fa-cilities. The Bank financed no health projects until 1986 and no addi-tional education (or health) project until the 1991 Human Resources Development Project.

By the mid-1980s the education system clearly exhibited the pattern of problems common in Africa, especially francophone Africa: high unit and aggregate costs, weak budget and personnel management, internal inefficiency (distorted budgets and high dropout or repeater rates), ex-ternal inefficiency (limited relevance and connection to the job market), and inequitable allocation of benefits. The health system shared many of these characteristics—notably weak management, inefficient allocation of resources, and concentration of benefits on the relatively well-off.

The Ivoirian problem is particularly severe. The RCI government spent (and spends) relatively more on education and health than most other countries; the social sector took more than half of budget outlays in the 1980s, and its share remained high at the end of the 1990s. Though social indicators improved, they remain uninspiring, and are below indicators in other countries at the same income level. Even in 1996 only half the primary school–age children were in school and only one-third of the population had access to health care. By some measures, even the urban health care system is less effective than it is in the much poorer Sahelian countries.[15]

These problems have absorbed the attention of reformers for more than a decade. They are considered here in two parts. First we describe briefly the main reforms and comment on their effectiveness. Education and health are treated separately. In the second part we analyze process issues and the role of aid. The main emphasis is on the dimension of public expenditure reform.

Reforms and Their Implementation

A major theme in education reform has been the imperative need to cut costs and in particular salary costs. Government had to pay high salaries to recruit the large number of teachers required by the expan-sion of the education system in the 1960s and 1970s, and to replace during the ensuing years the numerous expatriates present in the sec-tor.[16] The result was that by the mid-1980s the cost of a high school teacher was higher in Abidjan than in Madrid. In 1993 a primary school teacher was paid 13 times the country's average per capita GDP, five times the ratio in East Asia and 10 times that in industrial countries (World Bank 1999a: 73).[17]

Even after some cutting, in the early 1990s education accounted for half the total wage bill, which in turn claimed 60 percent of government revenues. Any policy to contain government expenditures (a key objective of macroeconomic reform) thus had to confront the issue of teacher salaries. It is no surprise that the education reform program was dominated by measures for cost-cutting, though in both health and education, resource reallocation and management strengthening were also priorities.[18]

An early measure was the reduction of salaries for new teachers. Teacher salary scales were reattached to the civil service scales, from which they had earlier been detached. (The premium over the civil service salary scale was 40 percent.) Salary rates were to be frozen at 1991 levels and the aggregate salary bill for teachers was to be limited to a 1 percent a year annual rise for the period of the HRDP (1991–94).

The limited rise in the salary bill was to be accomplished by relying more heavily on teaching assistants, reducing the number and cost of French TA providers, increasing workloads of teachers, and redeploying administrators to classrooms. Also, growth in numbers of secondary and university students and teachers was to be controlled. Transfer payments through the university support center and fellowships and transport subsidies were to be reduced and boarding facilities in Abidjan cut back.

Numerous other measures were introduced in both sectors—cost recovery, freezes on new construction, and introduction of generics, for example. But heavy emphasis was given to two sets of reforms of public expenditures, one substantive and the other procedural. The substantive reforms concerned raising the level of expenditures on primary education and primary health care and increasing the primary subsectoral *shares* of total sectoral spending. In education the primary enrollment rate was to be increased; in health, the share going to preventive, rural activities was to be increased.

The procedural reforms aimed at stronger management, especially financial and personnel management. To strengthen the budget process and also monitor implementation of reforms, annual programs and budgets were prepared, which brought together in a transparent way indicators of past budget performance, and established annual targets based on HRDP objectives. A lengthy set of budget performance indicators was established. This was to supplement the parallel general budget reforms being undertaken at the Ministry of Finance and the Ministry of Planning, such as nomenclature changes, some of them conceived with social sector budgeting deficiencies in mind.

Many of the individual reforms that were part of HRDP conditionality were implemented (World Bank 1995). For example, some fringe benefits were cut and salary rate increases were contained; expatriate TA teachers virtually disappeared; 1,100 assistant teachers were hired in 1996; aggregate transfer payments (scholarships, food, and transport subsidies) were reduced; 2,500 administrators were redeployed to classroom teaching at the primary level; locally financed construction costs in both education and health were put on hold; and sector programs were elaborated for both health and education. Health sector changes included the extension of cost recovery for medicines and consultations, encouragement of the use of generic drugs, and a start in defining a decentralized sector strategy based on primary care. (Most of the recommendations made in a joint donor health sector program in 1990 were also implemented.)[19]

Some of the HRDP spending targets were achieved.[20] In health, the ratio of nonsalary operating expenditures (mainly medicines) to salaries rose, from 39 to 45 percent between 1991 and 1995, and this trend continues.[21] Some cost recovery took place, though well below the program targets. And though the primary subsector's share in total health spending did not rise during the HRDP period (1991–95), it did increase (by 16 percent) in 1996 and 1997. The tertiary subsector, however, grew by twice as much.

Expenditure reforms also are visible in the education sector. Despite a rise of 10 percent in primary enrollments and a soaring university population (it rose from 26,000 in 1991 to 58,000 in 1995), the total education wage bill stayed constant between 1991 and 1994. The unit cost of primary school teachers fell from 13 times per capita GDP in 1993 to 9 times by 1995. Subsidies to university students (housing, scholarships, transport, and so on) were cut by 20 percent in real terms and by half in terms of budget share between 1992 and 1996. At the same time, nonsalary operating costs as a percentage of the overall education budget rose from 4 percent in 1992 to 13 percent in 1996. Unit education subsidies have become more efficient and equitable in RCI than in most other African countries.[22] Investment in education as a share of total public investment more than doubled to an average of 7 percent between 1994 and 1997.

In both sectors, however, achievements have fallen far short of objectives:

- *Social sector budget shares fell.* Education spending as a share of the total budget fell from 34 percent in 1992 to 27 percent in 1996. The health budget as a share of current expenditure fell from 7.4 percent to 6.7 percent between 1991–93 and 1994–97.
- *Social sector investment did poorly.* Investment in health declined in the same period from 7.7 percent of total public investment to un-

der 5 percent (World Bank 1999b, vol. 2: 27–28). More than 40 percent of the investment during 1992–94 went to administration; the share of the primary subsector fell from 17 to 14 percent during those years. A shift occurred in 1996 and 1997, but the primary subsector share of the 1997–99 PIP was only 20 percent compared with 26 percent for the tertiary.[23] Investment in education as a share of the total investment budget increased only slightly between 1991–93 and 1994–7, from 9 to 10 percent.

- *Reallocation in favor of primary education and primary health care did not occur.* Instead of rising, primary school expenditures fell from 52 percent of total education expenditures in 1991 to 47 percent in 1995. The trend continued at least through 1997. In health the primary subsector share of recurrent expenditures was supposed to rise from 35 percent in 1991 to 42 percent in 1995. Instead, it declined to 32 percent in 1995.[24] The gross enrollment rate in primary education was supposed to rise from 74 percent in 1991 to 77 percent in 1995. Instead it fell to 67 percent in 1994, from which it increased little by 1997.

- *The benefits of public spending on health and education remain unequally distributed.* The primary school gross enrollment rate is only 51 percent among the poorest 20 percent of households, while it is 99 percent among the richest 20 percent. Only 12 percent of eligible children in the poorest quintile of households attend secondary school, compared with 65 percent for the best-off 20 percent. Although 19 percent of the primary school subsidy goes to the poorest 20 percent (and 14 percent to the best-off), only 7 percent of the secondary school subsidy goes to the poorest quintile (37 percent to the richest). Only 12 percent of the tertiary subsidy goes to the poorest 20 percent, while 71 percent goes to the top quintile. Of the total education subsidy, the poorest quintile gets 13 percent, the richest 35 percent.[25]

- *Internal efficiency of the school system improved little.* The share of nonsalary recurrent costs in education and health budgets increased. In principle, this should be an indicator of greater efficiency; it would indicate that teachers and medical staff have more supplies to work with. In fact, however, the post-devaluation inflation has to be taken into account. Prices of imported goods rose sharply, and of import competing goods also; the consumer price index rose by 50 percent between 1993 and 1997. Deflated figures for nonsalary operating costs between 1994 and 1996 indicate that these fell by 50 percent in real terms at the primary level, 38 percent at the secondary level, and 20 percent at the university level. Moreover, the basic indicator of internal efficiency, repetition rates, shows that these have increased in most levels of the primary subsector and at many levels within the secondary school subsector between 1991 and 1995 (World Bank 1996).

- *External efficiency probably worsened.* The number of students in the public sector technical and vocational training schools declined during much of the 1990s, while private participation grew. The public sector had only 10,000 students, 5 percent of all secondary students, and less than the 15,000 in private professional schools in 1995. The subsector suffers from recruitment of uncommitted students. (Technical and professional training is a second choice for pupils, or a step to general secondary and then to university.) The subsector trains for nonexistent formal sector jobs. It is heavily underutilized, hence even more expensive than is standard for technical/professional systems. In 1993 there were five students per teacher.

- *Strengthening of sectoral management was uneven.* The reform programs of the 1990s contained important components aimed at stronger social sector administrative capacity. But budgets were poorly prepared and defended, and project development for investment, rehabilitation, and maintenance was especially weak. Inputs were the sole or main preoccupation; little monitoring or evaluation of outputs occurred. Staffing was poorly monitored, with inconsistencies between ministry payrolls and civil service rosters.

Some improvement has occurred, particularly in education. Officials interviewed say that personnel management is surer and budget preparation and implementation significantly better. There is some evidence for the latter. Implementation rates are much higher now than in the early 1990s, both for the overall budget and the Budget Spécial d'Investissement et Equippement (BSIE). The volume of unpaid *engagements (dépenses engagées non-ordonnances)* is much lower than it was until 1995, and the resulting unpaid bills problem is minimal. That is a strong indicator of better budgeting. Knowledge of aid flows and their management is much better.[26]

Nonetheless, the depth and sustainability of the budget reform remains to be demonstrated. Much of it is new. For example, the reform of budget nomenclature, which absorbed many months of TA time, was rejected by IMF experts as inadequate. This change, which should have been introduced in 1992 or 1993, did not arrive until 1998. The elaborate system of budget indicators worked out under HRDP seems to have been a one-shot exercise. It may have left some traces, but these were not readily visible in mid-1999.[27] This means that monitoring and evaluation capacity remains embryonic or nonexistent. Project preparation and screening capacities are also uncertain.[28]

Concrete evidence that gains in capacity in the health sector are not extensive can be found in the recent suspension of the World Bank's major integrated health project (PDSSIR) and in the story of misappropriation of European Union (EU) assistance, which became headline news early in 1999, and of which more will be said below.

Growth in capacity appears to have been more substantial in the education sector. There is a newly installed planning unit in the Ministère d'Enseignement Nationale et Formation de Base. But project preparation capacity is said to be much stronger at the tertiary level, at the Ministère d'Enseignement Superieur et Recherche Scientifique; they apparently prepare more and better projects for inclusion in the PIP than do the other education ministries. The dispersion of decision units makes sectoral planning and coordination difficult, a difficulty exacerbated by the frequent restructurings and shuffling of units between ministries.

Three factors seem to be most relevant in explaining the patchy implementation and unsatisfactory outcomes of Ivoirian social sector reform programs. First, the major donor efforts made early in the 1990s, notably the HRDP, were really part of the larger macroeconomic drama then in process. Everybody's focus was on the macro issues. It is no surprise that the HRDP was managed by the Ministry of Finance. It was intended to provide quick-disbursing, financial gap–closing assistance to the RCI. For its first two years little happened while the devaluation decision was pondered. Right after devaluation, disbursement occurred: 80 percent of the US$360 million credit was disbursed in 1994. The sideshow character of the health and education reform agenda meant that Ivoirian decisionmakers gave it limited time and energy.

The Bank and other donors had the same hierarchy of priorities as the government, and this is the second reason for poor performance. Macroeconomic stabilization was the highest priority by far. Supervision and concern over the substantive sectoral issues were not negligible, but the Bank side was preoccupied with keeping the money flowing. Attention to the conditionality in the social sectors was secondary, and assessments of performance perfunctory.

Finally, local decisionmakers believe only weakly in the major donor objective of shifting resources from tertiary levels to primary. Believers among politically aware elites are a distinct minority. Nor are all bilateral donors fully persuaded. On the Ivoirian side the argument is partly political. The enormous growth in numbers of university students was a potential time bomb. It had to be confronted. Moreover, there are economic rationales for continuing attention to the tertiary sector. It would be disastrous, they believe, to let the existing social infrastructure at that level continue its deterioration. The quality of university outputs has been declining, at great social cost.[29] It cannot be improved without additional spending.

Officials and other Ivoirians strongly disagree with judgments such as those incorporated in a recent Bank-financed health sector PIP review, which criticized six projects in the 1997–99 sectoral PIP, mainly renovation and re-equipment of university hospital centers in Abidjan (Shephard 1999). These six projects absorb 33 percent of the PIP and 40 percent of donor PIP financing. Almost 60 percent of their cost is to be financed by donor grants (Japanese and Spanish), a much higher ratio than other projects. Concerned officials and other Ivoirians question the validity of Bank recommendations to cut back on these projects (which are after all heavily grant-financed and likely to produce improved services) in favor of primary care–focused projects that are more dependent on local financing and may have uncertain outcomes.

Aid and Reform

Education reforms that began in the late 1980s in RCI were not entirely without precedent. Substantive reforms and strategy statements were drafted by Ivoirians and their advisers as early as 1972, and there were many internally generated ideas for change in both education and health in the 1980s, before there was a strong donor presence. So some reform proposals, for example in curriculum, teacher training, and nurse training, were already in the air, and provided some of the elements for the later reform proposals. Part of the reform program of the 1990s can thus be said to have been internally generated.

Moreover, Ivoirians provided inputs during the preparation of major projects like the Human Resources Development Program, which was almost four years in the making. Extensive consultations, formal and informal, marked this process. The companion TA project, the Human Resources Management Support Project (Projet d'Appui à la Gestion des Resources Humaines, PAGRH), had an even longer gestation period, involving even more local consultation. It was framed with great sensitivity to the problems of technical assistance delivery, which were then (in 1993) very much on the table. It emphasized use of local rather than resident expatriate TA.

So even the first round of social sector reforms, during the first half of the 1990s, had some domestic input. But it seems clear that the main trigger for the major reforms of the 1990s was the financial crisis and the need to contain social sector expenditures if macroeconomic stability was to be attained. Donors were the main bearers of this message. The significant planks of the reform program were focused on cost-cutting and on equity, donor preoccupations much more than local. The specific reforms were crafted mainly by donor staff, who also acted as their chief champions. Local technocrats in the core ministries, and some politicians, realized that the social sector budgets had to be constrained, and that this would involve strong salary restraint and sharp cutbacks in subsidies to students, among other changes. But the major impetus for these reforms came from outside, particularly the Bretton Woods institutions.

The outside impetus is clearest with respect to the idea that expenditures should be restructured in favor of primary education and primary health care. As noted above, the Ivoirian leadership was preoccupied until 1994 with debt crises and the devaluation issue. There was not much residual energy for, and only modest interest in, social sector expenditure reallocations. The Finance and Planning ministries negotiated adjustment credits and signed conditional agreements with detailed letters of development policy. The subject matter was education and health sector reform, but the pressure was to bring in the money. The Education and Health ministries participated relatively little in negotiations on the US$360 million adjustment credit begun in 1991, the HRDP; substantive concerns were in the back seat during its implementation.

As noted earlier also, very few Ivoirians had much conviction that the reallocation of spending in favor of primary subsectors was sensible, especially since it was easier to raise grant money for tertiary activities. This lack of conviction coexisted uneasily with the feeling, widespread at least since the mid-1990s, that more attention to primary schooling and health care was politically correct, the right thing to do.

These were not the only factors that made the donors the dominant players. There was also the fact that capacity in the government was too limited to enable it to take the lead. This changed in the late 1990s, when a stronger, more experienced corps of local technicians began to assert itself, drafting documents like the Policy Framework Paper and the comprehensive strategy statement called the "African Elephant." Local technicians also played important roles in the conception and implementation of sectoral investment or development programs in health and education after the mid-1990s. But for the first generation of sweeping reforms, the domestic contribution was much more limited.

Donors, then, bore the major responsibility for the adoption of the major reforms, from the expenditure reallocation objectives to strengthening of budget and personnel management. Local support existed in the core economic ministries for the management reforms and, less clearly, for the budgetary shift to primary subsectors. But few other local champions were apparent. Most of the actors—Education and Health ministry personnel, teachers, doctors, nurses, pharmacists, and others—were neutral or opposed. Their professional associations were in any event not vocal. Students at the secondary and tertiary levels were opposed.

One other environmental factor contributed in a basic way to the dominant donor role in the reform process. It is not clear that users of health and education services expressed at any stage great dissatisfaction with the status quo. A recent study surveyed 700 rural users of health facilities. It found that general satisfaction with respect to the care provided was rather good. The main complaint was lack of medicines (Côte d'Ivoire 1998a). This same lack of demand for change from the affected population has been noted in studies in Southern and East Africa (Mogedal, Hodne Steen, and Mpellmbe 1995). In the education sector user dissatisfaction is evident mainly in the technical and vocational subsector, where it finds expression in stagnant student numbers and movement to private providers.

The Major Hypotheses

What does the education and health reform experience in RCI tell us about the general hypotheses that inspire the research project of which this case study is part?

Take first the hypothesis that *nonfinancial aid generates more reform than money aid*. There is little or no evidence in support of this proposition in the institutional reform experience of the RCI. Two aspects of the education and health sector reforms in RCI raise doubts about it. First, "nonfinancial aid" in this study is defined as freestanding technical assistance, donor economic and sector research, or advisory services. But in the case at hand, technical assistance projects have been handmaidens of financial aid projects. The Human Resources Management Support Project, for example, was really a part of the HRDP, an adjustment credit. Nonfinancial aid that is untied to money seems to have been rare.

Secondly, financial aid projects themselves carry a great deal of nonfinancial baggage. In the RCI case many of the adjustment credits have had study components, training tours, training seminars, and so forth. More important is the long gestation period that has been typical for RCI projects. The HRDP was more than three years in preparation, and took several years to get off the ground after approval. Many studies and much dialogue occurred during this period. It is not only the Bank that has such long identification and appraisal periods for financial aid projects. The European Union Fond Européen de Developpement (FED), the European community development financing agency, does extensive program preparation that entails research and analysis and dialogue. For example, a number of basic studies and surveys formed the background for the health sector component of the upcoming Eighth FED. Ivoirians participated in and reviewed these studies, which generated intensive dialogue.

Studies and dialogue attached to money are a priori likely to be more effective than *freestanding* studies, which probably include most World Bank economic and sector work. The money is almost sure to make research and dialogue more action-oriented. It claims attention and concentrates minds in a way that freestanding studies do not. It is not clear, for example, that the 1996 Bank poverty assessment, which found sharp increases in the extent of poverty, had any effect in shaping education and health policy. Aside from the fact that the results have been contested, the political class is not unaware that many Ivoirians are very poor (Jones and Ye 1997). In any case the importance of a primary-level social sector focus in combating poverty has been part of public discourse for many years.

A second hypothesis is that *financial aid works when policy reforms and institution building are underway*. This is not an operational hypothesis. In the 1990s at least, reforms and institution building of some sort are almost everywhere and always "underway." In the RCI, reform of some kind was going on most years in the 1980s and every year in the 1990s.

The proposition is ambiguous in other respects. It can be taken as a sequel to the proposition that financial aid does *not* work when policy/institutional reform is *not* underway, which is unclear but probably incorrect in its extreme form, when applied to social sector–type reforms. Even in the worst policy/institutional environment, financial aid can have some positive effects if appropriately delivered, and in any case may be a prerequisite for getting a seat at the policy table. If the argument is that aid works *better* in good environments, that is surely true. In the RCI case a government more convinced and committed to expenditure reallocation in favor of primary education and health care would have gone further in that direction in the past decade.

Does the RCI social sector reform experience confirm the hypothesis that *governments choose to reform independently of the aid relationship?* This can be and has been expressed in various forms: that aid has no impact on policy, or that aid cannot buy reform. This view, a major conclusion of the World Bank's influential study *Assessing Aid* (1998a), is shared by some Ivoirian officials. One said that the Bank and others who believe that their efforts have induced reform are fooling themselves just like those who accepted Chanticleer's claim that his crowing makes the sun come up.

But it is not tenable to argue, in the case of institutional reforms for education and health, that aid has had no positive effects on reform. Even though implementation has been partial and some of the institutional reforms (performance budgeting in education, for example) did not "take," the reform program would have been different in content (less good), slower in implementation, probably less effective in results. The action-oriented studies, training, and study tours would have surely been fewer in number and probably less good had external financing been absent. The message about reallocation of spending to primary levels would have been much more muted.

Some of the least popular measures, such as salary cost containment and reductions in student subsidies, would have been less effective. The harmed interest groups were told that it was essential to follow this path because "the World Bank insists on it" and large aid inflows depended on it. The debt relief initiative is now cited by the government in all austerity-related discussions with stakeholders.

It seems no exaggeration to say that aid brought about such reforms in public expenditure management as have occurred. This was true of the process reforms in budget-making, cost-cutting efforts in student subsidies, staff redeployment, and, above all, in bringing formal acceptance of the idea of reallocation of spending in favor of primary education and primary health care.

Probably the most effective vehicle for aid influence was the dialogue, formal and informal, surrounding program preparation and supervision. When, during project preparation or supervision, the Health Ministry proposes that more nurses be recruited, Bank staff suggest concentrating more resources on training and supervision. When the ministry requests help for building up in-house maintenance capacity for biomedical equipment, the donor counterpart suggests contracting out that function. A *chef de service* says he needs an administrative secretary who knows all about the Ivoirian legal code. The donor spokesman asks why he needs that rare and costly competence.

Of course, not all donor staff suggestions are good. Not all donor project designs are well suited to the local environment. This raises the broader question of whether aid can retard reform. The aid presence does seem to have had some negative effects in the health sector. One is a distortion of priorities. Primary-level spending by the Ministry of Health has lagged badly behind plans and needs. The donor community has pushed hard to have the ministry spend faster and spend particularly on building up rural health infrastructure. A Bank review of the important Integrated Health Services Project (PDSSIR) comments as follows:

> The project undoubtedly has some perverse effects. Because of the large amounts of money available, and the resulting pressure to disburse, it shapes the priorities of responsible officials. It pushes them to invest in health facility construction and equipment, while the basic problems lie elsewhere, notably in the poor definition of responsibilities and the weakness of capacities to manage health facilities and properly organize work. (Côte d'Ivoire 1998c)

Those interviewed in our field visit took up this same theme: that while the Ministry of Health has much stronger intellectual capacity than it had a few years ago and many more cadres with training in public health, its implementing capacity remains extremely weak. Donor representatives pointed out, for example, that while the National Health Development Plan is a good document, it has been around for three years and little has been done to implement it. This is due in part to systemic problems that destroy incentives, such as low civil service pay and poor working conditions. And partly it is due to high turnover at senior levels within the ministry. Overfull plates are fundamental.

More dramatic evidence of implementing deficiencies is at hand. An audit of European Union programs in health at the end of 1998 discovered a large volume of improper transactions, spending that had not been adequately justified. The audit estimated that CFAF 18 billion–23 billion out of total program expenditures of CFAF 53 billion was involved. The government took no disciplinary action for some months, but finally six ministry officials were indicted and, after a further delay, the minister was sacked.

Two reasons are given to explain this unhappy incident. One is that the EU was pressed to spend, to speed up construction of rural facilities; otherwise the slow-moving administration would fail to meet the ambitious goals that had been established for health service provision. They urged government to loosen budget procedures, notably to raise the level of payment that could be made without going through all the laborious steps prescribed in the budget laws. The second is that too many goals were set for the program, not only building large numbers of health posts but also using small and medium-sized contractors to do the job. Capacity for managing all this was simply not there.

Similarly, after many warnings, the World Bank in August 1999 suspended its main health project, the PDSSIR. Two years after project effectiveness, with its completion date not far off, only 16 percent of the project budget had been disbursed. The underlying reason here was again excess optimism about local capacity to implement. But there were other explanations. Some critics say that in addition to being too ambitious, the project was put together too fast and had too short a time horizon.

Other critics, more severe, argue that the project was poorly conceived. It had two pillars, both new in RCI and both complicated: the focus on a "minimum activities package" (PMA in French), and the reorganization of health service structures along "district" lines. Definition of a PMA turned out to be far more difficult than anticipated. And more important, the district concept did not fit easily into existing structures, or indeed into existing decentralization programs supported by other donors. The ministry could not or would not implement.

Since 1993—that is, well before the Bank introduced its own decentralization approach in the PDSSIR—other donors had been pursuing another approach to deconcentration or decentralization. The EU, the French, and perhaps others, were trying to strengthen the Regional Health Directorates. The Bank introduced the different concept of "districts." It organized them quickly, ignoring the regionalization efforts of the other donors.[30] The Bank also pushed hard on the PMA approach, apparently assuming that it could be easily and quickly adopted. But it raised enormous problems of fit with existing structures, just as the district concept did.

All kinds of fundamental issues had to be resolved. How to reconcile existing regional structures with the district, which has no traditional counterpart in RCI? How to work out PMA delivery when the traditional system is vertical—a family planning unit, a maternal and child care unit, and so on. How to build sustainable capacity when different donors take over particular vertical slices. United Nations programs are completely vertical: UNICEF does vaccinations, the WHO information transfer, the UNFPA something else. How to bring about integrated service provision for primary health care when vertical structures remain dominant?

There was little coordination, little real dialogue to permit resolution of these basic matters of strategy and approach. Some donors appear to harbor strong resentment of the World Bank role. One view is that the Bank, seeking "leadership," tends to monopolize the dialogue. The example is given of a Bank project that contains a component on reform of medical school curriculum, which leads to a squeezing out of other donors. Dissatisfaction with the World Bank role in the health sector seems to be surprisingly lively, greater than is indicated in client survey data (World Bank 1998c).

LEGAL AND JUDICIAL REFORM

A predictable, efficient, and transparent judicial system is a cornerstone of good economic management, and critical for social equity, private sector development, and good governance in general. That sound legal and judicial institutions make these vital contributions has been recognized for decades. Because these institutions are weak in many developing and transition economies, aid donors have financed programs of legal/judicial (L/J) reform in many developing countries.

In the RCI, as in many low-income countries, legal reforms during the past decade have had a twin focus. One concern has been to remove legal obstacles to labor market flexibility, frequently regarded as a major reason for slow supply responses to stabilization and liberalization. The second concern is much broader: reform of the overall judicial system, strengthening its operational capacity and adapting it to the needs of a modern market economy.

Labor Market Reforms

The pre-reform situation (the late 1980s) was that the Labor Code and negotiated collective agreements made it difficult for employers to adjust work forces to fluctuating needs. Temporary workers were considered permanent after 90 days on the job. Overtime regulations were strict, and required prior authorization from the Ministry of Labor. It was very difficult to sack anyone; charges of "abusive" firing were common, and could lead to legal damages and reinstatement. Employers had to list staff by seniority, and unless they followed a last-in first-out policy in staff reductions their action could be considered "abusive."

The state-run labor exchange (Office de Main d'Oeuvre de la Côte d'Ivoire, OMOCI), a monopoly hiring agency, was another source of problems. Although in practice most firms did their own hiring, their choices needed OMOCI approval. Moreover, prior authorization by OMOCI was necessary for staff reductions. This gave rise to hassles and delays and opened opportunities for corruption.

Labor market reform was a major component of the Bank's 1991 Competitiveness and Regulatory Reform Adjustment Program (PASCO). Elimination of the OMOCI monopoly, elimination of constraints on hiring temporary or casual labor and on collective layoffs, and dropping prior administrative authorization for overtime were conditions of effectiveness for PASCO. Revision of the Labor Code and encouraging renegotiation of the central collective agreement were conditions of second-tranche release.

Many of these reforms were implemented. OMOCI's monopoly was abolished. Restrictions on temporary workers were lifted. Layoffs for economic reasons were made easier and the Labor Ministry's prior authorization was no longer needed for overtime. The Labor Code was liberalized and approved by the National Assembly in 1992.

Many of these changes had been introduced only under extreme Bank pressure, and with long delays that indicated obvious reluctance. The decrees implementing the Labor Code (21 of them) did not appear until 1996, four years after the National Assembly vote, and only after their issuance was made a tranche release condition of another adjustment loan (the Private Sector Development Adjustment Credit of 1996).

Also, while OMOCI's legal monopoly over hiring and firing was eliminated, the government created a new public placement agency, Agence d'Etudes de Promotion d'Emploi (AGEPE), which had many of the same employees as OMOCI.[31] AGEPE was supposed to monitor employment trends, but it has come to act as a regulatory body, and is said to be an unequal competitor with private recruitment agencies. It delivers work permits and operates as a recruitment agency itself for foreigners. Moreover, it charges a large fee, particularly for non-Africans. It is an expensive agency, and apparently inefficient.[32]

Despite revision of the Labor Code and institutional changes in the labor market, it is not certain that the actual functioning of these markets is much more flexible than in pre-reform days. One reason is that the extent of employer inability to adjust to fluctuating needs for labor was almost surely exaggerated. Subcontracting of parts of company operations was always possible; this was one way to meet seasonal needs, and was probably widespread. Also, some of the forces that stayed employer hands are still present. Collective bargaining agreements reflect (indirectly) government policies and concerns. The general judicial environment remains uncongenial. Employers are still vulnerable to legal challenges by fired workers claiming abusive action and to uncertain outcomes of court proceedings.

Nonetheless, new elements of flexibility have certainly been introduced into Ivoirian labor markets as a result of the reforms of the past decade. Employers appear to be more comfortable in this new environment. They say so, and the buoyancy of private foreign direct investment tends to confirm it.

General System Reform

Concerned donors and the RCI government turned to general judicial reform in the early 1990s. The prevailing diagnosis was that the quality of the L/J system had declined since the 1970s, and that by 1990 it was very weak, distrusted by the private sector, and a serious obstacle to market-oriented economic growth. The main elements of the common diagnosis were as follows:

- *Antiquated legal code.* Most of the laws relating to business dated from the nineteenth century. They were complex, anachronistic, and seriously deficient in such areas as contracts and credit, corporate financial and accounting regulations, and bankruptcy and liquidation.
- *Inadequate resources.* The Ministry of Justice (MOJ) budget was small, less than 2 percent of the state budget in the early 1990s, with almost no provision for nonsalary recurrent costs. Courts were too few in number: three-quarters of cases were handled by the Abidjan Court, inevitably clogging the system; only 6 first-level courts were in operation (of 10 that had been created), and 26 court sections out of 39. Judges were also too few. They numbered 253 for a population of 14 million, about one-twentieth of international standards. And the *greffiers* (clerks of court), who were responsible for administering the court's activity, were poorly trained. Only 47 of the 467 greffiers were *attachés* (had postsecondary education); the rest were assistants (301) and secretaries (120).
- *Inefficient and inequitable functioning.* Access to the courts was expensive and procedures burdensome. Respect for claims was irregular and contracts were frequently not enforced. Corruption was

said to be widespread, encouraged by the fact that judges frequently and without penalty failed to state the grounds for rulings, and by the fact that judgments were not published. Judges' decisions were often of low quality.[33] The poor administration of judicial arrangements was attributed to a shortage of judges, their weak general training, and their lack of specialized knowledge (in financial and accounting matters in particular), as well as to complex procedures and provisions that allowed defendants to adopt delaying tactics. Corruption, archaic working conditions, and inefficiency in the office of the clerk of the court (the greffier) was a major source of bottlenecks in the system.[34]

- *Lack of transparency.* Information about applicable regulations and procedures was dispersed and inaccessible, and procedures lacked transparency. This led to inconsistencies in treatment of claimants; uneven treatment of private sector agents was particularly harmful to business confidence.

The first major move in judicial reform in the RCI began in 1991 with the preparation of the World Bank's Economic Management Support Project (Projet d'Appui à la Gestion Economique, PAGE). The project was designed jointly with the French Ministry of Cooperation and emerged from a decision of the two aid agencies to divide responsibility in this reform area.

The French aid agency (Coopération Française) and the World Bank worked together through most of the 1990s, the Bank through judicial reform components in a succession of multi-component projects, the French by a US$1.3 million grant from the French Ministry of Cooperation.[35] The Ministry of Justice was to be strengthened. Better budgeting, organizational changes, computerization, and tighter inspection/control were to increase transparency and raise the productivity of existing resources. The court system would be expanded by hiring more judges and other staff and creating new courts in secondary cities. Training of judges and others would be intensified. An arbitration court for commercial dispute settlement would be created. Management and dissemination of legal data would be improved by creating a documentation center. Offices of the clerks of the court (greffiers) would be strengthened by modernizing offices in Abidjan and Dabou, training staff, acquiring computers, giving greater incentives to personnel, and simplifying legal forms. Major changes in the nature and management of the fees paid to the greffes would reduce corruption and raise money for court use (see below).

While these internal reform efforts were underway, the RCI government and the French government were moving along a second reform path. They were working on a multinational program to modernize laws covering economic and business affairs in participating African states. This was the Organisation pour la Harmonisation des Droits d'Affaires en Afrique, known by its acronym OHADA.

In 1993 the RCI signed the OHADA treaty with 14 other African countries (all francophone) to adopt a uniform system of business laws, covering general commercial codes, company law, bankruptcy, accounting rules, and various legal procedures. Draft laws were discussed by national commissions in each country. In 1997 and 1998 six "uniform acts" were adopted: on general commercial law, on company law, on surety, on simplified enforcement procedures, on bankruptcy, and on arbitration. All of these are now in effect.[36]

Judicial system strengthening remained on the reform table throughout the 1990s. It is still there. In addition to ongoing French judicial reform efforts, the World Bank 1998 capacity building project has legal/judicial components and the Ministry of Justice is seeking other donor support. The reform agendas were presented in various formal "action plans" in 1991, 1996, and 1999. The first two were produced to meet World Bank conditions in several of its projects. The most recent (1999–2001) is targeted for inclusion in the European Union's Sixth Adjustment Program that is part of the Eighth European Development Fund budget.

The specific reforms to be implemented have been more or less the same throughout the decade. Forward movement on these reforms was very slow in the five years that followed initial steps on judicial reform in 1991. In 1995 the World Bank cut back the amount allotted to judicial reform in its Economic Management Support Project because of lack of progress. Most of reforms proposed in the 1996 action plan were the same as those put forward in 1991; they were part of the conditionality in the 1996 Private Sector Adjustment Credit. The pace of change was quicker after 1996, but the reform agenda in the latest (1999–2001) action plan contains the elements familiar from past action plans: training for judges and other staff, speeding up the handling of litigation, computerizing the greffes and other entities, reinforcing infrastructure and equipment, creating an independent arbitration court, improving legal information flow, harmonizing RCI legal codes with the Uniform Acts of OHADA (Côte d'Ivoire 1999).

Many reform actions have been taken. Adoption of the OHADA "Uniform Acts" has meant a wholesale renovation of business law. More judges have been hired—50 a year from 1995 to 1997. Judges, greffiers, and other staff have benefited from 2,300 training days in 75 courses. There was significant training of trainers. At least 300 computers have been put in place in the MOJ and the courts. The Abidjan Arbitration Court (Cour d'Arbitrage de Côte d'Ivoire) has been set up, along with a National Legal Documentation Center (Centre National de Documentation Juridique) and a Central Legal Archives Service (Service Central des Archives Judiciaires). The General Inspectorate of judicial services was reinforced by appointment of four inspectors-general, provision of training seminars, and distribution of a circular on concepts and modalities of inspection.

Numerous other changes have been introduced, most of them small. A task force defined an improved methodology for drafting of laws. Judicial procedures were promulgated that are aimed at shortening the duration of cases, improving access, and lightening procedures. "Collegiality" (more than one judge present at hearings) was introduced. A law was passed creating a public prosecutor's office at Supreme Court level. The structure and functioning of the Supreme Court were changed. A new court building was constructed in Yopougon, a big Abidjan suburb.

Significant effects of the general judicial system reforms, however, seem few. The most fundamental effort—to sanitize the fee system and improve the operations of the greffes—led nowhere. Computerization in the greffes and elsewhere in the judicial structure is regarded by everybody as a failure. Observers talk of a fiasco; most of the computer stock is unused. It took from 1991 to 1997 for the Abidjan Arbitration Court to move from intention to reality; its case load is still (in 1999) very small and it will be some years before it is a significant actor. The birth of the national documentation center also took many years; hatched since 1995, it has had trouble finding financing.

Even some of the clear achievements of the reform program may have generated only limited effects. Some local lawyers criticize the training program on the grounds that it provided specialized training (mainly in business law) to judges who are unspecialized and mobile. They say that many judges will therefore make little use of what they learned. Resuscitation of the General Inspectorate's office has led to no energetic rooting out of wrongdoing or incompetence, no indictments for corrupt behavior by judges, greffiers or others. Some reforms may even have had counterproductive effects. For example, a new law specified that *chefs de juridiction* (presiding or chief judges) must preside in all litigation involving more than CFAF 100 million (about US$180,000). This is presumably intended to raise the quality of decisions. But some critics observe that it also reinforces the political dependence of the courts on the executive branch, since all chefs de juridiction are political appointees.

In evaluators' jargon, then, the L/J reform effort has produced numerous reform "inputs" or "results," but few "effects" or "impacts." This explains apparent paradoxes in performance assessment. For example, the Bank released the fourth tranche of its Private Sector Development project funds in September 1997, judging that the MOJ had implemented satisfactorily its 1996 action plan. But a year later, the evaluators of the PSD project stated flatly that the implementation of the action plan has not improved the functioning of the judicial system. To the contrary, they argued that deterioration has continued. They pointed out that magistrates are poorly motivated, operating budgets are insignificant, the clerks of court remain unaccountable, and rulings are slow and may even differ from decisions made during court proceedings. Businessmen often feel compelled to settle out of court when they are faced with abusive legal actions or when they try to enforce contracts (World Bank 1999d).

Plenty of reasons for the sparseness of effects are at hand, other than the time factor. First, institutional change in legal/judicial systems is notoriously difficult. One has only to skim some of the literature to understand that successful reforms in this area are few.[37]

Secondly, donor involvement was half-hearted, even perfunctory. French aid was limited in volume and in scope; its major theatre was OHADA. The Bank's commitment seems to have been lukewarm and partial, with intermittent involvement. Judicial component funds were cut from the PAGE project in 1995 for lack of activity. No conditionality was attached until 1996. Some Bank staff had questioned the wisdom of including judicial reform in the PAGE project on the grounds that Bank competence in the area was limited and resources for supervision were too thin, objections that proved to be well founded. Moreover, the projects within which judicial reform components were placed were too complex to be manageable. The PAGE, for example, had components on budget reform, civil service reform, privatization, and other matters. People on the ground, and Bank supervisors, had difficulty defining who was responsible for what.

More important, RCI commitment has also been half-hearted. Some of the literature on judicial system reform argues that it should not even be tried unless strong political commitment exists. Given the ambiguities in the concept of commitment, this is debatable. But lack of interest by the political leadership certainly seems to be a key factor in slow RCI progress. The slow, reluctant issuance of implementation decrees for some of the legal changes is one indication. The long gestation period for new institutions like the Arbitration Court is another. Budget appropriations have been derisory, even declining.[38]

The most striking manifestation is the unwillingness or inability of the government to change the structure and functioning of the clerks of court, the greffes, probably the main bottleneck to better judicial system performance. Part of the problem arises from cumbersome, nontransparent, and often ineffective procedures, from archaic working conditions, and from the poorly defined status and role of the greffier. He is paid as a *fonctionnaire* (civil servant) but he also receives legally specified percentages of service fees and fines. Money is the root of the problem—the nature of the fees and fines collected by the courts, the greffier's role as manager of these revenues, and the fact that these revenues provide the financial foundations of the judicial system, exceeding by far the budget appropriations to the courts.

As noted above, the budget allocation for the entire MOJ is a little more than CFAF 5 billion, or US$1.6 million.[39] This is for salaries, property amortization, operating costs, and maintenance. Each court jurisdiction gets tiny amounts: the section of Dabou, for example, received CFAF 100,000 in 1995, of which CFAF 30,000 was for gasoline.

The main source of funds is the revenue generated by fees and fines imposed on users for court services managed by the greffier. Thus the *greffier en chef* of the Tribunal d'Abidjan stated that he collected total emoluments in 1995 of CFAF 170 million, out of which he paid CFAF 50 million for salaries (mainly to so-called *bénévoles*, volunteers, serving as stenographers) and other court operating costs. The authors of a 1996 report on the greffes call the 120 million franc difference "profits." They note that in the same year this greffier sent CFAF 92 million in fees (*redevances et droits*) to the Treasury.[40]

The main source of revenue is the *droit proportionel d'enregistrement.* This is a fee paid by the plaintiff-creditor, amounting to 5 percent of the amount owed to him—in effect an ad valorum tax on the creditor. The purpose is to record a fixed date for the final court decision. This registration fee has been strongly and widely attacked, including by the World Bank in numerous reports. It has no real purpose; the date of final court decision is announced in other ways. It is simply a tax on the already-abused creditor. If he does not have the money to pay the fee his court award is not registered and he cannot receive the implementing document (the *gosse*) necessary for him to collect what he is owed.

Elimination of this registration fee was part of the conditionality of the Bank's 1991 Financial Sector Adjustment Credit. The fee was in fact eliminated by a law of 1992. But budget receipts from court service fees and fines fell by 90 percent in 1993. The registration fee was reimposed the following year, and remains on the books.

The main successes of the reform decade are OHADA and the Abidjan Arbitration Court, the first because it quickly created the foundations of modern business law in the RCI, the second because it facilitates the use of alternative methods of dispute settlement, which is probably the best way to improve the judicial environment in the short term. This is a slim yield, and new. And even here doubts nag.[41]

The Role of Aid

The main issues concern the causes and processes of the reforms and the relative roles of donors and internal actors in generating impetus for

Part of the problem is that the interest group entities do not have firm roots and solid organization. They have few staff members and little analytic capacity at their command, and modest commitment from their members. Part of the reason also is that the most vulnerable interest group, the least able to defend itself, consists of outsiders—Levantine businessmen and non-Ivoirian African commerçants. So the most likely source of support for reform is the one with the least political clout.

Local interest group organizations thus appear to have had a small part in the initiation of reform, and were not aggressive supporters once the reforms were underway. The defenders of the status quo, however, were much more forceful. They have been able, for example, to prevent reform of the greffe (clerk of court) arrangements, which contribute so heavily to the deficiencies of the L/J system.[42]

Design and Methods of Implementation

Several features related to design and implementation are relevant. First, aid coordination in L/J reform seems to have been unusually good. Coopération Française and the World Bank were the main, probably the only, donors involved. (The European Union is likely to participate after 2000.) They jointly planned their interventions, and where overlapping appeared, they addressed it fairly quickly. The OHADA exercise was entirely French-led, but the Bank has helped in its localization.

Second, effectiveness was undoubtedly reduced by inadequacies in design and implementation. The Bank's involvement was half-hearted and piecemeal. The L/J component clearly occupied second or third rank in priority in the PAGE project, its first vehicle. PAGE had many ambitious components other than L/J reform, notably budget and civil service reform, and privatization. These were the main concern in supervision and otherwise. Also, local leadership was diffuse; lines of authority between the overall project management and the component directors were complicated. It was not always easy to discern who was responsible for which tasks. The attack on the greffe problem, in particular elimination of the droit proportionel d'enregistrement, was pinned on to the Financial Sector Adjustment Credit of 1991. It did bring about a law that eliminated it. But as noted above, the fiscal impact was so severe that the law was withdrawn the following year. There seems to have been no Bank outcry, probably because until 1994, maintenance of government revenues was a major priority, and all reform questions were dominated by macroeconomic issues, especially exchange rate policy.

Moreover, PAGE attached no conditionality to the L/J component, while the other components had plenty. Evaluators of PAGE blamed the lack of progress in the L/J component on this factor. This is probably right in one sense. In a conditionality-heavy environment, tranche release conditions will monopolize government's attention and energy, especially where sizeable adjustment credits are at stake, but also where the stakes are smaller, as in PAGE. In the Bank's second round on L/J issues, it was again one of many components (in the Private Sector Development Adjustment Credit of 1996), but L/J reforms this time were made core conditions. Implementation of the required action plan of 1996 was better than earlier efforts, though, as noted above, only at a rather superficial level.

The Major Hypotheses

What light does the L/J reform experience shed on the three overarching hypotheses emerging from recent empirical research?

First, does it confirm the hypothesis that governments choose to reform independent of the aid relationship? The answer is yes and no, but with much stronger emphasis on the no. On the yes side, lack of political commitment or will clearly played a role in obstructing reform. It is a major reason why no fundamental restructuring of the L/J system occurred during this decade of reform. Very few of the basic problems were attacked, even fewer successfully. The labor market reforms required big-time arm-twisting and gave rise to some backsliding. The judiciary's lack of political independence, the methods of nominating judges for example, was never raised. The attempt to reform court administration, to transform the role of the greffiers en chef, was quickly abandoned when Treasury receipts plummeted; nobody seems to have tried to find a better way to raise receipts in compensation. Judicial corruption was never put on the table.

On the other hand, such progress as was made would have been much smaller without the aid presence. The modernization of business law through the OHADA exercise surely resulted in faster and better renovation of the legal codes affecting the market economy. Without donor presence, the labor market reforms would have been fewer and slower. The many small steps taken to rework laws and procedures, which resulted in some two dozen actions, were at least in part the result of donor-technocrat dialogue. Private sector participation in the internal dialogue, though limited, was greater than it would have been in the absence of donors. The increase in physical facilities, new and rehabilitated buildings, the introduction of computers, establishment of new institutions (the Arbitration Court and the documentation center) would not have occurred, or would have occurred more slowly, without aid donor pressures and money. In short, a government largely indifferent to L/J reform nonetheless adopted many progressive changes, thanks mainly to the aid presence.

The second hypothesis states that nonfinancial aid is better than money in generating policy reform (and, presumably, institutional change). Again the answer coming out of the L/J experience is a faint yes coupled to a loud no. Nonfinancial aid did play a role. The two Bank capacity building projects (in 1991 and 1998), and the 1991 French project, provided useful training, lots of equipment and some ideas. But except for OHADA and probably training, nonfinancial aid was small in amount and largely ineffective. Technical assistance inputs other than for OHADA were few; the most effective were probably the critical reviews provided by experienced legal scholars and practitioners from France.[43] Computerization has been largely a fiasco, particularly in the offices of the greffiers. In any event, the most effective actions came when L/J reform was part of financial transfers—the labor law reforms in the PASCO project and the general changes of the late 1990s in the Private Sector Development Adjustment Credit.

The third hypothesis is that financial aid works best when reform and institution building are underway. This is a reasonable proposition, hard to dispute a priori. But reflection on the L/J reform experience in the RCI yields no satisfactory insight into its validity. One problem is that as it is framed, the hypothesis is not really operational. The RCI has been in reform mode most of the time since 1980. Intensity has varied, and backsliding has occurred. But in the L/J case specifically, reforms have been "underway" virtually continuously since 1991.

Moreover, financial and nonfinancial aid are not separate and different instruments for institutional reform or capacity building. In the RCI case, L/J reform instruments came in nonfinancial form (French contributions to OHADA, and the 1991 grant for TA and training; World Bank economic management and capacity building projects) and as part of adjustment credits with multiple components, including L/J reform. The hypothesis thus cannot be assessed.

SUMMARY AND CONCLUSIONS

Côte d'Ivoire is one of the most "reformed" countries on earth, judging by the scope of its reform efforts and the time devoted to them. Reform programs have been present during most of the past two decades. Between 1980 and 1998 the RCI signed nine agreements with the IMF and received 22 policy loans from the World Bank (see tables 7.11 and 7.12). Numerous policy loans were also financed by other donors. Big sums changed hands. The World Bank disbursed approximately US$3 billion (in current dollars) on policy loans, the French government and the European Community hundreds of millions more. Between 1994 and 1997 the RCI was the World Bank's main policy reform customer; it received more than one-third of all the adjustment loans made by the Bank in Sub-Saharan Africa. It is hard to think of a single major policy area, sector, or institution that has not engaged in some reform operations.

In this paper we have summarized the institutional background and the political-economic context of the reform programs, described many of the specific reforms, and analyzed reform processes as well as—to a limited extent—their effectiveness. We have tried to answer three sets of questions. The first relates to the "causes" and processes of reform, the kinds of questions emphasized in the terms of reference. What "triggered" the reforms and who was primarily responsible for their conception, design, and implementation? To what extent were they externally generated? How much pressure for reform arose from domestic dissatisfaction with the status quo, from protests by local reformers? What was the nature and extent of dialogue, internal and external?

The second set of questions concerns the effectiveness of the aid for reform. Were the reforms implemented? To what extent are "effects" or impacts visible? Has Côte d'Ivoire become a more flexible, open, competitive economy? Have local institutions been made stronger, local capabilities enhanced? These issues are addressed in the sectoral chapters that produced the insights summarized in this concluding chapter.

The third set of questions respond to the broad generalizations proposed in the terms of reference for this study: that government decisions to reform are taken independently of the aid relationship, that nonfinancial aid stimulates reform more effectively than financial aid, and that financial aid is effective only when reform is underway.

Causes and Processes

It has been argued that three factors generate reform: local technocrats and politicians, the influence of reform in neighboring countries, and crises. In the Côte d'Ivoire case neighborhood influences seem to have been nil. And the role of local technocrats and politicians as initiators of reform was for a long time of secondary importance. The main exception was the role of the political team before and after the devaluation decision. Financial crisis was the main impetus for change, first in the late 1970s, then more profoundly in the late 1980s. It made all the actors aware that some reforms were imperative. It made technocrats and politicians willing to listen to their anxious external supporters.

In some reform areas, local technocrats and interest groups *were* early champions of change, and even where they did not initiate reforms, the reform process allowed considerable dialogue, giving scope for local inputs on reform design and priorities. But given the context of a need for change because of financial crisis, aid donors clearly played the lead role. They generated a sense of urgency about the need for reform, crafted most of the important reform proposals, and conditioned their aid on local agreement to support them. In this sense it is hard to deny donor primacy in the origin of these reforms. This is the conclusion of the analyses of trade liberalization, devaluation, social sector expenditure reforms, and efforts to strengthen legal/judicial institutions.

Trade Liberalization

In section 5 it is noted that trade liberalization was not adopted in reaction to demands by political elites or local interest groups. The prevailing political sentiment among decisionmakers was to resist these reforms. President Houphouët-Boigny thought that the RCI was sufficiently open, and neither he nor his main advisers really believed that levels of protection were excessive or biased against exports. They were not persuaded by World Bank–financed technical studies on patterns of effective protection. Nor did the private sector play a significant role in the trade reforms, though in recent years it has been more active and influential. (One example is its success in supporting World Bank demands that the public sector export promotion agency CCIA be replaced by the privately managed APEXCI.)

Trade reforms were adopted in response to the pressures of a severe financial crisis caused by a decline in world prices of cocoa and coffee, losses of foreign exchange and fiscal revenues, and heavy debt burden. The nature and, less clearly, the pace of trade liberalization were determined by the World Bank. It was generally opposed by the administration and by a well-sheltered business community fearful of external competition. The local reaction was to urge "prudence"—that is, a slower pace of reform than was pushed by the World Bank.

Moreover, indigenous reform-making capacity was too weak to generate a homegrown reform package. And internal dialogue on trade policy (and other reforms) was complicated by the existence of DCGTx, a Houphouët-created, French-managed parallel administration. It was staffed by numerous expatriates and had wage policy freedom that allowed it to recruit highly competent Ivoirians. In the internal debate DCGTx overpowered the technical ministries. Between 1986 and 1991, DCGTx was formally responsible for economic policies and programs, including the adjustment programs. This agency was generally suspicious of trade liberalization, reflecting French *dirigiste* traditions (and the sentiments of President Houphouët) in this matter.

Devaluation

The 1994 change in parity of the CFA franc was clearly an imposed reform. Its origin was in financial crisis, due mainly to changes in the RCI's terms of trade. The first financial crisis, in the late 1970s, had been (temporarily) resolved by favorable changes in terms of trade and exchange rates; world cocoa and coffee prices rose in 1984 and between 1980 and 1985 the French franc was devalued and the dollar appreciated. But financial crisis reappeared in the late 1980s, as the external environment moved unfavorably. Between 1988 and 1993 the country struggled to avoid falling into arrears on its external debt.

The political class and all urban groups in the RCI were strongly opposed to devaluation. Various reasons were given. Some argued that devaluation was not necessary, that policy changes focused on productivity improvements combined with probable improvements in world commodity prices would reestablish stability and growth. Many thought it would not work. Changing relative prices in this inflexible economy would not bring about the required supply responses. Devaluation would probably not be "effective" anyway, since the government was not strong enough to impose the fiscal discipline required if repeated devaluations were to be avoided. Rising prices for imported consumer goods would brutally reduce urban real incomes, with resulting high risk of political chaos. Above all, President Houphouët was perhaps the fiercest opponent, for reasons probably more political than economic.

In France, the major partner in the franc zone, many of these same ideas and concerns prevailed, and others as well. Many worried that the franc zone itself might not survive the turbulence that could be unleashed, especially since many member countries opposed any change in parity. They feared that, due to sociopolitical troubles, the lives and property of thousands of French citizens residing in the RCI could be endangered, as well as the investments of the numerous French enterprises operating there. Difficult practical problems existed, notably how to reach, secretly, a consensus on the timing and nature of the change without major exacerbation of capital flight.

For all these reasons a rearguard action was vigorously fought between 1988 and 1993 to maintain CFA parity. Four events led to change: the illness and death of Houphouët and the nomination of a more devaluation-friendly prime minister; the resounding failure of the 1990 effort to cut nominal wages; the deteriorating situation within the franc zone and the resulting financial costs being borne by France; and the unwillingness of major donors, especially the World Bank, to continue lending, as indicated by a sharp fall in aid disbursements in 1992–93.

Education and Health Sector Reforms

The main trigger for the social sector reforms of the 1990s, similarly, was the financial crisis and the need to contain social sector expenditures if macroeconomic stability was to be attained. Donors were the main bearers of this message. The reform program focused on cost-cutting, increased equity in social expenditures, and greater internal and external efficiency. The first two were donor preoccupations much more than local. The specific reforms were crafted mainly by donor staff.

The outside impetus is clearest with respect to the idea that expenditures should be restructured in favor of primary education and primary health care. The Ivoirian leadership was preoccupied until 1994 with debt crises and the devaluation issue. There was not much residual energy for, and only modest interest in, social sector expenditure reallocations. There was not much conviction that cutting back on tertiary-level social sector spending was the right policy, and little taste for the political risks involved in restricting university access. The need for general budget and balance of payments support was the main reform motor. The Finance and Planning ministries negotiated adjustment credits that were supposed to be about reform of education and health sectors. But the real purpose was to close financial gaps, to bring in the program money. Thus the Education and Health ministries participated relatively little in negotiations on the Human Resources Development Program, the US$360 million adjustment credit begun in 1991; substantive concerns were in the back seat during its implementation. Local ownership of major objectives (and conditionalities) was minimal.

Donor dominance also was due to the fact that capacity in the government was too limited to enable it to take the lead. This changed in the mid-1990s, when a stronger, more experienced corps of local technicians began to assert itself, drafting documents such as the Policy Framework Paper. But for the first generation of sweeping reforms, capacity constraints limited the domestic contribution. Moreover, few local champions were apparent. Most of the actors—Education and Health ministry personnel, teachers, doctors, nurses, pharmacists, and others—were neutral or opposed. This is hardly surprising, since the reforms involved many changes contrary to their economic interests. Their professional associations were in any event not vocal. Students at the secondary and tertiary levels were actively opposed.

Nor is there evidence of any popular insistence on reforms of the cost-cutting, equity-enhancing type. Users of health and education services expressed little dissatisfaction with the status quo, other than that services were too few and quality too low. This was particularly the case for health care. For example, a recent survey of users of health facilities found general satisfaction with respect to the care provided; the main complaint was lack of medicines.

Legal and Judicial System Reform

This reform arena had two segments: labor law modification and general system reform. In both the main initiatives came from aid donors. In labor market reform, the World Bank was without doubt the lead player. Its critique of labor legislation and administration in RCI was much the same as it applied to many countries, and its general reform targets the same: make it easier for employers to hire and fire and eliminate the monopoly of the state labor exchange (OMOCI). The Bank's 1991 PASCO program called for elimination of OMOCI's hiring monopoly, for elimination of constraints on hiring temporary or casual labor and on collective layoffs, and for dropping prior administrative authorization for overtime.

Very little consultation with the affected parties characterized the labor market reform process. The trade unions say they were not at all engaged in dialogue on the nature and scope of the reforms. The dialogue took place between the World Bank and government officials. And it was a contentious dialogue. Many of the reforms were introduced only under extreme Bank pressure, and with long delays that indicated obvious reluctance. The decrees implementing the Labor Code (21 of them) did not appear until 1996, four years after the National Assembly vote, and only after their issuance was made a tranche release condition of another adjustment loan (the Private Sector Development Adjustment Credit of 1996).

The general L/J system reforms were not aggressively contested as were the labor market reforms. Their problem was rather lack of government priority. But the triggers for reform in both cases differed in one important respect from those that energized the trade liberalization, exchange rate, and social sector reforms: their origin was not in financial crisis. It rather resulted from a simmering discontent with the operation of the labor laws and the overall judicial system. The impetus to undertake judicial system reform—as with most institutional reform, probably—came from the preoccupations of aid donors. After all, dysfunctional or degraded institutions often linger; political or ideological shifts are usually needed to generate internal demand for change. In their absence, institutional reform in poor country circumstances seems to require an outside push.

This was the case with judicial system reform in the RCI. A very small group of civil servants was pushing for reform in the late 1980s and early 1990s. Most were in the MOJ. Several became coordinators or project directors of judicial reform components in aid projects. According to one view, these officials had drawn up a reform program at the beginning of the decade, but could not get support for it from local sources. So they turned to donors for assistance.

There is no evidence at hand to confirm this version of the origins of the legal/judicial reform program. There is quite a lot of evidence suggesting that the main inspiration was from the two main donors, Coopération Française and the World Bank. Both had undertaken similar programs in other countries; it was part of their general reform agenda.

Debate within the World Bank in the early 1990s indicated staff concern about lack of RCI government commitment to this kind of reform. Very few government champions could be identified. The L/J reform component was added to the Economic Management Support Project (PAGE) because Bank staff not only believed it was warranted by the state of RCI legal/judicial institutions, but also because it was methodologically correct; a comprehensive approach to strengthening economic management required it.

Labor market reforms (flexibility in hiring and firing and elimination of the government hiring agency) were clearly hatched in Washington. No evidence is at hand that negatively affected local groups (employers, informal sector workers, and the unemployed) took any initiatives before the Bank's PASCO project identification and preparation. With respect to general L/J reforms, the MOJ action plans of 1991 and 1996 were drawn up at the urging of Coopération Française and the Bank, and their main elements reflected the agendas of these donors. The OHADA exercise was without question of French inspiration, and its main architects were French lawyers.

Participation of private actors, whether practicing members of the bar or representatives of private firms, was not extensive. The Ivoirian National Commission on OHADA, for example, consisted of six members appointed by the MOJ. The private sector appointed no one. The result, according to some local lawyers, was that they were unaware of the ongoing reform effort, and did not participate in any consensus-building activity.

The economic groups whose interests were badly served by the existing L/J system were formal sector employers, entrepreneurs in the small and middle-sized enterprise sector, and informal sector operators, especially traders (*commerçants*). Except for larger modern sector employers, these actors are poorly organized and have little political voice. Even professional organizations, like the bar association, play minor political roles, and played marginal roles in the reforms.

Part of the problem is that the interest group entities do not have firm roots and solid organization. They have few staff members and little analytic capacity at their command, and modest commitment from their members. Part of the reason also is that the most vulnerable interest group, the least able to defend itself, consists of outsiders—Levantine businessmen and non-Ivoirian African commerçants. So the most likely source of support for reform is the one with the least political clout. Local interest group organizations thus appear to have had a small part in the initiation of these reforms, and were not aggressive supporters once the reforms were underway. The defenders of the status quo, however, were much more forceful—beneficiaries of the greffe fee system in the courts, for example.

Effectiveness

How effective have the reforms been? The question can be discussed at many levels; we focus on three. First, have the promised or targeted reforms actually been implemented? This involves looking at reform "inputs" or "results." Second, have the implemented reforms led to any real changes in the way things work? In evaluators' jargon, these are "effects." Finally, were the reform concepts and designs appropriate and were implementation approaches sound?

Reform Inputs ("Results")

Scores of reform measures have been adopted by the RCI in the past decade. The extent to which they have been implemented varies among sectors.

The record seems best in exchange rate reform (the change in parity) and in trade liberalization. Devaluation has reduced the real effective exchange rate—by some 30 percent in 1997—and this has augmented competitiveness. Tariff levels and dispersion have been reduced. The weighted average tariff rate fell from 37 percent in 1990 to 27 percent in 1995. Nontariff barriers have been removed, tariff exemptions cut back, and the rate of effective protection lowered. Far-reaching institutional changes have magnified the private sector role. Cocoa and coffee marketing has been liberalized, as has rice importing and marketing. Large-scale agriculture (oil palm, rubber, sugar) has been privatized, as have public utilities and some industrial enterprises. It is the same in maritime transport and key trade-related institutions such as the export promotion agency.

In the social sectors numerous reforms were implemented. Education sector costs were contained by cuts in teacher salaries and benefits and near-freezes on increases. Expatriate TA teachers virtually disappeared, 1,100 assistant teachers were hired, and 2,500 administrators were put back in primary classrooms. Student subsidies (for scholarships, food, transport) were cut by 20 percent in real terms and by half in terms of budget share between 1992 and 1996. Efforts were made to increase quality at the primary level by creating "pilot schools." Nonsalary operating costs tripled as a share of the education budget. In the health sector some cost recovery was introduced and use of generic drugs encouraged. In both sectors intensive management improvements were undertaken, notably by introducing sector plans, annual programs and budgets, and performance indicators.

However, implementation with respect to the achievement of expenditure targets was poor. Instead of rising, education's share of the total budget fell from 34 percent in 1992 to 27 percent in 1996, and the health sector share of recurrent spending also fell. The primary health care sector received a falling share of the Public Investment Program until the mid-1990s, and in 1997 its share (20 percent) remained below the share of the tertiary sector (hospitals, administration). Most significant, the promised reallocation of spending in favor of primary education and health did not occur. Primary school spending actually fell, from 52 percent of the education budget in 1991 to 47 percent in 1995. Primary health was supposed to rise from 35 percent of the current budget in 1991 to 42 percent in 1995. Instead, it fell to 32 percent. The benefits of public spending on health and education remain unequally distributed. Only half of the poorest fifth of households receive a benefit for having children in primary school. Of the total education subsidy, the poorest fifth gets 14 percent, the richest 35 percent.

Many reform actions have also been undertaken or agreed to in the legal/judicial area. The labor codes have been revised, hiring and firing was made more flexible, and the state labor exchange monopoly was ended. Business law has undergone a wholesale renovation by adoption of the OHADA Uniform Acts. More judges were hired—50 a year from 1995 to 1997. Judges, greffiers, and other staff have benefited from 2,300 training days in 75 courses. At least 300 computers have been put in place in the MOJ and the courts. The Abidjan Arbitration Court has been set up, as well as a National Legal Documentation Center and a Central Legal Archives Service. The General Inspectorate of judicial services was reinforced by appointment of four inspectors-general, provision of training seminars, and distribution of a circular on concepts and modalities of inspection. A law was passed creating a public prosecutor's office at Supreme Court level, and the structure of the Supreme Court was revised. A new court building was constructed in an Abidjan suburb. And numerous other, less visible changes have been introduced, such as an improved methodology for drafting laws and rules aimed at shortening the duration of cases, improving access, and lightening procedures.

Effects ("Impacts")

The determination of inputs (or "results") is the first step in reform assessment. It answers the question: Were the specific reform actions that were agreed to or planned undertaken? The next step is to ask whether the reform inputs were "effective."

This has two senses. First, were the reform actions undermined by contrary actions or policies? Fiscal and monetary looseness can frustrate an exchange rate devaluation. Tariff reductions can be offset by changes in commodity classifications or imposition of minimum ("reference") prices. Some of this kind of reform backpedaling has occurred in the RCI. One example is the government's creation of a substitute labor market institution (AGEPE) following elimination of OMOCI. There appears also to have been some customs behavior that offsets tariff reductions, but we do not know how much. Also, agencies and/or officials have in some instances subjected traders to price controls, demanding price information or imposing fines despite price deregulation.

Second, did the reforms bring about changes in performance or functioning? Did macroeconomic and trade policy changes have positive effects on growth? Did quality of social services increase? Are labor markets more flexible, is the legal/judicial system more transparent and efficient?

These are difficult questions to answer. Some hints nonetheless emerge from our sectoral reform studies. There is, for example a strong presumption that the change in CFA parity and trade liberalization have stimulated growth and had other positive effects. The economy has grown at 5–6 percent a year during the past five years, much faster than before. Investors have returned more enthusiastically to the RCI than to any other African country. These positive changes are not due to policy reforms alone. Favorable terms-of-trade movements and large post-devaluation aid inflows also contributed. But the reforms were critical.

Trade and price liberalization has been effective, though local opinion has some reservations. The playing field is not even; there is some discriminatory and unequal treatment linked to political and family connections. Also, there are cases where insufficient information about decontrolled prices subjects small private actors in trading activities to the corrupt practices of civil servants. The business community is favorable to liberalization with equal treatment for everybody. Tariff reductions and price decontrol have not hurt local businessmen. Spokesmen for 31 percent of the firms questioned in a mid-1998 survey thought that liberalization had had a positive impact and 55 percent reported no impact. Very few (3 percent) indicated negative effects.

One important reform that was strongly contested by Ivoirians has proved successful in terms of effects on market operation. This is the liberalization of coffee marketing. The 1998/1999 marketing season was the first under new, liberalized trading rules. It was a clear success. A widely held expectation was that marketing margins would rise, with traders and exporters expropriating more of the value of the crop. In fact, marketing margins fell in absolute terms and the price received by producers rose both as a percentage of the f.o.b. price (from 52 percent to 67 percent) and in absolute terms. Producers thus benefited; traders and government lost. This result was facilitated by the small coffee harvest in 1998, but nonetheless demonstrated that the markets worked competitively. Liberalization also has encouraged efficiency-enhancing changes in marketing structures.

In social sector reform, we have already seen that most equity-enhancing objectives were not attained; primary education and health care have not been favored in public expenditure allocations. Moreover, the internal efficiency of the educational system has improved little. While in nominal terms, for example, nonsalary budget shares rose sharply, they fell in real terms because of devaluation-induced price increases. Repetition rates have not declined, pupil-teacher ratios have not fallen, public sector professional/vocational training has improved little. In health, investment in urban hospital facilities remains high. And while higher education continues to receive large budget shares, the general view is that quality of instruction has seriously deteriorated. Management reform has been slow and uneven, particularly in the health sector. The major programming and budgeting exercises introduced as part of the conditionality of the early 1990s have left few traces.

As for legal/judicial reforms, not many effects are observable yet. A recent World Bank evaluation found that reform efforts have not improved the functioning of the judicial system. To the contrary, the evaluators argued that deterioration has continued. They pointed out that magistrates are poorly motivated, operating budgets are insignificant, and the clerks of court remain unaccountable. Rulings are slow and may even differ from decisions made during court proceedings. Businessmen often feel compelled to settle out of court when they are faced with abusive legal actions or when they try to enforce contracts.

The judgment may seem harsh. There have been some forward steps and all institutional reforms take time. But the yield from the decade of effort in judicial reform in RCI nonetheless seems slender. The most fundamental effort—to sanitize the fee system and improve the operations of the greffes—led nowhere. Computerization in the greffes and elsewhere in the judicial structure is regarded as a failure by everyone; the word fiasco is used. Most of the computer stock is unused. It took from 1991 to 1997 for the Abidjan Arbitration Court to move from intention to reality; its case load is still (in 1999) very small and it will be some years before it is a significant actor. The birth of the National Legal Documentation Center also took many years; since its inception in 1995, it has had trouble finding financing. Most important, no anticorruption policies or programs have been introduced.

Part of the explanation for partial implementation and sparse effects can be found in design flaws or faulty methods of implementation. These will be outlined below. But other important factors were at work. Until 1994, avoidance of arrears and maintenance of donor inflows was the overriding Ivoirian objective, diverting official energies from agreed reform programs. So many reforms had little government ownership; they were the price to be paid for external support. In addition, many Ivoirians were unconvinced that some of the reforms were soundly conceived. For example, few agreed with donors that expenditures should be reallocated from tertiary to primary education. Changes in the environment made implementation extremely difficult in some cases; the vast expansion in numbers of university students after 1990, for example, made expenditure reallocations particularly unmanageable. In some instances donor supervision capacity was inadequate. This was so in the case of legal/judicial reforms.

Reform Program Design and Methods of Implementation

There is broad agreement that the content of the reform programs has been pertinent. Questions can be raised of course about priorities and the realism of objectives. It was probably utopian to expect major reallocations of expenditure to primary education and health care at a time when university enrollments rose from 20,000 to 50,000 and university infrastructure and teaching was deteriorating, and when donors were willing to provide grant funding for urban hospital rehabilitation. Similarly, the contradiction between cutting teacher salaries and raising educational quality may not have been given enough attention.

There was also some possible misreading of institutional contexts, as in the case of the World Bank attempt to restructure health sector organization by creating health "districts," despite its novelty and lack of fit with other donor operations. Another example may be the focus on business law in the training program for judges, despite their unspecialized responsibilities. Also, the strong and early emphasis on labor market reforms may have been ill advised. It used up lots of donor political capital for what were likely small benefits; private employers probably had adapted to the old system and the reforms did not in the end mark a great improvement in flexibility and freedom from harassment. But much of this is second-guessing and debatable. In general, the reforms have been well targeted on needed and important structural reforms.

Other design or implementation weaknesses are less debatable. First, key elements of the reform program were so closely integrated into adjustment operations that the substantive reforms became a sideshow to the main drama—obtaining program money to close financial gaps. A recent World Bank project paper (1998d) summarized the problem this way:

> The main lesson of the Human Resources Development Project and the parallel TA project, the Human Resources Management Support Project, is that programs must be fully owned and carefully developed by *sectoral* [my emphasis] stakeholders for budgetary objectives to be met. The HRDP was prepared largely through the Finance Ministry. It consisted more of a series of economic interventions rather than of substantive sectoral interventions, and did not address issues such as the quality of education or human resource management. Sectoral management felt little incentive to achieve goals that did not reflect its own priorities.

Related to this, implementation of some of the programs was perfunctory. In judicial system reform each of the donor partners (France
and the World Bank) had other preoccupations. French attention was
concentrated on broader regional reforms in the franc zone—the OHADA
operation. The Bank had too little capacity to adequately supervise the
program; it focused on other components of projects into which judicial
reform had been inserted. The RCI government was equally half-hearted
in its implementation. It made one effort to reform the greffier fee system, retreated when that negatively impacted on budget revenues, and
never tried again.

Finally, too many reforms were to be implemented at the same time
without due attention to the government's limited absorptive capacity.
A classic example is the European Union program of accelerated construction of rural health posts. The program demanded faster spending
than was customary in the Health Ministry. It also included a secondary
objective, of stimulating local construction entrepreneurs. An audit of
the program in early 1999 revealed improper procedures for perhaps a
third of expenditures. Officials have been fired and jailed and the program put on hold.

With respect to conditionality, prevailing wisdom holds that there is
too much of it, and that it is ineffective. Both propositions seem in accord with empirical observation. However, the Ivoirian experience does
not altogether confirm these generalizations. First, it is not clear that all
projects or programs have too many conditions. The Bank worked hard
to limit the number of conditions, for example in the Human Resources
Development Program, which had "floating" conditionality; tranche releases were numerous and spread out, each depending on implementation of two conditions, only one of which was a core condition. (It should
be noted that there is no evidence that this made much difference in the
unfolding of the program.)

Given the large number of programs in operation at any moment,
even when individual project conditionality is restrained, the aggregate
burden of conditionality is heavy, at least on core economic ministries.
The real problem derives from the marriage of weak technical ministries
and ardent donors. Weak ministries often find large aid programs unmanageable. In the RCI the health sector provides only the most striking
example. The dilemma is that donors often have their greatest enthusiasm for projects in weak ministries.

The RCI case suggest also that conditionality may be more effective
than is commonly thought. An odd feature of many of our interviews
was the repeated argument that *more,* not *less,* conditionality was needed.
Officials make this argument because they believe that only aid that is
conditioned will reach their ministry. More generally, there is throughout the political system a pervasive skepticism about the reality of

government's interest in reform. Virtually all representatives of civil society we spoke with (trade unionists, journalists, lawyers, university professors, students, and private businessmen) expressed doubts about the government's commitment to true reform. Similar doubts circulate among technocrats in the civil service. These champions of more aggressive reform not only distrust the government, but typically have a strong sense of their own political powerlessness. Since they see the political system as unresponsive to internal demands for reform, they believe donor-imposed reform is the only option. Hence the reliance on external players, especially the Bank, and calls for broader and deeper conditionality, more vigorously monitored and sanctioned for nonperformance.

The Major Hypotheses

We summarize here the sectoral analyses of the three "major hypotheses" set out in the terms of reference: that governments choose to reform independent of the aid relationship; that nonfinancial aid is better than money in generating policy reform (and presumably institutional development also); and that aid works best when reform and institution building are underway. What does the reform experience of the RCI tell us about these hypotheses?

Did Côte d'Ivoire's Government Choose
to Reform Independently of Aid Donors?

This hypothesis has been expressed in various forms: that aid has no impact on policy, or that aid cannot buy reform. This view, a major conclusion of the World Bank's influential study, *Assessing Aid,* is shared by some Ivoirian officials. One said that the Bank and others who believe that their efforts have induced reform are fooling themselves, much like Chanticleer, who thought his crowing made the sun come up.

In its more extreme versions, this is not a tenable argument. Until the mid-1990s at least, donors conceived, designed, financed, helped implement, and evaluated the vast majority of reforms. Certainly there were more reforms, and probably better ones, because of the aid presence.

In the devaluation case, it is evident that government did not decide first against devaluation, then later in its favor, independently of aid relationships. In the pre-1994 period, some reforms were adopted because they were necessary to win donor support of the no-devaluation policy. External assistance allowed retention of the existing parity until 1994, and it was the suspension of aid and promises of abundant post-devaluation donor support that provoked the devaluation.

In the case of institutional reforms in education, health, and the judicial system, aid has had positive effects on reform even though implementation has been partial and some of the institutional reforms (performance budgeting in education, for example, or computerization of the greffes) did not "take" or were not sustainable. For all their imperfections, the reform programs would have been different in content (less good), slower in implementation, and probably less effective in results, in the absence of donors. Action-oriented studies, training, and study tours would have surely been fewer in number and probably less good had external financing been absent. Reform messages, such as the need to make the economy more open, encourage the private sector, strengthen public expenditure management, and reallocate spending to primary levels, would have been much more muted.

Some of the least popular measures, such as salary cost containment and reductions in student subsidies, would have been less effective. The harmed interest groups were told that it was essential to follow this path because the World Bank insisted on it and large aid inflows depended on it. The debt relief initiative is now cited by the government in all austerity-related discussions with stakeholders.

Probably the most effective vehicle for aid influence has been the dialogue, formal and informal, surrounding program preparation and supervision. When, during project preparation or supervision, the Health Ministry proposes that more nurses be recruited, donor staff suggest concentrating more resources on training and supervision. When the ministry requests help for building up in-house maintenance capacity for biomedical equipment, the donor counterpart suggests contracting out that function. A chef de service says he needs an administrative secretary who knows all about the Ivoirian legal code. The donor spokesman asks why he needs that rare and costly competence. These are positive examples; of course not all donor staff suggestions are good.

Can it be seriously argued that the government introduced, independent of aid relationships, the reforms in trade policy, in labor market operation, in liberalization, and in privatization (especially in areas of hard-core domestic opposition such as cocoa and coffee marketing and maritime transport)? Can it be doubted that such progress as was made would have been much smaller without the donor ideas, pressures, and money—that modernization of business law would have been slower, civil society participation in the internal dialogue even less active, increases in physical facilities and equipment smaller, and innovations like the Arbitration Court fewer?

The hypothesis that aid has had no effect on reforms can perhaps be partially resuscitated by framing it more restrictively. If it is taken to mean that decisions on basic political or ideological choices are determined by governments independent of the aid relationship, it is more credible. Lack of political commitment clearly played a role in obstructing reform. It helps explain why no expenditure restructuring took place in the social sectors, why there occurred no fundamental restructuring of the L/J system, why the labor market reforms required big-time arm-twisting and gave rise to some backsliding. The judiciary's lack of political independence, the methods of nominating judges for example, was never raised. The attempt to reform court administration, to transform the role of the greffiers en chef, was quickly abandoned when Treasury receipts plummeted; nobody seems to have tried to find a better way to raise receipts in compensation. Judicial corruption was never put on the table.

These are areas not reached by the largely externally driven reform efforts of the past decade. They involve matters decided by government, not donors. But it is nonetheless true that in numerous instances, aid did lead an indifferent or unwilling government to adopt growth and equity-enhancing reforms.

Did Nonfinancial Aid Generate More Reform than Money Aid?

In this study "nonfinancial aid" is defined as freestanding technical assistance, donor economic and sector research, or advisory services. Nonfinancial aid did play some role. Studies done by the World Bank for the competitiveness project (PASCO) provided analytic support useful in the intense dialogue of the late 1980s and early 1990s. Also, the two Bank capacity-building projects with legal/judicial components (in 1991 and 1998) and a 1991 French project for judicial system reform, provided useful training, lots of equipment, and some ideas. The numerous studies on social sector reforms also played some role, according to local testimony. But generally the RCI experience provides thin support for this hypothesis.

Nonfinancial aid, for example, did not have a stronger impact than conditioned financial aid on the decision to devalue. The devaluation decision was made at the highest political levels. It might have been influenced by economic ideas, analysis, or the simulations done in Washington or in France on the anticipated effects in the RCI. But given the nature of the decision, its close link to fiscal imperatives, and its eminently political dimension, financial aid surely played the essential role.

In the L/J arena nonfinancial aid was small in amounts, and largely ineffective. It does not seem to have been significant except for OHADA. The most effective actions came when L/J reform was part of financial transfers—the labor law reforms in the PASCO project, the general changes of the late 1990s in the Private Sector Development Adjustment Credit.

The same is true in other areas of institutional reform. In the education and health sector reform programs technical assistance projects were handmaidens of financial aid projects. Nonfinancial aid that is untied to money seems to have been rare. Also, financial aid projects themselves carried a great deal of nonfinancial baggage. The adjustment credits have had study components, training tours, training seminars, and so forth. Many studies and much dialogue occurred during the long project gestation periods—commonly three or four years.

Studies and dialogue attached to money are a priori likely to be more effective than *freestanding* studies such as most of those in World Bank economic and sector work. The money is almost sure to make research and dialogue more action-oriented. It claims attention, and concentrates minds in a way that freestanding studies do not.

Did Financial Aid Work Best When Reform and Institution Building Were Underway?

This is not an operational hypothesis. In the 1990s at least, reforms and institution building of some sort are almost everywhere and always "underway." In the RCI, reform of some kind was going on most years in the 1980s and every year in the 1990s. Moreover, financial and nonfinancial aid are not separate and different instruments for institutional reform or capacity building.

The proposition is ambiguous in other respects. It can be taken to be a sequel to the proposition that financial aid does *not* work when policy/institutional reform is *not* underway, which is unclear but partially correct. It applies in cases where there exist fundamental macroeconomic disequilibria, for example the 1988–93 situation of the overvalued CFAF. In fact structural reforms moved forward very slowly during this period. But the hypothesis is incorrect in its extreme form. Even in the bad macro policy/institutional environment before 1994, financial aid had some positive effects, and would have had more if appropriately delivered. In any event, if the argument is that aid works *better* in good environments, it is surely true but not very interesting.

Concluding Observations

The reform history of Côte d'Ivoire has been uncommonly contentious—a bruising experience for all parties. The World Bank, chief agent of these reforms, is regarded by many Ivoirians as an organization with an arrogant staff, ideologically motivated, and poor at assessing institutional conditions and constraints. Distrust and hostility exist on both sides—a surprising amount on the Ivoirian side, given the more positive views recorded in the 1998 World Bank Client Survey. On the donor side many believe that the record shows persistent weakness in the commitment to reform; some suspect promotion of private interests and corrupt inclinations lie behind reform postures.

The rough path to reform in the RCI is not surprising, given its unique historical experience. Ghana, Uganda, and most reformers of the 1980s and 1990s came to the reform table not only with wrecked economies but with discredited policy models or strategies of development. Not so Côte d'Ivoire. The Ivoirians came with a history of brilliant growth. And they were convinced that the "Ivoirian miracle" had come about because their policies were right: monetary and exchange rate stability and openness based on membership in the franc zone; priority to agriculture, reflected in the fixing of high producer prices, state-controlled marketing, and creation of large state plantations; protection and price controls to stimulate investment. For many years into the reform process, most of the political class continued to believe that this model was still valid.

The external reformers' policy models were of course in fundamental disagreement with that of the Ivoirians. The resulting confrontation was more combative than elsewhere because the Ivoirians continued to believe that their model was tested and successful, while that of the Bretton Woods institutions was ideological and of uncertain applicability.

The contentiousness of the reform experience derived also from more general sources. Even with committed, reforming governments, donors almost always regard the pace of reforms as too slow and their reach too shallow. This happens because in all cases reforming governments are less sure than donors about the appropriateness of donor prescriptions. Reforms can also be restrained because local political leaders question their political feasibility or judge their risk to be too big. Donors, with less on the line, are less risk-averse, and can be expected to have more expansive views about where the edge of the envelope lies. Where donors have large political and economic interests at stake, as was the case with France on the devaluation issue, they are, unsurprisingly, more cautious.

Despite distrust and suspicion in RCI-donor relations, the contentiousness that has marked the past decade of reform, and continuing doubts about the extent of local political commitment, the RCI is a much different economy than it was in 1989. It is more open, far less dirigiste, more congenial to private activity. Much of this has to be credited to the country's external partners/financiers.

Many worries remain. The demand for more conditionality expressed by technocrats and members of civil society reflects a pervasive lack of confidence in the openness and responsiveness of the political system, a problem that has grown more ominous in recent months. The industrial sector remains highly protected; it has not yet been exposed to serious competitive pressures, so the extent to which real adjustment has taken place in that sector is unknown.

Finally, there is the problem of excessive donor expectations and potentially harmful missteps. Where there is fundamental disagreement, as for example in the case of reallocating public expenditures to primary health and education and away from urban hospitals and universities, donor expectations are unlikely to be met. Donors should distinguish between wishful thinking and real objectives. It would be wrong to give the RCI a bad grade for failure to meet ambitious, externally generated goals, especially when the effort to meet those goals distorts priorities, as in the social sectors. Constraints on implementing capacity have been systematically underestimated in the past, and are being neglected in some present planning. The expansion of rural facilities in the health sector in the clearest example (see section 6). The stories of the European Union's failed effort to accelerate spending in the primary health care sector and the 1999 suspension of the World Bank's main health project illustrate two of the main conclusions of this paper—that aid *can* buy reform, but only *some* reform. No matter how strong the commitment, unless reforms are soundly conceived and well implemented, they will be ineffective and possibly counterproductive.

APPENDIX 7.1
CÔTE D'IVOIRE: CHRONOLOGY
OF POLITICAL AND ECONOMIC DEVELOPMENTS

1960	The country won its independence from France.
1960–1977	The economy enjoyed its period of high growth (average 6 percent per year).
1976–1977	Cocoa and coffee prices boomed, and there was a sharp increase in public sector borrowing.
1978–1980	The country experienced a financial crisis when there was a significant slowdown of the economy as a result of the decline in the prices of cocoa and coffee and a consequent fall in public investment.
1981	The country received a succession of IMF and World Bank loans: an Extended Fund Facility (EFF) agreement with the IMF in 1981 and the first of three successive World Bank structural adjustment loans (SALs).
1984–1986	The economy saw stabilization and resumption of growth.
1987 (May)	The government failed to meet debt service payments.
1988–1989	Under IMF standby agreements there was an attempt at "internal adjustment" by cutting producer prices and civil service salaries. Government abandoned salary cut attempt following strikes and social protests.
1989–1991	Six World Bank sectoral adjustment loans were introduced, but there was little disbursement until 1994.
1991	Labor market reforms and general legal/judicial reforms were introduced.
1990–1993	Alassand Ouattara was named Prime Minister, and general political liberalization (press freedom, legalized political parties) occurred.
1993 (September)	The French government refused to give any more aid without a Fund agreement.
1993 (December)	The death of Félix Houphouët-Boigny ended a 40-year reign.
1994 (January)	The CFA franc was devalued.
1994–1999	The economy experienced renewed growth (average 5 percent per year).
1995	Konan Bédié was elected President.

1999	A military coup ousted Bédié.
2000	After a popular revolt against the military junta, the country elected Laurent Gbagbo President, but political unrest, exacerbation of ethnic tensions, and a stagnant economy still troubled the new government.

APPENDIX 7.2
INTERVIEWS IN CÔTE D'IVOIRE, AUGUST 1999

Mme. Kouadio, Ministère d'Enseignement Nationale et Formation de Base

M. Koumenan Mougo, Ministère de Développement Industriel & PME

M. Seka Seka, FIPME

M. Jacques Kouassi Kaouadiom , Ministère de Justice

M. Mian Phillippe, Primature

M. Flinde Albert, MEF

M. Jean-Paul Monne, MEF

M. Alexandre Assemien, MPPD

M. Sain Oguie, Chambre de Commerce

Mlle Yman Ginette, MPPD

M. Kone Mamadou, Ministère de Santé

Ministre Ahoua N'Doli

M. Yao Francois, FESACI

M Lylla Lansana, MEF

M. Toure Theophile, Ministère d'Enseignement Nationale et Formation de Base

M. Bernard Laborderie, European Union

M. Bruno Assemien, Ministère d'Enseignement Nationale et Formation de Base

M. Honorat Kacou, METFP

M. Kouassi Kouame, D.G. Budget

M. Koffi Koffi

M. Prosper Akmel Akpa, CEPCI

M. Legelin, Coopération Française

M. Eno Ephrem, Primature

M. Adiko Niamkey, UGTCI

M. Honorat Kacou, MET

M. Coullibaly Alassane, UGTCI

M. M. Guy Mbengue, APEXCI

Me N'Gata, Batonier

M. Desire Conde, FENADYS

M. Guy Terracol, Agence Française de Développement

M. Pierre Ewenczyk, International Monetary Fund

M. Aka Narcisse, Cour d'Arbitrage de Côte d'Ivoire

M. Traore Soungalo, CNPI

Students and faculty, CIRES, Université d'Abidjan

M. Demazere, Coopération Française

M. Aurelien Agbenouci, United Nations Development Programme

M. Seydou Ba, CCA de OHADA

Ministre Tidjane Thiam, PPPD

M. N'Doumi, Ministère d'Enseignement Superieur et Recherche Scientifique

Ministre Guy-Alain Gauze, Com Ext.

M. Francis Declerc, Pres. Comptables

S.E.M. Daniel Kablan Duncan

APPENDIX 7.3
CÔTE D'IVOIRE: STATISTICAL TABLES AND FIGURES

TABLE 7.8 CÔTE D'IVOIRE: TOTAL NET ODA BY DONOR TYPE, 1960–97

| | Millions of current U.S. dollars | | | Millions of 1996 constant U.S. dollars | | |
	Bilateral	Multilateral	Total	Bilateral	Multilateral	Total
1960	0.0	0.0	0.0	0.0	0.1	0.1
1961	1.0	2.1	3.1	6.5	13.7	20.2
1962	2.0	6.2	8.3	13.1	40.5	53.6
1963	2.1	5.8	7.9	13.7	37.5	51.2
1964	31.8	6.3	38.1	206.2	41.1	247.3
1965	27.8	9.7	37.4	180.0	62.8	242.8
1966	25.8	9.1	34.9	167.4	59.0	226.4
1967	27.4	5.6	33.0	171.4	35.2	206.6
1968	33.2	0.0	33.2	202.7	0.0	202.7
1969	37.4	12.3	49.7	218.5	71.9	290.4
1970	36.7	16.0	52.7	202.1	87.8	289.9
1971	39.5	11.7	51.2	201.0	59.5	260.5
1972	36.7	11.7	48.4	166.6	52.9	219.5
1973	49.4	14.1	63.5	189.2	53.8	243.0
1974	51.6	24.4	76.0	178.4	84.5	262.9
1975	71.7	28.9	100.6	217.5	87.7	305.2
1976	75.6	32.5	108.2	222.2	95.5	317.7
1977	75.2	31.1	106.3	201.8	83.5	285.3
1978	85.7	45.6	131.4	196.0	104.3	300.3
1979	138.6	22.9	161.5	284.3	47.0	331.4
1980	151.9	58.5	210.3	283.9	109.3	393.2
1981	91.2	32.5	123.7	178.6	63.7	242.3
1982	102.3	34.5	136.8	206.5	69.6	276.1
1983	140.7	15.0	155.8	286.5	30.6	317.1
1984	114.2	9.2	123.4	238.2	19.2	257.4
1985	110.5	7.1	117.6	228.2	14.6	242.8
1986	137.9	36.9	174.8	228.0	60.9	288.9
1987	221.3	19.5	240.8	316.3	27.9	344.2
1988	226.3	199.1	425.4	300.8	264.6	565.4
1989	260.1	135.4	395.5	349.5	182.0	531.5
1990	530.6	158.7	689.3	635.7	190.1	825.9
1991	434.7	198.0	632.7	503.4	229.3	732.7
1992	527.4	230.5	757.8	574.5	251.0	825.5
1993	708.7	56.5	765.1	790.6	63.0	853.6
1994	820.4	773.8	1594.2	877.8	827.9	1705.7
1995	726.7	485.8	1212.5	709.2	474.1	1183.3
1996	449.2	518.4	967.6	449.2	518.4	967.6
1997	232.7	211.3	444.0	250.5	227.4	478.0

Source: OECD-DAC.

TABLE 7.9 CÔTE D'IVOIRE: EDA FLOWS BY TYPE, 1970–96

	Millions of current U.S. dollars			Millions of 1996 constant U.S. dollars		
	Loans	Grants	Total	Loans	Grants	Total
1970	42.9	32.8	75.6	236.0	180.3	416.3
1971	39.1	34.0	73.0	198.8	172.9	371.7
1972	37.7	61.4	99.1	171.0	278.4	449.4
1973	64.2	49.4	113.6	245.7	188.9	434.6
1974	92.2	64.6	156.9	319.2	223.6	542.8
1975	95.9	72.0	167.9	291.1	218.5	509.7
1976	136.1	69.7	205.8	399.9	204.7	604.6
1977	190.2	74.7	264.9	510.6	200.5	711.1
1978	213.3	73.4	286.7	487.8	167.7	655.5
1979	281.0	107.8	388.7	576.5	221.1	797.6
1980	231.1	126.5	357.6	432.1	236.4	668.5
1981	516.0	73.5	589.4	1011.1	144.0	1155.1
1982	547.7	64.9	612.5	1105.7	131.0	1236.7
1983	552.1	97.2	649.3	1124.1	197.8	1321.9
1984	402.0	69.6	471.6	838.2	145.0	983.3
1985	218.6	59.0	277.6	451.3	121.8	573.1
1986	278.5	144.6	423.1	460.3	239.0	699.3
1987	561.2	119.3	680.5	802.2	170.5	972.7
1988	409.7	296.9	706.6	544.6	394.6	939.3
1989	432.8	275.5	708.3	581.7	370.2	951.9
1990	911.4	417.8	1329.2	1092.0	500.6	1592.6
1991	711.7	366.6	1078.3	824.2	424.6	1248.8
1992	650.8	323.5	974.3	708.9	352.4	1061.3
1993	628.7	336.6	965.4	701.5	375.6	1077.0
1994	918.1	798.3	1716.4	982.4	854.2	1836.6
1995	668.6	576.1	1244.7	652.4	562.2	1214.7
1996	464.8	609.0	1073.7	464.8	609.0	1073.7

Source: Chang, Fernández-Arias, and Servén 1999.

TABLE 7.10 CÔTE D'IVOIRE: TOTAL DISBURSEMENTS BY DONORS, 1970–96

	Millions of current U.S. dollars		Millions of 1996 constant U.S. dollars	
	Bilateral	Multilateral	Bilateral	Multilateral
1970	52.7	22.9	290.0	126.3
1971	54.2	18.9	275.6	96.1
1972	75.9	23.2	344.1	105.3
1973	81.5	32.0	312.0	122.6
1974	69.2	61.3	239.5	212.0
1975	101.6	66.3	308.4	201.2
1976	121.1	42.7	355.6	125.6
1977	175.8	89.1	471.9	239.2
1978	157.5	112.9	360.1	258.1
1979	291.5	97.3	598.0	199.6
1980	209.6	148.0	391.9	276.7
1981	137.8	75.3	269.9	147.6
1982	183.3	301.8	370.0	609.4
1983	249.5	234.2	507.9	476.8
1984	179.4	249.7	374.0	520.7
1985	119.8	96.5	247.3	199.2
1986	164.3	199.5	271.6	329.8
1987	234.5	446.0	335.1	637.5
1988	137.9	448.1	183.4	595.6
1989	330.1	340.6	443.7	457.7
1990	554.7	621.5	664.6	744.7
1991	439.2	593.8	508.7	687.7
1992	462.0	512.3	503.3	558.1
1993	767.7	197.5	856.5	220.3
1994	982.3	734.0	1051.0	785.4
1995	829.2	415.6	809.2	405.6
1996	622.8	450.9	622.8	450.9

Sources: OECD-DAC; Chang, Fernández-Arias, and Servén 1999.

TABLE 7.11 CÔTE D'IVOIRE: WORLD BANK POLICY-BASED LOANS, 1980–98

Loan	Type	Millions of U.S. dollars		Approval year
		Commitment	Disbursement	
SAL I	SAL	150	150	1981
SAL II	SAL	250.7	250.7	1983
SAL III	SAL	250	250	1986
Agriculture	SAD	150	150	1989
Energy	SAD	100	100	1989
Water	SAD	80	80	1990
Banking	SAD	300	200	1991
Human resources	SAD	335	235[a]	1991
Competitiveness	SAD	150	100	1991
Human resources	SAD	100	100	1994
Human resources	SAD/5th	85	85	1994
Financial sector	SAD	100	100	1994
Economic recovery	SAL	100	100	1994
Regulatory reform	SAL	50	50	1994
Economic recovery	SAD/5th	77.9	77.9	1994
Agricultural sector	SAD	150	150	1995
Agricultural sector	SAD/5th	73.6	73.6	1995
Private sector	SAD		180	1996
Private sector	SAD/5th	54.6	54.6	1996
Debt reduction	SAL	70	70	1997
Private sector	SAD/5th	36.6	36.6	1997
Transport sector	SAD	180	45[b]	1998

Note: SAL = Structural Adjustment Loan/Credit. SAD = Sector Adjustment Credit. SAD/5th = Supplemental credit with 5th dimension.
a. The US$100 million committed under the second and third tranches of the IBRD loan were canceled after the devaluation and restored as an IDA credit of US$100 million.
b. Credit not yet closed which has an investment component equivalent to US$80 million.
Source: World Bank.

TABLE 7.12 CÔTE D'IVOIRE: IMF POLICY-BASED LOANS

Loan	Time	Year	Millions of SDR		Millions of U.S. dollars	
			Amount approved	Amount drawn	Amount approved	Amount drawn
Enlarged Facility	3 years	1981		484.5		571.3
Stand by	1 year	1984		82.7		84.8
Stand by II	1 year	1985		66.2		67.2
Stand by III[a]	2 years	1986		24.0		28.2
Stand by IV	1 year	1988		94.0		126.3
Stand by V	2 years	1989	146.5	117.2	187.8	150.2
Stand by VI	1 year	1991	82.8	33.0	113.2	45.2
ESAF	3 years	1994	333.5	333.5	477.5	477.5
ESAF	3 years	1998	286.0		388.0	

a. Loan cancelled.

Sources: IMF; *Marchés Tropicaux.*

TABLE 7.13 CÔTE D'IVOIRE: MULTILATERAL DEBT AGREEMENTS WITH OFFICIAL CREDITORS, 1980–98

Date of agreement	Contract cutoff date	Consolidation period for current maturities		Consolidation includes		Share of debt consolidated (%)	Amount consolidated (millions of U.S. dollars)	Repayment terms	
		Start date	Length, months	Arrears	Previously rescheduled debt			Maturity years/ months	Grace years/ months
4 May 84	1 July 83	1 Dec 83	13	—	—	100	265	8/6	4/0
25 Jun 85	1 July 83	1 Jan 85	12	—	—	100	215	8/6	4/0
27 Jun 86	1 July 83	1 Jan 86	36	—	—	Variable	157	8/7	4/1
18 Dec 87	1 July 83	1 Jan 88	16	Yes	Yes	100	931	9/4	5/10
18 Dec 89	1 July 83	1 Jan 90	16	Yes	Yes	100	1,116	13/4	5/10
20 Nov 91	1 July 83	1 Oct 91	12	Yes	Yes	100	768	14/6	8/0
22 Mar 94	1 July 83	1 Mar 94	37	Yes	Yes	100	1,943	Menu[b]	Menu
24 Apr 98	1 July 83	1 Apr 98	36	Yes	Yes	100	1,402	Menu	Menu

— Not available.

a. 80 percent of principal due in 1986, 70 percent of principal due in 1987, and 60 percent of principal due in 1988.
b. "Menu" terms refer to the option agreed to at the 1988 Toronto economic summit meeting.
Source: World Bank, Global Development Finance 1997.

FIGURE 7.7 CÔTE D'IVOIRE: BILATERAL OFFICIAL DEVELOPMENT
FINANCE FLOWS, 1975–96

Millions of 1996 constant U.S. dollars

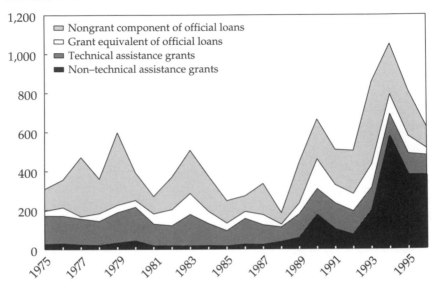

Source: Chang, Fernández-Arias, and Servén 1999.

FIGURE 7.8 CÔTE D'IVOIRE: MULTILATERAL DEVELOPMENT
FINANCE FLOWS, 1975–96

Millions of 1996 constant U.S. dollars

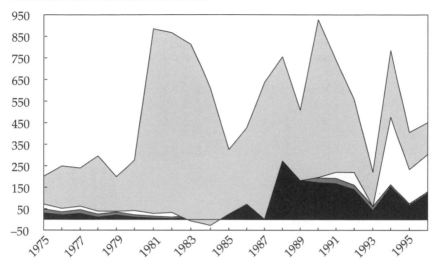

☐ Nongrant component of official loans
☐ Grant equivalent of official loans
▨ Technical assistance grants
■ Non–technical assistance grants

Notes: Official loans include IMF concessional loans (SAF and ESAF) and nonconcessional loans (enhanced facility and standby agreement).
Source: Chang, Fernández-Arias, and Servén 1999.

FIGURE 7.9 CÔTE D'IVOIRE: COMPOSITION OF NET PRIVATE
FLOWS, 1960–97

Millions of 1996 constant U.S. dollars

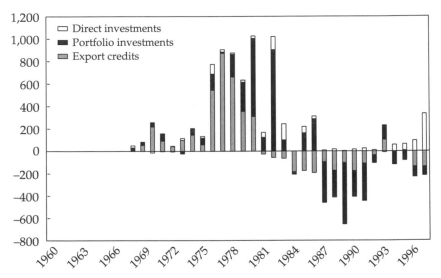

Source: OECD-DAC.

FIGURE 7.10 CÔTE D'IVOIRE: DEBT RATIOS, 1975–96

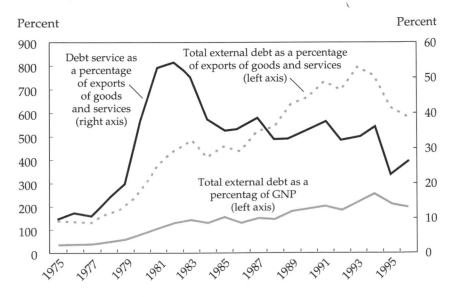

Source: World Bank, *Global Development Finance 1998.*

NOTES

1. "All official loans" excludes bilateral loans made for military and defense purposes.

2. Conventional net ODA accounts for debt relief by recording a fictitious disbursement matched with an equally fictitious loan repayment, with no effect on net ODA totals.

3. These data come not from the tables but from "Report and Recommendations of the President of the International Development Association to the Executive Directors on Assistance to the Republic of Côte d'Ivoire under the HIPC Debt Initiative" (World Bank 1998e).

4. In the four-year period 1994–97, the RCI received more than a third of all the adjustment lending that the Bank provided to Sub-Saharan Africa (World Bank 1999a: 8).

5. Interview with the Mission d'Aide et de Coopération in Abidjan in August 1999.

6. The other member states are Benin, Burkina Faso, Guinea Bissau (since 1997), Mali, Niger, Senegal, and Togo.

7. Caisse Française de Coopération Economique later became Caisse Française de Développement Economique and then Agence Française de Développement.

8. These figures come from research at the Centre de Recherche sur le Développement International (CERDI), Université de l'Auvergne, which estimated real effective exchange rates (as the ratio of consumer prices in Côte d'Ivoire to those of its main trading partners for import, expressed in the same currency).

9. The level reached in 1992 was about 36 percent of the average level during the first half of the 1970s.

10. Staff of the IMF, who are accustomed to working under tighter discipline, seem to have been more discreet.

11. French policymakers reasoned that it was important that Côte d'Ivoire continue its payments and also that France maintain its role of guarantor that it had assumed in relation to the Bretton Woods institutions when it pushed them in 1991 to start lending again.

12. See the analysis of these measures in Guillaumont and Guillaumont Jeanneney 1994.

13. Law 60-273 of September 1960, revised by law of December 21, 1964. These controls had three modalities or regimes: taxation, "homologation," and market determination. Under the taxation regime, prices were set by government decrees based on average cost and profit margins. This price regime concerned a limited number of basic necessity goods. In the homologation regime, the administration approved the price set on the basis of elements justified by appropriate documentation. Under the market-determined regime, buyers and sellers were free to set their prices.

14. See Bamba, Kouassy, and Pegatienan 1999. The investment code and the tariff reform of 1973 were testimony to the political objective of industrialization. This political resolve to industrialize was taken in the context of a competition between Côte d'Ivoire and Senegal in the former French West Africa. Senegal was the former capital of this political entity. It had a good port and a relatively advanced industrial base. There was also political competition between socialist-type economic policies favored by, among others, Senegal, Guinea, and Ghana, and capitalist-type economic policies adopted by Côte d'Ivoire. Finally, there was personal competition for regional leadership between Houphouët-Boigny and his African colleagues.

15. According to a 1996 study, the rate of maternal mortality (deaths during pregnancy, at delivery, or up to six weeks after) in Abidjan was 428 per 100,000 live births. Although this was half the rate estimated for rural areas in the RCI, it was substantially higher than that in Ouagadougou, Bamako, Nouakchott, and Niamey (Brunet-Jailly 1999: 82).

16. In 1981 French TA personnel in education numbered 3,247, and there were 255 in health (and social development). By 1990 the numbers were 1,273 and 94; and by 1998 there were only 130 in education and fewer than 25 in health.

17. Teachers' wages absorbed three times as much of government revenue in RCI as they did in East Asia and 10 times as much as in industrial countries.

18. The main source of reform measures in the first half of the 1990s was the conditionality in the Human Resources Development Project, which was designed in the late 1980s. Disbursements on the US$360 million project began in 1991. The Bank was the main designer and funder, but other donors participated.

19. These included calls for more cost recovery, for creation of health districts to manage resources allocated to the regions, and for some budget changes, notably more transparent presentation and definition of a core investment program with simplified financial procedures that would allow speedier implementation (World Bank and others 1995).

20. This discussion draws on World Bank 1999b, vol. 1, and World Bank 1995.

21. Its efficiency-enhancing impacts, however, were undercut by relative price changes. Because of the devaluation-induced increase in prices of traded goods, the purchasing power of nonsalary budgets actually fell in real terms between 1993 and 1997.

22. In the mid-1990s, each secondary student received a subsidy of CFAF 118,000 a year, or 1.8 times the amount received per primary student. According to a recent comparative study, only Tanzania's ratio was smaller (1.1 times), while in Ghana, Uganda, and Kenya the ratio was close to 3. At the tertiary level the RCI subsidized each student to the tune of CFAF 348,000, or 5.4 times the primary subsidy. This is far better than Ghana (16 times), Guinea (55 times), Kenya (31 times), or Uganda (32 times). See Castro-Leal and others 1999.

23. The primary subsector investment share rose to 23 percent in 1996, then to 30 percent in 1997. Investment in the tertiary subsector fell from 51 percent in 1996 to 41 percent in 1997 (Shephard 1999).

24. This refers to recurrent budgets. The primary subsector share of the total health budget remained around 28 percent between 1991 and 1996, before rising to 32 percent in 1996 and 1997.

25. This is about the same distribution of benefits as in Uganda (Castro-Leal and others 1999).

26. World Bank 1994 presents a devastating analysis of the way things were.

27. According to one observer of the Projet d'Appui à la Gestion des Resources Humaines (PAGRH) in 1995, despite the new approach to technical assistance embodied in this project (give the tools and the process to the people concerned and let them do the work themselves), the responsible local staff in the recipient agencies and the national counterparts are not always involved in the work done by the experts.

28. Continuing management weakness is underscored in the Programme Nationale pour le Développement de la Santé, 1996–2005, which observes: "Because of the absence of planning and methodological weaknesses in programming and budgeting we are unable to control personnel numbers, our budget preparation remains thin and the monitoring of budget implementation inadequate" (Programme Nationale pour le Développement de la Santé, 1996–2005, vol. 1: 28, cited in World Bank 1998f).

29. The case of magistrates is cited. As part of judicial reform 50 magistrates a year were to be hired in the late 1990s. But according to one report, not one of the numerous candidates received a passing grade on the qualifying examination—that is, a grade that was above the normal bar. The best candidates have nonetheless been hired.

30. This account comes from interviews with only a few people, most of them critical of the Bank. Its reliability has to be judged accordingly. Much is surely left out.

31. AGEPE had 90 employees in 1995, 70 percent of whom came from OMOCI.

32. According to the Implementation Completion Report of the Private Sector Development Adjustment Credit (World Bank 1999d): "AGEPE's . . . fees are retained by the agency for funding its programs, including credit for employment creation. These programs are a waste of resources. The repayment rate under its credit schemes is less than 10 percent. It is not monitoring employment satisfactorily. Its analysis of employment in the modern sector for 1996 was not available in October 1998. . . . The government should commission an audit of AGEPE, and consider reallocating its resources (about CFAF 2.5 billion a year, i.e., about one-half of the budget allocated to the Ministry of Justice) to more useful purposes."

33. The Chambre des Comptes of the Supreme Court, one of the three *chambres* comprising the Court, received in 1993 some 150 financial accounts from municipalities and public enterprises for approval. It passed on 30 of them, sug-

gesting a five to six year backlog. Misfiling and lost pieces of files were common. After hearings, *arrêts* were not public and parts of the file were returned to the parties.

34. According to a November 1995 Ministry of Justice analysis: "It has to be admitted that lawyers, judges, private operators and even some *greffiers* are unanimous in their denunciation of the functioning of the *greffes* as a major— probably *the main*—obstacle to rapid and transparent justice: the dossiers or the *greffiers* themselves do not show up for hearings, forcing their postponement; important papers from files get lost and can never be found, dossiers are not kept up to date; numerous court decisions await typing, and final disposition of cases usually takes one to two years, even more if the *greffier* is not paid off (*motivé*)."

35. At least five World Bank projects had relevant components: PASCO, a competitiveness and regulatory reform project (1991); PAGE, economic management support (1991); financial sector adjustment (1992); PSD, private sector development (1996); and PSD capacity building (1998).

36. Revision of commercial and company law was a major reform component that had been the Bank's responsibility under the Economic Management Support Project of 1991 (PAGE). This was taken over by OHADA.

37. See, for example, Messick 1999: 117–136; Berg 1977: 492–530; Blair and Hansen.

38. In 1996 the MOJ budget request was CFAF 9.3 billion. It received CFAF 5.7 billion. Its 1997 request was for CFAF 12.1 billion, and it received CFAF 5.3 billion. The entire operating budget is 0.4 percent of the national budget. The Cours d'Appel receives CFAF 750,000 (US$12,500) a year. Each court *section* is allocated CFAF 120,000 (US$200) for operating costs. Most of the financing of court operations comes from fees and tax-like charges imposed on plaintiffs and defendants (Côte d'Ivoire 1999). Fee charges are discussed below, where greffier problems are considered.

39. The following paragraphs draw on Ghelber 1996.

40. The amounts collected, estimated salaries for bénévoles and other operating costs, and "net profits" to greffiers vary enormously from court to court.

41. In many industrial countries 30 percent of private arbitration awards are contested by one of the parties. The case is then submitted to some appeals procedure and if procedures are judged appropriate and the award well founded, it goes to the courts for implementation. Judging from existing practices in the RCI, more than 30 percent of awards may be contested and require court action. This may dilute its effectiveness. More pertinent probably is the concern about the prospects for OHADA's institutions. The Magistrate's School is located in Benin. It may not have the resources needed for high-quality training, and the costs of bringing participants from distant UMEOA member countries may be excessive. Similarly, the Common Court of Justice and Arbitration, which is in Abidjan, may compete with the Cour d'Arbitrage de Côte d'Ivoire, and maintenance of its complement of seven judges may be very expensive. Costs of travel

to and subsistence in Abidjan also may restrict use of the court by other UMEOA countries to a few large cases.

42. The Ghelber report (1996) put it as follows: "That the present [greffe] system has become so well entrenched and has been able to survive so much criticism means that it benefits somebody. Most legal professionals believe that the *greffier-en-chef* is the key to it. In addition to his salary, he collects and manages various service fees that are not monitored or controlled, and for which there is no detailed accounting . . . The government and those who must use judicial services are the losers in this arrangement. The clear gainers (other than the *greffiers*) are those who have been judged liable but do not pay what they owe, partly because they resort to delaying tactics permitted by existing procedures, and partly because of the neglect or actual complicity of implementing agents who discreetly share the revenues of the *greffier-en-chef*, directly or by devices like personal loans . . .

"There are also those people called *margouillats*, informal intermediaries who promise to help plaintiffs or defendants for a price. It is depressing to observe the spectacle in the corridors and environs of the Palais de Justice, where bribery propositions fill the air . . . The large array of Mercedes and other luxury cars occupying the places reserved for judges on the parking lot of the Palais de Justice poses the question of the honesty of magistrates whose style of life is far more luxurious than can be financed by their official remuneration."

43. Much of the TA provided was local. The value added is presumably the energizing of otherwise poorly motivated local expertise. But net impact must take account of diversion of local skills from important assignments, for example, when a senior civil servant becomes a project director or adviser.

REFERENCES

Bamba, N., O. Kouassy, and H. J. Pegatienan. 1999. "Policy-Making and Implementation in Côte d'Ivoire: Example of Selective Trade and Strategic Industrial Policies." Abidjan.

Blair, Harry, and Gary Hansen. 1994. "Weighing in on the Scales of Justice: Strategic Approaches for Donor-Supported Rule of Law Programs." Program and Operations Assessment Report 7. U.S. Agency for International Development, Washington, D.C.

Bohoun, B. 1996. "Politiques industrielles et commerciales et croissance economique." Centre Ivoirien de Recherch Economique et Social (CIRES), Abidjan.

Brunet-Jailly, J. 1999. "Santé en Capitales. La Dynamique des systèmes de santé des capitales ouest-africaines." Coopération Française, Abidjan.

Burg, Elliot M. 1977. "Law and Development: A Review of the Literature and a Critique of Scholars in Self-Estrangement." *American Journal of Comparative Law* 25: 492–530.

Calipel, Stéphanie, and Sylvanie Guillaumont Jeanneney. 1996. "Dévaluation, chocs externes et politique économique en Côte d'Ivoire. Analyse de leurs effets respectifs à partir d'un modèle d'équilibre général calculable." *Revue d'Economie du Développement* 4 (3): 65–97.

Castro-Leal, Florencia, Julia Dayton, Lionel Demery, and Kalpana Mehra. 1999. "Public Social Spending in Africa: Do the Poor Benefit?" World Bank Research Observer *14 (1): 49–72.*

CERDI (Centre de Recherche sur le Développement International). 1996. *Etude macroéconomique de la Côte d'Ivoire après la dévaluation.* Study coordinated by Patrick Guillaumont, Sylvanie Guillaumont Jeanneney, and G. Chambas for the Ministère de la Coopération. Université de l'Auvergne, Clermont-Ferrand, France. 299 pp.

Chang, Charles C., Eduardo Fernández-Arias, and Luis Servén. 1999. "Measuring Aid Flows: A New Approach." Policy Research Working Paper 2050. World Bank, Development Research Group, Washington, D.C.

Contamin, B. 1997. "Competivité et promotion des exportations des produits ivoiriens." CIRES, Abidjan.

Côte d'Ivoire. 1989. "Schema directeur du développement industriel de la Côte d'Ivoire." Ministère de l'Industrie. Abidjan.

———. 1998a. "La qualité des services de santé; enquête preliminaire." By Michel Garenne and others. Ministère de la Santé Publique, Commission Européenne, VIIIème FED.

———. 1998b. *Rapport Annuel 1997.* Comité de mobilisation des financements extérieures et de suivi des investissements publics. Abidjan.

———. 1999. "Table Ronde sur la Justice; Project de Document Preparatoire." Ministère de Justice, Abidjan.

Geourjon, A. M. 1996. In CERDI, *Etude macroéconomique de la Côte d'Ivoire après la dévaluation.* Study coordinated by Patrick Guillaumont, Sylvanie Guillaumont Jeanneney, and G. Chambas for the Ministère de la Coopération. Université de l'Auvergne, Clermont-Ferrand, France.

Ghelber Consultants. 1996. "Etude sur les greffes en Côte d'Ivoire." Draft report. Paris.

Guillaumont, Patrick, and Sylvanie Guillaumont Jeanneney. 1994. "La zone franc, les Institutions de Bretton-Woods et la conditionnalité." *Revue d'économie financière* (December): 443–57. Numéro spécial Bretton-Woods. *Mélanges pour un cinquantenaire.* Also published in *La France et les Institutions de Bretton-Woods 1944–1994.* Ministère de l'Economie, dês Finances et de l'Industrie, Paris. 1998. Pp. 197–201.

———. 1995a. "Ebranlement et consolidation des fondements des francs CFA." *Revue d'économie du développement* (3): 87–111.

———. 1995b. "La conditionnalité à l'épreuve des faits." In R. Rainelli, ed., *La négociation commerciale et financière internationale.* Economica. Paris.

Hinkle, Lawrence E., and Peter J. Montiel. 1999. *Exchange Rate Misalignment Concepts and Measurements for Developing Countries.* New York: Oxford University Press.

Hopkins, Michael. 1989. "Adjustment and Poverty in Côte d'Ivoire, 1980–1989." World Bank, Washington, D.C.

Jones, Christine, and Xiao Ye. 1997. "Issues in Comparing Poverty Trends Over Time in Côte d'Ivoire." Policy Research Working Paper 1711. World Bank, Development Research Group, Washington, D.C.

Messick, Richard E. 1999. "Judicial Reform and Economic Development: A Survey of the Issues." *World Bank Research Observer* 14 (1): 117–36.

Mogedal, S., S. Hodne Steen, and G. Mpellmbe. 1995. "Health Sector Reform and Organizational Issues at the Local Level: Lessons from Selected African Countries." *Journal of International Development* 7 (3): 349–67.

Ouayogode, B., and Jacques Pegatienan. 1994. "The Relations between the World Bank and Côte d'Ivoire." A study for the World Bank History Project. Abidjan.

Serageldin, Ismail. 1988. "La Banque Mondiale en Afrique: L'ajustement, voie de la croissance et de l'équité." *Le Courrier CEE-ACP* (September–October): 54–61.

Shephard, Donald S., coordinator. 1999. "Analyse du Programme des Investissements Publics du Secteur Santé de la Côte d'Ivoire." Ministère de Santé, Abidjan.

World Bank. 1994. "Côte d'Ivoire. Revue des Investissements Publics: 1994." Abidjan.

———. 1995. "Implementation Completion Report: Human Resources Development Program." Report 14841. Washington, D.C.

———. 1996. "Examen des Dépenses Publiques en Côte d'Ivoire. Secteur Education." Abidjan.

———. 1997. "Côte d'Ivoire Country Assistance Review." Washington.

———. 1998a. *Assessing Aid: What Works, What Doesn't, and Why.* New York: Oxford University Press.

———. 1998b. "Côte d'Ivoire: Bilan et Perspectives, 1991–2000." Washington.

———. 1998c. "Côte d'Ivoire: Client Feedback Survey, 1997." Africa Region, Washington, D.C.

———. 1998d. "Côte d'Ivoire: Education and Training Support Project." Project Appraisal Report 17770. Washington, D.C.

———. 1998e. "Report and Recommendations of the President of the International Development Association to the Executive Directors on Assistance to the Republic of Côte d'Ivoire under the HIPC Debt Initiative." Project Appraisal Report P7229. Washington, D.C.

———. 1998f. "Revue Annuelle du Projet de Développement des Services du Santé Integrés et du Recensement." Abidjan.

———. 1999a. "Côte d'Ivoire Country Assistance Review." Report 19422. Operations Evaluation Department, Washington, D.C.

———. 1999b. "Côte d'Ivoire, Revue des Dépenses Publiques, 2 vols, 1991 à 1998." Abidjan.

———. 1999c. "Examen des Dépenses Publiques en Côte d'Ivoire. Secteur Education." Abidjan.

————. 1999d. "Implementation Completion Report. Private Sector Development Adjustment Credit (PSDAC)." Washington, D.C.

————. 1998c. "Revue Annuelle du Projet de Développement des Services de Santé Integrés et du Recensement." Abidjan.

————. Union Européenne, Coopération Française, and Coopération Belge. 1995. "Revue des dépenses publiques de Santé. Documents intermediaires." Bruxelles.

Kenya

F. S. O'Brien
Washington, D.C.

Terry C. I. Ryan
University of Nairobi
Nairobi, Kenya

ACRONYMS AND ABBREVIATIONS

ADF	African Development Fund
AfDB	African Development Bank
ASAO	Agricultural Sector Adjustment Operation
BOP	Balance of payments
CBK	Central Bank of Kenya
CG	Consultative Group
CPI	Consumer price index
DAC	Development Assistance Committee (of the OECD)
EAC	East African Community
EC	European Commission
EDA	Effective development assistance
EDP	Export Development Program
EDSAC	Education Sector Adjustment Credit
ESAF	Enhanced Structural Adjustment Facility (of the IMF)
FY	Fiscal year
GDP	Gross domestic product
GPCO	General Price Control Order
IBRD	International Bank for Reconstruction and Development (of the World Bank Group)
ICOR	Incremental capital-output ratio
IDA	International Development Association (of the World Bank Group)
IMF	International Monetary Fund
KANU	Kenya African National Union
KSh	Kenya shilling
LIBOR	London interbank offered rate
NCPB	National Cereals and Produce Board
ODA	Official development assistance
OECD	Organisation for Economic Co-operation and Development
QR	Quantitative restriction on imports
SAC	Structural Adjustment Credit
SAL	Structural Adjustment Loan
SAP	Structural adjustment program
SDR	Special drawing right (of the IMF)
SECAL	Sectoral Adjustment Loan/Credit
SOE	State-owned enterprise
SP	Sessional paper
SPA	Special Program of Assistance (for Sub-Saharan Africa)
SPCO	Specific Price Control Order
SSA	Sub-Saharan Africa
TA	Technical assistance
UNCTAD	United Nations Conference on Trade and Development
UNDP	United Nations Development Programme

This study focuses on the years between 1980 and 1998, the period in which the Kenyan government was engaged in implementing a program of structural adjustment reforms with financial support from the World Bank, the International Monetary Fund, and other multilateral and bilateral donors. It also presents background on political and economic trends in Kenya during the earlier post-independence years, from 1963 to 1980, in order to explain the economic problems and policy framework that prevailed in Kenya when structural adjustment programs were introduced at the beginning of the 1980s.

Section 2 of the paper describes the trend of aid flows to Kenya between 1970 and 1996, emphasizing the policy-based lending linked to structural adjustment reforms that became a major component of Kenya's resource inflow after 1980. Section 3 examines the broad outlines of political and economic developments in Kenya, first for the 1963–80 period and then for the period of structural adjustment, 1980–98. It presents an overview of the economic policy reform agenda as it evolved during the latter period, followed by details of specific reforms in the areas of macroeconomic management, trade policy, public sector management, and agricultural policy, and their time path and sequencing. This section concludes with a discussion of the part that key Kenyan individuals and institutions played in generating policy reform initiatives, in translating reform proposals into policy actions, and in implementing reform programs. Finally, section 4 explores linkages between the timing and volume of aid flows and the adoption of policy reforms in Kenya.

AID FLOWS

Between 1970 and 1996, Kenya experienced a strong, steady buildup in nominal flows of official development assistance (ODA).[1] Gross ODA inflows increased from an annual average of US$205 million in the 1970s to more than US$630 million in the 1980s, and to slightly over US$1 billion in 1990–96 (see table 8.5 in Appendix 8.3). In per capita terms, nominal gross aid flows rose from an annual average of $15 in the 1970s to $34 in the 1980s and almost $40 in the1990s. At the peak in 1990–91, net ODA inflows were equivalent to 14 percent of Kenya's gross domestic product (GDP) and to approximately 45 percent of the government budget.

This impressive growth in nominal aid inflows shows that Kenya has followed the pattern for Sub-Saharan Africa (SSA) as a whole. Kenya's share of total development aid to SSA remained remarkably stable over this entire period, as shown in table 8.1.

These data tell only part of the story, however. Certain qualifications must be added in order to see the whole picture. On the positive side,

471

TABLE 8.1 KENYA'S SHARE OF TOTAL ODA TO SUB-SAHARAN
AFRICA, 1970–96
(billions of U.S. dollars)

Period	Kenya's ODA	Africa's ODA[a]	Kenya's share (percent)
1970–79	2.055	39.157	5.2
1980–89	6.732	127.644	5.3
1990–96	7.069	136.635	5.2
1970–96	15.856	302.836	5.2

Note: ODA (official development assistance) includes both concessional loans (those with a grant element of at least 25 percent according to the DAC definition) and grants. Grants include both technical cooperation and debt relief on previous ODA loans. All data in current prices.
a. Data cover the 49 principal aid-receiving countries in Sub-Saharan Africa.
Sources: Loan data from World Bank Debtor Reporting System; grant data from OECD-DAC.

Kenya benefited from the fact that the terms of its ODA softened over this period. The share of grants increased, rising from 48 percent in the 1970s to 53 percent in the 1980s and to more than 63 percent in the 1990s.[2] The breakdown of ODA into loans and grants is shown in table 8.6 in Appendix 8.3. (In this regard Kenya has lagged slightly behind the overall trend in Sub-Saharan Africa: the grant share in ODA to all of SSA increased from 52 percent in the 1970s to 67 percent in the 1990s.) On the negative side, the gross ODA data for the 1986–92 period are overstated because they include debt relief from bilateral donors on past ODA loans of approximately US$700 million (which the Development Assistance Committee includes in grant aid in the year that relief is provided). The data on gross ODA excluding debt relief are given in table 8.7 in Appendix 8.3, which also provides data on net ODA in current and constant prices.

Two important conclusions can be drawn from these data series. First, while there was a dramatic buildup in nominal aid flows during the 1980s, in both gross and net terms, there has been a slackening of donor support in the 1990s, resulting in a sharp decline in inflows since the peak in 1989–90. Second, when aid flows are measured in real terms, this decline has brought aid inflows in recent years down to a level well below that of the middle and late 1980s, and even below the real value of aid disbursements in 1980.

Bilateral/Multilateral Breakdown of ODA

Table 8.8 in Appendix 8.3 provides a breakdown of gross aid disbursements to Kenya according to their multilateral and bilateral sources over the 1970–96 period. Kenya received approximately three-fourths of its total aid from bilateral donors, with no distinct trend toward greater reliance on either multilateral or bilateral aid. The share of multilateral aid increased moderately in the 1980s, primarily due to the large disbursements of World Bank adjustment lending, but the bilateral share rose again in the 1990s with the decline in new adjustment lending after 1991.

Bilateral aid has been mainly in the form of grants (72 percent of the total), with the share of grants actually increasing in recent years, whereas multilateral aid has been mainly in the form of loans (86 percent). The principal source of multilateral loans has been the World Bank Group, accounting for almost 80 percent of total loans in the 1970–96 period.[3] The African Development Bank (AfDB) accounted for 11 percent.

While the overall shares of multilateral and bilateral aid sources have not changed markedly over time, there have been significant changes within the two categories. Table 8.9 in Appenidx 8.3 shows the shares in total ODA by periods for the major donors/creditors. The World Bank, which accounted for 20 percent of total flows in the 1970s and 1980s, saw its share of total disbursements fall to 16 percent in the 1990s because of the growing importance of certain bilateral donors, the significant reduction in disbursements for balance of payments support since the early 1990s, and a shrinking portfolio of project loans. The other principal multilateral agencies, the AfDB and the European Commission (EC), have each contributed a much smaller share of Kenya's ODA.

With respect to bilateral assistance, Kenya has for many years received aid from virtually all aid-giving nations and agencies. In addition to those shown in table 8.9 in Appendix 8.3, Kenya has also received aid from Australia, Austria, Belgium, China, Ireland, the Republic of Korea, Spain, Switzerland, and various Middle Eastern governments and aid agencies.

Among the notable trends within the bilateral group has been the decline in the share of the United Kingdom, which was Kenya's leading development partner in the immediate post-independence years of the 1960s and early 1970s. The nominal value of U.K. aid has risen only modestly over the years, from an average of US$37 million per year in the 1970s to US$62 million per year in the 1980s, falling back to US$55 million per year in the 1990s. Over this same period Japanese aid increased from 4 percent of gross ODA in the 1970s to 17 percent in the 1990s. Japan's annual average ODA to Kenya increased from insignificant levels in the early 1970s to US$60 million per year in the 1980s and to US$170 million per year in the 1990s. This is not an unmixed blessing, however, since Japanese aid (like French aid) has a high share of loans to grants compared to the rest of Kenya's ODA (60 percent loans in the 1990s). Another significant trend has been the declining share of many medium-size donors, including the Scandinavian countries, Canada, and the Netherlands. Sweden's aid has actually fallen in nominal terms, from an average of US$25 million per year in the 1980s to US$23.5 million per year in 1990–96. The trend is even more pronounced for Norway, with which Kenya actually broke diplomatic relations during 1990–95: Norwegian aid disbursements fell from US$25 million per year in the 1980s to US$2.5 million per year in 1992–96.

There are obvious reasons why Kenya has received such a large inflow of aid over many years from such a wide range of aid partners. Generally speaking, the primary motivations for providing aid are developmental (to promote economic growth and poverty alleviation in poor countries); commercial (to cement commercial and financial relations with the aid recipient, open markets, and ensure opportunities for investors, contractors, and suppliers from the aid-giving country); and political (to maintain the allegiance of governments that are politically aligned with the donor, an especially prominent feature of aid relationships during the Cold War era). Kenya, since independence in 1963, was a logical candidate to receive aid for all of the above reasons. First, the government's management of the economy was prudent and the economic track record was relatively good, at least through the 1970s. Despite a mixed record on economic policy reform and macroeconomic outcomes in the 1980s, Kenya still performed better than most African countries. Second, Kenya was for many years a relatively attractive locale for foreign investment, at least within the SSA context; it especially attracted consumer goods industries targeted at the East African market before the collapse of the East African Community (EAC) in 1977. Third, throughout the Cold War years Kenya consistently aligned itself with the West both economically and politically.

However, the end of the Cold War in 1989, which essentially eliminated the geopolitical motivation for aid, coincided with a weakening of economic reform efforts. Kenya's economic performance deteriorated between 1989 and 1992. There was, as well, a hardening of political lines within the country just as donors were adding "good governance" and democratization to their criteria for judging the worthiness of aid recipients. The result was an intensification of the "stop-go" relationship between donors and the Kenyan government, which has persisted to the present. This is discussed in more detail below.

Technical Assistance

Table 8.10 in Appendix 8.3 provides annual data on grant aid for technical assistance (TA). In the 1970s a high proportion of bilateral grant aid (58 percent for the decade) was devoted to TA; at that time donors were financing most development *projects* through loans. During the 1980s, as bilateral donors shifted an increasing proportion of their project assistance to grant terms, the share of technical assistance in total grant assistance began to decline, to 39 percent in the 1980s and 36 percent in the 1990s. However, the absolute amounts expended for TA have remained extremely high, averaging US$140 million per year in the 1980s and US$225 million per year in the 1990s.

Since 1970 Kenya has received more than US$3.5 billion of grant assistance for TA. Much of this, of course, is money that the Kenyan government itself does not receive, since it is paid directly to resident advisers, or to education and training institutions outside Kenya, by the aid-giving country or international agency. And it is certainly open to question whether overall human resource capacity building and institutional strengthening in the Kenyan government has been commensurate with this level of expenditures. There are many well documented causes of the generally disappointing record of technical assistance in Africa on both the donor and recipient sides, but any discussion of these deficiencies is beyond the scope of this paper (see, for example, Berg 1993).

Nevertheless, within this massive amount of TA finance one component stands out as important for the focus of this study: the assistance that has been provided for more than 30 years for the training of Kenyan economists and other officials from the key economic ministries and agencies (Finance, Planning, and the Central Bank) and for the provision of foreign advisers and advisory teams to these core agencies. This TA has undoubtedly influenced the analytical capabilities of Kenyan technocrats and institutions and their approach to analyzing economic issues, as is discussed more fully below.

Adjustment or Program Lending

Kenya, like many other African countries, has received a very sizable amount of lending for balance of payments support, also referred to as program lending, and, since 1980, identified with structural adjustment programs (SAPs). Most of this lending has come from the World Bank and the International Monetary Fund (IMF), with smaller amounts from the AfDB and bilateral donors, the latter often linked to World Bank–supported adjustment programs. A complete listing of IMF and World Bank/International Development Association (IDA) adjustment lending to Kenya is provided in table 8.2. Data on total disbursements of adjustment loans from all sources is provided in table 8.11 in Appendix 8.3.

Kenya first received loans for balance of payments support in the mid-1970s in response to the first "oil crisis." These included a US$30 million program loan from the World Bank and US$128 million from the IMF through the Special Oil Facility, Compensatory Financing Facility, and Extended Fund Facility. (The IMF credits were not fully used and were allowed to lapse when the balance of payments situation improved following the coffee boom of 1976–77.) Such program loans were not a com-

TABLE 8.2 IMF AND WORLD BANK/IDA POLICY REFORM LOANS
TO KENYA, 1974–96

		IMF	
Year	Loan type	Amount (millions of SDRs)	Comments
1974	Oil Facility	63.9	Drawn during 1974–76.
1975	Extended Facility	67.2	Only SDR 7.7million drawn.
1975	Standby	12.0	Drawn and fully repaid in same year.
1976	Compensatory Facility	24.0	
1978	Standby	17.25	Fully disbursed by August 1979.
1979	Standby	122.5	Not drawn, canceled 14 October 1980.
1979	Supplemental Facility	70.7	Not drawn, canceled 14 October 1980.
1979	Compensatory Facility	69.0	
1980	Standby	241.5	Only SDR 90 million drawn, canceled 7 January 1982.
1980	Supplemental Facility	184.8	Only SDR 50.1 million drawn, canceled 7 January 1982.
1982	Standby	151.5	Only SDR 90 million drawn, canceled 7 January 1983.
1982	Supplemental Facility	96.8	
1982	Compensatory Facility	60.4	
1983	Standby	175.9	
1985	Standby	85.2	
1986	Compensatory Facility	37.9	
1988	Standby	85.0	Only SDR 62.6 million drawn, canceled 15 May 1989.
1988	Structural Adjustment Facility	99.4	Only SDR 28.4 million drawn, replaced by ESAF 15 May 1989.
1989	Enhanced Structural Adjustment Facility	261.4	SDR 216.2 million drawn prior to November 1991, was suspended January 1992, expired March 1993. Balance renegotiated December 1993, drawn by December 1994.
1996	Enhanced Structural Adjustment Facility	149.6	Only SDR 25.0 million drawn, suspended July 1997, expired April 1999.

(continued on next page)

mon practice for the World Bank at that time, having been confined
largely to India and Bangladesh. This mid-1970s program lending and
associated IMF drawings carried very low conditionality since the
Kenyan economy had been performing well up to that point, economic

TABLE 8.2—*continued*

		World Bank	
Year	Loan type	Amount (millions of U.S. dollars)	Comments
1975	Program Loan	30.0	
1980	Structural Adjustment Loan I	55.0	IDA lending terms.
1982	Structural Adjustment Loan II	130.9	$70.0 million on IDA terms, $60.9 million on IBRD terms.
1986	Agricultural Sector Adjustment Operation I	40.0	IDA terms. Also IDA reflows of $20.8 million.
1988	Industrial Sector Adjustment	102.0	IDA terms. Also IDA reflows of $63.1 million.
1989	Financial Sector Adjustment	120.0	IDA terms. Also IDA reflows of $114.6 million.
1990	Export Development Program	100.0	IDA terms. Also IDA reflows of $53.0 million.
1991	Agricultural Sector Adjustment Operation II	75.0	IDA terms. Only $30.9 million of balance of payments support disbursed, balance canceled December 1992.
1991	Education Sector Adjustment Credit	100.0	IDA terms. 2nd and 3rd tranches affected by November 1991 aid freeze, credit not fully disbursed until 1995. Also IDA reflows of $96.2 million.
1996	Structural Adjustment Credit I	90.0	IDA terms. Only $44.5 million of credit and $35.3 million of IDA reflows disbursed. Balance of credit and $42.1 million of IDA reflows canceled June 1998.

Sources: IMF annual reports; World Bank, *World Debt Tables;* World Bank country program files; government of Kenya budget data.

management was generally sound, and the World Bank and IMF were reconciled to the established market interventions of the government that included a fixed exchange rate and interest rates, price controls, and a sizable and growing state-owned enterprise sector.[4]

In the late 1970s and early 1980s the Kenyan economy experienced a series of shocks. Some of them affected all developing countries, but others were specific to Kenya. In response to these shocks the World

Bank, the IMF, and other donors responded with a substantial commitment of structural adjustment lending. Kenya was, in fact, the first Sub-
Saharan African country to receive structural adjustment funding from
the World Bank, and, later, the first to receive an Enhanced Structural
Adjustment Facility (ESAF) loan from the IMF. The Bank committed an
IDA Structural Adjustment Credit (SAC) of US$55 million in March 1980
and a second combined Structural Adjustment Loan/Credit of US$130.9
million in July 1982. However, because of Bank dissatisfaction with the
government's progress in meeting the policy reform conditions, release
of the US$50 million second tranche of the 1982 operation was delayed
for nine months, until early 1984. These funds were finally disbursed
even though the conditions, especially those dealing with cereals market liberalization, were not fully met.

While the World Bank and the Kenyan government had earlier discussed a possible third structural adjustment operation, this did not
materialize. Despite Kenya's continuing balance of payments deficit there
was a hiatus in further adjustment loan commitments and disbursements
until 1986, although the decline in this form of assistance was offset to
some extent by a large volume of food aid in response to a devastating
drought in 1984. This stop-go pattern in adjustment lending, resulting
from donor dissatisfaction with the pace and extent of policy reforms
and the strained relations between the government and donors that ensued, was repeated in the early 1990s and again since 1996.

Economic reform in Kenya gained renewed momentum in 1986 following the government's adoption of parliamentary Sessional Paper No.1
(SP #1) of that year, "Economic Management for Renewed Growth"
(Kenya 1986). Policy dialogue with the World Bank and IMF had re-
sumed during 1985 while this comprehensive policy reform document
was in preparation. As implementation of the policy reform proposals
set out in SP #1 got underway, the IMF and World Bank responded. The
IMF initiated a program of lending under the SAF, later converted to an
ESAF, and the World Bank undertook a new program of IDA Sectoral
Adjustment Credits (SECALs). Loans and grants from bilateral and other
multilateral donors for balance of payments support supplemented these
World Bank/IMF initiatives.

Between 1986 and 1991 the World Bank approved six SECALs (two
based on agricultural sector policy reforms, one supporting industrial
sector reforms, one in the financial sector, an export development program, and an educational sector policy support operation). The total
original commitment of these six IDA credits was US$537 million, but
they were supplemented by an additional US$348 million in "IDA
reflows"—additional IDA lending disbursed to offset debt repayments
on previously contracted World Bank loans. IDA reflows are only disbursed to eligible countries that have ongoing adjustment programs, and

they are linked to disbursements under the associated adjustment credits. Most of these commitments were disbursed in 1987–91. During this same period the IMF disbursed US$360 million of SAF and ESAF funds.

As described below, this infusion of balance of payments support, along with continued project lending, contributed to a recovery in the growth rate of the Kenyan economy in the second half of the 1980s. However, donor frustration began to build over lagging implementation of the government's commitments under the adjustment program, and there were increasing donor concerns over corruption and governance issues. This led, at the Consultative Group (CG) meeting of November 1991, to a suspension of already committed adjustment lending and a refusal to commit any new adjustment support until "substantial" progress was seen on all of the above fronts.[5]

It has been estimated that this freeze, which lasted until mid-1993, and later for some donors, affected more than US$400 million in financial support that would otherwise have been disbursed during 1991–93. This included the undrawn balance of the IMF ESAF, for US$63.2 million; second tranches of the World Bank Second Agricultural Sector Adjustment Operation credit (ASAO II), for US$33 million, and Export Development Program (EDP), for US$25 million plus US$53 million in IDA reflows; second and third tranches of the Education Sector Adjustment Credit (EDSAC), for US$65 million plus US$52 million in reflows[6]; an African Development Fund credit of US$35.3 million; and bilateral grant aid from Japan, US$77.3 million, and Germany, US$18.2 million, along with smaller amounts from the United Kingdom, the European Community, and the Netherlands. In addition, U.S. commodity and military aid of around US$43 million was frozen, while the U.S. Department of Agriculture canceled negotiations of a proposed US$100 million wheat import program under U.S. PL 480. Finally, a STABEX grant of US$26 million equivalent from the EC, which was not formally linked to the structural adjustment program, was also held up until the end of 1992. Again, as in 1984, some of this withheld aid was offset by inflows of emergency relief and food aid in response to the severe drought of 1992–93, but this relief assistance was far below the amount of aid suspended.

While some of the frozen commitments were subsequently canceled or simply never renegotiated—including the second tranche of ASAO II, the German grant, and the USAID commodity support—about half of the total affected by the freeze was eventually disbursed to Kenya in 1993–95, after the government renewed its reform efforts and made substantial progress in liberalization of both external trade and the domestic economy. In response to these renewed reform efforts of 1993–95, the IMF renegotiated and disbursed the US$63 million balance of the suspended 1989 ESAF, and in April 1996 agreed to a new ESAF arrangement for SDR 150 million (US$220 million) over three years. The World

Bank disbursed the outstanding tranches of the EDP and EDSAC and associated IDA reflows between mid-1993 and the end of 1995, and in June 1996 the Bank approved a new Structural Adjustment Credit of US$90 million, plus IDA reflows of US$35 million.

Since 1996, however, the performance of the Kenyan government in the implementation of structural adjustment policies has again been disappointing to the World Bank and IMF. They have seen, as in 1990–91, a slackening of reform efforts and failure to meet fully the SAC and ESAF conditions. As a result, the ESAF program was suspended in mid-1997, after only SDR 25 million had been drawn, and was allowed to expire in February 1999; while the second tranche of the SAC was canceled in mid-1998 and associated 1996–97 IDA reflows of US$42 million were allowed to lapse. The total amount of balance of payments support forgone by the Kenyan government since 1997—assuming that fully satisfactory implementation of the ESAF and SAC would have led to follow-on operations from the World Bank and IMF—is probably very close to the total amount of financial aid that was frozen in November 1991 (Barkan 1998: 218). This up-and-down, on-off experience with adjustment support to Kenya over the entire 1980–99 period is discussed in detail in the next section.

A summary of the entire 1970–96 period for which detailed data have been provided shows clearly the growing importance of program or structural adjustment lending to Kenya. Total ODA loans plus IMF drawings provided as balance of payments support totaled almost US$3 billion, rising from just over US$290 million in the 1970s to US$1.6 billion in the 1980s, and to US$934 million, or US$133 million per year, in 1990–96. The share of gross ODA plus IMF drawings provided as balance of payments support rose from 12.8 percent in 1970–79 to 21 percent in 1980–89, dropping back to 12.8 percent in 1990–96. For the World Bank, adjustment lending over the 1980–96 period, including IDA reflows, totaled US$1.08 billion, equivalent to 43 percent of total IBRD and IDA lending, and for the period of intensive sectoral adjustment lending, 1987–91, it represented 61 percent of total disbursements. Of course the *net* flow of adjustment lending over the entire period was much less than the totals cited above, due to repayments of principal and interest charges.[7]

Aid Coordination

Given the multiplicity of multilateral and bilateral donor agencies active in Kenya, donor coordination has been a continuing challenge. Each donor has its own program priorities, procurement and disbursement procedures, and regular program and policy discussions with the government. All of these make heavy demands on the time of senior government officials. At the same time the Kenyan government has demonstrated little effort or inclination to better coordinate donor activities.

In an effort to enhance donor coordination the World Bank organized a Consultative Group (CG) for Kenya in the early 1970s. This group met regularly throughout the 1970s and 1980s, normally once every two years.[8] In the early 1990s, as donor concerns grew over economic management, economic policy reforms, political reforms, and corruption, CGs were held in both 1990 and 1991, as well as meetings of donors without the government's presence. Following the suspension of program aid in November 1991 a formal CG was not held again until November 1993, but several informal, donors-only meetings were held in the interim to review progress, or lack of progress, in reforms. Following the resumption of the formal CG process in late 1993, meetings were held in 1994 (two), 1995 (informal), and 1996; but with the slowing of reforms since 1996 there have been no further formal CG meetings since that year.

The formal CG process is supplemented by regular meetings in country of the local donor community, comprising the heads of donor and U.N. agencies and their staffs in Nairobi. This local coordination group is co-chaired by the World Bank and the United Nations Development Programme (UNDP). In addition, there are sector coordination subgroups for all the major sectors receiving significant donor aid, such as health, education, and agriculture, and including a "good governance" or "democratic development" group. The Kenyan government participates regularly in some, but not all, of these sectoral coordination meetings. Periodically the government has convened meetings in Nairobi to inform donor representatives and ambassadors of its plans and progress in economic reforms, poverty alleviation, governance, and so forth. In general, throughout the structural adjustment period there has been broad agreement within the donor community on the priorities for economic reform in Kenya and, accordingly, on whether withholding aid or proceeding with disbursements and new commitments of policy-based lending is warranted.[9]

Debt and Debt Relief

After growing slowly until the late 1970s, Kenya's external debt more than doubled in the 1980s, rising from US$3.4 billion in 1980 to US$7.1 billion in 1990. Total foreign debt peaked at US$7.5 billion in 1991 but was reduced modestly thereafter, to US$6.9 billion in 1996. However, within the total debt stock the share of public and publicly guaranteed debt has grown more rapidly, from US$2.1 billion in 1980 to US$4.8 billion in 1990 and to US$5.9 billion in 1995, before dropping to US$5.6 billion in 1996.[10] While some of this debt was contracted on commercial terms, especially in the late 1970s, most of it was aid-related. As a low-income country Kenya qualified for conversion of a substantial part of bilateral aid to a grant basis, which occurred in the 1980s as mentioned above.

Between 1986 and 1992 bilateral donors also provided debt forgiveness of prior ODA debt of US$700 million. The principal sources of ODA debt relief were the United States (US$118.5 million, while an additional US$38.7 million was revoked in connection with the 1991 aid freeze), Germany (DM 600 million), Canada (US$90 million), the Netherlands, and the United Kingdom. The Japanese government has not provided debt forgiveness, but has offset debt repayments with supplemental grant aid.

Until the 1990s the Kenyan government had always serviced the country's official external debts, including those on commercial terms. The country had avoided arrears and had never been forced to seek debt relief from the Paris Club, London Club, or individual creditors. However, as the economy fell into recession in the early 1990s, with accompanying severe balance of payments constraints and shortages of foreign exchange, and with the curtailment of donor balance of payments support in late 1991, the government began to accumulate arrears on official debt, both to ODA donors and to Paris and London Club creditors. By mid-1993 arrears on external debt peaked at approximately US$750 million, close to 15 percent of the outstanding stock of official debt. However, with the re-establishment of a strong reform program and the resumption of balance of payments support in 1993, the foreign exchange crisis was alleviated and regular debt repayments resumed. In January 1994 Kenya was able to negotiate with the Paris Club a highly favorable refinancing (of arrears only) over an eight-year repayment period. A similar refinancing of arrears was subsequently negotiated with the London Club.

Special Program of Assistance

In the late 1980s the World Bank organized a special program to assist the heavily indebted countries in Sub-Saharan Africa, primarily through debt relief and conversion of aid flows from project finance to quick-disbursing balance of payments support linked to SAPs. All the major bilateral and multilateral donors to Africa were invited to participate in the program, which included biannual meetings to discuss the status of the heavily indebted low-income countries in Africa, closer aid coordination, and support for additional program aid and debt relief. The Special Program of Assistance (SPA) was influential in inducing the Paris Club to adopt more favorable terms in its reschedulings, in increasing both bilateral and multilateral debt relief, and in mobilizing additional lending to offset debt payments such as the IDA reflows program.

The criteria for inclusion in this program for low-income African countries were an unsustainable debt burden (defined as a debt service to export ratio of over 30 percent), one or more prior debt reschedulings with the Paris Club, and adherence to a program of structural adjustment supported by the World Bank and IMF. Initially Kenya was not included in the SPA group because its debt service ratio was slightly below 30 percent and Kenya had neither defaulted on external debt nor applied to the Paris Club for rescheduling. Nevertheless, the donor community agreed in 1989 to include Kenya in the SPA, a decision that helped to augment the flow of program aid to the country. In the early 1990s, given the rising debt service ratio and the buildup of arrears on official external debt, Kenya qualified for the SPA on these criteria. However, the status of Kenya's structural adjustment program was in question from late 1991 until mid-1993.

POLICY REFORMS AND INSTITUTIONAL DEVELOPMENT

Political Developments 1963–80

Kenya gained independence from Great Britain in 1963. For the next 15 years the country was led by President Jomo Kenyatta, the foremost leader of the independence movement, and by his political party, the Kenya African National Union (KANU). The Kenyatta government rapidly Africanized the civil service and other public sector appointments in order to consolidate national sovereignty. Since the president's ethnic group, the Kikuyus, had been the main beneficiaries of education and employment in the formal sector during the colonial period, they were the logical candidates for appointments to public sector jobs (Barkan 1994: 17). (They were also favored by the new government in the allocation of agricultural land and credit.) Other ethnic groups attempted to organize opposition parties but these either failed or were suppressed, and by 1969 Kenya had become a de facto single-party state (Throup and Hornsby 1998: ch. 2).

Nevertheless, within this single-party framework Kenyan politics was relatively democratic, with parliamentary and presidential elections on a regular five-year cycle, open and competitive primary races at the district level, and a high turnover of parliamentary seats. Normally some two-thirds of sitting members of Parliament, and one-third of those holding cabinet posts, were voted out of office at each election, a trend that has continued throughout Kenya's history. Following the death of President Kenyatta in 1978 and the accession to the presidency of Vice President Daniel arap Moi, who comes from one of the smaller ethnic groups, the Kalenjin, there began a gradual shift in the balance of power within the ruling party that is reflected in the framework of Kenyan politics to the present day.

From the standpoint of economic policymaking, the most significant political factor in the first years of independence was the concentration of decisionmaking authority in the central government and, in particular, in the Office of the President (Throup and Hornsby 1998: ch. 2). The first national election, in 1963, decided the basic political question of whether Kenya should have a strong central government or should be a federal state (referred to locally as *majimboism*). KANU stood for strong central authority, and won. Following from this, a series of laws and constitutional amendments in the 1960s increased the power of the president in relation to the cabinet, Parliament, judiciary, civil service, local government, and civil society organizations such as labor unions, cooperatives, and women's groups (Ng'ethe and Owino 1998: ch. 2).[11] The president also expanded his political power through the control of institutions inherited from the colonial regime (described below) that could be used for political patronage and provided a source of economic rents for ministers and other political supporters.

Such a concentration of authority meant that the adoption and implementation of any major economic policy initiative would always require the agreement of the president. Thus any analysis of the process of policy formulation and implementation in Kenya must recognize the central role of the president and the circle of key advisers and associates who control access to him. However, despite the existence of this highly centralized and authoritarian structure, in the early years of the Kenyatta presidency the cabinet, Kenyan technocrats, and a small coterie of foreign advisers played an important role in policy formulation. Policy issues were seriously debated, the civil service maintained a reasonable degree of professionalism (Barkan 1994: 17), the president listened to and followed many of the recommendations of his advisers, and the policy framework was sufficiently predictable to encourage investment.

Economic Developments 1963–80

In the early post-independence years economic policymaking was managed by the Cabinet Economic Subcommittee, which had substantial influence. It was chaired by Minister of Planning Tom Mboya, one of the most creative and dynamic members of the new government. Also beginning to have influence were young Kenyan economists such as Philip Ndegwa and Harris Mule, whose impact on policy continued in the 1970s and 1980s.

The framework of the economy in the early post-independence years was only moderately influenced by the prevailing development paradigm of the period. At the time of Kenya's independence most newly independent African countries were following the path of "African socialism." The Kenyan government accepted the label, but opted for a mixed economy that was more market-based, supportive of the private sector, and open to foreign investment than was the strict socialist model followed in other African countries such as Tanzania (see Kenya 1964, 1965; Barkan 1984).

Nevertheless, the government did wish to achieve "economic sovereignty": that is, to expand the participation of the African population in economic life and economic benefits while reducing the role of the former colonialists, resident Asians, and multinational corporations. Given the lack of entrepreneurial and other job-related skills in the indigenous population, policymakers believed that this would require a strong government role in the economy for some time to come.

Such a strong central role was also a natural continuation of the economic policies of the colonial regime (Lehman 1995: 203). The colonial government had supported the creation of institutions specifically designed to deliver benefits to the settler community. These included public agencies to control (and sometimes subsidize) economic activities, such as the Maize Board, Wheat Board, Dairy Board, Tea Board, Meat Commission, Pyrethrum Board, and so forth, as well as producers' organizations established to interact with the government in the interest of their constituents, such as the Kenya Farmers' Association and the Kenya Cooperative Creameries. (Several of these had their roots in the economic controls imposed during World War II.) Following independence these public institutions were maintained and the private associations or cooperatives were converted into quasi-public bodies.[12] During this early post-independence period the government also expanded its involvement in productive activities through the establishment of new state-owned enterprises (SOEs) and joint public/private ventures in manufacturing and commerce.

Government authority over the economy was also increased through the regulatory framework and the steady expansion of controls on domestic prices, interest rates, foreign exchange, imports, and exports. Some of these controls were introduced in response to shocks, such as the capital flight that followed the assassination of Minister Mboya in 1969 and the first oil shock in 1973. Finance Minister Mwai Kibaki, who served in that capacity from 1971 to 1982, addressed these crises primarily through the imposition of additional controls and an expansionary fiscal policy, reflecting his *dirigiste* mind-set. While some circles in government argued that many of these interventions, in particular the commercial SOEs, were temporary, there were clearly differences of opinion between technocrats and politicians on the issue of controls versus economic liberalization. It must also be recognized that controls, regulations, and state ownership of enterprises opened up opportunities for rent-seeking.

Another important aspect of Kenyan economic policy in the 1960s and 1970s was the industrialization strategy that, as in many other developing countries, was based on import substitution—trade protection for domestic "infant industries" that were set up to produce substitutes for previously imported consumer goods. The view that developing countries should follow an industrial development policy based on import substitution rather than export promotion was grounded in large part in the "export pessimism" argument—that their prospects for breaking into global markets for manufactured products were poor. The policy was promoted, in the 1960s and 1970s, by U.N. organizations such as the United Nations Conference on Trade and Development (UNCTAD) and the Economic Commission for Latin America.

This overall economic policy framework—significant government intervention in directly productive activities and in management of the economy, combined with an import substitution approach to industrialization—was developed by Kenyan technocrats and politicians, supported by advisers funded by donor technical assistance, and endorsed by the World Bank/IMF and the larger donor community. Financial support of the strategy from multilateral and bilateral donors is evident in the amount of aid channeled to and through SOEs, and also in the fact that early World Bank/IMF program lending in the mid-1970s basically accepted the existing controls on prices, interest rates, and foreign exchange, and did not impose conditions requiring the divestiture of state enterprises.

The Kenyan economy performed well over most of the 1964–80 period. The GDP growth rate averaged 5.8 percent per year in 1965–73 and 5.3 percent in 1974–80. The agricultural sector grew at nearly 5 percent, with growth based primarily on smallholder farmers who benefited from the conversion of former colonial estates to African ownership.[13] The manufacturing sector expanded at 10 percent per year, fueled by the growth in domestic rural incomes and the expansion of exports to Tanzania and Uganda under the common market created by the EAC. The domestic savings rate averaged 16 percent in the 1970s. The efficiency of investment was relatively high, with an incremental capital-output ratio (ICOR) of 3 in the 1960s and 4 in the 1970s. The tax/GDP ratio was rising steadily, from 12 percent in the mid-1960s to 20 percent in 1979–80, and while expenditures were rising equally rapidly, the fiscal deficit was contained in most years to 3–6 percent of GDP. The overall balance of payments deficit was also manageable, at 3–4 percent of GDP.

Within this generally quite positive set of economic trends there were some disruptions. Economic growth slowed in the mid-1970s to an average of 3.4 percent per year in 1973–76. One of the principal causes was the negative impact of the fivefold increase in oil prices in 1973; this first oil shock was a serious blow to the Kenyan economy given the country's total dependence on imported petroleum products (Kenya 1975).

Then, in the late 1970s, further severe shocks adversely affected Kenya's economic situation and prospects. The first was the boom-and-bust cycle in coffee and tea prices in 1976–79. The boom sparked a ratcheting up of both consumer and government spending (the fiscal deficit rose to 9.5 percent of GDP in 1975–76). The government then proved unable to reduce spending sufficiently when coffee and tea export revenues fell sharply after 1977. The economy was also set back by the August 1977 breakup of the EAC, which ended the favored access for Kenyan exporters to the Ugandan and Tanzanian markets, raised infrastructure costs, and forced the Kenyan government to absorb much of the work force of the overstaffed EAC railways, ports, and posts and telecommunications agencies. Yet another contributing factor was the second oil shock in 1979.

As a direct result of this rapid succession of economic shocks, the balance of payments current account deficit rose from 3 percent of GDP on average in 1975–77 to 10–11 percent in 1978–82. While concessional loans and grants from aid donors were rising, some of the deficit was financed with a commercial loan at a floating interest rate,[14] contributing to a rise in the debt service ratio from 2.6 percent of export revenues in 1977 to 14 percent in 1983. Inflationary pressures were also increasing, despite the now comprehensive price controls.

By the beginning of the 1980s the Kenyan economy had suffered, within a short span of only three to four years, a series of economic shocks that were far more severe than any problems previously confronted in the post-independence era. At the same time the country had other difficulties that compounded the challenges facing economic policymakers. Economic management had begun to weaken during the policy "drift" of the late Kenyatta years and the corresponding loss of influence of the cabinet and civil service technocrats. The productivity of private investment was declining, reflected in a steadily rising ICOR. Manufacturing sector growth was slowing as the limits to import substitution in the local market were reached, access to EAC markets was curtailed, and domestic industries were neither oriented toward, nor competitive in, overseas markets. Job creation in the formal sector lagged well behind the growth in the labor force. In the agricultural sector there was little scope for further expansion of land under cultivation. The public sector, and public employment in particular, had been growing much faster than the economy, and the rising share of government tax revenue and expenditure, as well as the low productivity of the large SOE sector, were becoming a drag on economic performance.

By the end of the 1970s it had become clear to many Kenyan technocrats, if not to politicians, that significant changes in the direction of economic policy would be required to address these complex problems. During the 1978–82 period the government, with the help of a few foreign advisers, reviewed virtually all its economic policies; these reviews

were incorporated in the 1979 Development Plan and in various working party reports and sessional papers.[15] In 1979 Philip Ndegwa, who
had close contacts with both President Kenyatta and President Moi,
chaired a working party that highlighted the shortcomings of public
enterprises (Kenya 1979). He chaired a second working party on government expenditures in 1982 that addressed the problems of fiscal indiscipline in macroeconomic management (Kenya 1982b). These two
reports indicate a clear awareness of the adverse consequence of the
decline of public sector institutions in the country. As discussed in the
following section, these internal reviews did produce a framework for
addressing the country's economic crisis, but it remained uncertain
whether there was sufficient conviction and political will to implement
the recommendations in the reports.

The Reform Period (1980–present)

Political Developments

As previously stated, President Kenyatta centralized decisionmaking
authority in the Office of the Presidency. His successor, Daniel arap Moi,
who took office in 1978 and has been president for more than 20 years,
has maintained, if not increased, the concentration of power in the executive branch. An unsuccessful coup attempt against the Moi government in 1982 severely disrupted political and economic affairs for a time,
but did not weaken the president's grip on the reins of authority.[16] A
constitutional amendment was adopted in 1982 making Kenya a de jure
single-party state. In 1988 the constitution was further amended to give
the president power to remove members of the Public Service Commission, the Judicial Service Commission, and the judiciary, although these
provisions were later modified. President Moi also used his authority to
reduce the preponderance of Kikuyu civil servants, especially in the
higher ranks of the public service. His argument was that Kikuyu domination of institutions was undermining social cohesion, and that their
replacement, even with less qualified candidates, was necessary to ensure stability in the country. However, this policy had the unfortunate
effect of further undermining efficiency in the public sector and, to a
degree, replacing one group of rent-seekers with another, many of whom
lacked the experience to run the organizations they inherited (see Throup
and Hornsby 1998: ch. 3).

National elections under the single-party regime were held in 1979,
1983, and 1988, but with greater party control over the selection of candidates than in the Kenyatta era. Still, a high rate of turnover of parliamentary seats at each election continued. To further consolidate party

control over the election process, the secret ballot was replaced in the 1988 election by a system of queue voting. This proved so unpopular that only 23 percent of eligible voters participated. Following a process of nationwide consultations led by Vice President Saitoti during 1990, the government decided to give up the queue voting system and to restore the independence of the judiciary. There was, nevertheless, growing domestic discontent with the political situation, essentially with the monopoly of political power held by KANU, and this culminated in riots in July 1990. The internal pressure for multiparty politics received strong support from the donor community, in particular the outspoken U.S. ambassador, Smith Hempstone (Hempstone 1997). The desire to see a more democratic system introduced in Kenya was one of the principal reasons for the unanimous decision by the donor community in November 1991 to suspend balance of payments support.

While the leaders of government and of KANU appeared to be adamantly opposed to multi-partyism, the decision was taken in early December 1991, by a KANU national convention and by the all-KANU Parliament, to amend the constitution to allow for the formation of multiple political parties. Whether this move was made in response to donor pressures or domestic political protests can be endlessly debated; it probably resulted from the combination of forces, but the timing undoubtedly bore some relationship to the outcome of the November 1991 donor meeting.[17]

This constitutional opening led to the first genuine multiparty election in Kenya's history. The vote was held a year later, on December 29, 1992, following a full year of frenetic political campaigning. In the end, because the opposition split into three major and several minor parties along essentially ethnic lines, because the government controlled access to the media, and because KANU had greater access to financial resources, President Moi was reelected with a plurality of 37 percent of the votes (see Throup and Hornsby 1998: ch. 9). KANU also kept control of the Parliament with an initial margin of 112 seats to 88 (100 elected plus 12 nominated by the president). In the second multiparty election in December 1997, Moi was reelected with a slightly higher plurality, but KANU gained only a narrow majority of parliamentary seats over an even larger number of still-divided opposition parties.[18]

In this new era of multiparty politics, the political parties have evolved almost entirely on ethnic lines. The inability of contending opposition factions to unite behind a single candidate, whether for the presidency or for parliamentary seats, has been the primary reason for the ruling party's continued hold on power. Also, personalities have been much more important than ideology or any other set of issues. While various parties have published manifestos setting out their political, social, and economic goals (and generally the opposition parties have been openly in favor of economic liberalization through structural adjustment, criticizing the government for weak implementation of SAPs) these policy documents have received little notice during the campaigns and have likely had little or no influence on voter behavior.

Macroeconomic Developments and Growth Performance

The record of macroeconomic performance in Kenya since 1980 has been extremely mixed, with fluctuations in the GDP growth rate, fiscal deficit, balance of payments deficit, and inflation. In general, the best macroeconomic performance has occurred during and immediately following the periods of stronger implementation of reform measures (1986–89 and 1993–96), but all the macroeconomic indicators have not necessarily moved in unison.

The period begins with attempts to adjust to the economic shocks of the late 1970s. The fiscal deficit rose to 9.3 percent of GDP in FY 1981, the balance of payments current account deficit reached 11–12 percent of GDP in 1980–81, and the inflation rate—measured by the consumer price index (CPI)—increased from an average of 12 percent in 1977–81 to 18 percent in 1982–83. These economic strains contributed to the pressures that precipitated the coup attempt of August 1982. In response, the government undertook a stabilization program with IMF support that succeeded in reducing the fiscal deficit to 3 percent in FY 1983, but at the expense of investment and growth. GDP growth averaged only 2.3 percent per year during 1982–84, with a severe drought in 1984 also affecting the growth rate adversely. For the entire 1980–85 subperiod the average growth rate was only 3.6 percent. In retrospect it seems clear that the fiscal squeeze was too great and proved unsustainable. The government was pushed by the IMF to adopt an excessively tight demand management policy.

Recovery in the second half of the 1980s brought the average GDP growth rate up to 5 percent, but in the 1990s the GDP growth record was highly erratic. In the early 1990s the economy fell into severe recession, with the growth rate plunging from 4.2 percent in 1990 to 0.5 percent in 1992 and 0.2 percent in 1993. With the renewed reform efforts in 1993 the economy began to recover, attaining an average growth rate of 4.2 percent in 1994–96. However, the economy fell again into recession toward the end of the decade, with the growth rate declining to 2.4 percent in 1997 and 1.8 percent in 1998. It is important to remember that with Kenya's past high rate of population growth—3.9 percent in the 1970s, 3.7 percent in the 1980s, and 2.8 percent in the 1990s—there has been very little improvement in per capita income over the past 30 years. The annual growth in per capita income, which had been a healthy 2.8 percent during 1964–70, averaged only 1.1 percent in the 1970s and 0.6

percent in the 1980s, and it was negative in the 1990s. In addition, with modest per capita income growth over this entire period, the incidence of poverty has increased since 1980 (World Bank 1994).

On the fiscal front the record has also been mixed. It has proven difficult for the government to sustain fiscal stabilization, and there have been substantial swings in the fiscal deficit over the past 20 years. The ratio of total revenue to GDP remained fairly stable at around 22 percent from 1979/80 to 1992/93, but increased sharply to 27 percent in 1993/94, where it remained through fiscal year 1997/98; however, expenditure growth outpaced that of revenues. Following the stabilization of 1982–84 fiscal management weakened in the second half of the 1980s, with deficits averaging over 5 percent of GDP. In the early 1990s the fiscal position remained difficult, with the average deficit rising to almost 6 percent in fiscal years 1991–94.

Inflation was contained in the mid-1980s but began to rise in the last years of the decade before accelerating dramatically in the early 1990s. Fueled by excessive monetary expansion to finance the fiscal deficit and the 1992 election, the inflation rate rose to 34 percent in 1992 and 55 percent in 1993. But these annual averages do not convey the full severity of the situation. In the second quarter of 1993 the annualized inflation rate reached 101 percent—far beyond anything Kenya had ever experienced in the past. Money supply growth and the resulting inflation were finally brought under control in the second half of 1993, with the CPI reduced to an annualized rate of 16 percent by year's end through the floating of massive amounts of short-term Treasury bills at very high interest rates. This, however, has left the government with a heavy overhang of domestic debt that has risen from KSh 40 billion in 1990 to KSh 160 billion in 1998. (Another form of domestic debt is unpaid or "pending" bills for goods and services provided to the government, which expanded from an estimated KSh 1.2 billion in 1990 to an estimated KSh 7.3 billion in January 1998.)

Following the balance of payments crisis of the early 1980s, the external accounts were held in reasonable balance until the late 1980s, when the deficit rose to around 6 percent of GDP on average in 1987–90. Then, in the 1991–93 period Kenya faced even more severe balance of payments problems, compounded by the suspension of donor balance of payments support in 1991. Before the full liberalization of the trade and exchange regime in 1993–94 the government coped with this crisis primarily by maintaining tight controls on import licenses and on access to foreign exchange, and through the accumulation of arrears on external debt. During the 1993 crisis described above, and following the partial liberalization of the exchange rate, the value of the Kenya shilling to the U.S. dollar fell from 50:1 at the end of 1992 to 81:1 in July 1993. It stabilized and then strengthened dramatically as the liberalization led to a massive inflow of foreign exchange, much of which was of a short-term speculative nature.

Overview of Economic Policy Reforms

The concept of "structural adjustment," comprising a set of economic reform policies, was introduced in 1979.[19] The basic objectives of SAPs, as initially conceived, were to restore developing countries to macroeconomic stability following the disruptions of the 1970s (primarily the two oil shocks), and to revive economic growth through increased resource mobilization and more efficient utilization of resources. Efficiency gains would be achieved through greater reliance on market forces and on the private sector, and, in most developing countries, by reducing the role of government in the economy.

This meant, first of all, "getting the prices right": eliminating market distortions and increasing competition in the domestic economy. Greater competition was to be achieved through deregulation; phasing out public sector monopoly control in markets for foreign exchange, credit, and agricultural commodities; and privatization of commercial state enterprises. SAPs also called for eliminating barriers to foreign trade and foreign investment. Steps would be taken to promote export-led growth instead of import substitution by reducing protection and controls on access to foreign exchange, adopting a flexible exchange rate policy, and possibly providing additional incentives for exporters. As SAPs have evolved from this essentially "quick fix" approach of the early 1980s, their scope has expanded to include institutional reforms and the social aspects of adjustment. This includes, for example, the impact of budget rationalization on the allocation of resources to the health and education sectors. However, SAPs have only a medium-term focus, and are not intended to deal directly with more fundamental development priorities such as poverty alleviation, reducing unemployment, and human capital development.

Much of aid conditionality in the 1980s was focused on persuading sometimes reluctant governments to adopt and then implement this policy framework of liberalization and reorientation of the government's role. While the World Bank and IMF initially assumed that structural adjustment programs could be implemented, and growth momentum restored, within three to five years, this proved to be excessively optimistic for almost all developing countries. For such countries, many facing more severe economic crises than Kenya, the total SAP reform agenda proved to be extremely demanding. Undertaking major policy reforms simultaneously across the entire span of the economy proved beyond the capacity of many developing country governments, even if the need for the full package of reforms was generally accepted. Furthermore, even a well designed and faithfully implemented program could be thrown off track by a decline in the terms of trade, adverse weather conditions, public resistance, or political shocks such as the 1982 coup attempt in Kenya.

Since 1980 Kenya has been carrying out, with varying degrees of success, a comprehensive structural adjustment program. Virtually all of the macroeconomic and sectoral policy recommendations found in SAPs in other countries can be found in the Kenyan program. In the Kenyan context structural adjustment meant unbundling the pervasive control system and reducing the prominent role of government in the economy. There has been much less ideological bias against liberalization in Kenya than in most other SSA countries. Indeed, by the late 1970s, as suggested earlier, while the reform program had not yet been launched, technocrats and advisers in the Kenyan government were advocating greater reliance on markets, elimination of price controls, and measures to improve efficiency in the public sector as part of the response to the economic crisis.

The Kenyan government and the World Bank were already working in 1979 on an industrial sector policy operation intended to support the outward-oriented industrial development strategy set forth in the 1979–83 Development Plan. This industrial sector operation, with only slight modifications, became the first Structural Adjustment Credit to Kenya (SAC I). The focus was on reducing protection of the manufacturing sector and promoting manufactured exports. The primary policy actions were replacement of quantitative restrictions on imports (QRs) with equivalent tariffs and rationalization of the tariff structure to reduce the wide variations in effective protection to different industries. An IMF program focused on fiscal and monetary management was negotiated in 1979, but was canceled because of the government's failure to meet the agreed credit ceilings. It was replaced by a new program in October 1980.

Following these initial operations the government entered into a continuing series of adjustment programs with the World Bank and IMF between 1982 and 1996. The policy framework throughout emphasized macroeconomic stabilization through fiscal and monetary and exchange rate management—the purview of the IMF—and trade liberalization supported by the World Bank. But the policy agenda also encompassed a range of other measures: interest rate deregulation; domestic price decontrol; cereals market liberalization; decontrol of markets for agricultural inputs and other agricultural outputs such as meat, dairy products, cotton, and sugar; export incentive schemes; reform of financial sector management and regulatory reforms; and even family planning and financing for reforms in the health and education sectors. Midway through the first decade of structural adjustment the Kenyan government articulated its analytical framework for this comprehensive reform program in Sessional Paper No. 1 of 1986, "Economic Management for Renewed Growth." This paper presented the broad outlines of the increasingly liberalized economy that was to take shape in the 1990s.[20]

Throughout the entire SAP period the timing and sequencing of the various reform measures varied significantly. For example, in the area of public sector management, although the government working party reports issued between 1978 and 1982 made the case for civil service reforms and reform or divestiture of SOEs, these problems were not confronted until the 1990s. Also, reforms have been implemented at an extremely uneven pace with respect to both different policy reform areas and time periods, with intervals of steady, and sometimes rapid, progress followed by stagnation and occasional reversals. Therefore it is difficult to come to an overall judgment regarding Kenya's performance as a reformer, or to compare Kenya with other reforming countries in Sub-Saharan Africa. As discussed below, if one adds up all the reforms in economic policy carried out over the past 20 years the extent of change is impressive, with backtracking only on trade liberalization (for valid reasons in 1980–82), on cost sharing, and on cereals market reforms. But if one looks at the time it has taken to achieve various reforms in relation to the government's own timetable or the specific conditionalities of adjustment operations, as most critics have done, Kenya can be made to fit the mold of a reluctant reformer whose overall record has been no better than the SSA average.[21] The distinct phases of the reform effort in Kenya are summarized in table 8.3.

Path and Sequencing of Specific Reforms

MACROECONOMIC MANAGEMENT. Fiscal, monetary, and interest rate policies, and the decontrol of domestic prices were all important components of the government's structural adjustment program throughout the period. They were also core elements in the conditionality of World Bank and IMF adjustment operations. Under the implicit division of labor between the World Bank and the IMF, the Fund took responsibility for negotiating conditionalities relating to total government spending and the fiscal deficit, credit ceilings, and overall monetary policy, while the Bank's programs dealt with the composition of public expenditures, in particular the development budget, budgetary management reforms, monitoring of external debt, and financial market reforms. Interest rate policy was treated jointly. Normally the Bank would require that the overall macroeconomic situation receive IMF endorsement before releasing structural adjustment funds, particularly for sectoral adjustment operations for which the Bank did not always conduct its own macroeconomic assessment. However, this has not always been the case.

Table 8.3 Stages in Kenya's Structural Adjustment Program

Period	Description
1980–83	Loss of fiscal discipline followed by successful, but possibly too abrupt, macro/fiscal stabilization; fiscal control restored by FY 1983; start of flexible monetary and exchange rate policy; beginning attempts at trade liberalization but limited success due to lack of coordination with macroeconomic policies; little progress in cereals market liberalization.
1984–85	Hiatus in reform efforts and in donor balance of payments support.
1986–91	Government SP #1 of 1986 defines policy objectives. Period of *sectoral* adjustment programs in agriculture, industry, trade, and finance, with renewed donor support. Slow but steady progress in domestic price decontrol and trade liberalization (further elimination of QRs, tariff reform, more active exchange rate management, liberalization of interest rates, improvements in management of financial sector, some initial steps in cereals market liberalization); but decay in fiscal discipline.
1991–93	Slowing of reform effort. Reversals of cereals market liberalization but continued progress in domestic price decontrol; tariff rationalization plus introduction of ad hoc measures for limited liberalization of foreign exchange market. But weak overall reform effort, growing political problems, and donor concerns over governance and corruption lead to suspension of balance of payments support from November 1991 to mid-1993.
1993–95	Resumption of reform effort, particularly trade and exchange rate policy. Complete liberalization of foreign exchange market, end to import licensing, further tariff reform; completion of domestic price decontrol; only limited progress in reform/privatization of state-owned enterprises, civil service reform. Resumption of donor balance of payments support from mid-1993.
1996–98	Again, slowing of reform effort. Government maintains liberalized trade and exchange regime, interest rates, decontrol of domestic prices. Fiscal and monetary policy are reasonably well managed, but structural problems in budget, state enterprise sector, civil service, and agricultural sector institutions are not adequately dealt with. Result is suspension of new IMF ESAF in July 1997, cancellation of World Bank SAC in June 1998.

The government's growing fiscal problems were thoroughly analyzed by the 1982 Working Party on Government Expenditures led by Philip Ndegwa, which examined the expansion in overall government spending, the rising share of the wage bill, and growing inefficiency in the public sector, including the public enterprises (Kenya 1982b). The report made a strong case for improved fiscal management, and recommended that the bulk of the fiscal adjustment should be achieved through expenditure reductions: restricting government functions, limiting recruitment into the public services, improving efficiency in managing recurrent expenditures, and introducing cost sharing for government services in higher education, health care, roads, and agricultural support services. On the side of the development budget the report argued that no project should be included in the budget without an assessment of its recurrent cost and staffing implications, and that no project should receive public funds unless it had been included in the budget. In its comprehensive and frank assessment of public finance issues and its cogent recommendations, this report anticipated virtually all the issues later raised by the World Bank in its series of public expenditure reviews in the 1990s. The timing of the report's publication was unfortunate, however, since it appeared only a few months before the August 1982 coup attempt. For this reason as well as other political factors, little action was taken on most of these proposals until some years later.

As indicated earlier, the government did undertake, at IMF urging, a strong stabilization program during 1982–84 that succeeded in sharply reducing the fiscal deficit. However, in the second half of the 1980s the government was less successful in managing fiscal policy. IMF program targets were often not met, the fiscal balance deteriorated, and inflation accelerated. While donor budgetary support covered a substantial part of the annual deficit there was a slow accumulation of domestic debt in the form of Treasury bills, which grew to KSh 40 billion in 1990 as mentioned earlier. Some observers have characterized the first half of the 1980s as stabilization without much structural adjustment and the second half as structural adjustment without adequate stabilization. Fiscal policy weakened further in the early 1990s, with the fiscal deficit rising to over 7 percent of GDP in fiscal year 1993. However, since that time the deficit has been substantially reduced, averaging only 1.2 percent over fiscal years 1995–98. The decision of the IMF to suspend the 1996 three-year ESAF arrangement in July 1997 was not because of disagreements regarding the size of the overall budget deficit.

Monetary policy was both rigid and passive throughout the 1960s and 1970s. Interest rates were fixed, and the Central Bank of Kenya (CBK) had as its primary function the accommodation of the deficit financing requirements of the government through the sale of Treasury bills. (For many years the Treasury was heavily subsidized as Treasury bill rates were pegged well below inflation.) In fact, interest rates have not been utilized as a primary tool for economic management in Kenya. The government imposed fixed minimum or maximum interest rates on the financial sector throughout the period up to 1990. In the 1970s the minimum rate on savings was gradually increased from 3 percent in 1974 to 10 percent in 1981–82, but this minimum rate remained negative in real terms throughout the period. Over the same time span regulated maximum lending rates were allowed to rise from 10 percent to 16 percent, but were also negative in real terms in most years.

Finally, in the 1980s the government and the CBK, under its new governor, Philip Ndegwa, adopted a more flexible and market-based interest rate policy, with more frequent adjustments in savings and lending rates to reflect inflation. From 1984 onward real lending rates at least remained positive. One of the objectives of the World Bank's 1989 financial sector SECAL was the full liberalization of interest rates. By 1990 the minimum rate on savings had been raised to 12.5 percent and the maximum lending rate to 19 percent, but with banks permitted to charge additional fees, meaning that lending rates were de facto freed. Treasury bill rates were allowed to float from November 1990 and in 1991 all interest rates were fully deregulated.

Despite the progress made on interest rate deregulation, other aspects of monetary policy and monetary management deteriorated in the late 1980s and early 1990s, following the replacement of Philip Ndegwa by Eric Kotut as governor of the CBK in 1988. The quality and effectiveness of bank supervision declined, adherence to prudential regulations was lax, and a number of smaller banks failed and had to be put into receivership, or were propped up with public funds. Growth in the money supply began to outpace demand. In the second half of 1992 the money supply expanded at an annualized rate of 63 percent (for the full year growth was 34 percent) against an IMF program target of 10 percent, fueling the inflation that peaked at an annualized rate of 101 percent in the second quarter of 1993. As the money supply/inflation situation appeared to be spiraling out of control in early 1993, the government initially rejected IMF advice to mop up excess liquidity by selling Treasury bills at a fixed interest rate of 45 percent, but two months later opted to auction Treasury bills at market-determined rates that briefly soared to over 80 percent. By late 1993 the financial crisis was contained and Treasury bill rates had declined to the 20–30 percent range, where they remained for a long period before falling further to a range of 7–15 percent in 1999.

Another policy objective was decontrol of prices. As discussed earlier, pervasive price controls had become an important part of Kenyan economic life in the 1970s and early 1980s. The prices of almost all goods were controlled under either the General or the Specific Price Control

Orders (GPCO and SPCO) established under regulations dating as far back as 1956 and amended in the Price Control Act of 1972. The coverage of the SPCO was extended four times during the 1970s; the GPCO was first introduced in 1971 as a temporary measure but was made permanent in 1974. The system was complex and bureaucratic, and businesses often experienced long delays in obtaining clearance to raise prices. At the same time, the cost-plus principles employed in justifying price increases did not promote economic efficiency. Price controls were one of the two primary concerns of the business sector, the other being the import and foreign exchange control system.

By the 1980s there was growing sentiment even within government for reducing or eliminating price controls, although the 1979 and 1982 working party reports did not explicitly mention price decontrol, and Sessional Paper No. 1 of 1986 argued that some price controls should be maintained, only suggesting that they be "streamlined" (Kenya 1986: 100–103). However, following the publication of SP #1 quite rapid progress was made in reducing the number of goods controlled under both general and specific orders, usually by listing the goods to be decontrolled in the finance minister's annual budget speech. By 1994 all price controls had been eliminated. This was one of the more successful efforts at policy reform that was possible because a small group of technocrats within the key ministries continued to chip away at the issue year after year, and because of the strong support for decontrol from the private sector.

TRADE POLICY. Trade policy has been a central aspect of structural adjustment reforms in Kenya since 1980. While progress in liberalization of the trade regime has been sporadic, with periods of significant progress followed by slower movement and even reversals, the final position achieved following the major reforms of 1993–94 has brought Kenya firmly into the group of developing countries with the most liberal trade and foreign exchange regimes. In contrast to the pervasive controls maintained through the 1970s and 1980s and even into the early 1990s, and the inefficiencies and rent-seeking that the control system perpetuated, the current situation can be regarded as a revolutionary change.

As with other aspects of the structural adjustment program, there was a division of labor between the World Bank and IMF in dealing with the external trade and payments system. Conditionalities relating to the overall balance of payments gap and its financing, and the exchange rate, were incorporated in IMF programs, while quantitative restrictions on imports, tariffs, and foreign exchange licensing were incorporated in policy agreements with the World Bank. This did not always lead to perfect coordination of policy advice or the timing of policy actions.

As mentioned earlier, the Bank's SAC I in 1980 evolved out of a proposed industrial sector operation, the objective of which was to support the policy shift from import substitution to export expansion set forth in the 1979–84 Development Plan. This decision was initially made operational in November 1981 with the adoption of a program for the removal of "no-objection certificates" from domestic producers, a phased replacement of QRs with equivalent tariffs, and subsequent tariff reductions and rationalization. At the same time the level of export compensation, intended to offset tariffs and other taxes on imported inputs, and established in 1974 at 10 percent, was raised to 20 percent. However, with the fiscal and balance of payments deficits not yet under control, trade liberalization had to give way to macroeconomic stabilization and the program was suspended in mid-1982. Export compensation was restored in December 1982, but at the original rate of 10 percent. The remaining components of the trade liberalization program were reinstated in late 1983 but progress from that point was slow; QRs still applied to approximately 50 percent of imports in 1986 and rates of effective protection had been modified only slightly. The removal of no-objection certificates was the one clear success of SAC I.

In retrospect it was unwise for the Bank to push for a rapid pace of import liberalization in the face of large macroeconomic imbalances, and at a time when the exchange rate was not yet being used to close the trade gap. (More active exchange rate management urged by the IMF had begun in 1982 under new CBK Governor Philip Ndegwa, with the introduction of a crawling peg in 1983, but the early, modest nominal devaluations were overwhelmed by domestic inflation.) The response to this initial effort at trade liberalization was disappointing. Exports of goods and services as a share of GDP, which had declined steadily from 45 percent in the mid-1960s to around 30 percent in 1980–81, fell further during 1980–85. This weak response was undoubtedly due in large part to the global recession of the early 1980s, but must also be attributed to the limited amount of import liberalization and export incentives actually implemented and the on-off nature of the reform process.

The second push to liberalize the trade regime began in 1988 and was more successful. SP #1 of 1986 made a strong case for export promotion over import substitution (Kenya 1986: ch. 6). Another reason for success may be the fact that a World Bank study on the structure of industry and of effective protection provided a better information base for setting tariffs than had previously existed. In the event, steady progress was made in eliminating QRs and in reducing tariffs; between 1987/88 and 1997/98 the maximum tariff was reduced from 170 percent to 25 percent, the number of tariff bands was reduced from 24 to 4, and the average tariff was lowered from 49 percent to 17 percent. Also, a more active exchange rate policy was implemented in the second half of the 1980s. Kenya's terms of trade declined by about 50 percent from the mid-1970s to 1990, and this was partially offset by a 40 percent depreciation in the real exchange rate in 1985–90. Export compensation was raised again to 20 percent in 1985 and manufacturing under bond was introduced in 1988. In this period there was a strong supply response to liberalization; between 1986 and 1991 the quantum index of exports rose on average by 10 percent per year. (Horticultural exports, which remained relatively free of any government interference, expanded sevenfold during the 1980s.)

The area that proved most difficult to reform was the import and foreign exchange licensing system. The licensing procedures, involving both the Ministry of Commerce and the CBK, were cumbersome and open to rent-seeking. Long delays in issuing both import and foreign exchange licenses led to a buildup in the queue of applications in the late 1980s, to which the business community reacted defensively by submitting multiple applications for the same imports. The inability of the authorities to meet all legitimate requests for foreign exchange forced business firms to hold large inventories that raised costs. Foreign investors were constantly frustrated by the inability to obtain foreign exchange for remittance of dividends to foreign shareholders.

The World Bank–financed Export Development Program (EDP), introduced in 1990, set as an objective only improvement in the management of the import and foreign exchange licensing systems, not their elimination. And little progress was made in achieving even this limited goal during the difficult years of 1991–92. Still, while the government was moving slowly and reluctantly to meet the EDP conditionalities, it did take independent steps to open a legal parallel market for foreign exchange. In October 1991 foreign exchange bearer certificates that could be resold to private parties were introduced, and currency declaration forms were abolished in November 1991. In August 1992, 100 percent export retention accounts were permitted for exporters of nontraditional goods, and the import licensing regulations were revised to permit automatic issuing of import licenses to those holding their own foreign exchange. In November 1992 the export retention scheme was extended to provide 50 percent retention for traditional exporters, and it was further expanded to cover the services sector in February 1993. These partial liberalization measures, while welcomed by the business community, did not attack the basic structure of the import and foreign exchange licensing system. This fundamental reform came about as part of the wave of trade and domestic market liberalization and financial sector reforms that began in mid-1993, on the heels of the financial crisis in the first half of the year. Within a year from the initiation of these new reforms virtually all transactions in both the current and capital accounts of Kenya's balance of payments had been fully liberalized.

PUBLIC SECTOR MANAGEMENT. Two key reform areas within public sector management are civil service reform and the reform and privatization of state-owned enterprises. These are adjustment issues that the Kenyan government only began to address in the 1990s; they did not feature at all in the policy dialogue or conditionality surrounding the structural adjustment program during the first decade of reforms.

In the 1960s and 1970s the Kenyan public service was relatively well paid and the government could attract qualified staff. In addition, following the recommendation of a 1970–71 commission of inquiry chaired by then CBK Governor Duncan Ndegwa, civil servants were permitted to have private business interests as long as these were publicly declared (Kenya 1971). This controversial measure has been subject to much criticism on the grounds of conflict of interest, despite the adoption of a code of ethics for civil servants in 1979. However, permitting outside sources of income did offset to a limited extent the long-term decline in public sector real wages, which fell by some 65 percent between 1970 and 1994.

The falling real wages were a direct result of much more rapid growth in public sector employment than in available resources. Throughout the 1970s and 1980s public employment grew much faster than the economy or the government budget. For example, in the 1980s, despite uneven growth of the economy and increasing fiscal constraints, civil service employment continued to grow at 7.4 percent per year, rising from 160,000 in 1979 to a peak of 277,600 in 1989. The share of the public sector in formal wage employment rose from 32 percent in 1964 to 50 percent in 1990 (Collier and Gunning 1999: 10). Contributing to the excessive growth of the civil service were a government guarantee of employment to anyone passing through a government training institute and a de facto guarantee of a public sector position to all university graduates. (The latter policy was discontinued in the late 1980s, when it was clearly no longer sustainable in the face of a government decision to implement a fivefold expansion in university enrollment.)

While the Kenyan government in the 1980s faced growing budget pressures arising from the total civil service wage bill, at the same time that falling real wages made it more difficult to fill professional and managerial positions, the problem was still less serious for Kenya than for most other SSA countries. The large amount of budgetary and balance of payments support that the government was receiving in the second half of the 1980s also made it easier to avoid confronting the problem in any fundamental way. Furthermore, retrenchment, or even the cessation of new hiring, was politically sensitive given the problem of high and growing urban unemployment. Instead the government used workshops, task forces, review commissions, and the like essentially as a means of buying time and avoiding action.

By 1993, however, action on this issue had become imperative, in large part due to the fiscal dimensions of the economic crisis that erupted in the first half of that year. A civil service reform program was launched in 1993, supported by the World Bank, UNDP, and several bilateral donors, but progress to date has been limited. A central component of the program has been the retrenchment of workers in the lower-wage categories through a voluntary retirement incentive scheme; some 50,000 low-wage employees were retired between fiscal 1993 and 1998, contributing to a reduction in the overall civil service rolls to 214,000 in 1998. However, in terms of total public sector employment these retrenchments in the civil service have been largely offset by expansion in the employment of teachers. The civil service reform program has also achieved the computerization of the employment rolls and the payroll and has been fairly successful in eliminating "ghost workers." Other more fundamental components of the program, such as a comprehensive review, ministry by ministry, of the appropriate role and functions of government, have lagged. Finally, as a corollary to civil service reform the government has moved some critical public functions, such as revenue collection under the Kenya Revenue Authority, outside the public service system in order to offer better pay and other incentives and, it is hoped, enforce performance standards.

The "Report of the Working Party on Government Expenditures" also discussed at some length the problems of state-owned enterprises (Kenya 1982). It characterized the SOEs as highly inefficient because of government pressure to carry out public, noncommercial functions and absorb more workers than needed, and because of protection from competition, declining standards of management and financial control, and lack of proper budgetary review. The report recommended forming a committee to oversee the divestiture of commercial enterprises. Such a committee was established in 1983 and continued to operate until 1987, but it failed to divest anything and only produced papers that provoked a hostile reaction from the Office of the President. This was one issue on which then Chief Secretary Simeon Nyachae was not prepared to push a reform agenda.[22] SP #1 of 1986, while emphasizing the preeminent role of the private sector, did not deal explicitly with SOEs beyond suggesting that they would have to become more efficient (Kenya 1986: 18). The authors of SP #1 recognized that there was as yet no political support for divestiture: leaders had strong vested interests in continued control over these enterprises as sources of political power and jobs for constituents, as a direct source of income from appointments to the boards of corporations, and as an easily exploitable source of rents. Consequently, the SOE sector continued to expand rather than contract in the 1980s, accounting for 11 percent of GDP by 1990.

A program of enterprise reform and privatization was finally announced in 1991. Up to then efforts to reform or divest individual enterprises, primarily in the agricultural sector, had been incorporated in some of the sectoral adjustment credits of the late 1980s, but with very limited results. The 1991 program was the first acknowledgment by the government that the problem was comprehensive, involving the entire sector which had by then expanded to include some 240 enterprises. Of these, 207 were to be divested, with the remaining 33 retained by government as "strategic." A policymaking board was set up under the chairmanship of Vice President and Minister of Finance George Saitoti, and a privatization unit was created with competent leadership but very limited staff. Later a unit was established in the Ministry of Finance to deal with the reform of the strategic enterprises—their arrears on taxes or other debts to government, performance plans, phasing out explicit and implicit subsidies, and so forth—and later these two units were merged under a single manager.

Initial progress was slow because politicians could not agree on the objectives of the exercise and because powerful vested interests favored keeping enterprises in the public sector. In subsequent years the pace of privatization picked up and a substantial number of transactions were completed, mainly for smaller firms and for those joint ventures in which the private partner held a preemptive right to buy the government shares. More recently the pace of privatizations has slackened again. And badly needed reforms in the major strategic enterprises, especially the railway, port, post and telecommunications, and power company, have proven extremely difficult to carry out. Within this mixed picture the one outstanding success was the reform and privatization of Kenya Airways during 1991–95.

AGRICULTURAL PRICING AND MARKETING. Another important area of Kenya's adjustment program is the attempted reform of agricultural pricing and marketing. This has been perhaps the most difficult and contentious area of policy reform throughout the entire period of structural adjustment. It is the area of economic policy that has created the most misunderstanding and ill will between donors and government, and probably the area where the gap between agreed policy conditions and implementation has been widest. However, given that the extensive interventions of government in agricultural pricing and marketing are longstanding and are tightly linked to the basic structure of the Kenyan economy, and given that previous efforts to reduce the government role had been unsuccessful, it is not surprising that the problems encountered during the structural adjustment period proved so difficult for all parties involved.

As described earlier, the government had established a number of public or quasi-public institutions that operated as monopolies or regulatory bodies in agricultural markets. Many of these evolved from organizations, such as the Wheat Board, that were created in the colonial period to serve the interests of the large-scale settler farmers. The most deeply entrenched of all these institutions has been the National Cereals and Produce Board (NCPB), established in 1979 as the successor to the maize and wheat boards. It has been for many years the monopsonist buyer of maize, the basic food grain of the Kenyan diet, produced by large, medium, and small-scale farmers. The NCPB monopsony was sustained by tightly restricting inter-district movement of cereals by private traders. NCPB paid a high fixed price, normally in excess of export parity, and guaranteed to purchase all maize supplied. The government controlled the price of maize at the producer, wholesale, and retail levels. In order to maintain "affordable" prices for urban consumers the government subsidized the price of maize in urban markets, in effect covering NCPB's losses in purchasing, storing, and marketing maize and smaller amounts of wheat and other food crops. This usually unpredictable drain on the exchequer subverted efforts to maintain fiscal discipline. On the other hand, because of its dependence on government subventions through the annual budgets, NCPB often suffered cash flow problems. Despite these problems, NCPB made every effort to ensure prompt payment to large-scale farmers in order to maintain their political support. But small farmers might have to wait months for payment, or might have to pay a bribe or sell at a distress price to larger farmers. This was often a critical problem for poor farmers who needed immediate cash to purchase inputs, pay debts, purchase other foodstuffs, and pay school fees.

Because NCPB was inefficient its losses were often heavy, and frequently exceeded the amounts included in the annual budgets for subventions to NCPB. By 1987 the accumulated debts of NCPB were equivalent to 5 percent of GDP. There was, moreover, corruption within the organization and a desire within parts of government, particularly the Ministry of Finance, to reduce the direct cost to government of maintaining the cereals monopoly and to promote the private sector's role in agricultural marketing. For all these reasons, there were frequent proposals to downsize, privatize, or end the life of NCPB. In fact, seven studies of the cereals market were carried out by special commissions of inquiry between the end of World War II and the 1980s, and all of them recommended reducing the role of the state in grain marketing (Mosley 1986b: 110). These recommendations were not followed, however, and inter-district movements of maize continued to be tightly controlled. The World Bank had attempted to promote limited deregulation of the cereals market through agricultural projects in the 1970s, but without success.

Liberalization of the grain market became stated government policy in the 1979–84 Development Plan and in a sessional paper on "National Food Policy" (Kenya 1981). On the basis of these policy statements dedicated officials in the Treasury such as Harris Mule encouraged the World Bank to make another effort at supporting liberalization, and cereals policy became a component of SALs I and II. When the straightforward approach did not work in SAL I the Bank and the government agreed, in SAL II, that government "would undertake a review of maize marketing and implement its recommendations." When this was not accomplished by the anticipated time of the second tranche release the Bank held up the release for nine months, finally agreeing to release the tranche on government assurance that the agreement would be carried out. It was, but only to the letter, and controls were reimposed subsequently. It was primarily this failure that led to the decision by the World Bank not to proceed with a SAL III.

The Bank returned to this issue in both ASAO I and II. ASAO I called for the restructuring of NCPB but this was not carried out.[23] ASAO II called for the introduction of annual performance contracts for NCPB and provided for the gradual liberalization of inter-district maize movements, starting with waiver of the permit requirement for movements of up to 44 bags (one truckload), then moving to 88 bags, and so forth. Permission to move 44 bags without a permit was announced in April 1991 by the Ministry of Supplies and Marketing, but was revoked in July 1991 by NCPB. The gradual deregulation was put back on track in early 1992 but canceled in November by a presidential decree that cited fear of a worsening drought as the rationale. At this point the World Bank canceled the second tranche of ASAO II.

Both the Bank and the government have been criticized for the failure to achieve meaningful reforms in cereals marketing during most of the SAP period.[24] On the other hand, Paul Mosley suggests that the result should have been expected, given past experience with this policy issue.[25] Since 1992 some progress has been made in opening up the cereals trade to private traders and in reducing the role of NCPB. But it is legitimate to ask whether the final achievement is commensurate with the efforts expended over so many years by the World Bank and reformers within the Kenyan government. In retrospect it might be questioned why the World Bank in particular was so consumed with cereals market liberalization, or indeed the liberalization of other agricultural markets in Kenya, given that the government-introduced distortions in such markets in Kenya were much less serious than in many other SSA countries (Mosley 1986a).

Origins of Reforms: Who Were the Reformers?

The first question to be considered here is the origin of the reform proposals that have been incorporated in Kenya's adjustment program over the past 20 years. There is no doubt that policy dialogue with both multilateral and bilateral donors, during the cycle of primarily project lending before 1980 and during the post-1980 era of SAPs, was important in highlighting problems and indicating approaches to their solutions. Technical assistance was also important, not least for the exposure to neoclassical economics that it provided to large numbers of Kenyan technocrats, including most of the key actors mentioned below. TA was also responsible for providing a cadre of economic advisers to the core economic ministries and agencies throughout the post-independence period. Individual advisers or advisory teams in the key economic bodies—Finance, Planning and the CBK—have been funded for more than 30 years by the Ford Foundation, UNDP, the Swedish International Development Authority, the United Kingdom, the World Bank, and a few other bilateral donors. While they were always few in number, several of these advisers, having gained the full confidence of their counterparts in government, have remained involved with the country over many years and have had a continuing influence on the direction of policy thinking.

An important point to be made, so far as economic policy reform is concerned, is that it is not the total dollar amount of technical assistance that is important. Rather, it is whether this total has included funding for needed advisory personnel in the central economic agencies, whether these funds have been employed to engage competent and committed advisers, and whether their advice has been utilized effectively. While the overall record of Kenya and its aid donor partners in utilizing TA across the full range of government functions can be criticized, a few influential advisers have had a positive impact on the economic policymaking process in the Kenyan government.

Although outsiders may have influenced the priority given to various economic policy issues, it is nevertheless clear that most of the reform agenda implemented over the past 20 years has been developed internally. Despite the progressive weakening of the civil service over a long period due to falling real wages and politicization, Kenya has always had a core of competent technocrats who could analyze the country's economic problems and propose solutions. The economic crises at key points in Kenya's post-independence economic development have provided openings for these technocrats, supported in their analysis by trusted advisers, to propose fundamental changes. The analysis and policy recommendations of these technocratic teams, on the full range of macroeconomic and sectoral issues, have been circulated within government in a continuing series of working party reports, reports of commissions of inquiry, sessional papers, annual budget speeches, national development plans and the like.

Key technocrats in this process, when new policy agendas were being articulated, have included Harris Mule in Treasury and Philip Ndegwa at the Central Bank in the early 1980s, and Nyachae, Mule, Ndegwa, and Ryan in 1984–86 when the second phase of the reform effort began with the publication of SP #1 of 1986.[26] In the trade and domestic market liberalization and financial sector reforms during1993–95, key actors included Governor Cheserem at the CBK, Ryan as economic secretary to the Treasury, and Benjamin Kipkulei as a supporter of education sector reforms under the EDSAC and later of the entire reform agenda as permanent secretary of the Ministry of Finance.

An important point to emphasize is that the economic policy formulation circle has always been of quite limited size and has been concentrated in the Finance and Planning ministries[27] and the CBK. Even within these agencies the policy formulation group has been small, and the internal discussion has been controlled and closed rather than open. Decisionmaking has been highly centralized, with limited dialogue and interaction with other branches of government. For example, when SP #1 of 1986 was in preparation in the Ministry of Finance and Planning, there was consultation but little interaction with other branches of the government in the later development of the policy paper. This was due to the generally passive response to earlier consultations, with the exception of the Agriculture and Energy ministries. After SP #1 received cabinet approval it was approved by Parliament with little debate.

This closed and often nontransparent approach has related in part to the desire of the core policymakers to prevent those, either within or outside government, who were potential losers from future policy actions from mobilizing opposition in advance. To a considerable degree Kenya has been successful in this strategy of introducing and implementing policy reforms through surprise or "stealth." But such an approach also has costs. When other branches of government, outside of the central economic agencies, have to be involved in policy implementation, the failure to include them in the policy development stage could dilute their sense of "ownership" of the policy measure in question. And this failure to obtain full ownership across the government can explain some cases in which good policies are implemented poorly, or not at all.

Another limitation in the policy formulation process has been the reluctance of government to involve "stakeholders" in the development of policy options. As noted above, in the era of multiparty politics since 1991 the government has made little or no response to the economic and social policy position papers prepared by opposition political parties or political action groups (For example, Gatheru and Shaw 1998; Ng'ethe and Owino 1998). The same can be said in general about government responsiveness to the private business community, the key stakeholder group for most of the policies discussed in this paper.

The business sector has made repeated efforts over the years to engage the government in economic policy dialogue, but with little or no success until recently. The key concerns of the business community for many years were price controls, foreign exchange rationing and import licensing, and taxes. The major business organizations, the Kenyan Association of Manufacturers and the Federation of Kenyan Employers, do transmit ideas from their membership to government on a regular basis, primarily by making annual submissions to the Finance Ministry in advance of the budget presentation. However, these and other stakeholder representatives have not always been satisfied that their views received an adequate hearing. Many Kenyan officials feel that the government should not discuss proposed policy changes with the business community; rather, they view the private business sector as a group that is always lobbying for its own vested interests, against whom it is the government's responsibility to represent the general public interest.

In 1980 a joint government-business consultative council was set up, co-chaired by Harris Mule, then permanent secretary of the Ministry of Finance, and Joe Wanjui, then chairman of the Kenyan Association of Manufacturers. While Mule was an excellent choice as chief government representative, the forum was not treated with sufficient seriousness by the rest of government, and its effectiveness soon evaporated. Only with the formation in 1992 of the Export Promotion Council, a body funded by government but with majority private sector membership on its board, including the chairman and a competent staff, has the business sector had an effective channel of communication for policy dialogue with government.

Another aspect of the policymaking process in Kenya has been the very limited use of local consultants, university researchers, or research institutes. Kenya has many qualified individuals working outside government who could be involved in advising government, but they have been almost irrelevant to the policymaking process. This assessment can be generalized to many other areas of government activity besides economic policy. Efforts have been underway in recent years to remedy this situation with regard to economic policy analysis through the creation of new research institutions such as the Institute of Policy Analysis and Research and the recently established Kenya Institute for Public Policy Analysis and Research, which is government-sponsored but independent. Both of these institutions have received funding from the African Capacity Building Foundation.

Policy proposals designed by technocrats and advisers must be "sold" to politicians if they are to be adopted. In Kenya the circle of key political actors for economic policy decisions is also small. At the center, obviously, is the president, who must be persuaded not only of the economic feasibility but also of the *political* soundness of any policy reform proposal. The finance minister is also critical, of course, as would be the relevant sector ministers for policy reforms in agriculture, commerce, energy, and so forth.

In the mid-1980s Simeon Nyachae played both technocratic and political roles as head of the civil service and also secretary to the cabinet. He was able to use his position and his access to the president to push adoption of the 1986 SP #1 and to outflank cabinet opposition to its implementation by ensuring that permanent secretaries reporting directly to him carried out the policies that were agreed for their ministries. George Saitoti, who came into government from the University of Nairobi in 1983 as an appointed member of Parliament and Minister of Finance and Planning, aligned himself with the reform agenda in the mid-1980s. At that time he was quite prepared to address the problems of inefficiency and high cost of government without regard for the rent-seeking privileges that had handicapped his predecessors. However, when he had to stand for election in 1988 and assumed responsibilities for a constituency, and then was appointed vice president in the following year, he was less able to give his attention to the economic reform agenda. His diminished support contributed to the slackening pace of reforms after 1989.

In the 1993–95 reform episode it was clearly the new finance minister, Musalia Mudavadi, who carried the burden of confronting the 1993 financial crisis in his first months in office and then pushing through a major trade liberalization and full deregulation of domestic prices. He came into the Finance Ministry in January 1993 without previous experience that would prepare him for the challenges he would face, but he listened carefully to his advisers, took stands on principle in support of reforms, and was not discouraged by occasional setbacks. His hand as a reformer was strengthened significantly by bringing Permanent Secretary Ben Kipkulei from the Ministry of Education to Finance, not so much because of Kipkulei's technical capacity as an economist but because of his access to the president and the president's confidence in him.

A question that must be considered regarding reformers and the policy reform process in Kenya is why the circle of political support for reforms has been so small. The key economic reformers have been confined largely to the Finance and Planning ministries and the CBK. It is much easier for this group to handle reforms in their own areas—fiscal and monetary policy, financial sector management, public debt, price controls, exchange and trade policies—than it is to deal with structural issues of agricultural marketing reforms, SOE reforms and privatization, or institutional capacity building for reform implementation across the government. For success in these areas they require sustained support from counterparts in other ministries and departments. And this support did not develop as hoped in response to successful reforms in the macroeconomic, trade, and finance areas and the resulting positive economic outcomes.

Put another way, there has not been a significant "bandwagon" effect in Kenya. Periods of stronger reform efforts have brought positive economic results, yet these results do not seem to have won sizable numbers of converts to the cause of economic liberalization. The business community has been generally but not always supportive, while the political class within government appears to have preferred to guard its options and not line up squarely behind the reforms. One reason may be the inadequate consultation process referred to above; another may be the fact that sector ministers and their staffs seldom see the direct benefits of donor balance of payments support in the form of additional resources for their own ministries. In any event, Kenya's failure to build a broad constituency for reform within the government simply mirrors the experience of other SSA countries.

CONCLUSION: AID AND POLICY REFORMS

Results in Kenya

The economic results from almost 20 years of structural adjustment in Kenya must be considered disappointing. There have been periods (1985–90 and 1994–96) of reasonable recovery and respectable GDP growth, but overall the economic record has been mediocre. The structural adjustment era has failed to create the conditions for a sustained recovery of GDP growth to the levels attained in the 1960s and early 1970s. Even more worrying, with the slow growth of the economy poverty has been increasing and social indicators (life expectancy, child mortality, and primary school enrollment, among others) have shown negative trends in recent years (World Bank 1994).

Underlying the ups and downs in the economic growth record since 1980 has been the failure of structural adjustment to promote a sustained recovery of private investment or exports. This finding holds for both domestic and foreign investment. One of the stated objectives of the government, following periods of lagging reforms, has been to regain the confidence of donor countries, both to restore the flow of aid and to win the confidence of overseas investors, who come predominantly from the aid-giving countries. This has not happened, as shown in table 8.4, which gives annual data on foreign direct investment in Kenya since 1980. Several facts stand out in this data series. First, there has been a marked decline in the volume of foreign investment over this period, from an

TABLE 8.4 KENYA: FOREIGN DIRECT INVESTMENT, 1980–96
(millions of U.S. dollars)

Year	Amount	Year	Amount
1980	79	1989	62
1981	61	1990	57
1982	13	1991	19
1983	24	1992	6
1984	11	1993	2
1985	18	1994	4
1986	33	1995	32
1987	43	1996	13
1988	0		

Source: World Bank, *Global Development Finance* (formerly *World Debt Tables*), various years.

annual average of US$38 million in 1980–84 to only US$11 million in 1992–96. It is also striking that the major reforms in the trade and exchange area in 1993–95, which should have been of particular interest to foreign investors, elicited such a weak response.

On balance there appears to be little correlation between the periods of better-than-average reform performance and the inflow of foreign private investment. This can almost certainly be attributed to the fact that overseas investors are also concerned with factors other than the status of a country's SAP. While overseas investors might welcome the economic liberalization that Kenya has achieved, especially in the trade and exchange field, and may be reasonably confident that reforms will be sustained, they would also be conscious of the potential instability of the exchange rate given Kenya's high degree of aid dependency. Other factors influencing investor decisions, besides the predictability and sustainability of the policy framework, include political stability, the quality of infrastructure, and the incidence of corruption. On most of these factors Kenya has suffered from a deteriorating image in recent years. Thus, while Kenya's record of implementation of structural adjustment measures has been mixed, the disappointing economic track record of the 1980s and 1990s must also be attributed to deficiencies in these other essential prerequisites for higher investment and growth.

Despite shortcomings in performance and outcomes, it must nevertheless be acknowledged that Kenya has made major strides in economic reform over this period: decontrol of all prices, total liberalization of the trade and foreign exchange regime, decontrol of interest rates, and progress in reforms of the financial sector and of financial institutions, to mention the more important areas. In some cases the government has moved farther and faster than anticipated or stipulated in the conditionalities negotiated with aid donors. And these unanticipated reforms have been "homegrown" in the sense that they were developed and implemented independently. This applies to the limited foreign exchange liberalization measures introduced in 1991–92 at a time when relations with donors were strained, and the full extent of the trade liberalization measures adopted in 1993–94. However, fiscal problems have not been fully resolved, and the areas of structural or institutional reforms—civil service, judiciary, public enterprises, agricultural production and marketing agencies—have proved much more difficult.

While recurring economic crises over the past 20 years have provided the opening for Kenyan reformers to propose far-reaching policy changes, Kenya has proved more efficient in articulating policy reforms than in implementing them. Some of this gap may be explained by lack of adequate competence at middle and lower levels of the bureaucracy, and some by the lack of adequate internal consultation across the government. Admittedly, advanced consultations with either stakeholders or implementers is not required in every situation, and some of the most effective reforms in Kenya's experience have been introduced by "stealth," but the effectiveness of this approach is essentially limited to those "one-shot" reforms that can be carried out by decree and do not require an institutional structure for continuing implementation. Some of the implementation problems can be attributed to unrealistic assessments of the feasibility of certain reforms by Kenyan politicians and technocrats and by donors. Even when agreements were negotiated in good faith, they sometimes could not be fully implemented because of unanticipated political resistance, economic shocks, or similar factors. However, in a few cases implementation problems have resulted from Kenyan officials making commitments in the full knowledge that failure to meet the agreed conditions was inevitable.

Finally, some of the shortcomings in Kenya's implementation of structural adjustment measures in the past decade may be attributable to the introduction toward the end of the 1980s of the tripartite (government, IMF, World Bank) "Policy Framework Paper " as the prerequisite for accessing the IMF's SAF or ESAF resources. While these documents were supposed to be statements of *government* policy, it is well known that in the early years of their existence they were drafted by IMF and World Bank staff and presented to governments for review and acceptance. It is certain that some degree of government ownership was lost in this drafting process. However, while the regularly updated Policy Framework Paper is still a basic document underlying a country's adjustment program, a more participatory approach is taken today to its preparation than was the case a decade ago.

Donor Conditionality

Kenya's economic reform efforts, ongoing but with slowdowns and re-starts over the past 20 years, have encompassed virtually all sectors of the economy. This is true also for the donor-supported adjustment lending agreements that the Kenyan government has negotiated. Given the scope and complexity of the successive adjustment phases it is perhaps not surprising that the conditionalities attached to adjustment operations have been numerous, highly detailed, and challenging. Donors, and especially the World Bank, have been criticized for the breadth of conditionality applied in adjustment operations in many developing countries, including Kenya (Killick 1998). This overloading of conditions is often referred to as the "Christmas tree" effect. While it has been stated over and over that conditionality should be focused on a few priority measures, and this is generally accepted, putting it into practice has proved difficult.[28] If there are too many conditions it often becomes difficult to evaluate performance and determine whether a tranche of an adjustment support loan should be released, when, say, most conditions are met but a few are only partially met or not met at all. Other defects in conditionality include the specification of conditions in a form that is too general or too weak. For example, conditionality often focuses on studies or on developing "action plans." This approach often delays getting to any concrete *action*.

In the case of Kenya, follow-up on compliance with conditionality has been at times lax or erratic, at least in the 1980s, when release of funds sometimes occurred despite only partial or non-fulfillment of agreed conditions. The willingness of the World Bank to waive or accept partial implementation of certain conditions in SAL II and various of the late-1980s SECALs, coupled with similar actions on the part of the IMF and other donors, probably led the government to believe that full commitment to negotiated conditionalities was not required. Thus the government did not expect that something like the November 1991 aid freeze could ever occur, or if it did, it would only be a warning that would be quickly rescinded. Of course, in the 1980s Kenya represented a relative success story in Africa for the donor community, as Ghana was also seen then, and as Uganda is seen today. The donor community did not want to unduly penalize one of the better African performers.

However, with the end of the Cold War in 1989 and increased donor attention to good governance, human rights issues, political freedoms, and corruption, the donor community came together to close ranks against Kenya in 1991 (Barkan 1998). The expectation now is for full compliance with agreed conditions, with suspension or cancellation of funds as the penalty for failure, as evidenced in the IMF and World Bank actions in 1997–98. Thus, while Kenya today appears to fall at least in the middle rank of reforming countries in SSA, in terms of the full extent of reforms introduced since 1980, it is currently experiencing a sharp curtailment in total donor aid and a virtual cessation of structural adjustment lending, owing in part to weakening of the economic reform effort, but even more to donor perceptions about political and governance issues.

Aid and Reforms

Has donor financial support to Kenya given the donor community the leverage to strongly influence the shaping of Kenya's economic and social policies? Certainly Kenya has received massive amounts of aid over a sustained period of time—more than US$15 billion between 1970 and 1996. This substantial flow of financial and technical assistance has given donors leverage, but much less than the aggregate numbers might suggest. One important reason is that the amount of money that the donors disburse, through grants and loans, is greater than the amount of money that the government actually receives or "sees," for reasons partially explained in appendix 8.2. If aid flows into the country outside the government budget, or the government has less control over the use of the funds provided to it, the government is presumably less influenced by aid in these cases.

However, the more important question is whether one specific type of aid—conditional balance of payments financing tied to implementation of a structural adjustment program—has had a significant impact on the timing, strength, and sustainability of Kenya's reform efforts. Did such aid induce the Kenyan government to adopt reforms that it might not otherwise have undertaken? Kenya received huge amounts of aid in return for policy reform agreements—almost US$3 billion over the entire 1970–96 period. How effective was this aid in "buying" reforms? We would argue that at times of severe economic crisis, as in 1980–82 and 1993, the government's need for financial support was sufficiently desperate that the promise of such support did induce the government to come to agreement relatively quickly on far-reaching reform programs. However, as noted above, these agreements were not always implemented. Sometimes the probability of successful implementation was low from the outset. Other times the lenders or donors may have aligned themselves with well-intentioned technocrats who wished to achieve the results contracted for but lacked the political support to do so. It is our view, therefore, that donor aid can have an influence on the form of agreement reached and on the agreed timetable for implementation, but whether implementation is carried out depends in the end much more on domestic political and economic factors than on donor money (see Burnside and Dollar 1997; World Bank 1998).

If aid has had only limited impact on the implementation of reforms, is it possible that a large volume of aid could make it easier for a government to ride out a crisis without undertaking needed reforms? It is probable that the heavy infusion of budget support Kenya received during the 1980s helped the government to finance the budgetary cost of an overstaffed civil service and inefficient public enterprises, thus enabling the government to defer reforms in these areas until the 1990s. Finally, can the threat or actuality of an aid cutoff induce a government to restart a reform effort that has stalled or gone into reverse? In such circumstances the pressure of debt obligations on past ODA or commercial loans would presumably give added leverage to the donor/creditor community to induce a return to the reform program. In the early 1990s Kenya faced exactly such pressures, with mounting debt arrears to donors and commercial creditors. Yet in this case, as in other instances of weakening or backtracking on reforms, the government did not respond quickly with a renewal of reforms. Rather, a significant time lag intervened. The first hiatus in adjustment lending, following the disappointing results of SALs I and II, lasted from the beginning of 1984 to 1986. The second, the freeze in balance of payments support following the November 1991 CG meeting, lasted until mid-1993, and the mid-1997 suspension of the IMF ESAF program persisted for three years without a new agreement. On balance, we conclude that government ownership and political will have more to do with the timing, extent, and sustainability of the reform program than does the volume of donor aid.

APPENDIX 8.1
KENYA: CHRONOLOGY OF POLITICAL
AND ECONOMIC DEVELOPMENTS

May 1963	First national election, won by KANU.
12 December 1963	Kenya's independence from the United Kingdom.
1965	Sessional Paper No. 10 of 1965, "African Socialism and Its Application to Planning in Kenya."
1966	Central Bank of Kenya established.
October 1969	Banning of Kenya People's Union; Kenya becomes a de facto single-party state.
October 1973	First oil crisis.
1976–77	Coffee boom results in erosion of fiscal discipline; subsequent decline in coffee prices worsens balance of payments deficits.
August 1977	Breakup of East African Community and common currency area linking Kenya, Tanzania, and Uganda.
August 1978	President Jomo Kenyatta dies; succeeded by Vice President Daniel arap Moi.
1979	Second oil crisis.
January 1980	Launch of structural adjustment program; first Structural Adjustment Credit from World Bank.
May 1982	Constitution amended to make Kenya a de jure single-party state.
1 August 1982	Attempted coup against Moi government led by members of the Air Force.
1984	Severe drought due to failure of rains, requiring massive food grain imports.
January 1986	Sessional Paper No. 1 of 1986, "Economic Management for Renewed Growth."
1986–87	Coffee boom, of lesser impact than 1976–77.
25–26 November 1991	Consultative Group meeting in Paris at which donors decide to suspend balance of payments aid.
10 December 1991	Constitution amended to permit formation of multiple political parties.
29 December 1992	First multiparty election since independence. President Moi reelected with 37 percent plurality of votes; KANU wins 100 of 188 contested parliamentary seats (plus 12 nominated MPs appointed by the president.)
December 1995	Repeal of Exchange Control Act to complete liberalization of trade regime.
December 1997	Second multiparty election. Moi reelected with larger plurality than in 1992 but KANU holds smaller majority in Parliament.

APPENDIX 8.2
KENYA: DATA SOURCES, DEFINITIONS,
AND CONSTRAINTS

The concept of aid used in this study is based on "official development assistance" as defined by the Development Assistance Committee (DAC) of the Organisation for Economic Co-operation and Development (OECD). ODA comprises both direct financial aid and technical cooperation or technical assistance. The latter consists largely of grants to nationals of aid-receiving countries for education or training, often conducted outside the national's country, and the cost of consultants, advisers, administrators, teachers, and so forth, hired to work in the aid-receiving country, as well as equipment provided to facilitate the transfer of skills. ODA comprises both grants and concessional loans for development purposes; the DAC considers concessional loans to be those having a grant element of at least 25 percent based on a discount rate or opportunity cost of 10 percent. Gross ODA measures total disbursements of aid, both grants and loans, to a country from all aid-giving sources in a given calendar year, as reported to the DAC by the donor country or agency. Net ODA measures disbursements minus amortization payments on past ODA loans.

In this study loan data are taken from the reports of the recipient countries to the World Bank's Debtor Reporting System; grant data are from the OECD-DAC. This enables us to break down the loan data by the purposes of the loan, that is, for projects in various sectors or for balance of payments support/structural adjustment lending. The DAC data for grants can only be subdivided into financial aid and technical cooperation. While this mix of dual sources for loan and grant data is reasonably consistent with the DAC data for gross and net ODA, including both grants *and loans* reported to the DAC by donors, it presents problems for the analysis in this paper.

The first problem is that because we cannot break out grant aid for balance of payments support, our estimate of the total amount of structural adjustment or policy-based lending is an understatement. It is likely that in addition to the US$2.8 billion of multilateral and bilateral *lending* for structural adjustment over the past 25 years, there has been several hundred million dollars of *grant* assistance for this same purpose from bilateral donors. However, we do not feel that this lack of information negates our basic conclusions regarding the influence, or lack of influence, of donor aid on policy reforms. Second, and possibly offsetting to some extent the lack of data on grant support for policy reforms, we have included under balance of payments aid all loans not linked to projects in specific sectors. This includes loans categorized as "balance of payments support" and as "contribution to financing current imports."

It is possible that some of the lending in this latter category, amounting to some US$140 million over the entire 1970–96 period, may not have been linked directly to economic policy reforms. However, this represents only 5 percent of the total balance of payments support, so the possible bias introduced is small. Third, we have included *all* IMF drawings under balance of payments support, both the more concessional lending under the SAF and ESAF programs and the conventional standby programs.

It has not been possible to reconcile the DAC data from donor sources with the aid figures in the Kenyan fiscal accounts. This is unfortunate, since it could have been one way to establish the volume of grant aid support for structural adjustment. One reason is the difference in reporting periods: calendar year reporting by the DAC and World Bank and fiscal year (July 1 – June 30) by the Kenyan government. However, the problem is greater than this difference in timing. Consistently over the entire period of this study the Kenyan fiscal accounts record a significantly smaller aid inflow, particularly for project-related investments, than donors are reporting to the DAC.

There are several possible explanations for this discrepancy. First, much assistance for TA does not pass to the Kenyan government but is paid directly to Kenyan students abroad, to overseas training institutions, or to the offshore bank accounts of resident advisers. Even if the donor agency is supposed to report the amount of such assistance to the Kenyan government, it is likely that a significant share of this is missed. Second, in the case of project aid a similar problem arises, since donor countries may procure goods offshore or pay contractors directly for work performed on behalf of the Kenyan government. Again, this should be recorded as aid furnished to Kenya, but some of it could be unreported or underreported. Third, as bilateral donor countries have converted an increasing proportion of their aid programs to a grant basis, for which they no longer require any government guarantee of repayment, they are providing a growing share of their assistance directly to nongovernmental agencies, including churches, citizens' associations, women's groups, the private business sector, and individuals. Much of this grant aid may not be reported to the host government. Fourth, donors report to the DAC as grant aid any debt relief provided on past ODA loans; it is quite likely that the aid-receiving country does not include this as new aid received. Finally, there may simply be a tendency of donors to overstate what they are providing and for the recipient to undervalue what has been received. (This could be cited as one reason why aid has not had as much influence as might be expected. If this is the case it would reinforce rather than undermine our principal thesis.)

In recognition of the fact that the DAC definition of concessional loans is arbitrary on several counts, including the use of a fixed 10 percent discount rate for all loans, and the inclusion or exclusion of the total value of loans based on the 25 percent grant element threshold, staff at the World Bank have developed an alternative concept known as effective development assistance (EDA) (Chang, Fernández-Arias, and Servén 1999). EDA incorporates only the grant component, not the total loan value, of a development loan, without regard to any grant element threshold such as the DAC-specified 25 percent, but with the grant element calculated based on an appropriate discount rate related to the cost of capital in the lending country. Annual data for total aid flows to Kenya during 1970–96, measured according to both ODA and EDA concepts, are shown in table 8.5. It can readily be seen that EDA is substantially lower than ODA; this is because the recalculated grant element is lower for most loans than the total value of those loans that qualify under the DAC 25 percent rule.

APPENDIX 8.3
KENYA: AID DATA

TABLE 8.5 TOTAL AID FLOWS TO KENYA, 1970–96
(millions of U.S. dollars)

Year	Total ODA	Total EDA
1970	66.1	31.8
1971	80.0	49.6
1972	141.5	92.8
1973	141.2	84.5
1974	150.7	105.1
1975	187.6	109.2
1976	258.7	147.4
1977	253.6	148.4
1978	343.4	226.6
1979	432.0	297.0
1980	480.9	370.1
1981	535.8	396.0
1982	578.0	406.1
1983	519.6	354.3
1984	655.6	416.4
1985	526.5	397.8
1986	637.1	452.0
1987	752.6	515.8
1988	954.4	737.7
1989	1,091.9	798.2
1990	1,615.0	1,442.2
1991	1,102.1	863.1
1992	987.1	798.3
1993	869.7	749.3
1994	731.3	611.9
1995	1,020.9	727.1
1996	743.3	575.0
Total	15,856.6	11,876.7

Note: ODA (official development assistance) includes both concessional loans (those with a grant element of at least 25 percent according to the DAC definition) and grants. Grants include both technical cooperation and debt relief on previous ODA loans. EDA (effective development assistance) includes all grants plus the grant element of all development loans recalculated according to the methodology in Chang, Fernández-Arias, and Servén (1999). All data in current prices.
Sources: Loan data from World Bank Debtor Reporting System; grant data from OECD-DAC. EDA from Chang, Fernández-Arias, and Servén (1999).

TABLE 8.6 KENYA: LOAN AND GRANT COMPONENTS OF ODA FLOWS, 1970–96

(millions of U.S. dollars)

Year	Loans	Grants	Total	% Grants
1970	35.5	30.6	66.1	46.3
1971	42.2	37.8	80.0	47.3
1972	55.7	85.8	141.5	60.1
1973	87.1	54.1	141.2	38.3
1974	77.8	72.9	150.7	48.4
1975	98.2	89.4	187.6	47.7
1976	148.8	109.9	258.7	42.4
1977	139.9	113.7	253.6	44.8
1978	168.8	174.6	343.4	50.8
1979	213.1	218.9	432.0	50.7
1980	232.1	248.8	480.9	51.7
1981	237.1	298.7	535.8	55.7
1982	317.8	260.2	578.0	45.0
1983	242.6	277.0	519.6	53.3
1984	373.5	282.1	655.6	43.0
1985	215.0	311.5	526.5	59.2
1986	287.9	349.2	637.1	54.8
1987	352.5	400.1	752.6	53.2
1988	387.3	567.1	954.4	59.4
1989	538.3	553.6	1,091.9	50.7
1990	429.7	1,185.3	1,615.0	73.4
1991	461.2	640.9	1,102.1	58.2
1992	327.5	659.6	987.1	66.8
1993	317.6	552.1	869.7	63.5
1994	227.5	503.8	731.3	68.9
1995	557.5	463.4	1,020.9	45.4
1996	342.8	400.5	743.3	53.9
Total	6,915.0	8,941.6	15,856.6	56.4

Sources: Total ODA from table 8.5. Loan data from World Bank Debtor Reporting System. Grant data from OECD-DAC.

TABLE 8.7 KENYA: GROSS AND NET ODA FLOWS, 1970–96
(millions of U.S. dollars)

Year	Gross ODA	Debt relief	ODA excluding debt relief	Net ODA[a]	Net ODA in 1995 prices
1970	66.1	0	66.1	57.5	—
1971	80.0	0	80.0	67.0	—
1972	141.5	0	141.5	72.3	—
1973	141.2	0	141.2	95.8	—
1974	150.7	0	150.7	119.4	—
1975	187.6	0	187.6	130.6	—
1976	258.7	0	258.7	160.0	—
1977	253.6	0	253.6	165.2	—
1978	343.4	0	343.4	242.5	—
1979	432.0	0	432.0	350.6	—
1980	480.9	0	480.9	396.5	771
1981	535.8	0	535.8	449.3	—
1982	578.0	0	578.0	484.9	—
1983	519.6	0	519.6	397.3	—
1984	655.6	0	655.6	411.1	—
1985	526.5	0	526.5	438.3	919
1986	637.1	14.0	623.1	458.0	775
1987	752.6	60.0	692.6	572.0	842
1988	954.4	13.0	941.4	809.0	1,107
1989	1,091.9	433.0	658.9	967.0	1,336
1990	1,615.0	84.0	1,531.0	1,053.0	1,473
1991	1,102.1	66.0	1,036.1	873.0	1,100
1992	987.1	30.0	957.1	894.0	1,000
1993	869.7	0	869.7	911.0	1,046
1994	731.3	0	731.3	677.0	743
1995	1,020.9	0	1,020.9	732.0	732
1996	743.3	0	743.3	606.0	626
Total	15,856.6	700.0	15,156.6	12,590.3	

— Not available.

a. Includes repayments of previous ODA loans.

Sources: Gross ODA from table 8.5. Debt relief data from World Bank, *World Debt Tables,* various years. Net ODA in current and constant prices from OECD-DAC annual reports, "Development Cooperation: Efforts and Policies of the Members of the DAC," various years.

TABLE 8.8 ODA TO KENYA BY SOURCE:
MULTILATERAL AND BILATERAL

Year	Total multilateral (millions of U.S. dollars)	Total bilateral (millions of U.S. dollars)	Multilateral percentage	Bilateral percentage
1970–79	502.3	1,552.3	24.5	75.5
1970	10.0	56.1	15.1	84.9
1971	11.0	69.0	13.7	86.3
1972	27.5	114.0	19.4	80.6
1973	33.4	107.8	23.7	76.3
1974	27.4	123.1	18.3	81.7
1975	57.4	130.2	30.6	69.4
1976	88.0	170.7	34.0	66.0
1977	73.2	180.4	28.9	71.1
1978	84.1	259.3	24.5	75.5
1979	90.3	341.7	20.9	79.1
1980–89	2,009.1	4,723.5	29.8	70.2
1980	159.8	321.1	33.2	66.8
1981	122.1	413.7	22.8	77.2
1982	205.9	372.1	35.6	64.4
1983	157.4	362.2	30.3	69.7
1984	198.5	457.3	30.2	69.8
1985	144.7	381.8	27.5	72.5
1986	124.5	512.6	19.5	80.5
1987	188.1	564.5	25.0	75.0
1988	273.3	681.1	28.6	71.4
1989	434.8	657.1	39.8	60.2
1990–96	1,758.4	5,310.7	24.9	75.1
1990	333.9	1,281.1	20.7	79.3
1991	242.5	859.6	22.0	78.0
1992	221.1	766.0	22.4	77.6
1993	272.8	596.9	31.4	68.6
1994	190.5	540.8	34.3	65.7
1995	280.5	740.4	27.5	72.5
1996	217.1	525.9	29.2	70.8
1970–96	4,269.8	11,586.5	26.9	73.1

Sources: Total ODA from table 8.5. Loan data from World Bank Debtor Reporting System. Grant data from OECD-DAC.

TABLE 8.9 SHARES OF MAJOR AID DONORS/LENDERS IN ODA
(percent)

Donor/lender	1970–79	1980–89	1990–96	1970–96
World Bank/IDA	19.9	20.4	16.2	18.5
Japan	4.0	8.6	17.0	11.8
Germany	11.3	6.6	12.6	9.8
United Kingdom	17.9	9.3	5.5	8.7
USAID	6.5	9.7	8.1	8.1
Netherlands	5.8	6.6	5.0	5.8
Canada	4.9	4.7	3.8	4.3
Sweden	8.6	3.7	2.3	3.7
European Community	1.3	4.1	4.1	3.7
Denmark	4.1	3.6	2.6	3.2
AfDB/ADF	0.9	3.0	2.7	2.6
Norway	4.2	3.7	0.6	2.4
Others	10.6	16.0	19.5	17.4
Total	100.0	100.0	100.0	100.0

Sources: Total ODA from table 8.5. Loan data from World Bank Debtor Reporting System. Grant data from OECD-DAC.

TABLE 8.10 GRANT AID TO KENYA FOR TECHNICAL ASSISTANCE, 1970–96
(millions of U.S. dollars)

Year	Grants for TA	Total grants	Percent for TA
1970–79	576.8	987.7	58.4
1980–89	1,385.3	3,548.3	39.0
1980	128.0	248.8	51.4
1981	128.0	298.7	42.9
1982	116.8	260.2	44.9
1983	122.1	277.0	44.1
1984	109.6	282.1	38.9
1985	116.9	311.5	37.5
1986	156.3	349.2	44.8
1987	154.5	400.1	38.6
1988	178.4	567.1	31.5
1989	174.7	553.6	31.6
1990–96	1,579.4	4,405.6	35.8
1990	208.3	1,185.3	17.6
1991	222.9	640.9	34.8
1992	281.5	659.6	42.7
1993	260.3	552.1	47.1
1994	192.6	503.8	38.2
1995	221.4	463.4	47.8
1996	192.4	400.5	48.0
1970–96	3,541.5	8,941.6	39.6

Note: ODA (official development assistance) includes both concessional loans (those with a grant element of at least 25 percent according to the DAC definition) and grants. Grants include both technical cooperation and debt relief on previous ODA loans. All data in current prices.
Sources: Grant data from OECD-DAC.

TABLE 8.11 BALANCE OF PAYMENTS AID TO KENYA:
MULTILATERAL, BILATERAL, AND IMF LOANS, 1970–96
(millions of U.S. dollars)

Year	Multilateral loans	Bilateral loans	IMF loans	Totals
1970–79	35.0	19.5	239.0	293.5
1970	0	0	0	0
1971	0	0	0	0
1972	0	0	0	0
1973	0	0	0	0
1974	0	6.6	38.0	44.6
1975	16.7	3.4	59.0	79.1
1976	13.3	0	31.0	44.3
1977	5.0	0.6	0	5.6
1978	0	1.8	0	1.8
1979	0	7.1	111.0	118.1
1980–89	510.9	202.4	886.0	1599.3
1980	68.4	18.5	94.0	180.9
1981	1.7	23.9	36.0	61.6
1982	83.7	18.2	166.0	267.9
1983	0	6.1	139.0	145.1
1984	50.0	59.3	47.0	156.3
1985	0	4.2	125.0	129.2
1986	0	15.6	0	15.6
1987	30.0	11.2	0	41.2
1988	95.5	5.1	176.0	276.6
1989	181.6	40.3	103.0	324.9
1990–96	605.7	50.3	284.0	940.0
1990	145.2	5.2	136.0	286.4
1991	124.6	0.7	48.0	173.3
1992	1.2	0	0	1.2
1993	160.6	0	32.0	192.6
1994	14.6	0	32.0	46.6
1995	79.7	44.4	0	124.1
1996	79.8	0	36.0	115.8
Total	1,151.6	130.4	1,409.0	2,832.8

Sources: Loan data from World Bank Debtor Reporting System. IMF loans from IMF, *Annual Report,* various years, and World Bank, *World Debt Tables,* various years.

APPENDIX 8.4
KENYA INTERVIEWS

James W. Adams	World Bank: Resident Representative in Kenya 1985–88, Country Director for Kenya 1995–96.
Edgar O. Edwards	Adviser to Kenyan government (Ministries of Finance and Planning), 1962–83.
Dr. Wilfred K. Koinange	Former civil servant: Director of Medical Services, Permanent Secretary, Ministries of Agriculture, Industry, Finance.
Joseph Magari	Former civil servant: Director of Fiscal and Monetary Affairs, Treasury; Permanent Secretary, Ministries of Finance, Agriculture.
Hon. Musalia Mudavadi	Minister of Agriculture, former Minister of Finance (1993–97).
Harris Mule	Former civil servant: Director of Planning (1970s) and Permanent Secretary, Ministry of Finance (1981–86).
Nicholas Muriuki	Former Managing Director, Shell Petroleum Company.
Peter Muthoka	Civil servant: Executive Director, Export Promotion Council.
Kurt M. Savosnick	Adviser to Kenyan government (Ministries of Finance and Planning) during late 1960s, early 1970s.
Robert Shaw	Kenyan businessman, journalist.
John Simba	Former civil servant, banker: former Executive Secretary of unit in charge of divestiture of public enterprises.
Gurushri Swamy	World Bank: economist working on Kenya 1980s, early 1990s.
Gene Tidrick	World Bank: seconded adviser to Kenya government 1979–80.
Joseph Wanjui	Former Managing Director, East African Industries.

NOTES

1. For details on definitions and sources of the data used in this study, see appendix 8.2.

2. Loan terms have also softened because the World Bank, the major provider of development loans, phased out lending on IBRD terms in 1986. Since then all World Bank loans have been on IDA terms.

3. Total cumulative World Bank and IDA lending commitments to Kenya as of June 30, 1998 were US$4.0 billion, consisting of US$1.2 billion in IBRD loans and US$2.8 billion in IDA credits.

4. The so-called "Washington consensus" on the virtues of liberalization and a substantially reduced role for government in economic affairs only evolved during the era of structural adjustment in the 1980s. See "What Washington Means by Policy Reform" in Williamson (1990).

5. This donor action at the November 1991 CG meeting has been widely misunderstood. It has often been assumed that donors froze *all* aid, but in fact aid for ongoing and new development projects, technical assistance, and emergency relief continued as before.

6. This credit was approved, and the first tranche of US$34 million disbursed, in September 1991, only two months before the donor meeting of November 1991 that imposed the freeze on balance of payments support.

7. In the case of the IMF, all drawings, including the more concessional SAF and ESAF, have much shorter grace and repayment periods than other concessional loans. When repayments to the IMF are taken into account, the net flow of IMF resources during 1970–96 was only US$115 million. When interest charges are included the net balance was negative.

8. Formal CG meetings chaired by the World Bank were held in fiscal years 1972, 1974, 1977, 1979, 1982, 1984, 1986, and 1989.

9. As stated earlier, the donor consensus underlying the freeze of balance of payments support that was imposed in November 1991 was essentially maintained until the subsequent CG meeting in November 1993. While the World Bank and IMF began release of suspended funds in mid-1993 based on the new policy agreement reached in May of that year, bilateral donors held up on similar releases until receiving the World Bank/IMF report on Kenya's renewed reform efforts at the 1993 CG. The one exception was Japan's release before the CG of US$75 million, which had been tied to release of the second tranche of the World Bank Export Development Program. This "premature" release came in for some criticism from other donors, but the criticism was mild and not of lasting significance.

10. See annual editions of the World Bank's *World Debt Tables* and *Global Development Finance*.

11. Constitutional amendments 1–7 and 9–10, adopted between 1964 and 1969, abolished the position of prime minister, abolished the pre-existing powers of the regional authorities, abolished provincial councils and gave the presi-

dent more powers in setting provincial and district boundaries, entrenched the Preservation of Public Security Act, expanded the authority of the president in a state of emergency and the authority to detain without trial, gave the president authority to nominate 12 members of Parliament, and gave the president authority to appoint and dismiss civil servants and to appoint the members of the electoral commission, a responsibility previously held by the speaker of Parliament.

12. "For Kenyatta and his government, the development challenge was to continue, modify, and augment the institutions inherited from the colonial period, not replace them" (Barkan 1994: 16).

13. Between 1962 and 1976 almost 2 million hectares were purchased from former white settlers and transferred to African owners.

14. A US$200 million loan in June 1979 had 7 years maturity and interest of LIBOR plus 1.5 percent.

15. The 1978–83 Fourth Development Plan was written prior to the second oil shock and had to be amended subsequently through Sessional Paper No. 4 of 1980 and Sessional Paper No. 4 of 1982.

16. This coup attempt was an additional shock to the economy as it caused a massive fall in private investment. It also increased President Moi's reliance on members of his own ethnic group.

17. The decision to remove Minister Nicholas Biwott, the closest associate of President Moi, from the cabinet and to place him under arrest temporarily in connection with the investigation of the 1990 murder of another minister, while the November 1991 donor meeting was in progress, can certainly be ascribed to donor pressure.

18. The smaller parliamentary majority was due in part to a constitutional change that provided that nominated seats would be apportioned according to all parties' shares of elected seats, rather than going entirely to the majority party.

19. World Bank president Robert McNamara announced the Bank's intention to launch a new program of lending in support of structural adjustment at the Manila UNCTAD conference in April 1979.

20. A precursor of this important policy statement was a speech by President Moi in September 1982, shortly after the coup attempt, in which he admitted that the government had been too involved in economic affairs and stated that the private sector should henceforth assume a greater role.

21. Kenya's mixed record on the implementation of policy reforms led Gurushri Swamy to title her report on the country's adjustment performance "Kenya: patchy, intermittent commitment" (Swamy 1994). See also the chapter on Kenya in volume 2 of Mosley, Harrigan, and Toye (1991), in which Kenya receives a low score on implementation of reforms in the 1980s.

22. Nyachae's full title was Chief Secretary, Secretary to the Cabinet, and Head of the Civil Service. In this composite role during the mid-1980s he was extremely powerful.

23. One problem was that while the World Bank and USAID were trying to influence the Kenyan government to reduce the role of NCPB, other donors were financing a major expansion of its facilities and staff (Mosley 1986b). NCPB expanded its staffing threefold between 1980 and 1987.

24. Paul Collier comments, "Consider, for example, the astonishing story of relations between the Government of Kenya and the World Bank. During a fifteen year period, the Government of Kenya sold the same agricultural reform to the World Bank four times, each time reversing it after the receipt of the money" (Collier 1997: 60).

25. "The World Bank was attempting, from outside the country, a feat of political muscle which had defeated all liberalizing pressures from inside for over 40 years" (Mosley, Harrigan, and Toye 1991, 2: 284).

26. Philip Ndegwa, who died in 1996, was at the center of policymaking in Kenya for more than thirty years. He was permanent secretary of planning under Minister Mboya in the 1960s, permanent secretary of finance under Minister Kibaki in the 1970s, and CBK governor in the 1980s. Even after leaving the CBK in 1988 for the private sector, he continued to advise President Moi and other senior officials, and he served as chairman of the board of Kenya Airways during the period of rehabilitation and privatization of the national airline. He became active in politics in KANU in the final years of his life. He was not always a strong reformer but was an outstanding analyst of Kenya's economic problems.

27. The Ministry of Finance and the Ministry of Planning were merged and separated many times over the years; thus in some time periods the reference is to the Ministry of Finance and Planning.

28. An example of this problem of conditionality overload arose in the preparation of ASAO II. The World Bank organized a workshop with Kenyan authorities for the sole purpose of reaching an agreement on a small set of meaningful conditions; however, the final document prepared in Washington was, in the eyes of the Kenyan officials, another "Christmas tree."

REFERENCES

Barkan, Joel. 1998. "Toward a New Constitutional Framework in Kenya." *Africa Today* 45 (2): 213–26.

―――, ed. 1984. *Politics and Public Policy in Kenya and Tanzania.* Revised edition. New York: Praeger.

―――, ed. 1994. *Beyond Capitalism vs. Socialism in Kenya and Tanzania.* Boulder: Lynne Rienner.

Berg, Elliot. 1993. *Rethinking Technical Cooperation: Reforms for Capacity Building in Africa.* New York: United Nations Development Programme.

Burnside, Craig, and David Dollar. 1997. "Aid, Policies and Growth." Policy Research Working Paper 1777. World Bank, Development Research Group, Washington, D.C.

Central Bank of Kenya. Various years. *Annual Report.* Nairobi.

Chang, Charles C., Eduardo Fernández-Arias, and Luis Servén. 1999. "Measuring Aid Flows: A New Approach." Policy Research Working Paper 2050. World Bank, Development Research Group, Washington, D.C.

Collier, Paul. 1997. "The Failure of Conditionality." In Catherine Gwin and Joan M. Nelson, eds., *Perspectives on Aid and Development.* Washington, D.C.: Overseas Development Council.

Collier, Paul, and Jan Willem Gunning. 1999. "Why Has Africa Grown So Slowly?" *Journal of Economic Perspectives* 13 (3): 3–22.

Gatheru, Wamuyu, and Robert Shaw, eds. 1998. *Our Problems, Our Solutions: An economic and public policy agenda for Kenya.* Nairobi: Institute of Economic Affairs.

Hempstone, Smith. 1997. *Rogue Ambassador: An African Memoir.* Sewanee, Tenn.: University of the South Press.

International Monetary Fund. Various years. *Annual Report.* Washington, D.C.

Kenya. 1964. "Foreign Investment Protection Act." Nairobi.

———. 1965. "African Socialism and Its Application to Planning in Kenya." Sessional Paper No.10. Nairobi.

———. 1971. "Report of the Commission of Inquiry 1970–71." Public Service Structure and Remuneration Commission. Nairobi.

———. 1975. "On Economic Prospects and Policies." Sessional Paper No. 4. Nairobi.

———. 1979. "Review of Statutory Boards: Report and Recommendations of the Committee Appointed by His Excellency the President." Nairobi.

———. 1980. "Economic Prospects and Policies." Sessional Paper No. 4. Nairobi.

———. 1981. "National Food Policy." Sessional Paper No. 4. Nairobi.

———. 1982a. "Development Prospects and Policies." Sessional Paper No. 4. Nairobi.

———. 1982b. "Report and Recommendations of the Working Party on Government Expenditures." Nairobi.

———. 1986. "On Economic Management for Renewed Growth." Sessional Paper No. 1. Nairobi.

Kenya, Ministry of Finance. Various years. "Budget Estimates and Accounts." Nairobi.

Killick, Tony. 1998. *Conditionality: The Political Economy of Policy Change.* London: Routledge.

Lehman, Howard P. 1995. "Empowering the African State: Economic Adjustment Strategies in Kenya and Zimbabwe." In Kidane Mengisteab and B. Ikubolajeh Logan, eds., *Beyond Economic Liberalization in Africa: Structural Adjustment and the Alternatives.* Cape Town: Southern African Political Economic Series. London and Atlantic Highlands, N.J.: Zed Books.

Mosley, Paul. 1986a. "Agricultural Performance in Kenya Since 1970: Has the World Bank Got It Right?" *Development and Change* 17 (3): 513–30.

————. 1986b. "The Politics of Economic Liberalization: USAID and the World Bank in Kenya, 1980–84." *African Affairs* 85 (338): 107–19.

Mosley, Paul, Jane Harrigan, and John Toye. 1991. *Aid and Power: The World Bank and Policy-Based Lending*. Vol. 2: *Case Studies*. London and New York: Routledge.

Ng'ethe, Njuguna, and Wasunna Owino, eds. 1998. *From Sessional Paper No. 10 to Structural Adjustment: Towards Indigenising the Policy Debate*. Nairobi: Institute of Policy Analysis and Research.

Swamy, Gurushri. 1994. "Kenya: Patchy, Intermittent Commitment." In Ishrat Husain and Rashid Faruqee, eds. *Adjustment in Africa: Lessons from Country Case Studies*. Washington, D.C.: World Bank.

Throup, David, and Charles Hornsby. 1998. *Multi-Party Politics in Kenya*. Oxford, U.K.: James Currey.

Williamson, John, ed. 1994. *The Political Economy of Policy Reform*. Washington, D.C.: Institute for International Economics.

————. 1994. *Kenya: Poverty Assessment*. Washington, D.C.

————. 1998. *Assessing Aid: What Works, What Doesn't, and Why*. New York: Oxford University Press.

————. Various years. *World Debt Tables*. Washington, D.C.

————. Various years. *Global Development Finance*. Washington, D.C.

Zambia

Lise Rakner
Christian Michelsen Institute
Bergen, Norway

Nicolas van de Walle
Michigan State University
East Lansing, Michigan

Dominic Mulaisho
Lusaka, Zambia

ACRONYMS AND ABBREVIATIONS

CG	Consultative Group
EDA	Effective development assistance
EIU	Economist Intelligence Unit
ESAC	Economic and Social Adjustment Credit (of the World Bank)
ESAF	Enhanced Structural Adjustment Facility (of the IMF)
GDP	Gross domestic product
GNP	Gross national product
HIPC	Heavily indebted poor countries
IBRD	International Bank for Reconstruction and Development (of the World Bank Group)
IDA	International Development Association (of the World Bank Group)
IFI	International financial institution
IMF	International Monetary Fund
Kw	Kwatcha (local currency)
MMD	Movement for Multiparty Democracy
ODA	Official development assistance
RAP	Rights Accumulation Program (of the IMF)
UNDP	United Nations Development Programme
UNIP	United National Independence Party
UP	United Party
UPP	United Progressive Party
USAID	U.S. Agency for International Development
ZCCM	Zambia Consolidated Copper Mines
ZCTU	Zambia Congress of Trade Unions
ZIMCO	Zambia Industrial and Mining Corporation

In Zambia, more than in most other Sub-Saharan African countries, financial aid from the international donor community over the last two decades has been tied to the implementation of economic policy reform. Zambia's experiences with economic policy reform can be divided into two main periods. During the 1980s, under the one-party rule of the United National Independence Party (UNIP) and President Kenneth Kaunda, the structural adjustment reforms advocated by international donors were largely discontinued. Most observers argue that these economic reforms constituted a threat to the privileges of the large urban community that provided the main support for UNIP (Bates and Collier 1993; Callaghy 1990; Hawkins 1991; West 1992). The UNIP government had a long tradition of subsidizing urban consumer commodities and was vulnerable to urban protest. Faced with "food riots" in the urban areas each time comprehensive reforms were attempted, President Kaunda abandoned the economic reform programs. But an escalating debt burden together with increasing donor coordination meant that by the late 1980s, Zambia was ineligible for financial assistance from the international financial institutions (IFIs). In 1989 the Kaunda government again approached the IFIs for a structural adjustment agreement.

In the early 1990s, economic events were overtaken by political events as the continuous decline of the Zambian economy became the main rallying cry of forces opposed to the one-party regime. In 1991, the Movement for Multiparty Democracy (MMD), an opposition drawn from a broad coalition of trade unions, business interests, intellectuals, and students, won an overwhelming electoral victory over the UNIP, which had been in power for 17 years. Zambia thus became one of the first countries in Sub-Saharan Africa to experience a peaceful transition to multiparty rule. One of the most significant aspects of the transition was the fact that the MMD had promised to implement an ambitious economic reform program (MMD 1991).

The peaceful transition to multiparty democracy, as well as the economic policies promoted by the new government of President Frederick Chiluba, made Zambia a model for Africa in the eyes of both the international donor community and much of the academic community (Bratton 1992; Joseph 1992; Bonnick 1997). With donors eager to promote one of the few African "success stories" of dual reforms, Zambia experienced substantial growth in official development assistance in the 1990s. Contrary to the experiences in the 1980s, Zambia has maintained a structural adjustment program throughout the period known as the "Third Republic" (1991–).

The political transitions begun in 1991 and the economic policy changes implemented in the first years thereafter were expected to signify a major shift in Zambia's economic policy regime. However, we argue that the notion of discontinuity from the policies of the Kaunda era may have been overstated. Rather, events since the mid-1990s point to a disturbing degree of *continuity*, in terms of uneven implementation and limited commitment to policy reform. After almost a decade of continuous structural adjustment programs, the record on Zambian policy reforms in the 1990s is exceedingly complex and mixed.

On the one hand, during the 1990s the foundation has been laid for a shift from a state-oriented to a market-based economy. Most importantly, despite several exogenous shocks and uneven implementation, none of the reform measures implemented has been reversed. On the other hand, several key reforms have not been implemented, including civil service reform and the privatization of the copper industry. The MMD government has displayed genuine commitment to liberalization and stabilization with the implementation of the cash budget, the establishment of the Zambia Revenue Authority, and the freeing of exchange controls as significant examples. However, commitment to a long-term strategy of growth, which would have included a proactive position on the mines from the very beginning as well as a strategy to enhance tourism and nontraditional agriculture, has not been displayed. The failure to restructure the civil service remains an example of the government's limited commitment to reform. The net result is that the Zambian economy has not experienced any growth in the 1990s. Most alarmingly, social indicators have regressed within the last decade. From our perspective in 1999 it is therefore difficult to argue that the Zambian economy is heading in the right direction and that a resumption of growth is an immediate prospect.

New evidence on aid effectiveness in developing countries suggests that aid transfers to date have not been effective either in promoting growth or in inducing policy reform, except in good policy environments (Burnside and Dollar 1997; Killick 1998). We argue that the Zambian case supports these findings. Throughout the 1980s, the UNIP government rejected policy reform. The cutoff of IFI finances following the cancellation of reform agreements in 1983 and 1987 was largely offset by bilateral aid flows. After Zambia's performance in the 1980s as a classic "nonreformer," the reformist government coming to power in 1991 was rewarded by substantial increases in aid. Despite external support, however, the MMD government's commitment to reform waned over time, in part because the reforms achieved so little in terms of stemming the continued economic decline.

Because of their intellectual influence as well as their financial impact, international donors have played a central role in Zambia's economic policy development in the last decade. Financial aid has been instrumental for implementing some policy reforms and sustaining other reform measures. Nonetheless, we argue that the donors, as well as the Zambian government, have failed to express a coherent strategy of economic growth. A donor-promoted growth strategy would have placed the mining industry at the center of negotiations with the MMD government much earlier than 1997. Instead, in the 1990s both the government and the external donors have made fiscal austerity an end in itself and a measure of reform commitment. As a result, stabilization is today threatened, as there has been no growth to support continued austerity.

Much as in the 1980s, donor conditionality has proved unable to stem the waning reform commitment witnessed in the latter half of the 1990s. The experiences in Zambia indicate that the specific targeting of certain reform elements and the technically formulated benchmarks offered the authorities relatively wide room to maneuver. Furthermore, the singular focus on meeting the conditionality benchmarks made the Zambian government a *receiver* of a policy rather than an initiator. The government has indicated commitment to various elements of the policy reform package and little ideological opposition has been displayed. Yet ownership of the reform process remains weak, and the government appears to justify policy implementation as a means to generate aid funds rather than as part of a domestically argued development strategy. As government commitment to political and economic reforms has declined, donors have seemed unable to apply the conditionality instruments in a coherent manner. The result has been a "partial reform" syndrome reflecting continuity rather than a shift in donor-government relations.

Zambia nevertheless presents a challenging case study for the Aid and Reform in Africa project. As an alternative to conditionality-based aid, the *Assessing Aid* report (World Bank 1998) recommends that recipient countries should be selected on the basis of good policy performance for aid to be effective. Based on Zambia's experiences with conditionality aid and policy reform, we argue that *Assessing Aid* underestimates the difficulty of donor coordination when calling for aid selectivity. The model of selectivity presented is essentially a one-donor model, which assumes that donor preferences are singular rather than plural. However, in the Zambian case a range of conflicting interests within the international donor community complicated the pursuit of unified action when commitment to reform appeared to be waning.

A major aim of the operations of the International Monetary Fund (IMF) and the World Bank is to enable indebted nations to repay their debt. In the case of Zambia, large amounts of the balance of payments support contributed by the donor community over the past decade have been used to service old debts to the same donor institutions. Both the Zambian government and the IFIs may therefore have had an incentive to exaggerate the results of the reform effort in order to maintain a constant flow of financial aid. Furthermore, the multilateral donors have high financial and intellectual stakes in the policy reform processes in Africa. A mixed, or even slipping, policy performance is not easily dismissed as the costs involved in entering yet another aid agreement six months ahead are exceedingly high.

The bilateral donors have tended to take a somewhat different view in the 1990s. Most bilateral donors have emphasized political reforms as a condition for financial support. Answering back to their local constituencies and taxpayers, the bilateral donors have become increasingly wary of supporting undemocratic Third World governments. Since 1995, Zambia's bilateral donors have shown an increasing willingness to exercise political conditionality over such issues as corruption, drug-related activities, and the struggle over revision of the constitution. However, pointing to the progress made on basic economic reforms and the need to support a government that has gone a distance on reform, the multilateral donors have advocated continued support of Zambia's economic reform process. Thus, underscoring the notion of continuity from the Kaunda era, the Zambian case study shows that donor differences largely diluted the impact of conditionality instruments.

The main findings of this report are based on research carried out in Zambia by Lise Rakner between 1991 and 1997. Nicolas van de Walle and Dominic Mulaisho carried out additional field research in May 1999. In addition to the recent fieldwork, the study draws on two earlier studies by the authors: "Reform as a Matter of Political Survival: Political and Economic Liberalisation in Zambia 1991–1996" (Rakner 1998) and "Democratization and Economic Reform in Zambia" (van de Walle and Chiwele 1994).

This case study draws on quantitative data provided by the World Bank for the Aid and Reform in Africa project. In addition, it presents qualitative interview data to promote a deeper understanding of the relationship between policy reform and aid in the case of Zambia. It may not be possible to draw general conclusions from this study due to the case study format and the data material. But the Zambian case supports a number of the findings reported in recent cross-national analyses of aid and reform carried out by, among others, Killick (1995, 1998), Collier (1997), Nelson and Eglington (1993), Burnside and Dollar (1997), and the World Bank (1998). This case study can therefore be read as an attempt to provide "a story behind the numbers," or as an attempt to supplement and question some of the general findings appearing in the cross-national surveys.

Section 2 of this paper assesses the aid flows that Zambia has received since the early 1980s. Section 3 analyzes the institutional developments and policy reforms in the period since 1980. The main emphasis is on the years following the introduction of the Third Republic in 1991, as this represents the period of continuous economic reform in Zambia. In section 4 we focus on the relationship between policy reform and conditionality-based aid. The World Bank and the terms of reference for this study have emphasized economic conditionality issues; however, in Zambia a combination of political and economic conditionalities influenced reform implementation and the strength of donor cohesion in the 1990s. Political developments and political conditionalities will therefore be assessed together with the economic issues. The concluding section summarizes the main findings.

AID TO ZAMBIA

Aid flows to Zambia have grown rapidly during the period under study, and in the last two decades multilateral aid levels have been substantially higher than bilateral aid. In Zambia, more than in most other Sub-Saharan African countries, foreign aid since the early 1980s has predominantly been tied to structural adjustment loans and programs.

Definitions of Aid and Measures Applied

The standard concept of aid used in most studies is official development assistance (ODA), consisting of financial aid and technical cooperation. Financial aid includes grants and concessional loans with a grant element of 25 percent or higher. But it has long been acknowledged that the standard ODA measure tends to overestimate aid flows because it does not provide an accurate measure of the grant element in official loans. As a result, the World Bank has produced a new aid measure, effective development assistance (EDA), which provides a more accurate measure of actual aid flows.[1] EDA is defined as the sum of grant equivalents and grants, excluding technical assistance and bilateral debt forgiveness. This adjusted measure uses the same conventional grant data but aggregates the grant equivalent of loans rather than the full face value of all loans deemed concessional.

In this paper we use the EDA measure when presenting the overall aid trends in Zambia. However, the World Bank EDA figures are only provided until 1996. We therefore present aid figures compiled by the Zambian Ministry of Finance as well to cover the period until 1999. These aid measures include technical assistance and bilateral debt forgiveness and are therefore higher than the World Bank estimated EDA figures.

Trends in Zambia's Relationship to External Partners

Zambia has received financial aid since the mid-1960s. A major leap was experienced in the mid-1970s and another significant increase took place in 1991. Due to the poor performance of the Zambian economy since the mid-1970s, the dependence on development assistance has increased both on a per capita basis and as a percentage of gross domestic product (GDP). The importance of aid to Zambia cannot be overstated. At their peak in 1992 the disbursements from multilaterals and 22 bilaterals amounted to US$1,479 million, equal to 67 percent of export earnings and 77 percent of total public expenditure. More than 35 percent of the government's budget is financed by the donor community, and donor financing accounts for on average 80 percent of the budget for capital expenditure, according to the Zambian government's 1999 budget address. The donor community is large and influential, with approximately 150 international donor agencies working in Zambia.

The agriculture, infrastructure, health, and education sectors received most of the Western bilateral aid in the 1970s and 1980s (see tables 9.6 and 9.7 in Appendix 9.5). Due to the worsening foreign exchange situation facing Zambia in the 1980s, a number of donors shifted substantial parts of their aid from project aid to program aid. Balance of payments support, or program aid, has become an increasingly important part of Zambia's aid portfolio, accounting for more than half of total aid to Zambia by the early 1990s (Saasa 1996). It has mainly been linked to the ongoing structural reform efforts, and to a large extent has been used to service Zambia's debt and maintain existing levels of imports. Zambia's external debt has grown rapidly since 1970 (see table 9.11 in Appendix 9.5). It presently stands at US$6.6 billion—one of the highest debt figures on a per capita basis in Sub-Saharan Africa. The external debt service burden has been reduced in the 1990s through Paris Club debt forgiveness. Nevertheless, in the mid-1990s the debt service flow has absorbed close to 80 percent of the balance of payments support provided by donors. An evaluation of Swedish development assistance to Zambia concludes that:

> Essentially, Zambia used non-concessional monies to repay borrowing from creditors and is now receiving grants and concessional funds to repay these non-concessional debts. Aid flows have thus for the most part been a large scale debt rescheduling. (White and Edstrand 1994: 286)

In 1999 the Paris Club, grouping Zambia's major bilateral donors, agreed to restructure its loans to Zambia by writing off 67 percent of the debt and rescheduling the remaining 33 percent on more concessional terms. The Paris Club negotiations have been considered the first step toward further debt reductions through the Heavily Indebted Poor Countries (HIPC) Debt Initiative, which will cover the bulk of Zambia's multilateral debt stock. The World Bank is currently lobbying the bilateral donors and the IMF to ensure that Zambia qualifies for the HIPC Initiative, suggesting that some criteria for entry should be waived (EIU 2nd quarter 1999).

The Relationship to Multilateral Donors

The first big leap in aid flows to Zambia dates back to the downturn of the copper industry in the mid-1970s. From 1973 on, Zambia drew on IMF financial resources. Due to the country's high copper earnings, Zambia borrowed from the World Bank on International Bank for Reconstruction and Development (IBRD) terms until 1978. It was only in that year that Zambia was declared eligible, that is poor enough, to qualify for World Bank funds on International Development Association (IDA) terms. Zambia was a "blend" country, drawing on both IDA and IBRD terms, from 1978 until 1984. Since then, the country has borrowed on IDA terms only.

The first two IMF standby agreements in 1973 and 1976 were fully drawn, but balance of payments was not restored to equilibrium. From 1978 on, Zambia depended on the IMF and the Consultative Group (CG) of donors for its foreign exchange requirements (West 1989). The World Bank and the IMF have been the most important providers of external support to Zambia's reform efforts. Yet neither the World Bank nor the bilateral donors took an active part in policy discussions concerning Zambia until 1980. In the 1970s, therefore, the IMF was the main external advocate for liberal economic reforms in Zambia. However, since the early 1980s the operations of the World Bank and IMF in Zambia have been marked by steady increases in borrowing, matched by more stringent conditions.

In the early 1980s the World Bank presented a new development strategy (World Bank 1981). From this time on, Zambia's development assistance from the IFIs has predominantly been adjustment lending, which has accounted for approximately 60 percent of World Bank commitments and close to 80 percent of disbursements since the mid-1980s (Bonnick 1997). This figure is substantially higher for Zambia than for other Sub-Saharan African countries, including Tanzania, Kenya, and Uganda.

Zambia was a controversial country with respect to adjustment lending throughout the 1980s. Despite the great concentration on adjustment-related programs, the economic reform programs in Zambia have been marked by frequent interruptions. Due to the accumulation of arrears, the IMF and the World Bank canceled their programs in 1983 and again between 1987 and 1990. In 1991 the World Bank and the bilateral donors were able to clear Zambia's arrears on their multilateral debt and lending resumed.

In the Third Republic (1991–), Zambia has remained committed to the economic reform program agreed to with its international partners to the extent that the country has kept current on its international debt payments (see table 9.1). The main achievement of the Zambian government in terms of economic liberalization after 1991 was the completion

TABLE 9.1 POLICY-BASED LOANS TO ZAMBIA FROM MULTILATERAL INSTITUTIONS

Institution	Year and loan	Requirements
World Bank	1991: Economic Reform Credit	Phase out maize subsidies, begin liberalizing maize markets, limit bank credits, remove tariff bans, eliminate surplus civil service staff, announce privatization policy and offer at least six parastatal companies for sale, complete studies of Zambia Airways.
World Bank	1992: Privatization and Industrial Reform Credit (PIRC I)	Improve fiscal and monetary performance, harmonize sales taxes, broaden tax base, reduce tariffs, retrench 10,000 civil service workers, enact privatization law, offer additional 10 parastatals for sale, restructure ZIMCO.
World Bank	1993: Privatization and Industrial Reform Credit (PIRC II)	Improve fiscal and monetary performance, reduce tariffs, develop plans for land markets, reform Investment Act, offer for sale 60 companies, establish Privatization Trust Fund, study options to privatize ZCCM.
World Bank	1994: Economic and Social Adjustment Credit (ESAC I)	Redirect budget to social sectors (health and education), eliminate export ban on maize, create legal basis for land leasehold and begin sale of state-owned farms, adopt acceptable financial plan for Zambia Airways.

World Bank	1995: Economic Recovery and Investment Project (ERIP)	Introduce value added tax, improve budget management procedures, meet minimum budget and spending targets for key social services, reform social security, adopt and implement plans to privatize ZCCM.
World Bank	1996: Economic and Social Adjustment Credit (ESAC II)	Maintain a social sector budget of at least 35 percent, privatize ZCCM, implement 1995 Land Act, implement National Housing Policy of 1995, amend Employment and Industrial and Labour Relations Act, formulate policy on collaboration with NGOs in welfare service delivery.
IMF	1992–95: Rights Accumulation Program (RAP)	Restore macroeconomic stability, eliminate arrears to international creditors, implement Economic Recovery Program in collaboration with multinational finance institutions.
IMF	1995–98: Enhanced Structural Adjustment Facility (ESAF)	Quantitative benchmarks: increase net domestic assets of Bank of Zambia, increase international reserves, reduce government domestic arrears. Structural performance criteria: reform civil service, publish banking regulations, privatize ZCCM.
World Bank	1999: Structural Adjustment Fund	Structural performance criteria: reform civil service, publish banking regulations, privatize ZCCM.

Sources: World Bank 1996d; IMF 1995.

FIGURE 9.1 ZAMBIA: TOTAL GRANTS (EDA), 1980–96

Millions of U.S. dollars

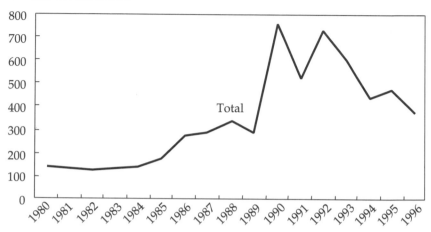

Source: Based on table 9.8.

of the Rights Accumulation Program (RAP) with the IMF in December 1995. By completing the RAP, Zambia gained access to an IMF Enhanced Structural Adjustment Facility (ESAF). This again meant that the IMF lifted Zambia's ineligibility to draw on IMF resources. The significance of this is underscored by the fact that it was the first time Zambia had completed any agreement entered into with the IMF. Zambia has now entered into its second ESAF program (1999–2001) as the completion of the previous program (1995–98) has been postponed and the program period extended.

Since the early 1980s the operations of the World Bank and the IMF have become increasingly tied. Nevertheless, the IMF, more than the World Bank, has maintained a narrow mandate: to restore macroeconomic stabilization and growth through the introduction of a set of macroeconomic policies. IMF loans, while on concessional terms, are conditioned on closely monitored macroeconomic and structural performance benchmarks (Killick 1997; Collier 1997).

The World Bank, adhering to similar performance criteria, has a wider "conditionality agenda" that includes governance issues as well as policy goals linked to poverty reduction and sectoral performance. Connecting the lack of success of the first decade of structural adjustment programs to domestic policy issues, the World Bank introduced the concept of "good governance" in the early 1990s (Kapur 1997). The Bank has emphasized issues of governance considered "non-political," such as accountability, transparency, and the rule of law, as necessary ingredients for successful implementation of economic reforms. This way, both the World Bank and the IMF have sought to avoid tying their assistance to the issues of democracy and human rights advocated by the bilateral donors.

In contrast to the stop-go character of the relationship between the Zambian government and the multilaterals in the 1980s, in the 1990s no multilateral adjustment loans have been canceled. World Bank balance of payments support continued in 1997, but in 1998 there was no multilateral balance of payments financing because no World Bank adjustment loan was scheduled until the second half of 1998. Another World Bank adjustment operation was approved in early 1999.

The Relationship to Bilateral Donors

As a result of the financial impact and the large concessional element of bilateral aid, bilateral donors have been influential in Zambian policymaking. The main bilateral donors have included Canada, Denmark, Finland, Germany, Japan, the Netherlands, Norway, Sweden, the United Kingdom, and the United States. In the 1980s, in the absence of aid coordination, the majority of bilateral aid was disbursed independently of policy reform. Some of the major bilateral contributors to Zambia remained unconvinced of the economic reform programs advocated by the World Bank and IMF and even increased their aid portfolios when Zambia canceled the agreements with the IFIs. In the first decade of structural adjustment lending, therefore, the bilateral donors represented a countervailing influence to that of the World Bank and IMF (Bates and Collier 1993; Sandberg 1990; West 1989; Saasa 1996).

In the 1990s the coordination of aid as well as ideology has been much tighter. Most bilateral donors have tied their program aid to a previous agreement with the IMF and the World Bank. Furthermore, the Consultative Group meeting process has brought greater coherence to the operations of the various donors than was the case in the 1980s. Zambia's bilateral donors are not a homogenous group in terms of the size of their aid portfolios or their policy goals, but they display a number of similarities. Most of the large Western bilateral donors have since the early 1990s explicitly tied their aid policies to the promotion of good governance, democratic development, and adherence to human rights.[2] Observers have attributed this emphasis to the growing aid fatigue in the Western world (Killick 1996; Havnevik and van Arkadie 1996). In the 1990s differences between Zambia's multilateral and bilateral donors have been most clearly expressed with regard to governance issues.

The majority of Zambia's bilateral donors withheld balance of payments support from 1996 through 1998. In June 1996, the United States, Norway, Sweden, the Netherlands, Germany, and Japan cut off balance of payments support to protest the exclusion of Kenneth Kaunda from the presidential elections. At the CG meeting in July 1997, US$150 million was pledged in balance of payments support, conditional on governance reform. However, no bilateral donors disbursed their balance of payments support, and all cited poor performance on governance issues as their reason for withholding funds. At the May 1998 CG meeting, Zambia's donors again pledged US$530 million in balance of payments support, but the disbursement was made contingent on sale of the copper mines and further improvements in the governance record. Most bilateral support was again held back.

It should be noted that the financial cuts have in most instances affected program aid, or balance of payments support, while project aid has continued.[3] Debt rescheduling and debt cancellations have also continued. Statistics compiled by the Ministry of Finance indicate that while virtually no bilateral balance of payments support was disbursed between 1996 and 1998, project support in the same period *increased* from the 1991–94 levels. Project support, continued multilateral balance of payments support, and debt relief have meant that net aid transfers to Zambia have remained relatively constant, as shown in table 9.2.

The governance situation in Zambia has not improved significantly in recent years. Furthermore, the privatization of Zambia Consolidated Copper Mines (ZCCM) has not been finalized. Yet the bilateral donors now appear to be moving toward the position of the IFIs and to view Zambia's achievements in a more positive light. The turbulent situations in neighboring Angola, the Democratic Republic of Congo, and Zimbabwe have induced a number of donor governments to invoke regional security concerns in explaining their aid portfolios in Zambia.

During the 1970s and 1980s, regional concerns in the Cold War context prompted the bilateral donor governments to assist Zambia financially. As the Cold War ended, regional concerns became less salient, and donors united in their focus on issues of governance and human rights. Since 1996, however, the Great Lakes crisis and the Congo war have again brought regional issues to the forefront of bilateral donor concerns. Recently, Zambia's president has taken initiatives toward peace building in Congo. At the May 1999 CG meeting for Zambia, Zambia's regional role was stressed to justify continued aid to the country. The long-anticipated influx of balance of payments support from the donors began in March 1999 and it is expected that continued unrest in the region will induce the bilateral donors to continue their support (EIU 2nd quarter 1999).

TABLE 9.2 NET AID TRANSFERS TO ZAMBIA, 1991–99
(millions of U.S. dollars)

Type of aid	1991	1992	1993	1994	1995	1996	1997	1998 (estimated)	1999 (estimated)
Total external assistance	926	928	623	556	559	445	422	322	827
Balance of payments support	586	491	299	278	304	142	120	0	359
World Bank	202	165	144	148	160	121	111	0	173
Other	384	326	155	130	144	21	9	0	186
Commodity aid	74	246	90	26	40	34	0	3	10
Drought	16	146	40	34	0	0	2	—	—
Other	58	100	50	26	0	34	0	1	10
Project finance	266	191	234	252	215	269	302	319	458
Debt relief	1,158	551	359	260	234	310	159	122	219
Total external financing	2,084	1,491	982	816	793	755	581	444	1,046
Gross debt service	–1,841	–926	–710	–616	–578	–453	–352	–286	–309
Net transfers	243	553	272	200	215	302	229	155	737

Source: Zambia Ministry of Finance 1999.

Aid Coordination and the Evolution
of Conditionality-Based Lending

Until the early 1980s, aid carried few conditions and involved little co-ordination. It consisted mainly of project support. Increasingly, the do-nors assumed full responsibility for planning, preparing, and implementing their own programs in Zambia. In the absence of any do-nor coordination, donors took the initiative without a framework for setting national priorities (Bonnick 1997: 116).

In the 1980s, multilateral donors began to focus on policy reforms and formal conditions for assistance. However, little attention was paid to the coordination of donor efforts. In an attempt to meet the growing balance of payments problems facing many Sub-Saharan African na-tions, the World Bank in the early 1980s shifted a large proportion of its lending portfolio from project aid to program aid. By tying the disburse-ment of program aid to an a priori stabilization agreement with the IMF, the Bank linked its operations more closely to those of the IMF. Toward the late 1980s, the evolution toward cross-conditionality increasingly included the bilateral donors. Thus a stronger degree of cohesion and coordination emerged within the international donor community around the principles of economic policy reform, based on the promotion of ex-ports through market-friendly economic policies.[4]

FIGURE 9.2 ZAMBIA: TOTAL AID IN EDA LOANS, 1980–96

Millions of U.S. dollars

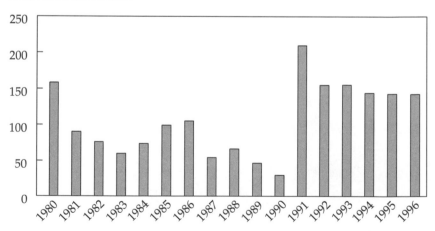

Note: Covers effective development assistance loans.
Source: World Bank.

Consultative Group meetings chaired by the World Bank began in the mid-1980s as a mechanism to improve coordination among donors and cooperation with the recipient governments in the field of macroeconomic and structural policy reforms. In addition to the Roundtable meetings hosted by the United Nations Development Programme (UNDP), the CG meetings hosted by the World Bank are intended to serve as "pledging sessions" to help close financing gaps for the aid-recipient countries. Since the 1980s, the CG meeting process has increasingly become the main channel through which indebted recipient governments raise external support to meet their balance of payments needs and debt servicing obligations. As a result, recipient governments have had great incentive to participate in these meetings (van de Walle and Johnston 1996: 50).

In 1989 the World Bank assumed leadership of the CG meeting for Zambia. Since then, the Bank has played a crucial role in mobilizing donor support for Zambia through an unusually active dialogue with the donor community and the client country. The Zambian government has used the periodic CG meetings as one of its principal mechanisms to facilitate aid mobilization and coordination (Saasa 1997: 197). The main task of the World Bank has been to mobilize assistance to close financial gaps and to provide the documentary and analytical basis for discussions and negotiations. According to the Bank's own evaluation, it has also played an advocacy role by educating donors and convincing them of the merits of structural adjustment (Bonnick 1997: 9). Another important measure of aid coordination in the 1990s relates to debt rescheduling and debt cancellations that have taken place within the Paris Club. In the 1990s, Zambia has seen a net fall in interest burden as indicated in table 9.2. Over time, however, the share of multilateral debts has increased (table 9.3).

Donor coordination has improved in the 1990s with respect to policy-based lending. However, a key feature of the aid relationship in Zambia still appears to be lack of coordination both among the donors themselves and within the government. Analyses of donor involvement and various bilateral donor programs in Zambia have revealed a diversity of external agencies and organizations involved in supporting the same sectors and subsectors, suggesting the need for better collaboration (Saasa 1996: 126). Attempts at sectoral coordination among donors began in 1992. Sweden was given the lead role for the education sector, health was to be the main area of Dutch project aid, and water supply and sanitation were assigned to Germany and Norway. In recent years, considerable efforts have gone into a coordinated and integrated approach for the health and agricultural sectors in particular. In agriculture, sectoral coordination has centered around the Agricultural Sector Investment Program initiated by the World Bank. According to a World Bank

TABLE 9.3 CONSULTATIVE GROUP MEETINGS ON ZAMBIA, 1991–99

Date	Issues of debate
March 1992	■ the economic reform program (main) ■ the drought and food security situation ■ the external debt situation
December 1992	■ inflation ■ implementation of a cash budget ■ corruption ■ the slow pace of privatization
April 1993	■ composition of public spending ■ social sector spending ■ subsidies to Zambia Airways ■ inflation ■ the state of emergency ■ corruption
December 1993	■ governance, corruption, and drug trafficking ■ slow pace of privatization (ZIMCO) ■ government expenditure priorities
March 1994	■ "renewed partnership" ■ continued high interest rates ■ slow progress on privatization ■ the external debt situation
December 1994	■ continued slow pace of privatization ■ delayed closure of ZIMCO ■ limited progress on the Public Sector Reform Program ■ governance and corruption ■ poverty
December 1995	■ governance issues (the constitution) ■ privatization of ZCCM ■ poverty alleviation
July 1997	■ "renewal of partnership" ■ budget balance and discipline ■ the external debt situation ■ privatization of ZCCM ■ the Public Sector Reform Program ■ poverty reduction ■ governance issues ■ aid dependency
May 1998	■ privatization of ZCCM ■ the Public Sector Reform Program ■ poverty reduction ■ governance issues
May 1999	■ privatization of ZCCM ■ the Public Sector Reform Program ■ poverty reduction ■ governance issues ■ regional stability

evaluation, the Bank has sought to limit itself to a catalyst role, but has faced conflicting pressures—on the one hand, a desire to promote local ownership, and on the other hand, a need to offset institutional weaknesses in public sector management to maintain momentum of the process (Bonnick 1997). In the health sector, the Ministry of Health, which has adopted a very open and transparent approach with the donors, has driven the Health Sector Support Project (Graham 1995; Bonnick 1997).

Earmarking aid expenditures to specific sectors or projects like health and education may improve expenditure outcomes. Evidence from Zambia suggests that sector reform can have a significant impact even in the absence of commitment to macroeconomic reform. Comparative studies of sector reforms in education and health suggest that competent ministers who manage to work well with donors and assemble a good team can bring reform processes far without much initial support from the rest of the government (Graham 1995). Yet the problem of aid fungibility raises the question of whether aid in the form of project grants or loans may dilute policy conditionality in the sense that money can be reallocated, thereby lessening the need to follow through on the reform program. Thus, the question is whether or not budgetary support, with more coherent and strict conditionality, would work better.

As indicated in table 9.2, increases in project aid to Zambia from 1996 on reduced the impact of reductions in balance of payments support in terms of overall aid transfers. This issue is explored further in section 4, where we discuss the impact of donor divisions on conditionality. However, with regard to sector support, we find the fungibility issue to be of limited relevance in fiscally strapped countries like Zambia that essentially lack a development budget. If donors fail to finance health or education, the fear is that very little will take place beyond the most basic administration. Thus, donor support to sectoral reform may be meaningful even in the absence of macroeconomic reforms.

INSTITUTIONAL DEVELOPMENT AND POLICY REFORM

During the first ten years after independence in 1963, the Zambian economy expanded fairly rapidly, with GDP increasing at an average of 2.3 percent annually in real terms as shown in table 9.4 (World Bank 1984). However, Zambia's modest luck ran out in 1974, and according to estimates, between 1975 and 1990 the country experienced a 30 percent decline in real per capita growth (World Bank 1990). Starting in the early 1970s, Zambia suffered one of the greatest and most rapid economic declines of any nation of Sub-Saharan Africa. Copper prices fell sharply on the world market after 1974, and this coincided with an enormous increase in oil prices. Zambia's revenues plunged with the decline in the

TABLE 9.4 ZAMBIA: MACROECONOMIC INDICATORS, 1973–90

Year	Terms of trade[a]	Reserves[b]	Current account[c]	Budget balance[d]	GDP growth[e]	Copper prices[f]
1973	301.8	185.5	113.3	–315.4	– 0.9	80.58
1974	215.5	164.4	8.4	70.0	6.7	93.23
1975	126.3	142.0	–726.1	–340.8	– 2.4	56.10
1976	139.6	92.7	–132.8	–231.3	4.3	63.64
1977	119.8	66.3	–232.3	–190.3	–4.8	59.41
1978	114.0	51.1	–321.1	–208.8	0.6	61.92
1979	135.9	80.0	4.7	–139.9	–3.0	89.49
1980	125.5	78.2	–544.6	–295.0	3.0	99.12
1981	100.1	56.2	–766.6	–210.2	6.2	79.05
1982	88.9	58.2	–592.6	–276.5	–2.8	67.21
1983	97.8	54.5	–310.0	114.6	–2.0	72.23
1984	—	54.2	–162.7	–120.1	–0.4	62.66
1985	—	200.1	–404.1	–232.7	1.6	64.29
1986	—	70.3	–372.1	–388.1	0.6	62.13
1987	—	108.8	–256.7	–232.3	–0.2	80.79
1988	—	134.0	–324.7	–205.2	6.7	117.93
1989	—	116.2	–292.0	–71.7	–1.1	129.15
1990	—	193.1	–489.8	–43.8	–0.4	120.72

— Not available.
a. 1987 index.
b. Total reserves minus gold in millions of U.S. dollars.
c. Current account balance before official transfer in millions of U.S. dollars.
d. Government balance in millions of kwatchas.
e. Annual growth rates of GDP at constant prices.
f. London Metal Exchange copper prices in U.S. cents per pound.
Sources: World Bank, *World Debt Tables*, various years; IMF, *International Financial Statistics Yearbook 1992*.

price of its major export. Although diversification of the economy away from copper had been an expressed political goal since independence, Zambia remained dependent on copper for 90 percent of its exports and 40 percent of its GDP throughout the 1970s and 1980s.

Declining ore grades and technical production difficulties led to a lower volume of copper exports and reduced export revenues, exacerbating the effects of the price decline. Adding to the problem was disorder in the copper industry resulting from the government's assumption of management of the mines in 1969. With declining revenues from copper, other productive industries were starved of foreign exchange. The inevitable government market and price controls triggered shortages and decreased production (Hawkins 1991; Bates 1981).

In the years that followed, the Zambian economy essentially collapsed. GDP growth was either negative or weak for the period 1975–80, reserves declined, and the budget balance was negative. By 1977 the government had completely exhausted its foreign reserves (Hawkins 1991: 844). Thus from 1975 on, Zambia was caught in a classic bind: the weakening market for its main export cut into foreign exchange earnings, hampering the country's ability to pay for increasingly more expensive industrial and consumer goods.

Economic Policy Reforms in the Kaunda Era (1974–91)

Economic decline in Zambia coincided with implementation of the one-party state constitution (the Second Republic, 1973–91). Responses to the economic decline from UNIP and President Kaunda's leadership and from major interest associations and the international donor community can be divided into three periods.

1974–83: Economic crisis without reaction. Through commercial and public borrowing Zambian consumers were shielded from the effects of economic decline. From the late 1970s onward Zambia accumulated large arrears on international loan repayments. Despite increasingly strong demands for economic restructuring from the international donors, no sustainable reform program was implemented. The World Bank and a majority of the bilateral donors appeared to share Zambia's optimism with regard to the copper industry and were therefore uncritical of the country's industrial development strategy (West 1989; Bonnick 1997).

1983–87: External pressure for reform faces internal opposition. By 1983, "soft options" in terms of nonconcessional borrowing were no longer available. Increasingly, IMF and World Bank conditionalities guided economic policymaking. From 1985 onward the implementation of a substantial structural adjustment program was attempted. However, external pressure for change met with internal opposition, and in May 1987 the structural adjustment program was abandoned.

1987 to 1989: Homegrown reform is hampered by the magnitude of crisis. In this period Zambia sought to implement an economic recovery program without economic assistance from the international donor community. The economic crisis and escalating international debt, however, forced the Zambian leadership to enter new aid agreements with the IFIs in 1989. The new economic restructuring program was adhered to until the political pressures of the 1991 election campaign led the UNIP government to again abandon reforms and international debt obligations.

Reform in the 1980s: Lack of Ownership

A large literature exists on Zambia's failure to implement structural adjustment policies in the 1980s.[5] The majority of these analyses explain the collapse of reform with reference to the overwhelming domestic resistance to the structural adjustment actions. The strong and vocal trade union movement (the Zambia Congress of Trade Unions, ZCTU) has been singled out as a major element in the 1987 decision to abandon economic reforms. At this time, donor pressure to reduce maize-meal subsidies caused prices to triple, and riots broke out in Lusaka and in the copper belt towns. Others, however, have pointed to the strong opposition to reform found within the ruling party and its bureaucracy (Bates and Collier 1993; Geddes 1995).

We argue that the failure of reform in the 1980s should be attributed in part to the ideological resistance to orthodox reform found within the Zambian state. At the time, high-level politicians, bureaucrats, and party officials simply did not believe that copper prices would not eventually recover. A fascinating account of the economic reform efforts in the 1980s ties the limited understanding of the economic crises to optimism regarding the copper industry (West 1989). Furthermore, neither top bureaucrats nor politicians believed that an outward economic orientation would result in growth. It should be emphasized here that the inward-looking strategy based on import substitution industrialization was partly justified by the fear of South Africa and by the entire ideology of the Frontline states. Moreover, the structuralist economic ideas were widely supported by influential bilateral donors and development economists in the Western world as well (Helleiner 1986). The 1980s witnessed an intense ideological debate between socialist and capitalist economic models within the party, the government, and the bureaucracy at large (West 1989; Sandberg 1990). By the mid-1980s, a technocratic core team within the Ministry of Finance and the Bank of Zambia was present. However, these technocrats had very limited support from the political leadership as neither President Kaunda nor the central elements of the UNIP cadre were convinced of the necessity or virtue of economic reform.

According to one observer, Zambia was effectively bankrupt before agreeing to undertake a comprehensive structural adjustment program put forth by the IFIs in 1985 (West 1992). Again, however, the economic reform measures threatened to undermine the welfare of the main constituencies of the increasingly weaker UNIP party. In April 1986, President Kaunda changed his economic team from the group who had negotiated the program with the IFIs to some of the strongest critics of the market-based economy, and the program was discontinued. UNIP's attempts to compromise between externally expressed demands for economic liberalization and an increasingly outspoken trade union movement were overtaken by political events on an international scale toward the end of 1989. Increasingly, economic dissatisfaction and discontent with UNIP's reign were translated into demands for a return to multiparty politics and a new government. However, it should be emphasized that UNIP's heterodox experiment had already failed and been replaced by an IFI-led reform program in 1990, more than a year before the political transition that led to UNIP's and Kaunda's resignation from the government.

As a result of the government's failure to adjust to the changing economic conditions, by 1991 Zambia was considerably worse off than it had been in 1964. Per capita income in 1991 was US$390, down sharply from the 1964 figure of US$540. Basic social service schemes barely functioned; hospitals lacked drugs, beds, and personnel, while schools had no desks or books. Zambia's 1989 agreement with the World Bank and IMF was canceled in the summer of 1991 when President Kaunda refused to cut maize subsidies right before the 1991 elections. In the pre-election atmosphere, Kaunda abandoned spending limits set by the economic reform program, raised salaries for civil servants, and increased subsidies on maize and housing. When Zambia failed to make a US$20 million payment to the World Bank in July 1990, the IMF and the World Bank suspended a scheduled disbursement of US$75 million. According to one observer, by this point even the Scandinavian donors appeared reluctant to finance further operations (Graham 1994: 155). This was the legacy of UNIP and the starting point for the new government. The Movement for Multiparty Democracy and President Chiluba entered office on October 31, 1991.

Economic Policy Reforms in the Third Republic (1991–)

Considering the fact that UNIP's loss of popularity stemmed in part from its attempt to reduce food subsidies, it is ironic that MMD was overwhelmingly elected to office despite a clear promise to implement a structural adjustment program. However, after 27 years of Kaunda and UNIP—the latter years marked by precipitous economic decline—the Zambian people appeared willing to accept what was then perceived to be short-term austerity in return for the promise of future economic stability and growth. The political and economic reform processes that began in 1991 had strong domestic support at the outset. Most notably, the MMD government included committed policy reformers in all the key economic ministries. Throughout its election campaign, MMD advocated a complete shift in economic policies, involving a change from the system of public monopolies to a greater reliance on markets, private networks, and institutions. The 1991 election manifesto spelled out the party's commitment to fostering private sector growth and a limited role for government:

> The government restricts itself to rehabilitate and build socioeconomic infrastructure with a small public sector in the midst of a basically private enterprise economy. (MMD 1991: 14)

The manifesto did not, however, enter into details of MMD's future economic program. Soon after winning power, the MMD government adopted a structural adjustment program agreed with the IMF and the World Bank.[6] Based on its 1991 manifesto and the Policy Framework Paper agreed with its multilateral financial partners, MMD had three main economic goals: first, to restore macroeconomic stability through monetary and fiscal reforms; second, to facilitate private sector growth by withdrawing the state from price and exchange-rate regulations and import/export restrictions; and, finally, to shift the industrial and agrarian sectors from a system of public monopolies to one of private and decentralized institutions.

Macroeconomic Stabilization through Monetary and Fiscal Measures

In its task of economic reconstruction, the government identified the attainment of macroeconomic stabilization as its most immediate objective (McPherson 1995). An attack on inflation was identified as the most urgent step to restore macroeconomic equilibrium. To achieve this, the government instituted thoroughgoing monetary and fiscal reforms to cut fiscal deficits and growth in money supply. As indicated by the chronology of economic reforms in appendix 9.4, the government immediately started to address the issue of subsidies as a drain on the government budget. After only a few months in office, in December 1991, the government eliminated subsidies on mealie-meal, the main staple food in Zambia.[7] This was a significant political action, considering the fact that all attempts to reduce subsidies earlier had resulted in major internal uprisings and break-offs in the relationship with the international finance institutions. The sharp reduction in food and parastatal subsidies achieved by these measures caused the fiscal deficit to decline from 7.4 percent to 2.2 percent of GDP in the MMD's first year of government (table 9.5).

However, while 1992 was a year of promise in terms of economic reforms, the economy was adversely affected by a number of external and internal factors. The most serious was a severe drought that reduced agricultural output by 39.3 percent (Zambia 1993: 3). By late 1992, it was becoming evident both to the Ministry of Finance and to the donor community that lack of budgetary control constituted a major impediment to the attainment of macroeconomic stabilization (Zambia 1993: 5–6). While the elimination of expensive programs such as the consumer maize subsidies was critical to reducing the budget deficit, the most important measure to strengthen budgetary control was taken in the 1993 budget when the MMD government implemented a *cash budget system*. This key institutional innovation meant that the Bank of Zambia would deny any government transaction unless adequate funds had been made

TABLE 9.5 ZAMBIA: MACROECONOMIC INDICATORS, 1991–98

Indicator	1991	1992	1993	1994	1995	1996	1997	1998
GDP growth (%)	-4.0	-2.8	6.8	-8.6	-4.3	6.4	3.5	6.6
Exchange rate Kw:US$	127.3	172.2	600.4	687.3	878.9	1,213.0	1,336.0	1,862.0
Inflation (%)	92.6	165.1	187.3	54.6	34.9	43.5	22.1	22.0
Interest rates (%)[a]	25.0	47.0	133.3	80.9	39.8	52.5	25.6	—
Total reserves (millions of U.S. dollars)[b]	184.6	184.2	192.3	—	133.4	163.4	237.0	92.0
Money supply (%)[c]	99.2	128.5	87.6	44.3	55.6	30.1	27.5	—
Investment/GDP	11.1	11.9	15.0	13.4	13.9	15.1	—	—
Consumption/GDP	85.5	93.6	87.0	90.4	79.8	103.5	—	—
Current account (millions of U.S. dollars)	-307	-117	-88	-185	-314	-472	-257	-301
Copper output[d]	387	432	403	354	307	320	325	293
Total external debt (billions of U.S. dollars)	7.27	7.04	6.82	6.61	6.85	6.85	7.10	7.19
Debt service/GDP	51.4	29.3	34.9	31.7	205.3	25.7	—	—

— Not available.
a. 1991–92: prime lending rate (percent); 1993–97: Treasury bills average (percent).
b. Excluding gold.
c. Change from previous year.
d. Thousands of metric tons.
Sources: International Monetary Fund, *International Financial Statistics Yearbook 1997*; Zambia Investment Center 1997; Zambia Ministry of Finance budget addresses, 1992–98.

available, that is, unless there was enough revenue to support it at the time.[8] Thus the government could no longer resort to printing money in order to cover expenses. With the new budgetary procedures, extraordinary expenditures could only be financed from additional tax increases or expenditure cuts (Zambia 1993: 10). In order to put the new rule into effect, the Ministry of Finance and the Bank of Zambia created a joint committee to monitor fiscal and monetary conditions; it met three days a week to oversee virtually all checks going out of the Finance Ministry's accounts. The cash budget provided the government with capacity to curb fiscal deficits, and inflation was reduced from almost 300 percent to 30 percent within two years. Initially the measure also helped instill a perception that the fiscal regime was coming under control (Bolnick 1997).

Of equal importance in terms of reducing the growth in money supply was the auctioning of Treasury bills. This measure was introduced in the 1993 budget to provide a market mechanism for determining interest rates and siphoning off large amounts of excess liquidity. The Treasury bill tender implied that domestic debt was to be financed by the sale of new Treasury bills to members of the public. On the domestic revenue side, the creation of the semi-autonomous Zambia Revenue Authority in 1994 constituted an equally important development. Through the revenue authority, computerized tax records were implemented and the former government-employed tax collectors were retrained. A value added tax instituted in 1995 replaced the former cumbersome system of sales tax and was also an important mechanism in terms of broadening the tax base.

Liberalization of Imports, Trade, and Exchange Rates

The MMD government also wanted to encourage the private sector to take the lead in productive activities. A range of liberal reforms were implemented soon after the new government came to power in 1991, and evaluations of Zambia's adjustment efforts after 1991 have emphasized the pace of economic liberalization as one of the government's most remarkable achievements (van de Walle and Chiwele 1994; Seshamani 1996; World Bank 1996a, 1996c).

In order to encourage foreign investments and enhance the confidence of the local business community, the new government soon started to decontrol foreign exchange. A system of foreign exchange bureaus was introduced in October 1992, and by December that year the official exchange rate was unified with the bureau rate (Zambia 1993). With these changes, the exchange rate became fully market determined, and the government abandoned the practice of seeking to control the exchange rate through administrative means. Such practice had been maintained throughout the Second Republic, save for a short spell of foreign exchange auctioning in 1985–86. The 1994 budget further eliminated the Exchange Control Act and thus allowed both citizens and noncitizens to open foreign currency accounts (Zambia 1994). From early 1994 onward, Zambia made its national currency, the kwatcha, fully convertible, one of the very few countries on the African continent to do so. Funds now flowed freely into and out of Zambia. The final restriction in the foreign exchange field was removed in April 1996, when the Bank of Zambia allowed ZCCM to retain 100 percent of its foreign exchange receipts to supply the market directly (Bank of Zambia 1997; Kani 1996). Since the nationalization of the mines in the late 1960s, the mining company's lack of access to foreign exchange generated from mining had meant that only limited capital was reinvested into the mining industry. This decision was therefore considered to be of great political significance.[9]

Reforms in the domestic money market constituted another significant area of reforms implemented in the first few years of the MMD government. In 1993, the Bank of Zambia removed all restrictions on bank lending and deposit rates. The liberalization of the money market resulted in the entry of several commercial banks and nonbank financial institutions, ranging from insurance companies to pension funds. Furthermore, with the introduction of weekly Treasury bills, from 1993 onward the official interest rates were freed from administrative controls.

The government moved equally fast to liberalize the commodity market and trade. The liberalization meant that all goods could be bought from or sold to any buyers locally or abroad, freely and at market-determined prices. Free imports of consumer goods meant that the choice of commodities widened and the queues for basic commodities, which had become a daily occurrence in the Second Republic, were effectively ended. Extensive reforms within the external trade regime began in 1992. Over the five-year period, all licensing and quantitative restrictions on imports and exports were eliminated. The tariff structure was compressed and simplified. Customs duty rates, which before 1991 ranged from 0 to 100 percent with 11 tariff bands, by 1996 ranged from 0 to 25 percent with only 4 bands (Zambia 1996; Seshamani 1996; Taylor 1997). The trade liberalization meant that local firms were no longer protected by the state but had to compete with imported products. In terms of changing its economic policy regime and its regulatory environment, despite exogenous factors such as the severe drought, Zambia could by mid-1994 claim to have one of the most liberal foreign exchange regimes in Africa, and an impressive record in terms of inflation and fiscal probity.

Institutional Reforms

Alongside the stabilization and economic liberalization measures, several institutional reforms were initiated. These involved both the creation of new institutional frameworks and the dissolution of existing ones in order to facilitate private sector–led growth. Zambia's record in this area proved much more varied than in the areas of stabilization and liberalization.

A Public Sector Reform Program (PSRP) was launched in 1993. The program promised to cut 25 percent of the civil service within three years and to improve conditions of service for the remaining staff in order to retain and attract the best candidates (Zambia 1993). However, while 15,000 contract daily employees with no job security were retrenched in 1992, no retrenchment of civil servants had taken place by early 1999.[10] The contentious nature of this reform and its potential political implications were highlighted when the minister of finance announced in March 1996 that the PSRP had been put on hold indefinitely (*Times of Zambia*, 22 March 1996). Based on interviews with senior policymakers in Zambia, the main obstacle to the PSRP exercise appears to be the cost of reforms. Since the legally mandated retrenchment costs amounted to 10 years' salary for each employee, the most economical approach for the government has simply been to retain workers rather than retrench them. According to estimates by the Central Statistical Office, the civil service, rather than growing leaner as promised by MMD in its election campaign, instead grew by 19 percent between 1989 and 1994 (see table 9.13). Most observers have regarded the continued failure to address the issue of a large and inefficient public sector as the main obstacle to economic growth, in addition to the decline in copper production and the successive droughts (McPherson 1995; Seshamani 1996; World Bank 1996a, 1996b, 1996c).

Agricultural Liberalization

The agricultural liberalization process has been the most contentious issue of the economic restructuring program in Zambia to date. Throughout the Second Republic, political factors dictated policies that hampered growth in the agricultural sector. After independence, the UNIP government increased and broadened maize subsidies substantially, in part to keep both producers and consumers satisfied and in part to adhere to its development doctrine. Agricultural subsidies had their origin in the 1974/75 agricultural season when the government introduced uniform national producer prices (pan-territorial prices). This resulted in maize production dominating the agricultural sector, accounting for approximately 70 percent of land cropped and 85 percent of crop production (World Bank 1993).

The MMD government set out to alter this long-standing arrangement. Announcing its withdrawal from the marketing of agricultural inputs in 1993, the government appointed a small number of principal buying agents and allowed private traders to enter the maize market. This meant that cooperative societies were no longer allocated government funds for handling marketing or for the purchase of maize from farmers (Zambia 1995: 3). However, a combination of continued intervention by the government, the effects of the stabilization measures on credits and interest rates, and, finally, the size of the 1993 crop recovering from the disastrous drought in 1992, left the private sector unresponsive to the liberalized market for grain marketing and purchase.

With hindsight, it appears that the largest transitional problem may have been that the agricultural liberalization was carried out before the economy was stabilized. In 1993 the government liberalized the exchange rate and interest rates, introduced Treasury bills, and committed to a cash budget. However, with interest rates running as high as 300 percent, private investors tended to neglect the risk-prone and politically sensitive agricultural sector and invest instead in the lucrative, and virtually risk-free, government Treasury bills. On the one hand, the bumper crop tested the capacities of the new production and marketing structures that were evolving. On the other hand, farmers entered the 1992–93 season with pressing financial needs after a devastating drought the previous year. The combination of extremely high interest rates and the cash budget put a strain on the government-allocated finances for marketing the 1992–93 crop, which in turn had dire consequences for the 1993–94 crop. The lack of private sector response forced the government back into the market as a buyer. However, due to the restrictions of the cash budget, the funding was given in the form of promissory notes, or forward sales contracts. The financial obligation this imposed on the 1994 budget in turn put a severe strain on the cash budget.

Thus, as a consequence of market liberalization taking place simultaneously with macroeconomic stabilization, the newly emerging agricultural trade sector faced a harsh financial environment. Throughout the Third Republic, agricultural liberalization has had a destabilizing effect on the industry. However, none of the major liberalization measures within agriculture has been reversed despite the fact that growth continues to be hampered by poor implementation practices, limited supply response, and adverse external conditions. It should also be noted that some product diversification has taken place as a result of the liberalization efforts. Marketed production of tobacco, cotton, wheat, and groundnuts, among other products, has increased in the last decade (see table 9.14 in Appendix 9.5).

Privatization of the Parastatal Industries

Under UNIP and President Kaunda, the majority of the parastatals were managed by the state under an umbrella management institution, the

Zambia Industrial and Mining Corporation (ZIMCO). Under pressure from the donors, Zambia had begun to sell state-owned companies during the last stages of the Second Republic. A Technical Committee on Privatization was set up within the Ministry of Commerce, Trade and Industry in 1990 and carried out some preliminary work. However, by the time of the political transition in 1991, no privatization transactions had taken place.

In its 1991 manifesto, the MMD government committed itself to privatizing the parastatal sector (MMD 1991: 4). The process of privatization followed an implementation pattern very different from that of agricultural liberalization. The liberalization of the agricultural sector was implemented in a so-called "shock-therapy" manner. In contrast, the process of privatizing the public enterprises that accounted for some 80 percent of GDP in 1991 and employed 140,000 workers was a very slow process that only gathered momentum in 1995. From its inception, apart from some key ministers, the privatization process had only lukewarm support even within the cabinet. As a result, neither the mines nor the utility companies were included in the government's original privatization portfolio (Rakner 1998). While some government ministers had argued for the inclusion of the mines from an early stage, the general feeling within the MMD government at the time was that the issue was too controversial to include so soon. Instead, the government opted for a careful process in which the smaller companies were privatized first.

Despite the lack of support and slow beginning of the privatization process—and most notably, the failure to take action toward the mining sector—by 1996 the privatization program in Zambia was cited as one of the government's key successes. By 1997, 224 companies of a total of 275 offered for sale had been sold, and the government had committed itself to tender the mining conglomerate by February 28, 1997. The World Bank attributed the success of the privatization program to the fact that the process through the Zambia Privatization Agency was predominantly private sector–driven, with little interference from the government (*World Bank Findings*, October 1996; *Times of Zambia*, 15 October 1996).[11]

Because of Zambia's dependence on copper, the privatization of the mining conglomerate was the main issue in terms of a potential economic turnaround. It was only in 1996 that the government accepted the advice to begin the process of privatizing the Zambia Consolidated Copper Mines in unbundled units by open tender, with the aim of reaching agreements before June 1997. This decision was made during a fierce debate with the bilateral donors over the new constitution. The move on privatization of the mines was decisive in securing funding from the multilateral donors and, subsequently, the bilateral donors.

However, when tenders came in February 1997, the government's negotiating team declined all offers. In November 1997 the Kafue Con-

sortium presented a bid that was considered good by independent observers, considering the fact that copper prices had fallen by 35 percent
since earlier in the year.[12] But the government turned down the bid. As
copper prices continued to fall, in March 1998 the consortium made a
new and lower offer. Again, the Zambian government turned down the
offer. After substantial pressure from the IFIs and two years of reduced
balance of payments support, the government has since early 1999 en-
tertained the uncertain possibility of a much lower offer from Anglo
American Corporation, on the condition that Anglo can find a partner.
As of mid-1999, no sale has been finalized. The view among the donors
in Lusaka is that the negotiations failed because of a combination of incompetence and corruption on the part of the MMD government.

Economic Reforms in the 1990s: Opportunities Lost

After almost a decade of uninterrupted policy reforms, the record in
terms of economic growth, employment creation, investments, and poverty reduction remains weak. In terms of macroeconomic growth indicators, the Zambian economy has shrunk and is now smaller than it was
in 1991. Over the last decade, with a 25 percent increase in population,
per capita income has dropped by 4 percent per year, thus extending the
long period of economic decline that began in the 1970s (van der Heijden
1999). Mineral production has declined throughout the decade (table
9.5), formal employment has been reduced in all sectors except public
administration (table 9.13 in Appendix 9.5), and poverty and infant mortality have increased since the 1980s (table 9.15 in Appendix 9.5). Zambia's
most notable success in terms of macroeconomic stabilization has been
to bring inflation under control. And while inflation—pronounced "national enemy number one"—has been subdued during this period, it
has not disappeared completely, and since 1998 has increased again
slightly.[13]

Despite the rather dismal record in terms of results attained, it cannot
be argued that the direction of the government's overall economic policies has been altered, as was so often the case during the Kaunda era.
The Zambian government has, in principle, remained committed to stabilization and the economic liberalization process throughout its first
electoral period and now into its second period. None of the reform
measures implemented has been reversed and no aid agreement with
the IFIs has been canceled. However, other aspects of the reform program, most notably institutional reforms, have lagged behind. Midway
through the second and, according to the present constitution, last electoral term of the Chiluba government, the Public Sector Reform Program, deemed essential both to balancing the budgets and to enhancing
the capacity of the bureaucracy, has not been implemented. Furthermore,

the postponement of the privatization of the mining industry is considered to have had enormous adverse consequences for the economy as a whole (World Bank 1996b, 1996c; *Profit*, July 1998). The effect on the economy has been exacerbated by the decline in international copper prices and the donors' decision to withhold balance of payments support both in 1997 and 1998 in response to the government's failure to privatize the largest mines.

Thus, after a promising start as "one of the most important and hopeful transitions anywhere in Africa," as U.S. Secretary of State for African Affairs Chester Crocker phrased it, Zambia in 1999 is once again depicted a "poor reformer" by its external aid partners (World Bank 1998) and international investors. The quote from a South African investment firm illustrates how international investors regard Zambia. Under the heading: "What a Difference a Year Can Make," the South African Merchant Bank, Investec Securities, stated:

> The transformation in less than a year is startling. Twelve months ago Zambia seemed set for a rosy economic future. Inflation was falling and with it domestic interest rates, the external value of the kwatcha was stable, the government was running a budget surplus (albeit after significant contributions from foreign aid) and the keystone of the government's privatization program—the sale of ZCCM—was imminent. The contrast between those optimistic days and the situation today in Lusaka is marked. Where there was once hope, there is now despair. As the political situation has deteriorated, foreign aid has dried up, leaving the government desperately short of funds. Inflation, interest rates and the currency have all reacted negatively, whilst the sale of ZCCM has all but collapsed. (*Profit*, July 1998: 16)

A fundamental question in the case of Zambia is why a government committed to reform, with a wide mandate for change from its population and with donor finances to support it, achieved so little in terms of growth. A number of explanations for the limited supply response have been offered, ranging from claims that the government's commitment to reform has waned, to sequencing errors, investor insecurity, exogenous factors, and Zambia's landlocked status. We argue that most of these explanations point to a key underlying problem: the failure of the MMD government to set forth a genuine strategy for economic development. As detailed in section 4, long-term development goals have also largely been absent from the donors' strategy.

A Waning Commitment to Reform?

A number of factors suggest that the Zambian government's commitment to economic reform may have waned in the second half of the decade. While no reform measures have been reversed, it is evident that the major reform initiatives, such as the liberalization, the implementation of the cash budget, and the establishment of Zambia Revenue Authority, happened in the first years after the 1991 transition. Since 1991, macroeconomic stability has been a major problem. Since 1993 the MMD government has maintained, and in principle has remained committed to, a cash budget. According to analyses of monthly spending data the government has generally adhered to a rule of prohibiting monetary financing of fiscal deficits, but it has on several occasions violated its zero monetary financing rule (Stasavage and Moyo 1999: 10). Following each of these episodes, the government has imposed severe expenditure reductions. The period since 1994 has seen a regular pattern of fiscal performance going off-track in the early part of the year, with the problem being resolved later in the year by squeezing expenditures and/or introducing ad hoc revenue measures. Thus, evidence suggests that Zambia has failed to solve commitment problems in fiscal policy. As argued by Stasavage and Moyo (1999: 11): "It is important to note that in most of the above cases, violations of the zero monetary financing rule were prompted by excess expenditure by central authorities (such as wage hikes) rather than being due to expenditure overruns by line ministries."

In addition, the Zambian government has run sizeable primary domestic deficits, financed by increased holdings of government securities in commercial banks (Stasavage and Moyo 1999: 11). Thus after some years, the cash budget, which was meant to curb fiscal deficits, appears to have become a mere window-dressing activity. Budgetary constraints appear to be obeyed, but at the same time the government fails to pay suppliers. The government's failure to pay its bills was a subject of constant complaint by both members of the Zambian business community interviewed. It may therefore be argued that the cost of a compressed economy in Zambia today is not carried by the government through reduced spending, but rather by the private business sector. Despite austerity measures introduced and maintained, budget allocations also indicate that government consumption levels remain high, a view that was expressed repeatedly by our respondents from the Zambian business community and the bilateral donors.

Most respondents interviewed in Lusaka expressed the opinion that the government's commitment to economic reform had declined. Pointing to a series of watershed events—beginning in 1993 with the replacement of agriculture minister Guy Scott and finance minister Emmanuel Kasonde and culminating with the sacking of finance minister Ronald Penza in 1997—respondents argued that experienced, competent, and reform-minded ministers had been removed from the cabinet.[14] With hindsight, it is clear that the MMD leadership that entered the statehouse in 1991 included some exceptional people with regard to reform commitment as well as capacity. Increasingly, junior staffers, displaying a stronger commitment to the MMD president than to an economic development strategy, have replaced the experienced and reform-minded ministers. However, it is important to disaggregate commitment. Commitment to reform in Zambia has varied across issues and across parts of the cabinet. The MMD government was united in its resolve to attain stabilization in 1991. Furthermore, there was relatively strong support for the liberalization measures implemented and the re-invigoration of the private sector, including some privatization. But the public debates in the early 1990s indicate that the MMD government was never united over the privatization of ZCCM (Rakner 1998). The reactions to the agricultural liberalization from various cabinet ministers from 1994 on further indicate that few in the MMD government had thought through the implications of substantive agricultural reform.

With growth prospects still appearing dismal after nearly a decade of continuous austerity measures, a waning commitment to reform may be expected. Yet at some levels the Zambian government still appears committed to reform, and many of the reforms now seem irreversible, such as privatization, liberalization, and much of the opening of the economy. On the other hand, stabilization measures by their very nature are reversible, as balancing a budget one year in no way ensures that a government will balance the budget again the next year. As argued above, with regard to budgetary discipline it is evident that the government's commitment to the economic reform process has waned over the last five years. The government denies this and argues instead that donors have kept "moving goal posts" by introducing new conditionalities and failing to recognize the difficulties of what they are asking the government to achieve. Such disputes do, however, invariably point to uneven government commitment to policy reform. More and more, the MMD government's policy choices appear justified or criticized in terms of donor conditionality rather than in terms of an indigenous development strategy.

Investor Uncertainty and Sequencing Dilemmas

The government's lack of commitment to key reform measures such as privatization of the mines and reform of the public service has constituted a major impediment to growth in the last decade. However, as commitment to these reform measures was weak and uneven from the start, it is not clear that a waning commitment to the reform process can explain the limited supply response witnessed in Zambia during the last decade of continuous reform. Responding to the paradox of why a seemingly "good reformer" appeared unable to generate growth and sectional "winners," a World Bank report summarized the reform process in Zambia as follows:

Persistent uncertainty has caused investors to be hesitant to commit themselves in a significant way. While there have been many positive signs of market liberalization, decontrol of prices, and a lower Government role in the economy, there was still high inflation, tight credit, reduced protection and uncertainties about whether these policies would continue. Agricultural market reform has left producers with transitional increase in uncertainty. Privatization has brought more anxiety and conflict in the short term than tangible results in terms of companies sold or turned around. Based in part on conflicting signals, the stop-go experiences of the 1980s and the fear that donor fatigue or government intransigence on some issue could lead to a cessation of international support, many investors adopted a wait and see attitude before making major changes. (World Bank 1996a: 48)

Seconding the views expressed by World Bank staff, our Zambian respondents in the private sector cited lack of investor confidence in the irreversible nature of the reform process as the main reason for the limited supply response. We find this explanation plausible. However, the persistent budgetary problems have also affected the business community's confidence (Stasavage and Moyo 1999). Added to this, anecdotal evidence suggests that corruption and government enrichment have increased in the Third Republic, which again has led investors to question the government's credibility.

Not disregarding the issue of investor confidence, a recent external evaluation of the IMF's ESAF funding to Sub-Saharan Africa concludes that the current adjustment program in Zambia has been weakly designed (Botchwey and others 1998). First, the move to capital account convertibility and interest rate liberalization prior to the attainment of stabilization created an avoidable bout of inflation; this in turn led to a credit crunch of the private sector, delaying the emergence of rural food markets and reducing the private investments required for structural change. Second, the IMF evaluation argues that the structural reforms needed to be sequenced in a particular fashion to produce growth. Copper and agriculture in particular should have received early policy attention. The privatization of the ZCCM has still not been implemented, and agricultural growth would have required early improvement of rural roads. With hindsight, the argument put forth by the ESAF evaluators seems justified: Liberalization carried out in the early phases of the reform program created economic distortions that, coupled with a devastating drought, hampered growth in the agricultural sector.

On the other hand, it can also be argued that the MMD government chose to take advantage of the "honeymoon" offered by its election victory and implemented the liberalization measures as a shock therapy. It might not have been possible to carry through the liberalization measures later, when the political opposition would have reorganized. Emmanuel Kasonde, who was minister of finance from 1991 to 1993, later explained in an interview:

> I was lucky as prior to taking office Chiluba has told me that I would be offered the Ministry of Finance if we were to form a government. I therefore had a year in which I followed economic events very closely and when we formed government we were able to hit the road running in order to implement my ideas quickly. I was also aware of MMD's popularity; if I had to make unpopular decisions it had to be done during the honeymoon period, otherwise it would be very difficult. In other words, necessary but unpopular decisions had to be quick. I was very interested in using the political status of the MMD government to make economic advancements. . . . I use the singular "I" because the cabinet did not contain many economically trained brains and I myself had to train them. (Interview, Kasonde, 1996)

Most of the above explanations point to a precarious lack of a coherent long-term strategy of growth. The MMD immediately implemented stabilization measures to curb fiscal deficits. However, the one factor that would have reduced government consumption drastically, public service reform, did not enter into the early restructuring plan. For this major reform effort, the "honeymoon" from public opposition was apparently not enough to carry the process through. Similarly, investments in agriculture and tourism depended on investment capital. This could only have come from one source, apart from donor funds, namely a reinvigorated, privatized mining industry. Again, this reform did not enter into the government's immediate restructuring plan. In the absence of any kind of long-term growth strategy on the part of the government, in the 1990s fiscal austerity appears to have become a goal in itself and the focal point in discussions with the international donors in terms of adhering to a structural adjustment program.

So far, the discussion has centered on economic reforms. Yet, as we have seen, in Zambia since the mid-1990s governance issues have played a central role in terms of souring relations both among Zambia's donors and between the donors and the government. The MMD government's commitment to good governance waned during its first electoral term, culminating with the signing of the 1996 constitution that denied the main opposition candidate access to the presidential elections. A question to be addressed is whether or not commitment to economic reform has co-varied with commitment to political reform.

A Note on the Political Reform Process

In 1991 the MMD manifesto laid out an ambitious plan to strengthen the democratic gains won in the 1991 elections. However, by 1996 the early euphoria had largely given way to conflict. The government appeared more and more isolated and reacted in a paranoid manner to criticism from external donors, the press, interest groups, and opposition parties. The individuals who had entered politics in 1991 displayed a strong commitment to the values of democracy and human rights. By 1996 these ministers had largely been replaced by young and inexperienced politicians with loyalties to the president and consolidation of the MMD party rather than to the development of a democratic political system.

In May 1996, a unified bilateral donor community decided to withhold balance of payments support and in some instances new project aid pledges. The decision was based on what the external donors interpreted as declining adherence to the principles of good governance by the MMD government. The passing of a constitutional amendment that effectively barred former president Kenneth Kaunda from contesting the 1996 elections became the crucial issue in a long chain of events leading to the bilateral donors' decision. However, despite loud protests from the donor community and the domestic opposition—consisting of a large number of nongovernmental organizations (NGOs), interest groups, the independent press, and opposition parties—the MMD government went ahead and conducted the elections on the basis of a contentious voter registration system and a constitution denying the main opposition candidate the opportunity to compete.

The 1996 general elections were considered flawed by many observers (Bratton, Alderfer, and Simutanyi 1997; Baylies and Szeftel 1997). The MMD took advantage of its control over government resources to promote its electoral prospects. The conduct of the elections proved that the Chiluba government was intolerant of criticism, willing to compromise the rule of law, and willing to exploit its majority position and control of government resources to undermine its opponents. In terms of political reform, progress over the five-year period and the holding of a second election were not sufficient, therefore, to conclude that a process of democratic consolidation had taken place in Zambia. In 1996, the separation between the incumbent MMD party and the government was increasingly blurred. After five years of political liberalization, no opposition party had emerged that was remotely capable of challenging the ruling party and winning either a parliamentary majority or the presidency. The capacity of the political opposition and of civic associations to shape the political agenda was limited.

Since the 1996 elections, the governance situation in Zambia appears to have deteriorated even further. Negative highlights include the police shooting and wounding of Kenneth Kaunda in August 1997, the detention of Kaunda and other high-profile politicians, the declaration of a state of emergency in October 1997 following a failed coup by junior officers, and increasing harassment of the private press and human rights organizations. In 1998 the Zambian Parliament approved a discretionary fund of approximately US$5 million for the president of the republic, and in 1999 the government refused to announce the amount allocated to the presidential fund, raising speculation of abuse (Afronet 1999). Commonly referred to as the "slush fund," the pool of money has no disbursement criteria, nor is a system of accountability in place to ensure it is used for legitimate purposes. Local observers therefore viewed the presidential fund as a means for the president to enhance his own public standing.

Most observers of Zambian politics characterize the negative trends in governance performance as a return to the politics of the past. NGOs, the press, and the political opposition all point to the high levels of government corruption and to the increased powers and resources of the presidency, despite the stated intention to reduce presidential power in 1991. Nonetheless, the period since 1991 has not witnessed a complete reversal of the process of political liberalization. The independent press still exists, and manages to continue its critical and independent reporting. Judicial rulings in favor of press freedom and opposition candidates in detention continue to indicate that the courts operate with a considerable degree of independence. During the first electoral term, 48 by-elections were conducted freely and fairly. Despite the high levels of conflict, international criticism, and declining levels of aid, the 1996 parliamentary and presidential elections were conducted peacefully and the turnout of registered voters actually increased compared to 1991 (Bratton, Alderfer, and Simutanyi 1997; Electoral Commission of Zambia 1996). The 1998 local elections were also carried out peacefully, albeit with alarmingly low participation figures as a result of serious deficiencies in the registration process.

To what extent, then, has commitment to good governance co-varied with commitment to economic policy reform within the last decade? Recent research carried out by the World Bank shows that the rates of return for World Bank projects are correlated with the indices of political and civil rights collected by Freedom House (Pritchett 1998). The Zambian experiences over the last decade support this general finding. The original reformist cabinet of the MMD was committed to both economic and political reform, and it appears that the commitment to both processes waned at the same time. The new politicians who replaced the original reformist cabinet have viewed both economic and political reform with much less enthusiasm, and in 1996 economic policymaking became subordinated to political objectives—most notably, winning the 1996 elections.

Yet, despite the lack of economic growth, and the fact that no sectors of society had emerged as clear "winners" of the economic reform measures implemented, the MMD government faced no serious challenge to its popularity in the 1996 elections. No party or politician lobbied for a return of the controlled exchange rate regime or protection of local industry. As a result, the 1996 elections represented a significant departure from the Zambian policy debates in the 1980s when opposition to the various structural reform programs centered around the *desirability* of economic reform programs as such. Based on the 1996 election results, it cannot be argued that the Zambian voting population displayed strong resistance to the economic changes carried out by the MMD government. Indeed, one of the most striking features of Zambia's first electoral period under a multiparty constitution is the decline in influence of key economic interest groups. In Zambia the process of political liberalization appears to have weakened the relative position of interest groups in relation to the government on account of the proliferation of associations and the various associations' weak membership base (Rakner 1998).

Turning now to the relationship between the Zambian government and the external donor community, the next section will show that the deteriorating political situation largely cooled off the bilateral donors' enthusiasm for the Zambian political reform process from 1993 onward. From about 1996 on, the bilateral donors increasingly began to question the economic policy record as well, despite the multilateral donors' claim that Zambia's "economic house" was largely in order. We argue that the disagreements within the donor community regarding how much weight to attach to economic performance and governance weakened the clout of the donors' conditionality weapon.

AID AND REFORM

The Aid-Reform Relationship in the 1980s: Lack of Ownership

As argued above, economic reform efforts in the Kaunda era failed because the reform objectives of the international donors were at odds with the interests and ideology of the political leadership and its main political constituents. Furthermore, during the 1980s the politicians, the press, and even the opposition forces such as the trade union movement consistently blamed the country's economic misfortunes on external forces, most notably the IFIs. The lack of domestic ownership, within both the political elite and society at large, resulted in increasingly strong conditionality measures from the aid community. Western donor institutions had insisted since the early 1980s that market mechanisms should replace state controls. The demands and conditions became ever more pronounced and insistent. Zambia's ability to ignore these demands was limited as a result of its financial need and lack of alternative financial sources for securing foreign exchange. In theory, therefore, the leverage of the Western financial institutions and donor governments was high.

However, when one looks at the efforts to implement reforms in the 1985–87 period, the lack of influence of the external institutions in the face of unraveling agreements is striking (West 1989; Sandberg 1990; Callaghy 1990). The implementation of the 1985 structural adjustment program indicated that the international donors were virtually powerless and unable to interfere after the president changed his economic team in April 1986 from the group who had negotiated the program to some of the strongest critics of a market-based economy. Experiences in Zambia in the 1980s highlight the importance of local ownership of the reform process: The conditionality mechanisms were unable to bring about policy change as these measures were at odds with the economic ideology prevailing at the time, and therefore were not supported by the political leadership.

Imperfect donor coordination further reduced the credible threat of the conditionality instruments. While a number of bilateral donors from the early 1980s onward tended to link part of their commitments to Zambia's policy reform measures, as defined by a prior agreement with the IFIs, not all bilateral donors responded in the same way. Some bilateral aid flows followed the multilateral aid flows, some increased regardless of policy reforms, and lastly, some bilateral aid actually flowed in the opposite direction of the multilateral aid flows. According to estimates by Saasa (1996: 54), aid flows from Norway, Japan, and the UNDP increased when Zambia canceled the structural adjustment agreement with the IMF and World Bank both in 1983 and in 1987–89. Thus, Zambia received substantial levels of external assistance in the form of both concessional loans and grants throughout the 1980s, rendering the conditionality instruments less than credible. As figure 9.1 indicates, despite multilateral aid cancellation in 1983 and between 1987 and 1989, aid levels to Zambia increased gradually during the 1980s.

The Aid-Reform Relationship Since 1991

The 1990s signified a new era in donor-government relations in Zambia. A democratically elected government, committed to economic reform, set out to work closely with the international donor community in an attempt to turn the Zambian economy around.

The relationship between the Zambian government and the international donor community in the Third Republic appears to have passed through four stages:

- In the first phase the level of enthusiasm was high, as the donor community was eager to support the new reformist government on the basis of the 1991 manifesto.
- However, it quickly became apparent that the MMD government was very diverse. In this phase, donors sought to support the pro-reform ministers in the cabinet, still within a pro-reform partnership.
- From 1994 onward the relationship became characterized by hard negotiations and increasing use of conditionality instruments. This tactic was particularly evident in terms of the privatization process, but also with regard to governance issues.
- Finally, since the 1996 election the international donor community appears to have lost faith in the effectiveness of the conditionality instruments. The Zambian government for its part has adopted a rather skeptical attitude toward the donors, increasingly viewing the process of policy reform as externally imposed and charging the donors with moving goal posts.

Thus, within just a few years the international donor community's view of Zambia appears to have shifted significantly. Viewed earlier as a most promising reformer, the country now is labeled a most reluctant reformer. The following section examines the processes leading to these changes.

Liberalization as a Signal of Commitment to Reform

The political transition in 1991 offered a new situation as the democratically elected government indicated its intention to reform the economic system and work with the international donor community. As argued by the Zambian local press, for the MMD government facing an escalating economic crisis the question was not whether to adopt an IMF/World Bank–approved structural adjustment program, but rather which steps to take to meet the requirements of the IMF/ World Bank policies (*Financial Mail*, 21–27 April 1992). The emphasis on restoring Zambia's international financial reputation was underscored by one observer:

> Economic reform is meant to fundamentally alter a country's growth prospects. In principle, reform is not primarily a means of satisfying external creditors. But because of Zambia's poor credit standing, a practical precondition for the resumption of sustained

growth is for Zambia to re-establish a reputation of responsible financial behaviors. Thus, a major objective for the reform effort has been to gain regular access to international finance as due to its debt overhang Zambia could not finance its economic imbalances independently of donor support. (McPherson 1995: 14)[15]

In retrospect, it can be argued that the initial period after the 1991 elections reflected an almost uncritical acceptance of the donor policy agenda. Particularly in the area of trade reforms, the MMD government is seen as having overcommitted and carried out reforms too rapidly. As argued in section 3, financial liberalization was carried out in Zambia prior to the achievement of fiscal balance. This increased the fiscal costs of stabilization. According to the ESAF evaluation (Botchwey and others 1998), the MMD government went ahead with its decision to liberalize the economy at an early stage against the IMF's advice.[16] Adam argues that the government hoped to signal its commitment to economic reform to the international donor community through decisive moves in the area of financial liberalization:

> In the absence of other mechanisms to signal its commitment to reform, the government chose to accelerate the liberalization measures, even though it distorted the logical sequence of reforms and imposed significant costs on the economy later in the stabilization process. (Adam 1995: 738)

Adam's argument appears plausible. During the UNIP era the Kaunda regime failed on a number of occasions to implement the agricultural and financial liberalization measures strongly advocated by the external donors. These areas of reform were the ones pushed most consistently by the new MMD government almost from the start. The government used its honeymoon to implement far-reaching reforms in the areas of liberalization because these reforms would signal the MMD's clear commitment to implement "new" economic policies in contrast to the former regime. Liberalization measures are also relatively easy reforms in the sense that they do not require a large administrative apparatus or the consent and participation of a large group of stakeholders (Nelson 1993).

Arguably, the main reward for carrying out these reform measures was witnessed in the relationship with the international donor community. The negotiations carried out at the various Consultative Group meetings between Zambia and external donors indicate that the commitment displayed in the areas of financial and agricultural liberalization was an instrumental factor in the donor community's decision to reward the Zambian government with extraordinary levels of financial assistance in the 1992–94 period. Similarly, in 1993, when the government accepted the donors' advice to implement a cash budgeting system, a new strong "commitment barometer" was established. The adherence to the cash budget, with a resulting decline in inflation, became a significant policy measure in terms of donor support.

Presenting the 1993 budget to Parliament, Minister of Finance Emmanuel Kasonde emphasized the importance of international credibility and of attracting donor finance. He defended the decision to remove subsidies on maize meal and fertilizer and made no secret of the main rationale for the decision. Pointing out that the move would save the government around US$10 million, the finance minister stressed that the main result would be to secure an estimated US$600 million in donor support required by Zambia that year (Zambia 1993). Commenting on the fact that few of the economic targets set for 1992 had been met, the minister nevertheless noted that

> Our commitment to policy reform has yielded substantial benefits already. For example, we have been able to reactivate our Rights Accumulation Program with the International Monetary Fund, which paved the way for external assistance amounting to US$1.5 billion. This amount is unprecedented in our history. (Zambia 1993)

Donor Leverage in the Area of Privatization

The issue of privatization was raised in the meetings between the Zambian government and its external donors from the very beginning. According to observers, the urgency expressed by the donors regarding privatization in part reflected the lack of results achieved under Kaunda. But it also reflected a desire to take advantage of the support and legitimacy enjoyed by the MMD in the early stages of the reform period.[17] Reflecting the changes from a cooperative relationship to a conditionality-based relationship, the external donor community used stronger conditionality measures in order to push the privatization program forward after 1994.

Privatization had a small group of influential supporters in Zambia. However, it should be noted that even the Zambian business community was divided on the issue. Many emerging business owners with a background in the public sector were unable to reap the benefits of privatization and felt threatened by the prospect of foreign takeovers of indigenous businesses (Rakner 1998). As a result, in the first half of the 1990s there was no coherent domestic lobby group that favored privatization.

Comparing the internal policy debates on the process of privatization to the external debate between donors and the government at the various

Consultative Group meetings, it can be argued that external pressure, through a combination of "promotion" mechanisms and economic conditionality, played a significant role in moving the privatization process forward. In interviews with approximately 40 representatives of various multilateral donor organizations and bilateral donor governments, all respondents cited the privatization process as either the principal or one of two principal adjustment achievements of Zambia during the period in question. The interviews also indicated that in terms of the donors' leverage—and thus the success of their economic conditionality policies—the progress achieved in privatization was considered the principal area of success.

In late 1994, for the first time since coming to power, the MMD government ran into serious conflict with the IMF when it failed to meet the monetary benchmarks set for advancement to an ESAF agreement in March 1995. Slippage on a number of macroeconomic indicators led the international donors to question the MMD government's continued commitment to economic liberalization. The new benchmarks negotiated with the IMF for the postponement of the ESAF agreement strongly emphasized progress in the area of parastatal reform. Incidentally, it was only when encountering these problems that the government made the policy decision that appeared to secure progress in the process of privatization, namely to liquidate the holding company, ZIMCO.

Furthermore, it was only when faced with increasing donor pressure and reduction of funds due to governance issues that the Zambian government officially announced a date for the sale of the copper mines. The MMD government's commitment in 1996 to a February 28, 1997 date for privatization of the mining industry was a major reason for the decision by the multilateral finance institutions in 1996 to continue financing the Zambian reform program. It was also the prospect of the sale of the mines, and associated investments expected to flow from that action, that induced most bilateral donors to pledge new funding to Zambia at the July 1997 CG meeting. Again, the failure of the MMD government to finalize the sale of the mines in 1998 has held back large amounts of bilateral donor funds until 1999.

Political Conditionality

The relationship between the MMD and the international donor community was very positive in the first years of the MMD's electoral term. The donor community shared the political and economic visions of the new Zambian government as set forth in the 1991 manifesto. The MMD manifesto committed the new government to improve accountability, strengthen the legislature and the Parliament in relation to the cabinet, delink the party from the state, grant freedom of speech and association, and adopt a new constitution based on the principle of consensus. On the basis of its manifesto, the MMD was given a large electoral majority in the 1991 elections. However, the manifesto also functioned as the basic document, or "contract," between the new government and its external supporters, and as such it became significant in terms of securing the resumption of high levels of financial support from the international donor community. As a result, as the conflicts unfolded between the Zambian government and the international donor community in the period leading up to the 1996 elections, the question of adherence to the principles laid out in the 1991 manifesto became key.[18]

In retrospect it can be argued that the cabinet reshuffles and the introduction of state of emergency laws in the spring of 1993 ended the honeymoon between the domestic opposition and the government. Perhaps not surprisingly, the very same issues changed the relationship between the MMD government and the external donors from one of cooperation to one of conflict. Governance first appeared as an issue of conditionality between the Zambian government and its external partners at the Consultative Group meetings in 1993. Concerns were raised about the state of emergency laws in March 1993 and later about issues of corruption and drug trafficking at high political levels. In an apparent response to demands made by the donors at this stage, several high-ranking cabinet members, including the minister of foreign affairs, were dismissed from the cabinet.

In 1995, as the work on the constitutional review increasingly became tied to Kenneth Kaunda's return to the presidency of UNIP, the relationship between the donors and the Zambian government again became conflictual. According to donor representatives in Lusaka, late 1995 witnessed a distinct decline in the commitment to good governance by the Zambian government. Most saw the quality of governance as having deteriorated sharply and linked this development to Kaunda's return, as well as the stagnant economy and increasing levels of unemployment.

At the December 1995 Consultative Group meeting governance was once again the main topic of debate. But whereas the use of political conditionality and threats of aid withdrawal had produced "results" in 1993, this time the government did not bow to donor pressure. The constitution was ratified by the Parliament and later signed into law by the president, despite the conflicts raised over the issue of "the Kaunda clause," among other things. During the spring and summer of 1996, a majority of the bilateral donors announced that they were either withholding balance of payments support, freezing discussions on new aid grants, or cutting ongoing project aid to Zambia. All bilateral donors cited the lack of progress on governance issues, in particular the signing of the constitution banning Kenneth Kaunda from contesting the elections, as their main reason for withholding financial support.[19]

Divisions among the External Partners

Following the bilateral aid reductions over issues of governance, an intense debate unfolded during the summer of 1996 between the bilateral donors and the multilateral agencies of the World Bank and the IMF. Attempting to reach a compromise between the bilateral donors' concerns regarding governance issues and the economic assessments conducted by the IMF in October 1996, the Board of the World Bank decided to release US$45 million in balance of payments support. The remaining sum would be released in February 1997, pending a solution to the impasse over the constitutional issue in the upcoming elections between the Zambian government and the bilateral donor community.

The 1996 elections did not resolve the stalemate between the domestic opposition and the government in Zambia. Furthermore, the elections did not bring an end to the chill in relations between the external donor community and the Zambian government. However, in January the MMD government began a process of confidence building. During the spring of 1997, the Zambian government and its external partners met on several occasions to discuss governance issues. At the Consultative Group meeting in Paris in July 1997, the donors acknowledged the initiatives taken by the MMD government toward reconciling with the opposition. Expressing satisfaction with the positive developments, the meeting concluded that the groundwork was laid for the donors to engage in more active cooperation with the Zambian government.

Bilateral donors lifted the aid freeze on Zambia by granting US$435 million to the country for 1997, pending the privatization of the mines and progress on the governance situation. The donor enthusiasm experienced in 1991 was largely gone, but Zambia and the external donors resumed "business as usual" in the summer of 1997. The government had maintained the economic reform program, but refused to meet the demands raised in terms of the voter registration procedure and the constitutional amendment process. And while the mutual goodwill and high aid levels of the early 1990s have not been restored, a comment by the Economist Intelligence Unit seems to capture an essential ingredient of the donor-government relationship:

> The government's risky policy stand of standing firm on these issues and waiting out the bilateral donor aid freeze has paid off in a spectacular fashion. (EIU 3rd quarter 1997: 9)

Since 1997, governance issues and the failure to finalize the sale of ZCCM have again resulted in a withholding of bilateral balance of payments support. However, as argued earlier, at the 1999 CG meeting regional concerns induced a number of donors to resume their lending to

Zambia. The current arguments for increasing bilateral aid levels are fear of regional instability and the potential for instability within Zambia caused by a cancellation of donor funds rather than economic and political reform.

Conditionality Reconsidered

The change from positive cooperation to mutual distrust between the government and the donors resulted from a combination of economic slippage and reversals in the field of political liberalization. However, it was first and foremost governance issues that generated the heated conflicts. This related to what donor representatives felt was a breach of the contract expressed in the 1991 manifesto. Zambia had presented an ambitious agenda promising an economic turnaround within the context of democratic governance procedures. Based largely on the manifesto, the international donor community had expected far more progress in terms of adherence to both democratic principles and economic reforms. The Zambian government for its part had expected that several years of fiscal austerity measures and economic hardship would produce results in terms of growth, employment creation, and substantially increased levels of foreign investment. With both sides disappointed, many donors present in Lusaka in 1996 described a feeling of betrayal, a loss of trust between the Zambian government, the people, and the country's external partners.

A number of studies have pointed to the dilemmas of political conditionality and the potential conflicts between the application of conditionality and the building and consolidation of democratic institutions (Mkandawire 1996, 1998; Havnevik and Arkadie 1996; Collier 1997; Gwin and Nelson 1997). The case of Zambia's dual reform processes in the period after 1991 reflects these general concerns. The conflicts between the need for consistency in aid flows to sustain and secure the processes of reform and the increasing application of donor conditionality from 1993 onward strained the relationship between the government and its external partners. The donor community, in particular the various bilateral donors present in Lusaka, judged the declining performance of the MMD government on both political and economic reforms against the goals presented in the 1991 manifesto. The MMD government asked to be judged in comparison with other developing nations as well as Zambia's previous economic and political record.[20] Echoing the sense of betrayal felt among the international donors, a number of government officials who had participated in designing and implementing the reform program expressed anger toward the external donors as they felt the MMD was being judged much more harshly than Kenneth Kaunda had been during his 27 years in office.

The Zambian government refused to bow to the demands—raised by both the international donors and the local opposition—to postpone the debate on the constitution to the next electoral term and to scrap the use of the voter registry and instead let people vote on the basis of their national registration cards. Choosing to abide, in principle, by the conditions set in terms of economic reforms, yet refusing to abide by the political conditionality ties, the Zambian government presented the bilateral donor community with a dilemma. The use of political conditionality and the withdrawal of balance of payments support had not produced the intended political response from the MMD government. By continuing and extending the withholding of financial support, the bilateral donors risked causing the structural adjustment program to fail at a time when the benefits of the copper mine privatization were in sight.

In the press, as well as in negotiations with external donors, the Zambian government indicated that it saw its commitment to carry out economic reforms as more important than the process of political liberalization. Increasingly, government representatives presented the situation as one in which Zambia had committed itself to carry out an economic reform program. From the government's perspective, it was the bilateral donor community that changed the agenda by deciding also to include issues of governance. From 1996 on, members of the MMD government criticized the external actors for introducing new hurdles, for "blackmailing the government to follow an external dictate," and for "interfering with Zambia's principal rights as a sovereign nation."[21] The multilateral institutions were portrayed as the real partners of Zambia because of their main focus on the economic reform process.

The conduct of the 1996 elections, and the fact that the multilateral finance institutions insisted that Zambia's "economic house was in order," to a certain extent shifted the burden of proof from the Zambian government to the bilateral donors. Given the tension between the short-term goals of debt reimbursement and the long-term goal of sustained economic development, the rhetorical question of ownership of the debt problem had no clear answer in the case of Zambia. A statement by the chief economic adviser at the Swedish embassy illustrated the conflicts and dilemmas for all parties:

> The whole situation is a bit absurd. The Bretton Woods institutions are of course very keen that we as bilateral donors pay Zambia's debt; we are in reality paying to them. As a result, they tend to take a much more positive view assessing the economic situation than the bilateral donors tend to do. They [the multilateral donors] naturally want to see Zambia on its feet; however, it is we that pay the credits and as a result, they gloss over economic realities. In addi-

tion, we have an additional criterion for evaluating the results, as we also have put in political conditionalities … Everybody will have to page in. Who is in the driver's seat is difficult to say. (Interview, Aagren, 1996)

The Swedish diplomat's comment highlights several of the conflicting motivations and incentives facing the bilateral and multilateral donors. The emphasis on debt repayment by their member governments has made the multilateral institutions prone to defensive lending (Gordon 1993). Furthermore, the multilateral institutions have invested much intellectual prestige in the African adjustment programs (Kapur 1997). Bilateral donors in the West, on the other hand, are increasingly facing domestic parliaments that demand a stronger emphasis on democratic development and, thus, political conditionality.

In sum, in terms of political reforms, the international donor community was not able to reverse the regressive trends that were especially marked from 1995 onward. The influential position of the World Bank throughout Sub-Saharan Africa in the 1990s was also clearly reflected in the case of Zambia. However, despite the strong coordination function, the donors did not appear to achieve a positive influence in the areas of governance stressed by the World Bank—institution building to ensure accountability and transparency and a limit to corrupt practices. The combined effects of the continued disbursements from the multilateral donors and the debt rescheduling agreements, which were not affected by the bilateral aid freeze, reduced the impact of the freeze.

The figures from the Ministry of Finance (table 9.2) provide a key to understanding the limits of donor conditionality and the potential conflicts of interest between the principles of political liberalization and economic liberalization. The bilateral donor agencies presented an unusually unified and coherent policy reaction to the political actions of the MMD government. However, the fact that substantial amounts of their aid had been tied to the multilateral finance institutions and the implementation of economic rescheduling programs at least in the short run rendered a purely bilateral reaction of limited effect. Thus, the aid freeze in 1996–98 represents a clear parallel to the situation in the 1980s, when continued bilateral funding diluted the impact of aid cancellations by the multilateral donors.

In the case of Zambia, it can be argued that concern for the economic reform program won over the principle of political liberalization and democratic consolidation. For the IMF and the World Bank, arguably, the key credibility point was the continuation of the process of privatization and the continued adherence to a stable macroeconomic framework. For the multilateral institutions, Zambia's proven ability to carry through a conditionality program in the context of political turmoil became a crucial determining factor for continued support. Because they placed so much importance on cultivating Zambia as a success story of structural adjustment, the multilateral donors were unlikely to withdraw funding unless Zambia started to slide on its debt service obligations. If the government were to stop meeting its debt service commitments, and thus risk the collapse of the ESAF agreement with IMF, a real financial crisis would be looming. As argued by the Economist Intelligence Unit:

> It remains the case that the donor community in general, and the Bretton Woods institutions in particular, need Zambia to look successful as an example to the rest of the continent of the workability of structural adjustment. (EIU 4th quarter 1996: 4)

Commitment and Conditionality

The question remains, however, to what extent the international donor community exercised real influence and leverage over the economic policies of the Zambian government during the period under study. Increasingly, the academic literature has argued that the economic reform programs of the Bretton Woods institutions do not increase economic growth or levels of investments (Killick 1995; Collier 1997; Burnside and Dollar 1997). As argued above, Zambia has in principle remained committed to stabilization and fiscal discipline by adhering to a cash budgeting procedure. However, it has suffered from significant month-to-month volatility of expenditures. Zambia's several lapses in fiscal discipline have invariably been followed by drastic cuts in expenditure, and nonwage expenditures and capital expenditures have suffered the largest reductions. This situation has meant that inflation remains relatively low. However, accumulation of arrears on domestic debt has increased, and unbudgeted wage hikes and retirement packages for civil servants have not convinced the private sector of the government's commitment to fiscal discipline. Yet the swift fiscal adjustments have sent a positive signal to the IFIs:

> Ultimately, the most convincing explanation for the fiscal policy outcomes observed in Zambia may be the simple need to meet IMF government saving targets. In fact, corrective measures taken after the emergence of monthly deficits in Zambia have frequently coincided with months at the end of which IMF targets for the change in net claims of the banking sector on government need to be met. (Stasavage and Moyo 1999: 15)

Similarly, members of the Zambian business community and bilateral donor representatives expressed concerns in interviews that the

MMD government showed a lack of budgetary discipline, despite seeming to adhere to a cash budget and the macroeconomic benchmarks set by the donors. This problem also affected the bilateral donors. As argued by the economic adviser at the German Embassy in Lusaka:

> Coming to 1997 it is our view that the budget situation is not a sane one, budget discipline is not being observed. Through our bilateral cooperation project we have been supporting Lusaka Sewage Company for more than a decade. However, this last year the Zambian government has not paid their water bill, as this payment was suppressed in order to balance the budget. But a budget is not in balance if you do not pay your bills, it is like shopping and refusing to pay and claiming you have saved money ... The simple idea that if you do not have money you cannot spend is not adhered to. (Interview, Zeidler, 1997)

The arguments put forth here address the dilemmas of conditionality-based aid in the absence of genuine government ownership. Swift adjustments ensure that benchmarks are met. Yet no real fiscal discipline, which could provide the basis for investor confidence, investments, and ultimately growth, has been achieved. The MMD government's emphasis on maintaining a good relationship with the IFIs by, at least in principle, meeting the benchmarks stands in contrast to the conduct of economic reform in the 1980s and the 1990s and ultimately represents policy learning. Despite the macroeconomic problems encountered from 1995 on, Zambia has remained current on its external debt service payments throughout the first electoral term and also for 1997 and 1998. Debt servicing has been maintained even though balance of payments support was withheld in response to the postponement of the privatization of the mining industry. In the eyes of the international donor community, the progress of the economic restructuring program therefore justified continued support to Zambia despite the regression in the areas of democracy and good governance. It can therefore be argued that the government in the 1990s used adherence to the economic reform demands of the donor community as a "trump card" with the bilateral donors when conflict arose over the issues of respect for human rights and political liberties.

With hindsight, it seems that the commitment to both the political and economic processes of reform waned within the MMD government midway through the first electoral term. For a number of reasons, Zambia appears to have returned to the "politics of the past," in which officials made promises at CG meetings with no intention of sticking to them. We find that Zambia, both in the 1980s and 1990s, fit a more general portrait of a country in which policy choices are driven by donor funding rather than domestically formulated development concerns. The recent developments in the privatization of the mines illustrate both the effects and the limits of donor conditionality in the absence of a firm and strong government commitment to the reform measures.

LESSONS ABOUT CONDITIONALITY AID FROM ZAMBIA

The point of departure for the Aid and Reform project has been new evidence on aid effectiveness indicating that aid transfers to date have been ineffective both in promoting growth and in inducing policy reform except in good policy environments. The Zambian case supports these findings. Throughout the 1980s, the UNIP government rejected policy reform. However, the cutoffs from IFI finances following the cancellation of reform agreements were offset by continued bilateral aid flows and poor aid coordination. Viewed in the 1980s as a classic "nonreformer," Zambia gained a new image when a reformist government came to power in 1991 with the firm intent to undertake policy reform. The donors rewarded this local ownership of a policy process with substantial increases in aid. Influential ministers in key positions in the initial MMD cabinet clearly favored economic policy reform. The high levels of aid received initially reflected the mutual interests and understanding shared by Zambia's key policymakers and the donor community. While the prospect of aid was not the main motivation for the government's reform effort, the financial and nonfinancial support from the donors was nevertheless important. The experiences of frequent cancellations of agreements with the IFIs in the 1980s had contributed to policy learning before the 1991 transition. Both politicians and technocrats acknowledged that an agreement with the IFIs, entailing servicing the country's international debt, was essential in order to receive external financial aid.

Over time, however, the MMD government's commitment to reform waned despite external support, in part because the reforms achieved so little in terms of stemming the continued economic decline. While the government did display genuine commitment to liberalization and stabilization, there was no evidence of commitment to a long-term strategy of growth—one that would include privatization of the mines and a restructuring of the public sector. The donors for their part also failed to express a coherent strategy of economic growth. A donor-promoted growth strategy would have placed the mining industry at the center of negotiations with the MMD government much earlier than 1997. Instead, in the 1990s both the government and the external donors made fiscal austerity an end in itself and a measure of reform commitment.

Thus, nearing the end of the decade, the similarities and continuity with the policy practices of the Second Republic appear more striking than the policy shifts. In line with the findings of the *Assessing Aid* report, in Zambia donor finances and donor conditionality have proved unable to stem the waning reform commitment witnessed in the last half of this decade. Reflecting continuity rather than a shift of practices, the inability of donors to apply the conditionality instruments in a coherent manner has led to a partial reform syndrome.

The Limits of Conditionality

In terms of actual results achieved, however measured, Zambia's reform experience cannot be depicted as a success. With a basis in comparative research, Tony Killick raises the question of whether the effect of financial aid for structural adjustment purposes has been to *postpone* real adjustment by allowing governments to avoid politically sensitive decisions (Killick 1996, 1998). This observation appears relevant to the Zambian case.

In Zambia the economic reform process progressed far after 1991, and major areas of reform appear irreversible. However, two important reform processes were postponed to the second electoral term at considerable economic cost: the reforms within the large public sector and the privatization of the mining industry. Considering Zambia's dire economic situation in 1991 and the complete run-down of the country's foreign reserves and food reserves, it may be appropriate to ask whether the large civil service, as well as the loss-making mines and national airline, could have been sustained in the absence of increased balance of payments support from the donor community. Supporting the argument raised by Killick, a number of Zambian businessmen suggested that the abundance of aid in the 1991–94 period in fact hindered real economic adjustment by making it possible for the MMD government to postpone difficult decisions. In 1996 Zambia was able to meet its international debt obligations despite reduced levels of aid through increased mobilization of internal resources. This indicates that large inflows of foreign exchange to weak economies may create economic distortions that hinder actual economic restructuring. The Zambian case therefore supports findings by Burnside and Dollar (1997) suggesting that the high volumes of aid to Africa during the 1980s may in fact have slowed the adjustment process by acting as a substitute for private capital.

However, the Zambian case also suggests that the *Assessing Aid* report, and ongoing work to reform conditionality-based aid, underestimates the difficulty of donor coordination when calling for aid selectivity. The model of selectivity presented is essentially a one-donor model that assumes donor preferences to be singular rather than plural. Yet in the Zambian case, a range of conflicting interests within the international donor community complicated the conduct of unified action when a waning commitment to reform was witnessed.

Throughout the 1990s, bilateral donors have emphasized political rights and given much attention to democratic reform in their aid allocations. In Zambia, the bilateral donors' focus on policy reform and governance issues led them to reduce aid allocations at a time when the multilateral donors claimed that the government's good economic reform record qualified for increases in donor funding. Approaching the second general elections in 1996, the bilateral donors started to openly question the multilateral institutions' judgment of Zambia's economic policy record as well. The numerous different, and often inconsistent, motivations of the various donor agencies diluted the impact of the conditionality measures imposed. As a result, the Zambian government to an extent succeeded, as in the 1980s, in pitting the various donor agencies against each other.

The paradox of more and more conditions leading to less and less effective conditionality has been referred to as the "nonreform paradox" (Gordon 1993; Collier 1997). The real problem of the "conditionality game"—in which a donor tries to "buy" as much reform as possible while recipient governments attempt to get as much money from the donor as possible—is that it draws government attention away from the serious need for economic restructuring and development. That is, the benefits of reform are sometimes defined more in terms of increased donor aid than improved economic performance. In Zambia, we argue that the much-delayed processes of privatizing the mines and reforming the public sector in recent years have been pursued in order to fulfill Consultative Group meeting demands rather than because these reforms are part of a domestically formulated development strategy. We are concerned that the World Bank's preoccupation with debt service has diverted resources and time—including management time—away from development issues, and that the debt situation has been improved at the expense of focusing on real sector issues.

The terms of reference for the Aid and Reform study argue that the World Bank in particular has a large role to play in persuading governments of the virtues of reform, and that this role ultimately is more important than the Bank's role as a provider of finance. Particularly in the absence of a political leadership committed to reform, it is now assumed that nonfinancial aid will have a greater impact than financial aid.

The Zambian case study reinforces findings from across Africa that commitment to reform is at best thin and confined to a few political leaders. In many cases, as in Zambia, the shallow support for reform indicates that the reform processes and commitment to these processes can regress with a few changes in the cabinet. However, based on our analysis in Zambia we do not believe that aid in its present form has generated much policy learning. It does not appear that donors have communicated their views effectively to governments, let alone to the general population.

First, as the Zambian case illustrates, poor donor coordination means that the donor community does not send a single clear message about reform. Governments receive policy advice from a full ideological spectrum, ranging from the so-called Washington consensus to NGOs advocating a new international economic order. Second, and most importantly, the process of aid, and in particular adjustment aid, is such that the recipient government is essentially a passive participant and the larger population is completely absent. Technical assistance to a country's central bank and ministry of finance typically provide ammunition to reformist technocrats. But very little of their work is disseminated, and more time is spent briefing donor missions than promoting policy learning in the country.

Indeed, in aid-dependent countries such as Zambia, donor conditionality undermines genuine policy learning. Once they understand that donors mean to set policy, ministries become passive. Individual officials have negative incentives to disagree with the donors since this will only serve to delay the arrival of the much-needed resources. Most ministries in Zambia appear paralyzed by the austerity under which they have performed now for two decades. They appear to be so desperate for donor money that they will agree to any proposal received from the external donors. In sum, we do not think nonfinancial aid will result in much policy learning in Zambia in the foreseeable future unless current delivery mechanisms are altered.

APPENDIX 9.1
ZAMBIA: CHRONOLOGY OF POLITICAL
AND ECONOMIC DEVELOPMENTS, 1964–91

October 1962	Self-government under UNIP/ANC coalition.
24 October 1964	First Republic of Zambia inaugurated. UNIP forms government, led by Kenneth Kaunda.
November 1965	Unilateral declaration of independence by Rhodesia; road and rail links to Zambia affected.
July 1966	United Party formed.
April 1968	Mulungushi economic reforms.
August 1968	Presidential and parliamentary elections.
August 1969	Macroeconomic reforms. Government purchases 51 percent controlling share of mining corporations.
August 1971	United Progressive Party formed; Simon Kapwepwe leaves UNIP to head UPP.
February 1972	UPP banned; Kapwepwe and 122 party members detained.
December 1972	Legislation passed introducing a "one-party participatory democracy" constitution.
August 1973	Second Republic (one-party state) inaugurated.
December 1973	First presidential and parliamentary election in the Second Republic.
Summer 1974	Copper prices begin to fall.
October 1977	Kaunda addresses emergency meeting of the National Assembly on the state of the economy. Dissidents organize within UNIP in opposition to the government's economic management.
January 1978	Austerity budget introduced.
September 1978	UNIP General Conference amends constitution, excluding Nkumbula and Kapwepwe from contesting the presidency.
October 1978	Presidential and parliamentary elections.
October 1980	Failed coup attempt involving business and labor.
July 1981	Detention of labor leaders, followed by strikes.
October 1983	Presidential and parliamentary elections.
August 1984	Third National Convention of UNIP. Restructuring of the economy and an "economic crusade" are announced.
October 1985	Government announces a foreign exchange auction and import liberalization.
April 1986	Kaunda changes the economic team negotiating the 1985 economic reforms.

December 1986	Copper belt riots.
January 1987	Labor unrest.
May 1987	Labor Day speech. Kaunda announces break with the IMF and World Bank and the introduction of New Economic Recovery Program.
December 1988	Presidential and parliamentary elections.
June 1989	Agreement between the government and IMF/World Bank on Policy Framework Paper involving devaluation of the kwatcha and removal of price controls.
June 1990	Riots in Lusaka and Kitwe following announcement of increase in maize prices; 27 people killed.
30 June 1990	Coup attempt.
August 1990	Formation of opposition alliance, the Movement for Multiparty Democracy.
August 1990	Constitutional change, lifting article 4 of the 1973 constitution which banned opposition parties.
25 October 1991	Presidential and parliamentary elections involving opposition parties and presidential candidates.

APPENDIX 9.2
ZAMBIA: CHRONOLOGY OF
ADJUSTMENT PROGRAMS, 1973–91

1973	One-year standby agreement with IMF.
1976	One-year standby agreement with IMF.
1978	Two-year standby agreement with IMF.
1981	Three-year Extended Fund Facility with IMF.
1982	IMF plan canceled as objectives are not met.
April 1983	Return to the IMF after failure to find alternative sources of funds; one-year standby agreement.
May 1984	Consultative Group meeting on external aid.
July 1984	Paris Club agreement on debt rescheduling.
July 1984	21-month standby agreement.
December 1984	London Club commercial bank rescheduling.
April 1985	IMF agreement suspended for noncompliance.
June 1985	Consultative Group meeting on external aid.
December 1985	Consultative Group meeting on external aid.
February 1986	"Shadow program" transformed into 24-month standby agreement with IMF.
March 1986	Paris Club agreement on debt rescheduling.
December 1986	Consultative Group meeting on external aid.
January 1987	Kaunda backs away from reform measures; IMF and World Bank programs are suspended.
March 1987	Discussions with IMF to get program back on track.
May 1987	Kaunda announces suspension of IMF reform effort and introduces New Economic Recovery Program.
1988	Informal talks with IMF and World Bank.
August 1989	Policy Framework Paper 1989–93 announced.
February 1990	Zambia reaches preliminary agreement with IMF and World Bank.
September 1991	IMF and World Bank suspend agreement in response to Zambia's failure to make payments in July.

Sources: Nelson 1991; Gertzel 1984; West 1991; Graham 1994; Jones 1994.

APPENDIX 9.3
ZAMBIA: CHRONOLOGY OF PRINCIPAL
ECONOMIC REFORMS, 1991–99

November 1991   First comprehensive set of data on Zambia's external debt produced.

December 1991   Priority program to rehabilitate infrastructure begun.

MMD announces that responsibility for the privatization process is transferred from ZIMCO to the Ministry of Commerce, Trade, and Industry.

Substantial reductions of subsidies on maize meal and fertilizer.

January 1992   Nontraditional exporters allowed 100 percent foreign exchange retention.

Official exchange rate devalued by 30 percent (155 percent through 1992).

Subsidies on maize meal removed.

Program to reduce military expenditure in real terms over 1992–94 announced.

Commitment is announced to limit net borrowing by government from the banking system to zero.

Subsidies, loans, and loan guarantees eliminated for all parastatals, except Zambian Airways and Zambian Consolidated Copper Mines.

Import preferences (except for PTA) revoked.

Debt Management Task Force created within Ministry of Finance to coordinate all issues related to external debt.

Zambia's arrears to the World Bank cleared.

February 1992   Zambian government, IMF, and World Bank reach agreement on a Policy Framework Paper for 1992–94, focusing on subsidy removals, privatization of the parastatal enterprises, and liberalization of markets.

March 1992   First evidence of major failure of maize crop due to drought. Efforts begin to mobilize increased donor support.

Controls on exports of petroleum eliminated.

June 1992   Subsidies on maize meal (roller meal) removed.

Controls on all prices eased, most eliminated.

Fertilizer market opened up for full competition.

	Pan-territorial pricing for maize eliminated in favor of pricing to reflect differential transport costs.
July 1992	Privatization bill passed in Parliament. Zambia Privatization Agency established.
	Legislation enacted to increase autonomy of Local Councils.
	Investment Act amended to make incentives automatic and transparent.
	The IMF approves a restructured Rights Accumulation Program enabling clearance of Zambia's arrears to the IMF.
August 1992	Agreement with Paris Club on rescheduling of bilateral debt on enhanced Toronto terms.
	Rescheduling and debt cancellation reduce Zambia's external debt burden by US$1.5 billion.
September 1992	First phase of government redundancy program. 12,000 contract daily employees within civil service are made redundant.
October 1992	Foreign exchange bureaus introduced.
	Open General License System changed from a positive to a negative list.
	Tax Policy Task Force recommends sweeping changes in the tax system.
December 1992	Joint Ministry of Finance/Bank of Zambia Data Monitoring Committee established.
	Exchange rates unified (with ZCCM selling at the market exchange rate).
	First tranche of 19 state companies offered for sale.
January 1993	Cash budget introduced.
	Weekly Treasury bill tender begun.
	Announcement that Exchange Control Act will be repealed.
	General reduction in tariffs and excises, shift to Harmonized Code for trade classification.
	Reduction in corporate tax rate, modification of personal income tax rates and bands.
	Budget Heads established for defense and security forces.
	Elimination of import and export licenses announced; import license levy abolished.
	Company tax reduced from 40 to 35 percent.
	Special fund set up to accelerate road rehabilitation.

March 1993	All bilateral (Paris Club) agreements finalized. Negotiations on interest rate reductions and additional debt write-off produce savings of US$100 million.
June 1993	Import and export licenses eliminated. Establishment of Zambia Revenue Authority.
July 1993	Formal establishment of the Lusaka Stock Exchange. Markets for maize and fertilizer opened to full competition.
November 1993	Beginning of Public Sector Reform Program.
January 1994	Exchange controls removed. Manufacturing-in-bond permitted. Duty drawback extended to include third-party exporters. Property transfer tax reduced from 7.5 percent to 2.5 percent. Monitoring of ministry's commitments begins. Provision for countervailing duties if unfair trade practices can be proved.
April 1994	Zambia Revenue Authority begins operations. Privatization Fund account established.
June 1994	Retirement package for civil servants determined.
August 1994	Mineral Tax Act revoked and replaced by Mineral Royalty Tax Act (bringing Zambia into line with international norms).
September 1994	Commercial debt buyback operation (ongoing since 1992) completed. Approximately US$652 million in debt eradicated.
October 1994	Proposed Land Act converting customary tenure to leasehold is deferred by Parliament pending further consultations.
December 1994	Zambia Airways and United Bus Company put into receivership. The government announces that ZIMCO will be dissolved by March 31, 1995.
January 1995	Conversion of most commercial banks' statutory reserve deposits to medium-term government debt as a means of reducing the interest rate spread. Adjustment of personal income tax limits to overcome "bracket creep." Fuel levy increased to finance road funds (further increased in 1996 budget).

February 1995	Meridian Bank supported by the Bank of Zambia and the government after a major run on its deposits.
March 1995	ZIMCO put into voluntary liquidation.
May 1995	Sale by public flotation of shares of Chilanga Cement to the general public.
	Meridian Bank and African Commercial Bank put into receivership.
	Mid-term review of ESAF postponed to December.
July 1995	Value added tax introduced, sales tax repealed.
	Sale of Zambia Sugar Company Ltd.
	Revised Land Act passed by Parliament, enabling unused land to be purchased by new investors (Land Act 1995).
August 1995	Temporary revenue measures are introduced to close budget deficit created in first half of budget year, including increases in the excise duty on petroleum (from 30 to 45 percent), the rate on withholding tax (from 10 to 25 percent), the excise tax on electricity (from 3 to 10 percent), and the excise sugar tax (from 10 to 20 percent).
September 1995	Cash budget moved from daily observance to monthly observance.
	Road license taxes increased.
December 1995	The IMF recognizes Zambia's successful completion of the Rights Accumulation Program and approves a three-year Enhanced Structural Adjustment Facility.
January 1996	Customs duty exemptions, including government purchases, eliminated. Customs duty tariffs reduced on most goods by 15 percent.
February 1996	IMF finds a number of year-end benchmarks (6 out of 10) have been missed by the Zambian government. As the March ESAF targets will not be met, a delay of ESAF is proposed.
	A tentative agreement reached with the Paris Club on Naples terms being applied to Zambia's external debt obligations. The agreement implies a 67 percent debt cancellation, pending the IMF's mid-term review evaluation.
April 1996	Bank of Zambia allows ZCCM to retain 100 percent of its foreign exchange receipts to supply the market directly.

May 1996	Cabinet endorses plan and timetable for ZCCM's privatization and announces the proceeds of sales to begin on February 28, 1997.
June 1996	ZCCM Board approves the ZCCM privatization plan.
	Increased parliamentary gratuities passed in Parliament (but withdrawn by president in July).
July 1996	Zambia passes IMF's mid-term review of ESAF's first year.
October 1996	World Bank Board releases first tranche of US$90 million structural adjustment facility.
February 1997	Closing date for tenders for the privatization of ZCCM in unbundled units.
	Zambia passes IMF's mid-term review of ESAF. The 1996 Paris Club agreement on debt rescheduling on Naples terms is formalized.
July 1997	Consultative Group meeting. Donors promise US$150 million in balance of payments support as well as US$285 for general financing. However, bilateral donors make it clear that disbursements are conditional on governance reform.
	The Zambian government announces the resumption of the Public Sector Reform Program.
November 1997	The Kafue Consortium presents a bid for major ZCCM units, but the government turns down the bid.
March 1998	A new and lower bid is presented by the Kafue Consortium. The government again rejects the bid.
May 1998	Consultative Group meeting. Donors pledge US$530 million for balance of payments support, but make disbursement contingent on the sale of ZCCM and progress on governance issues.
May 1999	Consultative Group meeting. Citing regional concerns, most bilateral donors express a willingness to disburse balance of payments funds.

APPENDIX 9.4
ZAMBIA: CHRONOLOGY OF PRINCIPAL
POLITICAL DEVELOPMENTS, 1991–99

October 1991	MMD wins presidential and parliamentary elections by a clear majority.
	Inauguration of the Third Republic under President Frederick T. Chiluba.
January 1992	Chiluba declares Zambia a Christian nation.
May 1992	A pressure group, Caucasus for National Unity, is created within MMD. All members asked to leave the party.
July 1992	United Democratic Party formed.
	Kaunda announces that he will resign from politics.
August 1992	500 striking bank workers dismissed. Zambia Congress of Trade Unions criticized for being too close to MMD.
	MMD ministers Baldwin Nkumbula and Aka Lewanika resign from the cabinet, citing growing corruption within the government as reason for their departure.
November 1992	UDP is dissolved and its leader, Enoch Kavindele, rejoins MMD and is immediately appointed to the MMD party finance committee.
February 1993	"Zero Option Plan" to overthrow the MMD government discovered. Government detains 26 opposition members with a base in UNIP, among them the son of Kenneth Kaunda.
March 1993	President Chiluba announces the reintroduction of state of emergency laws. They are lifted after 82 days (May 1993).
April 1993	Major ministerial reshuffle. Key "reform ministers," Emmanuel Kasonde (Finance), Guy Scott (Agriculture), Arthur Wina (Education), and Humphrey Mulemba (Mines), are dismissed from cabinet. No official explanation offered.
June 1993	Roger Chongwe removed from the Ministry of Legal Affairs; the move is interpreted as connected to his criticism of the introduction of state of emergency laws.
August 1993	Catholic churches issue a pastoral letter, "Hear the Cry of the Poor," criticizing the social consequences of the government's economic policies. The National Party is registered.

November 1993	National Party captures 4 seats in 8 by-elections. Mwankatwe constitutional commission established.
December 1993	Bilateral donors threaten to withhold balance of payments support unless something is done to curb drug trafficking.
January 1994	A number of ministers attending the December 1993 Consultative Group meeting, including the minister of health (Kavimbe) and deputy minister of finance (Mung'omba), are dismissed from the cabinet.
	The foreign affairs minister (Vernon Mwaanga), community development and social welfare minister (Nakatindi Wina), and deputy speaker of Parliament (Sikota Wina), resign their positions in response to repeated allegations that they are involved in drug trafficking.
April 1994	The managing director (Fred M'membe) and a reporter of *The Post* newspaper are arrested and charged with defaming the president, but no conviction results.
July 1994	Chiluba publicly criticizes the economic policies of the MMD, arguing that unless problems within the agricultural sector are solved, MMD will not be able to win the upcoming elections.
	"The Young Turks," a group of young dissenters within MMD, issue their vision statement criticizing the governance record and economic policies of the MMD.
August 1994	Amendment of the Land Bill, intended to transform land from customary to private land tenure, is rejected by the National Assembly.
September 1994	Kenneth Kaunda announces his return to national politics, citing opposition to the economic policies of MMD as the main reason for ending his retirement.
October 1994	ZCTU's quadrennial congress in Livingstone. Five unions leave the labor congress after losing elections for leadership positions.
December 1994	The ZCTU leadership claims that MMD has failed workers more than Kenneth Kaunda and UNIP ever did.
January 1995	*The Post* newspaper claims President Chiluba is not a true Zambian.

February 1995	Kenneth Kaunda replaces Kebby Musoktwane as president of UNIP.
March 1995	Friction between the "young Turks" led by Derrick Chitala and "the old guard" led by Michael Sata are brought to the fore.
June 1995	Mwanakatwe Constitutional Review Commission releases its report.
	Derrick Chitala and Dean Mung'omba, associated with the "young Turks" dissenters, are expelled from MMD.
August 1995	Baldwin Nkumbula, president of the National Party and former minister of sports in the MMD government, is killed in a car accident in which President Chiluba's son, Castro Chiluba, is implicated. The independent press link Chiluba to Nkumbula's death.
September 1995	Zambia Democratic Congress (ZDC) formed by Derrick Chitala and Dean Mung'omba.
	Government issues a white paper on the procedure for adopting the new draft constitution, rejecting recommendations of the Constitutional Review Commission that the draft be adopted through a constitutional assembly and a national referendum.
October 1995	UNIP, reinvigorated by Kaunda's return, wins 3 seats in 8 by-elections. The National Party fails to win any seat.
	Incidents of harassment of nongovernmental organizations and their leaders increase. 17 Catholic priests are arrested together with three other civil society leaders for campaigning against the constitutional amendment process.
November 1995	An Israeli firm, Nikuv computers, is offered the contract for the voter registration process.
February 1996	The first bilateral donors announce partial withdrawal of aid, citing the governance situation as their main reason.
	Three journalists from *The Post* are arrested and jailed on charges of libel and contempt for the Parliament by the speaker of the House. They are released without charges after three weeks by a High Court ruling.
March 1996	The minister of finance, Ronald Penza, announces that MMD is suspending the implementation of the Public Sector Reform Program.

May 1996	The government white paper on the new constitution is ratified by the National Assembly and signed into law by President Chiluba on May 28.
June 1996	Eight opposition party leaders, including UNIP's vice-presidential candidate, are arrested and charged with treason after a spate of bombings in Lusaka and the copper belt.
October 1996	The government announces the second national and presidential elections in the Third Republic to take place on November 18.
	UNIP and 6 smaller opposition parties announce that they will boycott the presidential and parliamentary elections because of the constitution and the voter registration process.
November 1996	MMD wins 60 percent of national vote in the parliamentary elections. President Chiluba wins 71 percent of the vote in presidential elections. Some local and international election monitoring groups characterize the elections as flawed on account of the voter registration and constitutional amendment barring Kaunda from contesting. Others, focusing on the actual voting process, endorse the elections as free and fair.
August 1997	Police shoot and wound former president Kenneth Kaunda.
	Bilateral donors do not disburse, citing poor performance on governance issues.
October 1997	Failed coup by junior officers. Kaunda is detained and a state of emergency declared.
February 1998	Finance minister Ronald Penza is fired, purportedly on grounds of corruption, and replaced by Edith Nawakwi.
	Charges against Kenneth Kaunda dropped.
November1998	Former finance minister Ronald Penza assassinated in his Lusaka home.
	Most bilateral balance of payments support held back.
January 1999	Trial of 77 soldiers starts in Lusaka
2001	Elections scheduled. According to the current constitution, President Chiluba must resign.

TABLE 9.6 ZAMBIA: TOTAL AID IN LOANS BY SECTOR, 1980–96

(millions of U.S. dollars)

Sector	1980	1981	1982	1983	1984	1985	1986	1987	1988	1989	1990	1991	1992	1993	1994	1995	1996
Agriculture, forestry, fishing	7.71	6.83	5.89	9.52	6.54	15.89	30.49	4.09	14.94	11.15	15.17	24.23	6.60	18.71	7.90	6.06	18.78
Balance of payments support	0	0	21.98	1.81	1.78	0.16	0.06	21.05	0.27	0.00	0.00	154.28	79.76	15.86	3.66	1.72	0.89
Communication	1.44	0.65	0.52	3.38	1.39	0.51	1.37	-0.86	-1.85	-0.27	-0.95	-0.13	-0.64	-0.10	-0.05	-0.33	-0.01
Community, social, personal, and environmental services	26.63	15.83	0.64	16.96	16.96	7.49	4.79	1.36	5.80	7.93	10.04	18.78	3.37	8.79	96.62	112.27	97.55
Construction	0	0	0	0	0	0	0	0	0	7.68	0	0.61	1.09	0	0	0	0
Contribution to finance current imports	78.06	33.85	11.12	4.50	1.98	15.25	11.30	3.44	9.29	0.16	0	0	3.12	0	0	0	0
Electricity, gas, and water production	0.10	1.51	0.27	2.96	4.02	3.94	5.06	6.68	20.79	9.84	1.26	5.41	4.21	3.75	7.05	5.43	4.15
Financial, insurance, real estate, business	-0.40	0.81	1.45	1.14	0.21	-0.02	0.00	0.00	0.66	0.00	0.04	0.36	54.44	103.82	17.09	4.54	3.15
General purpose contributions	9.41	0	2.98	0.17	0.01	0	0	0	0	0	0	0	0	0	0	0	0
Manufacturing	10.29	16.86	8.86	5.12	17.63	37.76	39.42	8.57	2.71	3.52	1.20	3.78	1.55	0.40	2.92	6.16	11.72
Mining, quarrying	0.95	1.44	0.32	-0.11	11.04	10.31	8.19	4.12	1.23	0.51	0.56	0.22	0.59	3.55	3.61	5.25	2.92
Not available	0	0	0	0	0	0	0	0	0	0	0	-1.89	0	0	0	0	0
Other contributions	6.81	0	0	0	0	0	0	0	0	0	0	0	0	0	0	0	0
Pension payments	0	0	3.32	0	0	0	0	0	0	0	0	0	0	0	0	0	0
Trade, restaurants, lodging	1.75	0.61	0.06	0.02	-0.07	0	-0.11	0	-0.18	-0.04	0	-0.07	0	0	0	0	0
Transport and storage	15.65	11.79	18.93	14.33	12.18	7.78	4.70	5.85	12.59	5.97	2.39	4.40	1.29	0.87	5.46	1.86	3.41
Total	158.40	90.18	76.34	59.80	73.67	99.07	105.27	54.30	66.31	46.45	29.71	209.98	155.38	155.65	144.26	142.96	142.56

Note: Covers effective development assistance loans.
Source: Chang, Fernández-Arias, and Servén 1999.

TABLE 9.7 ZAMBIA: TOTAL DISBURSEMENTS BY SECTOR, 1980–96
(millions of U.S. dollars)

Sector	1980	1981	1982	1983	1984	1985	1986	1987	1988	1989	1990	1991	1992	1993	1994	1995	1996
Agriculture, forestry, fishing	15.329	10.808	12.916	15.119	12.436	23.558	39.484	6.712	23.152	18.346	20.164	33.801	9.632	26.994	11.496	8.311	29.452
Balance of payments support	0	0	54.300	2.429	2.403	0.211	0.076	27.284	0.358	0	0	202.380	112.466	51.324	4.948	2.320	1.199
Communication	15.114	9.354	3.457	9.455	7.002	0.904	2.449	7.107	18.181	2.263	7.834	1.062	5.333	0.863	0.435	2.745	0.094
Community, social, personal, and environmental services	47.565	54.956	8.151	40.015	25.508	57.482	42.985	34.748	23.906	13.668	42.905	38.866	6.825	19.422	146.727	258.309	147.566
Construction	0	0	0	0	0	0	0	0	3.369	26.457	0.283	1.210	2.186	0	0	0	0
Contribution to finance current imports	113.518	57.033	18.452	11.559	8.412	23.160	21.042	6.776	16.457	0.321	0	0	4.365	0	0	0	0
Electricity, gas, and water production	1.595	2.453	0.54	6.256	7.353	7.133	8.060	10.116	39.379	20.415	2.373	8.550	10.673	7.213	11.633	9.416	6.348
Financial, insurance, real estate, business	7.477	12.502	12.129	6.688	2.768	1.076	0.080	0.012	1.227	0	0.076	0.605	76.910	147.134	24.952	6.804	4.771
General purpose contributions	14.858	0	4.697	0.262	0.023	0	0	0	0	0	0	0	0	0	0	0	0
Manufacturing	20.006	46.379	18.623	6.335	31.846	71.882	67.734	24.542	33.464	10.708	30.251	13.228	2.124	0.557	4.070	8.838	16.613
Mining, quarrying	32.204	33.002	11.027	2.121	67.608	44.222	36.180	31.562	7.795	4.671	8.715	4.129	23.227	22.945	27.532	9.205	5.480
Not available	0	0	0	0	0	0	0	0	1.505	0	0	0	0	0	0	0	0
Not available	22.556	0	0	0	0	0	0	0	0	0	0	18.747	0	0	0	0	0
Other contributions	0	0	0	0	0	0	0	0	0	0	0	0	0	0	0	0	0
Pension payments	0	0	41.342	0	0	0	0	0	0	0	0	0	0	0	0	0	0
Trade, restaurants, lodging	2.035	0.709	0.074	0.021	1.500	0	2.250	0	3.750	3.279	0	1.415	0	0	0	0	0
Transport and storage	22.037	21.587	28.262	31.668	29.740	30.745	24.681	17.585	31.137	20.194	4.656	13.984	6.886	2.647	8.516	3.474	7.062
Total	314	249	214	132	197	260	245	166	204	120	117	338	261	279	240	309	219

Source: Chang, Fernández-Arias, and Servén 1999.

TABLE 9.8 ZAMBIA: TOTAL GRANTS BY CREDITOR, 1980–96
(millions of U.S. dollars)

Creditor	1980	1981	1982	1983	1984	1985	1986	1987	1988	1989	1990	1991	1992	1993	1994	1995	1996
African Development Bank	0	0	0	0	0	0	0	0	0	0	0	0	0	0	0	0	0
Canada	8.1	5.2	4.7	3.7	10.0	8.4	12.7	25.5	30.4	15.9	87.8	23.2	26.0	13.6	10.1	18.7	9.5
Commission of the European Communities	11.6	17.9	5.0	8.2	16.5	28.8	15.6	19.7	34.9	23.5	19.9	24.2	97.8	133.5	43.4	69.2	36.0
Switzerland	0.2	0.1	0.2	0.3	0.5	4.4	0.2	1.6	0.2	0.6	0.4	0.9	2.5	0.5	0.5	0.9	0.5
Germany	13.1	10.4	14.9	10.2	9.9	12.1	11.7	16.8	14.8	15.2	329.7	13.8	54.7	74.3	39.2	71.0	79.7
Denmark	4.2	2.9	3.2	1.8	1.8	3.1	4.5	2.7	11.2	6.4	22.1	17.3	38.6	15.6	17.7	25.6	25.8
Finland	8.3	6.4	8.6	10.2	9.4	11.8	16.6	16.1	23.8	25.1	24.9	25.4	31.1	15.2	13.1	11.9	11.7
France	0.8	0.5	1.0	0.8	1.0	0.7	1.0	1.2	1.4	1.4	21.4	20.0	14.5	14.4	11.5	8.4	2.1
United Kingdom	29.3	25.8	18.6	16.9	14.9	15.5	41.2	38.9	29.6	27.6	42.6	67.1	102.5	44.2	76.2	70.1	56.6
Italy	0.1	3.7	1.0	0.7	3.5	1.3	4.3	15.5	10.6	11.7	8.6	7.0	6.3	37.0	2.4	6.0	1.0
Japan	1.4	4.2	10.2	11.4	4.8	16.2	23.2	31.9	71.4	62.9	40.1	61.5	73.7	68.9	87.3	62.0	48.3
Netherlands	11.8	11.4	13.6	11.8	19.8	15.7	48.5	28.4	24.4	21.1	60.6	29.5	46.0	30.2	36.6	42.0	26.6
Norway	10.5	8.7	13.8	16.1	16.0	16.7	28.7	31.9	40.2	34.9	55.3	51.6	50.4	31.3	51.2	35.1	30.6
Sweden	31.1	28.8	27.5	29.4	20.4	22.9	36.1	25.4	35.8	36.1	37.2	90.0	79.5	34.5	35.5	32.4	31.1
United States	11.0	6.0	4.0	11.0	11.0	23.0	30.0	31.0	6.0	7.0	7.0	90.0	106.0	89.0	17.0	23.0	18.0
World Bank	0	0	0	0	0	0	0	0	0	0	0	0	0	0	0	0	0
IMF	25.0	0	0	0	0	0	0	0	0	0	0	0	0	0	0	1,265	—
Total	141.5	132	126.3	132.5	139.5	180.6	274.3	286.6	334.7	289.4	757.6	521.5	729.6	602.2	441.7	476.3	377.5

Source: Chang, Fernández-Arias, and Servén 1999.

TABLE 9.9 ZAMBIA: TOTAL DISBURSEMENTS BY CREDITOR, 1980–96
(millions of U.S. dollars)

Creditor	1980	1981	1982	1983	1984	1985	1986	1987	1988	1989	1990	1991	1992	1993	1994	1995	1996
African Development Bank	9.429	4.888	6.826	12.231	5.225	22.850	34.144	27.474	45.342	6.820	90.045	36.858	52.884	34.729	31.950	26.950	21.387
Canada	15.346	1.024	12.68	5.245	10.732	2.023	0.846	0.482	0	0	0	0	0	0	0	0	0
Commission of the European Communities	0	0	0	0.141	0.114	1.453	0	0	0.95	0	0	0.885	0.583	0.408	0.233	0	0
Germany	26.012	6.577	10.674	18.982	9.313	6.871	12.250	19.929	39.67	8.627	0	16.938	7.674	0	0	0	0
Denmark	0	0.599	4.300	2.429	2.403	1.646	7.568	1.296	0.510	0.027	0	0	0	0	0	0	0
Finland	0	0	0	0	0	0	0	0	0	0	0	0	0	0	0	0	0
France	0	0	0	0	0	0.712	2.316	0	0.514	0	0	18.747	0	0	0	0	0
United Kingdom	53.845	24.862	11.564	3.497	28.609	16.396	7.053	25.145	2.407	3.279	0.264	5.927	0	0	0	0	0
Italy	0	0	0	0	0	0	7.644	3.059	61.685	25.607	5.157	12.105	4.973	0	0	56.744	0
Japan	14.654	28.814	2.791	3.454	8.535	23.034	25.651	10.764	0.914	0	0	0	0	0	0	0	0
Netherlands	20.809	7.435	1.675	0.311	0	0.036	0	2.904	0	1.333	2.502	0	0	0	0	0	0
Sweden	0	0	0	0	0	0	0	0	0	0	0	0	0	0	0	0	0
United States	99.584	35.006	20.731	12.281	19.235	22.595	10.720	1.197	12.395	0.497	2.260	0	0	0	14	0	0
World Bank	42.508	32.692	35.266	28.351	56.225	113.026	116.630	55.260	13.734	4.168	2.827	209.668	173.696	174.187	186.062	208.942	181.098
IMF	25.000	0	0	0	0	0	0	0	0	0	0	0	0	0	0	01.265.000	—
Total	307.187	141.897	106.507	86.922	140.391	210.642	224.822	147.510	178.121	50.358	103.055	301.128	239.810	209.324	232.245	1,557.636	202.485

Source: World Bank.

TABLE 9.10 ZAMBIA: TOTAL DISBURSEMENT, BILATERAL AND MULTILATERAL, 1980–96
(millions of U.S. dollars)

Creditor type	1980	1981	1982	1983	1984	1985	1986	1987	1988	1989	1990	1991	1992	1993	1994	1995	1996
Bilateral	563.6	270.7	178.5	134.8	253.0	386.4	394.8	245.8	269.8	85.2	116.1	547.6	418.5	383.5	432.3	3088.3	383.6
Multilateral	2543.6	2251.7	2160.5	2117.8	2237.0	2371.4	2380.8	2232.8	2257.8	2074.2	2106.1	2538.6	2410.5	2376.5	2426.3	5083.3	2379.6
Total	3107.2	2522.4	2339.1	2252.6	2490.0	2757.9	2775.7	2478.7	2527.5	2159.5	2222.1	3086.2	2829.0	2760.0	2858.6	8171.6	2763.2

Source: Chang, Fernández-Arias, and Servén 1999.

TABLE 9.11 ZAMBIA: EXTERNAL DEBT, 1990–98
(millions of U.S. dollars)

Type of debt	1990	1991	1992	1993	1994	1995	1996	1997	1998 (estimated)
Total external debt	6,898	6,827	4,981	5,102	6,397	7,041	7,085	6,971	6,613
Medium and long-term debt	6,517	6,435	4,738	4,58	6,156	6,817	6,880	6,924	6,613
Multilateral	2,969	2,843	2,714	2,734	3,127	3,251	3,381	3,397	3,412
IMF	1,362	1,326	1,238	1,188	1,216	1,239	1,198	1,138	1,132
Other	1,607	1,517	1,476	1,546	1,911	2,086	2,182	2,259	2,280
Bilateral official	3,265	3,348	2,117	2,107	2,945	3,272	3,345	3,431	3,141
Paris Club	2,508	2,362	1,583	1,674	2,361	2,863	2,936	3,022	2,732
Other	757	986	434	433	584	409	409	409	409
Suppliers and other	283	244	7	17	84	220	155	95	60
Short-term debt	381	392	243	244	241	224	205	47	0

Source: Bank of Zambia.

TABLE 9.12 ZAMBIA: GOVERNMENT EXPENDITURES, 1990–98

(millions of kwatcha)

Category of expenditure	1990	1991	1992	1993	1994	1995	1996	1997	1998
Total expenditures and net lending	37.3	87.7	212.0	531.0	854.0	1,000.0	1,213.0	1,406.0	1,943.0
Current expenditure	30.3	63.9	155.0	390.0	624.0	727.0	869.0	1,017.0	1,262.0
Interest due	8.9	18.5	49.0	183.0	260.0	259.0	322.0	326.0	421.0
Agricultural expenditure	0	5.3	16.8	35.6	31.9	25.6	30.3	3.1	15.3
Capital expenditure	7.1	23.8	57.0	141.0	230.0	273.0	345.0	390.0	680.0
Financed by GRZ	4.0	6.3	9.7	18.2	36.7	58.2	40.6	70.0	113.0
Foreign-financed	3.1	17.5	47.3	123.0	193.0	215.0	304.0	319.0	567.0

Source: International Monetary Fund.

TABLE 9.13 ZAMBIA: EMPLOYMENT BY ECONOMIC SECTOR, 1990–98
(thousands of employees)

Sector	1990	1991	1992	1993	1994	1995	1996	1997	1998
Agriculture	79	77	82	83	79	69	68	58	57
Mining	65	65	62	58	51	52	48	45	39
Manufacturing	77	75	74	68	57	56	47	47	43
Electricity	7	7	8	6	5	5	4	5	5
Construction	33	33	27	22	17	10	13	17	18
Transportation and communications	34	34	31	29	29	36	47	49	50
Distribution and trade	55	53	51	49	50	41	38	46	46
Finance and insurance	33	36	39	37	34	42	37	38	38
Public administration	159	162	171	168	174	173	176	170	168
All sectors	543	544	546	520	497	485	479	475	465

Source: Zambia Central Statistical Office.

TABLE 9.14 ZAMBIA: MARKETED PRODUCTION OF SELECTED CROPS, 1990–98
(metric tons)

Crop	1990	1991	1992	1993	1994	1995	1996	1997	1998
Maize	601.0	603.0	259.0	930.0	476.0	345.0	668.0	315.0	182.0
Tobacco (Virginia)	2.7	0.8	1.2	4.1	5.0	2.2	1.9	3.5	3.8
Tobacco (Burley)	1.5	0.8	1.0	2.5	1.1	1.6	1.9	0.9	5.1
Sugarcane	1,137.0	1,126.0	1,136.0	1,255.0	1,222.0	—	—	—	—
Mixed beans	0.4	6.0	11.7	15.9	13.7	13.7	13.0	6.9	7.4
Groundnuts	4.2	8.8	8.0	23.1	13.7	13.2	14.5	17.6	24.1
Cotton	33.5	48.7	25.8	47.8	33.0	16.5	40.8	74.6	100.0
Soya beans	7.0	24.3	23.5	27.3	20.6	17.3	37.5	23.1	13.1

— Not available.
Source: Zambia Central Statistical Office.

TABLE 9.15 ZAMBIA: SOCIAL INDICATORS, 1986–95

Year	GNP per capita (U.S. dollars)	Total population (thousands)	Population growth rate (percent)	Life expectancy (years)	Infant mortality (per thousand)	Per capita supply of calories (per day)	Secondary school enroll- ment rates (percent)	Energy consumption per capita (kilogram of oil equivalent)
1986	470	6.429	3.2	51.6	84.8	—	17	422.2
1987	300	6.945	3.3	52.0	84.0	2.126	17	412.0
1988	240	7.196	3.3	53.0	93.0	2.126	19	412.0
1989	290	7.490	3.7	53.1	80.0	—	19	379.4
1990	390	7.840	3.7	53.7	76.6	2.026	17	379.4
1991/92	420	8.110	3.7	49.7	82.1	2.007	20	378.8
1993	460	8.319	3.3	49.0	106.0	—	20	379.0
1994	450	8.272	3.0	48.0	107.0	—	20	159.0
1995	380	8.936	3.3	48.0	103.0	—	37	149.0

— Not available.
Source: Bonnick 1997.

APPENDIX 9.6
INTERVIEWS IN ZAMBIA AND WASHINGTON, D.C.

Christer Aagren. Economic adviser, Embassy of Sweden. Lusaka, September 1996.

Theo Bull. Board member, Zambia Chamber of Commerce and Industry. Lusaka, January 1997 and May 1999.

I. Chamwere. President, Zambia Chamber of Commerce and Industry. Lusaka, October 1996.

Ellah Chembe. Resident economist, World Bank. Lusaka, June 1995, September 1996, and January 1997.

Hans Hedlund. Program coordinator, Economic Expansion in Outlying Areas, Richard Woodrofe and Associates. September 1996.

Hendrik van der Heijden. External financing adviser, Ministry of Finance and Economic Development. Lusaka, October 1996, December 1996, January 1997, and May 1999.

P. Henriot. Jesuit Centre for Theological Reflection. Lusaka, November 1996.

Akihiko Ishimoto. First secretary, Embassy of Japan. Lusaka, May 1999.

Elisabeth Jere. Managing director, Social Impact Division, Zambia Privatisation Agency. Lusaka, December 1996.

Emmanuel Kasonde. Minister of finance and economic development in the MMD government 1991–93. Lusaka, October 1996 and May 1999.

Robert Keller. Economic adviser, Embassy of Sweden. Lusaka, September 1996.

Cornia van der Laan. Economic adviser, Embassy of the Netherlands. Lusaka, January 1997.

Aka Lewanika. Member of Parliament 1991–96; cabinet minister 1991–92; MMD 1991–93; National Party 1993–96; Agenda for Zambia 1996–. Lusaka, June 1995 and September 1996.

Jon Lomøy. Ambassador, Embassy of Norway. Lusaka, May 1999.

Francis Mbewe. Coordinator, World Bank programs, Ministry of Finance. Lusaka, May 1999.

Abel Mkandawire. Board chairman, Zambia Privatisation Agency; vice chairman, Zambia Chamber of Commerce and Industry. Lusaka, January 1997.

Charles Moen. Chief economist, USAID. Lusaka, September 1996.

P. E. Mulenga. Director, Zambia Congress of Trade Unions. Lusaka, October 1996.

Nganda Mwanajiti. Executive director, Afronet. Lusaka, January 1997 and May 1999.

Bright Mwape. Managing director, *The Post*. Lusaka, January 1996.

Ben Mwene. Secretary to the Treasury, Ministry of Finance and Economic Development. Lusaka, December 1996 and January 1997.

Mushimba Nyamazana. Resident economist, Zambia Resident Mission, World Bank. Lusaka, May 1999.

Phyllis Pomerantz. Country director, Africa Region, World Bank. Washington, D.C., March 1997.

Guy Scott. President, Lima Party; Minister of Agriculture 1991–93. Lusaka, September 1996.

A. C. Sichinga. Permanent secretary, Ministry of Agriculture, Food and Fisheries. Lusaka, January 1997.

Lucy Sichone. Director, Zambia Civic Education Association. Lusaka, January 1997.

Emily Sikazwe. Executive director, Women for Change. Lusaka, June 1995.

Robinson Sikazwe. Regional consultant (Africa), Norwegian Confederation of Trade Unions. Lusaka, November 1996.

Moses Simemba. Deputy executive director, Secretariat, Zambia Chamber of Commerce and Industry. Lusaka, November 1996.

Neo Simutanyi. University of Zambia, Institute of African Studies. Lusaka, September 1996.

Jopeph Stepanek. Director, USAID. Lusaka, September 1996.

Helge Svendsen. Second secretary, business and energy sector, Embassy of Norway. Lusaka, September 1996.

E. Taha. Resident representative, IMF. Lusaka, December 1996.

John Todd. Principal economist, Macroeconomics Southern Africa, World Bank. Lusaka, January 1996, and Washington, D.C., March 1997.

Oliver C. Campbell White. Senior public enterprises specialist, World Bank. Washington, D.C., March 1997.

C. F. Wolters. Program officer, USAID. May 1999.

Abdon Yesi. Foundation for a Democratic Process. Lusaka, January 1997.

Mitsunori Yuuki. First secretary, Embassy of Japan. Lusaka, August 1996.

Axel Zeidler. First Secretary, Embassy of the Federal Republic of Germany. Lusaka, January 1997.

Simon Zukas. Minister of Agriculture, Food and Fisheries 1993–95. Cabinet member until 1996. Lusaka, December 1996.

NOTES

1. For a critique of ODA measures and presentation of the methodology used in measuring EDA, see Chang, Fernández-Arias, and Servén (1999).

2. The Scandinavian countries, the Netherlands, and Canada were among the first to tie their aid to adherence to human rights principles (Selbervik 1997; Stokke 1995, 1996).

3. As one of the few examples of cuts in project aid, USAID reduced its governance aid program as a reaction to the exclusion of Kaunda from the presidential elections in 1996.

4. The concept of donor cohesion refers to the level of agreement among representatives of the states and multilateral organizations within the international donor community (Sandberg 1990).

5. Zambia's relationship with the IMF and most notably its much-publicized decision to break the relationship in 1987 have received much scholarly attention. For useful presentations, see Akwetey 1994; Bates and Collier 1993; Callaghy 1990; Gulhati 1989; Mwanza 1992; West 1989 and 1992; Loxley and Young 1990; Sandberg 1990.

6. The previous government had already negotiated a complete reform program with the donors, which remained viable despite the suspension in September 1991. The new structural adjustment agreement was, therefore, essentially the same as the 1989 Policy Framework Paper that the Kaunda government had agreed to with the donor community after a short spell of homegrown economic reforms. The MMD and the multilateral institutions in early 1992 nevertheless produced a new Policy Framework Paper (Zambia 1992). This program differed little from the earlier programs and included all the significant reform measures advocated by the MMD during its election campaign.

7. This resulted in a price increase of almost 700 percent as a 25-kilogram bag of maize meal increased from Kw. 225 to Kw. 1,800 between October 1991 and October 1992 (Seshamani 1996).

8. For a useful account of the initiation and early experiences with the cash budget, see Bolnick (1997). Stasavage and Moyo (1999) provide a comparative analysis with the experiences in Uganda and also a more detailed analysis of the effects of the cash budget in the second half of the 1990s.

9. The economic significance of this decision in 1996 is more questionable because of the low copper production and ZCCM's debt estimated at US$800 million (*Financial Mail*, 4 March 1997).

10. According to a recent World Bank evaluation study of the Zambian structural adjustment program, the Zambian government is still required by law to hire recent graduates in the teaching and medical professions (World Bank 1996b: 28).

11. The success of the privatization program was further highlighted by most respondents, including external donors, government officials, and independent local analysts.

12. See "Trouble in Lusaka," *Institutional Investor* (international edition), December 1998; Theo Bull, "An Incredible Country," *Profit*, July 1998; Theo Bull, "The mines—Where are we now?" *Profit*, April 1999.

13. The minister of finance at the time, Emmanuel Kasonde, first named inflation as the nation's number one enemy in his 1992 budget address.

14. However, as both Scott and Kasonde were replaced by pro-reform ministers (Simon Zukas in Agriculture and Ronald Penza in Finance), the 1993 reshuffle cannot be interpreted as a reversal of the reform process.

15. Malcolm McPherson was the leader of the Harvard team working as advisers within the Ministry of Finance from 1990 until spring 1996.

16. An earlier confidential evaluation of the implementation of the RAP by the International Monetary Fund (1995) seconds this view. World Bank and IMF staff also raised this issue in interviews with the author (interview, Chembe, 1995; interview, Taha, 1996).

17. Interview, White, 1997; interview, van der Heijden, 1996.

18. Before the Consultative Group meeting scheduled for December 15, 1995, the donors and the Zambian government met in Lusaka for a preparatory meeting on December 5. The minister of finance, Ronald Penza, stressed the government's economic achievements and urged the donors to judge Zambia relative to other developing nations. When a representative of the donor community stated that Zambia should be judged according to the 1991 manifesto, which constituted a contract between the government and its citizens as well as between the government and its external partners, a representative of the Zambian government responded with a loud laugh.

19. The United Kingdom was the first bilateral donor to announce the suspension of US$10 million in balance of payments support shortly after the constitution was signed into law on May 28. Norway then suspended all of its nonproject aid on June 5, amounting to US$40 million per year. The United States followed shortly after, suspending 10 percent (approximately US$3.5 million) of its aid to Zambia on July 16. Over the next weeks and months, Japan, the Netherlands, Sweden, Denmark, and Finland followed suit.

20. This was the main argument presented by the minister of finance in his opening statement to the December 1995 Consultative Group meeting. It was repeated by various members of the MMD government throughout the 1996 election campaign (*The Post*, 13 August 1996).

21. Such criticisms appeared frequently in the local press. See, for example, *The Post*, 9 April 1996; *The Post*, 19 June 1996; *Times of Zambia*, 21 May 1996.

REFERENCES

Adam, Christopher. 1995. "Fiscal Adjustment, Financial Liberalization, and the Dynamics of Inflation: Some Evidence from Zambia." *World Development* 23 (5): 735–50.

Adam, Christopher, Per-Åke Andersson, Arne Bigsten, Paul Collier, and Steve O'Connell. 1994. "Evaluation of Swedish Development Co-operation with Zambia." Gothenburg University and Oxford University. Processed.

Afronet (Inter-African Network for Human Rights and Development). 1999. *Annual Report.* Lusaka.

Akwetey, Emmanuel Obliteifio. 1994. "Trade Unions and Democratisation: A Comparative Study of Ghana and Zambia." Ph.D. diss., University of Stockholm.

Andreassen, Bård Anders, Gisela Geisler, and Arne Tostensen. 1992. "Setting a Standard for Africa? Lessons from the Zambian 1991 Elections." Report Series R5. Christian Michelsen Institute, Bergen, Norway.

Arkadie, Brian van, and Harris Mule. 1996. "Some Comments on Recent Developments in Donor Conditionality." In Kjell Havnevik and Brian van Arkadie, eds., *Domination or Dialogue? Experiences and Prospects for African Development Cooperation.* Uppsala, Sweden: Nordic Africa Institute.

Bank of Zambia. 1997. *Annual Report.* Lusaka.

Bates, Robert. 1981. *Markets and States in Tropical Africa.* Berkeley and Los Angeles: University of California Press.

———. 1988. "Governments and Agricultural Markets in Africa." In Robert Bates, ed., *Toward a Political Economy of Development: A Rational Choice Perspective.* Berkeley and Los Angeles: University of California Press.

Bates, Robert, and Paul Collier. 1993. "The Politics and Economics of Policy Reform in Zambia." In Robert Bates and Anne Krueger, eds., *Political and Economic Interactions in Economic Policy Reform: Evidence from Eight Countries.* Oxford, U.K., and Cambridge, Mass.: Blackwell.

Bates, Robert, and Anne Krueger, eds. 1993. *Political and Economic Interactions in Economic Policy Reform: Evidence from Eight Countries.* Oxford, U.K., and Cambridge, Mass.: Blackwell.

Baylies, Carolyn, and Morris Szeftel. 1984. "Elections in the One-Party State 1973–1980." In Cherry Gertzel, Carolyn Baylies, and Morris Szeftel, eds., *The Dynamics of the One-Party State in Zambia.* Manchester: Manchester University Press.

———. 1992. "The Rise and Fall of Multiparty Politics in Zambia." *Review of African Political Economy* 19 (54): 75–91.

———. 1997. "The 1996 Zambian Elections: Still Awaiting Democratic Consolidation." *Review of African Political Economy* 24 (71): 113–28.

Bolnick, Bruce. 1997. "Establishing Fiscal Discipline. The Cash Budget in Zambia." In Merilee Grindle, ed., *Getting Good Government: Capacity Building in the Public Sectors of Developing Countries.* Cambridge: Harvard University Press.

Bonnick, Gladstone G. 1997. "Zambia Country Assistance Review: Turning an Economy Around." World Bank Operations Evaluation Study. Washington, D.C.

Boone, Peter. 1996. "The Politics and Effectiveness of Foreign Aid." *European Economic Review* 40 (June): 289–329.

Botchwey, Kwesi, Paul Collier, Jan Willem Gunning, and Koichi Hamada. 1998. "External Evaluation of the ESAF Report by a Group of Independent Experts." International Monetary Fund, Washington D.C.

Bratton, Michael. 1992. "Zambia Starts Over." *Journal of Democracy* 3 (2): 81–94.

———. 1994. "Economic Crisis and Political Realignment in Zambia." In Jennifer Widner, ed., *Economic Change and Political Liberalization in Sub-Saharan Africa*. Baltimore: Johns Hopkins University Press.

Bratton, Michael, and Beatrice Liatto-Katundu. 1994. "Political Culture in Zambia: A Pilot Survey." MSU Working Papers on Political Reform in Africa. Michigan State University, East Lansing, Mich.

Bratton, Michael, and Daniel Posner. 1998. "A First Look at Second Elections in Africa with Illustrations from Zambia." In Richard Joseph, ed., *State, Conflict and Democracy in Africa*. Boulder: Lynne Rienner.

Bratton, Michael, and Nicolas van de Walle. 1992. "Popular Protest and Reform in Africa." *Comparative Politics* 24 (4): 419–42.

———. 1997. *Democratic Experiments in Africa: Regime Transitions in Comparative Perspective*. New York: Cambridge University Press.

Bratton, Michael, P. Alderfer, and N. Simutanyi. 1997. "Political Participation in Zambia, 1991–1996: Trends, Determinants and USAID Program Implications." Zambia Democratic Governance Project, Special Study 5. Michigan State University, East Lansing, Mich.

Brautigam, Deborah. 1991. "Governance and Democracy: A Review." Policy Research Working Paper 815. World Bank, Development Research Group, Washington, D.C.

Bull, Theo. 1996. "Boom, Doom or Merely Gloom?" *The World Today* 52 (10).

Burdette, Marcia. 1988. *Zambia Between Two Worlds*. Boulder: Westview.

Burnside, Craig, and David Dollar. 1997. "Aid, Policies, and Growth." Policy Research Working Paper 1777. World Bank, Development Research Group, Washington, D.C.

Callaghy, Thomas. 1990. "Lost between State and Market: The Politics of Economic Adjustment in Ghana, Zambia and Nigeria." In Joan M. Nelson, *Economic Crisis and Policy Choice: The Politics of Adjustment in the Third World*. Princeton, N.J.: Princeton University Press.

Callaghy, Thomas, and John Ravenhill, eds. 1993. *Hemmed In: Responses to Africa's Economic Decline*. New York: Columbia University Press.

Chang, Charles C., Eduardo Fernández-Arias, and Luis Servén. 1999. "Measuring Aid Flows: A New Approach." Policy Research Working Paper 2050. World Bank, Development Research Group, Washington, D.C.

Collier, Paul. 1997. "The Failure of Conditionality." In Catherine Gwin and Joan M. Nelson, eds., *Perspectives on Aid and Development*. Washington, D.C.: Overseas Development Council.

Collier, David, and Steven Levitsky. 1997. "Democracy with Adjectives: Conceptual Innovation in Comparative Perspective." *World Politics* 49 (3): 430–51.

Donge, Jan Kees van. 1998. "Reflections on Donors, Opposition and Popular Will in the 1996 Zambian General Elections." *Journal of Modern African Studies* 36 (1): 71–101.

Electoral Commission of Zambia. 1996. "Presidential and Parliamentary General Elections 1996." November 25. Lusaka.

Engberg-Pedersen, Poul, ed. 1995. *Limits of Adjustment in Africa: The Effects of Economic Liberalization, 1986–1994.* London: Zed Books.

———. 1996. "The Politics of Good Development Aid: Behind the Clash of Aid Rationales." In Kjell Havnevik and Brian van Arkadie, eds., *Domination or Dialogue? Experiences and Prospects for African Development Cooperation.* Uppsala, Sweden: Nordic Africa Institute.

Foundation for Democratic Process. 1992–96. By-election reports. Lusaka.

Fundanga, Caleb M. 1996. "Practical Effects of Economic and Political Conditionality in Recipient Administration." In Kjell Havnevik and Brian van Arkadie, eds., *Domination or Dialogue? Experiences and Prospects for African Development Cooperation.* Uppsala, Sweden: Nordic Africa Institute.

Geddes, Barbara. 1995. "The Politics of Economic Liberalization." *Latin American Research Review* 30 (2): 195–214.

Gertzel, Cherry. 1979. "Industrial Relations in Zambia to 1975." In Ukandi Damachi, Dieter Seibel, and Lester Trachtman, eds., *Industrial Relations in Africa.* New York: St. Martin's Press.

Gertzel, Cherry, Carolyn Baylies, and Morris Szeftel, eds. 1984. *The Dynamics of the One-Party State in Zambia.* Manchester: Manchester University Press.

Gibbon, Peter. 1992. "Structural Adjustment and Pressures toward Multipartyism in Sub-Saharan Africa." In Yussuf Bangura, Peter Gibbon, and Arve Ofstad, eds., *Authoritarianism, Democracy and Adjustment: The Politics of Economic Reform in Africa.* Uppsala, Sweden: Nordic Africa Institute.

———. 1993. "The World Bank and the New Politics of Aid." In Georg Sørensen, ed., *Political Conditionality. European Journal of Development Research* 5 (1).

Gordon, David. 1993. "Debt, Conditionality, and Reform: The International Relations of Economic Policy Restructuring in sub-Saharan Africa." In Thomas Callaghy and John Ravenhill, eds., *Hemmed In: Responses to Africa's Economic Decline.* New York: Columbia University Press.

———. 1996. "Sustaining Economic Reform under Political Liberalization in Africa: Issues and Implications." *World Development* 24 (9): 1527–37.

Graham, Carol. 1994. *Safety Nets, Politics and the Poor: Transitions to Market Economies.* Washington, D.C.: The Brookings Institution.

———. 1995. "The Political Economy of Adjustment and Sectoral Reforms in Zambia: A Stakeholders' Approach?" The Brookings Institution, Washington, D.C. Processed.

Grindle, Merilee, and John Thomas. 1991. *Public Choices and Policy Change: The Political Economy of Reform in Developing Countries.* Baltimore: Johns Hopkins University Press.

Gulhati, R. 1989. *Impasse in Zambia: The Economics and Politics of Reform.* Development Political Case Series 2. World Bank, Economic Development Institute, Washington, D.C.

Gwin, Catherine, and Joan M. Nelson, eds. 1997. *Perspectives on Aid and Development.* Policy Essay 22. Washington, D.C.: Overseas Development Council.

Haggard, Stephan, and Robert R. Kaufman. 1992. "The Political Economy of Inflation and Stabilization in Middle-Income Countries." In Stephan Haggard and Robert R. Kaufman, eds., *The Politics of Economic Adjustment.* Princeton, N.J.: Princeton University Press.

Haggard, Stephan, and Robert R. Kaufman, eds. 1995. *The Political Economy of Democratic Transitions.* Princeton, N.J.: Princeton University Press.

Haggard, Stephan, and Stephen B. Webb, eds. 1994. *Voting for Reform: Democracy, Political Liberalization, and Economic Adjustment.* New York: Oxford University Press.

Harvey, Charles. 1976. "The Structure of Zambian Development." In Ukandi Damachi, Guy Routh, and Abdel-Rahman E. Ali Taha, eds., *Development Paths in Africa and China.* London: Macmillan.

Havnevik, Kjell, ed. 1987. *The IMF and the World Bank in Africa: Conditionality, Impact and Alternatives.* Uppsala, Sweden: Nordic Africa Institute.

Havnevik, Kjell, and Brian van Arkadie, eds. 1996. *Domination or Dialogue? Experiences and Prospects for African Development Cooperation.* Uppsala, Sweden: Nordic Africa Institute.

Hawkins, Jeffrey. 1991. "Understanding the Failure of IMF Reform: The Zambian Case." *World Development* 19 (7):839–49.

Healey, John, and Mark Robinson. 1992. *Democracy, Governance, and Economic Policy: Sub-Saharan Africa in Comparative Perspective.* London: Overseas Development Institute.

Helleiner, Gerhald K., ed. 1986. *Africa and the International Monetary Fund.* Washington, D.C.: International Monetary Fund.

Hellman, Joel S. 1998. "Winners Take All: The Politics of Partial Reform in Postcommunist Transitions." *World Politics* 50 (2): 203–35.

Henley, Andrew, and Euclid Tsakalotos. 1993. *Corporatism and Economic Performance.* Aldershot, U.K., and Brookfield, Vt.: Edward Elgar.

Herbst, Jeffrey. 1990. "The Structural Adjustment of Politics in sub-Saharan Africa." *World Development* 18 (7): 949–58.

Hewitt, Adrian P., and Tony Killick. 1996. "Bilateral Aid Conditionality and Policy Leverage." In Olav Stokke, ed., *Foreign Aid Toward the Year 2000: Experiences and Challenges.* London: Frank Cass.

IMF (International Monetary Fund). 1995. "Zambia: Staff Report for Accumulation of Rights and Economic Program for 1995–1998." Washington, D.C.

Johnson, John, and Sulaiman Wasty. 1993. "Borrower Ownership of Adjustment Programs and the Political Economy of Reform." Discussion Paper 199. World Bank, Washington, D.C.

Joseph, Richard. 1992. "Zambia: A Model for Democratic Change." *Current History* (May): 199–201.

Joseph, Richard, ed. 1998. *State, Conflict and Democracy in Africa*. Boulder: Lynne Rienner.

Kahler, Miles. 1990. "Orthodoxy and Its Alternatives: Explaining Approaches to Stabilization and Adjustment." In Joan M. Nelson, ed., *Economic Crisis and Policy Choice: The Politics of Adjustment in the Third World*. Princeton, N.J.: Princeton University Press.

———. 1992. "External Influence, Conditionality, and the Politics of Adjustment." In Stephan Haggard and Robert Kaufman, eds., *The Politics of Economic Adjustment*. Princeton, N.J.: Princeton University Press.

Kanyinga, Karuti. 1993. "The Social-Political Context of the Growth of Nongovernmental Organisations in Kenya." In Peter Gibbon, ed., *Social Change and Economic Reform in Africa*. Uppsala, Sweden: Nordic Africa Institute.

Kaplan, Irving, ed. 1979. *Zambia: A Country Study*. Washington, D.C.: American University.

Kapur, Devesh. 1997. "The Weakness of Strength: The Challenge of Sub-Saharan Africa." In Devesh Kapur, John P. Lewis, and Richard Webb, *The World Bank: Its First Half Century*. Vol. 1. Washington, D.C.: The Brookings Institution.

Kapur, Devesh, John P. Lewis, and Richard Webb. 1997. *The World Bank: Its First Half Century*. 2 vols. Washington, D.C.: The Brookings Institution.

Killick, Tony. 1995. *IMF Programmes in Developing Countries: Design and Impact*. London and New York: Routledge.

———. 1996. "Principals, Agents and the Limitations of BWI Conditionality." *World Economy* 19 (2): 211–30.

———. 1997. Principals, Agents and the Failings of Conditionality." *Journal of International Development* 9 (4): 483–97.

———. 1998. *Aid and the Political Economy of Policy Change*. London and New York: Routledge.

Lancaster, Carol. 1993. "Governance and Development: The Views from Washington," *IDS Bulletin* 24 (1).

———. 1997. "The World Bank in Africa since 1980: The Politics of Structural Adjustment Lending." In Devesh Kapur, John P. Lewis, and Richard Webb, eds., *The World Bank: Its First Half Century*. Vol. 2. Washington, D.C.: The Brookings Institution.

Landell-Mills, Pierre. 1992. "Governance, Cultural Change, and Empowerment." *Journal of Modern African Studies* 30 (4): 543–67.

Lehman, Howard, and Jennifer McCoy. 1992. "The Dynamics of the Two-Level Bargaining Game: The 1988 Brazilian Debt Negotiations." *World Politics* (July): 600–44.

Leith, Clark, and Michael Lofchie. 1993. "The Political Economy of Structural Adjustment in Ghana." In Robert Bates and Anne O. Krueger, eds., *Political and Economic Interactions in Economic Policy Reform: Evidence from Eight Countries*. Oxford, U.K., and Cambridge, Mass.: Blackwell.

Lemarchand, Rene. 1992. "Africa's Troubled Transitions." *Journal of Democracy* 3 (4).

Lewanika, Aka, and Derrick Chitala. 1990. "The Hour Has Come! Proceedings from the National Conference on the Multiparty Option." Zambia Research Foundation, Lusaka.

Lewis, Peter. 1996. "Economic Reform and Political Transition in Africa: The Quest for a Politics of Development." *World Politics* 49 (1): 92–129.

Loxley, John, and Roger Young. 1990. *Zambia: An Assessment of Zambia's Structural Adjustment Experience.* Ottawa: North-South Institute.

McPherson, Malcolm F. 1995. "The Sequencing of Economic Reforms: Lessons from Zambia." Development Discussion Paper 516. Harvard Institute of International Development, Harvard University, Cambridge, Mass.

Mkandawire, Thandika. 1996. "Economic Policy-Making and the Consolidation of Democratic Institutions in Africa." In Kjell Havnevik and Brian van Arkadie, eds., *Domination or Dialogue? Experiences and Prospects for African Development Cooperation.* Uppsala, Sweden: Nordic Africa Institute.

———. 1998. "Crisis Management and the Making of 'Choiceless Democracies' in Africa." In Richard Joseph, ed., *State, Conflict and Democracy in Africa.* Boulder: Lynne Rienner.

Mkandawire, Thandika, and Adebayo Olukoshi. 1995. *Between Liberalisation and Oppression: The Politics of Adjustment in Africa.* Dakar: CODESRIA.

MMD (Movement for Multiparty Democracy). 1991. "Party Manifesto 1991–1996." Lusaka.

Mwanza Allast, M., ed. 1992. *The Structural Adjustment Program in Zambia.*

1991 Manifesto of the Movement for Multiparty Democracy. Lusaka.

Nelson, Joan M. 1991. "Organized Labor, Politics, and Labor Market Flexibility in Developing Countries." *World Bank Research Observer* 6 (1): 37–56.

———. 1993. "The Politics of Economic Transformation: Is Third World Experience Relevant in Eastern Europe?" *World Politics* 45 (3): 433–63.

——— 1994. "The Political Economy of Stabilization: Commitment, Capacity and Public Response." *World Development* 12 (10).

———, ed. 1989. *Fragile Coalitions: The Politics of Economic Adjustment.* New Brunswick: Transaction Books.

———. 1990. *Economic Crisis and Policy Choice: The Politics of Adjustment in the Third World.* Princeton, N.J.: Princeton University Press.

Nelson, Joan M., and Stephanie Eglington. 1992. "Encouraging Democracy: What Role for Conditioned Aid?" Policy Essay 4. Overseas Development Council, Washington, D.C.

———. 1993. "Global Goals, Contentious Means: Issues of Multiple Aid and Conditionality." Policy Essay 10. Overseas Development Council, Washington, D.C.

Olukoshi, Adebayo. 1996. "The Impact of Recent Reform Efforts on the African State." In Kjell Havnevik and Brian van Arkadie, eds., *Domination or Dialogue? Experiences and Prospects for African Development Cooperation.* Uppsala, Sweden: Nordic Africa Institute.

Panter-Brick, Keith. 1994. "Prospects for Democracy in Zambia." *Government and Opposition* 29 (2): 230–47.

Pausewang, Siegfried, and Hans Hedlund. 1986. *Zambia: Country Study and Norwegian Aid Review.* Bergen, Norway: Christian Michelsen Institute.

Please, Stanley. 1984. *The Hobbled Giant: Essays on the World Bank.* Boulder: Lynne Rienner.

Pritchett, Lant. 1998. "Patterns of Economic Growth: Hills, Plateaus, Mountains, and Plains." Policy Research Working Paper 1947. World Bank, Development Research Group, Washington, D.C.

Rakner, Lise. 1998. "Reform as a Matter of Political Survival: Political and Economic Liberalisation in Zambia 1991–1996." Ph.D. diss. University of Bergen (Norway).

Roberts, Andrew D. 1976. *A History of Zambia.* London: Heinemann.

Roberts, Kenneth M. 1995. "Neoliberalism and the Transformation of Populism in Latin America: The Peruvian Case." *World Politics* 48 (October): 82–116.

Saasa, Oliver. 1996. "Policy Reforms and Structural Adjustment in Zambia: The Case of Agriculture and Trade." Technical Paper 35. U.S. Agency for International Development, Washington, D.C.

———. 1997. "Reducing Africa's Aid Dependence: Lessons from Zambia on Capacity Building and External Support." In Henock Kifle, Adebayo O. Olukoshi, and Lennart Wohlgemuth, eds., *A New Partnership for African Development: Issues and Parameters.* Uppsala, Sweden: Nordic Africa Institute.

Sachs, Jeffrey, ed. 1989. *Developing Country Debt and Economic Performance.* Chicago: University of Chicago Press.

Sandberg, Eve. 1990. "International Foreign Aid, Donor Cohesion, and Donor Bounded Decision Making in Zambia's Agricultural Sector." Ph.D. diss., Yale University.

———, ed. 1994. *The Changing Politics of Non-Governmental Organizations and African States.* Westport: Praeger.

Sandbrook, Robert. 1985. *The Politics of Africa's Economic Stagnation.* Cambridge: Cambridge University Press.

Selbervik, Hilde. 1997. "Aid as a Tool for the Promotion of Human Rights: What Can Norway Do?" Report no. 7. Norwegian Ministry of Foreign Affairs, Oslo.

Seshamani, V. 1996. "The Macro Development Context of Macroeconomic Policy in Zambia." University of Zambia, Department of Economics, Lusaka. Processed.

Sichone, Owen, and Bornwell C. Chikulo, eds. 1996. *Democracy in Zambia: Challenges for the Third Republic.* Harare: SAPES Books.

Simutanyi, Neo. 1996a. "Organised Labour, Economic Crisis and Structural Adjustment in Africa: The Case of Zambia." In Owen Sichone and Bornwell C. Chikulo, eds., *Democracy in Zambia: Challenges for the Third Republic.* Harare: SAPES Books.

———. 1996b. "The Politics of Structural Adjustment in Zambia." *Third World Quarterly* 17 (4): 825–39.

Stasavage, David, and Dambisa Moyo. 1999. "Are Cash Budgets a Cure for Excess Fiscal Deficits (and at What Costs)?" Working Paper Series 99-11. University of Oxford, Center for the Study of African Economies, U.K.

Stokke, Olav, ed. 1995. *Aid and Political Conditionality.* London and Portland, Ore.: Frank Cass.

———. 1996. *Foreign Aid Towards the Year 2000: Experiences and Challenges.* London and Portland, Ore.: Frank Cass.

Taylor, Scott. 1997. "Open for Business? Business Associations and the State in Zambia." Paper presented at the Business Associations and the State in Africa Project, American University, Washington, D.C., 6 February.

van der Geest, Willem, ed. 1994. *Negotiating Structural Adjustment in Africa.* London: James Currey.

van der Heijden, Hendrick. 1999. "Losing the Decade or Getting Things Going for the Next Millennium." Zambian Ministry of Finance, Lusaka. Processed.

van de Walle, Nicolas. 1994. "Political Liberalization and Economic Policy Reform in Africa." *World Development* 22 (4): 483–500.

———. 1998. "Globalization and African Democracy." In Richard Joseph, ed., *State, Conflict and Democracy in Africa.* Boulder: Lynne Rienner.

van de Walle, Nicolas, and Dennis Chiwele. 1994. "Democratization and Economic Reform in Zambia." MSU Working Papers on Political Reform in Africa 9. Michigan State University, East Lansing, Mich.

van de Walle, Nicolas, and Timothy A. Johnston. 1996. *Improving Aid to Africa.* Policy Essay 21. Washington, D.C.: Overseas Development Council.

West, Eugenia. 1989. *The Politics of Hope: Zambia's Structural Adjustment Program, 1985–1987.* Ph.D. diss., Yale University.

———. 1992. "Politics of Implementation of Structural Adjustment in Zambia, 1985–1987." In *Politics of Economic Reform in Sub-Saharan Africa.* Washington, D.C.: U.S. Agency for International Development.

White, Gordon. 1996. "Civil Society, Democratization and Development." In Robin Luckham and Gordon White, eds., *Democratization in the South: The Jagged Wave.* Manchester: Manchester University Press.

White, H., and T. Edstrand. 1994. "Aid Impact in a Debt Stressed Economy: The Case of Zambia." In Howard White, ed., *The Macroeconomics of Aid: Case Studies of Four Countries.* Stockholm: SASDA.

Widner, Jennifer A., ed. 1994. *Economic Change and Political Liberalization in Sub-Saharan Africa.* Baltimore: Johns Hopkins University Press.

Wiseman, John, ed. 1995. *Democracy and Political Change in Sub-Saharan Africa.* London: Routledge.

Williamson, John, ed. 1994. *The Political Economy of Policy Reform.* Washington, D.C.: Institute for International Economics.

Williamson, John, and Stephan Haggard. 1994. "The Political Conditions for Economic Reform." In John Williamson, ed., *The Political Economy of Policy Reform.* Washington, D.C.: Institute of International Economics.

Wohlgemuth, Lennart, ed. 1994. *Bistånd på Utvecklingens Villkor.* Uppsala, Sweden: Nordic Africa Institute.

Woods, David. 1992. "Civil Society in Europe and Africa: Limiting State Power through a Public Sphere." *African Studies Review* 2 (35): 77–100.

World Bank. 1981. "Accelerated Development in Sub-Saharan Africa: An Agenda for Action." World Bank, Washington, D.C.

———. 1984. *Towards Sustained Development in Sub-Saharan Africa.* Washington, D.C.

———. 1988. "Adjustment Lending." Washington, D.C.

———. 1989. "From Crisis to Sustainable Growth." Washington, D.C.

———. 1990. *The Long-Term Perspective Study for Sub-Saharan Africa.* 4 vols. Washington, D.C.

———. 1991. *World Bank Debt Tables 1990–91.* Washington, D.C.

———. 1993. "Zambia: Prospects for Sustainable and Equitable Growth." Report 11570-ZA. Washington, D.C.

———. 1994. "Zambia: Poverty Assessment." 5 vols. Report 12985-ZA. Washington, D.C.

———. 1995. "Zambia: Agricultural Sector Investment Program." Report 13518-ZA. Washington D.C.

———. 1996a. "Zambia: Prospects for Sustainable Growth 1995–2005." Report 15477-ZA. Washington, D.C.

———. 1996b. "Implementation Completion Report. Zambia: Economic and Social Adjustment Credit (credit 2577-ZA)." Washington, D.C.

———. 1996c. "Zambia: Country Assistance Strategy." Report 15761-ZA. Washington, D.C.

———. 1998. *Assessing Aid: What Works, What Doesn't and Why.* New York: Oxford University Press.

Zambia. 1992–99. Budget addresses by the Minister of Finance. Ministry of Finance, Lusaka.

———. 1992. "Policy Framework Paper 1992–95." Prepared by the government of Zambia in collaboration with the International Monetary Fund and the World Bank. Lusaka.

———. 1995. "The Adjustment by the Cooperative Sector to the Liberalised Marketing Environment." Market Liberalization Impact Studies, no. 6. Ministry of Agriculture, Food and Fisheries, Lusaka.

Zambia Independent Monitoring Team. 1991. "Parliamentary and Presidential Election Results." Lusaka.

Zambia Investment Center. 1997. *Annual Report.* Lusaka.

Zambia Privatisation Agency. 1992–97. Status reports.

Periodicals (all various years)

EIU (Economist Intelligence Unit). *Country Report: Zambia.*
EIU (Economist Intelligence Unit). *Country Profile: Zambia.*
The Post (daily newspaper, Lusaka).
Profit (magazine, Lusaka).

Times of Zambia (daily newspaper, Lusaka).
The Weekly Post (weekly newspaper, Lusaka).
World Bank Findings
ZACCI Business Line (publication of Zambia Chamber of Commerce and Industry, Lusaka).

Nonreformers

Democratic Republic of Congo

Gilbert Kiakwama
Jerome Chevallier

ACRONYMS AND ABBREVIATIONS

GECAMINES	Générale des Carrières et des Mines
GDP	Gross domestic product
IMF	International Monetary Fund
PIP	Public Investment Program
PFP	Policy Framework Paper
SAC	Structural Adjustment Credit
SDR	Special drawing right (of the IMF)
UMHK	Union Minière du Haut Katanga

During its first years of independence, the country now known as the Democratic Republic of Congo plunged into anarchy and became a hot spot in the Cold War between the Soviet Union and the West. In 1965, Mobutu Sese Seko took power in a bloodless coup supported by Western governments. A stabilization plan was prepared in 1967 with the help of the International Monetary Fund (IMF). With favorable terms of trade, restoration of private sector confidence, and sound macroeconomic management, the country (renamed Zaire) enjoyed a few years of solid growth. Four shocks, two external (the oil price increase in 1973–74 and copper price decline in 1975), and two self-administered ("Zairianization" of all economic activities in 1973 and heavy debt financing of nonviable projects in 1973–74) led to a period of steady decline and accumulation of arrears.

After several unsuccessful attempts at financial stabilization, Zaire implemented a comprehensive and far-reaching reform program in 1983–85. The economy recovered. It is unfortunate, however, that during this period the international community did not find ways to help Zaire address its heavy debt burden. Fiscal discipline in the face of negative net transfers in favor of bilateral lenders became increasingly difficult to justify. In 1986 the reform program stalled. Fiscal management deteriorated further in 1987 and 1988, despite strong support from the international community. A last attempt at reform was made in 1989. It was short-lived, however, and the World Bank decided to discontinue support to adjustment in early 1990. Lack of control over public expenditure led the country into hyperinflation.

While the responsibility for the failure of the Democratic Republic of Congo as a state lies squarely with the political elite under President Mobutu, which ruled the country until 1997, it is clear also that the interaction with the international donor community has not been as helpful as it could have been. The major donors were also the major creditors. By financing nonviable projects under commercial credit conditions in the early 1970s, and not providing appropriate debt relief ten years later when the country was in the process of reforming, they contributed to making adjustment difficult to sustain.

This chapter is in two parts. The first section presents the economic performance of Congo/Zaire and the reform programs from independence in 1960 to the end of the Mobutu era in 1997. The second discusses some key issues in the interaction between the donor community and the attempts at reform in Mobutu's Zaire.

The case study was conducted by a team of two researchers, including Gilbert Kiakwama, who was Congo's Minister of Finance in 1983–85, and Jerome Chevallier.

ECONOMIC POLICY AND PERFORMANCE

The Chaotic Post-Independence Years

Independence of the Congo in June 1960 was followed by a long period of political instability and civil strife. The country was ill prepared for independence, with only a handful of university graduates available. Together with Cuba and Vietnam, Congo had the dubious privilege of being a hot spot in the conflict between the Soviet Union and the West during the Cold War. Its vast resources, particularly in the mining sector, its huge size, and its strategic location at the center of the continent made it a coveted prize in the East-West conflict.

The central instruments of a seemingly all-powerful colonial state decomposed rapidly. Anarchy prevailed after the breakdown of authority in 1960–61. Provincial fragmentation in 1962–63 led to armed rebellions in 1964–65. The economic toll of the first five years of independence was high. While mineral production, the mainstay of the economy, remained stable (copper production in 1965 stood at 282,000 tons, the same level as in 1959), commercial agriculture and the transportation network suffered from the pervasive lack of security. Their output was reduced by about one-third. Inflation, fueled by monetary financing of the budget deficit, soared to an annual average of 31 percent during the five-year period.

The Early Mobutu Years

On November 24, 1965, with the support of Western governments, Mobutu seized power in a bloodless coup. A new constitution was enacted in 1967 and the name of the country was changed to Zaire to make a symbolic break with the recent past.[1] A stabilization program prepared by the Central Bank with support from the IMF was announced in June 1967. It included a 300 percent devaluation and the replacement of the Congo franc by the zaire, the elimination of the dual exchange rate, a steep increase in export and import tariffs, the removal of import licensing, and the freeing of profit remittances. The stabilization plan was a success. The inflation rate declined rapidly to 2.5 percent in 1968, and economic growth resumed. The 1967–74 period was a favorable one for the economy, with steady growth supported by strong private investment and favorable terms of trade.

A generous investment code was enacted in 1969, offering exemption from import duties on capital equipment and a five-year corporate and real estate tax holiday. It triggered a strong wave of private investment, mostly in import substitution industries, including two vehicle assembly plants, a tire factory, and a flour mill. These industries relied heavily on imported inputs and protection from competing imports.

The Shocks of 1973–75

Two external shocks and two self-administered ones brought this period of economic expansion to an end. As an oil-importing country, Zaire suffered from the 1973–74 oil price hike. To make things worse, in 1975 the price of copper, the country's main export, fell dramatically, resulting in a 40 percent decline in its terms of trade. The self-administered shocks included the contracting of a large debt on commercial terms for the financing of nonviable projects in 1972–73, and the government's decision in late 1973 to transfer all economic activities to Zairian nationals. This latter policy was a major blunder that sapped private sector confidence. Its consequences were catastrophic, and by late 1975 and early 1976 the government had to abandon it in stages.

In 1972 the government launched two large projects, at an estimated cost of about US$250 million each, to make use of cheap energy produced at Inga, a site with a huge hydroelectric potential on the Zaire River west of Kinshasa. A steel mill was built with Italian financing, but never operated at more than 10 percent of capacity. The other project was the construction of the Inga-Shaba power line, partly financed by the U.S. Export-Import Bank. The objective of the project was to supply power from the Inga dam to the mining industry in Shaba, 1,800 kilometers away. Cheaper alternatives were available locally, but the project was launched for purely political purposes, as a means for the central authorities to keep control over the secession-prone province. Implementation of the project took much longer than expected and its final cost escalated to an estimated US$1.5 billion. For the next two decades, the debt for the Inga-Shaba project remained by far the largest part of Zaire's debt burden.

Recession Years and Early Attempts at Reform

By 1975, Zaire was unable to service its debt. A prolonged period of economic decline ensued, aggravated in 1977 and 1978 by rebel incursions in the Shaba region. Between 1975 and 1978, gross domestic product (GDP) declined at an average annual rate of 3.5 percent. The inflation rate reached on average 57 percent during this period. In 1978, the external current account deficit was the equivalent of 16 percent of GDP. Arrears on the external debt accumulated to US$1.2 billion at the end of 1978. With a view to correcting the growing imbalances, the government reinforced a number of controls across the economy. Most prices, including interest rates, were set administratively, the trade regime became highly restrictive, and the allocation of scarce foreign exchange came under the tight control of the Central Bank.

In March 1975 the World Bank approved a US$100 million loan to GECAMINES (Générale des Carrières et des Mines), the public enterprise responsible for most copper and all cobalt production, to increase production capacity from 470,000 to 590,000 tons of copper and from 16,000 to 20,000 tons of cobalt. The project was expected to be completed in mid-1978. Project implementation suffered from a number of factors, however, including the closing of the Benguela railway in Angola (which served as a major export route for Zaire's copper), foreign exchange shortages, and the hostilities in the Shaba region. In 1982, the GECAMINES production amounted to only 466,000 tons of copper and 5,600 tons of cobalt.

In 1979, the government adopted a stabilization plan supported by an 18-month standby arrangement with the IMF. The debt to official bilateral creditors (Paris Club) was rescheduled in December 1979, and to a syndicate of commercial banks (London Club) in May 1980. The reduction of the overall deficit from 4 percent of GDP in 1979 to less than 1 percent in 1980 brought inflation down from a rate of over 100 percent in 1979 to less than 50 percent in 1980. Real GDP increased by 2.5 percent. Debt service payments were met as rescheduled, absorbing about 20 percent of export earnings. The stock of external arrears was reduced by 35 percent between 1979 and end-June 1981.

In June 1981 the IMF approved a new program, supported by a three-year extended arrangement. The objectives were to achieve a 3 percent growth rate, reduce inflation to 25 percent, and limit the external current account deficit to 5 percent of GDP in 1983. The program included the lifting of most price controls, reorientation of the foreign exchange allocation system toward priority sectors, and a change in the interest rate structure. A Paris Club meeting in July 1981 rescheduled principal and interest falling due in 1981–82.

The program did not achieve its objectives. The terms of trade deteriorated further by over 20 percent from 1980 to 1983. Growth over the period was negligible, the inflation rate remained above 35 percent, and the external current account deficit remained at a high level of 13.7 percent of GDP.

The 1983 Reform

In September 1983 Zaire adopted a comprehensive and far-reaching reform program. After a steep devaluation, an interbank market was established to determine freely the value of the currency and the official exchange rate was set close to the interbank exchange rate at weekly fixing sessions. This key reform was accompanied by the liberalization of exchange restrictions, the freeing of interest rates, and the lifting of remaining price controls, except for petroleum products, water, electricity, and public transport. The program was supported by a 15-month standby arrangement extended by the IMF in December 1983. Under the program, the budget deficit was to be reduced by the equivalent of 5.5 percentage points of GDP in 1983–84, despite a sharp increase in external debt service payments.

The adjustment during 1983–85 was substantial. The overall budget deficit declined from 11 percent of GDP in 1982 to 5.9 percent in 1985, while the current account deficit was reduced to 4.9 percent in 1985. The inflation rate, which had reached over 100 percent in 1983, was sharply reduced to 20 percent in 1984, but increased again to 40 percent in 1985. Growth resumed at an average rate of 2.6 percent per year. Zaire resumed normal relations with its creditors. Debt service payments were made on schedule and external arrears were substantially reduced, but this failed to generate additional donor support.

Renewed Fiscal Laxity

In April 1986, the World Bank convened a Consultative Group meeting to shore up support to Zaire's reform program. Preparation for an Industrial Sector Adjustment Credit was initiated. The IMF supported a new program through a 22-month standby arrangement approved in May 1986. The objectives of the program were to contain the external account deficit to 6.4 percent of GDP, limit the budget deficit before rescheduling to 6.6 percent of GDP, and reduce inflation to 30 percent. Shortly after program approval, however, a new cabinet, much less committed to fiscal discipline, took over. The program went quickly off track. In 1986, expenditures increased by 56 percent, despite a sharp compression of investment, but revenues increased by less than 10 percent. Inflation accelerated as a result. In late 1986 Zaire suspended payments to Paris and London Club creditors. To hold down the depreciation of the currency, the Central Bank intervened heavily in the interbank foreign exchange market.

In June 1986 the World Bank extended the Industrial Sector Adjustment Credit in an amount equivalent to US$80 million. The credit supported a reform agenda aimed at increasing the inflow of private capital through the consolidation of the liberalization of the economy, reform of the incentive structure, and improvement of the business environment. The Public Investment Program (PIP) was reviewed with emphasis on rehabilitating infrastructure and improving the productivity of public enterprises in the mining, transport, and energy sectors.

The Promise of Structural Reforms

In early 1987, a consensus emerged among Zaire and its major donors on the need to develop a broad program aimed at restoring fiscal discipline and accelerating structural reforms in the context of a medium-term policy framework. To ensure its success, the donor community was to provide generous support that would offset Zaire's debt service obligations. A three-year Policy Framework Paper (PFP) was negotiated. The experience of 1986 showed that, despite the substantial reforms introduced since 1983, persistent structural weaknesses prevented Zaire from achieving a sustained rate of economic growth. The investment rate was at a low 12 percent of GDP, the economy was highly vulnerable to external shocks, infrastructure constraints were pervasive, the tax base was too narrow, and the debt burden was too heavy. A restructuring of the Zairian economy was needed to diversify exports, and substantial investment was required to improve infrastructure.

The objectives of the 1987–88/1989–90 PFP were to:

- Reach a growth rate of 3.5 percent;
- Increase the investment rate from less than 12 percent of GDP in 1986 to 18 percent in 1987 and onwards;
- Reduce the rate of inflation from 40 percent in 1987 to 20 percent in 1988 and less than 15 percent in 1990;
- Reduce the external current account deficit by 14 percent in SDR terms;
- Reduce the overall budget deficit from 16.3 percent to 12 percent of GDP; and
- Increase the share of foreign financing for the private sector.

The government intended to pursue a dual strategy, including promoting private initiatives in the productive sectors of the economy and improving the efficiency of public resource management.

The medium-term program included a broad range of actions. The liberalization of the economy initiated in 1983 was to be consolidated, particularly as regards the exchange rate, interest rates, and domestic prices. The business environment was to be enhanced through an even application of the investment code and adequate guarantees. The incentives system was to be streamlined through the elimination of export duties and the rationalization of import duties. The Public Investment Program was to focus sharply on the rehabilitation of infrastructure and the removal of constraints to increased productivity in key public enterprises in mining, energy, and transportation. The public enterprise sector was to be reformed through sales and liquidations as well by establishing performance contracts for enterprises slated to stay in the public sector. Finally, macroeconomic management was to be improved through the pursuit of strong fiscal, monetary, and external debt management policies.

A Consultative Group meeting was convened in April 1987 to mobilize funding for the 1987–90 Public Investment Program reviewed by the World Bank. In May 1987 the IMF approved a 12-month standby arrangement and the first annual arrangement under the Structural Adjustment Facility. One month later, the World Bank extended a two-tranche Structural Adjustment Credit (SAC) for the equivalent of US$149.3 million. The credit was cofinanced by Japan for the equivalent of US$15.2 million. No less than 128 actions were envisaged in the reform program supported by the credit. There were three broad categories of reforms in the program: (a) measures to strengthen macroeconomic management, including fiscal reform, financial sector policies, public expenditure programming and execution, and reform of public administration and public enterprises; (b) a reform of agricultural and transport sector policies; and (c) measures to strengthen the incentive framework for the private sector.

Disbursement of the second tranche of the credit was scheduled for February–March 1988. There were five conditions for second tranche release, as follows: (a) a satisfactory macroeconomic framework, including the level and composition of the 1988–91 PIP; (b) establishment of an oversight structure for the supervision of public enterprises and the appointment of its administrator; (c) classification of enterprises to be maintained in the state portfolio, liquidated, or wholly or partially privatized; (d) finalization of a restructuring and reorganization program for public enterprises remaining in the state portfolio; and (e) completion of financial and administrative arrangements for the retirement of eligible public employees.

Implementation of the program ran into difficulties from the outset. Fiscal discipline did not improve and the domestic financing of the budget deficit led to a high inflation rate of over 100 percent in 1987. Performance deteriorated further in 1988. Government revenue as a share of GDP fell to a low 13.2 percent, while expenditures rose significantly in real terms. Spending in all major categories exceeded original budget allocations by a wide margin. As a result, the overall budget deficit climbed to over 22 percent of GDP. Despite a strong rise in copper prices, external imbalances worsened. The spread between the official and parallel market exchange rates widened. Arrears on external debt accumulated.

The Last Attempt

In November 1988, President Mobutu appointed Leon Kengo wa Dondo, artisan of the successful reforms of 1983–85, as the new prime minister.

The new government quickly demonstrated its commitment to reform by taking a series of difficult measures. Petroleum prices and public transportation tariffs were adjusted, interest rates were increased, the currency was devalued, and a tight budget was prepared for 1989. A new medium-term program was prepared for 1989–92. The macroeconomic objectives of the program were to achieve a growth rate of 3.3 percent rising to 4 percent in 1992, increase investment from 11 percent of GDP in 1988 to 14 percent in 1992, reduce inflation gradually from triple digits in 1987–88 to 15 percent in 1991, halve the budget deficit as a share of GDP (on a cash basis and before debt relief) from 24 percent in 1988 to 12 percent in 1992, and reduce the external account deficit from 14.2 percent of GDP in 1990 to 11.3 percent in 1992.

Taking account of past experience, a ceiling was set on foreign expenditure by government, and to prevent recurrence of excessive contributions imposed by the government on GECAMINES, a dividend policy was formulated with the help of the World Bank. Before finalization of the program, however, in a one-on-one meeting with the World Bank's vice-president for the Africa region in March 1989, President Mobutu was asked to make a personal commitment that there would be no expense outside the budget and the Public Investment Program. He was also warned that failure to implement the program would make it impossible for the World Bank to continue its support to adjustment. The president gave his word as a soldier that he would respect the program. The second tranche of the SAC was released, and the IMF approved a new standby arrangement in June 1989.

Good progress was made in 1989. The rate of inflation was reduced sharply and the spread between the official and parallel exchange rates was maintained within the target band of 10 percent. Government revenues as a share of GDP increased from 13.2 percent in 1988 to 17.5 percent in 1989. Interest rates became positive in real terms in June 1989. Government expenditure was stabilized in the first half of 1989, but increased steadily in the second half.

In June 1989, President Mobutu became the first African head of state to make an official visit to the Bush White House. At that time, there were signs that expenditures outside the budget and the Public Investment Program were being initiated by the presidency. Again, senior management of the World Bank warned President Mobutu of the dire consequences of not respecting his commitment. This warning failed to impress him, however, and several months later, in March 1990, with evidence that he had indeed not respected his word as a soldier, the World Bank informed the Zairian authorities that it would reduce its lending program to a core mode, with emphasis on direct support to local initiatives in the social sectors.

For lack of expenditure control, inflation sprang up again and rapidly turned into hyperinflation, with an annual rate jumping from 39 percent in 1989 to over 4,000 percent in 1991. The economy went into a free fall. In 1996, the year before the demise of the Mobutu regime, GDP per capita was estimated at about US$150, less than 40 percent of the 1958 level. The production of copper barely reached 40,000 tons, less than one-tenth the level achieved in the mid-1980s.

Without maintenance, infrastructure has deteriorated to such an extent that most regions are now completely isolated. Poverty has become widespread, and social indicators, which used to compare favorably with those in the rest of Sub-Saharan Africa, have steadily declined.

AID AND REFORM

The next section will discuss a series of issues at the core of the relationship between aid and reform, including the role of financial flows in reform, the adequacy of the reform agenda, the management of public resources, and the political dimension of reform.

Financial Flows and Reform

During the 1967–97 period, Zaire made two genuine attempts at economic reform. Both programs were formulated through close cooperation between the IMF and the Central Bank. The first one, in 1967, enabled the Congo to recover from the difficult post-independence years. The international community strongly backed the reform program and provided financial support through the IMF. At that time, the Central Bank was in control of macroeconomic management with little interference from the government. The 1967 reform reestablished private sector confidence, and the economy quickly bounced back. The reform program was supported by an IMF standby agreement, but the financial flows involved were quite limited.

The second ambitious reform initiated by Zaire took place in 1983–85. After a steep devaluation, the government liberalized the exchange rate, interest rates, and most prices. Again, this reform was supported by an IMF standby arrangement, but little additional support came from the donor community. Improved fiscal management allowed Zaire to pay its external debt as rescheduled, resulting in a net transfer of resources in favor of its creditors. In 1984–85 the debt service actually paid by Zaire increased by 88 percent over the previous two years. Whereas in 1982 and 1983, Zaire was a net beneficiary of transfers from its creditors for a total of US$42 million, it transferred the equivalent of US$369 million to its creditors in 1984–85, or about 2.6 percent of its GDP.

The net negative transfer situation in which Zaire found itself in 1984–85 gave strong ammunition to the opponents of fiscal rigor. The reform program was abandoned in late 1985, but the donor community, reacting with delay to the net transfer problem, stepped up its assistance. Net transfers became positive in 1986, averaging about US$133 million annually during the period 1986–88. This was mostly due to large disbursements from multilateral creditors, which averaged US$244 million annually, despite a steady deterioration in Zaire's fiscal performance during the same period. The net transfers in favor of bilateral creditors continued, however, but at a much lower level (US$12 million per year, compared with US$127.5 million per year during 1984–85).

The debt burden was a serious problem for Zaire in the late 1970s and early 1980s. The debt-to-GDP ratio increased from about 60 percent on average in 1975–78 to about 120 percent in 1985. This sharp increase was the result not so much of new debt incurred as of the early debt rescheduling agreements, which brought temporary relief but at the cost of higher debt in the future. Debt service absorbed a growing share of resources. The ratio of debt service actually paid to exports sharply increased from about 12 percent to about 30 percent during the same period.

Arrears became a chronic issue. They steadily increased from the equivalent of about 50 percent of exports of goods and services in 1975–78 to 76 percent in 1979. Debt rescheduling agreed to at the Paris Club and London Club meetings in 1979 and 1980 brought a temporary solution to the problem, but arrears increased again to reach 61 percent of exports of goods and services in 1982. Implementation of the 1983–85 reform program brought down the level of arrears to about 7 percent of exports of goods and services in 1986.

Lack of financial discipline in 1986–88 contributed to the resurgence of the arrears problem, despite generous transfers from the donor community and significant debt relief provided by bilateral creditors. In 1988 external arrears reached about 44 percent of exports of goods and services. A temporary reduction of this ratio to 24 percent took place in 1989, but arrears started to accumulate again. As exports of goods and services declined in the 1990s, the ratio jumped to 286 percent in 1992 and to a whopping 436 percent in 1996.

The debt burden was a major factor that contributed to making the stabilization program of 1983–85 difficult to sustain. Debt service absorbed an excessive amount of resources, leaving little for essential domestic programs. During the period 1978–82, on average, external debt service represented about 18 percent of government revenues. In 1985 this percentage climbed to about 48 percent, which is far beyond what would be considered reasonable today. In retrospect, bilateral creditors by being too shortsighted undermined the efforts of the only government team that was committed to fiscal stabilization and economic adjustment. By 1988, debt service absorbed 35 percent of government revenue, but adjustment support provided by the international community reduced this ratio to only 11 percent. The debt service burden was much reduced, but during that period the debt issue was used by the political leadership as an excuse for not reforming economic management.

Adequacy of the Reform Agenda

The first economic reform program in 1967 was highly successful. Private sector investment, which had been on average equivalent to about 16 percent of GDP during the 1950s, bounced back and became the driving force for a solid economic recovery in the late 1960s and early 1970s. The nationalization of Union Minière du Haut Katanga (UMHK), the copper mining company, in 1967 did not erode private sector confidence. The Belgian owners of UMHK received a profitable compensation package, including rights to the marketing of copper. The nationalization took place during a period of favorable international prices and did not affect copper production. It allowed a large number of Zairians to gain managerial skills. On the other hand, it also opened the door to government interference, which nonetheless remained limited in the early years of GECAMINES, the new company that took over from UMHK. The enactment of an investment code in 1969 triggered a strong private sector response. Investment, however, was mostly in highly protected import substitution activities with little real value added.

In 1972, one year before the "Zairianization" of all economic activities, the government initiated the establishment of marketing agencies to monopolize the purchase of major export crops. This policy was a major departure from the liberal approach to economic activities, which had served the country well in earlier years. As in many other African countries, however, this policy did not bring about its intended benefits of giving the farmers a higher price for their products. On the contrary, poor management led to lower prices and payment delays, which discouraged the producers.

To deal with the consequences of the financial crisis of 1975, which was partly of its own making, the government imposed a series of controls over economic activities. This new approach addressed some of the symptoms of the crisis, but not its root causes. It did not work, and Zaire became increasingly dependent on the goodwill of its creditors. The international community relied on the IMF to help stabilize the economy, and posted advisors in key management positions in the public sector, including the Central Bank, to help control the damage being done to the country's infrastructure and institutions. The country was kept on a short leash. Some improvements were made locally, but they were short-lived and not sustainable. Zaire's economy and social fabric continued to deteriorate.

The 1983–85 stabilization program was successful in removing the major controls established in the late 1970s. Foreign exchange became more readily available, but this was not sufficient to generate sustained growth. Both the Zairian authorities and the IMF agreed that a comprehensive adjustment program was needed. Private investment was at a low level (about 6–7 percent of GDP), and a major effort was deemed necessary to remove a number of constraints to private activity. An Industrial Sector Adjustment Credit was approved in June 1986 by the World Bank to support a reform program aimed at reducing effective protection, streamlining business taxes, and eliminating ex-post price controls. A number of measures were taken, but many of them were quickly circumvented thereafter. The reform program was not particularly relevant. It addressed issues considered not very important by the business community, but failed to address their real constraints, mainly infrastructure difficulties and the low purchasing power of the population. The foreign exchange made available under the credit was used by local enterprises to increase inventories, not so much to boost output. There was a modest growth in industrial production in 1987, but it was followed by a decline of similar importance in 1988 and 1989.

In June 1987 the World Bank approved a Structural Adjustment Credit. The reform program supported by the credit was far too complex, however, including measures in the areas of tariff, tax, the Public Investment Program, civil service, public enterprises, financial sector, agricultural sector, and transport sector. It was long on action plans and processes, but short on actual changes. It was not bold enough, as it did not seek to make irreversible changes to the ownership structure of key public enterprises. Its implementation ran into considerable difficulties from the outset. Even before the credit was declared effective, large uneconomic investments were initiated outside the agreed- upon PIP. The reform program failed and Zaire missed an opportunity to reestablish its economy on a sound footing.

During the 1983–89 period, policy dialogue with the authorities was conducted by the IMF in the early years, then by the IMF and the World Bank on behalf of the donor community. The dialogue with technicians and high officials was open and productive. There was a broad consensus on the reform agenda at this level, but, as became increasingly clear, President Mobutu had no intention of making any change in his ways of managing the country. In his view, the reform program was fine as long as it did not impose any limits on his prerogatives.

Management of Public Resources

Improved public resource management was a key objective of the stabilization and adjustment programs during the period 1983–89. Despite considerable efforts to improve the tax system and the programming of expenditures, the management of public resources deteriorated steadily over the period. The ratio of revenue to GDP increased modestly from a low of 8 percent in 1982–83 to an average of about 10 percent during the 1984–89 period. During this period, the government relied increasingly on contributions from GECAMINES (from about 20 percent in 1984–86 to about 40 percent in 1988–89). The share of income taxes and taxes on goods and services in total revenue declined from an average of 60 percent at the beginning of the period to an average of 35 percent in 1988–89.

Serious weaknesses in the tax and customs departments were not corrected. Improvements were made when competent administrators were appointed, but quickly forgotten when they were replaced. The tax and customs systems were undermined by a considerable number of exemptions and widespread fraud. A multitude of taxes with negligible yields for the Treasury, but representing a substantial burden for the business community, continued to be levied. Without counting local taxes, no less than 1,300 fiscal and quasi-fiscal instruments have been inventoried

The modest increase in revenue during the 1983–89 period allowed for an expansion in expenditures. Nondebt current expenditure increased from about 8 to 11 percent of GDP during the period. This increase was not used for development purposes, however. The share of defense, security, foreign affairs, and administrative and political functions increased from 38 to 62 percent of the total during the period, while the share of education and health declined from 39 to 22 percent. Allocations for sovereignty functions were routinely exceeded, while actual expenditures for development activities were consistently lower than budgetary allocations.

The government's use of resources rose from 11 percent of GDP in 1984–86 to 14 percent in 1987–89, with a peak of 17 percent in 1988. This increase was made possible by the availability of external resources, which represented 39 percent of government absorption in 1987–89 compared to 5 percent in 1984–86. As indicated earlier, net transfers on account of the external debt became highly negative in the early part of the 1984–89 period, but highly positive in the latter part of it. Government absorption was in reality substantially higher than indicated in official data. Expenditures were made outside the budgetary process and financed through a variety of means, such as extra contributions from GECAMINES and other public enterprises.

Public investment programming improved over the 1983–89 period. The public investment programs became more realistic and focused increasingly on the rehabilitation of infrastructure and productive facilities, and on human development. Starting in 1987, the PIPs became three-year rolling plans. Their implementation was monitored quarterly. Financial execution ratios improved steadily from a low of 43 percent in 1981–83 to a high of 92 percent in 1988–89. These improvements were seriously undermined, however, by the continued support that President Mobutu, in spite of explicit commitments made by his government, gave to his pet projects, which were financed through recourse to expensive sources of credit. One such project was the Mobaye dam and hydroelectric plant established on the Ubangui River to supply the presidential town of Gbadolite at an extravagant unit cost.

Increased availability of foreign assistance during the second half of the 1980s gave the government the opportunity to spend more. As indicated earlier, higher public spending benefited nondevelopment activities almost exclusively. By funding development sectors, the donor community in effect gave the government more latitude to spend for nondevelopment purposes, and to disengage itself from its developmental responsibilities.

Efforts to improve the management of public resources were doomed. They clashed with the political realities of an increasingly voracious regime. To maintain his hold on the country, President Mobutu needed either coercion, or a growing amount of resources with which to buy the support of influential people all around the country, or a combination of both. He also needed to remain in good standing with the international community. Open coercion was becoming less of an option in the 1980s as the international community was less prone to tolerate it, even when the excuse of "fighting communism" was used. Sensing this change in values, President Mobutu established a Ministry of Human Rights to placate Western public opinion. The only option left, therefore, was to maintain his direct control over a large quantity of resources. That objective was not consistent with the adjustment program, however. The program sought to eliminate a great number of practices that were not part of a sound public management system, but little was achieved in this area.

President Mobutu paid lip service to the adjustment program, but continued his raids on the Treasury, the Central Bank, GECAMINES, and other institutions. He was convinced that he would continue to be courted by world leaders even if he did not mend his ways. Experience shows that he was right. Even after the fall of the Berlin Wall in 1989, he was perceived by Western governments as the only person capable of keeping the country together. He presented himself as the only alternative to chaos, even after he brought chaos to his country by encouraging the army riots in 1991.

The Political Dimension of Reform

The Mobutu regime lasted for more than three decades. Its exceptional longevity stands in sharp contrast to the instability of its institutions and governments. During the 1980s Zairian governments lasted on average less than one year. Political considerations were paramount in the decisionmaking process. The consolidation of his regime was consistently President Mobutu's main concern. In 1967 he established a one-party system to consolidate his grip on power. The party included all Congolese nationals from their birth date. It was the center of power, and all public institutions, including the government, were under its dominance.

The regime could not tolerate any sign of dissent. In the late 1960s, the Central Bank, the business community (which was dominated by foreigners), and the Catholic Church still had too much autonomy for the regime's comfort. The governor of the Central Bank was replaced by a member of the president's office. The "Zairianization" launched in 1973 was meant to create *ex nihilo* a Zairian business class that would be forever grateful to the regime for its rapid enrichment. This initiative was part of a broader plan to mobilize all national energies through a cultural revolution process calling for a return to "African authenticity." This process was specifically aimed at curbing the enormous influence of the Catholic Church, which controlled most of the education and health facilities in the country.

In this context, economic reforms were adopted as long as they did not threaten the dominance of the regime. They were introduced in response to immediate pressures, not to address the root causes of economic problems, and were viewed as a means to placate the international community and extract more aid. They were not meant to last and were circumvented most of the time. They were running against a patrimonial way of governance, that was, incidentally, part of the heritage left by the so-called Congo Free State, the property of King Leopold of Belgium in the late nineteenth century.

CONCLUSION

The Democratic Republic of Congo and its citizenry have paid a heavy price for the country's strategic importance, its extraordinary mineral wealth, and its role in the Cold War. Independence in 1960 was poorly prepared and the chaotic years that followed it gave Cold War protagonists ample opportunities to manipulate local factions. When Mobutu took over through a bloodless coup in 1965, the country was longing for peace and tranquility. With Western support and IMF guidance, the Mobutu regime succeeded in restoring the conditions for economic growth, and its first years brought about positive changes for the country's population. The external shocks of 1973–75, however, and the decisions made during the same period to "Zairianize" all economic activities and to launch high-cost and nonviable projects with the support of commercial lenders and bilateral credit institutions, brought the process of economic recovery to a halt.

During the late 1970s and early 1980s the country struggled to recover from these shocks, but without much success. Chronic shortages of foreign exchange crippled economic activities, and infrastructure deteriorated. The donor community provided financial and technical assistance to help run public institutions and the large public enterprise sector, which was in charge of most mining and infrastructure activities. Technical advisers were in line positions. Some progress was made but it could not be sustained, mostly because of an inappropriate macroeconomic framework. There were some bright spots, particularly in those institutions where systematic on-the-job training took place. A number of Zairian technicians were trained in various sectors and they became the backbone of the economy.

Economic reform started in earnest in 1983 with IMF assistance. After a long slide the economy showed signs of bouncing back. It was a short episode, however. Bilateral creditors, who were also the major supporters of the country and its regime, did not seize the opportunity to help establish the reform process on a sound footing. They got paid, but for lack of sufficient resources the reform program fizzled out. External support came too late, and was indirectly used to enlarge the capacity of the regime to spend for nondevelopment purposes. The reformers who counted on the help of the international community had great difficulties fighting against the populist sentiments that were stirred up by the regime as a means to better maintain its staying power. After the fall of the Berlin Wall, the regime managed to stay in power for seven more years, but at a terrible cost to the population. It bought chaos to the country, a full-circle trip back to the early years of independence.

NOTES

1. We use the name Zaire in this chapter to refer to the country during the Mobutu years, which lasted until 1997.

Nigeria

Jeffrey Herbst
Princeton University
Princeton, New Jersey

Charles C. Soludo
University of Nigeria
Nsukka, Nigeria

ACRONYMS AND ABBREVIATIONS

GDP   Gross domestic product
GNP   Gross national product
IFI   International financial institution
IMF   International Monetary Fund
N   Naira (Nigerian currency)
ODA   Official development assistance
OPEC   Organization of Petroleum Exporting Countries
SAP   Structural adjustment program
SFEM   Second-tier Foreign Exchange Market

Recent discussions of the effectiveness of foreign aid have focused on Africa because it has received the greatest amount of aid on a per capita basis of any world region, yet policy reform has been the weakest there (Holmgren 1998: 1). Nigeria must have a critical role in any analysis of why economic performance has been so ineffective because the country's 118 million people account for roughly 20 percent of Sub-Saharan Africa's total population (World Bank 1998a: 191). Despite its bountiful oil resources, Nigeria's economic performance has been startlingly poor. Per capita income has suffered a significant erosion since the peak in the early 1980s that occurred, not coincidentally, when oil prices were at a historic high (see figure 11.1). The country has not been able to escape dependence on petroleum exports. The World Bank's judgment that "almost nothing positive has happened . . . in Nigeria in the past three decades" is harsh but not inaccurate (World Bank 1998b: 103).

Nigeria has received less foreign aid on a per capita basis than other countries in Sub-Saharan Africa. While average net real official development assistance (ODA) for African countries in 1990–96 was US$52 per person, Nigeria received just US$2.20 per person. As a percentage of gross national product (GNP), net ODA for Sub-Saharan Africa averaged 14 percent, while for Nigeria it was less than one percent of GNP in the period (O'Connell and Soludo 1999). Debt rescheduling, including the rescheduling of private debt (again, unusual for Africa), has been as important or more important than foreign aid flows during most periods of Nigeria's economic history. As a result, the power of the international financial institutions (IFIs) in relation to Nigeria comes from their unique ability to provide the "certificate of good health" that is a necessary element of private debt rescheduling.

This paper examines the relationship between foreign assistance, debt rescheduling, and policy performance between 1970 (when the civil war ended and oil began to dominate the Nigerian economy) and 1998. It places particular emphasis on the reforms attempted during the presidency of Ibrahim Babangida (1985–93) because these were the most comprehensive reforms ever attempted in Nigeria and because at times during this period, Nigeria was receiving more aid on a per capita basis than the average for other countries in this study. The lessons of the previous major episode of reform will be particularly relevant to future governments because Nigeria still faces the fundamental challenge of removing policy distortions and lessening its dependence on petroleum exports.

The rest of the paper is organized as follows. First, a brief discussion of Nigerian political economy is presented. The next section is an overview of aid flows, sources, and uses, focusing on how the character of aid can affect policy design and implementation. We then evaluate the context and environment for policy reforms, paying attention to the poli-

FIGURE 11.1 NIGERIA: PER CAPITA INCOME, 1970–97

Current U.S. dollars

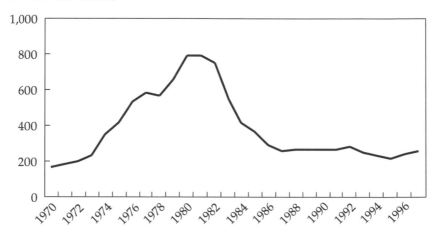

Source: World Bank, Africa Database on CD-ROM, 1999.

tics of policy choice, the specific policies, and the implementation record. We also examine the interaction between aid and the nature and effectiveness of reforms. The conclusions present lessons derived from the Nigerian case.

NIGERIAN POLITICAL ECONOMY

Chief Obafemi Awolowo noted in 1947 that one of the fundamental problems facing Nigeria at the time was that it was, in many ways, little more than "a geographic expression" (Joseph 1987: 184).[1] During the postcolonial period, far-reaching political, economic, and social programs were aimed at accelerating the processes of nation building within a federal system. Today, Nigeria is much more than a geographic expression and has taken on many of the characteristics of a modern nation-state. Nevertheless, a constellation of ethnic, regional, religious, and class conflicts continue to pose tremendous problems and still have the potential (as demonstrated in the civil war of 1967–70) to seriously threaten national unity. These conflicts have had a significant impact on economic policymaking and on the reform process. Indeed, many of the economically inefficient public investment projects that successive governments have launched since the early 1970s can be attributed directly to the myriad ethnic, regional, and religious competitions that are always a component of Nigerian politics.

As a result, resource allocation has always been central to Nigerian politics. Nigerian governments have had to assuage fears in southern Nigeria of Hausa-Fulani political domination while at the same time attempting to win the confidence of the peoples of the relatively under-developed north through the deliberate allocation of industrial, infra-structure, and commercial assets. Indeed, the peoples of the south, especially in the oil-producing areas, sometimes openly protest the "en-richment" of the north via the state at the expense of the south.

The oil windfall that Nigeria received in the early 1970s as a result of increases in production and the OPEC price hike greatly aggravated the tendency toward clientelism and patrimonialism. In 1970, oil exports were valued at N510 million; a decade later they had increased to N14,187 million. Since almost all of the oil revenue was funneled through the state, government expenditures increased by more than 3,000 percent during the same period (Nigeria 1991: 7–8). As a result, control of the state became exceptionally valuable and the explosion of oil revenue fueled the creation of ever larger and more elaborate patron-client net-works. Indeed, the oil boom greatly expanded the ranks of the indig-enous trading, contracting, and manufacturing classes, many of whose members were utterly dependent on the state for their continued exist-ence. With the robust flow of oil revenue, it seemed in the 1970s and early 1980s that government revenue could finance public projects indefinitely at what was, for a still-poor African country, an extravagant level.

The great inflow of revenue caused by the oil boom also created other strong constituencies that continue to lobby the central government for significant budgetary allocations. The state greatly expanded its public expenditures program so that utilities and social services could be deliv-ered relatively cheaply. For instance, primary education was made free and mandatory, creating an enormous market for school building con-struction and textbooks, all of which had to be allocated through the state. A strong exchange rate also made possible the importation of cheap food and consumer goods for the population. Moreover, speculators, contractors, commission agents, importers of all commodities, local and foreign manufacturers, and the urban working class all benefited to vary-ing degrees from the massive increase in state expenditures. Finally, the military was well rewarded, especially in terms of imported equipment and other expensive perquisites.

As a result, the availability of government revenue to reward con-stituencies, fund public works programs, and buy off opponents is the central consideration for any Nigerian ruler. Leaders in Nigeria are vi-tally concerned that they have access to the maximum amount of rev-enue possible in the short term. There are many good reasons for this, such as the desire to build schools and roads. However, since government revenue also buys support for leaders and, at some fundamental level, national unity, leaders also want to ensure their immediate access to revenue for political reasons. Indeed, given the history of coups and instability in Nigeria, it is understandable that members of the elite view the fluctuations and availability of government revenue in the short term as literally a life-or-death matter. The notion that any Nigerian leader can champion reform, as the World Bank (1998b: 104) now says is necessary, is particularly problematic given the political pressures that leaders face.

A model of Nigerian leadership behavior must take politics into account. Otherwise, explanations of Nigeria's failure to reform fall short, as is the case with Moser, Rogers, and van Til (1997: 45). We argue later in this paper that given the objective conditions of the Nigerian economy, the issue was not *whether* to reform but *how* to reform, that is, which model of reform to pursue. The choice was between tinkering on the margin—intensifying the austerity measures of the previous regimes—or embarking on the type of reforms advocated by the World Bank and International Monetary Fund (IMF).

The choice to adopt the Bank-Fund type of adjustment was not necessarily made because the Nigerian government and people had faith in that model's superiority over alternative ones. Rather, it was made principally because of the leverage exercised by the IFIs. That leverage stems from their ability to provide a basis for debt rescheduling, and therefore to provide the government with the direly needed fiscal space to operate. To measure the pressure that government leaders were under to adopt the Bank-Fund reforms, we use nonconcessional debt as a percentage of total exports (see figure 11.2). This serves as a relatively good indicator of how much revenue government leaders had available in light of their almost complete dependence on oil for government revenue and given the repayment schedule to which they had committed. Note that the model explicitly assumes that debt rescheduling and oil revenue are essentially interchangeable, a realistic provision given the need of Nigerian rulers for maximum revenue in the short term.

AID INTENSITY, SOURCES, AND USES

Aid has been a much less important component of Nigeria's political economy than has been the case in other African countries. There are three reasons for this. First, the well-known bias of donors against countries with large populations tends to work heavily against Nigeria given its status as the giant of Africa (World Bank 1998b: 41–2). Second, Nigeria's extravagant oil wealth caused many donors to assume that the

FIGURE 11.2 NIGERIA: NONCONCESSIONAL EXTERNAL DEBT
TO EXPORTS, 1980–96

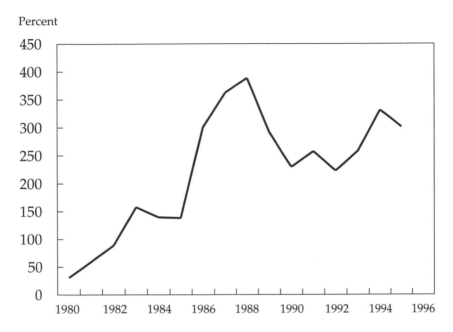

Percent

Source: World Bank, Africa Database on CD-ROM, 1999.

country did not need aid. This perception was occasionally encouraged
by Nigerian leaders who, especially in the 1970s, portrayed their country as the superpower of Africa. As a result, Nigeria agreed not to demand significant concessionary inflows as part of the Lomé agreements.
Finally, the outrageous level of corruption and the sheer difficulty of
working in Nigeria has undoubtedly deterred many aid agencies.[2]

Figure 11.3 displays net overseas development assistance by all donors on a per capita basis to Nigeria and the average for the nine other
countries in the study (Côte d'Ivoire, Democratic Republic of Congo,
Ethiopia, Ghana, Kenya, Mali, Tanzania, Uganda, and Zambia). For most
of the last 25 years, Nigeria has received far less aid on a per capita basis
than the other countries studied. As figure 11.4 indicates, donors did not
direct funds to Lagos during the oil boom years. However, Nigeria is
not immune to trends in foreign assistance; indeed, Nigeria's trajectory
clearly tracks the average of the rest of the sample for most of the period. The late 1980s and early 1990s are a dramatic break from the general pattern. In those years Nigeria received far more money on a per
capita basis from all donors than was the case for the rest of the sample.

FIGURE 11.3 NIGERIA: NET ODA PER CAPITA, ALL DONORS

U.S. dollars

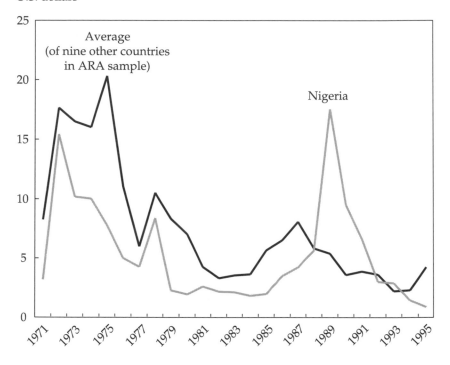

Source: World Bank Effective Development Assistance database.

Figure 11.4 indicates that donors were responding, in part, to the fall in oil revenue. When both the economic reforms and the political transition proposed by the Babangida government began to unravel after 1993, aid to Nigeria declined sharply, reverting to its historic position below the rest of the sample.

Inflows from multilateral donors display much the same pattern. Nigeria received far less on a per capita basis than the average for the rest of the study sample, except for the period in the late 1980s and early 1990s and an extremely brief spike in the late 1970s (see figure 11.5). It is clear that the multilateral and bilateral donors approached Nigeria (in relation to the rest of the sample) in much the same manner over the last 25 years.

When funding is disaggregated by source, it is clear that Nigeria received far more funds from the World Bank, as a percentage of its total flow of disbursements from all creditors between 1970 and 1997, than

FIGURE 11.4 NIGERIA: OIL EXPORTS AND NET ODA

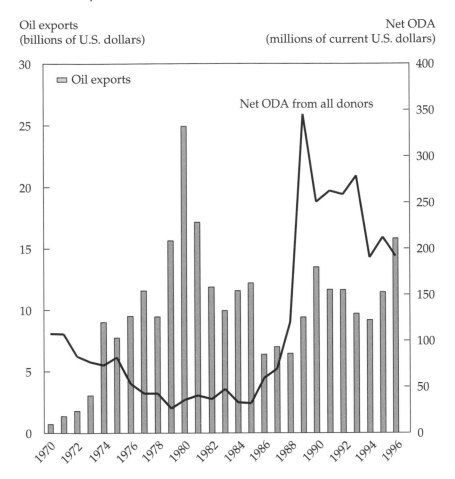

Oil exports
(billions of U.S. dollars)

Net ODA
(millions of current U.S. dollars)

Source: World Bank Effective Development Assistance database.

was the case for the average of the sample (see table 11.1). Not surprisingly, very few of the small donors chose to work in Nigeria because they prefer countries where they can make some impact.

Nor did Nigeria receive any concessional IMF flows during these years. Even in the Babangida period, when reform was nominally at the top of the government's agenda, Nigeria refused an IMF loan, despite the Fund's formal role in monitoring the program. The government could not take the IMF loan principally because Nigerians had, in a national debate, rejected the loan and its conditionalities.

FIGURE 11.5 NIGERIA: NET ODA PER CAPITA,
MULTILATERAL DONORS

U.S. dollars

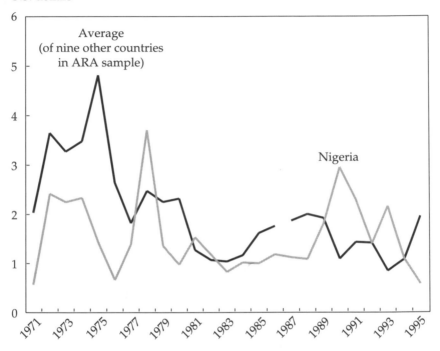

Source: World Bank Effective Development Assistance database.

Furthermore, Nigeria has become progressively more dependent on World Bank loans throughout the period as grants from the bilateral donors have gradually declined (see figure 11.6). For instance, United States aid fell from US$30 million in grants in 1970 to US$1 million in 1977 and did not increase significantly again until the early 1990s (the high point was 1991, when U.S. grants totaled US$44 million). After the Babangida program failed, American aid plunged to zero. A major reason for the gyrations in the aid from major donors such as the United States could be the interests of the donors. Since the end of the Cold War, the United States has conditioned much of its aid on the promotion of democracy, and the 1990–93 period was the high point of Babangida's democratic transition program. The three largest industrial economies—the United States, Japan, and Germany—have been the largest bilateral donors to Nigeria. This presence of the largest econo-

TABLE 11.1 NIGERIA: CONTRIBUTIONS BY DONOR, 1970–97
(percentage of disbursements by all creditors)

Donor	Nigeria	Nine other countries[a]
African Development Bank	18.8	14.3
Canada	0.6	1.7
European Union	0	0.4
Denmark	0	0.8
Finland	0	0.3
France	0	8.0
Germany	3.3	4.5
Italy	0	3.8
Japan	5.0	6.0
Netherlands	0.2	0.7
Norway	0.4	0.3
Sweden	0	0.7
Switzerland	0	0.1
United Kingdom	0.8	2.3
United States	6.1	5.5
World Bank	63.6	52.3

a. The average for the nine other countries in the Aid and Reform in Africa study: Côte d'Ivoire, Democratic Republic of Congo, Ethiopia, Ghana, Kenya, Mali, Tanzania, Uganda, and Zambia.
Source: World Bank Effective Development Assistance database.

FIGURE 11.6 NIGERIA: GRANTS AS A PERCENTAGE
OF TOTAL DISBURSEMENTS

Percent

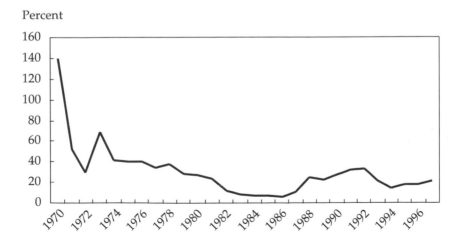

Source: World Bank Effective Development Assistance database.

mies might well be related to the donors' strategic interests in exerting some influence in Nigeria.

As figure 11.6 indicates, grants as a percentage of disbursements declined significantly throughout the 1970s and 1980s. The 1970s were the years of the oil boom and foreign aid was almost unnecessary. It was not until the late 1980s, when Nigeria demonstrated some seriousness about reforms, that donors began to reward the government with further inflows. Grants did rise when total aid increased in the late 1980s and early 1990s as many bilateral donors who had fled Nigeria returned to support the Babangida program. However, when the political and economic reforms began to collapse, grants declined even more than total disbursements. After General Sani Abacha took control in November 1993, Nigeria became increasingly isolated from the international community.

As is the case for all other countries in the sample, the distribution of disbursements to Nigeria by sector has evolved over time (see table 11.2). At least two factors are at work: the changing needs of Nigeria and changes in the overall aid regime. Not surprisingly, in the early 1970s sectors associated with basic infrastructure received the greatest amount of money as development thinking was still guided by the two-gap model. Transport and storage, electricity, gas, and water production, and communications dominated disbursements, accounting for 74 percent of all aid in 1970. By 1979, when the basic human needs philosophy was probably at its operational high point, those three sectors received only 14 percent of total disbursements to Nigeria, while community, social, personal, and environmental services hit a high point of 50 percent (up from 13 percent in 1970). In the late 1980s and early 1990s, the period when Nigeria was receiving significant inflows on a per capita basis, balance of payments support, which had been almost nonexistent before 1986, came to dominate overall disbursements. When the reform program collapsed, balance of payments support returned to almost zero.

As a result of Nigeria's relatively low inflows of official aid and its ability to borrow, however briefly, in the 1970s and 1980s against its then-robust oil revenues, debt rescheduling is far more important to Nigeria than foreign aid. In the critical seven-year period of adjustment between 1986 and 1993, total rescheduling of principal and interest payments was US$18.5 billion, averaging about US$2.6 billion per year. Of these, average annual rescheduling of private debt was US$2.0 billion, with the residual annual average of US$596 million rescheduled from official debt. Put differently, the total annual debt service payment due was about US$3.6 billion, which was about 10 percent of GNP, 40 percent of oil export receipts, and more than 70 percent of government spending (see table 11.3).

Were it not for the debt rescheduling arrangements that reduced the actual service payments to about US$1.0 billion annually, it is difficult to see how the Nigerian government could have coped. By contrast, a number of the other countries in the sample—the Democratic Republic of Congo, Côte d'Ivoire, Mali, Tanzania, and Uganda—had private debt flows of close to zero. Private flows as a percentage of official (excluding IMF) flows are 21 percent for Ethiopia, 28 percent for Ghana, and 26 percent for Zambia. However, private flows were 88 times larger than official flows for Nigeria between 1992 and 1996 (US$617 million compared to US$7 million). Only Kenya, where private flows are 92 percent of official flows, had a remotely similar ratio, but Kenya is coded as a moderately indebted low-income country while all the others (including Nigeria) are severely indebted low-income countries (World Bank 1999: 10). Indeed, Nigeria is the only African country whose net transfer to the creditors was substantially negative (–US$8.6 billion) for the seven-year period of reform between 1986 and 1992 (O'Connell and Soludo 1999).

ADJUSTMENT IN NIGERIA

The characteristics of the Nigerian economy for the period 1981–85 (that is, immediately before the adjustment reforms) suggest a classic case of an economy in fundamental disequilibrium. The collapse of oil prices from about US$40 per barrel in 1980 to US$9 in 1985/6, together with the sharp cut in the OPEC production quota for Nigeria, left the economy in crisis. Government revenue fell from about 24 percent of gross domestic product (GDP) in 1980 to 12 percent in 1985. Major macroeconomic imbalances appeared and persisted as a result of the neglect and decay of the non-oil sectors, an inward-looking industrialization regime that depended heavily on imported inputs, a highly overvalued exchange rate regime, and the bloated public consumption and investment patterns of the 1970s (especially for distributional purposes and massaging of patronage networks).

Budget deficits increased from a mere 0.5 percent of GDP in 1980 to 9.5 percent in 1981, while the external current account went from a modest surplus of 4.5 percent in 1980 to a deficit of 7.5 percent in 1981. Fiscal deficits were financed mainly by money creation, and inflation soared. External reserves were quickly run down, and external borrowing intensified to the extent that external debt rose from 5 percent of GDP in 1980 to 23 percent in 1985. The scarcity of foreign exchange and stringent but cumbersome import licensing procedures led to sharp declines in availability of imported inputs for the manufacturing sector. Capacity utilization in the sector fell from 73 percent in 1980 to 38 percent in 1981, and urban

TABLE 11.2 SECTORAL DISTRIBUTION OF AID TO NIGERIA, 1970–96
(percent of total aid)

Sector	1970	1971	1972	1973	1974	1975	1976	1977	1978	1979	1980	1981	1982
Agriculture, forestry, fishing	0	0	0	0	0	0	26	36	40	30	29	36	49
Balance of payments support	0	0	5	0	0	0	0	0	0	0	0	0	0
Communication	33	11	2	8	3	0	1	1	0	0	1	15	24
Community, social, personal, and environmental services	13	36	47	17	12	13	12	11	17	50	27	7	3
Construction	0	0	0	0	0	0	0	0	0	0	0	0	0
Contributions to finance current imports	0	12	4	0	9	0	0	0	0	0	0	0	0
Electricity, gas, water production	24	11	8	6	25	36	30	25	15	0	11	24	4
Finance, insurance, real estate, business	5	3	2	3	2	0	0	0	0	3	14	14	7
Manufacturing	8	4	5	8	3	5	3	11	5	3	2	1	0
Mining, quarrying	0	0	0	0	0	0	0	0	0	0	0	0	0
Other contributions	0	0	0	0	0	0	0	0	0	0	0	0	0
Transport and storage	17	22	28	59	44	45	28	16	23	14	16	2	14

Sector	1983	1984	1985	1986	1987	1988	1989	1990	1991	1992	1993	1994	1995	1996
Agriculture, forestry, fishing	16	26	22	11	18	21	19	24	17	27	28	28	14	13
Balance of payments support	0	0	0	34	38	24	58	46	17	3	0	0	2	3
Communication	2	0	10	3	3	0	0	0	2	0	0	0	1	1
Community, social, personal, and environmental services	13	11	11	11	12	29	8	8	10	23	20	26	32	30
Construction	0	0	0	0	0	0	0	0	0	0	0	0	1	1
Contributions to finance current imports	0	0	0	0	0	0	0	0	0	0	0	0	0	0
Electricity, gas, water production	6	13	16	15	12	18	9	8	14	18	31	31	31	20
Finance, insurance, real estate, business	1	2	6	6	6	3	4	7	9	5	1	6	2	4
Manufacturing	9	45	34	19	11	3	1	2	15	2	7	2	7	14
Mining, quarrying	0	0	0	0	0	0	0	0	15	15	8	2	0	0
Other contributions	52	0	0	0	0	0	0	0	0	0	0	0	0	0
Transport and storage	1	3	1	1	1	1	0	6	1	5	5	5	11	13

Source: World Bank Effective Development Assistance database.

TABLE 11.3 NIGERIA: EXTERNAL DEBT SERVICE PROFILE
(millions of U.S. dollars)

Year	Principal			Interest			Total rescheduled	Repayments plus rescheduling	Principal repayments	Net transfers	Total debt stock
	Principal rescheduled	Official rescheduled	Private rescheduled	Interest rescheduled	Official rescheduled	Private rescheduled					
1981	0	0	0	0	0	0	0	634	634	1,305	12,108
1982	0	0	0	0	0	0	0	833	833	1,607	12,815
1983	0	0	0	0	0	0	0	1,148	1,148	407	18,422
1984	0	0	0	0	0	0	0	2,217	2,217	(2,183)	18,435
1985	21		21	7		7	28	3,546	3,518	(3,702)	19,324
1986	3,673	44	3,629	343	23	321	4,016	5,241	1,225	427	23,164
1987	5,459	71	5,388	500	40	460	5,959	6,389	430	552	30,039
1988	0	0	0	0	0	0	0	812	812	(1,448)	30,718
1989	2,879	684	2,194	1,206	569	637	4,085	4,692	607	(499)	30,122
1990	1,280	1,090	191	169	149	21	1,449	2,629	1,180	(2,376)	33,440
1991	1,731	589	1,142	834	568	266	2,565	3,427	862	(2,130)	33,527
1992	327	277	51	60	49	11	387	2,265	1,878	(3,174)	29,019
1993	0	0	0	0	0	0	0	579	579	(897)	30,699
1994	0	0	0	0	0	0	0	746	746	(1,223)	33,092
1995	0	0	0	0	0	0	0	918	918	(1,344)	34,093
1996	0	0	0	0	0	0	0	1,418	1,418	(2,153)	31,407
Total (1986–92)	15,349	2,755	12,595	3,112	1,398	1,716	18,461	25,455	6,994	(8,648)	
Average (1986–92)	2,193	394	1,799	445	200	245	2,637	3,636	999	(1,235)	

Sources: World Bank, World Debt Tables 1989–1990: 282–5; World Bank, Global Development Finance 1998: 408–11.

unemployment grew rapidly. It is not surprising therefore that the average GDP growth rate was negative for the period 1981–85.

The crisis had a dramatic impact on the external sector. For example, between 1981 and 1982 the average monthly import bill was US$2.0 billion while exports averaged US$1.5 billion. The ratio of debt service to exports ratio soared from 9.0 percent in 1981 to 18.5 percent in 1982, 23.6 percent in 1983, and 39 percent in 1985. Arrears on letters of credit accumulated, and in 1983 some US$2.1 billion of such arrears had to be refinanced over a 30-month period. A second refinancing was done in 1984. Still, the arrears continued to accumulate between 1984 and 1987 through open account and bills for collection as well as arrears on dividends, royalties, technical fees, airline remittances, and so on, amounting to US$3.85 billion. Together with capitalized interest of US$1.05 billion, this brought the total to US$4.9 billion (Nigeria 1997). These developments underscored the fact that some reforms were imperative.

In fact, Nigeria has never lacked for "reforms," and since the 1970s various governments have tried to respond to the observed disequilibria through all kinds of ad-hoc measures. These responses were due in part to the misreading of developments in the international oil market and the mistaken inference that the shocks were temporary. For example, a decline in oil prices in 1977–78 led to the first jumbo loan of US$1 billion from the international capital market as well as the introduction of some austerity measures by the Obasanjo regime. In late 1979 the oil market recovered, whereupon the government relaxed the austerity measures and resumed its ostentatious consumption patterns.

As the crisis became full blown in the early 1980s, the Shehu Shagari regime (1979 to 1983) contemplated adjustment. The Shagari administration enacted the Economic Emergency and Stabilization Act of 1982, which targeted the manifest excesses in government spending and tried to curb the persistent deficit in the balance of payments through stringent import and exchange rate controls. The fiscal retrenchment consisted of a freeze on capital expenditure, the curtailment of low-priority public investment projects, an increase in petroleum product prices and utility tariffs, a freeze on wages and salaries in the public sector, and a restriction of foreign borrowing by state and local governments. Despite these measures, real GDP still contracted in 1982–83 and inflation soared from 7 percent in 1982 to 39 percent in 1983; but the external current account improved slightly in 1983 due to the severe import compression (Moser, Rogers, and van Til 1997). Negotiations with the World Bank and the International Monetary Fund began in 1983 as the crisis deepened, but as it was an election year, the government did not dare even to give the impression that it was going to institute tougher reforms.

Shagari was toppled in a military coup by General Muhammadu Buhari at the end of 1983. Among the reasons given for the overthrow of the regime were the enduring economic crisis and the hardship it entailed, corruption, and the decay of social services. Buhari suspended negotiations with the international financial institutions and instead embarked on a stringent fiscal retrenchment program, initiated an anti-corruption crusade, and imposed stricter import and exchange rate controls. The heightened austerity measures entailed further tightening of financial, exchange rate, trade, and administrative controls. Taxes were increased and spending was cut drastically, resulting in a retrenchment of more than 10,000 public service workers (5 percent of the civil service work force). Under this regime, possession of foreign currency was a crime.

Without an agreement with the international financial institutions, debt service payments could not be rescheduled, but the government could also only partially service the debt. Unpaid interest arrears on external debt accumulated and the stock of debt grew fivefold. The economy groaned under the weight of the austerity measures, and there were no explicit measures to ensure long-term viability. Some positive outcomes of the austerity regime included the reduction of inflation to just one percent, balance in the current account, and a jump in GDP growth rate to 9.5 percent, ostensibly because of the favorable weather and upward revision of the OPEC production quota for Nigeria. These depressive stabilization measures were clearly unsustainable without efforts to fundamentally restructure the economy and eliminate the myriad distortions. As Moser, Rogers, and van Til (1997: 10) note, "The extensive system of direct controls suppressed market signals and discouraged private sector activity. Crippling import shortages and growing social and political discontent set the stage for another military coup."

By the time General Ibrahim Babangida took over in a palace coup in August 1985, the economy was in dire straits and the government was starved for revenue. Nonconcessional debts as a percentage of exports reached 138 percent that year, up from only 31 percent in 1980. In 1986 it soared still higher, to 301 percent. The government was facing a profound fiscal challenge that also challenged all of Nigeria's traditional political practices of state-centered clientelism.

Babangida faced many possibilities but one real choice: he could opt to continue with the austerity measures and strengthen direct controls. However, a major reason that such measures had not succeeded in the past was that they were implemented in the context of extreme foreign exchange scarcity. Donors did not sanction the measures and therefore did not give the government the kind of fiscal relief it so badly needed. To obtain any relief on debt servicing obligations, it was imperative that the government reach an agreement with the IMF, both to receive new funds and, critically, to enable it to begin debt rescheduling talks with the private lenders. At the same time, however, the government faced a different dilemma: there was no discernible domestic constituency for the kind of reforms preferred by donors (that is, the Bank-Fund type of reforms that required more wide-ranging measures including privatization, devaluation, trade and financial liberalization, and so on). In an economy where ordinary citizens as well as the ruling elite had become accustomed to cheap and easy imports, subsidies, and patronage or rents from public enterprises, the Bank-Fund reforms were a tough sell.

Furthermore, if there was anything the average Nigerian loathed, it was the thought that an outside institution was dictating policies to the country. Having been champions of anti-imperialism and liberation struggles throughout much of Africa, Nigerians tended to see any program endorsed by the IMF or the World Bank as a neocolonialist or imperialist agenda that must be resisted. Also, there was no real reason for the government to be enthusiastic about the Bank-Fund reforms because such reforms compromised the patron-client networks and would cut the government's profligate use of spending to pander to diverse interests. Government weighed the options carefully and realized that its survival hinged on the availability of revenues, which in turn depended upon its ability to negotiate a rescheduling of debt service payments. Without this kind of binding constraint (debt overhang), it is debatable whether the government would have willingly embarked upon the Bank-Fund reforms.

Babangida's strategy for dealing with the dilemma was to try to sell the reforms as "Nigerian-made" and not externally driven. In a clever maneuver to prepare Nigerians for the painful adjustment to come, Babangida orchestrated a national debate that was somewhat deceitfully couched in terms of whether or not Nigeria should take the IMF loan and the accompanying conditionalities. When the outcome of the debate was announced in early 1986, it was predictable. Nigerians, it was said, had rejected the IMF loan and conditionality, but instead agreed to embark on their own "homegrown" adjustment measures designed to ensure "economic reconstruction, social justice, and self-reliance." Consequently, Babangida went on to declare a 15-month national economic emergency. As he told Nigerians in his December 1985 budget speech:

> In my silver jubilee address to you on 1st October 1985, I declared a state of national economic emergency for a period of 15 months. This action was dictated by the serious economic problems facing us: huge foreign and domestic debts, a rapidly declining per capita income, a high rate of unemployment, severe shortages of raw materials and spare parts for our industries, and a high rate of inflation. We Nigerians all agreed the solution to these serious social and economic problems must be found through our own efforts at own pace and our volition, consistent with our own voluntary

national interest. We are determined more than ever before to har-
ness our own homegrown efforts to solve our problems and set a
new path for the future. (Babangida 1985)

Much of the motivation for this convoluted strategy was derived from
movement in the oil spot market from US$27 per barrel in December
1985 to US$9 per barrel in May 1986 (Biersteker and Lewis 1997: 308).
    While this speech pandered to the emotions of the eminently proud
Nigerians who hated to have any external agency intervene in their internal affairs, Babangida did not tell them two things. First, he did not
tell Nigerians how this "homegrown" program would be fundamentally different from the typical IMF program (or whether the difference
would simply be that it was designed or copied by Nigerians). Second,
Babangida did not explain how the supposedly "unique" program would
be sustained without reaching an agreement with the international financial institutions and, critically for Nigeria, private creditors—agreements that would be crucial in order to reschedule debt as well as garner
possible new financing, given the binding budget and balance of payments constraints. Subsequent events showed that this political strategy, while clever in the short term, was not viable because at some point
the government had to take ownership of what was, in the final analysis, a very conventional program if the reforms were to be supported by
the IFIs. In retrospect, it is clear that Babangida should not have been
considered the type of reformer that the World Bank now says is necessary: one with a "long-term vision at the local or national level" (World
Bank 1998b: 116). His limited and halting embrace of reform was simply
too problematic.
    While the 1986 budget committed the government to the general prin-
ciples of a typical structural adjustment program (fiscal retrenchment,
monetary controls, devotion of 30 percent of exports to debt servicing),
the regime still insisted on "not devaluing the naira overnight," and thus
maintaining the import licensing system. However, by July 1986, the limited success of the stabilization program was obvious. Babangida admitted in his broadcast of June 27, 1986, that

> We were aware that the successful outcome of the economic stabi-
> lization program depended on a favorable and stabilized foreign
> market; good weather for agricultural production; effective imple-
> mentation by the public bureaucracy; and an inherent political
> understanding and mass support. Our experience on each of these
> factors has so far been a mixed one. (Babangida 1986)

This admission paved the way for further actions and an intensification of negotiations with the multilateral institutions.

However, while Nigeria effectively embarked on what appeared to be the standard reform package backed by the World Band and the IMF around the world, the official rhetoric insisted that it was adjustment Nigerian-style. Even as Babangida was launching the reforms in June 1986, he told Nigerians:

> Our international creditors appreciate our commitments in the path of agro-structural adjustment which we have started for ourselves. They have remained in useful dialogue with us to ensure successful implementation of our programs. We are particularly gratified that the major international financial institutions have come to recognize and to agree with this administration's position not to take the IMF loan, and not to devalue the naira overnight. (Babangida 1986)

Babangida evidently sensed the increasing cynicism of Nigerians to the claims of full "ownership" of the reforms. In his budget speech of January 1, 1987, he assured them that

> Once again, the real or assumed roles of the international institutions in the conduct of our affairs must be put in their right perspectives. In my Republic Day address last 1st October, I affirmed that we have neither sought nor obtained any loan from the International Monetary Fund, but in line with our normal rights and entitlements, the World Bank, of which we are a member, has assisted us with a moderate resource backing to help the kick off of SFEM. Our structural adjustment program was produced by Nigerians for Nigerians. (Babangida 1987)

It was, in fact, obvious that the Nigerians had the technical ability to design an adjustment program. Unlike many Sub-Saharan countries, Nigeria, which has a population 10 times larger than the average African country, has a critical mass of trained technocrats who can readily accomplish much of the preparatory and technical work that the IMF and World Bank are forced to do elsewhere on the continent. Indeed, in 1987, in spite of the huge brain drain that had occurred over the years, Nigeria set up a technical aides corps scheme to assist African countries which regularly requested Nigerian personnel in specific fields. Under this scheme, young Nigerian professionals in such fields as medicine, engineering, surveying, teaching, law, agriculture, veterinary medicine, and others were sent to other African countries requesting assistance to work for a period of two years in the first instance (Babangida 1987).

There was also a clear understanding within the bureaucracy of the structural problems that Nigeria faced. Indeed, Finance Minister Dr. Kalu

Idika Kalu captured this sense when, during one of his many interventions in the debate over structural adjustment, he stressed that the question was not whether Nigeria should take the IMF loan and the accompanying conditionality but whether it could afford not to do so. The annual reports of the Central Bank of Nigeria and analysis in the independent business press also indicated that there was no shortage of economists with technical skills who had a persuasive diagnosis of what was wrong with the Nigerian economy and prescriptions to fix the problem that fell well within the emerging "Washington consensus."

To assist in implementing the economic recovery program, the president also relied on a core group of officials from the key economic ministries and the presidency. Particularly prominent were the ministers and director-generals of the ministries of Finance and Planning, the governor of the Central Bank, the secretary to the Federal Military Government, and their advisers. Besides this core group, the president also established the Presidential Advisory Committee, independent of all ministerial control and located in the presidency. Headed by a prominent economist, this advisory committee became a key part of the economic policy formulation and budget production process, providing a platform for internal debates on policies and ways to manage their repercussions. This "change team"—to use the language of the day—was designed to be independent of politics but team members had to report to a leader who was still deeply embedded in the Nigerian political system.

The problem for Nigeria had less to do with ignorance of the "right economics" than with the consistent derailing of attempts at policy implementation. Some useful technical assistance was provided by the IFIs but the Nigerian government had the basic technocratic capability to design the reforms. Indeed, the government's strategy of denying that it was adopting an IMF-type program essentially prevented it from developing a relationship in which technical assistance could have become even more important. Technical assistance, as the Nigerian case clearly shows, is a political matter in African countries given the widespread distrust of the IFIs. Those who believe that technical expertise can be provided in an apolitical manner until a country is ready for structural adjustment can easily underestimate how controversial these reforms still are, even in theory, in African countries—certainly the case in Nigeria. There was and is a lingering debate in much of Africa, not about whether or not to reform, but about what kinds of reforms are desirable given the structural problems of these economies.

Implementation of Reforms

Reforms in Nigeria, as in many developing countries, were implemented in a stop-go manner. This underlines the point that regardless of the level and sophistication of technical skills in the bureaucracy, the conviction and commitment of the political leadership to the process are indispensable. Where there is lack of domestic ownership of the reforms, implementation will almost always falter.

The structural adjustment program (SAP) was underpinned by three standby arrangements with the International Monetary Fund between 1986 and 1992, spanning a noncontinuous period of 42 months. The major reason for the adoption of the SAP by Nigeria, as indicated earlier, was to open the door to official debt rescheduling which was the topmost priority of the government (Moser, Rogers, and van Til 1997; Nigeria 1997). Consequently, the standby arrangements led to three debt rescheduling agreements with the Paris Club of creditor countries: (a) a 1986 agreement that rescheduled/refinanced debt worth about US$4.6 billion ; (b) a 1989 agreement that rescheduled about US$5.2 billion; and (c) a 1991 agreement that rescheduled about US$3.3 billion (Ikem 1996). Summing up the implementation record, Moser, Rogers, and van Til (1997: 12) observe that "the first Fund program (January 1987– January 1988) quickly went off track; the second (February 1989–May 1990) was successfully implemented; and the third (January 1991–April 1992) also went off track soon after its approval." The reasons for this lackluster implementation record will be examined later.

A striking observation, however, is that aside from 1986, there is no discernible strong correlation between the implementation of reforms and the years that debt rescheduling agreements were signed (see table 11.4). One would have expected that a government eager to secure a rescheduling agreement would do everything to show stronger "commitment," especially in the year right before the next rescheduling meeting. Table 11.4 does not show any clear indication of that.

In general, the broad objectives of the reform program were to: (a) restructure and diversify the productive base of the economy in order to reduce dependence on the oil sector and on imports; (b) achieve fiscal and balance of payments viability over the period; (c) lay the basis for sustainable noninflationary or minimally inflationary growth; and (d) lessen the dominance of unproductive investments in the public sector, improve the sector's efficiency, and intensify the growth potential of the private sector.

The policy strategies in terms of the main measures to be adopted were, first, a realistic exchange rate policy coupled with the liberalization of the external trade and payments system, and second, appropriate pricing policies in all sectors with greater reliance on market forces and reduction in complex administrative controls. Further rationalization and restructuring of public expenditure and custom tariffs was also included (Central Bank of Nigeria 1986).

With these objectives, an initial two-year structural adjustment program was announced on July 1, 1986. The high point was the promulga-

TABLE 11.4 NIGERIA: STRUCTURAL ADJUSTMENT AND IMPLEMENTATION RECORD

Area of reform	1986	1987	1988	1989	1990	1991	1992	1993	1994
Structural/policy reforms									
Foreign exchange market[a]	*	*		*	*		*	x	x
Import liberalization[b]	*	*	x	x	x	x			
Export promotion[c]	*	x	*x	x					
Debt conversion	*						*		
Prices							*	*	*
Privatization/commercialization			*						
Interest rates[d]	*	*		x		x	*		x
Credit guidelines	*	*					*		
Financial sector					*	*		*	
Budget (tax/expenditure)									
Policy implementation									
Inflation	—	+	+	+	-	+	+	+	—
Fiscal deficit/GDP	+	+	+	-	-	+	+	+	-
Petroleum subsidy		>	>	>	>	>	>	>	>
Fertilizer subsidy	>	>	>	>	>	>	>	>	>
Extrabudgetary expenditures	—	+	+	+	+	+	+	+	-
Growth in broad money	-	+	+	-	+	-	+	-	-
Real effective exchange rate (+ appreciate)	-	-	+	-	-	-	-	+	+
Official and parallel exchange rate spread	-	-	-	+	+	+	-	+	+
External current account	-	+	-	+	+	-	-	-	-

Note: * indicates reform; x indicates reversal of reform (change relative to previous year); - indicates a decline; + indicates an increase; > indicates variable was positive; and — indicates figure is zero, or that the item does not exist.

a. Prorated allocation of foreign exchange by Central Bank of Nigeria in 1993, fixed exchange rate in 1994.

b. During 1981–91 higher tariffs or import bans were introduced.

c. In 1987 export bans on grains were introduced, and bans were extended to other commodities in 1988 and 1989. In 1989 the rediscount/financing facility for exports was introduced by the Central Bank of Nigeria.

d. On November 10, 1989, the Central Bank of Nigeria introduced a maximum interest rate spread between saving and prime lending rates, the prime and the highest lending rates, and the interbank prime lending rates. Ceilings were imposed on maximum lending rates at the beginning of 1991 and 1994.

Source: Moser, Rogers, and van Til 1997: 13.

tion of the decree establishing the Second-tier Foreign Exchange Market (SFEM). SFEM took effect in September 1986 and instantly caused the depreciation of the naira by 66 percent. Liberalizing the foreign exchange market was considered the linchpin of subsequent reforms affecting the financial sector, trade, and the product markets. With the introduction of the SFEM, the import licensing system was effectively abolished, and the large depreciation of the real exchange rate substantially reduced the black market premium on the naira. These changes were important steps toward a more open trade regime. Another important institutional reform was the abolition of the marketing boards in order to eliminate the implicit over-taxation of the agricultural sector by the exploitative boards.

Enactment of the structural adjustment measures was met with mass rioting (especially in 1988 and 1989) and unrelenting and venomous criticisms from all sectors of the society. The massive opposition was led by university students, labor, and various social groups who stood to lose from the reforms. At the same time, the pro-reform coalition was extremely limited. Even those who might benefit from the reforms had a significant problem identifying themselves as winners. The structural problems in the Nigerian economy (including a deficient infrastructure, limited credit system, and an extremely difficult business environment) prevented entrepreneurs from becoming enthusiastic about price reforms, no matter how much the government needed their support.

The implementation of the reform program was therefore uneven and plagued by frequent reversals. Several factors accounted for this inconsistency. First, the reform measures were technically hard to implement, sometimes contradictory, and vied for resources and leadership attention with the political transition that was occurring at the same time. Indeed, many analysts contend that from 1989, the political transition grossly overshadowed economic reforms. With a regime that was especially sensitive to public opinion and eager to please the opposition, public resources were freely used to bribe the opposition. Some extravagant but politically savvy programs, such as the creation of more state and local governments, were implemented. Second, it was not clear how determined the government was to reform the economy as opposed to simply lifting the constraint on resources that it faced. Finally, as mentioned above, the reforms were politically unpopular.

The Babangida government's response to the riots of 1988 and 1989 was to embark on a set of reflationary measures designed to cushion the effects of the policy changes. The government raised the minimum wage, unfroze wages in the public sector, and removed the ban on civil service recruitment. Furthermore, in reaction to the demand for economic reform with a "human face," the government embarked on a series of initiatives to aid vulnerable groups and sectors. This effort included the establishment and funding of the National Directorate of Employment; the People's Bank (for lending to artisans, petty traders, and all those without the usually required collateral); the Directorate of Food, Roads and Rural Infrastructure; the Better Life program (designed to empower rural women); and a variety of urban mass transit schemes. While these programs consumed significant public resources and were politically popular, their impact on the poor was dubious.

Of course, the government was able to spend more because, as debts were rescheduled, the amount owed as a percentage of oil revenue began to decrease. Inevitably, however, the budget deficit soared, money supply rocketed, and inflation and balance of payments deteriorated as the Babangida government became less concerned about enforcing austerity. The fungibility issue is particularly severe in Nigeria because the preferences of the Nigerian government are strikingly different from those of the international donors (World Bank 1998b: 63). Certainly, it is absolutely clear from Nigeria that, absent a constructive policy environment, aid and debt rescheduling are useless and possibly counterproductive. For reform to be institutionalized, government leaders must be motivated by something other than the amount of government revenue that is immediately available.

The consequences of these stop-go reforms were mixed. Inflation generally averaged more than 40 percent per year but the trade balance remained positive (though the current account still deteriorated). The GDP growth rate averaged about 5 percent per year during the period. However, the economy remained essentially monocultural, depending on oil for exports and agriculture for employment. The budget deficit as a percentage of GDP also gyrated from year to year, and in 1993 it soared to about 13 percent of GDP.

The effects of the reforms were always problematic because the halting nature of the effort meant that initiatives, when they were implemented, had to be large-scale in order to make up for the policy slippage of the previous period. Correspondingly, the dead-weight losses associated with the abruptly introduced measures were large as individuals and businesses were unable to adjust quickly (Moser, Rogers, and van Til 1997: 44). In other words, reform had begun to make a difference in some areas but it was hardly institutionalized four years after adoption.

Did Aid Make a Difference?

We have argued that Nigeria sustained huge negative transfers to the donors during the entire period of reforms. Aid, if any, was miniscule and the huge debt service payments more than outweighed the inflows. In several instances, Nigeria deliberately refused to accept certain resources. For example, as part of the standby arrangements, the IMF committed to grant Nigeria a total of 1.44 billion in special drawing rights. The Nigerian government declined to draw the resources ostensibly because of the verdict of a national referendum that rejected any such offers. Since the early 1990s, Nigeria also has not had any program with the World Bank and thus had no concessional loans from it. Rather, during most of the 1990s, Nigeria made an annual transfer of US$1 billion to the Bank to service existing debt. As noted earlier, technical assistance has never been important, especially in policy design. This is understandable given the extra sensitivity of Nigerians to such overt "external intervention" in the country's internal affairs. Such technical assistance would have belied the government's insistence that the reforms were designed by Nigerians for Nigerians. In any case, it bears repeating that Nigeria's problem was not in not knowing what to do, but in trying to implement programs without much commitment to them and in a difficult political-economic context.

For Nigeria, therefore, the key element that determined the adoption of the Bank-Fund type of reforms was the pressure to reach agreements on debt rescheduling. The second key element was the particular leadership in power and its convictions and commitment to the reform process. Given the political economy of the country described earlier, the government has dragged its feet on those aspects of reforms that interfered with its ability to dispense rents: privatization, a dual exchange rate regime, and control over government spending. It is little wonder that once the fiscal constraint was relaxed somewhat (as during the oil windfall in 1990–91), spending was difficult to curtail. It should be noted, however, that once reforms in some critical areas were started, they assumed a life of their own and it became difficult to sustain a reversal. For example, the liberalization of the exchange rate, prices, financial sector liberalization, and so forth were temporarily reversed at one point or another, but the reversals did not last. Important constituencies have begun to organize to defend these reforms. Without debt rescheduling, perhaps increased aid could have played a critical role as was the case in most African countries. In the Nigerian experience so far, it was the conditionality tied to debt rescheduling rather than aid inflows that pushed the country to the Bank-Fund type of reforms.

1990–91: Coping with the Oil Windfall

The oil "boomlet" of 1990–91, following the Iraqi invasion of Kuwait in August 1990, provided an excellent test of the degree of institutionalization of key aspects of the economic reform program (see Herbst and Olukoshi 1994). Given that the weak link in Nigeria's structural adjustment program had been fiscal policy (due to the importance of government revenue to leaders), the oil windfall presented an ideal opportunity to test the extent to which the Babangida government had been able to institutionalize controls on spending. Certainly, the sudden rapid rise in oil prices after August 1990 had a profound effect on Nigerian finances. The World Bank estimates that total oil export revenue in 1990 was US$14 billion, a 49 percent increase over the 1989 level (World Bank 1991: 404). As figure 11.2 shows, the ratio of nonconcessional debt to oil exports declined from 292 percent in 1989 to 230 percent in 1990. Relative to previous years, there was suddenly far less fiscal pressure, and as a result the leverage that the IFIs had achieved through influencing debt rescheduling was severely reduced.

From the start of the Gulf crisis, the Nigerian government said that it would treat the increase in revenue as a temporary exogenous shock that would have no long-term effect on the level of spending. Indeed, General Babangida, in his 1991 budget address, went out of his way to stress that his administration had learned the lessons of the 1973 and 1979 oil windfalls and was committed to handling the huge revenue increase in a responsible manner. Babangida said that "most of the extra earnings [from the oil windfall] were in fact sterilized in building up the nation's foreign exchange reserves" (Babangida 1991: 5–6). If the money had in fact been treated in such a manner, it would have been nothing short of a revolution in Nigerian finances given the fiscal irresponsibility of previous regimes over the past 20 years.

As it happened, the Babangida regime came under powerful pressure to increase spending after the invasion. First, as noted, opposition to the structural adjustment program was still strong and a visible pro-reform coalition had not developed. Indeed, the manufacturers' association had announced in April 1990 that first-quarter capacity utilization had actually decreased below the 1989 level. The regime therefore felt the need to increase expenditures in order to buy popular acquiescence.

Second, in April 1990 there was an amateurish coup attempt by junior officers that came surprisingly close to succeeding. While the coup-makers' grievances revolved around ethnic and religious issues (they declared that the states in northern Nigeria were expelled from the federation), Babangida felt it necessary to buy more support from the military. As a result, the government launched a large spending program for the rehabilitation of the police and military barracks, increased spending on security (including a controversial National Guard), procured new weapons, and approved special grants to improve the welfare of officers. For instance, in February 1992, the government allocated US$50 million to purchase 3,000 Peugeots for the private use of captains and majors in the Nigerian army. Similar presidential gifts were promised to the officers of the Navy and the Air Force.

Third, the states made a strong appeal for their share of the oil revenue. And finally, more money may have been needed to grease the wheels of the political transition program.

In the face of this increased spending, the IFIs were essentially powerless. As there was suddenly more revenue available to the Babangida government, its desire to reform the economy automatically declined. Funds from the outside—aid that was largely used for balance of payments support, debt relief, and oil inflows, which were treated as largely fungible by the Nigerian government—were no longer moving in lockstep with reform. The World Bank (1998b: 51) has noted that in Ghana and elsewhere, the receipt of outside funds had to be correlated with reform to make the new initiatives successful. However, an oil producer can receive a windfall that will make other sources of outside funds (aid, debt rescheduling) much less important than is the case in most African countries. Indeed, as the beneficial effects of the rescheduling and the oil boomlet occurred at roughly the same time, the government in Lagos may have felt particularly unmotivated to carry on with the politically unpopular and technically difficult adjustment exercises.

In fact, it appears that the government ratcheted up spending almost as soon as the spot oil market responded to the Iraqi invasion by dramatically increasing the price of crude. Total expenditures as a percentage of GDP increased from 21.2 percent in 1989 to 26.4 percent in 1990 (Herbst and Olukoshi 1994). This caused the overall deficit to increase, despite the revenue windfall, from 7.9 percent to 10.1 percent of GDP (Central Bank of Nigeria 1991: 2). The government increased expenditure massively by funding the intervention in Liberia and the purchase of new military equipment (estimated at US$250 million to $500 million), failing to curb spending on the Ajaokuta steel plant (initial price US$1.4 billion, final price estimated at US$4.0 billion), continuing the commitment to a dubious aluminum smelter (US$2.4 billion), and sponsoring the 1990 Organization of African Unity summit (US$150 million) (Keeling1991: 4). A World Bank report completed in early 1991 also noted that there was

> a breakdown in fiscal and monetary discipline in 1990 . . . not only characterized by additional spending and monetary expansion but also by a major surge in expenditures bypassing budgetary mechanisms for expenditure authorization and control. (Quoted in Holman 1992: 14)

The report noted that "significant domestic currency spending appears to have occurred without any apparent budgetary authorizations." In particular, the report noted that inconsistencies in the Federal Stabilization Account, if they are equivalent to actual expenditures, "imply spending outside normal accounting and budgetary mechanisms which exceed total budgetary non–debt service spending of the Federal government in 1990" (quoted in Holman 1992: 14).

That is, the reform package essentially came apart. At this point it should have become clear that Babangida was not a champion of reform, if there was any doubt beforehand. Similarly, our simple model of Nigerian leadership behavior appears to be vindicated.

Any notion of Nigerian reform finally ended when General Abacha had the political transition program aborted in June 1993 and took power directly a few months later. Abacha had extremely bad relations with the IFIs and the major bilateral donors because of disagreements over human rights and poor economic policies. Debt rescheduling and foreign assistance dropped to zero as Nigeria became isolated from Africa, the Commonwealth, and the international community. The new leader coped with the decline in oil revenue by printing money to finance the government deficit (Moser, Rogers, and van Til 1997: 39). Abacha also ruled with particular brutality, in large part because the traditional levers of Nigerian politics that had been available through the creative use of government revenue disappeared after the donors began to boycott Lagos. The ratio of debt to exports climbed perceptibly until the government and economy were in crisis. Abacha died in 1998 and now the Obasanjo government must start over again to try to reform the Nigerian economy.

CONCLUSIONS

Nigerian leaders before 1985 understood the economic crisis they faced but failed to address it. The Babangida government attempted to address the complex issues that contributed to the impoverishment of Africa's largest country, but failed to implement a coherent program. These failures came about because the logic of austerity and economic reform is anathema to the clientelistic system of Nigerian politics. Of course, the money provided by donors gave the Babangida government some breathing room. However, in an odd manner, it was both inadequate and too much. It was inadequate because the government still faced a grave fiscal crisis and was under a far greater revenue constraint than in the early 1980s. As a result, some patronage opportunities were not available to the new government, and for this and other reasons it became deeply unpopular. At the same time, the money provided through assistance and rescheduling was too much because when these inflows combined with the additional oil revenue following the invasion of Kuwait in 1990, it allowed the Babangida government to try to revert to politics as usual. The government did not have enough money to return to the status quo ante but the immediate impetus for adopting the reform program was no longer there. The donors could never have provided enough money for Babangida to get the reform program through the old-fashioned way, via bribes and patronage. As a result, the program foundered on its own contradictions.

The mantra of the latest study on aid effectiveness (World Bank 1998b: 58) is "if commitment, money—if not, ideas." This is a laudable notion and represents a substantial rethinking by the World Bank. By 1991, it was clear that the Nigerian government was not committed to the reform package and therefore the money from the IFIs and the donors was not consequential. However, the Nigerian program did not fail because of a lack of ideas. Discussions between Nigerian authorities and the International Monetary Fund, the World Bank, and the bilateral donors were useful but not nearly as important as in other African countries where there is a near-absolute lack of technocratic knowledge. What is needed is to develop new ideas about how Nigerian politics should operate, something that the World Bank, the IMF, and the bilateral donors cannot provide. Only the Nigerians can do that.

APPENDIX 11.1
NIGERIA: CHRONOLOGY OF POLITICAL
AND ECONOMIC DEVELOPMENTS

October 1960	Nigeria wins independence.
1963	First Republic.
1966	Coup d'etat led by General Johnson Ironsi.
	Coup d'etat led by Yakubu Gowon.
May 1967	Civil war begins.
1970	Civil war ends.
1973	Oil windfall due to OPEC pricing decisions.
1975	Coup d'etat led by General Murtala Muhammed.
1976	Coup d'etat led by General Olusegun Obasanjo.
1979	Shehu Shagari elected to power.
1980–85	Collapse of oil prices.
1983	Coup d'etat; General Muhammad Buhari overthrows Shagari.
1985	General Ibrahim Babangida overthrows Buhari.
1985–93	Babangida presidency.
1 October 1985	Babangida declares a state of national economic emergency for 15-month period.
1 July 1986	Two-year structural adjustment program launched.
September 1986	Establishment of SFEM.
April 1990	Coup attempted by junior officers.
June 1993	Moshood Abiola wins election only to have them abrogated by Babangida.
November 1993	Coup d'etat led by General Sani Abacha.
1998	General Abdulsalami Abubakar succeeds General Sani Abacha upon his death.
May 1999	Obasanjo wins presidential elections.

NOTES

1. This section is partly based on Herbst and Olukoshi (1994).

2. In 1998, Transparency International, which ranks countries by the level of corruption as perceived by business people, risk analysts, and others familiar with each country, ranked Nigeria 81st out of 85 countries, or among the most corrupt. See Transparency International at http://www.gwdg.de/~uwvw/icr.htm.

REFERENCES

Babangida, Ibrahim. 1985. "Excerpts from broadcast of President Babangida's speech in Lagos on 31st December 1985." British Broadcasting Corporation Summary of World Broadcasts, 14 January 1986.

———. 1986. "Nigerian president's 27th June address: economic and social issues." British Broadcasting Corporation Summary of World Broadcasts, 1 July 1986.

———. 1987. "Excerpts from address by Nigerian President Ibrahim Babangida presenting the 1987 national budget in Lagos on 1st January 1987." British Broadcasting Corporation Summary of World Broadcasts, 13 January 1987.

———. 1991. Budget speech. Lagos.

Biersteker, Thomas, and Peter M. Lewis. 1997. "The Rise and Fall of Structural Adjustment in Nigeria." In Larry Diamond, Anthony Kirk-Greene, and Oyeleye Oyediran, eds., *Transition without End: Nigerian Politics and Civil Society under Babangida*. Boulder: Lynne Rienner.

Central Bank of Nigeria. 1986. *Annual Report and Statement of Accounts*. Lagos.

———. 1991. *Annual Report and Statement of Accounts*. Lagos.

Herbst, Jeffrey, and Adebayo Olukoshi. 1994. "Nigeria: Economic and Political Reforms at Cross Purposes." In Stephan Haggard and Steven B. Webb, eds., *Voting for Reform: Democracy, Political Liberalization and Economic Adjustment*. New York: Oxford University Press.

Holman, John. 1992. "'Inconsistencies' in State Funds." *Financial Times*, 16 March.

Holmgren, Torgny. 1998. "Aid and Reform in Africa: Terms of Reference." World Bank, Development Research Group, Washington, D.C. Processed.

Ikem, A. O. 1996. "The Paris Club and Nigeria's Debt Rescheduling: The Way Forward." *Central Bank of Nigeria Debt Trends* 2 (1).

Joseph, Richard A. 1987. *Democracy and Prebendalism in Nigeria*. Cambridge: Cambridge University Press.

Keeling, William. 1991. "Concern at the use of Lagos oil windfall," *Financial Times*, 27 June: 4.

Moser, Gary, Scott Rogers, and Reinhold van Til. 1997. "Nigeria: Experience with Structural Adjustment." International Monetary Fund, Washington, D.C.

Nigeria. 1991. "Nigeria's Principal Economic and Financial Indicators, 1970–1990." Federal Office of Statistics. Lagos.

———. 1997. "The Evolution and Management of Nigeria's External Debt: The Way Forward." Ministry of Finance. Lagos.

O'Connell, S., and C. C. Soludo. 1999. "Aid Intensity in Africa." Forthcoming in *World Development*.

World Bank. 1998a. *World Development Report 1998*. New York: Oxford University Press.

———. 1998b. *Assessing Aid: What Works, What Doesn't, and Why*. New York: Oxford University Press.

———. 1999. *Global Development Finance 1999*. Vol. 2. Washington, D.C.

Index

Abacha, Sani, 656, 674
Abbey, Joe, 10, 64–65, 67
Abidjan Arbitration Court, Côte d'Ivoire, 422, 425, 438, 440
Acheampong, Ignatius Kutu, 58–59, 71, 95n2
Adjustment programs. *See* Structural policies/adjustments
African Capacity Building Foundation, 508
African Development Bank
    Ethiopian aid, 180, 196
    Kenyan aid, 473
    Mali aid, 244
    Tanzanian aid, 292
    Ugandan aid, 111
African socialism. *See also* Post-Socialist reformers
    Tanzania, 314–16
Agence d'Etudes de Promotion d'Emploi (AGEPE), Côte d'Ivoire, 419, 453n32
Agence Française de Développement (AFD), 379
Agency for International Development, U.S.
    Ghana and, 55
    Mali aid, 256, 257, 264–65, 266
    Zambia aid, 612n3
Aggregate net transfers, 371–72
Aggregate official development finance (ODF), 231. *See also* Official development finance (ODF)

Agriculture
    Kenyan pricing and marketing, 503–5
    Ugandan policy, 131
Aid. *See also* Effective development assistance (EDA); Official development assistance (ODA)
    concepts, 230–33
    coordination, 21–22
    definition of, 36
    for mixed reformers, 17–18
    for nonreformers, 18–19
    for post-Socialist reformers, 16–17
    for successful reformers, 14–16
    as technical assistance and nonfinancial aid, 19–21
    trends, 12–14
Aid and reform, 22–33
    good policy regimes, 31–33
    pre-reform phase, 23–28
    rapid reform period, 28–31
Aid and reform, Congo. *See* Aid and reform, Zaire/Congo
Aid and reform, Côte d'Ivoire
    causes and processes, 431–36
    CFA parity hypotheses, 398–99
    decentralization and, 417–18
    effectiveness, 437–41
    impacts, 438–41
    implementation results, 437–38
    legal and judicial system, 425–30

679